THE
ART
OF
FACT

A HISTORICAL ANTHOLOGY
OF LITERARY JOURNALISM

EDITED BY

KEVIN KERRANE
AND BEN YAGODA

A TOUCHSTONE BOOK
PUBLISHED BY SIMON & SCHUSTER

TOUCHSTONE
1230 Avenue of the Americas
New York, NY 10020

First Touchstone Edition 1998

TOUCHSTONE and colophon are registered trademarks of Simon & Schuster Inc.

DESIGNED BY ERICH HOBBING

Text set in Fairfield

Manufactured in the United States of America

10

The Library of Congress has cataloged the Scribner edition as follows:

The art of fact: a historical anthology of literary journalism /
[compiled by] Kevin Kerrane and Ben Yagoda.
p. cm.
Includes index.
1. Literature—Collections. 2. Reporters and reporting. 3. Reportage literature.
I. Kerrane, Kevin. II. Yagoda, Ben.
PN6014.A76   1997
081—dc21   97–8497
CIP

ISBN-13: 978-0-684-83041-4
ISBN-10:   0-684-83041-8
ISBN-13: 978-0-684-84630-9 (Pbk)
ISBN-10:   0-684-84630-6 (Pbk)
See page 553 for text permissions.

*To the writers
collected herein,
with intense admiration*

Acknowledgments

∞

Many people helped bring this book into being, some by suggesting possible selections, others by graciously accepting scandalously low fees for their splendid work. What we found almost everywhere, and what spurred us on more than anything else, was a firm conviction that the book needed to exist. Particular thanks to: Jerry Beasley, Mark Bowden, Rosie Boycott, Jimmy Breslin, Bill Buford, Hodding Carter, Roy Peter Clark, Richard Ben Cramer, Grace Darby, Carl Dawson, Henry Dunow, Carla Field, Don Fry, Martha Gellhorn, Alan Halpern, Steve Helmling, Michael Herr, Godfrey Hodgson, Kate Kerrane, Quinn Kerrane, Dennis Jackson, Alan Jenkins, Robert Lucid, Sheila McGrath, Norman Mailer, the late Joseph Mitchell, Daniel Okrent, Chip Scanlan, Bonnie Kime Scott, David Simon, Bill Stempel, Chuck Stone, Arch Tait, Gay Talese, John Ware, and Jon Winokur.

Thanks, also, to Katharine and to Gigi, for support above and beyond the call.

Contents

CONTENTS

THE REPORTER TAKES THE STAGE

STYLE AS SUBSTANCE

CONTENTS

Preface

∞

If anything is less pleasant than long periods of standing in front of a photocopying machine, it is haggling over copyright permissions, which explains in part how this book came to be. Kevin Kerrane and I both found, when we taught courses on what is called, for lack of a better term, "literary journalism," that there was no appropriate textbook to assign to our students. So they would end up having to buy copies of Truman Capote's *In Cold Blood* and John Hersey's *Hiroshima* and Joseph Mitchell's *Up in the Old Hotel*, while we spent hours securing the rights to, reproducing, and distributing copies of pieces by Liebling, Orwell, Lillian Ross, and other worthies we had treasured for years or delightedly discovered over the previous summer. We finally decided to take matters into our own hands; you are holding the result in yours.

Putting the anthology together has been a bracing and sometimes exhilarating experience, like planning and executing a dinner party with all the best guests. The challenge, of course, was to winnow the guest list from the thousands of potential invitees to the few dozen who made the final cut, and the key to this process was to bring some definitions to literary journalism, a profoundly fuzzy term. Most people are not acquainted with it; those who are tend to use it to signify different things. It sometimes seems to refer to nothing more specific than laudable nonfiction. For us, definition begins with the second half of the formulation, that is, with "journalism." And so for a piece of writing to be included in this anthology, it must first of all be factual. We do not mean to say that we guarantee the veracity of every statement in every piece in the collection. But we did disqualify works that were not, in our view, informed and animated by the central journalistic commitment to the truth (not just The Truth). So we did not include Joseph Mitchell's *Old Mr. Flood*, admittedly about a composite character, or John Gregory Dunne's *Vegas*, admittedly a pastiche of fact and fancy, or such factually problematic recent books as *Midnight in the Garden of Good and Evil* and *Sleepers*.

Journalism also implies a process of active fact-gathering—not just working from memory or sensory observation but doing what reporters call reporting. And this requirement was most helpful of all in winnowing the

13

candidates for the anthology to manageable size. It eliminated volume after volume of laudable nonfiction: memoir, essay (even the distinguished journalistic essays of a Murray Kempton), nature writing, and travel writing (though we did excerpt Rosemary Mahoney's *Whoredom in Kimmage* and Rebecca West's *Black Lamb and Grey Falcon,* both of which offer substantially more than a literate account of the writer's wanderings).

Our final journalistic criterion is currency—that a writer get on the story soon after it happened. The longer the gap, the more the resulting work edges into the realm of history, which is where we place such admittedly groundbreaking and worthy books as *The Longest Day, Praying for Sheetrock,* and *Young Men and Fire.*

So much for journalism. But just what kind of journalism is "literary"? Our five-word answer would be: thoughtfully, artfully, and valuably innovative. The "innovative" is key, for two reasons. First, it is our view that like much else in the twentieth century, journalism has been an object of mass production, turned out according to codified standards and in agreed-upon shapes. These standards are in many ways useful, yet they are also limiting, and for a writer to cast one or more aside can be liberating.

Think of one of the most time-honored journalistic conventions, the direct quotation. Thousands of editors have told a hundred thousand reporters that quotes add essential liveliness to a story, and at the same time help cover your posterior: if someone else provides the information, you don't have to stand by it. The reporters, for their part, know quotes are a splendid way to take up space. All true; yet as tempting as they can be, after-the-fact quotes, sound bites from the interview room, are antiliterary. They take the reader away from the moment in question to some vague and indeterminate present in which the quote is uttered. They take the writer away from his or her voice. And they take away from the writing the deep-down appeal of once-upon-a-time storytelling. Compare: *"I knew I had to get out of there," said firefighter Ken Jones* with *Jones knew he had to get out of there.* The first is the boilerplate; the second, a cobblestone in the road to art.

Quotes can be as hard to give up as any addiction. Verification becomes an overarching issue (you can be sure what Jones said, but can you be sure what he knew?), as does marshaling and structuring your data (quotes plug in so easily!). But going inside Ken Jones's head is so extraordinary, it is worth the effort. Even if you are not prepared to make that particular journey, there are others: with the addition of some props, stage directions, and body language, his quotes can turn into *dialogue* and his entire account of the fire becomes a *scene.*

Innovation is also important because, like portrait painting, rebounding, playing blues guitar, or doing quantum physics, high-level literary journalism is a tradition, with each practitioner standing on the shoulders of his or her predecessors. Thus, with *In Cold Blood,* Truman Capote was taking off from the innovations of John Hersey's *Hiroshima,* the first serious work to attempt a novelistic factual narrative on a large scale. And thus Tom Wolfe would add his own wrinkle to this strain in *The Electric Kool-Aid Acid Test* by eschewing Capote's uninflected and rather stiff narrative voice for a wigged-out hip patois that mirrored his characters' sensibility. It took a distinguished novelist like Piers Paul Read, in *Alive,* to present real events with the kind of suspense and emotion one expects from the best realistic fiction. And, to bring this tale up to the present day, the woefully underrecognized Gary Smith bores deep into his subjects' consciousness, emerging with an intimacy and empathy that let him write the journalistic equivalent of Raymond Carver short stories.

Our premium on innovation also allowed us to pare our list of possible inclusions, eliminating, for example, Alex Kotlowitz's *There Are No Children Here* and Darcy Frey's *The Last Shot,* both of them outstanding books but neither displaying techniques or approaches that hadn't been seen before. Similarly, although more fine writing is being done for newspapers today than ever, including some labeled explicitly as literary journalism, we found that even the finest tended to be too traditional for our purposes. A newspaper article has to cover the bases, and even the best pieces we looked at had long stretches of background, exposition, reaction and, yes, quotes.

As we read and debated, the pieces we selected fell into three principal categories, which—along with the pre-twentieth-century pioneers that anticipated them—constitute the anthology's sections. (Because of our historical emphasis, each section proceeds in chronological order.) The first is narrative journalism, and the first of its two substrains is the novelistic tradition mentioned above—works of journalism where the reporter gathers as much information as possible about an event, then uses it to re-create what happened in the manner of narrative fiction. In the other strain, the model is not the novel but the movie or play: the reporter is on the scene and more or less matter-of-factly relates what happens, in the manner of a script. Much of the artistry here lies in the reporter's retreat from our vision, whether as partial or full-scale "fly on the wall." It is, in any case, much less factually problematic than re-creation, which has always had to grapple with this question: can one definitively assert that X happened or Y said Z if one was not there to witness it? The dramatic set piece has long been a favorite of newspaper columnists, who have found that it lets them be ironic, sardonic, or sentimental without openly editorializing; practitioners represented in the anthology are Ben Hecht, Jimmy Cannon, Jimmy Breslin, and Bob Greene. In the 1940s, magazine writers like W. C. Heinz, Lillian Ross, and Walter Bernstein wove scenes together into long articles. Ross's 1952 *Picture,* about the making of John Huston's *The Red Badge of Courage* and not included here, applied the technique in a book, but no one confidently stood on her shoulders until about thirty years later, when Tracy Kidder's *The Soul of a New Machine* inaugurated a new wave of "process" books.

As obvious as this approach's strengths is its main drawback: the near-impossibility—especially in these days of limited access—in most newsworthy stories of a reporter's being present at all the important scenes. As a result, the I-am-a-camera school has tended to focus on the less significant but far more accessible and frequently no less interesting tales. Kidder's books, for example, deal with the engineering of a particular model of computer, the building of a house, and a year in the respective lives of a grade-school classroom and a nursing home.

Our second category consists of works with the reporter at the forefront—which, as anyone who has ever taken Journalism 101 knows, violates not only a formula but one of the guiding principles of the profession. It turns out that, when done intelligently, violation can lead to inspiration. James Boswell, George Orwell, A. J. Liebling, Hunter Thompson, Norman Mailer, and James Fenton would seem to have little in common besides literary eminence. One other thing they share is an understanding that outsized and unabashed subjectivity can be a superb route to understanding. The disembodied, measured voice of classic journalism is a kind of flimflam; the pure objectivity it implies is probably unattainable by humans. By stepping out from the shadows and laying bare his or her prejudices, anxieties, or thought processes the reporter gives us something firmer and truer to hold on to as we come to our own conclusions.

There is a distinct possibility for abuse here: the reporter's forgetting that he is not the story, just a means to it. And where the use of "I" should offer the reporter a means to construct a multidimensional and memorable character, in magazine journalism today it has become a reflexive cliche. Still, the narrative presence has unquestionably given to journalism more than it has taken away.

The last category, Style as Substance, shows that the road to literary journalism has many more than two lanes. Some writers (James Agee, Joseph Mitchell, Tom Wolfe, Joan Didion, John McPhee) have crafted distinctive *voices* that elevate their work to the level of literature. Others (Orwell, John Steinbeck, David Simon, Svetlana Alexiyevich, Ryszard Kapuściński) have artfully and fruitfully experimented with structure or chronology or even syntax. And for some selections, like Rebecca West's heartbreaking and prescient account of the people of the Bosnian town of Travnik, the criterion for inclusion is little more than prose of a remarkably high order.

It would certainly be possible to organize this anthology differently—by theme, for example. But here it stands, for better or worse, and we will be satisfied if it does one thing: make the case that literary journalism exists, and is not an oxymoron.

—BEN YAGODA

Making Facts Dance

∞

In 1973, when Tom Wolfe coedited a wonderful anthology called *The New Journalism,* he naturally emphasized differences between traditional reportage and the creative nonfiction of his own day. New journalists, Wolfe said, combined in-depth reporting with literary ambition: they wanted to make the nonfiction story shimmer "like a novel" with the pleasures of detailed realism. As an afterthought, Wolfe noted that this journalism had been prefigured, in a shadowy way, by earlier novelist-reporters like Charles Dickens, George Orwell, and John Hersey.

Our anthology reverses Wolfe's emphasis by giving prominence to such pioneers, and by connecting their work to the journalism of the 1960s and '70s—and beyond. Our very first selection honors a great factual storyteller, perhaps the first true modern literary journalist: Daniel Defoe, whose 1725 tract on the criminal Jonathan Wild offers a prototype of the modern true-crime narrative. Later excerpts from Hickman Powell, Truman Capote, and David Simon show striking modifications of that genre over the last sixty years.

Another genre—we might call it tales of the city—has been popularized by such newspaper writers as Jimmy Breslin and Rick Bragg. It is the human-interest story as social parable: a narrative form that can be traced back to Morris Markey and Ben Hecht, through Abraham Cahan at the turn of the century, and ultimately to Victorian social reporters such as Dickens, Henry Mayhew, and W. T. Stead.

The term "new journalism," in fact, was originally coined by Matthew Arnold in 1887 to describe the style of Stead's *Pall Mall Gazette:* brash, vivid, personal, reform-minded—and occasionally, from Arnold's conservative viewpoint, "featherbrained." The Victorian social reporters, and the American muckrakers who followed them, aimed at a factual literature of modern industrial life. Their literary touches came less from artistic design than from the writers' sense of moral or political urgency: a determination to dramatize the reality of poverty, prostitution, and prejudice. Looking for news amid the daily struggles of the unknown poor, Henry Mayhew edited his interviewees' responses into sustained dramatic monologues. Exploring the urban abyss, Jack London became a character in his own story: the narrator as dropout, undertaking a secret journey to the cultural interior.

The downwardly mobile reporter reappears here in the writing of George Orwell, Marvel Cooke, Lawrence Graham, and Ted Conover—and can also be found in many other brave works of investigative journalism, from John Howard Griffin's *Black Like Me* (an American white passing as black) to Yoram Binur's *My Enemy, My Self* (an Israeli living as a Palestinian). In every case, the narrative point of view is possible only because of the writer's complete immersion in the world of the story.

Similarly, war reporting has evolved from nineteenth-century scene painting to close-ups of direct experience. When the great Victorian journalist William Howard Russell wrote his 1854 dispatch on the charge of the Light Brigade, he was watching from a ridge two miles away. Seven years later, covering the Battle of Bull Run, Russell arrived late—and so was caught in the middle of a Union retreat. Most New York correspondents had left the scene early, to file dispatches of an apparent Union victory. Russell's account described "a miserable, causeless panic" in a way that no other report could, and for that reason it generated huge controversy.

Modern correspondents aim for a startling image of what Martha Gellhorn called the face of war. To capture that image, they may try all kinds of experiments. Richard Harding Davis slows the pace to an agony of anticipation; John Hersey replays the same moments from the viewpoints of six victims; John Steinbeck fragments the events of one day into a sequence of brute sensations; Michael Herr internalizes the paranoia of combatants; Svetlana Alexiyevich creates a fugue of dramatic monologues. Gellhorn herself breaks up a war story with parenthetical memories that reveal the dimensions of civilian suffering. She typifies the outlook of the modern correspondent in treating war not as a matter of strategic weapons or mass movements, but as a cruelty inflicted on individuals, one after another.

New trends in sports writing are also evident here. An old-fashioned style, based on florid description and moral pronouncement, was fading by the 1940s. Jimmy Cannon's account of the second Joe Louis–Billy Conn fight in 1946 relied instead on photographic realism and startling subjectivity to create a total picture of the event. Later selections from Al Stump, Gay Talese, Gary Smith, and Bill Buford show how the modern sports story can open out into a psychological profile or a cultural parable.

A topical approach to literary journalism highlights what was really new in the nonfiction of the 1960s and '70s. Tom Wolfe stressed stylistic innovations: scene-by-scene narration, dramatic dialogue, experiments in point of view, and attention to the symbolic details of social life. But much of this fresh writing was, first and foremost, a direct response to the transforming events of the era: war protests, race riots, assassinations, and countercultural challenges to all proprieties. The reporting of Norman Mailer or Hunter Thompson, or of Wolfe himself, shows that the "genteel voice" of traditional reportage was no longer sufficient to articulate public reality.

*   *   *

Wolfe's anthology included only one non-American writer: Nicholas Tomalin, whose reporting from Vietnam in 1966 caught the manic bravado of U.S. Army officers. In 1973, covering the Yom Kippur War, Tomalin was killed by a stray shell. But between stints as a war correspondent, he had coauthored—with Ron Hall—one of the most intriguing nonfiction works of the period: *The Strange Last Voyage of Donald Crowhurst* (1970).

Trying to "combine the techniques of the novelist with those of the journalist," Tomalin and Hall told of the madness and suicide of a competitor in a round-the-world sailing race. They were writing for the London *Sunday Times*, Crowhurst's sponsor in the race, and their investigative reporting included complex analysis of Crowhurst's several logs (all but one false), as well as a convincing reconstruction of his final days at sea. "The actual sequence of events," they observed, "had the shape and inevitability of fictional tragedy." (Robert Stone later used many details of the story in his novel *Outerbridge Reach*.) For two decades Crowhurst's family has refused permission to reprint any part of the book, and yet it remains at the center of what might be called the British new journalism.

We have included work by several British writers—Norman Lewis, Piers Paul Read, John Simpson, and James Fenton—to illustrate an alternate tradition of literary reportage. More examples could be found in almost any issue of *Granta* or the British edition of *Esquire*. Such stories may be less mannered or self-conscious than their American equivalents, but they are no less dramatic. Built on ironic details and edgy dialogue, they proceed with a rapid pace and a compelling voice, often politically engaged. In many respects, they illustrate the legacy of George Orwell.

Orwell is also a model for journalists, even outside Britain, who have created a genre of postcolonial reportage. In 1939 Orwell's "Marrakech" was a prescient essay, in the form of five vignettes, on the coming demise of empire. His imagistic and transitionless style, his focus on poverty, and his preoccupation with the "consciousness" of colonialism (often marked by a literal inability to *see* natives)—all are operative in the reports of Ryszard Kapuściński on civil war in Angola, Rian Malan on apartheid in South Africa, and Svetlana Alexiyevich on the Russian conflict in Afghanistan.

The critic B. T. Oxley describes Orwell's nonfiction books of the 1930s—*Down and Out in Paris and London*, *The Road to Wigan Pier*, and *Homage to Catalonia*—as "documentaries." He means that these social reports are sustained investigations, suffused with atmosphere and carried forward by a far more personal voice than any straightforward sociological survey would allow. Today, of course, "documentary" usually refers to nonfiction on film, and in the last twenty-five years the boundaries of factual cinema have been stretched to accommodate just such qualities of atmosphere and personality.

A quarter-century ago, when "new journalism" was a new term, the most interesting documentary movies were in the fly-on-the-wall style of Frederick Wiseman's *High School* or the Maysles brothers' *Salesman*. The flat

19

objective manner of these films was like the reportorial tone of Ernest Hemingway or W. C. Heinz. Today documentaries are closer to exploratory essays, and some explicitly follow the lead of literary reportage. Director George Butler describes his documentary about hunters, *In the Blood*, as cinematic new journalism: "I'm trying to take the facts and adhere to truth, but to give it a dramatic structure—just as Tom Wolfe, Norman Mailer, and Gay Talese gave a dramatic structure to nonfiction."

Butler uses his thirteen-year-old son as a pivotal character in the movie. Other directors, like Michael Moore (*Roger and Me*) or Nick Broomfield (*Heidi Fleiss: Hollywood Madam*), become pivotal characters themselves: gonzo reporters trying to get the impossible interview. But even third-person documentaries now emulate the stylistic exuberance of literary journalism. Such nonfiction films as *The Thin Blue Line*, *Crumb*, or *Hoop Dreams*—a true-crime narrative, a portrait of an artist, a sports story in counterpoint—borrow storytelling ideas from print reporting even while adding their own cinematic flair.

Literary journalism also sets the standard for documentary in its extraordinary range of subject matter. *The Art of Fact* includes reports on huge public events such as John F. Kennedy's funeral, Richard Nixon's resignation, the Tiananmen Square massacre, and on the private underside of experience, including the most apparently mundane or eccentric details of life. Barrooms, for example, become brilliant dramatic settings in the writing of Walter Bernstein, Ted Conover, and Rosemary Mahoney.

John Grierson, the father of the British nonfiction film, defined documentary as "the creative treatment of actuality." Ben Yagoda, my coeditor, describes literary journalism as "making facts dance." Both formulations point to the double pleasure of true stories artfully told.

But the print journalist still enjoys one great advantage over the filmmaker. Despite continuous improvements in equipment—ever more lightweight and portable, with less need for special lighting—the camera's presence subtly alters the very reality it would show. By contrast, the eye of the writer is an omnipresent lens, no more and no less intrusive than the mind behind it. The literary journalist enjoys greater freedom in researching a story and greater flexibility in telling it, often refocusing in an instant to take us beneath the surface and into the psyche, either a character's or the writer's own.

As a result, the stories stay with us and, as this book suggests, they may even read better over time. And so the best characterization of literary journalism may ultimately be the definition that Ezra Pound gave for literature itself: "news that stays news."

—KEVIN KERRANE

PIONEERS

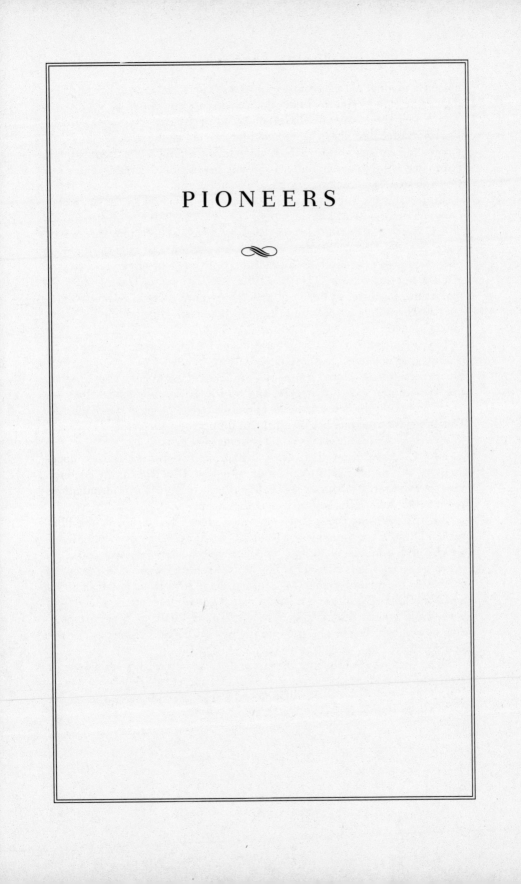

From *The True and Genuine Account of the Life and Actions of the Late Jonathan Wild*

DANIEL DEFOE

∞

Daniel Defoe (1659–1731) built a writing career in the zone between fiction and fact. His novels, rich in realistic detail, read like documentary reports, while his journalism shines with literary quality. This generic ambiguity is typified by *A Journal of the Plague Year* (1722), which purports to be a survivor's memoir of the 1665 London epidemic; in fact, the book is a clever composite of Defoe's family history, early childhood memories, and very extensive reading.

In 1704 Defoe wrote the first modern work of "disaster journalism," *The Storm,* an eyewitness account of terrible devastation along the southern coast of England. That same year he became editor of *The Review,* a newspaper blending party politics and honest reporting. For the next decade, three times a week, Defoe single-handedly produced the paper and wrote every article.

The literary dimension of Defoe's journalism is evident in his 1725 tract about Jonathan Wild, the infamous confidence man who had been executed a few months earlier. Defoe insisted that the story was "Not made up of fiction and fable, but taken from his [Wild's] own mouth, and collected from papers of his own writing." The tract included Defoe's own brief encounter with Wild, but it drew primarily on interviews with victims and jailers, and even with the underlings in Wild's crime ring. Moll King, mentioned at the beginning of this excerpt, was a source for Defoe's novel, *Moll Flanders.*

Defoe was modern not only in the thoroughness of his reporting but in the scenic organization of his story. One long conversation, reprinted here, provides a dramatic reconstruction of Wild's chicanery, showing how he played on the sympathies of well-to-do robbery victims even as he terrorized the thieves in his employ. Literary details abound, such as the "Calli-mancoe night-gown"—the woolen robe in which Wild conducted his business, and in which he was later hanged. That execution scene is memorable not for any description of the hanging but for its images of a doped-up prisoner and an impatient crowd.

Defoe's tract helped to make Jonathan Wild a legendary figure. In 1728 Wild was incarnated as Peachum in John Gay's play *The Beggar's Opera*. In 1742 he became the protagonist of Henry Fielding's novel *The Life of Mr. Jonathan Wild the Great,* which turned his criminality into political satire. Defoe's goal was more modest—a factual story with occasional moral observations—but in achieving it, he created a prototype of the modern true-crime narrative.

—K. K.

∞

[W]hen ever any person came to enquire for his goods lost, he could make a tolerable guess at the thief by the quarter of the town you lived in, or where you were when you lost it. . . .

[One] case related to a gold watch, with trinkets and some diamonds about either the watch, and the lady offered very considerably for the restoring it, as I remember, £30, but no advertisements had been published. Mr. Wild, after the usual enquiries of when it was lost, and where; and being told it was at St. Ann's church, Westminster, pauses a while, and calls up a servant and asks aloud, "where was M——ll K——g last Sunday?" "About Westminster," says the man, "but the bi——h would not tell where." "Was she crank [pulling a confidence trick]?" says Mr. Wild. "I don't know," says the fellow. However, turning to the lady, says he, "Madam, I fancy I shall be able to serve you, and perhaps for less money than your ladyship speaks of. If it be M——ll K——g, that woman I have in my thoughts, as I believe 'tis, for she is a dexterous jade at the work, I'll have her safe before morning." The lady, full of compassion returns, "O sir! Don't take her up. I assure you I won't prosecute, I'll rather lose my watch than have any poor wretch hanged for it." "Why, madam," says Mr. Wild, "We can't talk with her but by threatening. We must not make a bargain with her; that would be to compound a felony. If I can persuade her to come and bring your watch and ask your pardon, will that satisfy you?" "Nay," says the lady, "I don't know whether that would be safe neither. If she will send it me, I had rather. And I'll forgive her, without asking pardon." "Well, madam, will you take it and give the porter that brings it 20 guineas, if you please, but not to oblige you to it." "Whatever you say, Mr. Wild," says the lady. "Well madam," says Mr. Wild, "if I may have the honour to see your ladyship again."

Lady: Will it not do if I send anybody?

Wild: Why, truly, no madam: People that deal in these things do not care for witnesses.

Lady: Well, well, that's true. I'll come myself. What day would you have me come?

Wild: On Thursday, madam.

Lady: Well, Mr. Wild, what must I do? What will satisfy you for your trouble?

Wild: It is time enough, madam, to speak of that when I am sure I can do you any service. These creatures are very loose, and I can't tell you how it may be.

Lady: Well, Mr. Wild, I'll come furnished to pay my respects to you.

Wild: Madam, your most obedient servant.

(Waits on her to her coach.)

Accordingly, Thursday coming, the Lady appears. Mr. Wild in his Callimancoe night-gown, (the same he was hanged in) receives her; and with a pleasant look tells her he is very glad to be able to say that he believes he shall serve her. That it was the same woman he suspected, and that the jade had already pawned the watch for some money, but that it was but a little, and he was glad she had.

Lady: Why, Mr. Wild?

Wild: Because, madam, if she had kept it all this while, it would have been ten to one but she had broke something about it, or done it some mischief.

Lady: That's true, indeed. Pray, what has she pawned it for?

Wild: Not much, madam, she has got but seven guineas upon it yet.

Lady: Well, Mr. Wild, what must be done?

Wild: Why, madam, if the people that have it, bring it safe and sound to your ladyship, will you give me your honour that you will ask no questions, or stop the person that comes with it?

Lady: I promise you, on my word, I will not.

Wild: The man that brings it may be a poor innocent fellow that knows nothing of it.

Lady: Well, well, he shall have no harm or interruption from me.

Wild: Then I believe your ladyship may hear something of it tonight.

Lady: And what must I give him?

Wild: I don't yet know, madam, but I'll bring them as low as I can. Not above 20 guineas, to be sure, madam.

Lady: That is very kind indeed. Well, Mr. Wild, then I'll make it up to you. *(So the lady pulls out her purse in order to give him some money.)*

Wild: No, madam, not a farthing. Besides, you have not got your watch yet. Pray stay till you see whether the jade will perform; though I think, indeed, I am pretty sure of her.

Lady: Well, I'll take your word, Mr. Wild.

(Offers him money again.)

Wild: By no means, madam. Let me see if I can serve you.

Lady: Well, Mr. Wild, if it must be so, I must come again then.

Wild: It may be not. Will your ladyship be pleased to stay about half an hour?

Lady: Ay, with all my heart.

In about half an hour, Jonathan having been called hastily out, comes in again immediately. "Madam," says he, "if your ladyship pleases to go into your coach, and drive gently up ———street, perhaps a messenger may desire to speak with you as you go along."

"Very well, Mr. Wild, I understand you."

Upon the lady's going along ———street, a ticket-porter, with his hat in his hand, shows himself by the coach-side, and the lady taking the hint, stops her coach and lets down the glass, and speaking to the fellow, says, "Would you speak with me, friend?"

The fellow says not a word, but delivers into her hand the watch with all the trinkets and diamonds perfectly safe; and when she had looked upon it a little, gives her a note, wherein was written nothing but thus in words at length,

Eighteen Guineas.

The lady immediately tells out the money to the porter, and he was going away. "Hold, honest friend," says the lady, "there's somewhat for yourself," and gives him half a guinea, and so dismissed him.

A day or two after she makes Mr. Wild a visit, and presents him with 15 guineas more. But with great difficulty made him accept of it; telling her it was a great deal too much; that he would not take it by any means, but at last accepts it, with the ceremony of saying he would not take it on account of the watch, but for having been at some trouble in serving her ladyship, in which she was pleased to reward him much more than he deserved. When at the same time 'twas very likely [Wild] had part of the 18 guineas too from M——ll K——g, who he frighted out of the watch with threatening to have her put into Newgate for stealing of it. . . .

. . . We come now to his behaviour after this condemnation, and at the place of execution; at which last place he indeed scarce said a word to God or man, being either dozed with the liquid laudanum which he had taken, or demented and confused by the horror of what was before him, and the reflection of what was within him. Nor even before he took the dose of laudanum was he in any suitable manner sensible of his condition, or concerned about it, very little sign appeared of his having the least hope concerning his future state. But as he lived hardened, he seemed to die stupid. He declined coming to the chapel, either to the sermon or prayers, pleading his lameness by the gout, but chiefly the crowds and disorders of the people discomposing or disordering him. In the condemned hold, or place where malefactors are kept after their sentence, they had prayers as usual; and he seemed to join with them in a kind of form, but little or nothing of the penitence of a criminal, in view of death, appeared upon him. His principal enquiries seemed to be about what kind of state was to be expected after death, and how the invisible world was to be described; but nothing of the most certain judgement which is there to be expected, righteous and terrible, according to the deeds done in the body, or of a saviour to whom to have recourse, as the slayer in the old law had to the city of refuge, to save him from the avenger of blood. As his time shortened he seemed more and more confused, and then began to entertain discourses of the lawfulness of dismissing ourselves out of the present misery, after the example of the ancient Romans, which, as he said, was then esteemed as an act of bravery and gallantry, and recorded to their honour.

This kind of discourse was indeed sufficient to have caused the keepers to have had an eye to him, so as to prevent any violence he might offer to himself, and they did watch him as narrowly as they could. However, he so far deceived them, as that the day before his execution he found means to have a small bottle with the liquid laudanum conveyed to him unseen, of which he took so large a quantity, that it was soon perceived by the change it made upon him, for he was so drowsy that he could not hold up his head, or keep open his eyes, at the time of reading the prayers. Upon this two of his fellow prisoners endeavoured to rouse him (not suspecting that he had taken enough to hurt him) and taking him by the hands, they persuaded him to stand up, and walk a little about the room, which he could not do without help because of his gout. This walking, though it did a little waken him, had several other operations at the same time. For first it changed his countenance, turning it to be exceeding pale, then it put him into a violent sweat, which made them apprehend he would faint, upon which they offered to give him something to keep up his spirits, but he refused it, telling them he was very sick; soon after which he vomited very violently, and this in all probability prolonged his life for the execution. For by their stirring him, and making him vomit, he brought up the greatest part of the laudanum which he had taken, before it had been long enough in his stomach to mix with the animal spirits or blood, which if it had done but one hour more, he would certainly have taken his last sleep in the prison. But nature, having thus discharged itself of the load, he revived again, and though still dozed and insensible of what he said or did, yet he was able to walk about, speak, and act sufficiently for the part that remained to him, namely, for the last scene of his life at the gallows.

Accordingly on Monday the 24th of May, he was conveyed in a cart to Tyburn, and though it was apparent he was still under the operation of the laudanum, and that which was left in his stomach had so far seized upon his spirits as to make him almost stupid, yet it began to go off, and nature getting the mastery of it, he began to be more sensible of what he was going about; but the scene was then short, and he had little to do but to stand up in the cart, and, the needful apparatus being made, be turned off with the rest, which was done about 3 a-clock in the afternoon. The rudeness of the mob to him, both at his first going into the cart, and all the way from thence to the place of execution, is not to be expressed, and shows how

27

notorious his life had been, and what impression his known villainies had made on the minds of the people. For, contrary to the general behaviour of the street in such cases, instead of compassionate expressions, and a general cast of pity, which ordinarily sits on the countenances of the people, when they see the miserable objects of justice go to their execution; here was nothing to be heard but cursings and execrations. Abhorring the crimes and the very name of the man, throwing stones and dirt at him all the way, and even at the place of execution; the other malefactors being all ready to be turned off, but the hangman giving him leave to take his own time, and he continuing setting down in the cart, the mob impatient, and fearing a reprieve, though they had no occasion for it, called furiously upon the hangman to dispatch him, and at last threatened to tear him to pieces, if he did not tie him up immediately.

In short there was a kind of an universal rage against him, which nothing but his death could satisfy, or put an end to, and if a reprieve had come, it would have, twas thought, been difficult for the officers to have brought him back again without his receiving some mischief, if not his death's wound from the rabble. So detestable had he made himself by his notorious crimes, and to such a height were his wicked practices come.

Thus ended the tragedy, and thus was a life of horrid and inimitable wickedness finished at the gallows, the very same place where, according to some, above 120 miserable creatures had been hanged whose blood in great measure may be said to lie at his door, either in their being first brought into the thieving trade, or led on in it by his encouragement and assistance; and many of them at last betrayed and brought to justice by his means, upon which worst sort of murder he valued himself, and would have had it passed for merit, even with the government itself.

From *The Life of Samuel Johnson*

JAMES BOSWELL

∞

In the era when journalism was defined by distanced objectivity, the writings of James Boswell (1740–1795) would not have qualified: he was eager to express his opinions; he thrust himself into the narrative spotlight; and on occasion he blatantly stage-managed the action. It wasn't until the iconoclastic new journalism of the 1960s and '70s that reporters started permitting themselves such license, and Boswell deserves to be recognized as a progenitor of the movement. *The Life of Samuel Johnson* (1791), Boswell's masterwork, also anticipated what Tom Wolfe, in his essay "The New Journalism," called "scene-by-scene construction": the biography proceeds largely through theatrical set pieces, with copious dialogue and Wolfean "status details." Finally, Boswell's fascination with fame (he confessed to a "desire of being acquainted with celebrated men of every description") has a contemporary feel, prefiguring the rampant celebrity journalism of today.

Theorists of journalism have long noted parallels to Heisenberg's uncertainty principle in physics: by reporting on something, one subtly but irrevocably changes it. In this excerpt, Boswell throws subtlety aside and unabashedly tricks Dr. Johnson into having dinner with an archenemy, John Wilkes. Among the charms of the passage are the toothsome description of Wilkes serving veal to Johnson, Boswell's testiness over the anti-Scottish humor, and his (again) unabashed pleasure at his feat of matchmaking: "I exulted as much as a fortune-hunter who has got an heiress into a post-chaise with him to set out for Gretna-Green."

—B. Y.

∞

I am now to record a very curious incident in Dr. Johnson's life, which fell under my own observation; and which I am persuaded will, with the liberal-minded, be much to his credit.

My desire of being acquainted with celebrated men of every description, had made me, much about the same time, obtain an introduction to Dr. Samuel Johnson and to John Wilkes, Esq. Two men more different could perhaps not be selected out of all mankind. They had even attacked one another with some asperity in their writings; yet I lived in habits of friendship with both. I conceived an irresistible wish, if possible, to bring Dr. Johnson and Mr. Wilkes together. How to manage it, was a nice and difficult matter.

My worthy booksellers and friends, Messieurs Dilly in the Poultry, at whose hospitable and well-covered table I have seen a greater number of literary men, than at any other, except that of Sir Joshua Reynolds, had invited me to meet Mr. Wilkes and some more gentlemen on Wednesday, May 15. "Pray (said I,) let us have Dr. Johnson."—"What, with Mr. Wilkes? not for the world, (said Mr. Edward Dilly:) Dr. Johnson would never forgive me."— "Come, (said I,) if you'll let me negociate for you, I will be answerable that all shall go well." DILLY: "Nay, if you will take it upon you, I am sure I shall be very happy to see them both here."

Notwithstanding the high veneration which I entertained for Dr. Johnson, I was sensible that he was sometimes a little actuated by the spirit of contradiction, and by means of that I hoped I should gain my point. I was persuaded that if I had come upon him with a direct proposal, "Sir, will you dine in company with Jack Wilkes?" he would have flown into a passion, and would probably have answered, "Dine with Jack Wilkes, Sir! I'd as soon dine with Jack Ketch." I therefore, while we were sitting quietly by ourselves at his house in an evening, took occasion to open my plan thus:—"Mr. Dilly, Sir, sends his respectful compliments to you, and would be happy if you would do him the honour to dine with him on Wednesday next along with me, as I must soon go to Scotland." JOHNSON: "Sir, I am obliged to Mr. Dilly. I will wait upon him—" BOSWELL: "Provided, Sir, I suppose, that the company which he is to have, is agreeable to you." JOHNSON: "What do you mean, Sir? What do you take me for? Do you think I am so ignorant of the world, as to imagine that I am to prescribe to a gentleman what company he is to have at his table?" BOSWELL: "I beg your pardon, Sir, for wishing to prevent you from meeting people whom you might not like. Perhaps he may have some of what he calls his patriotick friends with him." JOHNSON: "Well, Sir, and what then? What care I for his *patriotick friends*? Poh!" BOSWELL: "I should not be surprised to find Jack Wilkes there." JOHNSON: "And if Jack Wilkes should be there, what is that to *me*, Sir? My dear friend, let us have no more of this. I am sorry to be angry with you; but really it is treating me strangely to talk to me as if I could not meet any company whatever, occasionally." BOSWELL: "Pray forgive me, Sir: I meant well. But you shall meet whoever comes, for me." Thus I secured him, and told Dilly that he would find him very well pleased to be one of his guests on the day appointed.

Upon the much-expected Wednesday, I called on him about half an hour before dinner, as I often did when we were to dine out together, to see that he was ready in time, and to accompany him. I found him buffeting his books, as upon a former occasion, covered with dust, and making no preparation for going abroad. "How is this, Sir? (said I.) Don't you recollect that you are to dine at Mr. Dilly's?" JOHNSON: "Sir, I did not think of going to Dilly's: it went out of my head. I have ordered dinner at home with Mrs. Williams." BOSWELL: "But, my dear Sir, you know you were engaged to Mr. Dilly, and I told him so. He will expect you, and will be much disappointed if you don't come." JOHNSON: "You must talk to Mrs. Williams about this."

Here was a sad dilemma. I feared that what I was so confident I had secured would yet be frustrated. He had accustomed himself to shew Mrs. Williams such a degree of humane attention, as frequently imposed some restraint upon him; and I knew that if she should be obstinate, he would not stir. I hastened down stairs to the blind lady's room, and told her I was in great uneasiness, for Dr. Johnson had engaged to me to dine this day at Mr. Dilly's, but that he had told me he had forgotten his engagement, and had ordered dinner at home. "Yes, Sir, (said she, pretty peevishly,) Dr. Johnson is to dine at home"—"Madam, (said I,) his respect for you is such, that I know he will not leave you unless you absolutely desire it. But as you have so much of his company, I hope you will be good enough to forego it for a day; as Mr. Dilly is a very worthy man, has frequently had agreeable parties at his house for Dr. Johnson, and will be vexed if the Doctor neglects him to-day. And then, Madam, be pleased to consider my situation; I carried the message, and I assured Mr. Dilly that Dr. Johnson was to come, and no doubt he has made a dinner, and invited a company, and boasted of the honour he expected to have. I shall be quite disgraced if the Doctor is not there." She gradually softened to my solicitations, which were certainly as earnest as most entreaties to ladies upon any occasion, and was graciously pleased to empower me to tell Dr. Johnson, "That all things considered, she thought he should certainly go." I flew back to him, still in dust, and careless of what should be the event, "indifferent in his choice to go or stay"; but as soon as I had announced to him Mrs. Williams's consent, he roared, "Frank, a clean shirt," and was very soon drest. When I had him fairly seated in a hackney-coach with me, I exulted as much as a fortune-hunter who has got an heiress into a post-chaise with him to set out for Gretna-Green.

When we entered Mr. Dilly's drawing room, he found himself in the midst of a company he did not know. I kept myself snug and silent, watching how he would conduct himself. I observed him whispering to Mr. Dilly, "Who is that gentleman, Sir?"—"Mr. Arthur Lee."—JOHNSON: "Too, too, too," (under his breath,) which was one of his habitual mutterings. Mr. Arthur Lee could not but be very obnoxious to Johnson, for he was not only a *patriot* but an *American*. He was afterwards minister from the United States at the court of Madrid. "And who is the gentleman in lace?"—"Mr. Wilkes, Sir." This information confounded him still more; he had some difficulty to restrain himself, and taking up a book, sat down upon a window-seat and read, or at least kept his eye upon it intently for some time, till he composed himself. His feelings, I dare say, were awkward enough. But he no doubt recollected his having rated me for supposing that he could be at all disconcerted by any company, and he, therefore, resolutely set himself to behave quite as an easy man of the world, who could adapt himself at once to the disposition and manners of those whom he might chance to meet.

The cheering sound of "Dinner is upon the table," dissolved his reverie, and we *all* sat down without any symptom of ill humour. . . . Mr. Wilkes placed himself next to Dr. Johnson, and behaved to him with so much attention and politeness, that he gained upon him insensibly. No man eat more heartily than Johnson, or loved better what was nice and delicate. Mr. Wilkes was very assiduous in helping him to some fine veal. "Pray give me leave, Sir:—It is better here—A little of the brown—Some fat, Sir—A little of the stuffing—Some gravy—Let me have the pleasure of giving you some butter—Allow me to recommend a squeeze of this orange;—or the lemon, perhaps, may have more zest."—"Sir, Sir, I am obliged to you, Sir," cried Johnson, bowing, and turning his head to him with a look for some time of "surly virtue," but, in a short while, of complacency. . . .

Talking of the great difficulty of obtaining authentick information for biography, Johnson told us, "When I was a young fellow I wanted to write the *Life of Dryden,* and in order to get materials, I applied to the only two persons then alive who had seen him; these were old Swinney, and old Cibber. Swinney's information was no more than this, 'That at Will's coffee-house Dryden had a particular chair for himself, which was set by the fire in winter, and was then called his winter-chair; and that it was carried out for him to the balcony in summer, and was then called his summer-chair.' Cibber could tell no more but 'That he remembered him a decent old man, arbiter of critical disputes at Will's.' You are to consider that Cibber was then at a great distance from Dryden, had perhaps one leg only in the room, and durst not draw in the other."

Mr. Arthur Lee mentioned some Scotch who had taken possession of a barren part of America, and wondered why they should choose it. JOHNSON: "Why, Sir, all barrenness is comparative. The *Scotch* would not know it to be barren." BOSWELL: "Come, come, he is flattering the English. You have now been in Scotland, Sir, and say if you did not see meat and drink enough there." JOHNSON: "Why yes, Sir; meat and drink enough to give the inhabitants sufficient strength to run away from home." All these quick and lively sallies were said sportively, quite in jest, and with a smile, which showed that he meant only wit. Upon this topick he and Mr. Wilkes could perfectly assimilate; here was a bond of union between them, and I was conscious that as both of them had visited Caledonia, both were fully satisfied of the strange narrow ignorance of those who imagine that it is a land of famine. But they amused themselves with persevering in the old jokes. When I claimed a superiority for Scotland over England in one respect, that no man can be arrested there for a debt merely because another swears it against him; but there must first be the judgement of a court of law ascertaining its justice; and that a seizure of the person, before judgement is obtained, can take place only, if his creditor should swear that he is about to fly from the country, or, as it is technically expressed, *in meditatione figae:* WILKES: "That, I should think, may be safely sworn of all the Scotch nation." JOHNSON: (to Mr. Wilkes,) "You must know, Sir, I lately took my friend Boswell and shewed him genuine civilised life in an English provincial town. I turned him loose at Lichfield, my native city, that he might see for once real civility: for you know he lives among savages in Scotland, and among rakes in London." WILKES: "Except when he is with grave, sober, decent people like you and me." JOHNSON: (smiling,) "And we ashamed of him."

They were quite frank and easy. Johnson told the story of his asking Mrs. Macaulay to allow her footman to sit down with them, to prove the ridiculousness of the argument for the equality of mankind; and he said to me afterwards, with a nod of satisfaction, "You saw Mr. Wilkes acquiesced."

After dinner we had an accession of Mrs. Knowles, the Quaker lady, well known for her various talents, and of Mr. Alderman Lee. Amidst some patriotick groans, somebody (I think the Alderman) said, "Poor old England is lost." JOHNSON: "Sir, it is not so much to be lamented that Old England is lost, as that the Scotch have found it." Mr. Wilkes held a candle to shew a fine print of a beautiful female figure which hung in the room, and pointed out the elegant contour of the bosom with the finger of an arch connoisseur. He afterwards, in a conversation with me, waggishly insisted, that all the time Johnson shewed visible signs of a fervent admiration of the corresponding charms of the fair Quaker.

This record, though by no means so perfect as I could wish, will serve to give a notion of a very curious interview, which was not only pleasing at the time, but had the agreeable and benignant effect of reconciling any animosity, and sweetening any acidity, which in the various bustle of political contest, had been produced in the minds of two men, who though widely different, had so many things in common—classical learning, modern literature, wit, and humour, and ready repartee—that it would have been much to be regretted if they had been for ever at a distance from each other.

Mr. Burke gave me much credit for this successful *negociation;* and pleasantly said, that "there was nothing to equal it in the whole history of the *Corps Diplomatique.*"

Watercress Girl

HENRY MAYHEW

❧

The literary career of Henry Mayhew (1812–1887) included stints as a novelist, travel writer, educator, magazine editor, and satirist. In 1841 Mayhew cofounded *Punch,* the great Victorian comic weekly. In 1849, when he became "Metropolitan Correspondent" for the London *Morning Chronicle,* he discovered his true vocation.

Mayhew's tales of the city focused on lives stunted by economic hardship, illuminating them through vivid details and fresh reporting. According to the novelist William Thackeray, Mayhew presented "a picture of human life so wonderful, so awful, so piteous and pathetic, so exciting and terrible, that readers of romances own they never read anything like to it."

One of Mayhew's innovations resulted from the limits of newspaper space: he edited out his own questions and wove the interviewee's words into a continuous testimony, a kind of life statement, a dramatic monologue in prose. He preserved authentic tones and turns of phrase ("I bears the cold—you must") but reorganized them for dramatic emphasis, especially at the end of each story. Today Mayhew's method is most familiar in the books of Chicago journalist Studs Terkel (*Working*), but it also underlies the whole genre of oral history.

Mayhew saw his work as a venture in practical social science, and in 1861–62 he published *London Labour and the London Poor,* a four-volume survey of the city's "street people," categorized by occupation and caste. But his style remained more literary than sociological, informed by respect for "the heroism of the unknown poor" and by an artist's eye for archetypes rather than stereotypes.

—K. K.

❧

The little watercress girl who gave me the following statement, although only eight years of age, had entirely lost all childish ways, and was, indeed, in thoughts and manner, a woman. There was something cruelly pathetic in hearing this infant, so young that her features had scarcely formed themselves, talking of the bitterest struggles of life, with the calm earnestness of one who had endured them all. I did not know how to talk with her. At first I treated her as a child, speaking on childish subjects; so that I might, by being familiar with her, remove all shyness, and get her to narrate her life freely. I asked her about her toys and her games with her companions; but the look of amazement that answered me soon put an end to any attempt at fun on my part. I then talked to her about the parks, and whether she ever went to them. "The parks!" she replied in wonder, "where are they?" I explained to her, telling her that they were large open places with green grass and tall trees, where beautiful carriages drove about, and people walked for pleasure, and children played. Her eyes brightened up a little as I spoke; and she asked, half doubtingly, "Would they let such as me go there—just to look?" All her knowledge seemed to begin and end with watercresses, and what they fetched. She knew no more of London than that part she had seen on her rounds, and believed that no quarter of the town was handsomer or pleasanter than it was at Farringdon-market or at Clerkenwell, where she lived. Her little face, pale and thin with privation, was wrinkled where the dimples ought to have been, and she would sigh frequently. When some hot dinner was offered to her, she would not touch it, because, if she eat too much, "it made her sick," she said; "and she wasn't used to meat, only on a Sunday."

The poor child, although the weather was severe, was dressed in a thin cotton gown, with a threadbare shawl wrapped round her shoulders. She wore no covering to her head, and the long rusty hair stood out in all directions. When she walked she shuffled along, for fear that the large carpet slippers that served her for shoes should slip off her feet.

"I go about the streets with water-creases, crying, 'Four bunches a penny, water-creases.' I am just eight years old—that's all, and I've a big sister, and a brother, and a sister younger than I am. On and off, I've been very near a twelvemonth in the streets. Before that, I had to take care of a baby for my aunt. No, it wasn't heavy—it was only two months old; but I minded it for ever such a time—till it could walk. It was a very nice baby, not a very pretty one; but, if I touched it under the chin, it would laugh. Before I had the baby, I used to help mother, who was in the fur trade; and, if there was any slits in the fur, I'd sew them up. My mother learned me to needle-work and to knit when I was about five. I used to go to school, too; but I wasn't there long. I've forgot all about it now, it's such a time ago; and mother took me away because the master whacked me, though the missus use'n't to never touch me. I didn't like him at all. What do you think? he hit me three times, ever so hard, across the face with his cane, and made me go dancing down stairs; and when mother saw the marks on my cheek, she went to blow him up, but she couldn't see him—he was afraid. That's why I left school.

"The creases is so bad now, that I haven't been out with 'em for three days. They're so cold, people won't buy 'em; for when I goes up to them, they say, 'They'll freeze our bellies.' Besides, in the market, they won't sell a ha'penny handful now—they're ris to a penny and tuppence. In summer there's lots, and 'most as cheap as dirt; but I have to be down at Farringdon-market between four and five, or else I can't get any creases, because every-one almost—especially the Irish—is selling them, and they're picked up so quick. Some of the saleswomen—we never calls 'em ladies—is very kind to us children, and some of them altogether spiteful. The good one will give you a bunch for nothing, when they're cheap; but the others, cruel ones, if you try to bate them a farden less than they ask you, will say, 'Go along with you, you're no good.' I used to go down to market along with another girl, as must be about fourteen, 'cos she does her back hair up. When we've bought a lot, we sits down on a door-step, and ties up the bunches. We never goes home to breakfast till we've sold out; but, if it's very late, then I buys a penn'orth of pudden, which is very nice with gravy. I don't know hardly one of the people, as goes to Farringdon, to talk to; they never speaks to me, so I don't speak to them. We children never play down there, 'cos we're thinking of our living. No; people never pities me in the street—excepting one gen-tleman, and he says, says he, 'What do you do out so soon in the morning?' but he gave me nothink—he only walked away.

"It's very cold before winter comes on reg'lar—specially getting up of a morning. I gets up in the dark by the light of the lamp in the court. When the snow is on the ground, there's no creases. I bears the cold—you must; so I puts my hands under my shawl, though it hurts 'em to take hold of the creases, especially when we takes 'em to the pump to wash 'em. No; I never see any children crying—it's no use.

"Sometimes I make a great deal of money. One day I took 1s. 6d., and the creases cost 6d.; but it isn't often I get such luck as that. I oftener makes 3d. or 4d. than 1s.: and then I'm at work, crying, 'Creases, four bunches a penny, creases!' from six in the morning to about ten. What do you mean by mechanics?—I don't know what they are. The shops buys most of me. Some of 'em says, 'Oh! I ain't a-goin' to give a penny for these'; and they want 'em at the same price as I buys 'em at.

"I always give mother my money, she's so very good to me. She don't often beat me; but, when she do, she don't play with me. She's very poor, and goes out cleaning rooms sometimes, now she don't work at the fur. I ain't got no father, he's a father-in-law. No; mother ain't married again—he's a father-in-law. He grinds scissors, and he's very good to me. No; I don't mean by that that he says kind things to me, for he never hardly speaks. When I gets home, after selling creases, I stops at home. I puts the room to rights: mother don't make me do it, I does it myself. I cleans the chairs, though there's only two to clean. I takes a tub and scrubbing-brush and flannel, and scrubs the floor—that's what I do three or four times a week.

"I don't have no dinner. Mother gives me two slices of bread-and-butter and a cup of tea for breakfast, and then I go till tea, and has the same. We has meat of a Sunday, and, of course, I should like to have it every day. Mother has just the same to eat as we has, but she takes more tea—three cups, sometimes. No; I never has no sweet-stuff; I never buy none—I don't like it. Sometimes we has a game of 'honey-pots' with the girls in the court, but not often. Me and Carry H——carries the little 'uns. We plays, too, at 'kiss-in-the-ring.' I knows a good many games, but I don't play at 'em, 'cos going out with creases tires me. On a Friday night, too, I goes to a Jew's house till eleven o'clock on Saturday night. All I has to do is to snuff the candles and poke the fire. You see they keep their Sabbath then, and they won't touch anything; so they gives me my wittals and 1 1/2d., and I does it for 'em. I have a reg'lar good lot to eat. Supper of Friday night, and tea after that, and fried fish of a Saturday morning, and meat for dinner, and tea, and supper, and I like it very well.

"Oh, yes; I've got some toys at home. I've a fire-place, and a box of toys, and a knife and fork, and two little chairs. The Jews gave 'em to me where I go to on a Friday, and that's why I said they was very kind to me. I never had no doll; but I misses little sister—she's only two years old. We don't sleep in the same room; for father and mother sleeps with little sister in the one pair, and me and brother and other sister sleeps in the top room. I always goes to bed at seven, 'cos I has to be up so early.

"I am a capital hand at bargaining—but only at buying water-creases. They can't take me in. If the woman tries to give me a small handful of creases, I says, 'I ain't a goin' to have that for a ha'porth,' and I go to the next basket, and so on, all round. I know the quantities very well. For a penny I ought to have a full market hand, or as much as I could carry in my arms at one time, without spilling. For 3d. I has a lap full, enough to earn about a shilling; and for 6d. I gets as many as crams my basket. I can't read or write, but I knows how many pennies goes to a shilling, why, twelve, of course, but I don't know how many ha'pence there is, though there's two to a penny. When I've bought 3d. of creases, I ties 'em up into as many little bundles as I can. They must look biggish, or the people won't buy them, some puffs them out as much as they'll go. All my money I earns I puts in a club and draws it out to buy clothes with. It's better than spending it in sweet-stuff, for them as has a living to earn. Besides it's like a child to care for sugar-sticks, and not like one who's got a living and vittals to earn. I ain't a child, and I shan't be a woman till I'm twenty, but I'm past eight, I am. I don't know nothing about what I earns during the year, I only know how many pennies goes to a shilling, and two ha'pence goes to a penny, and four fardens goes to a penny. I knows, too, how many fardens goes to tuppence—eight. That's as much as I wants to know for the markets."

The *Great Tasmania*'s Cargo

CHARLES DICKENS

❧

Charles Dickens (1812–1870) started his career as a reporter of debates in the house of Commons, and a certain journalistic fervor informs his novels, as they insinuate their way into the hidden cracks of society and shine a great light on them. In 1860, having achieved international success as a novelist, he returned to nonfiction in a series of articles published in his weekly periodical *All the Year Round*, adopting the persona "the Uncommercial Traveller." ("Figuratively speaking, I travel for the great house of Human Interest Brothers," he wrote in the preface to the collection of these pieces.) In "The *Great Tasmania*'s Cargo," he tries to find the truth behind a well-publicized incident in which British soldiers in India, after perceived insubordination, had been imprisoned and shipped home under very hard conditions.

Dickens is an unmistakable presence in his journalism, and not only because, as with the Circumlocution Office, transposed from *Little Dorrit* to "The *Great Tasmania*'s Cargo," he reprises conceits used in his novels. We also recognize the moral fervor, the rhetorical flights, the Manichaean world populated by obfuscating scoundrels and put-upon saints. Less expected (but not surprising, considering those days in Commons) is his reportorial rigor. Dicken's interlocution of the good sergeant toward the end of the piece could be used as a model in a journalism school lecture on interviewing. And while his "official friend" Pangloss is a composite character named for the incurably optimistic tutor in Voltaire's *Candide*, and thus not kosher by today's standards, he shows Dickens's mastery of the classic reporter's strategy of simultaneously eliciting and deriding the official view.

—B. Y.

❧

I travel constantly, up and down a certain line of railway that has a terminus in London. It is the railway for a large military depôt, and for other large barracks. To the best of my serious belief, I have never been on that railway by daylight, without seeing some handcuffed deserters in the train.

It is in the nature of things that such an institution as our English army should have many bad and troublesome characters in it. But, this is a reason for, and not against, its being made as acceptable as possible to well-disposed men of decent behaviour. Such men are assuredly not tempted into the ranks, by the beastly inversion of natural laws, and the compulsion to live in worse than swinish foulness. Accordingly, when any such Circumlocutional embellishments of the soldier's condition have of late been brought to notice, we civilians, seated in outer darkness cheerfully meditating on an Income Tax, have considered the matter as being our business, and have shown a tendency to declare that we would rather not have it misregulated, if such declaration may, without violence to the Church Catechism, be hinted to those who are put in authority over us.

Any animated description of a modern battle, any private soldier's letter published in the newspapers, any page of the records of the Victoria Cross, will show that in the ranks of the army, there exists under all disadvantages as fine a sense of duty as is to be found in any station on earth. Who doubts that if we all did our duty as faithfully as the soldier does his, this world would be a better place? There may be greater difficulties in our way than in the soldier's. Not disputed. But, let us at least do our duty towards *him*.

I had got back again to that rich and beautiful port where I had looked after Mercantile Jack, and I was walking up a hill there, on a wild March morning. My conversation with my official friend Pangloss, by whom I was accidentally accompanied, took this direction as we took the up-hill direction, because the object of my uncommercial journey was to see some discharged soldiers who had recently come home from India. . . . [T]here were men who had been in many of the great battles of the great Indian campaign, among them; and I was curious to note what our discharged soldiers looked like, when they were done with.

I was not the less interested (as I mentioned to my official friend Pangloss) because these men had claimed to be discharged, when their right to be discharged was not admitted. They had behaved with unblemished fidelity and bravery; but, a change of circumstances had arisen, which, as they considered, put an end to their compact and entitled them to enter on a new one. Their demand had been blunderingly resisted by the authorities in India; but, it is to be presumed that the men were not far wrong, inasmuch as the bungle had ended in their being sent home discharged, in pursuance of orders from home. (There was an immense waste of money, of course.)

Under these circumstances—thought I, as I walked up the hill, on which I accidentally encountered my official friend—under these circumstances of the men having successfully opposed themselves to the Pagoda Department of that great Circumlocution Office on which the sun never sets and the light of reason never rises, the Pagoda Department will have been particularly careful of the national honour. It will have shown these men, in the scrupulous good faith, not to say the generosity, of its dealing with them, that great national authorities can have no small retaliations and revenges. It will have made every provision for their health on the passage home, and will have landed them, restored from their campaigning fatigues by a sea-voyage, pure air, sound food, and good medicines. And I pleased myself with dwelling beforehand, on the great accounts of their personal treatment which these men would carry into their various towns and villages, and on the increasing popularity of the service that would insensibly follow. I almost began to hope that the hitherto-never-failing deserters on my railroad would by-and-by become a phenomenon.

In this agreeable frame of mind I entered the workhouse of Liverpool.— For, the cultivation of laurels in a sandy soil, had brought the soldiers in question to *that* abode of Glory.

Before going into their wards to visit them, I inquired how they had made their triumphant entry there? They had been brought through the rain in carts, it seemed, from the landing-place to the gate, and had then been carried up-stairs on the backs of paupers. Their groans and pains during the performance of this glorious pageant, had been so distressing, as to bring tears into the eyes of spectators but too well accustomed to scenes of suffering. The men were so dreadfully cold, that those who could get near the fires were hard to be restrained from thrusting their feet in among the blazing coals. They were so horribly reduced, that they were awful to look upon. Racked with dysentery and blackened with scurvy, one hundred and forty wretched soldiers had been revived with brandy and laid in bed.

My official friend Pangloss is lineally descended from a learned doctor of that name, who was once tutor to Candide, an ingenious young gentleman of some celebrity. In his personal character, he is as humane and worthy a gentleman as any I know; in his official capacity, he unfortunately preaches the doctrines of his renowned ancestor, by demonstrating on all occasions that we live in the best of all possible official worlds.

"In the name of Humanity," said I, "how did the men fall into this deplorable state? Was the ship well found in stores?"

"I am not here to asseverate that I know the fact, of my own knowledge," answered Pangloss, "but I have grounds for asserting that the stores were the best of all possible stores."

A medical officer laid before us a handful of rotten biscuit, and a handful of split peas. The biscuit was a honeycombed heap of maggots, and the excrement of maggots. The peas were even harder than this filth. A similar handful had been experimentally boiled six hours, and had shown no signs of softening. These were the stores on which the soldiers had been fed.

"The beef—" I began, when Pangloss cut me short.

"Was the best of all possible beef," said he.

But, behold, there was laid before us certain evidence given at the Coroner's Inquest, holden on some of the men (who had obstinately died of their treatment), and from that evidence it appeared that the beef was the worst of possible beef!

"Then I lay my hand upon my heart, and take my stand," said Pangloss, "by the pork, which was the best of all possible pork."

"But look at this food before our eyes, if one may so misuse the word," said I. "Would any Inspector who did his duty, pass such abomination?"

"It ought not to have been passed," Pangloss admitted.

"Then the authorities out there—" I began, when Pangloss cut me short again.

"There would certainly seem to have been something wrong somewhere," said he; "but I am prepared to prove that the authorities out there, are the best of all possible authorities."

I never heard of any impeached public authority in my life, who was not the best public authority in existence.

"We are told of these unfortunate men being laid low by scurvy," said I. "Since lime-juice has been regularly stored and served out in our navy, surely that disease, which used to devastate it, has almost disappeared? Was there lime-juice aboard this transport?"

My official friend was beginning "the best of all possible—" when an inconvenient medical forefinger pointed out another passage in the evidence, from which it appeared that the lime-juice had been bad too. Not to mention that the vinegar had been bad too, the vegetables bad too, the cooking accommodation insufficient (if there had been anything worth mentioning to cook), the water supply exceedingly inadequate, and the beer sour.

"Then the men," said Pangloss, a little irritated, "were the worst of all possible men."

"In what respect?" I asked.

"Oh! Habitual drunkards," said Pangloss.

But, again the same incorrigible medical forefinger pointed out another passage in the evidence, showing that the dead men had been examined after death, and that they, at least, could not possibly have been habitual drunkards, because the organs within them which must have shown traces of that habit, were perfectly sound.

"And besides," said the three doctors present, one and all, "habitual drunkards brought as low as these men have been, could not recover under care and food, as the great majority of these men are recovering. They would not have strength of constitution to do it."

"Reckless and improvident dogs, then," said Pangloss. "Always are—nine times out of ten."

I turned to the master of the workhouse, and asked him whether the men had any money?

THE ART OF FACT

"Money?" said he. "I have in my iron safe, nearly four hundred pounds of theirs; the agents have nearly a hundred pounds more; and many of them have left money in Indian banks besides."

"Hah!" said I to myself, as we went up-stairs, "this is not the best of all possible stories, I doubt!"

We went into a large ward, containing some twenty or five-and-twenty beds. We went into several such wards, one after another. I find it very difficult to indicate what a shocking sight I saw in them, without frightening the reader from the perusal of these lines, and defeating my object of making it known.

O the sunken eyes that turned to me as I walked between the rows of beds, or—worse still—that glazedly looked at the white ceiling, and saw nothing and cared for nothing! Here, lay the skeleton of a man, so lightly covered with a thin unwholesome skin, that not a bone in the anatomy was clothed, and I could clasp the arm above the elbow, in my finger and thumb. Here, lay a man with the black scurvy eating his legs away, his gums gone, and his teeth all gaunt and bare. This bed was empty, because gangrene had set in, and the patient had died but yesterday. That bed was a hopeless one, because its occupant was sinking fast, and could only be roused to turn the poor pinched mask of face upon the pillow, with a feeble moan. The awful thinness of the fallen cheeks, the awful brightness of the deep set eyes, the lips of lead, the hands of ivory, the recumbent human images lying in the shadow of death with a kind of solemn twilight on them, like the sixty who had died aboard the ship and were lying at the bottom of the sea, O Pangloss, God forgive you!

In one bed, lay a man whose life had been saved (as it was hoped) by deep incisions in the feet and legs. While I was speaking to him, a nurse came up to change the poultices which this operation had rendered necessary, and I had an instinctive feeling that it was not well to turn away, merely to spare myself. He was sorely wasted and keenly susceptible, but the efforts he made to subdue any expression of impatience or suffering, were quite heroic. It was easy to see, in the shrinking of the figure, and the drawing of the bed-clothes over the head, how acute the endurance was, and it made me shrink too, as if I were in pain; but, when the new bandages were on, and the poor feet were composed again, he made an apology for himself (though he had not uttered a word), and said plaintively, "I am so tender and weak, you see, sir!" Neither from him nor from any one sufferer of the whole ghastly number, did I hear a complaint. Of thankfulness for present solicitude and care, I heard much; of complaint, not a word.

I think I could have recognised in the dismalest skeleton there, the ghost of a soldier. Something of the old air was still latent in the palest shadow of life I talked to. One emaciated creature, in the strictest literality worn to the bone, lay stretched on his back, looking so like death that I asked one of the doctors if he were not dying, or dead? A few kind words from the doctor, in his ear, and he opened his eyes, and smiled—looked, in a moment as if he would have made a salute, if he could. "We shall pull him through, please God," said the Doctor. "Plase God, surr; and thankye," said the patient. "You are much better today; are you not?" said the Doctor. "Plase God, surr; 'tis the slape I want, surr; 'tis my breathin' makes the nights so long." "He is a careful fellow this, you must know," said the Doctor, cheerfully; "it was raining hard when they put him in the open cart to bring him here, and he had the presence of mind to ask to have a sovereign taken out of his pocket that he had there, and a cab engaged. Probably it saved his life." The patient rattled out the skeleton of a laugh, and said, proud of the story, "Deed, surr, an open cairt was a comical means o' bringin' a dyin' man here, and a clever way to kill him." You might have sworn to him for a soldier when he said it.

One thing had perplexed me very much in going from bed to bed. A very significant and cruel thing. I could find no young man but one. He had attracted my notice, by having got up and dressed himself in his soldier's jacket and trousers, with the intention of sitting by the fire; but he had found himself too weak, and had crept back to his bed and laid himself down on the outside of it. I could have pronounced him, alone, to be a young man aged by famine and sickness. As we were standing by the Irish soldier's bed, I mentioned my perplexity to the Doctor. He took a board with an inscription on it from the head of the Irishman's bed, and asked me what age I supposed that man to be? I had observed him with attention while talking to him, and answered, confidently, "Fifty." The Doctor, with a pitying glance at the patient, who had dropped into a stupor again, put the board back, and said, "Twenty-four."

All the arrangements of the wards were excellent. They could not have been more humane, sympathising, gentle, attentive, or wholesome. The owners of the ship, too, had done all they could, liberally. There were bright fires in every room, and the convalescent men were sitting round them, reading various papers and periodicals. I took the liberty of inviting my official friend Pangloss to look at those convalescent men, and to tell me whether their faces and bearing were or were not, generally, the faces and bearing of steady respectable soldiers? The master of the workhouse, overhearing me, said he had had a pretty large experience of troops, and that better conducted men than these, he had never had to do with. They were always (he added) as we saw them. And of us visitors (I add) they knew nothing whatever, except that we were there.

It was audacious in me, but I took another liberty with Pangloss. Prefacing it with the observation that, of course, I knew beforehand that there was not the faintest desire, anywhere, to hush up any part of this dreadful business, and that the Inquest was the fairest of all possible Inquests, I besought four things of Pangloss. Firstly, to observe that the Inquest *was not held in that place*, but at some distance off. Secondly, to look round upon those helpless spectres in their beds. Thirdly, to remember that the witnesses produced from among them before that Inquest, could not have been selected because they were the men who had the most to tell it, but because they happened to be in a state admitting of their safe removal. Fourthly, to say whether the Coroner and Jury could have come there, to those pillows, and taken a little evidence? My official friend declined to commit himself to a reply.

There was a sergeant, reading, in one of the fireside groups. As he was a man of very intelligent countenance, and as I have great respect for non-commissioned officers as a class, I sat down on the nearest bed, to have some talk with him. (It was the bed of one of the grisliest of the poor skeletons, and he died soon afterwards.)

"I was glad to see, in the evidence of an officer at the Inquest, sergeant, that he never saw men behave better on board ship than these men."

"They did behave very well, sir."

"I was glad to see, too, that every man had a hammock."

The sergeant gravely shook his head. "There must be some mistake, sir. The men of my own mess had no hammocks. There were not hammocks enough on board, and the men of the two next messes laid hold of hammocks for themselves as soon as they got on board, and squeezed my men out, as I may say."

"Had the squeezed-out men none then?"

"None, sir. As men died, their hammocks were used by other men, who wanted hammocks; but many men had none at all."

"Then you don't agree with the evidence on that point?"

"Certainly not, sir. A man can't, when he knows to the contrary."

"Did any of the men sell their bedding for drink?"

"There is some mistake on that point too, sir. Men were under the impression—I knew it for a fact at the time—that it was not allowed to take blankets or bedding on board, and so men who had things of that sort came to sell them purposely."

"Did any of the men sell their clothes for drink?"

"They did, sir." (I believe there never was a more truthful witness than the sergeant. He had no inclination to make out a case.)

"Many?"

"Some, sir" (considering the question). "Soldier-like. They had been long marching in the rainy season, by bad roads—no roads at all, in short—and when they got to Calcutta, men turned to and drank, before taking a last look at it. Soldier-like."

"Do you see any men in this ward, for example, who sold clothes for drink at that time?"

The sergeant's wan eye, happily just beginning to rekindle with health, travelled round the place and came back to me. "Certainly, sir."

"The marching to Calcutta in the rainy season must have been severe?"

"It was very severe, sir."

"Yet what with the rest and the sea air, I should have thought that the men (even the men who got drunk) would have soon begun to recover on board ship?"

"So they might; but the bad food told upon them, and when we got into a cold latitude, it began to tell more, and the men dropped."

"The sick had a general disinclination for food, I am told, sergeant?"

"Have you seen the food, sir?"

"Some of it."

"Have you seen the state of their mouths, sir?"

If the sergeant, who was a man of a few orderly words, had spoken the amount of this volume, he could not have settled that question better. I believe the sick could as soon have eaten the ship, as the ship's provisions.

I took the additional liberty with my friend Pangloss, when I had left the sergeant with good wishes, of asking Pangloss whether he had ever heard of biscuit getting drunk and bartering its nutritious qualities for putrefaction and vermin; of peas becoming hardened in liquor; of hammocks drinking themselves off the face of the earth; of lime-juice, vegetables, vinegar, cooking accommodation, water supply, and beer, all taking to drinking together and going to ruin? "If not (I asked him), what did he say in defence of the officers condemned by the Coroner's Jury, who, by signing the General Inspection report relative to the ship *Great Tasmania*, chartered for these troops, had deliberately asserted all that bad and poisonous dunghill refuse, to be good and wholesome food?" My official friend replied that it was a remarkable fact, that whereas some officers were only positively good, and other officers only comparatively better, those particular officers were superlatively the very best of all possible officers.

My hand and my heart fail me, in writing my record of this journey. The spectacle of the soldiers in the hospital-beds of that Liverpool workhouse (a very good workhouse, indeed, be it understood), was so shocking and so shameful, that as an Englishman I blush to remember it. It would have been simply unbearable at the time, but for the consideration and pity with which they were soothed in their sufferings.

No punishment that our inefficient laws provide, is worthy of the name when set against the guilt of this transaction. But, if the memory of it die out unavenged, and if it do not result in the inexorable dismissal and disgrace of those who are responsible for it, their escape will be infamous to the Government (no matter of what party) that so neglects its duty, and infamous to the nation that tamely suffers such intolerable wrong to be done in its name.

From *Specimen Days*

WALT WHITMAN

〰

Walt Whitman's account of the 1863 Civil War battle of Chancellorsville (part of his book *Specimen Days*) unquestionably has literary qualities. Whitman (1819–92) shifts tenses, sputters out sentence fragments, tries out metaphors and similes, and unpacks a series of rhetorical questions, all to serve a central conceit—the difficulty of doing descriptive justice to reality's horror. ("What history, I say, can ever give—for who can know— the mad, determin'd tussle of the armies . . . ?")

But what makes the piece historically significant, and also gives intriguing overtones to the author's reiterated claims of narrative inadequacy, is the fact that Whitman wasn't there. At the time of the battle he was in Washington, D.C., and he got his facts from the wounded soldiers he tended as a hospital volunteer. As much as John Hersey in *Hiroshima,* Whitman was practicing the art of journalistic re-creation, and he deserves recognition as one of that genre's true pioneers.

Historical footnote: the battle in Stephen Crane's *The Red Badge of Courage* was largely based on Chancellorsville as well.

—B. Y.

〰

A NIGHT BATTLE, OVER A WEEK SINCE

May 12.—There was part of the late battle at Chancellorsville, (second Fredericksburgh,) a little over a week ago, Saturday, Saturday night and Sunday, under Gen. Joe Hooker, I would like to give just a glimpse of—(a moment's look in a terrible storm at sea—of which a few suggestions are enough, and full details impossible). The fighting had been very hot during the day, and after an intermission the latter part, was resumed at night, and kept up with furious energy till 3 o'clock in the morning. That afternoon (Saturday) an attack sudden and strong by Stonewall Jackson had gain'd a great advantage to the southern army, and broken our lines, entering us like a wedge, and leaving things in that position at dark. But Hooker at 11 at night made a desperate push, drove the secesh forces back, restored his original lines, and resumed his plans. This night scrimmage was very exciting, and afforded countless strange and fearful pictures. The fighting had been general both at Chancellorsville and northeast at Fredericksburgh. (We heard of some poor fighting, episodes, skedaddling on our part. I think not of it. I think of the fierce bravery, the general rule.) One corps, the 6th, Sedgewick's, fights four dashing and bloody battles in thirty-six hours, retreating in great jeopardy, losing largely but maintaining itself, fighting with the sternest desperation under all circumstances, getting over the Rappahannock only by the skin of its teeth, yet getting over. It lost many, many brave men, yet it took vengeance, ample vengeance.

But it was the tug of Saturday evening, and through the night and Sunday morning, I wanted to make a special note of. It was largely in the woods, and quite a general engagement. The night was very pleasant, at times the moon shining out full and clear, all Nature so calm in itself, the early summer grass so rich, and foliage of the trees—yet there the battle raging, and many good fellows lying helpless, with new accessions to them, and every minute amid the rattle of muskets and crash of cannon, (for there was an artillery contest too,) the red life-blood oozing out from heads or trunks or limbs upon that green and dew-cool grass. Patches of the woods take fire, and several of the wounded, unable to move, are consumed—quite large spaces are swept over, burning the dead also—some of the men have their hair and beards singed—some, burns on their faces and hands—other holes burnt in their clothing. The flashes of fire from the cannon, the quick flaring flames and smoke, and the immense roar—the musketry so general, the light nearly bright enough for each side to see the other—the crashing, tramping of men—the yelling—close quarters—we hear the secesh yells—our men cheer loudly back, especially if Hooker is in sight—hand to hand conflicts, each side stands up to it, brave, determin'd as demons, they often charge upon us—a thousand deeds are done worth to write newer greater poems on—and still the woods on fire—still many are not only scorch'd—too many, unable to move, are burn'd to death.

Then the camps of the wounded—O heavens, what scene is this?—is this indeed *humanity*—these butchers' shambles? There are several of them. There they lie, in the largest, in an open space in the woods, from 200 to 300 poor fellows—the groans and screams—the odor of blood, mixed with the fresh scent of the night, the grass, the trees—that slaughter-house! O well is it their mothers, their sisters cannot see them—cannot conceive, and never conceiv'd, these things. One man is shot by a shell, both in the arm and leg—both are amputated—there lie the rejected members. Some have their legs blown off—some bullets through the breast—some indescribably horrid wounds in the face or head, all mutilated, sickening, torn, gouged out—some in the abdomen—some mere boys—many rebels, badly hurt—

they take their regular turns with the rest, just the same as any—the surgeons use them just the same. Such is the camp of the wounded—such a fragment, a reflection afar off of the bloody scene—while over all the clear, large moon comes out at times softly, quietly shining. Amid the woods, that scene of flitting souls—amid the crack and crash and yelling sounds—the impalpable perfume of the woods—and yet the pungent, stifling smoke—the radiance of the moon, looking from heaven at intervals so placid—the sky so heavenly—the clear-obscure up there, those buoyant upper oceans—a few large placid stars beyond, coming silently and languidly out, and then disappearing—the melancholy, draperied night above, around. And there, upon the roads, the fields, and in those woods, that contest, never one more desperate in any age or land—both parties now in force—masses—no fancy battle, no semi-play, but fierce and savage demons fighting there—courage and scorn of death the rule, exceptions almost none.

What history, I say, can ever give—for who can know—the mad, determin'd tussle of the armies, in all their separate large and little squads—as this—each steep'd from crown to toe in desperate, mortal purports? Who know the conflict, hand-to-hand—the many conflicts in the dark, those shadowy-tangled, flashing moonbeam'd woods—the writhing groups and squads—the cries, the din, the cracking guns and pistols—the distant cannon—the cheers and calls and threats and awful music of the oaths—the indescribable mix—the officers' orders, persuasions, encouragements—the devils fully rous'd in human hearts—the strong shout, *Charge, men, charge*—the flash of the naked sword, and rolling flame and smoke? And still the broken, clear and clouded heaven—and still again the moonlight pouring silvery soft its radiant patches over all. Who paint the scene, the sudden partial panic of the afternoon, at dusk? Who paint the irrepressible advance of the second division of the Third corps, under Hooker himself, suddenly order'd up—those rapid-filing phantoms through the woods? Who show what moves there in the shadows, fluid and firm—to save, (and it did save,) the army's name, perhaps the nation? as there the veterans hold the field. (Brave Berry falls not yet—but death has mark'd him—soon he falls.)

From *If Christ Came to Chicago*

W. T. STEAD

❧

W. T. Stead (1849–1912) changed the face of British journalism as the editor of an evening newspaper, the *Pall Mall Gazette*, in the 1880s. He broke with traditional style by introducing bold type, eye-catching headlines, and highly readable bylined articles. He also popularized the feature-interview, personalizing the news with a foretaste of modern celebrity journalism, and transcending the question-answer format with details of atmosphere and descriptions of the interviewee's appearance and mannerisms.

Stead's innovations went beyond style. He launched civic and moral crusades, most notably when Parliament seemed unwilling to raise the age of sexual consent from thirteen to sixteen. To dramatize the widespread traffic in young girls, Stead experimentally "purchased" a thirteen-year-old from her mother and publicized the case as part of a sensational series: "The Maiden Tribute of Modern Babylon." Although he had no physical contact with the girl, Stead was prosecuted and served two months in jail. But he had persuaded Parliament to act.

When Matthew Arnold referred to Stead's "new journalism" in 1887, he criticized its appeals to mass taste and its often cavalier treatment of fact. Ironically, as Stead became more interested in international issues, he was forced out at the *Pall Mall Gazette*; in 1890 he assumed control of a monthly magazine, *Review of Reviews*. Stead remained a crusader, and during an 1893 visit to Chicago he declared the city an ideal test site for public reform.

As he looked at Chicago's labor strife, police corruption, and juxtaposition of great wealth and great squalor, Stead described the city as "a pretty fair section of mankind"—but with the fresh potential of the New World, especially in its "citizens full of a boundless elan." *If Christ Came to Chicago* (1894) takes its title from a James Russell Lowell poem. The book was too pragmatic to serve as a religious tract (it proposed decent saloons and well-managed brothels), and its editorial fervor was leavened by many storytelling touches, as in the portrayal of Maggie Darling. Stead's characterization overcomes sentimentality in sharply realized scenes and in Maggie's own profane anger.

In 1892 Stead wrote a short story about the sinking of an "unsinkable" ocean liner. Twenty years later he was a passenger on the *Titanic*. When last seen, Stead was standing calmly on the deck after giving up his life jacket to another.

—K. K.

∞

. . . Sure enough, the next day there was a new patrolman on the beat, and the girls were more cautious in their hustling. The routine of the day at Madame Hastings was monotonous enough. In the morning, just before 12, the colored girl served cocktails to each of the women before they got up. After they dressed, they took another refresher, usually absinthe. At breakfast they had wine. Then the day's work began. The girls sat in couples at the windows, each keeping watch in the opposite direction. If a man passed they would rap at the window and beckon him to come in. If a policeman appeared, even if it were their fat friend, the curtains would be drawn and all trace of hustling would disappear. But before the officer was out of sight the girls would be there again. They went on duty fifteen minutes at a time. Every quarter of an hour they were relieved, until dinner time. At five they dined, and then the evening's business began, with more drinking at intervals, all night through, to the accompaniment of piano playing with occasional step-dancing, and adjournments more or less frequent, as customers were more or less plentiful. About four or five in the morning, when they were all more or less loaded with drink, they would close the doors and go to sleep. Next day it would begin again, the same dull round of drink and hustling, debauch and drink. A dismal, dreary, monotonous existence broken only by quarreling and the constant excitement supplied by the police.

For a day or two the girls were discreet, but finding no harm came they relapsed a little, and "Redhead," the new policeman, saw them hustling at the window. So a warrant was sworn out at the police station and at five o'clock at night a posse of nine policemen sallied forth to "pull" Mary Hastings. The pulling of a house of this description is one of the favorite entertainments of the district. It attracts the floating and resident population as much as a first-class funeral draws the crowd in a country town. All unsuspecting the fate in store for them, the girls were preparing to sit down to dinner. Maggie was mixing the absinthe when the bell rang. Bohemian Mary—for here as elsewhere in Chicago, there are people of all nationalities under heaven—opened the door. A policeman placed his foot so the door could not be closed in his face and demanded Madame. When she came he produced his warrant and eight other officers filed into the house. Every door was guarded. There was no escape. Had there been but a few minutes warning the girls could have fled down the trap doors prepared for such an event, which led to the cellar from whence they could escape to a friendly saloon which frequently received them into its hospitable shelter. But it was too sudden. "Oh ———!" said Maggie, running up stairs, "we're pulled!" "Yes," said the officer, "and you'd better dress yourselves and make ready to go off to the station."

As Maggie was hastily putting on her dress one of the officers who had followed her to her bed-room touched her on the shoulder. "Would you mind making a date with me?" he said. The girl's appearance pleased him. "And though he was on pleasure bent," like John Gilpin, "he had a frugal mind." Policemen get their women cheap, and when you are arresting a woman she cannot haggle about terms. So Maggie said, "For sure." "Well," he said, "I am on Clark, can I meet you there some day next week?" "Certainly," she replied, "send me a message making the date and it will be all right."

By this time they were getting ready to start. Madame had thrust a roll of 300 dollar bills into her stocking. The girls, not less mindful of contingencies, had stuffed into their stockings small bottles of whisky and cigarettes and made ready to accompany their captors. There were six altogether. The housekeeper, the cook and one of the girls, a newcomer who was passed off as a servant, remained behind. Madame and her family of five stepped out amid the curious crowd which watched for the patrol wagon. "It makes a girl feel cheap," said Maggie, "let's start for the station." No sooner said than done. Bohemian Mary set off at a run followed by her cursing, panting custodian; then came the other girls, while Madame brought up the rear. It was no new thing to her. The house had been pulled only two months before and it was all in the day's work.

When they arrived at the police station they were taken down stairs and locked up all together in one of the iron barred cells. The policeman found a bottle of wine in a French girl's stocking and drank its contents to the immense indignation of its owner, who gave him in her own vocabulary "blue blazes." He only looked and laughed. "Here's to your health, Frenchie!" said the policeman as he drank the last drop. Madame in the meantime had dispatched a trusty messenger for a bondsman and as soon as he arrived she was bailed out. The girls in the cell amused themselves with shouting and singing and cursing and drinking, while Maggie and another tested their agility by climbing like monkeys up the iron bars of their grated door.

It was more like a picnic than an imprisonment. They had drink and cigarettes and company. They were as noisy and more lively and profane than if they had been at home.

In about an hour Madame bailed them all out, putting up $10 a head for their punctual appearance at the police court on Monday morning. Then the half dozen, more drunk than when they were pulled sallied out in triumph and resumed business as usual in the old premises as if nothing had happened.

Five or six hours afterwards, about midnight, I made Maggie Darling's acquaintance. I had been around several of the houses asking their keepers and their inmates to attend my meeting at the Central Music Hall the following day. A strange pilgrimage that was from house to house, to discuss what Christ would think of it, with landladies whose painted damsels in undress, were lounging all around! At last, well on to midnight, I came to Madame Hastings. The excitement of the "pulling" was still visible; Madame was indignant. She knew who it was that had put the "cops" on to her and she cursed them accordingly. Maggie was flushed and somewhat forward; both her eyes were blacked, the result of a fight with a French inmate of the house.

"I don't want anything," I said to Maggie. "Why can you not talk decently once in a while? Sit down and let us have a good talk."

Maggie looked at me half incredulously and then sat down.

"I want you to come to my meeting tomorrow night," I said, "at Central Music Hall."

"Yes," she said, "what kind of a meeting is it?"

"Oh, quite a new kind of meeting," I answered. "I am to speak on what Christ would think of all this, and I want you to know it all, to come to the meeting."

Maggie became serious; a dreamy look came over her face.

Then she said, "Oh, Christ! He's all right. It's the other ones, that's the devil." Then she stopped. "It's no use," she added, shortly.

"What's no use?" I asked, and after a time she told me the story which I repeated in brief at Central Music Hall next day.

It was a grim story; commonplace enough, and yet as tragic as life, that was told to me at midnight in that tawdry parlor. The old Jezebel flitted in and out superintending her business; the jingling piano was going in the next room where the girls were dancing, and the air was full of the reek of beer and tobacco. Maggie spoke soberly, in an undertone so that Madame might not hear what she was saying. Her narrative, which she told without any pretense or without any appeal for sympathy or for help, seemed a microcosm of the history of the human race. The whole of the story was there; from the Fall to the Redemption; from the Redemption to the Apostacy of the church, and the blighting of the hopes of mankind. I give it here as a page, soiled and grimy it may be, but nevertheless a veritable page torn from the book of life. Maggie Darling is a human document in which is recorded the ruin of one of the least of those of the brethren of Christ. It illustrates many things in our social organization, from the ruthless sacrifice of childhood, due to the lack of factory laws, to the murderous brutality of conventional Christianity, aping the morality without the heart of its Lord.

"No," said Maggie coldly. "It's no use! Don't commence no religion on me. I've had enough already. Are you a Catholic?"

"Why?" I asked. "No, I am not a Catholic."

"I'm glad," she said, "you're not a Catholic. I have no use for Catholics.

Least of all for Irish Catholics. I will never go near any of them any more, and if I could do them any harm, I would travel a thousand miles to do it."

Maggie was excited and troubled. Something in the past seemed to harass her, and her language was more vigorous than can be quoted here. After a little she became more restrained, and by degrees I had her whole history.

She was born of Irish-American parents, in Boston, in 1870. Her father was a carpenter by trade. Her mother died when Maggie was a mere child. Shortly after her death the family crossed the continent to California, where her father married again. He was a drunkard, a gambler and a violent tempered man, much given to drinking, and inclined to treat his children with great brutality. Maggie, after spending a year or two in a convent school in San Francisco, left before she had learned either to read or to write, and began to make her own living, at nine years of age. She was employed in a shoe factory, where she made from $4.50 to $7 a week at piece work. There were several children of only seven years of age in the factory. These infants were employed in picking shavings. They started work at six o'clock in the morning, had half an hour for dinner, and were dismissed at five. At the factory Maggie learned to read out of the newspapers, by the aid of her companions, and when she was eleven was sufficiently smart to obtain a situation as companion and reader to an old lady, who was an invalid, at $15 a month and her board. The place was comfortable. She remained there until she was eighteen.

From that situation she went as chambermaid to a private family in Golden Gate Avenue. She was eighteen, full of vigor and gaiety. She was a brunette with long dark hair, a lively disposition, and with all the charming audacity and confidence of inexperience. She fell in love. The man was older than she and for a time she was as happy as most young people in their first dream. Of course she was going to be married. If only the marriage day would come! But there are twenty-four hours in every day, and seven days in every week. Her betrothed, not less impatient, hinted that after all they were already united, why could they not anticipate the ceremony. Did she not trust him? He swore that it was all right, that everybody did it and they would be so much more to each other.

But why repeat the oft told story? At first Maggie would not listen to the suggestion. But after a time when he pressed her and upbraided her and declared that she could not love him if she did not trust him, she went the way of many thousands, only to wake as they have done with the soft illusion dissipated by the terrible reality of motherhood drawing near, with no husband to be a father to her child. When she told him of her condition, he said that it was all right; they must get married directly. If she would leave her place and meet him next day, at the corner of a certain street, he would take her to a church and they would be married. In all trusting innocence, relying upon his word, she gave up her situation, put up such things as she could carry and went next day to the trysting place. Of course the man was not there. After waiting till heartsick she went to make inquiries; she soon discovered the fatal truth. Her lover was a married man, and he had skipped the town followed by the brother of another of his victims.

Imagine her position! She had exactly fifteen cents in her pocket. If she had gone home her father, fierce and irascible as he usually was, would have thought little of killing the daughter who had brought disgrace upon the family. She dared not return to her old situation which she had left so suddenly. She had no character from her mistress and no references. Besides in six months she would be confined. What was she to do?

Her position is one in which some thousands of young women find themselves all over the world at this very moment. She was in the position of Eve after she had eaten the forbidden fruit and had been cast out of the Garden of Eden. It is a modern version of the Fall, and as the Fall led down to destruction, so it was with Maggie Darling. She seemed to be shut up to sin. She wandered about the town seeking work. Finding none all that day she walked about in the evening. She kept walking aimlessly on and on, until night came and she was afraid. When it was quite dark and she found a quiet corner she crouched upon a doorstep and tried to sleep. What was she to do? She was lonely and miserable; every month her trouble would grow worse. Where could she hide? She dozed off, only to awaken with a start. No one was near; she tried to sleep again. Then she got up and walked a little and rested again. When morning came she was tired out and wretched. Then she remembered the address of a girl she knew who was living in the neighborhood. She hunted her up and was made welcome. But her friend had no money. For one night she sheltered her, but all her efforts to find work were in vain.

What was to be done? On the third day she and her friend met a man who asked them if they wanted a job. They answered eagerly, yes. He gave them the address of a lady who he thought could give them something to do. They went there and found it was a house of ill-fame. The woman took them in and told them they might stay. Maggie hesitated. But what was she to do? She had lost her character and her place, and she had no friends. Here she could at least get food and shelter, and remain till her baby was born. It seemed as if she were driven to it. She said to herself that she could not help it, and so it came to pass that Maggie came upon the town.

Two years she remained there, making the best of it. Her baby fortunately died soon after it was born, and she continued to tread the cinder path of sin alone. This went on for three years, and then there dawned upon her darkened life a real manifestation of redeeming love. One day when she had a fit of the blues, a young man came into the house. He was very young, not more than twenty. Something in her appearance attracted him, and when they were alone he spoke to her so kindly that she marveled. She told him how wretched she was, and he, treating her as if she were his own sister, encouraged her to hope for release. "Take this," he said, as he left her, giving her five dollars. "Save up all you can until you can pay off your debts and then we will get you out of this."

He came again, and yet again, always treating her in the same brotherly fashion, giving her five dollars every time, and never asking anything in return. After she had saved up sufficient store to pay off that debt to the landlady, which hangs like a millstone round the neck of the unfortunate, her young friend told her that he had talked to his mother and his sister, and that as soon as she was ready they would be delighted to take her into their home until such time as they could find her a situation. Full of delight at the unexpected deliverance, Maggie made haste to leave. The young man's mother was as good as her word. In that home she found a warm welcome, and a safe retreat. Maggie made great efforts to break off the habit of swearing, and although she every now and then would make a bad break, she made such progress that at length it was deemed safe and prudent to let her take a place as a general servant. The short stay in that Christian home had been to her as a glimpse into an opening paradise. Hope sprang up once more in the girl's breast. She would be an honest woman once again. Thus, as we have seen her reproduce the Fall, so we see the blessed work of the Redeemer. Now we have to see the way in which His people, "the other ones," as she called them, shuddering, fulfilled their trust.

Maggie went to a situation in Oakland, Alameda Co., Cal. Her new mistress was a Mrs. McD——, an Irish Catholic of very devout disposition. She was general servant at $10 a month. She worked hard, and gave every satisfaction. Even the habit of profanity seemed to have been conquered. Gradually the memory of her past life with its hideous concomitants was becoming faint and dim, when suddenly the past was brought back to her with a shock. She was serving at table when she suddenly recognized in one of the guests a man who had been a customer in the old house. She felt as if she were going to drop dead when she recognized him, but she said nothing. The "gentleman," however, was not so reticent. "Where did you get that girl from?" he asked Mr. McD——. "Get her," said Mr. McD——; "why, she's a servant in our house." "Servant," sneered her guest; "I know her. She is a —— from San Francisco."

How eternally true are Lowell's lines:

> Grim-hearted world, that look'st with Levite eyes
>   On those poor fallen by too much faith in man,
> She that upon thy freezing threshold lies,
>   Starved to more sinning by thy savage ban,
> Seeking that refuge because foulest vice,
>   More God-like than thy virtue is, whose span
> Shuts out the wretched only, is more free
> To enter Heaven than thou wilt ever be!

Thou wilt not let her wash thy dainty feet
   With such salt things as tears, or with rude hair
Dry them, soft Pharisee, *that sitt'st at meat*
   With him who made her such, and speak'st him fair,
Leaving God's wandering lamb the while to bleat
   Unheeded, shivering in the pitiless air:
Thou hast made prisoned virtue show more wan
And haggard than a vice to look upon.

But in this case it was even worse. The lamb which had sought shelter was driven back into the wilderness.

Mr. McD——would not believe it, but said that he would tell his wife. Mrs. McD—— at once sent for Maggie. "If only I'd been cute," said she to me when telling the story, "I would have denied it, and they would have believed me. But I thought I had broken with all that, and that I had to tell the truth. So I owned up and said yes, it was true, I had been so, but that I had reformed, and had left all that kind of life. But the old woman, d—— her! she would listen to nothing. 'Faith, she would not have the disgrace of having a —— in her house!' that was all she said."

"Have you anything against me?" said Maggie. "Have I not done your work for you ever since I came?"

"No," was the reply, "I have nothing against you, but I cannot have a person of your character in my house. You must go."

Maggie implored her to give her a chance. "You are a Catholic," she said, "will you not give me a helping hand?"

"No," was the inexorable reply. "That does not matter. I cannot have a —— in my house."

Feeling as if she were sinking in deep water, Maggie fell on her knees sobbing bitterly and begged her for the love of God to have mercy on her and at least to give her a recommendation so that she might get another place.

It was no use. "I cannot do that, for if anything went wrong I would be to blame for it."

"Well then," said Maggie, "at least give me a line saying that for the four months I had been here I have worked to your satisfaction."

"No," she said.

"The old hound!" exclaimed Maggie to me. "My God, if ever I get the chance I'll knife the old she devil. Yes, if I swing for it. What does it matter? She's blasted my life. When I saw it was all no use, I lost all heart and all hope and I gave up there and then. There's no hope for such as me. No, I had my chance and she spoiled it, God d——n her for a blasted old hypocrite. And now it is no use. No use, never any more. I have taken dope, I drink. I'm lost. I'm only a ——. I shall never be anything else. I'm far worse than ever I was and am going to the devil as fast as I can. It's no use. But —— —— me to blue blazes if ever I come within a thousand miles of that old fiend if I don't knife her if I swing for it. When I think what I might have been but for her! Oh, Christ!" she cried, "What have they done with my life?"

What indeed? After the Fall the Redemption, after the Redemption the Apostacy, and now as the result, one of

The images ye have made of Me!

When Man Falls, a Crowd Gathers

STEPHEN CRANE

In the late nineteenth century and on into the twentieth, curiosity about the lives of the poor, and the conviction that traditional methods of investigation were inadequate, frequently led journalists to put on tattered clothes and try to *experience* how the other half lived. Whether changing one's point of view is as easy as changing one's wardrobe is debatable, but this approach did lead to some wonderful writing.

Stephen Crane's venture into the genre, published in the New York *Press* in 1894, when Crane (1871–1900) was a freelancer and had just completed the manuscript for *The Red Badge of Courage,* is less concerned with empathy or exposé than with language. Crane's decision to cast himself in the third person, and his use of epithets ("the seedy man," "the assassin") instead of actual names, the incessant visual imagery, the frequent similes and cunning adjectives ("a schooner of dark and portentous beer")—all mark "An Experiment in Misery" as a piece of writing that presses up against the border separating journalism from fiction. (In revising the piece for book publication in 1898—the version used here—Crane emphasized this by omitting an introduction explaining his project and a conclusion summing up what he had learned.)

"When Man Falls, a Crowd Gathers" is also from 1894 and is also a Cranean reworking of a traditional journalistic form, in this case the slice-of-life sketch. In pitilessly describing a rather unremarkable course of events—a man's epileptic fit, the gathering of a crowd of onlookers, the victim's seeming recovery—Crane presents a world in which a bloodthirsty curiosity has replaced any vestige of sympathy or dignity. (The omission of the indefinite article before "Man" in the title underscores this view.) Left unaddressed is the complicity of the author in all this. He was, after all, part of the crowd. And aren't we, his readers, crowding around the body and asking "What's the matter?" ourselves?

—B. Y.

A man and a boy were trudging slowly along an East-Side street. It was nearly six o'clock in the evening and this street, which led to one of the East River ferries, was crowded with laborers, shop men and shop women, hurrying to their dinners. The store windows were a-glare.

The man and the boy conversed in Italian, mumbling the soft syllables and making little quick egotistical gestures. They walked with the lumbering peasant's gait, slowly, and blinking their black eyes at the passing show of the street.

Suddenly the man wavered on his limbs and glared bewildered and helpless as if some blinding light had flashed before his vision; then he swayed like a drunken man and fell. The boy grasped his companion's arm frantically and made an attempt to support him so that the limp form slid to the side-walk with an easy motion as a body sinks in the sea. The boy screamed.

Instantly, from all directions people turned their gaze upon the prone figure. In a moment there was a dodging, pushing, peering group about the man. A volley of questions, replies, speculations flew to and fro above all the bobbing heads.

"What's th' matter? What's th' matter?"

"Oh, a jag, I guess!"

"Nit; he's got a fit!"

"What's th' matter? What's th' matter?"

Two streams of people coming from different directions met at this point to form a crowd. Others came from across the street.

Down under their feet, almost lost under this throng, lay the man, hidden in the shadows caused by their forms which in fact barely allowed a particle of light to pass between them. Those in the foremost rank bended down, shouldering each other, eager, anxious to see everything. Others behind them crowded savagely for a place like starving men fighting for bread. Always, the question could be heard flying in the air. "What's the matter?" Some, near to the body and perhaps feeling the danger of being forced over upon it, twisted their heads and protested violently to those unheeding ones who were scuffling in the rear. "Say, quit yer shovin', can't yeh? What d' yeh want, anyhow? Quit!"

A man back in the crowd suddenly said: "Say, young feller, you're a peach wid dose feet o' yours. Keep off me!"

Another voice said: "Well, dat's all right ———"

The boy who had been walking with the man who fell was standing helplessly, a terrified look in his eyes. He held the man's hand. Sometimes he gave it a little jerk that was at once an appeal, a reproach, a caution. And, withal, it was a timid calling to the limp and passive figure as if he half expected to arouse it from its coma with a pleading touch of his fingers.

Occasionally, he looked about him with swift glances of indefinite hope, as if assistance might come from the clouds. The men near him questioned him, but he did not seem to understand. He answered them "Yes" or "No," blindly, with no apparent comprehension of their language. They frequently jostled him until he was obliged to put his hand upon the breast of the body to maintain his balance.

Those that were nearest to the man upon the side-walk at first saw his body go through a singular contortion. It was as if an invisible hand had reached up from the earth and had seized him by the hair. He seemed dragged slowly, relentlessly backward, while his body stiffened convulsively, his hands clenched, and his arms swung rigidly upward. A slight froth was upon his chin. Through his pallid half-closed lids could be seen the steel-colored gleam of his eyes that were turned toward all the bending, swaying faces and in this inanimate thing upon the pave burned threateningly, dangerously, shining with a mystic light, as a corpse might glare at those live ones who seemed about to trample it under foot.

As for the men near, they hung back, appearing as if they expected it to spring erect and clutch at them. Their eyes however were held in a spell of fascination. They seemed scarcely to breathe. They were contemplating a depth into which a human being had sunk and the marvel of this mystery of life or death held them chained. Occasionally from the rear, a man came thrusting his way impetuously, satisfied that there was a horror to be seen and apparently insane to get a view of it. Less curious persons swore at these men when they trod upon their toes.

The loaded street-cars jingled past this scene in endless parade. Occasionally, from where the elevated railroad crossed the street there came a rhythmical roar, suddenly begun and suddenly ended. Over the heads of the crowd hung an immovable canvas sign. "Regular dinner twenty cents."

After the first spasm of curiosity had passed away, there were those in the crowd who began to consider ways to help. A voice called: "Rub his wrists." The boy and some one on the other side of the man began to rub his wrists and slap his palms, but still the body lay inert, rigid. When a hand was dropped the arm fell like a stick. A tall German suddenly appeared and resolutely began to push the crowd back. "Get back there—get back," he continually repeated as he pushed them. He had psychological authority over this throng; they obeyed him. He and another knelt by the man in the darkness and loosened his shirt at the throat. Once they struck a match and held it close to the man's face. This livid visage suddenly appearing under their feet in the light of the match's yellow glare, made the throng shudder. Half-articulate exclamations could be heard. There were men who nearly created a battle in the madness of their desire to see the thing.

Meanwhile others with magnificent passions for abstract statistical information were questioning the boy. "What's his name?" "Where does he live?"

Then a policeman appeared. The first part of the little play had gone on without his assistance but now he came swiftly, his helmet towering above the multitude of black derbys and shading that confident, self-reliant police face. He charged the crowd as if he were a squadron of Irish lancers. The people fairly withered before this onslaught. He shouted: "Come, make way there! Make way!" He was evidently a man whose life was half-pestered out of him by the inhabitants of the city who were sufficiently unreasonable and stupid as to insist on being in the streets. His was the rage of a placid cow, who wishes to lead a life of tranquillity, but who is eternally besieged by flies that hover in clouds.

When he arrived at the centre of the crowd he first demanded threateningly: "Well, what's th' matter here?" And then when he saw that human bit of wreckage at the bottom of the sea of men he said to it: "Come, git up outa that! Git outa here!"

Whereupon hands were raised in the crowd and a volley of decorated information was blazed at the officer.

"Ah, he's got a fit! Can't yeh see!"

"He's got a fit!"

"He's sick!"

"What th' ell yeh doin'? Leave 'm be!"

The policeman menaced with a glance the crowd from whose safe interior the defiant voices had emerged.

A doctor had come. He and the policeman bended down at the man's side. Occasionally the officer upreared to create room. The crowd fell away before his threats, his admonitions, his sarcastic questions and before the sweep of those two huge buckskin gloves.

At last, the peering ones saw the man on the side-walk begin to breathe heavily, with the strain of overtaxed machinery, as if he had just come to the surface from some deep water. He uttered a low cry in his foreign tongue. It was a babyish squeal or like the sad wail of a little storm-tossed kitten. As this cry went forth to all those eager ears the jostling and crowding recommenced until the doctor was obliged to yell warningly a dozen times. The policeman had gone to send an ambulance call.

When a man struck another match and in its meagre light the doctor felt the skull of the prostrate one to discover if any wound or fracture had been caused by his fall to the stone side-walk, the crowd pressed and crushed again. It was as if they fully anticipated a sight of blood in the gleam of the match and they scrambled and dodged for positions. The policeman returned and fought with them. The doctor looked up frequently to scold at them and to sharply demand more space.

At last out of the golden haze made by the lamps far up the street, there came the sound of a gong beaten rapidly, impatiently. A monstrous truck loaded to the sky with barrels scurried to one side with marvelous agility. And then the black ambulance with its red light, its galloping horse, its dull gleam of lettering and bright shine of gong clattered into view. A young man, as imperturbable always as if he were going to a picnic, sat thoughtfully upon the rear seat.

When they picked up the limp body, from which came little moans and howls, the crowd almost turned into a mob, a silent mob, each member of which struggled for one thing. Afterward some resumed their ways with an air of relief, as if they themselves had been in pain and were at last recovered. Others still continued to stare at the ambulance on its banging, clanging return journey until it vanished into the golden haze. It was as if they had been cheated. Their eyes expressed discontent at this curtain which had been rung down in the midst of the drama. And this impenetrable fabric suddenly intervening between a suffering creature and their curiosity, seemed to appear to them as an injustice.

He drew back, watching his neighbor from the shadows of his blanket edge. The man did not move once through the night, but lay in this stillness as of death, like a body stretched out, expectant of the surgeon's knife.

And all through the room could be seen the tawny hues of naked flesh, limbs thrust into the darkness, projecting beyond the cots; up-reared knees; arms hanging, long and thin, over the cot edges. For the most part they were statuesque, carven, dead. With the curious lockers standing all about like tombstones there was a strange effect of a graveyard, where bodies were merely flung.

Yet occasionally could be seen limbs wildly tossing in fantastic, nightmare gestures, accompanied by guttural cries, grunts, oaths. And there was one fellow off in a gloomy corner, who in his dreams was oppressed by some frightful calamity, for of a sudden he began to utter long wails that went almost like yells from a hound, echoing wailfully and weird through this chill place of tombstones, where men lay like the dead.

The sound, in its high piercing beginnings that dwindled to final melancholy moans, expressed a red and grim tragedy of the unfathomable possibilities of the man's dreams. But to the youth these were not merely the shrieks of a vision-pierced man. They were an utterance of the meaning of the room and its occupants. It was to him the protest of the wretch who feels the touch of the imperturbable granite wheels and who then cries with an impersonal eloquence, with a strength not from him, giving voice to the wail of a whole section, a class, a people. This, weaving into the young man's brain and mingling with his views of these vast and somber shadows that like mighty black fingers curled around the naked bodies, made the young man so that he did not sleep, but lay carving biographies for these men from his meager experience. At times the fellow in the corner howled in a writhing agony of his imaginations.

Finally a long lance point of gray light shot through the dusty panes of the window. Without, the young man could see roofs drearily white in the dawning. The point of light yellowed and grew brighter, until the golden rays of the morning sun came in bravely and strong. They touched with radiant color the form of a small, fat man, who snored in stuttering fashion. His round and shiny bald head glowed suddenly with the valor of a decoration. He sat up, blinked at the sun, swore fretfully and pulled his blanket over the ornamental splendors of his head.

The youth contentedly watched this rout of the shadows before the bright spears of the sun and presently he slumbered. When he awoke he heard the voice of the assassin raised in valiant curses. Putting up his head he perceived his comrade seated on the side of the cot engaged in scratching his neck with long finger nails that rasped like files.

"Hully Jee dis is a new breed. They've got can openers on their feet," he continued in a violent tirade.

The young man hastily unlocked his closet and took out his shoes and hat. As he sat on the side of the cot, lacing his shoes, he glanced about and saw that daylight had made the room comparatively commonplace and uninteresting. The men, whose faces seemed stolid, serene or absent, were engaged in dressing, while a great crackle of bantering conversation arose.

A few were parading in unconcerned nakedness. Here and there were men of brawn, whose skins shone clear and ruddy. They took splendid poses, standing massively, like chiefs. When they had dressed in their ungainly garments there was an extraordinary change. They then showed bumps and deficiencies of all kinds.

There were others who exhibited many deformities. Shoulders were slanting, humped, pulled this way and pulled that way. And notable among these latter men was the little fat man who had refused to allow his head to be glorified. His pudgy form, builded like a pear, bustled to and fro, while he swore in fish-wife fashion. It appeared that some article of his apparel had vanished.

The young man, attired speedily, went to his friend, the assassin. At first the latter looked dazed at the sight of the youth. This face seemed to be appealing to him through the cloud wastes of his memory. He scratched his neck and reflected. At last he grinned, a broad smile gradually spreading until his countenance was a round illumination. "Hello, Willie," he cried, cheerily.

"Hello," said the young man. "Are yeh ready t' fly?"

"Sure." The assassin tied his shoe carefully with some twine and came ambling.

When he reached the street the young man experienced no sudden relief from unholy atmospheres. He had forgotten all about them, and had been breathing naturally and with no sensation of discomfort or distress.

He was thinking of these things as he walked along the street, when he was suddenly startled by feeling the assassin's hand, trembling with excitement, clutching his arm, and when the assassin spoke, his voice went into quavers from a supreme agitation.

"I'll be hully, bloomin' blowed, if there wasn't a feller with a nightshirt on up there in that joint!"

The youth was bewildered for a moment, but presently he turned to smile indulgently at the assassin's humor.

"Oh, you're a d—— liar," he merely said.

Whereupon the assassin began to gesture extravagantly and take oath by strange gods. He frantically placed himself at the mercy of remarkable fates if his tale were not true. "Yes, he did! I cross m' heart thousan' times!" he protested, and at the time his eyes were large with amazement, his mouth wrinkled in unnatural glee. "Yessir! A nightshirt! A hully white nightshirt!"

"You lie!"

"Nosir! I hope ter die b'fore I kin git anudder ball if there wasn't a jay wid a hully, bloomin' white nightshirt!"

His face was filled with the infinite wonder of it. "A hully white night-shirt," he continually repeated.

The young man saw the dark entrance to a basement restaurant. There was a sign which read, "No mystery about our hash," and there were other age stained and world battered legends which told him that the place was within his means. He stopped before it and spoke to the assassin. "I guess I'll git somethin' t' eat."

At this the assassin, for some reason, appeared to be quite embarrassed. He gazed at the seductive front of the eating place for a moment. Then he started slowly up the street. "Well, goodby, Willie," he said, bravely.

For an instant the youth studied the departing figure. Then he called out, "Hol' on a minnet." As they came together he spoke in a certain fierce way, as if he feared that the other would think him to be weak. "Look-a-here, if yeh wanta git some breakfas' I'll lend yeh three cents t' do it with. But say, look-a-here, you've gota git out an' hustle. I ain't goin' t' support yeh, or I'll go broke b'fore night. I ain't no millionaire."

"I take me oath, Willie," said the assassin, earnestly, "th' on'y thing I really needs is a ball. Me t'roat feels like a fryin' pan. But as I can't git a ball, why, th' next bes' thing is breakfast, an' if yeh do that fer me, b'gawd, I'd say yeh was th' whitest lad I ever see."

They spent a few moments in dexterous exchanges of phrases, in which they each protested that the other was, as the assassin had originally said, a "respecter'ble gentlem'n." And they concluded with mutual assurances that they were the souls of intelligence and virtue. Then they went into the restaurant.

There was a long counter, dimly lighted from hidden sources. Two or three men in soiled white aprons rushed here and there.

The youth bought a bowl of coffee for two cents and a roll for one cent. The assassin purchased the same. The bowls were webbed with brown seams, and the tin spoons wore an air of having emerged from the first pyramid. Upon them were black, moss-like encrustations of age, and they were bent and scarred from the attacks of long forgotten teeth. But over their repast the wanderers waxed warm and mellow. The assassin grew affable as the hot mixture went soothingly down his parched throat, and the young man felt courage flow in his veins.

Memories began to throng in on the assassin, and he brought forth long tales, intricate, incoherent, delivered with a chattering swiftness as from an old woman. "—great job out'n Orange. Boss keep yeh hustlin', though, all time. I was there three days, and then I went an' ask'im t' lend me a dollar. 'G-g-go ter the devil,' he ses, an' I lose me job.

—"South no good. Damn niggers work for twenty-five an' thirty cents a day. Run white man out. Good grub, though. Easy livin'.

—"Yas; useter work little in Toledo, raftin' logs. Make two or three dollars er day in the spring. Lived high. Cold as ice, though, in the winter—

"I was raised in northern N'York. O-o-o-oh, yeh jest oughto live there. No beer ner whisky, though, way off in the woods. But all th' good hot grub yeh can eat. B'gawd, I hung around there long as I could till th' ol' man fired me. 'Git t'hell outa here, yeh wuthless skunk, git t'hell outa here an' go die,' he ses. 'You're a hell of a father,' I ses, 'you are,' an' I quit 'im."

As they were passing from the dim eating place they encountered an old man who was trying to steal forth with a tiny package of food, but a tall man with an indomitable mustache stood dragon fashion, barring the way of escape. They heard the old man raise a plaintive protest. "Ah, you always want to know what I take out, and you never see that I usually bring a package in here from my place of business."

As the wanderers trudged slowly along Park Row, the assassin began to expand and grow blithe. "B'gawd, we've been livin' like kings," he said, smacking appreciative lips.

"Look out or we'll have t' pay fer it t' night," said the youth, with gloomy warning.

But the assassin refused to turn his gaze toward the future. He went with a limping step, into which he injected a suggestion of lamb-like gambols. His mouth was wreathed in a red grin.

In the City Hall Park the two wanderers sat down in the little circle of benches sanctified by traditions of their class. They huddled in their old garments, slumbrously conscious of the march of the hours which for them had no meaning.

The people of the street hurrying hither and thither made a blend of black figures, changing, yet frieze-like. They walked in their good clothes as upon important missions, giving no gaze to the two wanderers seated upon the benches. They expressed to the young man his infinite distance from all that he valued. Social position, comfort, the pleasures of living, were unconquerable kingdoms. He felt a sudden awe.

And in the background a multitude of buildings, of pitiless hues and sternly high, were to him emblematic of a nation forcing its regal head into the clouds, throwing no downward glances; in the sublimity of its aspirations ignoring the wretches who may flounder at its feet. The roar of the city in his ear was to him the confusion of strange tongues, babbling heedlessly; it was the clink of coin, the voice of the city's hopes which were to him no hopes.

He confessed himself an outcast, and his eyes from under the lowered rim of his hat began to glance guiltily, wearing the criminal expression that comes with certain convictions.

The Death of Rodriguez

RICHARD HARDING DAVIS

∞

Richard Harding Davis (1864–1916) popularized the image of the war correspondent as romantic swashbuckler. Handsome and flamboyant, he traveled in style to battle sites all over the world, and then roughed it at the front. In the last twenty years of his life, Davis covered the Greek-Turkish War, the Spanish-American War, the Boer War, the Russo-Japanese War, the Mexican Revolution, and World War I.

Davis's mother, Rebecca Harding Davis, wrote naturalistic fiction (*Pig Iron*); his father, L. Clarke Davis, edited the Philadelphia *Public Ledger*. The young Davis published novels, plays, and travel books before finding his voice as a chronicler of war. "The Death of Rodriguez," one of his early dispatches, shows why he became famous as a descriptive writer.

A year before the Spanish-American War, William Randolph Hearst's New York *Journal* assigned Davis to report on insurrection in Cuba. One of the rebels was Adolfo Rodriguez, twenty, a farmer's son sentenced to death for bearing arms against Spanish authority. None of his friends or family could attend the execution. "Although Rodriguez could not know it," Davis later wrote, "there was one person present when he died who felt keenly for him, and who was a sympathetic though unwilling spectator."

Davis's report uses no dialogue at all. Its main impact is visual, establishing atmosphere through the eerie predawn light and the desolate landscape, and epitomizing the prisoner's bravery in his stride, posture, and quiet self-control. Davis seems to narrate in slow motion, which increases the tension while adding importance to each small particular. Rodriguez's spirit is symbolized by two objects, a cigarette (still burning after the execution) and a scapular. The story ends with sudden sunlight, cacophony, and a poignant tableau.

Some of the descriptions—of moon and sun, for example—are reminiscent of Davis's friend Stephen Crane. Other passages prefigure the reporting of Ernest Hemingway, especially in using a subdued tone and hauntingly precise details to eulogize chivalric courage.

—K. K.

∞

. . . There had been a full moon the night preceding the execution, and when the squad of soldiers marched from town it was still shining brightly through the mists. It lighted a plain two miles in extent, broken by ridges and gullies and covered with thick, high grass, and with bunches of cactus and palmetto. In the hollow of the ridges the mist lay like broad lakes of water, and on one side of the plain stood the walls of the old town. On the other rose hills covered with royal palms that showed white in the moonlight, like hundreds of marble columns. A line of tiny camp-fires that the sentries had built during the night stretched between the forts at regular intervals and burned clearly.

But as the light grew stronger and the moonlight faded these were stamped out, and when the soldiers came in force the moon was a white ball in the sky, without radiance, the fires had sunk to ashes, and the sun had not yet risen.

So even when the men were formed into three sides of a hollow square, they were scarcely able to distinguish one another in the uncertain light of the morning.

There were about three hundred soldiers in the formation. They belonged to the volunteers, and they deployed upon the plain with their band in front playing a jaunty quickstep, while their officers galloped from one side to the other through the grass, seeking a suitable place for the execution. Outside the line the band still played merrily.

A few men and boys, who had been dragged out of their beds by the music, moved about the ridges behind the soldiers, half-clothed, unshaven, sleepy-eyed, yawning, stretching themselves nervously and shivering in the cool, damp air of the morning.

Either owing to discipline or on account of the nature of their errand, or because the men were still but half awake, there was no talking in the ranks, and the soldiers stood motionless, leaning on their rifles, with their backs turned to the town, looking out across the plain to the hills.

The men in the crowd behind them were also grimly silent. They knew that whatever they might say would be twisted into a word of sympathy for the condemned man or a protest against the government. So no one spoke; even the officers gave their orders in gruff whispers, and the men in the crowd did not mix together, but looked suspiciously at one another and kept apart.

As the light increased a mass of people came hurrying from the town with two black figures leading them, and the soldiers drew up at attention, and part of the double line fell back and left an opening in the square.

With us a condemned man walks only the short distance from his cell to the scaffold or the electric chair, shielded from sight by the prison walls, and it often occurs even then that the short journey is too much for his strength and courage.

But the Spaniards on this morning made the prisoner walk for over a half-mile across the broken surface of the fields. I expected to find the man, no matter what his strength at other times might be, stumbling and faltering on this cruel journey; but as he came nearer I saw that he led all the others, that the priests on either side of him were taking two steps to his one, and that they were tripping on their gowns and stumbling over the hollows in their efforts to keep pace with him as he walked, erect and soldierly, at a quick step in advance of them.

He had a handsome, gentle face of the peasant type, a light, pointed beard, great wistful eyes, and a mass of curly black hair. He was shockingly young for such a sacrifice, and looked more like a Neapolitan than a Cuban. You could imagine him sitting on the quay at Naples or Genoa lolling in the sun and showing his white teeth when he laughed. Around his neck, hanging outside his linen blouse, he wore a new scapular.

It seems a petty thing to have been pleased with at such a time, but I confess to have felt a thrill of satisfaction when I saw, as the Cuban passed me, that he held a cigarette between his lips, not arrogantly nor with bravado, but with the nonchalance of a man who meets his punishment fearlessly, and who will let his enemies see that they can kill but cannot frighten him.

It was very quickly finished, with rough and, but for one frightful blunder, with merciful swiftness. The crowd fell back when it came to the square, and the condemned man, the priests, and the firing squad of six young volunteers passed in and the line closed behind them.

The officer who had held the cord that bound the Cuban's arms behind him and passed across his breast, let it fall on the grass and drew his sword, and Rodriguez dropped his cigarette from his lips and bent and kissed the cross which the priest held up before him.

The elder of the priests moved to one side and prayed rapidly in a loud whisper, while the other, a younger man, walked behind the firing squad and covered his face with his hands. They had both spent the last twelve hours with Rodriguez in the chapel of the prison.

The Cuban walked to where the officer directed him to stand, and turning his back on the square, faced the hills and the road across them, which led to his father's farm.

As the officer gave the first command he straightened himself as far as the cords would allow, and held up his head and fixed his eyes immovably on the morning light, which had just begun to show above the hills.

He made a picture of such pathetic helplessness, but of such courage and dignity, that he reminded me on the instant of that statue of Nathan Hale which stands in the City Hall Park, above the roar of Broadway. The Cuban's arms were bound, as are those of the statue, and he stood firmly, with his weight resting on his heels like a soldier on parade, and with his face held up fearlessly, as is that of the statue. But there was this difference, that Rodriguez, while probably as willing to give six lives for his country as was the American rebel, being only a peasant, did not think to say so, and he will not, in consequence, live in bronze during the lives of many men, but will be remembered only as one of thirty Cubans, one of whom was shot at Santa Clara on each succeeding day at sunrise.

The officer had given the order, the men had raised their pieces, and the condemned man had heard the clicks of the triggers as they were pulled back, and he had not moved. And then happened one of the most cruelly refined, though unintentional, acts of torture that one can very well imagine. As the officer slowly raised his sword, preparatory to giving the signal, one of the mounted officers rode up to him and pointed out silently that, as I had already observed with some satisfaction, the firing squad were so placed that when they fired they would shoot several of the soldiers stationed on the extreme end of the square.

Their captain motioned his men to lower their pieces, and then walked across the grass and laid his hand on the shoulder of the waiting prisoner.

It is not pleasant to think what that shock must have been. The man had steeled himself to receive a volley of bullets. He believed that in the next instant he would be in another world; he had heard the command given, had heard the click of the Mausers as the locks caught—and then, at that supreme moment, a human hand had been laid upon his shoulder and a voice spoke in his ear.

You would expect that any man, snatched back to life in such a fashion would start and tremble at the reprieve, or would break down altogether, but this boy turned his head steadily, and followed with his eyes the direction of the officer's sword, then nodded gravely, and, with his shoulders squared, took up the new position, straightened his back, and once more held himself erect.

As an exhibition of self-control this should surely rank above feats of heroism performed in battle, where there are thousands of comrades to give inspiration. This man was alone, in sight of the hills he knew, with only enemies about him, with no source to draw on for strength but that which lay within himself.

The officer of the firing squad, mortified by his blunder, hastily whipped up his sword, the men once more levelled their rifles, the sword rose, dropped, and the men fired. At the report the Cuban's head snapped back almost between his shoulders, but his body fell slowly, as though some one had pushed him gently forward from behind and he had stumbled.

He sank on his side in the wet grass without a struggle or sound, and did not move again.

It was difficult to believe that he meant to lie there, that it could be ended so without a word, that the man in the linen suit would not rise to his feet and continue to walk on over the hills, as he apparently had started to do, to his home; that there was not a mistake somewhere, or that at least some one would be sorry or say something or run to pick him up.

But, fortunately, he did not need help, and the priests returned—the younger one with the tears running down his face—and donned their vestments and read a brief requiem for his soul, while the squad stood uncovered, and the men in the hollow square shook their accoutrements into place, and shifted their pieces and got ready for the order to march, and the band began again with the same quickstep which the fusillade had interrupted.

The figure still lay on the grass untouched, and no one seemed to remember that it had walked there of itself, or noticed that the cigarette still burned, a tiny ring of living fire, at the place where the figure had first stood.

The figure was a thing of the past, and the squad shook itself like a great snake, and then broke into little pieces and started off jauntily, stumbling in the high grass and striving to keep step to the music.

The officers led it past the figure in the linen suit, and so close to it that the file closers had to part with the column to avoid treading on it. Each soldier as he passed turned and looked down on it, some craning their necks curiously, others giving a careless glance, and some without any interest at all, as they would have looked at a house by the roadside, or a hole in the road.

One young soldier caught his foot in a trailing vine, just opposite to it, and fell. He grew very red when his comrades giggled at him for his awkwardness. The crowd of sleepy spectators fell in on either side of the band. They, too, had forgotten it, and the priests put their vestments back in the bag and wrapped their heavy cloaks about them, and hurried off after the others.

Every one seemed to have forgotten it except two men, who came slowly towards it from the town, driving a bullock-cart that bore an unplaned coffin, each with a cigarette between his lips, and with his throat wrapped in a shawl to keep out the morning mists.

At that moment the sun, which had shown some promise of its coming in the glow above the hills, shot up suddenly from behind them in all the splendor of the tropics, a fierce, red disk of heat, and filled the air with warmth and light.

The bayonets of the retreating column flashed in it, and at the sight a rooster in a farm-yard near by crowed vigorously, and a dozen bugles answered the challenge with the brisk, cheery notes of the reveille, and from all parts of the city the church bells jangled out the call for early mass, and the little world of Santa Clara seemed to stretch itself and to wake to welcome the day just begun.

But as I fell in at the rear of the procession and looked back, the figure of the young Cuban, who was no longer a part of the world of Santa Clara, was asleep in the wet grass, with his motionless arms still tightly bound behind him, with the scapular twisted awry across his face, and the blood from his breast sinking into the soil he had tried to free.

Can't Get Their Minds Ashore

ABRAHAM CAHAN

Fleeing a pogrom in his native Lithuania, Abraham Cahan (1860–1951) emigrated to the United States at the age of twenty-one. After writing pamphlets for the Socialist Labor party, he turned to journalism, both in Yiddish and English. In 1897 he cofounded the *Jewish Daily Forward,* which would become the leading Yiddish newspaper in America. In 1898 he began working as a city reporter for the New York *Commercial Advertiser,* whose editor, Lincoln Steffens, wanted "to make a new kind of daily journalism, personal, literary and immediate."

One of Cahan's beats was the Barge Office at the foot of Manhattan, which for several years served as a receiving station for the newest immigrants. Here he developed a style of compassionate interviewing, and of reporting through extended dialogue. Without recourse to dialect spelling, Cahan captured the idiom and imagery, and the elation and bewilderment, of people from every corner of the world.

Another main beat was the Lower East Side, the center of Jewish immigrant life. Cahan's stories were filled with the rhythms of vernacular speech, the background sounds of pushcarts and peddlers' cries, and countless individual dramas, both tragic and comic, of cultural adaptation.

Cahan also wrote two books of fiction, and was a devoted reader (and occasional translator) of Tolstoy, Dostoyevsky, and Chekhov. Two of his American favorites, Stephen Crane and William Dean Howells, praised Cahan for extending the art of realistic storytelling in journalism. Cahan redefined "news" to include the felt life of the city itself—and in the process, he explored the larger question of what it means to be an American.

—K. K.

A score of immigrants of half a dozen different nationalities were this morning clustered about a young Italian who sat on one of the long benches at the Barge Office. His name was Farneti Albano, and he was quite a handsome fellow, but he spoke with a painful stutter, and as he went on answering the questions of his fellow-countrymen his ruddy cheeks twitched and his flashing black eyes blinked in a manner which made some of the bystanders smile, and made some others shake their heads sympathetically.

"What is the matter?" asked a visitor.

"Oh, he is an idiot," somebody answered. "Can't you see?"

A buxom Italian woman with a baby in her arms stood behind Albano chuckling. She was striving to catch the visitor's eyes, and when she succeeded she put her index finger to her forehead, saying, with a fresh giggle:

"He has no sense, *signore.* No more than a baby, *signore.* Si, *signore,* he is a born fool. God has punished his parents, *signore,* and he's the punishment."

Another woman, in a green kerchief, stood smiling and nodding assent. The visitor addressed himself to Albano.

"When did you arrive?"

"Day before yesterday, *signore,*" he stammered. "I have a father here. I have written to him and now I am waiting for his answer."

"How do you like America?"

The young immigrant smiled. "How do I know whether I like it or not?" he said. "I have not seen America. I have not been out of here since I came. The officers won't let me."

"Why, he is as sensible as any of the people I have seen around here," exclaimed the visitor.

"Of course," assented the green kerchief, ardently. "He is more sensible than she, anyhow," she added, with some indignation, as she pointed at the buxom woman with the child.

One of the other women in the crowd was a stout young Lithuanian, in a kerchief of red, yellow and white and a loose-fitting jacket of flaming blue. Her big fleshy face seemed to be bursting with fullness.

"What are you doing here?" was asked through an interpreter.

An ample grin overspread her massive face as she said:

"I am waiting for Joseph."

"Who is Joseph?"

"The son of Martin the blacksmith."

"Where is he?"

"In the smithy at home, far away from here."

"Who is in the smithy? Joseph?"

"No, Martin, his father. Joseph is in America. I am waiting for him to come for me."

"What is he to you?"

"My sweetheart," she said, the grin broadening over her flaming face.

"Is he going to marry you?"

"If he was not, why then did he send me a ticket? He has a good job in America, and he has saved lots of money. We shall live like noble folk in America."

Seated on their baggage by the wall were some Ruthenians, men, women and children. They looked forlornly about them from time to time, whispering to one another timidly.

"What makes you so downhearted?" was asked.

The eldest of the group, a portly, pleasant woman of fifty, getting up from her seat, folded her hands as if in prayer, and said, beseechingly:

"Good, merciful sir? Will our troubles ever come to an end? Will my husband and this woman's father, and the father of these girls, will they all come to us and take us out to America? The bailiffs here have been so kind to us, and they feed us well, but when, oh, when, will see our husbands and fathers?"

A bench nearby was occupied by several men in broad caps with huge visors and in heavy coats which had the effect of a tight-fitting jacket with a loose dangling skirt attached at the waist. They spoke good German, but they came from the Teutonic colonies in south Russia. The clerks at the Barge Office spoke of them as the most desirable class of immigrants.

"Our forefathers emigrated from Germany to Russia," said one of them, as he took snuff from an old "birchbark," "And now we are emigrating from Russia to a still better place—to America."

In a corner, a yard or two off, nestled a Jewish family from Volhynia, Russia. It was made up of a father, mother, and five daughters, all handsome, and all almost as robust as the Lithuanian girl. The eldest sister was a young woman of about twenty-six, and she sat with a beautiful little girl in her arms who bore striking resemblance to her.

"Are you married?" the visitor asked.

"No, sir. This is mamma's baby," was her reply.

"Oh, my dear little *Herr*," sighed the old man, "we have been over a week in this terrible place. They say I have not money enough, and they want to send us all back. God in heaven! I have ruined myself. I have sold my house and everything I had to pay my way, and now they will send us back a lot of beggars. But God will not forsake us. I have cousins in Philadelphia. They are good—ah, may God help them, they have the hearts of true Jews in them—and they came all the way from that city—is it a large town?—to try to get us out into the wide world, but—"

"But the officers here say the bonds they offer are not enough," the old woman interrupted him, anxiously. "They would have richer men to guarantee that we will earn our living in America. Don't we want to make a living ourselves?" she asked with a smile. She was about to say something else, but there it was her turn to be interrupted.

"Didn't we make a respectable living at home?" the eldest daughter broke in. "Father is a good tailor, and we all helped him. May no Jewish family fare worse than we did at home. They say America is a clever country. If they were clever they wouldn't keep us here for fear we might be poor. What fools they are! They want us to make money, and at the same time they won't let us go out and make it. They can't expect us to earn money here, can they?"

At this point dinner was announced, and the motley crowd threw itself at the long table, which was set with tin plates of soup and meat and long loaves of bread. There was no scramble. There was plenty of room and plenty to eat, and presently the room rang with jingling spoons and smacking lips.

"The soup is good! Very good! Would they had given us such soup on board the ship," a young Pole said to his neighbor. The neighbor was an Italian, and the Pole knew it, but he had to unbosom himself to somebody.

The Jewish family alone remained in their corner.

"Why don't you go to eat? Are you not hungry?" was asked. The girls smiled. The old man shook his head impressively. "We are Jews. The dinner is not *kosher,*" he said. "But we are not starving. We can live on bread and some *kosher* things, which we buy with our own money."

"We don't starve!" the eldest girl protested. "How can you live without a drop of soup? No wonder we look like corpses. Look how thin we are! There is not a drop of blood left in us, is there?"

As the visitor surveyed her plump, florid cheeks he felt like saying that there was, but he did not.

The large waiting room was thronged with people come for their newly arrived friends. The best-dressed woman in the crowd was a German servant girl. She wore a huge hat with a forest of ostrich feathers and a brand-new jacket of blue cloth overladen with trimmings of every color in the rainbow. Her landlady, a Bohemian, dressed much less majestically, was with her. The girl never ceased laughing, and every little while changed her place, dragging her landlady with her.

"What is she laughing about?" the visitor asked.

"Her brother has come, so she is glad," said the landlady, sympathetically.

Five or ten minutes later the young man came out, with his baggage. He was a husky-looking fellow, with some dignity in his walk and look.

"Here he comes! Here he comes! Hugo!" the servant girl said, with a ringing chuckle, and flinging herself upon her brother's shoulder, she burst out crying.

Pillelu, Pillelu!

ABRAHAM CAHAN

To those who stood on the corner of Hester Street and Ludlow last night the two intersecting marketplaces looked like a vast cross of flaring gold. It was the eve of the "second days" of the Jewish Passover. The sidewalks and the asphalt pavements were crowded with pushcarts, each with a torch dangling and flickering over it, and the hundreds of quivering flames stretched east and west, north and south, two restless bands of fire crossing each other in a blaze and losing themselves in a medley of fire, smoke, many-colored piles of fish and glimmering human faces.

"Get a move on you, housewives! Time is not waiting for you. It is flying. The holiday is in front of your noses. Buy fish—living fish, screaming, dancing fish!"

"Carrots, carrots, carrots! Buy carrots, good women! Carrots in honor of the holiday!"

"Passover prunes! Why tarry? The prunes melt in one's mouth. They are an ornament to the Passover table, a health to the stomach, a blessing to the family. Prunes, prunes—they are huge diamonds and pearls, not prunes! Prunes, good women! Buy them and be blessed!"

In one place, at the junction of Ludlow, Canal and Division Streets, there was a commotion. A knot of girls crowded about a consumptive street organ, and the market women were hurling curses at the spot.

"May his Passover be disturbed and darkened even as he disturbs and darkens our holiday trade. Beets, good women; blood-red, vivifying beets in honor of the second days! May he spend on doctor's bills a dollar for every cent of business we lose on account of his defiled bones. Beets, young women; beets, young and old!"

"Who is he?" asked a snooper.

"Who? The black and the bitter years know who he is, the Evil Visitation! Beets, sir? Beets that taste like wine, gentleman?"

The Evil Visitation proved to be a dashing young fellow in charge of fortune-telling mice and parrots. He wore a sack coat and trousers of gray corduroy, which, he said, he had bought in London; a collarless shirt, embroidered in the red and black of Little Russia, while glittering from under his coat sleeves were Rumanian cuffs, made of beads of half a dozen colors. His organ he bought at Algiers, and the "fortune tickets" in all languages were printed in Budapest, Hungary.

"Muy spake ulla laynguage!" he said, wagging his head in all directions and flashing his black eyes and dazzling teeth. "Aynd may balong to ulla countray. But excusay may, sayr, baseness bayfore playsure."

Here he went on jabbering in a sort of Yiddish, which the girls said was of the same quality as his English. As he spoke he gnashed his great teeth and squinted his eyes at the torch. This was his way of making himself look weird and wizardlike. But the girls never ceased laughing. The flickering light fell on his eyes, on his teeth, on his plump, dusky cheeks, but even this did not terrify them, they said. A newcomer, a little girl of fifteen, with a big hat, paid him two cents for her fortune. The young fellow screwed up his face to look like a Hungarian gypsy woman and said in a gentle, cooing voice, as he picked up one of the mice on his box:

"*Pillelu, pillelu, pillelu!* Dear little life, dear little soul, dear little sage! Go draw the lot of this little girl. Tell her the truth! Pick her the future! Tell her her fate! Pick it out! Pick it out! Pick it out! Tralla-la tralla-la tralla-la!"

The mouse pulled out the ticket upon which the wizard had pressed its snout, and the bit of printed paper was handed to the little girl with the big hat.

"Who can read?"

"I can, I can, I can!"

"Go ahead, Fanny!"

Fanny read aloud:

"You are often unhappy. You have enemies. ["How correct!" shouted the little girl.] Your greatest enemy is jealous of you. ["Holy words, as true as I wish to be well!"] But all her intrigues will avail her nothing. The young man is not so very, very tall, but those who know a thing or two about looks will tell you he is handsome and sugar-sweet. ["Never mind blushing; I know whom Mousie means and it is correct," declared the reader.] He is dead stuck on you. He is swooning away for you, but there are obstacles in your way. Never fear. Your enemy will burst with jealousy. The handsome man and the sweet girl will marry and be happy one hundred and twenty years. The wedding feast will be the talk of the town."

"*Mazel-tov.* [I congratulate you.] *Mazel-tov!*" laughed the maidens.

The next girl wanted an "English fortune," and she got a ticket which said, among other things, as follows:

"All this is because you kept part of the truth from your confessor. Still, your priest is your best friend, and it will all come right."

"What does it mean?" several girls asked, in consternation.

The wizard would not say. "Mousie ought to know what she is talking about," he answered.

"Who writes your tickets?" asked the snooper.

"They are not written, they are printed. *Pleellii—pleellii—li.*"

"Maybe you bought them of a Catholic or you got them mixed up with Catholic fortunes?"

"Mousie never mayx up nayting," the wizard answered, in haughty English. *"Trulitu-lu, trulilu-lu-lulu!"*

"Never mind your *trulilulu!*" screamed one of the girls. "What do you mean by working off ungodly fortunes on daughters of Israel?"

"I want my two cents!" stormed another.

"And I want mine!"

The wizard shouldered his burden, organ, mice, parrots, "Fortunes" and all, and fled.

"That's it! Let him fly to all the black years!" the market women shouted after him. "Now we will do some business in honor of the holiday."

"Carrots, carrots. Fish, living fish."

From *The People of the Abyss*

JACK LONDON

∽

Jack London (1876–1916) wrote more than fifty books before his tragic suicide at age forty. In addition to adventure stories and sociopolitical novels, London produced brilliant nonfiction, including war correspondence, sports writing, and documentary accounts of life at the margins. "Of all my books," London said, "I love most *The People of the Abyss*. No other book took so much of my young heart and tears as that study of the economic degradation of the poor."

In 1902 he lived for seven weeks in the East End of London, renowned as the worst slum in the world. His book about that experience brought together two strains of Victorian social reporting. First was the premise of *In Darkest England* (1890) by William Booth, founder of the Salvation Army: that the urban "interior" was as mysterious and forbidding as any colonial outpost. Second was the premise of such underground reports as James Greenwood's "A Night in a Workhouse" (1876): that the interior could be penetrated only in disguise. In America, the most daring underground reporter was Nellie Bly (the pen name of Elizabeth Jane Cochran), whose stratagems included feigning insanity to write an exposé of asylum abuses: *Ten Days in a Mad-House* (1887).

Far more than these predecessors, London identified with his downtrodden subjects. "The Descent," his opening chapter, is a narrative of initiation, ending with a kind of relief as his fear of the crowd drops away: "I had become part of it." His unorthodox socialism encourages a rhetoric of brotherhood.

But London also sees his fellow proletarians in a Darwinian light: as a "different race," stunted and devolved, apparently doomed by circumstance to lose in the struggle for existence. His controlling metaphor, the abyss, epitomizes this view. The present economic system makes the people of the East End expendable: "There are plenty, far fitter than they, clinging to the steep slope above and struggling frantically to slide no more."

London's use of the dropout narrator has inspired generations of reporters, from George Orwell ("The Spike") to Ted Conover (*Coyotes*). What later new journalists would call "immersion reporting" provides the very basis for *The People of the Abyss*—and becomes almost literal in London's initial descent: "The vast and malodorous sea had welled up and over me."

—K. K.

❧

Christ look upon us in this city,
And keep our sympathy and pity
Fresh, and our faces heavenward;
Lest we grow hard.
—THOMAS ASHE

"But you can't do it, you know," friends said, to whom I applied for assistance in the matter of sinking myself down into the East End of London. "You had better see the police for a guide," they added, on second thought, painfully endeavoring to adjust themselves to the psychological processes of a madman who had come to them with better credentials than brains.

"But I don't want to see the police," I protested. "What I wish to do, is to go down into the East End and see things for myself. I wish to know how those people are living there, and why they are living there, and what they are living for. In short, I am going to live there myself."

"You don't want to *live* down there!" everybody said, with disapprobation writ large upon their faces. "Why, it is said there are places where a man's life isn't worth tu'pence."

"The very places I wish to see," I broke in.

"But you can't, you know," was the unfailing rejoinder.

"Which is not what I came to see you about," I answered brusquely, somewhat nettled by their incomprehension. "I am a stranger here, and I want you to tell me what you know of the East End, in order that I may have something to start on."

"But we know nothing of the East End. It is over there, somewhere." And they waved their hands vaguely in the direction where the sun on rare occasions may be seen to rise.

"Then I shall go to Cook's," I announced.

"Oh, yes," they said, with relief. "Cook's will be sure to know."

But O Cook, O Thomas Cook & Son, pathfinders and trail-clearers, living sign-posts to all the world and bestowers of first aid to bewildered travellers—unhesitatingly and instantly, with ease and celerity, could you send me to Darkest Africa or Innermost Thibet, but to the East End of London, barely a stone's throw distant from Ludgate Circus, you know not the way!

"You can't do it, you know," said the human emporium of routes and fares at Cook's Cheapside branch. "It is so—ahem—so unusual."

"Consult the police," he concluded authoritatively, when I persisted. "We are not accustomed to taking travellers to the East End; we receive no call to take them there, and we know nothing whatsoever about the place at all."

"Never mind that," I interposed, to save myself from being swept out of the office by his flood of negations. "Here's something you can do for me. I wish you to understand in advance what I intend doing, so that in case of trouble you may be able to identify me."

"Ah, I see; should you be murdered, we would be in position to identify the corpse."

He said it so cheerfully and cold-bloodedly that on the instant I saw my stark and mutilated cadaver stretched upon a slab where cool waters trickle ceaselessly, and him I saw bending over and sadly and patiently identifying it as the body of the insane American who *would* see the East End.

"No, no," I answered; "merely to identify me in case I get into a scrape with the 'bobbies.' " This last I said with a thrill; truly, I was gripping hold of the vernacular.

"That," he said, "is a matter for the consideration of the Chief Office.

"It is so unprecedented, you know," he added apologetically.

The man at the Chief Office hemmed and hawed. "We make it a rule," he explained, "to give no information concerning our clients."

"But in this case," I urged, "It is the client who requests you to give the information concerning himself."

Again he hemmed and hawed.

"Of course," I hastily anticipated, "I know it is unprecedented, but—"

"As I was about to remark," he went on steadily, "it is unprecedented, and I don't think we can do anything for you."

However, I departed with the address of a detective who lived in the East End, and took my way to the American consul-general. And here, at last, I found a man with whom I could "do business." There was no hemming and hawing, no lifted brows, open incredulity, or blank amazement. In one minute I explained myself and my project, which he accepted as a matter of course. In the second minute he asked my age, height, and weight, and looked me over. And in the third minute, as we shook hands at parting, he said: "All right, Jack. I'll remember you and keep track."

I breathed a sigh of relief. Having built my ships behind me, I was now free to plunge into that human wilderness of which nobody seemed to know anything. But at once I encountered a new difficulty in the shape of my cabby, a gray-whiskered and eminently decorous personage, who had imperturbably driven me for several hours about the "City."

"Drive me down to the East End," I ordered, taking my seat.

"Where, sir?" he demanded with frank surprise.

"To the East End, anywhere. Go on."

The hansom pursued an aimless way for several minutes, then came to a puzzled stop. The aperture above my head was uncovered, and the cabman peered down perplexedly at me.

"I say," he said, "wot plyce yer wanter go?"

"East End," I repeated. "Nowhere in particular. Just drive me around, anywhere."

"But wot's the haddress, sir?"

"See here!" I thundered. "Drive me down to the East End, and at once!"

It was evident that he did not understand, but he withdrew his head and grumblingly started his horse.

Nowhere in the streets of London may one escape the sight of abject poverty, while five minutes' walk from almost any point will bring one to a slum; but the region my hansom was now penetrating was one unending slum. The streets were filled with a new and different race of people, short of stature, and of wretched or beer-sodden appearance. We rolled along through miles of bricks and squalor, and from each cross street and alley flashed long vistas of bricks and misery. Here and there lurched a drunken man or woman, and the air was obscene with sounds of jangling and squabbling. At a market, tottery old men and women were searching in the garbage thrown in the mud for rotten potatoes, beans, and vegetables, while little children clustered like flies around a festering mass of fruit, thrusting their arms to the shoulders into the liquid corruption, and drawing forth morsels, but partially decayed, which they devoured on the spot.

Not a hansom did I meet with in all my drive, while mine was like an apparition from another and better world, the way the children ran after it and alongside. And as far as I could see were the solid walls of brick, the slimy pavements, and the screaming streets; and for the first time in my life the fear of the crowd smote me. It was like the fear of the sea; and the miserable multitudes, street upon street, seemed so many waves of a vast and malodorous sea, lapping about me and threatening to well up and over me.

"Stepney, sir; Stepney Station," the cabby called down.

I looked about. It was really a railroad station, and he had driven desperately to it as the one familiar spot he had ever heard of in all that wilderness.

"Well?" I said.

He spluttered unintelligibly, shook his head, and looked very miserable. "I'm a strynger 'ere," he managed to articulate. "An' if yer don't want Stepney Station, I'm blessed if I know wotcher do want."

"I'll tell you what I want," I said. "You drive along and keep your eye out for a shop where old clothes are sold. Now, when you see such a shop, drive right on till you turn the corner, then stop and let me out."

I could see that he was growing dubious of his fare, but not long afterward he pulled up to the curb and informed me that an old clothes shop was to be found a bit of the way back.

"Won'tcher py me?" he pleaded. "There's seven an' six owin' me."

"Yes," I laughed, "and it would be the last I'd see of you."

"Lord lumme, but it'll be the last I see of you if yer don't py me," he retorted.

But a crowd of ragged onlookers had already gathered around the cab, and I laughed again and walked back to the old clothes shop.

Here the chief difficulty was in making the shopman understand that I really and truly wanted old clothes. But after fruitless attempts to press upon me new and impossible coats and trousers, he began to bring to light heaps of old ones, looking mysterious the while and hinting darkly. This he did with the palpable intention of letting me know that he had "piped my lay," in order to bulldose me, through fear of exposure, into paying heavily for my purchases. A man in trouble, or a high-class criminal from across the water, was what he took my measure for—in either case, a person anxious to avoid the police.

But I disputed with him over the outrageous difference between prices and values, till I quite disabused him of the notion, and he settled down to drive a hard bargain with a hard customer. In the end I selected a pair of stout though well-worn trousers, a frayed jacket with one remaining button, a pair of brogans which had plainly seen service where coal was shovelled, a thin leather belt, and a very dirty cloth cap. My underclothing and socks, however, were new and warm, but of the sort that any American waif, down in his luck, could acquire in the ordinary course of events.

"I must sy yer a sharp'un," he said, with counterfeit admiration, as I handed over the ten shillings finally agreed upon for the outfit. "Blimey, if you ain't ben up an' down Petticut Lane afore now. Yer trouseys is wuth five bob to hany man, an' a docker 'ud give two an' six for the shoes, to sy nothin' of the coat an' cap an' new stoker's singlet an' hother things."

"How much will you give me for them?" I demanded suddenly. "I paid you ten bob for the lot, and I'll sell them back to you, right now, for eight. Come, it's a go!"

But he grinned and shook his head, and though I had made a good bargain, I was unpleasantly aware that he had made a better one.

I found the cabby and a policeman with their heads together, but the latter, after looking me over sharply and particularly scrutinizing the bundle under my arm, turned away and left the cabby to wax mutinous by himself. And not a step would he budge till I paid him the seven shillings and sixpence owing him. Whereupon he was willing to drive me to the ends of the earth, apologizing profusely for his insistence, and explaining that one ran across queer customers in London Town.

But he drove me only to Highbury Vale, in North London, where my luggage was waiting for me. Here, next day, I took off my shoes (not without regret for their lightness and comfort), and my soft, gray travelling suit, and, in fact, all my clothing; and proceeded to array myself in the clothes of the other and unimaginable men, who must have been indeed unfortunate to have had to part with such rags for the pitiable sums obtainable from a dealer.

Inside my stoker's singlet, in the armpit, I sewed a gold sovereign (an emergency sum certainly of modest proportions); and inside my stoker's singlet I put myself. And then I sat down and moralized upon the fair years and fat, which had made my skin soft and brought the nerves close to the surface; for the singlet was rough and raspy as a hair shirt, and I am confident that the most rigorous of ascetics suffer no more than did I in the ensuing twenty-four hours.

The remainder of my costume was fairly easy to put on, though the brogans, or brogues, were quite a problem. As stiff and hard as if made of wood, it was only after a prolonged pounding of the uppers with my fists that I was able to get my feet into them at all. Then, with a few shillings, a knife, a handkerchief, and some brown papers and flake tobacco stowed away in my pockets, I thumped down the stairs and said good-by to my foreboding friends. As I passed out the door, the "help," a comely, middle-aged woman, could not conquer a grin that twisted her lips and separated them till the throat, out of involuntary sympathy, made the uncouth animal noises we are wont to designate as "laughter."

No sooner was I out on the streets than I was impressed by the difference in status effected by my clothes. All servility vanished from the demeanor of the common people with whom I came in contact. Presto! in the twinkling of an eye, so to say, I had become one of them. My frayed and out-at-elbows jacket was the badge and advertisement of my class, which was their class. It made me of like kind, and in place of the fawning and too-respectful attention I had hitherto received, I now shared with them a comradeship. The man in corduroy and dirty neckerchief no longer addressed me as "sir" or "governor." It was "mate," now—and a fine and hearty word, with a tingle to it, and a warmth and gladness, which the other term does not possess. Governor! It smacks of mastery, and power, and high authority—the tribute of the man who is under to the man on top, delivered in the hope that he will let up a bit and ease his weight. Which is another way of saying that it is an appeal for alms.

This brings me to a delight I experienced in my rags and tatters which is denied the average American abroad. The European traveller from the States, who is not a Crœsus, speedily finds himself reduced to a chronic state of self-conscious sordidness by the hordes of cringing robbers who clutter his steps from dawn till dark, and deplete his pocketbook in a way that puts compound interest to the blush.

In my rags and tatters I escaped the pestilence of tipping, and encountered men on a basis of equality. Nay, before the day was out I turned the tables, and said, most gratefully, "Thank you, sir," to a gentleman whose horse I held, and who dropped a penny into my eager palm.

Other changes I discovered were wrought in my condition by my new garb. In crossing crowded thoroughfares I found I had to be, if anything, more lively in avoiding vehicles, and it was strikingly impressed upon me that my life had cheapened in direct ratio with my clothes. When before, I inquired the way of a policeman, I was usually asked, "Buss or 'ansom, sir?"

But now the query became, "Walk or ride?" Also, at the railway stations it was the rule to be asked, "First or second, sir?" Now I was asked nothing, a third-class ticket being shoved out to me as a matter of course.

But there was compensation for it all. For the first time I met the English lower classes face to face, and knew them for what they were. When loungers and workmen, on street corners and in public houses, talked with me, they talked as one man to another, and they talked as natural men should talk, without the least idea of getting anything out of me for what they talked or the way they talked.

And when at last I made into the East End, I was gratified to find that the fear of the crowd no longer haunted me. I had become a part of it. The vast and malodorous sea had welled up and over me, or I had slipped gently into it, and there was nothing fearsome about it—with the one exception of the stoker's singlet.

TELLING TALES

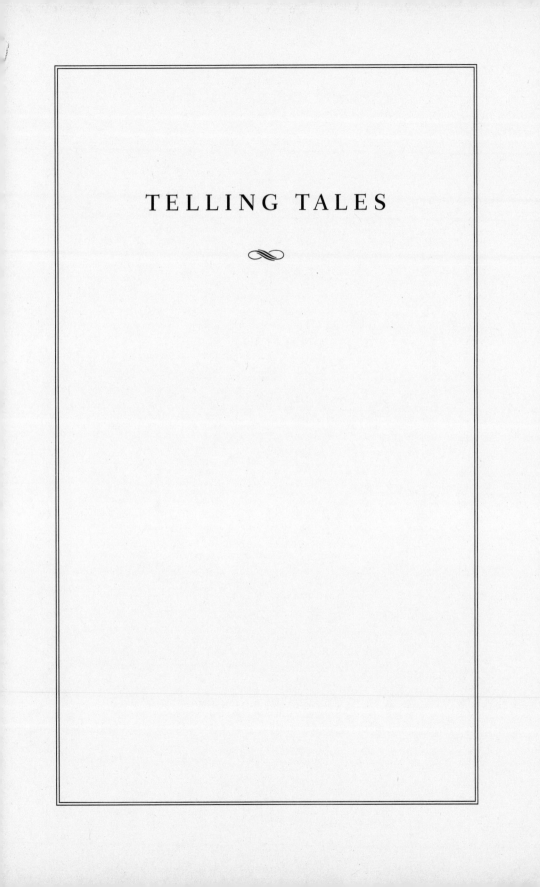

Drift

MORRIS MARKEY

∽

Since its founding in 1925, *The New Yorker* has had an unshakable reputation for airy sophistication in its humor, fiction, poetry, and journalism. The reputation is justified as far as it goes—but one place it does not go is the "Reporter at Large" pieces that Morris Markey (1899–1950) began turning out for the magazine in its very first year. Markey's work in the *New York World* had been spotted by founding editor Harold Ross, who hired him and gave him a simple charge: roam the city and write down what you see. That is what he did until 1931, when he left the magazine to pursue what turned out to be a spotty career as a Hollywood scriptwriter and freelance journalist.

Markey's articles did more than anything else to establish *The New Yorker* as a magazine that could be serious as well as light. He explored every stratum of society, and his presence as "I" or "we" in nearly all his pieces gave them an authority that the conventional reporting of the day usually lacked. In "Drift," published in 1931, Markey largely recedes from view and adopts the kind of "I am a camera" technique that *New Yorker* writer Lillian Ross would more fully exploit two decades later.

—B. Y.

∽

Detective Sergeant O'Keefe was on the assignment at the Morgue, and he was checking over the morning's instructions from Headquarters. He leaned over his desk in a pleasant room with a high ceiling, on the second floor of the old red building at Twenty-ninth Street and First Avenue, and thumbed the slips of paper. One of these slips, on pale-green paper, read "Release for Burial." The detective carried it to the head of the Mortuary Department.

"I've got a release on this one," he said. "Number 48,227."

"O.K.," said the superintendent. "We'll send him up on this afternoon's boat. But I thought that woman from Indianapolis was going to identify him."

"She kept coming back and looking," said the detective. "Finally made up her mind it wasn't her Willie. Willie had a scar on his arm where he fell out of a tree one time."

"She must have been around here nearly a month," said the superintendent. "And all the way from Indianapolis."

"They thought they had him identified once, down at Headquarters," said the detective. "Some fingerprints of a pickpocket that looked like his. But that was wrong, too."

"Did you ever hear of a pickpocket turning on the gas?" asked the superintendent.

He drew a slip of paper from a steel filing cabinet, and pinned it to the "Release for Burial." It contained the information that Number 48,227 was found dead in a Tenth Avenue rooming house, asphyxiation, apparently suicide. Number 48,227 was male, white, about twenty-eight years old, dark hair, blue eyes, five feet and eight inches tall, weight one hundred and fifty-four pounds. Hands not accustomed to manual work. Thirty-four dollars and seventy cents found on a dresser table. Good clothes. No papers or other means of identification in pockets. Took room twelve hours before death, giving no name and paying week's rent in advance.

The superintendent glanced over this data. "It's the depression," he said. "But it would save a lot of trouble if eggs like this would write their name and address on a piece of paper. Take that woman from Indianapolis. All that trouble and worry just because the description that was sent out sounded like her Willie boy. She must have had a nice trip east, all right."

Down in the cellar, the attendants prepared Number 48,227 in accordance with the release that the Medical Examiner's Office had furnished. The release meant that Number 48,227 had not been identified as a criminal from the voluminous records of fingerprints and measurements. It also meant that the hope of identification by relatives or friends might be given up. They sewed him in a sheet.

This was Wednesday, and burial day, and Number 48,227 was not alone in receiving the attentions of the busy workers. In the vast room, there were more than a hundred who lay beside him in long ranks. None other of these, however, were touched with the air of mystery that lay upon him. Their names were known, for they were the pauper dead gathered from all five boroughs of the city.

Some had crept with solitary misery into the city hospitals, and died there. Some had died in the dreadful squalor of the tenements. Some were dead-born infants from Bellevue next door. A division was perceptible in the ranks of this ghostly company. Some, about a third of the number, lay apart from the rest, and small crosses were imprinted on their shrouds. They were the Roman Catholics.

Somebody said: "Where does this unidentified go? Number 48,227?"

A clerk was sent upstairs to the office, and came back with word that

Number 48,227 wore a scapular when he was found. He belonged among the Catholics. But then somebody remembered that Catholics disapprove the interment of suicides in consecrated ground. Another messenger to the office upstairs brought back the final decision that no definite proof of suicide existed, that the poor fellow should have the benefit of the doubt, and it would be all right to bury him with the other Catholics.

Presently there was formed a long chain of stretcher-bearers, whose journey lay through a dim corridor and down a ramp to the deck of a weathered boat. The craft was thickly built, and squat, and painted black. Across its bows was written its name in white letters: *Riverside*. As the two men who bore Number 48,227 came aboard, shuffling with their burden, they were talking.

One of them said: "They ought to put in a new gangway. You bust your neck on them planks."

The other answered: "Maybe you better tell the Commissioner."

The trip up the East River was long and very slow. There was a shimmer on the water that hid its eternal filth of oil and refuse. The green lawns between the prisons and the hospitals on Welfare Island were bright in the sunshine, and very faintly from the nurses' home at the north end of the Island came the beat of dance music out of a radio. On the left the tall splendor of the buildings in Sutton Place and Beekman Place seemed quite immortal and even a little benign as we floated slowly past.

We pushed through the fairway that lies off Carl Schurz Park, turned, and beat toward the narrow channel of Hell Gate. Deep in the hold, the ancient engines chanted a dirge in monotone. Against a sky that was warm and blue our flag whipped at the half-mast. Coming into Hell Gate we passed very close to a tugboat that was driving ahead with a great show of foam at its bearded prow, and the man at the wheel of the tugboat took one hand from his wheel and lifted his hat stolidly from his head as we drew past.

Hart's Island is at the beginning of the Sound—low and flat and featureless. There are a few buildings huddled at one end, old buildings. The grass is green. It has been the Potter's Field for the town since 1869, and nearly two hundred and ninety thousand are buried there.

We came into a slip, and the unloading began. It was not long before Number 48,227 was brought ashore and they carried him at once to a long trench that was dug in the ground. The little crowd of still forms to which he was admitted because he had not forgotten his scapular lay on the grass, a considerable distance from the larger number who had not, in their lives, held with the Church of Rome. A priest in black vestments hovered over him for a moment, and very quickly he was lifted to the bottom of the pit. His motionless companions were lifted down to lie beside him, as close as the attendants could contrive, and soon men were working with shovels to cover them from the bright day. All of that lugubrious interment was accomplished in an incredibly short space of time.

Brief as were the ministrations of the priest in black over the Catholics, they were more than the others received. No man of God at all stood over them to repeat the formulas. Seventy of them were lifted rapidly down into one mammoth grave, and the shovellers were at work immediately.

The superintendent said: "The Catholic Church has consecrated the ground for its communicants, and they send a priest up twice a week. Nobody volunteers to give a ceremony to the others, and it is not the city's obligation."

There was no marking stone over the grave where Number 48,227 lay now. But in the office was a long slip of paper. It bore the number of the grave, and the names of all its occupants. Except, of course, that in one space it bore a numeral instead of a name.

The burials are conducted twice each week, on Wednesdays and Saturdays, and naturally it becomes a routine to the employees on the Island. About eight thousand a year are interred in the long trenches, and of these nearly five hundred are in the plight of Number 48,227—unidentified dead who carry no name into eternity.

In one spot on the Island, perhaps a little more carefully trimmed than the rest, there is an enclosure and the single monument that appears in all that level stretch of earth. It is the reservation for pauper dead among the veterans of the Civil War. Every year, on Decoration Day, representatives from posts of the G.A.R. come to hold ceremonies at the foot of the small granite shaft, and it is on this day alone in all the year that music sounds across the silent green, for the veterans always bring a band.

"Last year," said the superintendent, "they had twelve pieces."

There is no similar plot for veterans of the World War. "The American Legion or the government takes care of them," said the superintendent. "I don't know which. But occasionally we have an unidentified who is recognized from photographs after he has been buried, and if he is a veteran of the World War they come and get him and take him somewhere else."

About six bodies a week are disinterred and given over to relatives for burial in private cemeteries. But very rarely does this befall one of the unidentified dead, because it is unusual for one of these to be identified after interment. Generally, the bodies are taken away by people who have grown a little more prosperous since the day when their dead kin were taken to the Potter's Field.

The *Riverside* was leaving for the city. It turned slowly, and headed toward the spires that were lost in the haze above Manhattan.

Down at Police Headquarters a clerk was going through the routine which would permit the City Treasury to take over the thirty-four dollars and seventy cents that Number 48,227 had left behind when he decided he had enough of living.

From *Ninety Times Guilty*

HICKMAN POWELL

∞

In the first half of this century, readers would sometimes encounter dramatic reconstructions of actual events, but generally only in sports writing, in biographies for the children's market, and in true crime sagas—that is, on the other side of the literary tracks. *Ninety Times Guilty,* by Hickman Powell (1900–1966), is a cops and robbers tale—specifically, of Charles "Lucky" Luciano's prostitution racket, and New York prosecutor Thomas Dewey's successful attempt to bring it down—and thus did not get much credit for its literary attributes when it was published in 1939. But Powell, a New York newspaperman who based his narrative on court documents supplemented with extensive interviewing, was truly innovative in combining novelistic storytelling techniques with factual rigor. (Dewey was impressed enough to hire Powell as a staffer after becoming governor of New York, thereby ending his career as a journalist.)

Dave Miller was a "booker," an agent between the prostitutes and the madams, and would eventually prove to be a key witness in the prosecution of Luciano. In this excerpt, Miller gets shaken down for protection money, and thus experiences the first incursion of the mob into the New York prostitution trade.

—B. Y.

∞

DAVE FINDS PROSPERITY

By the dreadful depression summer of 1933, Dave Miller was one of the most prosperous citizens in New York. He had a string of very good-looking girls, and was booking them into an average of about twenty houses, scattered through Manhattan and Brooklyn. His ten per cent on the girls' earnings ranged from $300 to $400 a week, and the overhead of the business was not high. Also there were the presents he got from pimps who wanted him to put their girls into good jobs. He lived with his family in a fine house at 17

97

West Seventy-first Street, and did a lot of his business over the telephone from there. Most of his work was done on Saturday and Sunday, when he would go around to the various houses and collect his commissions.

One day in July, 1933, a fellow named Crazy Moe came to see Dave, bringing with him another man whom he called Charlie. This Crazy Moe had formerly run a joint up in Eighty-sixth Street and Dave had sent him girls.

But now it seemed he was getting into a tougher racket. He said that a combination was being formed and if Dave would put him and Charlie on his payroll he would see that Dave was not bothered. Dave was indignant. He didn't want to have anything to do with gangsters. Not even Crazy Moe.

Dave called in the housemaid and told her to take a good look at his two visitors in case she was ever needed for a witness. You would have thought that Dave was in the most respectable business in the world the way he went about it.

"What the hell did you get me into?" said the fellow named Charlie to Crazy Moe. He got very mad and walked out of the place. Then Dave told Crazy Moe to get out too.

One night a month later, Dave and his wife decided to go to the movies. There was a good gangster picture at the Rivoli. They parked their car in Fifty-fourth Street, by the Alba Hotel, between Seventh Avenue and Broadway, and started to walk toward the theatre.

Suddenly four men came up behind them in the darkness. One of them grabbed Dave by the shoulder, spun him around, and pinned him against the wall of the house they were passing. Another gave Ruth a little shove, and she walked on down the street a few steps, out of earshot. She knew enough not to ask questions, or make a commotion, or stick her nose too much into her husband's affairs.

Dave was dumbfounded for a minute, and just stood there not saying anything. He thought at first it was a stickup. Something poked him, and glancing down, he saw a glitter. The point of a long knife was held against his stomach.

"Say, what's this all about?" said Dave finally.

"Here's what it's about," said one of the men. "You got twenty-four hours to get out of town. You got to pick up and get out of town by midnight tomorrow night."

With that one of the men gave Dave a smack in the face, and with a renewed warning to get out of town, they walked off down the street and left him there.

Dave started to go on with his wife, but then turned and walked rapidly after the men.

"Hey," he called. "Wait a minute. What is all this about?"

"You know what the boss said," one of the four told the others. "We can't tell him nothing."

"Listen," said Dave, overtaking them. "What is all this about? Who can I see to straighten this out? Who are you guys and who can I see?"

"Well, who do you know?" asked the fellow that did most of the talking.

"I don't know anybody," said Dave. "But who are you, and I will have somebody see you."

They started naming a lot of names, haphazard, big shots that Dave didn't know; and they weren't getting anywhere.

"Do you know Moey?" Dave said finally, playing a hunch.

"What Moey?" said one of the fellows.

"The only name I know him by is Moey," said Dave. "All I know him by is Crazy Moe."

"I know Moey," said the fellow. "He is all right. You tell Moey to get in touch with me."

"Who will I ask him to get in touch with?" asked Dave.

"Just tell him to get in touch with Whitey," said Whitey.

And then the four fellows went away. They were Joey Levine, who Dave later knew was partners with Little Abie Wahrman, and Whitey and a fellow known as Jersey Ralph, and an Italian fellow that Dave never did know the name of.

Dave Miller went back to his wife, and they didn't think any more about going to the movies. He drove her home in his car, and then went back downtown looking for Crazy Moe.

He found Moe on the sidewalk near Broadway and Fifty-first Street, where he usually hung out. This little neighborhood of Broadway and Seventh Avenue, just above Times Square, might almost be called the capital of the underworld, of the half world, and of all the catch-as-catch-can industries of sport and entertainment. Stand on the corner, and sooner or later there will pass by everyone who amounts to anything in the fight and wrestling games, the kingdom of jazz and swing and tap dancing, the industries of gambling, narcotics, liquor, and of the strong-arm and the snatch. Around those streets there's always a lot of angles to be straightened out. This Crazy Moe hung out there, and knew a lot of people.

"Are these fellows the combination you were talking about?" asked Dave.

"No," said Moe. "That isn't the combination, but I think I know who they are."

Crazy Moe gave kind of a grunt, and then started down the street. They turned into Stewart's Cafeteria at Fiftieth Street and Broadway, and Crazy Moe went around speaking to this fellow and that. He talked for a while to a pimply faced fellow, and then came back to Dave, and they got in Dave's car, and Moe said to drive over to Brooklyn. So they drove downtown, and across the Manhattan Bridge, and way out on Myrtle Avenue to a little flyblown speakeasy, and there in a booth across from the bar was Whitey, with the Italian fellow that Dave didn't know the name of.

"Say, you got a lot of nerve," said Whitey to Dave. "You got just so long to get out of town."

"Lissen," said Crazy Moe. "This guy Dave Miller come in here with me, and I expect to take him out the same way I brought him in."

So then they began to talk business.

"I come over to find out what this is all about and try to straighten it out," said Dave.

"Well," said Whitey. "If you give us ten grand, we'll do the same to the fellow that we was supposed to do to you."

"What fellow?" asked Dave.

"You heard me," said Whitey. "You give us ten grand, we'll do the same to the fellow that we was supposed to do to you."

"Nobody carries ten grand in his pocket," said Dave. "Besides, I ain't got $10,000."

"Well," said Whitey, "that's our offer and that's the way it stands." And he wouldn't talk any more.

Dave and Crazy Moe drove back to Manhattan. Crazy Moe told Dave he would have to pay, for this was a tough crowd and meant business. Moe said he would see Dave the next day, and meantime he would see what he could do. Dave went home to bed, but did not sleep much.

Next day Dave had a telephone call from Whitey, putting on the heat, and Dave told him to be there at his meeting with Crazy Moe. So when Dave arrived at a speakeasy to meet Moey, there were the four fellows he had met on the street the night before. Dave and Moe tried to bargain with them, but they still held out for $10,000.

"You give us ten grand, and we'll make you the biggest man in New York," said Jersey Ralph.

"I'm satisfied the way I am," Dave said. "I like it this way. I don't want to be the biggest man in New York."

So they talked back and forth, and Dave tried to talk them down, but he could not make any headway.

"Well," said Jersey Ralph finally, "you still got till 12 o'clock tonight to get out of New York."

THE COPS

Dave Miller got in a cab and rode home. He was feeling pretty sore. Here he had worked for four years and built up a nice business, and now this gang of loafers wanted to take it away from him. Damned if he would stand for it! Damned if he would run! When he got home, he called up Abe Karp, his lawyer.

"Abe, make me out a will to sign, leaving everything to my wife. I got gangsters putting the arm on me," said Dave; and he told Karp how things were.

Karp came up to Dave's house with the will. Dave signed it. And then Karp took a surprising step.

This Karp was a wise apple. He had been dealing with cops, those with the vice squad at least, for a long time. There was no more accomplished operator in Women's Court and in spite of all the charges and evidence he had just brazened his way unscathed through the Seabury inquiry. He was very bold. Karp called up the West Sixty-eighth Street station and asked them to send over a couple of detectives. Within a few minutes Dave's doorbell rang, and there when he opened it, like a pair of human mountains stood two cops. Dave knew right away they were cops. When you are in his business, you can smell a cop a mile away.

"Mr. Miller?" said the cops, introducing themselves. "Mr. Karp said you had been threatened with grave bodily harm. We are here to protect you from bodily harm."

Dave told some sort of vague story about being threatened. He took the cops down to Stewart's Cafeteria and out to some places in Coney Island as if he was hunting for the gangsters. What he would have done if he had found any of them I don't know. It is hard to imagine Dave really going to bat on a complaint to the police.

The next two days were hell. In the side streets, if Dave were without the cops, lurked gangsters ready to pounce upon him. But here in his front parlor were two officers of the law. Good Lord! What if a cop should pick up a phone call and get an earful! If the cops caught on to him, Dave knew they could hand him five to ten, maybe twenty years.

When Dave went out in the street, the cops went along, and it was just as if he had leprosy. Nobody Dave knew would talk to him. He couldn't do any business. Those cops were poison.

The second day Dave's telephone rang.

"We know you've got coppers with you, but we are going to get you, coppers or no coppers," said a man on the wire and then hung up the phone.

Dave didn't know what to do. He was scared of the gangsters but quite as much afraid of the cops. He stood it for another day and then gave the cops the air. He told them he didn't need protection any more. That was all right with the cops. They had felt kind of foolish, for Dave wouldn't tell them anything much about himself.

PROTECTION

Rid of the cops, Dave felt easier. He moved about the city furtively, staying away from his usual haunts as much as possible. Next day he got a telephone call from a fellow named Six Bits.

"Say, Dave," said Six Bits, "I got a new package, and it's a honey. We're over on Broadway. Come on over and give a look."

Now this Six Bits was a pimp who usually had pretty snappy girls, so Dave said he would be right over to give a look at the package.

He went down in the elevator and out to his car, and he had just opened the door to get in, when Bang! it sounded as if a gun had gone off right close to his ears, which indeed was the case.

Dave dropped to the floor of his car. Two or three more bullets came spanging through the glass above him. Dave found himself thinking, vaguely, that it was a very good thing he had shatter-proof glass in his car. He lay quivering on the floor for a while, and then took a peek out. A car had been passing him, he knew, and now he saw it down the street, turning into Central Park West. He made a break and dashed back into the house.

Hardly anybody else was in the street at the time, and nobody did anything about this shooting. New York people don't like to meddle into matters that do not concern them.

Dave got in touch with Crazy Moe as soon as he could, and told him to renew negotiations with Joey Levine. This was a situation, Dave said, that had got to be straightened out.

It was several days before Moe could get an appointment, and Dave stayed in the house nearly all the time. Every time he started to go out, his wife, Ruth, went into hysterics. Finally Moey called him downtown, and Dave went to a restaurant at Sixth Street and Avenue C, on the lower east side. When he arrived, Moe was already there, with the four fellows who had put the arm on Dave.

"Well, what are you going to do about this?" said Joe Levine, tough-like, when Dave came in.

"What can I do?" asked Dave. "What do you want me to do?"

"Well, we decided to take $5,000 off you," said Joe, "and then you will pay us $200 a week protection money."

"Two hundred!" said Dave. "And what kind of protection do I get for that? Will you protect me from stick-ups? Will you protect me from the police if I get a grab?"

"No, we can't do that," said Joe. It was just as Dave thought, a shakedown, pure and simple.

"Why was I shot at?" asked Dave.

"That is the orders we got," said Joe.

"Who gave the orders? Who do you fellows represent?"

"Oh, we can't tell you that."

It went on that way for some time, and finally Dave saw he wasn't getting anywhere. He was in hot water, he was licked, and the only thing for him to do was take a powder.

"Let's have a drink," said Dave.

So Dave bought them all a drink, went home, put his furniture in storage, and took his family to California.

Thus protection came to the prostitution bookers of New York.

With the other bookers things went better. Cockeyed Louis, old, feeble, and nearly blind, paid $200 a week, and so did Nick Montana. Pete Balitzer, whose business was smaller, paid $100; but Jimmy Fredericks, who was running a small book with Danny Brooks, didn't have to pay, because there was a combination now and Jimmy was in the combination. Charlie Spinach paid. He had his hangout in the café at 121 Mulberry Street, which was also the office of Little Davie. But after a while Charlie Spinach disappeared, and we do not know what became of him.

Juke Joint

WALTER BERNSTEIN

❈

World War II had a salutary effect on nonfiction writing. Its unavoidable horrors not only banished much of the delicacy that remained in the collective journalistic sense of reality but, the old formulas proving inadequate, engendered new ways of representing the world. Although Walter Bernstein's marvelous "Juke Joint" was written just months after Pearl Harbor, it already displayed a new way of reporting on a new world. Bernstein (a twenty-two-year-old recent Dartmouth graduate at the time he wrote the piece) finds himself in a den of corruption but eschews euphemism, moralizing, and what-is-to-be-done? summation—all signal features of prewar journalism.

Bernstein in time would become a successful Hollywood screenwriter (he based *The Front* on his experience of being blacklisted), and "Juke Joint" has a strong cinematic feel, as it presents the mostly dispiriting sights and sounds of the place with minimal editorial comment; we are told a lot about smells, too, which goes the movies one better. Bernstein's ear was already superb: every single line of dialogue in the piece rings memorably true. Probably the most subtly cinematic touch of all is the jaunty sound track. The songs on the jukebox, as they segue from "You Are My Sunshine" to "Good-by, Dear, I'll Be Back in a Year," remind us that nearly all the denizens of Frankie's will be overseas before long, and that many of them will not return.

—B. Y.

❈

The principal industry of the small town of Phenix City, Alabama, is sex, and its customer is the Army. Located ten miles from Fort Benning, Georgia, the town is at least eighty per cent devoted to the titillation and subsequent pillage of that group it affectionately calls "Uncle Sam's soldier boys."

I became acquainted with Phenix following my initial month of recruit drill, when the selectees were first allowed to leave the post. During those thirty days we had heard approximately ninety-four lectures dealing with various sordid aspects of the town. There were some twenty thousand recruits at Benning for these talks. Our first free Saturday night, not more than ten, or at the most twelve, thousand hit the road to Phenix.

The first place to go in Phenix City is usually Frankie's. That is not the real name, but it will do. It is the name of the woman who owns the place, a determined and ageless female with red hair and a strong pioneer streak, only slightly perverted. Frankie's is reached by cutting off the paved main street after it has passed the town's two blocks of stores and climbed the hill past the new courthouse, and then hiking about a mile up a narrow dirt road. The place itself is like the other sagging frame houses that line the back streets of Phenix City, but it has a sign above the porch that says "Café" and on Saturday night there is a long line of taxicabs out front. Some of the soldiers walk from the Georgia town of Columbus, where the bus from camp stops, but only if they feel healthy. Too many bloody men have been found in Phenix alleys. The taxis only charge a quarter a head and for another quarter they will let you in on a number of other good things, and also include the transportation.

This Saturday night was a week after payday and the place was jammed. Frankie herself was behind the bar, seeing that the percentage of foam to beer was not more than half. Nothing harder than beer was sold at Frankie's; there was no necessity for anything else. The one square room that comprised the café was ugly and low-ceilinged. Now it was packed with soldiers. They stood five deep at the bar that ran across one side of the room. They filled the small dance floor and swallowed the juke box that stood in a corner. They sat on and around the dirty tables that dotted the rest of the room and spilled into the cubicle that had once been the kitchen, but now held three slot machines and a dice table.

There were about fifteen girls in the room. They were very young; some did not seem any more than sixteen or seventeen. They wore cotton dresses and low-heeled shoes and some did not even wear make-up. A few sat at tables, but most of them walked around, stopping every few feet to speak to one of the soldiers. Every so often one would talk a little longer with a soldier and then the two of them would walk out of the room, through the cubicle, and out a door at the other end. They were usually gone about ten minutes, and then they would return, the soldier grinning or shame-faced or defiant; and the girl would continue to walk around or perhaps sit at a table and have a Coca-Cola.

I finally got a bottle of beer from the bar and took it to a table at the edge of the dance floor, where there were some men from my company. They were drinking rye from a bottle and watching the girls. The juke box was screaming "You Are My Sunshine." It was hot and smoky in the room and I drank my beer quickly. As soon as I had finished, a girl came over and took the bottle. She looked very young and she was wearing a cheap housedress that ended an inch above her knee. "You want another beer?" she asked. I shook my head and one of the other soldiers said, "Sit down, Mary." The girl sat down without comment. She said something to the man next to her, who shook his head. She looked around at the rest of us and we all shook our heads. "Oh, well," Mary said.

"Have a beer," a soldier named Pat said.

"Don't mind if I do," Mary said. Pat got up and went to the bar and Mary reached down to loosen her saddle shoes. "My feet hurt," she said. She looked like the girls whom I had seen working in the town's textile mill.

"I know you," one of the men said. "You work in the dime store."

"That's Peggy," the girl said. "You boys always take me for Peggy."

"I could swear you were sisters," the man said.

"You're crazy," Mary said. Pat returned with the beers and the girl drank hers thirstily. "Well," she said when she was finished, "I got to get back to work."

"How's business?" Pat asked.

"Not good, not bad," Mary said. She stood up, glancing toward the door. Standing in the doorway were two M.P.'s, their eyes searching the crowd. Frankie waved to them from behind the bar and they waved back, still looking through the crowd. When they were satisfied they turned and went out. Mary jerked her head after them. "That don't hurt my business," she said scornfully. She walked off into the crowd and I stood up to stretch my legs. I said good-by to the other men, who were trying to decide what they could do and not be gypped, and went across the room to the cubicle. At the entrance was a blind man holding a cup. A sign in his hat said "God Bless You One and All." Whenever someone put a coin in his cup he would spill it into his hand, feel it very carefully, and then place it in his pocket.

There was a crowd of soldiers around the dice table that occupied most of the little gambling room. Three soldiers and two civilians in shirtsleeves were shooting craps. One of the civilians was the house man; the other looked like a shill of some sort, but I couldn't be sure. One of the soldiers, a corporal, had a pile of bills before him and his face was flushed and excited. The other two soldiers had some money, but not as much. The civilians kept their money hidden.

The corporal had the dice and was evidently riding a streak. He threw two passes and then made a four. The other two soldiers watched him enviously, but the civilians didn't seem very interested. The corporal threw another seven; he had about a hundred dollars in his pile. He threw a six and the spectators cheered. "He'll make that easy," whispered a soldier next to me. The corporal made his point on the next throw and the soldier nudged me happily. "Smart boy," he said. "Must be using his own dice." The corporal then threw a ten, and in rapid succession an eight, a five and a seven. Everyone sighed except the civilians, but the soldier next to me nodded wisely. "Just making it look good," he said. The dice went to one of the other soldiers and I slipped away from the table. There were no windows in the little room and the smoke made the air like lead. A slight draft blew from the door that kept opening at the other end of the cubicle, but that didn't help much. I watched some of the soldiers lose money in the slot machines, lost a few nickels myself, then returned to the main room.

Standing against a wall was a very fat man in civilian clothes. He wore an old windbreaker, a dirty pair of pants, and a slouch hat, pushed back on his head. He was leaning on a thick cane, watching the crowd. His feet were in carpet slippers. His name was Hancock and he was the bouncer. I had been introduced to him once, so I went over to say hello. He didn't remember me, but took my word that we had met. I asked him why he wore slippers and he pulled up his right trouser leg to show a bandage around his foot. "Got kicked by a G.I. boot," he said. I asked what was new. "Can't complain," he said. "For Saturday it's a quiet night." Just then one of the girls came over and said there was trouble by the juke box. "Excuse me," Hancock said, courteously. He limped across the room, his stomach running interference for the rest of his body. A soldier was drunk at the juke box and did not like the selection being played. He was hammering on the window when Hancock tapped him on the shoulder. He turned around full of fight, but Hancock spoke to him quietly and after a moment took him by the arm and walked him to the door. The soldier turned when they reached the door, but Hancock pushed him gently outside and shut the door after him. Then he limped back and resumed his place against the wall. "Boys that age shouldn't drink liquor," he said, shaking his head.

We stood for a while without talking. The room was still packed tight. Frankie's red head shone through the smoke. The girls still walked around, bored and weary, and the juke box still screamed "You Are My Sunshine." The soldiers stood in little knots or sat back at the tables, eyeing the girls. They were all dressed very carefully, with their insignia shining, but most of them looked as if they had gotten into the wrong place.

I stood against the wall wondering what to do. There was a burst of voices from the gambling room and Mary trotted out. "You better go in there," she said to Hancock. Hancock sighed and limped off. Mary stayed behind, taking his place against the wall. "My feet hurt," she said. She took one foot out of her shoe and wrinkled the toes appreciatively. I asked her how long she had been at Frankie's. "This is my first week," she said. "I used to be at Twin Oak." I asked why she had left. "You make more money here," she said. Twin Oak was a place like Frankie's, about six miles out of town. It was owned by the former chief of police, who also owned another place in town. He used to own them while in office, but quit the police department when asked by the respectable element to choose between business and pleasure.

I asked Mary if she preferred Frankie's and she shrugged. "At the other place we got officers." I admitted the distinction. "And this place you got to walk around all the time. But I like it here," she said. "It's more democratic."

I asked if the police ever bothered her and she laughed. "That don't hurt my business," she said loudly. She laughed again. "You know what? I'm a food handler. I got a card to prove it." She dug into the pockets of her dress, but came up empty-handed. "All the girls are food handlers," she said. "Every damned one of us." She seemed very proud of the fact, although all the girls who work in places like Frankie's are classified in Phenix City as food handlers. What this means is not exactly certain, since there were still 1082 new venereal disease cases at Benning in the past eight months. Lately, however, there had been a renewed vice crusade by the city authorities, and the F.B.I. was finally summoned. The Army is vehement in its demands that these places be abolished, but the responsibility is still a civil one. And when the lure of easy money and girls will bring thirty thousand paying customers to a town every night, the merchants who own the town are likely to consider health a peacetime luxury.

By now someone had broken the monopoly on the juke box and it was playing "I'm Walking the Floor Over You." Mary was whistling and tapping the floor to the music. "I'm walking the floor over you," she sang nasally. "Please tell me just what should I do." A soldier walking past told her what she should do, and she aimed a kick at him. The kick missed, but the momentum carried her away from the wall and she started her trip around the room again.

Hancock came out of the cubicle, leading another soldier by the arm. It was one of the soldiers from the dice table and he was very angry. He was gesturing wildly and making attempts to get back into the cubicle, but Hancock led him firmly to the door. He was not so gentle this time and tapped the soldier with his cane as he pushed him out. Then he limped back and leaned against the wall. "What kind of a home do these boys come from?" he asked me. "He says the dice were crooked. Why should they be crooked?"

I told him that the soldier wasn't the only one who felt that way.

"They're not smart," Hancock said. "They don't use their heads. Don't they know the odds against them in an honest game? Why should we make it crooked?"

There was no short answer to this, so I changed the subject and invited Hancock to the bar for a beer. The crowd had thinned there and we found a place at the end. Next to us a soldier with the high boots of a parachutist was arguing unsteadily with one who wore the patch of an armored division on his sleeve. "I wouldn't be seen in a tank for all the money in the world," the parachutist was saying emphatically. "Not for a hundred dollars."

"It's because you're old-fashioned," the other said.

"It's because a tank is uncomfortable," the parachutist explained patiently. "A tank is a messy machine."

"A tank is very useful," the other said.

"Now you take the sky," the parachutist said. "What could be cleaner?"

Frankie came over to serve us and Hancock introduced me. "Howdy,"

Frankie said, professionally. Her mouth opened and closed in a short smile, showing bad teeth. She had a huge, matronly front and her close bitten nails were painted blood-red. She looked like a suburban mah jong player who played for keeps. "You being treated all right?" she asked me.

"He's in my hands," Hancock said.

"Good," Frankie said. "Anything I can do for you, let me know." We ordered bottled beer and she had one of the girls behind the bar bring it to us. "Here's to the brave young men in the Army," Hancock said. I had the bottle tilted up when I saw four men in civilian clothes come through the front door. They stood for a moment in the doorway, looking around, and then walked slowly toward the bar. They all wore hats and their jackets were open and I had seen enough movies to know they were the Law.

I started to find the back door, but Hancock pulled me over to his old spot against the wall. Frankie had also seen the men and stood quietly behind the bar, not smiling as she had at the M.P.'s. No one else paid much attention to them. The men reached the bar and stopped and still the crowd did not notice them. Then they began pushing people away from the bar and the hush started there and spread through the room until the juke box was suddenly much louder than usual. All the soldiers stood up and a few made a quick break for the door. The men paid no attention to these. They cleared the crowd from the bar and one of the men took out a notebook and said, "O.K., Frankie." Frankie looked at him and then turned to the girls working behind the bar and said, "Get out the beer."

It was all very smooth and quick, as if it had been done many times before. The crowd settled back when they saw what the men were after, and now made a path for them as they carried the cases of beer outside. I noticed some soldiers slip out the back way, but none of the girls left and I could still hear the slot machines clicking. The man with the notebook took down figures as the beer went outside. Frankie talked to him as he wrote, but he kept shrugging his shoulders as if disclaiming any responsibility. After a few minutes the novelty and fear wore off and the room slid back to normal. The people who had been at the bar waited to resume their places, but the rest of the crowd moved off to other parts of the room. In about ten minutes the men had cleared the bar of beer. The man with the notebook wrote something on a piece of paper and handed it to Frankie. She said something in a low voice and he laughed. Then he tipped his hat and went out after the other men.

The crowd surged back against the bar as soon as they left and the girls served up Coca-Cola and Dr. Pepper. I turned to Hancock, but before I could speak he assured me that everything was all right. "It's only the State Liquor Control boys," he said. "They do this all the time." I said I thought the sale of beer was allowed in Alabama. "Not without no license," Hancock said.

Except for the absence of beer nothing seemed changed. Hancock went off in response to another girl's call and I walked around the room trying to find some fresh air. The juke box was playing "Good-by, Dear, I'll Be Back in a Year," and some soldiers stood around the machine giving each lyric a Bronx cheer. I wandered past the blind man into the little gambling room. The dice game was still going and there were five soldiers playing now instead of three. I recognized only the corporal who had been in the money. Now there were only a few dollars before him and he looked scared. The house man had also changed, but the other civilian was still there, pocketing his money as he won. He seemed to be winning more consistently now. The door at the far end of the cubicle had been left open and the trickle of cool air felt good. Occasionally one of the couples going through would close the door after them, and then the house man would walk patiently across the room and open it again.

After the dice game I put a few more nickels in the slot machines, then wandered back into the main room. I searched for someone I knew, but all the faces were strange in the familiar way most soldiers have to one another. A soldier hurried past me toward the front door, his face drawn and white. A girl came up, but I shook my head and she continued on around the room. There was a bad smell in this part of the room, so I moved away. The juke box was shrieking "We'll Have to Slap the Dirty Jap." I looked at my watch and was surprised to see it was not even midnight. I started to find Hancock when suddenly there was a loud whistle and I looked up to see the two M.P.'s standing in the doorway. "At ease!" one of them shouted. "All men of the 19th Engineers report to their barracks at once." He banged on the wall for emphasis and repeated the sentence. Then the two of them turned and went out.

This time the noise did not return to the room as quickly as it had when the Liquor Control men left. We had all seen this happen too often before, the same words in the same public places, and the next day an outfit gone from the post. The soldiers looked at each other and a few men stood up around the room and walked slowly to the door. The other soldiers watched them go and as soon as they were out everyone began to talk again and laugh, even more loudly than before. The air was getting more and more foul. I found Hancock and said good-night. He shook my hand warmly and told me to hurry back. As I left the room a soldier was being sick in a corner. The juke box was screaming "Good-by, Mama, I'm Off to Yokohama."

From *Hiroshima*

JOHN HERSEY

∞

The son of missionary parents, John Hersey (1914–1993) spent his child-hood in China. After studying at Yale and Cambridge, he became a secretary to novelist Sinclair Lewis, and then a correspondent for *Time* and *Life*. He reported on World War II in both the European and Pacific theaters, and was commended for bravery on Guadalcanal for helping to move wounded soldiers to safety. One of his most famous stories for *Life*, "Joe Is Home Now" (1944), relied on a composite character to dramatize the difficult adjustments of wounded servicemen, but Hersey later insisted that literary journalism must be factually authentic and absolutely reliable.

Hiroshima meets that standard. In clinical detail, the book follows six survivors through the aftermath of the atomic blast. On the strength of extensive interviews, Hersey reconstructs scenes and explores the survivors' thoughts and feelings in novelistic fashion. He restricts the story to the characters' sphere of knowledge—omitting, for example, any exploration of the physics of the bomb or President Truman's decision to use it.

The passage reprinted here exemplifies Hersey's descriptive power, his restrained narrative tone, and his focus on acts of quiet heroism. Mr. Tanimoto, a Methodist minister, was one of those who wandered to Asano Park on the first night of the atomic age. As he tries to help the most gravely injured, Tanimoto's reactions provide the story with a moral and psychological center. The other main characters include a German-Jesuit priest, two doctors, a young secretary, and a widow with a small child. Instead of a sociological cross section, Hersey offers American readers a series of sympathetic portraits. *Hiroshima* was first published in a single issue of *The New Yorker* (August 31, 1946), and historian John Toland recalls its impact: "Riveted by the ghastly details, those of us who had hated the Japanese for five years realized that Mr. Hersey's six protagonists were fellow human beings."

—K. K.

∞

Mr. Tanimoto found about twenty men and women on the sandspit. He drove the boat onto the bank and urged them to get aboard. They did not move and he realized that they were too weak to lift themselves. He reached down and took a woman by the hands, but her skin slipped off in huge, glovelike pieces. He was so sickened by this that he had to sit down for a moment. Then he got out into the water and, though a small man, lifted several of the men and women, who were naked, into his boat. Their backs and breasts were clammy, and he remembered uneasily what the great burns he had seen during the day had been like: yellow at first, then red and swollen, with the skin sloughed off, and finally, in the evening, suppurated and smelly. With the tide risen, his bamboo pole was now too short and he had to paddle most of the way across with it. On the other side, at a higher spit, he lifted the slimy living bodies out and carried them up the slope away from the tide. He had to keep consciously repeating to himself, "These are human beings." It took him three trips to get them all across the river. When he had finished, he decided he had to have a rest, and he went back to the park.

As Mr. Tanimoto stepped up the dark bank, he tripped over someone, and someone else said angrily, "Look out! That's my hand." Mr. Tanimoto, ashamed of hurting wounded people, embarrassed at being able to walk upright, suddenly thought of the naval hospital ship, which had not come (it never did), and he had for a moment a feeling of blind, murderous rage at the crew of the ship, and then at all doctors. Why didn't they come to help these people?

Dr. Fujii lay in dreadful pain throughout the night on the floor of his family's roofless house on the edge of the city. By the light of a lantern, he had examined himself and found: left clavicle fractured; multiple abrasions and lacerations of face and body, including deep cuts on the chin, back, and legs; extensive contusions on chest and trunk; a couple of ribs possibly fractured. Had he not been so badly hurt, he might have been at Asano Park, assisting the wounded.

By nightfall, ten thousand victims of the explosion had invaded the Red Cross Hospital, and Dr. Sasaki, worn out, was moving aimlessly and dully up and down the stinking corridors with wads of bandage and bottles of mercurochrome, still wearing the glasses he had taken from the wounded nurse, binding up the worst cuts as he came to them. Other doctors were putting compresses of saline solution on the worst burns. That was all they could do. After dark, they worked by the light of the city's fires and by candles the ten remaining nurses held for them. Dr. Sasaki had not looked outside the hospital all day; the scene inside was so terrible and so compelling that it had not occurred to him to ask any questions about what had happened beyond the windows and doors. Ceilings and partitions had fallen; plaster, dust, blood, and vomit were everywhere. Patients were dying by the hundreds, but there was nobody to carry away the corpses. Some of the hospital staff distributed biscuits and rice balls, but the charnel-house smell was so strong that few were hungry. By three o'clock the next morning, after nineteen straight hours of his gruesome work, Dr. Sasaki was incapable of dressing another wound. He and some other survivors of the hospital staff got straw mats and went outdoors—thousands of patients and hundreds of dead were in the yard and on the driveway—and hurried around behind the hospital and lay down in hiding to snatch some sleep. But within an hour wounded people had found them; a complaining circle formed around them: "Doctors! Help us! How can you sleep?" Dr. Sasaki got up again and went back to work. Early in the day, he thought for the first time of his mother, at their country home in Mukaihara, thirty miles from town. He usually went home every night. He was afraid she would think he was dead.

Near the spot upriver to which Mr. Tanimoto had transported the priests, there sat a large case of rice cakes which a rescue party had evidently brought for the wounded lying thereabouts but hadn't distributed. Before evacuating the wounded priests, the others passed the cakes around and helped themselves. A few minutes later, a band of soldiers came up, and an officer, hearing the priests speaking a foreign language, drew his sword and hysterically asked who they were. One of the priests calmed him down and explained that they were Germans—allies. The officer apologized and said that there were reports going around that American parachutists had landed.

The priests decided that they should take Father Schiffer first. As they prepared to leave, Father Superior LaSalle said he felt awfully cold. One of the Jesuits gave up his coat, another his shirt; they were glad to wear less in the muggy night. The stretcher bearers started out. The theological student led the way and tried to warn the others of obstacles, but one of the priests got a foot tangled in some telephone wire and tripped and dropped his corner of the litter. Father Schiffer rolled off, lost consciousness, came to, and then vomited. The bearers picked him up and went on with him to the edge of the city, where they had arranged to meet a relay of other priests, left him with them, and turned back and got the Father Superior.

The wooden litter must have been terribly painful for Father LaSalle, in whose back scores of tiny particles of window glass were embedded. Near the edge of town, the group had to walk around an automobile burned and squatting on the narrow road, and the bearers on one side, unable to see their way in the darkness, fell into a deep ditch. Father LaSalle was thrown onto the ground and the litter broke in two. One priest went ahead to get a handcart from the Novitiate, but he soon found one beside an empty house and wheeled it back. The priests lifted Father LaSalle into the cart and pushed him over the bumpy road the rest of the way. The rector of the Novitiate, who had been a doctor before he entered the religious order, cleaned the wounds of the two priests and put them to bed between clean sheets, and they thanked God for the care they had received.

Thousands of people had nobody to help them. Miss Sasaki was one of them. Abandoned and helpless, under the crude lean-to in the courtyard of the tin factory, beside the woman who had lost a breast and the man whose burned face was scarcely a face any more, she suffered awfully that night from the pain in her broken leg. She did not sleep at all; neither did she converse with her sleepless companions.

In the park, Mrs. Murata kept Father Kleinsorge awake all night by talking to him. None of the Nakamura family were able to sleep, either; the children, in spite of being very sick, were interested in everything that happened. They were delighted when one of the city's gas-storage tanks went up in a tremendous burst of flame. Toshio, the boy, shouted to the others to look at the reflection in the river. Mr. Tanimoto, after his long run and his many hours of rescue work, dozed uneasily. When he awoke, in the first light of dawn, he looked across the river and saw that he had not carried the festered, limp bodies high enough on the sandspit the night before. The tide had risen above where he had put them; they had not the strength to move; they must have drowned. He saw a number of bodies floating in the river.

Early that day, August 7th, the Japanese radio broadcast for the first time a succinct announcement that very few, if any, of the people most concerned with its content, the survivors in Hiroshima, happened to hear: "Hiroshima suffered considerable damage as the result of an attack by a few B-29s. It is believed that a new type of bomb was used. The details are being investigated." Nor is it probable that any of the survivors happened to be tuned in on a short-wave rebroadcast of an extraordinary announcement by the President of the United States, which identified the new bomb as atomic: "That bomb had more power than twenty thousand tons of TNT. It had more than two thousand times the blast power of the British Grand Slam, which is the largest bomb ever yet used in the history of warfare." Those victims who were able to worry at all about what had happened thought of it and discussed it in more primitive, childish terms—gasoline sprinkled from an airplane, maybe, or some combustible gas, or a big cluster of incendiaries, or the work of parachutists; but, even if they had known the truth, most of them were too busy or too weary or too badly hurt to care that they were the objects of the first great experiment in the use of atomic power, which (as the voices on the short wave shouted) no country except the United States, with its industrial know-how, its willingness to throw two billion gold dollars into an important wartime gamble, could possibly have developed.

The Day of the Fight

W. C. HEINZ

∾

W. C. Heinz (the initials stand for Winifred Charles) is the last surviving representative of a flowering of sports journalism that transpired in the pages of New York City's daily newspapers in the 1940s and '50s. Heinz, Frank Graham, Jimmy Cannon, and Red Smith, all of whom had read their Hemingway, brought irony and pity to their accounts of home-run hitters and club fighters; they could make an 800-word column into a set piece that brought tears to your eyes.

Heinz was set adrift from the demands of daily deadlines when his employer, the New York *Sun,* ceased publishing in 1950. Its notorious hardships notwithstanding, freelancing gave Heinz, then thirty-five, the opportunity to experiment with long forms. (In addition to his collected articles, *American Mirror,* Heinz has written two novels, *The Surgeon* and *The Professional.* Red Smith reported that Hemingway called the latter the only good book he'd ever read about a fighter.)

"The Day of the Fight," first published in *Cosmopolitan* in 1947 (those were the pre–Helen Gurley Brown days when it was a general-interest magazine), takes a more or less standard topic for a newspaper column, a boxer's routine in the hours before a prizefight, and centrifugally expands it into a 6,000-word tour de force. Like Lillian Ross in "Portrait of Hemingway" and *Picture* (but several years before those more widely known works), Heinz was attempting journalism in the form of a play. And a well-made play it is: the piece's steady accumulation of carefully chosen plain details one after another, the wonderfully *listened to* dialogue, the complete absence of editorial comment, the declarative irony of Heinz's sentences—all contribute to the steady buildup of nearly unbearable tension that the final paragraph magnificently releases.

—B. Y.

∾

The window was open from the bottom and in the bed by the window the prizefighter lay under a sheet and a candlewick spread. In the other bed

115

another prizefighter slept, but the first one lay there looking at the ceiling. It was nine-thirty in the morning and he would fight that night.

The name of the first prizefighter is Rocky Graziano, but you don't have to remember that. The thing to remember is that he is a prizefighter, because they said this was to be a piece telling what a fighter does, from the moment he gets up in the morning until the moment he climbs into the ring, on the day when he must fight.

"All right, Rock," Whitey Bimstein, his trainer, said. "If you don't want to sleep you can get up."

The suite is on the twelfth floor of a hotel in New York's West Eighties, off Central Park. In the other bedroom Eddie Coco, one of the fighter's managers, still slept. On the soiled striped sofa in the sitting room a young lightweight named Al Pennino lay on his right side, facing the room, a blanket over him and a pillow under his head.

"If he don't feel like sleepin'," Whitey said, "there's no sense of him lyin' there if he wants to get up."

He was walking around the sitting room, picking up newspapers and putting them on the table, fussing around the doors of the closetlike kitchenette. Graziano and Whitey had been living there in the long weeks Graziano had been training for this one. They do not let a fighter live at home when he is in training for a fight.

"What time is it?" Graziano said. He had come out of the bedroom and was standing just inside the sitting room. He was wearing a pair of brown checked shorts and that was all. There was sleep in his face and the black hair was mussed on his head.

"Nine thirty-five," Whitey said.

Pennino and Coco were awake and walking around now. The other fighter, Lou Valles, a welterweight, came out of the bedroom in a shirt and a pair of slacks.

"You sleep?" Coco said to Graziano.

"Yeah," Graziano said. "All right."

"We got a nice day."

Outside the window the sun shone a pale yellow and in the distance over the park there was a blue-gray haze. This one was to be held in Yankee Stadium and the weather is one of the things they worry about when they have an outdoor fight.

As they sat around the small sitting room now they said little, seeming reluctant to break the sleep that was still in their heads. Finally Valles got up and walked over to the table by the wall and picked up the morning newspapers. They were opened to the sports sections because Graziano was going to fight Tony Zale, the middleweight champion, and this one was an important fight.

"You see?" he said, showing one of the papers to Pennino. "That Rocky takes a good picture. Right?"

Graziano did not say anything.

"He's a good-looking guy," Pennino said.

"You know what I'm going to do if I win the title tonight?" Graziano said. "If I win the title, I'm gonna get drunk. You know what I mean by that?"

"Yeah," Whitey said. "I know what you mean. You remind me of another fighter I had. He said if he won the title he'd get drunk. He won the title and he had one beer and he was drunk."

"Who?" Graziano asked.

"Lou Ambers," Whitey said.

Graziano went to the bedroom and when he came out he had on a pair of gray sharkskin slacks, turned once at the cuffs, a basque shirt with narrow blue stripes,and over this a gray-blue sleeveless sweater. He had washed and his hair was combed back. At ten-thirty Jack Healey came in. He is another of Graziano's managers, a suave but nervous type they call "The Mustache."

"You all right?"

"Sure," Graziano said. "Relax. I'm all right."

They waited for Pennino and Coco to finish dressing and they sat around talking about Stanley Ketchel, Bob Fitzsimmons, and Joe Dundee, Healey and Whitey talking and the fighters gazing around the room and out the window.

They were ready to leave then because it was eleven-fifteen. At the door the maid, in a blue dress with white cuffs and collar, said she wished them luck, and the woman who ran the elevator smiled at them in a way implying that she knew it was a special day.

Graziano's car was waiting in front of the hotel. It is blue and buff, new, and on the front doors the small letters read "Rocky." They got in, Healey driving, Graziano in the middle, and Coco on the outside, Whitey and Pennino and Valles in the back.

When they reached Fifty-fourth Street they turned west and stopped in front of the side door to Stillman's Gym. They got out and left Pennino to watch the car and went upstairs and into the gym, gray and, but for Lou Stillman and a couple of others, deserted.

"Hey," Stillman said, coming across the floor from the front. "What you guys want anyway?"

"You know what we want," Whitey said.

"I'll punch you in the nose," Stillman said to Graziano. "I'll knock you out before tonight."

"You'll what?" Graziano said, feigning annoyance and taking a fighting pose.

"What's the matter?" Stillman said, smiling. "Can't you take a joke?"

They went back into a small partitioned room in the back. There was a scale and Graziano started stripping and they shut the door. In a couple of minutes they came out, Graziano fastening his belt.

"I'll bet you down there he'll weigh fifty-three and a half," Whitey said. "I'll bet you'll see."

"What did he weigh here?" Healey said.

"A little over fifty-four," Whitey said, "but he'll go to the toilet."

"He looks great," Healey said. "You can tell from his eyes."

In the car again they started around the block. Graziano shut off the radio which Pennino must have turned on while the rest were in the gym.

"You should listen to that," Healey said. "They might tell you about the fight."

Graziano said nothing. They drove west to the West Side Highway and south past the North River docks.

"Rock," Whitey said, "your old man still working down here?"

"No," Graziano said. "He's workin' down at the Fish Market instead."

It was 11:48 A.M. when they were looking ahead down the street to the mob around the rear entrance to the New York State building where Graziano and Zale would weigh in. There were about two hundred people there, men, kids, photographers, and even a few women standing on and around the steps.

"We'll park down in front of your grandmother's," Healey said.

He drove slowly across the intersection past the park and pulled up at the curb on the right in front of the building where Graziano, as a kid, had lived. This was his neighborhood, and when they got out of the car there was a cop standing there and he stuck out his hand to Graziano and shook his head.

"Well," he said, "you're still the same, aren't you?"

Graziano said something but by now some of the crowd, running, had caught up. They were men, young and middle-aged and a lot of kids, and one of the men had his left arm in a sling.

"You see this?" he was shouting at Graziano from the back and waving his right fist. "You see this? Think of this tonight."

"All right. All right," the cop was shouting. "Stand back."

They hustled the fighter, then, into the narrow doorway between two stores and, with the fighter leading, they climbed up three flights. He opened a door and there they followed him into the kitchen of an apartment.

"Hello," he said to the man standing there and then pausing and looking around. "Where's Grandma?"

"In the park maybe," the man, Graziano's uncle, Silvio, said. "Maybe shopping. She went out about half an hour ago."

Graziano sat on a chair by the window, his right elbow on the windowsill. He looked around the room and through the door and into one of the bedrooms and his uncle watched him.

"How you feel, Rocky?" Silvio said.

"I feel fine," Graziano said.

That was all they said. He sat there waiting, looking around occasionally, not saying anything to the others who had followed him in. The door to the hall was open and presently a couple of photographers came in.

"Do you mind, Rocky?" one of them said. "We'd just like to get a picture of you and your grandmother."

"That's all right," Graziano said. "She'll be in soon."

He looked out the window again and, leaning forward, at the street below. "Here she comes now," he said.

An old woman hurried across the street carrying a brown paper bag in one arm. She had been stout once and she had on a gray print house dress and a small black hat and when she came in, breathing heavily from climbing the stairs, she walked across the room, smiling, and took Graziano by the hands and the two of them stood there speaking in Italian and smiling.

Graziano took her then by the arms and led her to the chair by the window and she sat down and put her bundle on the floor and took off her hat. She sat there smiling at Graziano and looking occasionally at the others and nodding her head.

"Do you mind now?" the photographer said to Graziano.

"Oh," Graziano said, and then he turned to the old woman. "They want to take a picture for the newspapers of you and me."

"Picture?" the old woman said, and her face changed. "That's why you come?"

"Oh no," Graziano said, and his own face had changed and he was shaking his head. "Oh no. I'd have come anyway. They just came in."

"I put on black dress," the old woman said.

"No," the photographer said to Graziano. "Tell her no. We'll only take a minute. We haven't got time."

"No," Graziano said to her. "That dress is all right."

"I put on nice black dress," the old woman said.

They took several pictures, then, of Graziano showing his grandmother, in the house dress, his right fist, and then Graziano said good-by to her, taking her by the hands, and he and those who had followed him went downstairs where there was a crowd waiting.

They pushed through the crowd, kids grabbing at Graziano and trying to run along at his side, and men shouting at him, things like: "Hey, Rocky!" . . . "Good luck, Rocky!" . . . "Flatten him for me, Rocky!"

They swarmed, half-running, down the street and the bigger crowd around the steps of the State building shouted and pushed, the cops shoving them back, and the photographers' bulbs flashing and many in the crowd making fists. Inside they hurried into an elevator that was waiting. The room upstairs was a big one. It was crowded with men, some of them standing on chairs, and at the end of the room by the desk there was a scale and around that the crowd was tight-packed.

They pushed the fighter through, the crowd quiet, and when he got to the desk there was some milling around and conversation and then he started taking off his clothes and tossing them on the desk. The crowd stood back and watched him, and he stripped and took off even his wristwatch and his ring, and put on a pair of purple boxing trunks.

Mike Jacobs, the promoter, Nat Rogers, the matchmaker, Eddie Eagan, the chairman of the New York State Athletic Commission, Irving Cohen, another of Graziano's managers, Art Winch and Sam Pian, Zale's managers, Healey and Coco and Whitey—they all were there on the inside of the crowd. Outside of them were newspapermen and photographers and more commissioners, and then Graziano stepped on the scale and Eagan leaned forward and adjusted the weight on the bar and watched the bar settle slowly to rest.

"The weight," Eagan said, announcing it, "is exactly one hundred fifty-four. Graziano, one hundred fifty-four pounds."

Several of the newspapermen were crowding out to find telephones and there was the noise of conversation in the crowd.

"How much did Zale weigh?" Healey asked.

"A hundred and sixty," somebody said.

"Black trunks for Zale," Harry Markson, Jacobs' press agent, said, announcing it. "Purple trunks for Graziano."

Graziano sat on the desk and Dr. Vincent Nardiello, the commission physician, put a stethoscope to Graziano's chest. Then the doctor took the fighter's blood pressure and announced the heartbeat and blood pressure figures to the press.

"All right, Zale," Eagan said, raising his voice. "All right, Zale. Come out."

The other fighter, Zale, who would fight Graziano, came out through a doorway to the left of the desk. He was naked except for the black trunks and tan street shoes. The crowd moved back and he walked to the scales where Graziano stood. They did not look at each other.

"Take a pose. Make them pose," the photographers were hollering and Zale and Graziano faced each other, Graziano's arms cocked wide at the sides of his chest, Zale's arms drawn up in a fighting pose in front of his chest. They stood there holding the pose while the bulbs flashed again and their eyes met. Graziano smiled once and nodded; Zale smiled back.

The photographers were still working away, shouting for one more, swearing at each other, when Eagan stepped between the fighters and moved them over beside the desk.

"Now, I understand you're both good rugged fighters," Eagan said, "but I want a clean fight. I want no hitting in the breaks and that's one rule I'm going to caution the referee to observe."

He talked with them for another moment and then he turned and Zale went back through the door and Graziano went back to the desk and they both dressed. When they were finished dressing they walked, each with his group around him, through the crowd down the hall to another office where, in separate corners of the room, they tried on the gloves and alternate sets of gloves. One of the commissioners marked with a pen each fighter's name on the white lining of his gloves.

"He's got a bad eye," someone said to Graziano, nodding toward Zale who was waiting while the commissioner marked his set. "It's his left."

"No," Graziano said, looking over at Zale. "I noticed that. It's his right, not his left."

There were crowds again in the hall and outside the building, running after him and shouting the same things, a few of them different things, but most of them over and over again: "Hey, Rock!" . . . "Good luck, Rock!" . . . "I prayed for you last night."

They hurried down the street, photographers running ahead of them, and pausing to snap them, and the crowd pushed on behind. They passed the car parked at the curb and went into a small bar and restaurant on the right where a cop stood by the door to keep the crowd out.

They walked through the bar quickly into a small restaurant in the back. There were a half-dozen tables with red and white striped tablecloths on them and Graziano sat down at a table at the right. In the corner at the left there were two men and two women at a table, and one of the men said something to the others and they turned around quickly and watched Graziano as he sat there fingering a fork and waiting while the others, eight or ten, pulled up chairs around the table or stood in back.

"Look, Rock," Healey said, and he shoved a photograph of Graziano in a fighting pose across the table, "autograph this, will you?"

"Okay, Jack," Graziano said, looking at him and then reaching around for the pen someone handed him from in back. "Don't get excited. Relax."

"I know," Healey said, "I'm more excited than you are. I'll relax."

"Autograph it to Pete," someone said. "Pete is his first name. Pasca is the last. P-A-S-C-A."

Graziano wrote something on the photograph and Healey put another down in front of him.

"Sign that to Pat," he said. "P-A-T."

"What is it, a girl or a fella?" Graziano said.

"I don't know," Healey said. "Put 'Best Wishes, Rocky.' It don't matter. That covers it."

In the arched doorway they stood watching, about fifteen or twenty of them, and then the waitress came from the back, carrying on a tray a cup of tea with a slice of lemon on the saucer. She put those down and went away and when she came back she had toast and a soft-boiled egg broken into a cup.

Graziano sat there eating the egg and the toast, blowing on the tea and trying it. They had let those from the bar into the restaurant now and they stood, three and four deep around the table, not saying anything or speaking only in whispers, watching in almost complete silence the fighter as he finished the egg and toast.

There were the crowds outside again, then, shouting the same things and the cop had to clear a path through them to the car. There were many faces at the windows of the car, faces shouting and fists, and Healey pulled the car away from the curb and drove east and then north on Second Avenue and at Forty-ninth Street he turned west.

On Forty-ninth Street at Seventh Avenue they had to stop for a light. They sat there, not saying anything and waiting for the light to change, when a guy in a white shirt, in his twenties, came off the sidewalk and thrust his face into the open front window of the car where Graziano sat between Healey and Coco.

"Hey, Rock," he said, making a fist, "if you win I get married. If you lose she'll have to wait a couple more years."

He turned as if to leave the car and then he saw them inside starting to smile.

"I ain't kiddin'," he said, turning back and reaching into his pants pocket and coming out with a fist full of bills. "Fresh dough I just got from the bank."

Graziano said nothing. Healey drove over to Ninth Avenue where he had to swerve the car out to avoid a bus pulling wide from the curb.

"You see?" he said. "These bus guys think they got a license to do anything they want."

"Watch," somebody said. "He's gonna yap."

The bus driver was shouting out of the window at his side.

"Hey, Rock!" he was shouting. "Good luck tonight. I know you can flatten that guy."

"What do you make of that?" Healey said. "How do you like that?"

In front of the hotel they sat in the car waiting while Whitey went up to get a leather bag containing Graziano's robe, his boxing shoes, his trunks, and the other things he would need in the fight. While they waited Healey went across the street to a newsstand and came back with the afternoon newspapers. He tossed them down on the front seat and Graziano picked up the first one and turned to the sports page where the banner headline read: "Zale Picked to Knock Out Graziano in Eight Rounds."

"Look at this," he said to Healey, flatly, without emotion.

"That's okay," Healey said. "What a guy thinks, he should write."

They drove to Coco's house, which is in the Pelham Bay section of the Bronx. They parked the car in front of the house and walked down the concrete driveway to the back where there were eight or ten men and women and a couple of kids on the back porch.

"Rocky," Mrs. Coco said, "these are friends of ours from Utica. They'd like to meet you and they came down for the fight."

Graziano shook hands with them and they all smiled and tried not to look at him steadily. They studied him furtively, the way some men study an attractive girl on the subway. He sat there on the porch for a few minutes while the others talked around him and they took him downstairs for the dinner on which he would fight.

There was a bar at one end of the wood-paneled room and there was a long table set for twelve. He sat at the head of the table and some of the others sat watching him while they brought him his dish of spinach, his plate of lettuce, his toast, and his steak.

Graziano ate quickly, cutting large pieces, using his fork with his left hand, always holding the knife in his right. When he said he wanted some water, Whitey said he could have a little without ice. He had some hot tea and lemon and then he said he did not want to eat any more, pushing away the plate on which there was still a small portion of steak.

"That's all right," Whitey said. "If you feel satisfied, don't force yourself."

He went upstairs, then, and sat on the porch while the others ate. When they had finished, a half hour later, it was four-twenty and Whitey said they would take a short walk before Graziano took a nap.

They walked—Graziano and Pennino in front and Whitey and Healey in back—down the street and across the street under the elevated to the park. They walked through the park until four-thirty and then Whitey told them it was time to turn back. They walked past a barbershop where they saw Coco sitting down for a shave. Whitey said he would stop in the drugstore down the block and that he would be right back. Graziano and Pennino went into the barbershop and Graziano sat down in the barber chair next to the one in which Coco sat.

"I'll get a trim, Eddie," he said. "Is it all right if I just get a trim in the back?"

"Sure," Coco said. "Why not?"

A couple of girls in their teens and wearing sweaters and skirts came in then and stood by the chair looking at Graziano as he looked back at them.

"Are you Rocky Graziano?" one of them said.

"Yeah," Graziano said. "That's right."

"I could tell by your nose," one of them said. "You gonna win tonight?"

"Sure," Graziano said, smiling. "Why not?"

By now Whitey had come back.

"What are you doin' in the chair?" he said.

"I'm gettin' a trim," Graziano said.

"A what?"

"A trim. A trim just in the back."

"Listen," Whitey said, "get up out of there. It's time for you to rest."

"Look, Whitey," Graziano said, "I'm restin' here."

"C'mon," Whitey said.

When they got back to Coco's house they sat in the living room. At ten minutes to five Graziano went in the next room and phoned his wife and at five o'clock Whitey said it was time for Graziano to go upstairs and lie down.

"What difference does it make?" Healey said. "He'll flatten the guy anyway."

"I know," Whitey said, "but he goes upstairs and takes his nap."

Graziano and Whitey went upstairs then and Mrs. Coco showed them a small room with maple furniture and a single bed. When Mrs. Coco had turned the covers back she left and Graziano stripped down to his shorts and sat on the bed.

"See if they got any comic books, will you, Whitey?" he said. "Go downstairs and see, hey?"

Whitey went downstairs and came back with one comic book. Graziano took it and looked at the cover.

"Go out, hey Whitey?" he said, looking up. "Go out and get some others."

Whitey and Coco walked up the street to a candy store where they picked out ten books from the rack—"Buzzy" . . . "Comic Capers" . . . "Captain Marvel, Jr." . . . "Whiz Comics" . . . "Sensation Comics" . . . "Ace Comics" . . . "All-Flash" . . .

When they came back and opened the door to the bedroom Graziano was lying on his back under the covers reading the comic book and there was a towel over the pillow under his head.

"Hey!" Coco said. "What about that towel?"

"Yeah," Graziano said. "I got some grease on my hair."

"What of it?" Coco said. "We're gonna wash the sheets and pillow case."

They went downstairs, then, and left him. It was five-twenty and for the next hour and a half the men sat in the driveway at the back on chairs they had brought from the porch and the kitchen and they talked about fights.

At six-fifty Whitey got up and went into the house. He heard someone on the stairs and Graziano came into the kitchen, dressed, his hair combed back.

"Hey," Whitey said. "I was just gonna get you up. You sleep?"

"I don't know," Graziano said. "I think maybe I dropped off a little."

They went out into the back yard, then, and Graziano sat down on one of the chairs. Dusk was setting in, so one of them lighted the garage light so they could see a little better and they sat around waiting and not saying much. At seven twenty-five Whitey said they had to go.

The driveway, dark, seemed full of people. Some of them wanted to shake his hand and the rest kept calling the word "luck."

"If you hear any noise from section thirty-three," one woman yelled, "that's us."

"We've got an undertaker with us from Utica," another woman said, "so you don't have to worry and you can hit him as hard as you like."

"Excuse me, Rocky," Mrs. Coco said, "but this is my delivery boy and he wants to meet you."

"Sure. Hello," Graziano said.

They walked out the dark driveway and pushed through a lot of kids who had been waiting there all afternoon and got into the car. It took them twenty minutes to drive to Yankee Stadium. On the way Pennino, in the back seat, sang songs and Whitey told a couple of old jokes.

When they reached the Stadium, Healey pulled the car up in front of Gate Four and stopped.

"You can't stop here," a cop said.

"This is Graziano," Healey said.

"I can't help it," the cop said.

Healey did not argue with the cop but eased the car down a few feet in front of another cop. Now someone in the crowd had spotted Graziano in the front seat and the crowd stopped moving forward and started to gather around the car.

"This is Graziano," Healey said to the cop.

"You shouldn't stop here," the cop said.

"I know it," Healey said, "but we gotta stop somewhere. He's fightin' tonight."

"You better see the lieutenant," the cop said.

"C'mon," Whitey said. "Let's get out. Leave it here."

They got out and the cops were pushing the crowd back now and those in the crowd were calling the same things the other crowds had called before. The cops were clearing a way through and Whitey gave Pennino the bag and they pushed through to the gate.

Along the tunnel under the stands they led Graziano now into the clubhouse used by the visiting teams. It was divided lengthwise down the middle by a wood-framed partition covered with cheap lavender cloth. Just inside the door a half-dozen preliminary fighters were in various stages of preparation, getting into their ring clothes, having their hands taped, warming up. They led Graziano past them and, parting a heavy dark blue drape, into his own part of the room.

"What time is it now?" he said, looking around.

"Eight o'clock," somebody said.

He sat down on one of the folding chairs to wait. Whitey had opened the leather bag and was taking out the equipment—the ring shoes, the boxing trunks, the protective cup—and placing them on the rubbing table, when Commissioner Eagan and Commissioner Bruno came in. They shook Graziano's hand as he stood up and stood talking with him for a minute or so and then they left.

"You better warm up, Rock," Whitey said. "Just warm up a little."

Graziano moved around the room, clothed, throwing short punches for about five minutes, and then sat down again.

"Let's go," a voice outside said, calling to the preliminary fighters. "The first two bouts."

Graziano stood up again. He took off his sweater and his basque shirt and went to a locker and hung them up. He came back and sat down on the table, and took off his shoes and socks. He got off the table and put them in the locker and then he took off his trousers and shorts and hung them up. He came back and sat down, naked now, on the table, and Whitey handed him a new pair of white woolen socks. He put them on and then put on his boxing shoes. He started moving around the room again, throwing short punches, weaving and bobbing a little as he went. He did this for a couple of minutes and then Whitey called to him and he went over and tried on a pair of the purple trunks. He took them off and tried on another pair, which he seemed to like better.

Sol Bimstein, Whitey's brother, came in and walked over to the table and picked up a pair of the purple trunks.

"Ain't these a nicer color purple?" he said.

"I like these best," Graziano said.

"Whichever he likes best," Whitey said.

Graziano put on his basque shirt, then, and began shadowboxing around the room again. A couple of deputy commissioners came in to stand there and watch him and then Whitey took Graziano's robe—white with a green trim and with Graziano's name in green block letters on the back—and spread it over half the table. Graziano stopped the shadowboxing and took off his trunks and shirt and walked to the table and lay down on his back.

Whitey worked first over his upper body. He rubbed coco oil on Graziano's chest. Then he put a towel across Graziano's chest and Graziano turned over and lay facedown and Whitey rubbed the oil on his back. Then he sat up and Whitey went over his legs with rubbing alcohol. Whitey was sweating and he took off his own shirt. He worked hard on Graziano's legs and then he went back at his shoulders and chest. When he was finished Graziano got off the table and, once again stripped but for his shoes and socks, moved around throwing punches until Whitey stopped him and took him over to a corner where they talked together quietly and Whitey showed Graziano a move with his left. Then he told Graziano to sit down and put his feet up on the table and he put a towel across Graziano's back and another across his legs.

"What time is it?" Graziano said.

"Eight fifty-five," Sol Bimstein said.

"I thought it was later than that," Graziano said.

"How do you feel?" Whitey said.

"Tired," Graziano said.

At nine o'clock a couple of commissioners and Art Winch, one of Zale's managers, came in.

"Is it time?" Whitey said.

"Yes," Winch said. "We might as well get started."

Graziano got up, then, and Whitey helped him into the white and green satin robe. He sat on the table, his legs hanging over, and Whitey started bandaging Graziano's right hand, Winch and the commissioners watching. It took him about seven minutes to do the right hand. When he was starting the left hand Winch said something and Whitey raised his voice.

"Just what I'm allowed," he said. "No more. No less."

"All right. All right," Winch said.

They stood there watching until the job was done and then Sam Pian, Zale's other manager, came in.

"You stayin'?" Winch said.

"Right," Pian said. He sat down on a chair by the lockers and Winch and the commissioners went out. Graziano, the tape and gauze a gleaming white on his hands now, started moving around, shadowboxing again.

"I'm spying," Pian said as Graziano passed near him.

"Yeah. Sure," Graziano said. "I know."

He stopped throwing punches.

"This tape stinks," he said, looking at his hands.

"I know it does," Pian said.

"It peels off," Graziano said. He started moving around again, the leather of his shoes squeaking in the quiet room, the satin of his robe rustling. Mike Jacobs came in and Graziano stopped and spoke with him and then Jacobs went out and Healey came in.

"You got half an hour," he said.

"All right," Graziano said. He walked out through the drape.

"Where's he goin'?" Pian asked.

"Some of the preliminary fighters want to see him," Healey said. "They can't come in so he went out to see them."

"Oh," Pian said.

"He's a nice kid, ain't he, Sam?" Healey said.

"Yes," Pian said. "I guess he's a nice kid."

He got up to follow Graziano as Graziano came back in. Healey started out, and put his head back in between the curtains.

"I'll see you after, Rock," he said.

"Scram," Graziano said, looking up from where he was sitting by the table, his feet on the table, his hands on his lap. "Get out."

"I'll punch you in the eye," Healey said. He threw a kiss and pulled his head out as Sol Bimstein came in. "Main bout next," Sol said. "There's two rounds to go in the semifinal."

"Is it warm out?" Graziano said.

"Just nice," Sol said.

Graziano sat there waiting and Whitey came over to him and rubbed a little Vaseline on Graziano's face. It was ten minutes to ten. Whitey said something to him and he got up and went out. In a minute he came back and Whitey helped him off with his robe. He helped him into his protector and his trunks and then Graziano stood there rotating his shoulders, bending at the waist. When he stopped Whitey gave him a short drink from the water bottle. Then Whitey rubbed Graziano's chest and his stomach and his shoulders and Graziano took several deep breaths. Then Graziano began pacing back and forth, throwing short punches, breathing hard through his nose. He was doing this when a couple of the commissioners came in.

"Hey, Rock," one of them said to him. "What are you going to do with all the dough you get? The place is packed."

"All right," a voice shouted in from outside. "Main bout. Main bout."

"All right, Rocky," Whitey said. He moved over to his fighter and put the towel around his fighter's neck, crossing the ends in front, and he helped him back into his robe. Somebody took the pail and Whitey had his first-aid kit and, with Pian still watching them and following them, they moved out.

In the tunnel there were special cops and a couple of preliminary fighters who shouted something at Graziano. They moved quickly through the tunnel and down the steps to the lower level. Whitey's hand was on Graziano's back. Graziano kept exercising his arms, jigging a little now and then. They were close around him and they moved quickly along the lower level and then up the steps of the dugout where they hit him with the sound.

There were 39,827 people there and they had paid $342,497 to be there and when Graziano's head came up out of the dugout they rose and made their sound. The place was filled with it and it came from far off and then he was moving quickly down beneath this ceiling of sound, between the two long walls of faces, turned toward him and yellow in the artificial light and shouting things, mouths open, eyes wide, into the ring where, in one of the most brutal fights ever seen in New York, Zale dropped him once and he dropped Zale once before, in the sixth round, Zale suddenly, with a right to the body and a left to the head, knocked him out.

From "Portrait of Hemingway"

LILLIAN ROSS

When Lillian Ross's profile of Ernest Hemingway appeared in *The New Yorker* in 1950, five years after she had joined the staff of the magazine, it was widely thought to be a "devastating" portrait of the writer as an over-the-hill borderline alcoholic, whose mock-Indian lingo and constant base-ball and boxing references were sad affectations. Ross herself later professed to be mystified by this reaction. "Although I did not reveal my viewpoint directly," she wrote in a preface to a reprinting of the piece in book form, "implicit in my choice and arrangement of detail, and in the total atmosphere created, was my feeling of affection and admiration."

Readers can decide for themselves if the article is sympathetic, devastating, or somewhere in between. But the bifurcated reaction is in any case revealing. Like W. C. Heinz in "The Day of the Fight," Ross was perpetrating journalism as a series of scenes. In tagging along with Hemingway during a short visit to New York with his wife, Mary, she was working out what would later be called the "fly-on-the-wall" approach: for the most part she withdraws from the scene and meticulously describes carefully selected dialogue, action, and setting.

This technique can be heavy-handed and it can be deadly dull, as countless subsequent practitioners have demonstrated. In the hands of a master such as Ross, it is funny, sad, artfully crafted, and, in its lifelike ambiguity, oddly exhilarating. In the following excerpt, Ross observes Hemingway as he has lunch in his hotel room, buys a coat, looks at paintings, and meets with his publisher.

—B. Y.

After a while, Mrs. Hemingway came into the room. She was wearing gray flannel slacks and a white blouse, and she said she felt wonderful, because she had had her first hot bath in six months. Then she said she was going out to do her errands, and suggested that Hemingway get dressed and go out

129

and do his. He said that it was lunchtime, and that if they went out then, they would have to stop someplace for lunch, whereas if they had lunch sent up to the room, they might save time. Mrs. Hemingway said she would order lunch while he got dressed. Still holding his glass, he reluctantly got up from the couch. Then he finished his drink and went into the bedroom. By the time he came out—wearing the same outfit as the day before, except for a blue shirt with a button-down collar—a waiter had set the table for our lunch. We couldn't have lunch without a bottle of Tavel, Hemingway said, and we waited until the waiter had brought it before starting to eat.

Hemingway began with oysters, and he chewed each one very thoroughly. "Eat good and digest good," he told us.

"Papa, please get glasses fixed," Mrs. Hemingway said.

He nodded. Then he nodded a few times at me—a repetition of the sign for attention. "What I want to be when I am old is a wise old man who won't bore," he said, then paused while the waiter set a plate of asparagus and an artichoke before him and poured the Tavel. Hemingway tasted the wine and gave the waiter a nod. "I'd like to see all the new fighters, horses, ballets, bike riders, dames, bullfighters, painters, airplanes, sons of bitches, café characters, big international whores, restaurants, years of wine, newsreels, and never have to write a line about any of it," he said. "I'd like to write lots of letters to my friends and get back letters. Would like to be able to make love good until I was eighty-five, the way Clemenceau could. And what I would like to be is not Bernie Baruch. I wouldn't sit on park benches, although I might go around the park once in a while to feed the pigeons, and also I wouldn't have any long beard, so there could be an old man didn't look like Shaw." He stopped and ran the back of his hand along his beard, and looked around the room reflectively. "Have never met Mr. Shaw," he said. "Never been to Niagara Falls, either. Anyway, I would take up harness racing. You aren't up near the top at that until you're over seventy-five. Then I could get me a good young ball club, maybe, like Mr. Mack. Only, I wouldn't signal with a program, so as to break the pattern. Haven't figured out yet what I would signal with. And when that's over, I'll make the prettiest corpse since Pretty Boy Floyd. Only suckers worry about saving their souls. Who the hell should care about saving his soul when it is a man's duty to lose it intelligently, the way you would sell a position you were defending, if you could not hold it, as expensively as possible, trying to make it the most expensive position that was ever sold. It isn't hard to die." He opened his mouth and laughed, at first soundlessly and then loudly. "No more worries," he said. He picked up a long spear of asparagus with his fingers and looked at it without enthusiasm. "It takes a pretty good man to make any sense when he's dying," he said.

Mrs. Hemingway had finished eating, and she quickly finished her wine. Hemingway slowly finished his. I looked at my wristwatch, and found that it was almost three. The waiter started clearing the table, and we all got up.

Hemingway stood looking sadly at the bottle of champagne, which was not yet empty. Mrs. Hemingway put on her coat, and I put on mine.

"The half bottle of champagne is the enemy of man," Hemingway said. We all sat down again.

"If I have any money, I can't think of any better way of spending money than on champagne," Hemingway said, pouring some.

When the champagne was gone, we left the suite. Downstairs, Mrs. Hemingway told us to remember to get glasses fixed, and scooted away.

Hemingway balked for a moment in front of the hotel. It was a cool, cloudy day. This was not good weather for him to be out in, he said sulkily, adding that his throat felt kind of sore. I asked him if he wanted to see a doctor. He said no. "I never trust a doctor I have to pay," he said, and started across Fifth Avenue. A flock of pigeons flew by. He stopped, looked up, and aimed an imaginary rifle at them. He pulled the trigger, and then looked disappointed. "Very difficult shot," he said. He turned quickly and pretended to shoot again. "Easy shot," he said. "Look!" He pointed to a spot on the pavement. He seemed to be feeling better, but not much better.

I asked him if he wanted to stop first at his optician's. He said no. I mentioned the coat. He shrugged. Mrs. Hemingway had suggested that he look for a coat at Abercrombie & Fitch, so I mentioned Abercrombie & Fitch. He shrugged again and lumbered slowly over to a taxi, and we started down Fifth Avenue in the afternoon traffic. At the corner of Fifty-fourth, we stopped on a signal from the traffic cop. Hemingway growled. "I love to see an Irish cop being cold," he said. "Give you eight to one he was an M.P. in the war. Very skillful cop. Feints and fakes good. Cops are not like they are in the Hellinger movies. Only once in a while." We started up again, and he showed me where he once walked across Fifth Avenue with Scott Fitzgerald. "Scott wasn't at Princeton any more, but he was still talking football," he said, without animation. "The ambition of Scott's life was to be on the football team. I said, 'Scott, why don't you cut out this football?' I said, 'Come on, boy.' He said, 'You're crazy.' That's the end of that story. If you can't get through traffic, how the hell are you gonna get through the line? But I am not Thomas Mann," he added. "Get another opinion."

By the time we reached Abercrombie's, Hemingway was moody again. He got out of the taxi reluctantly, and reluctantly entered the store. I asked him whether he wanted to look at a coat first or something else.

"Coat," he said unhappily.

In the elevator, Hemingway looked even bigger and bulkier than he had before, and his face had the expression of a man who is being forcibly subjected to the worst kind of misery. A middle-aged woman standing next to him stared at his scraggly white beard with obvious alarm and disapproval. "Good Christ!" Hemingway said suddenly, in the silence of the elevator, and the middle-aged woman looked down at her feet.

The doors opened at our floor, and we got out and headed for a rack of topcoats. A tall, dapper clerk approached us, and Hemingway shoved his hands into his pants pockets and crouched forward. "I think I still have credit in this joint," he said to the clerk.

The clerk cleared his throat. "Yes, sir," he said.

"Want to see coat," Hemingway said menacingly.

"Yes, sir," said the clerk. "What kind of coat did you wish to see, sir?"

"That one." He pointed to a straight-hanging, beltless tan gabardine coat on the rack. The clerk helped him into it and gently drew him over to a full-length mirror. "Hangs like a shroud," Hemingway said, tearing the coat off. "I'm tall on top. Got any other coat?" he asked, as though he expected the answer to be no. He edged impatiently toward the elevators.

"How about this one, sir, with a removable lining, sir?" the clerk said. This one had a belt. Hemingway tried it on, studied himself in the mirror, and then raised his arms as though he were aiming a rifle. "You going to use it for *shooting,* sir?" the clerk asked. Hemingway grunted, and said he would take the coat. He gave the clerk his name, and the clerk snapped his fingers. "Of course!" he said. "There was *something* . . ." Hemingway looked embarrassed and said to send the coat to him at the Sherry-Netherland, and then said he'd like to look at a belt.

"What kind of belt, Mr. Hemingway?" the clerk asked.

"Guess a brown one," Hemingway said.

We moved over to the belt counter, and another clerk appeared.

"Will you show Mr. Hemingway a belt?" the first clerk said, and stepped back and thoughtfully watched Hemingway.

The second clerk took a tape measure from his pocket, saying he thought Hemingway was a size 44 or 46.

"Wanta bet?" Hemingway asked. He took the clerk's hand and punched himself in the stomach with it.

"Gee, he's got a hard tummy," the belt clerk said. He measured Hemingway's waistline. "Thirty-eight!" he reported. "Small waist for your size. What do you do—a lot of exercise?"

Hemingway hunched his shoulders, feinted, laughed, and looked happy for the first time since we'd left the hotel. He punched himself in the stomach with his own fist.

"Where you going—to Spain again?" the belt clerk asked.

"To Italy," Hemingway said, and punched himself in the stomach again. After Hemingway had decided on a brown calf belt, the clerk asked him whether he wanted a money belt. He said no—he kept his money in a checkbook.

Our next stop was the shoe department, and there Hemingway asked a clerk for some folding bedroom slippers.

"Pullman slippers," the clerk said. "What size?"

" 'Levens," Hemingway said bashfully. The slippers were produced, and he told the clerk he would take them. "I'll put them in my pocket," he said. "Just mark them, so they won't think I'm a shoplifter."

"You'd be surprised what's taken from the store," said the clerk, who was very small and very old. "Why, the other morning, someone on the first floor went off with a big roulette wheel. Just picked it up and—"

Hemingway was not listening. "Wolfie!" he shouted at a man who seemed almost seven feet tall and whose back was to us.

The man turned around. He had a big, square red face, and at the sight of Hemingway it registered extreme joy. "Papa!" he shouted.

The big man and Hemingway embraced and pounded each other on the back for quite some time. It was Winston Guest. Mr. Guest told us he was going upstairs to pick up a gun, and proposed that we come along. Hemingway asked what kind of gun, and Guest said a ten-gauge magnum.

"Beautiful gun," Hemingway said, taking his bedroom slippers from the clerk and stuffing them into his pocket.

In the elevator, Hemingway and Guest checked with each other on how much weight they had lost. Guest said he was now down to two hundred and thirty-five, after a good deal of galloping around on polo ponies. Hemingway said he was down to two hundred and eight, after shooting ducks in Cuba and working on his book.

"How's the book now, Papa?" Guest asked as we got out of the elevator.

Hemingway gave his fist-to-the-face laugh and said he was going to defend his title once more. "Wolfie, all of a sudden I found I could write wonderful again, instead of just biting on the nail," he said slowly. "I think it took a while for my head to get rebuilt inside. You should not, ideally, break a writer's head open or give him seven concussions in two years or break six ribs on him when he is forty-seven or push a rear-view-mirror support through the front of his skull opposite the pituitary gland, or, really, shoot at him too much. On the other hand, Wolfie, leave the sons of bitches alone and they are liable to start crawling back into the womb or somewhere if you drop a porkpie hat." He exploded into laughter.

Guest's huge frame shook with almost uncontrollable laughter. "God, Papa!" he said. "I still have your shooting clothes out at the island. When are you coming out to shoot, Papa?"

Hemingway laughed again and pounded him on the back. "Wolfie, you're so damn big!" he said.

Guest arranged to have his gun delivered, and then we all got into the elevator, the two of them talking about a man who caught a black marlin last year that weighed a thousand and six pounds.

"How do you like it now, gentlemen?" Hemingway asked.

"God, Papa!" said Guest.

On the ground floor, Guest pointed to a mounted elephant head on the wall. "Pygmy elephant, Papa," he said.

"Miserable elephant," said Hemingway.

Their arms around each other, they went out to the street. I said that I had to leave, and Hemingway told me to be sure to come over to the hotel early the next morning, so that I could go with him and Patrick to the Metropolitan Museum. As I walked off, I heard Guest say, "God, Papa, I'm not ashamed of anything I've ever done."

"Nor, oddly enough, am I," said Hemingway.

I looked around. They were punching each other in the stomach and laughing raucously.

The following morning, the door of the Hemingway suite was opened for me by Patrick, a shy young man of medium height, with large eyes and a sensitive face. He was wearing gray flannel slacks, a white shirt open at the collar, Argyle socks, and loafers. Mrs. Hemingway was writing a letter at the desk. As I came in, she looked up and said, "As soon as Papa has finished dressing, we're going to look at pictures." She went back to her letter.

Patrick told me that he'd just as soon spend the whole day looking at pictures, and that he had done a bit of painting himself. "Papa has to be back here for lunch with Mr. Scribner," he said, and added that he himself was going to stay in town until the next morning, when the Hemingways sailed. The telephone rang and he answered it. "Papa, I think it's Gigi calling you!" he shouted into the bedroom.

Hemingway emerged, in shirtsleeves, and went to the phone. "How are you, kid?" he said into it, then asked Gigi to come down to the Finca for his next vacation. "You're welcome down there, Gigi," he said. "You know that cat you liked? The one you named Smelly? We renamed him Ecstasy. Every one of our cats knows his own name." After hanging up, he told me that Gigi was a wonderful shot—that when he was eleven he had won second place in the shoot championship of Cuba. "Isn't that the true gen, Mouse?" he asked.

"That's right, Papa," said Patrick.

I wanted to know what "true gen" meant, and Hemingway explained that it was British slang for "information," from "intelligence." "It's divided into three classes: gen; the true gen, which is as true as you can state it; and the really true gen, which you can operate on," he said.

He looked at the green orchids. "My mother never sent me any flowers," he said. His mother was about eighty, he said, and lived in River Forest, Illinois. His father, who was a physician, had been dead for many years; he shot himself when Ernest was a boy. "Let's get going if we're going to see the pictures," he said. "I told Charlie Scribner to meet me here at one. Excuse me while I wash. In big city, I guess you wash your neck." He went back into the bedroom. While he was gone, Mrs. Hemingway told me that Ernest was the second of six children—Marcelline, then Ernest, Ursula, Madelaine, Carol, and the youngest, his only brother, Leicester. All the sisters were named after saints. Every one of the children was married; Leicester was living in Bogotá, Colombia, where he was attached to the United States Embassy.

Hemingway came out in a little while, wearing his new coat. Mrs. Hemingway and Patrick put on their coats, and we went downstairs. It was raining, and we hurried into a taxi. On the way to the Metropolitan, Hemingway said very little; he just hummed to himself and watched the street. Mrs. Hemingway told me that he was usually unhappy in taxis, because he could not sit in the front seat to watch the road ahead. He looked out the window and pointed to a flock of birds flying across the sky. "In this town, birds fly, but they're not serious about it," he said. "New York birds don't climb."

When we drew up at the Museum entrance, a line of schoolchildren was moving in slowly. Hemingway impatiently led us past them. In the lobby, he paused, pulled a silver flask from one of his coat pockets, unscrewed its top, and took a long drink. Putting the flask back in his pocket, he asked Mrs. Hemingway whether she wanted to see the Goyas first or the Breughels. She said the Breughels.

"I learned to write by looking at paintings in the Luxembourg Museum in Paris," he said. "I never went past high school. When you've got a hungry gut and the museum is free, you go to the museum. Look," he said, stopping before "Portrait of a Man," which has been attributed to both Titian and Giorgione. "They were old Venice boys, too."

"Here's what I like, Papa," Patrick said, and Hemingway joined his son in front of "Portrait of Federigo Gonzaga (1500–1540)," by Francesco Francia. It shows, against a landscape, a small boy with long hair and a cloak.

"This is what we try to do when we write, Mousie, " Hemingway said, pointing to the trees in the background. "We always have this in when we write."

Mrs. Hemingway called to us. She was looking at "Portrait of the Artist," by Van Dyck. Hemingway looked at it, nodded approval, and said, "In Spain, we had a fighter pilot named Whitey Dahl, so Whitey came to me one time and said, 'Mr. Hemingway, is Van Dyck a good painter?' I said, 'Yes, he is.' He said, 'Well, I'm glad, because I have one in my room and I like it very much, and I'm glad he's a good painter because I like him.' The next day, Whitey was shot down."

We all walked over to Rubens' "The Triumph of Christ Over Sin and Death." Christ is shown surrounded by snakes and angels and is being watched by a figure in a cloud. Mrs. Hemingway and Patrick said they thought it didn't look like the usual Rubens.

"Yeah, he did that all right," Hemingway said authoritatively. "You can tell the real just as a bird dog can tell. Smell them. Or from having lived with very poor but very good painters."

That settled that, and we went on to the Breughel room. It was closed, we discovered. The door bore a sign that read "NOW UNDERTAKING REPAIRS."

"They have our indulgence," Hemingway said, and took another drink from his flask. "I sure miss the good Breughel," he said as we moved along. "It's the great one, of the harvesters. It is a lot of people cutting grain, but he uses the grain geometrically, to make an emotion that is so strong for me that I can hardly take it." We came to El Greco's green "View of Toledo" and stood looking at it a long time. "This is the best picture in the Museum for me, and Christ knows there are some lovely ones," Hemingway said.

Patrick admired several paintings Hemingway didn't approve of. Every time this happened, Hemingway got into an involved technical discussion with his son. Patrick would shake his head and laugh and say he respected Hemingway's opinions. He didn't argue much. "What the hell!" Hemingway said suddenly. "I don't want to be an art critic. I just want to look at pictures and be happy with them and learn from them. Now, this for me is a damn good picture." He stood back and peered at a Reynolds entitled "Colonel George Coussmaker," which shows the Colonel leaning against a tree and holding his horse's bridle. "Now, this Colonel is a son of a bitch who was willing to pay money to the best portrait painter of his day just to have himself painted," Hemingway said, and gave a short laugh. "Look at the man's arrogance and the strength in the neck of the horse and the way the man's legs hang. He's so arrogant he can afford to lean against a tree."

We separated for a while and looked at paintings individually, and then Hemingway called us over and pointed to a picture labelled, in large letters, "Catharine Lorillard Wolfe" and, in small ones, "By Cabanel." "This is where I got confused as a kid, in Chicago," he said. "My favorite painters for a long time were Bunte and Ryerson, two of the biggest and wealthiest families in Chicago. I always thought the names in big letters were the painters."

After we reached the Cézannes and Degas and the other Impressionists, Hemingway became more and more excited, and discoursed on what each artist could do and how and what he had learned from each. Patrick listened respectfully and didn't seem to want to talk about painting techniques any more. Hemingway spent several minutes looking at Cézanne's "Rocks— Forest of Fontainebleau." "This is what we try to do in writing, this and this, and the woods, and the rocks we have to climb over," he said. "Cézanne is my painter, after the early painters. Wonder, wonder painter. Degas was another wonder painter. I've never seen a bad Degas. You know what he did with the bad Degas? He burned them."

Hemingway took another long drink from his flask. We came to Manet's pastel portrait of Mlle. Valtesse de la Bigne, a young woman with blond hair coiled on the top of her head. Hemingway was silent for a while, looking at it; finally he turned away. "Manet could show the bloom people have when they're still innocent and before they've been disillusioned," he said.

As we walked along, Hemingway said to me, "I can make a landscape like Mr. Paul Cézanne. I learned how to make a landscape from Mr. Paul Cézanne by walking through the Luxembourg Museum a thousand times with an empty gut, and I am pretty sure that if Mr. Paul was around, he would like the way I make them and be happy that I learned it from him." He had learned a lot from Mr. Johann Sebastian Bach, too. "In the first paragraphs of 'Farewell,' I used the word 'and' consciously over and over the way Mr. Johann Sebastian Bach used a note in music when he was emitting counterpoint. I can almost write like Mr. Johann sometimes—or, anyway, so he would like it. All such people are easy to deal with, because we all know you have to learn."

"Papa, look at this," Patrick said. He was looking at "Meditation on the Passion," by Carpaccio. Patrick said it had a lot of strange animals in it for a religious painting.

"Huh!" Hemingway said. "Those painters always put the sacred scenes in the part of Italy they liked best or where they came from or where their girls came from. They made their girls the Madonnas. This is supposed to be Palestine, and Palestine is a long way off, he figures. So he puts in a red parrot, and he puts in deer and a leopard. And then he thinks, This is the Far East and it's far away. So he puts in the Moors, the traditional enemy of the Venetians." He paused and looked to see what else the painter had put in his picture. "Then he gets hungry, so he puts in rabbits," he said. "Goddam, Mouse, we saw a lot of good pictures. Mouse, don't you think two hours is a long time looking at pictures?"

Everybody agreed that two hours was a long time looking at pictures, so Hemingway said that we would skip the Goyas, and that we would all go to the Museum again when they returned from Europe.

It was still raining when we came out of the Museum. "Goddam, I hate to go out in the rain," Hemingway said. "Goddam, I hate to get wet."

Charles Scribner was waiting in the lobby of the hotel. "Ernest," he said, shaking Hemingway's hand. He was a dignified, solemn, slow-speaking gentleman with silvery hair.

"We've been looking at pictures, Charlie," Hemingway said as we went up in the elevator. "They have some pretty good pictures now, Charlie."

Scribner nodded and said, "Yuh, yuh."

"Was fun for country boy like me," Hemingway said.

"Yuh, yuh," said Scribner.

We went into the suite and took off our coats, and Hemingway said we would have lunch right there. He called room service, and Mrs. Hemingway sat down at the desk to finish her letter. Hemingway sat down on the couch with Mr. Scribner and began telling him that he had been jamming, like a rider in a six-day bike race, and Patrick sat quietly in a corner and watched his father. The waiter came in and passed out menus. Scribner said he was going to order the most expensive item on the menu, because Hemingway was paying for it. He laughed tentatively, and Patrick laughed to keep him company. The waiter retired with our orders, and Scribner and Hemingway talked business for a while. Scribner wanted to know whether Hemingway had the letters he had written to him.

Hemingway said, "I carry them everyplace I go, Charlie, together with a copy of the poems of Robert Browning."

Scribner nodded and, from the inner pocket of his jacket, took some papers—copies of the contract for the new book, he said. The contract provided for an advance of twenty-five thousand dollars against royalties, beginning at fifteen per cent.

Hemingway signed the contract, and got up from the couch. Then he said, "Never ran as no genius, but I'll defend the title again against all the good young new ones." He lowered his head, put his left foot forward, and jabbed at the air with a left and a right. "Never let them hit you solid," he said.

Scribner wanted to know where Hemingway could be reached in Europe. Care of the Guaranty Trust Company in Paris, Hemingway told him. "When we took Paris, I tried to take that bank and got smacked back," he said, and laughed a shy laugh. "I thought it would be awfully nice if I could take my own bank."

"Yuh, yuh," Scribner said. "What are you planning to do in Italy, Ernest?"

Hemingway said he would work part of each day and see his Italian friends and go duckhunting in the mornings. "We shot three hundred and thirty-one ducks to six guns there one morning," he said. "Mary shot good, too."

Mrs. Hemingway looked up. "Any girl who marries Papa has to learn how to carry a gun," she said, and returned to her letter-writing.

"I went hunting once in Suffolk, England," Scribner said. Everyone waited politely for him to continue. "I remember they gave me goose eggs to eat for breakfast in Suffolk. Then we went out to shoot. I didn't know how to get my gun off safe."

"Hunting is sort of a good life," Hemingway said. "Better than Westport or Bronxville, I think."

"After I learned how to get my gun off safe, I couldn't hit anything," Scribner said.

"I'd like to make the big Monte Carlo shoot and the Championship of the World at San Remo," Hemingway said. "I'm in pretty good shape to shoot either one. It's not a spectator sport at all. But exciting to do and wonderful to manage. I used to handle Wolfie in big shoots. He is a great shot. It was like handling a great horse."

"I finally got one," Scribner said timidly.

"Got what?" asked Hemingway.

"A rabbit," Scribner said. "I shot this rabbit."

"They haven't held the big Monte Carlo shoot since 1939," Hemingway said. "Only two Americans ever won it in seventy-four years. Shooting gives me a good feeling. A lot of it is being together and friendly instead of feeling you are in some place where everybody hates you and wishes you ill. It is faster than baseball, and you are out on one strike."

The telephone rang, and Hemingway picked it up, listened, said a few words, and then turned to us and said that an outfit called Endorsements, Inc., had offered him four thousand dollars to pose as a Man of Distinction. "I told them I wouldn't drink the stuff for four thousand dollars," he said. "I told them I was a champagne man. Am trying to be a good guy, but it's a difficult trade. What you win in Boston, you lose in Chicago."

Two Generals

NORMAN LEWIS

❧

Even after thirteen novels, Norman Lewis is best known in England as a travel writer and world reporter. He considers his most important work to be a long article, "Genocide in Brazil," published in the London *Sunday Times* in 1968, which drew international attention to the treatment of Amazonian Indians and the deforestation of their land.

During World War II, Lewis worked for British intelligence in the south of Italy. A memoir, *Naples '44,* re-creates the confusion of that time as it describes a city without electricity—or rules. *The Honoured Society,* a non-fiction study of the Sicilian Mafia, was serialized in *The New Yorker.*

What interests Lewis most as a journalist, he says, is "the background and style of life in a country, rather than the colour of threads in the political web." He wrote "Two Generals" in 1958, shortly before Fidel Castro took power in Cuba. It illustrates the charm of Lewis's writing, particularly his use of dialogue to convey personalities in both the present and the past. With genial humor and sad wisdom, the two generals look back six decades—evoking a sense of bygone elegance, and putting their own heroism in perspective, as they confront an implacable enemy: time.

—K. K.

❧

General Enrique Loynaz took me to see General Garcia Velez, the other surviving hero of Cuba's War of Independence against Spain. General Velez sat in the cool, vaulted marble of his library, in his pyjamas surrounded by piles of magazines, mostly English. He had been ambassador to Great Britain for twelve years. A softly groaning symphony of distant car horns and loudspeakers came through the open window. There was a big military parade on in the city.

"I'm commonly stated in the press to be 94," General Velez said. "It's not true. I'm only 93." General Loynaz was in his late eighties. Before leaving his house he had shown me a slightly bent Toledo sword. "It's out of shape from whacking cowards on the backside," he said. "To keep their faces to the enemy."

"The very opposite in fact, of my own methods," Garcia Velez said. "*He* used to bully his men. I believed in kidding them along. In my opinion he was guilty of faulty psychology. How none of them ever had the guts to shoot him in the back I shall never understand."

These two old men had sat quietly in the shadows for sixty years, watching with sardonic eyes the comings and goings of the politicians and the big business men who had gathered like vultures over their victories. They had sat through the revolutions and the *coups d'état,* had seen tyrants rise to power and fall, seen poor, honest men become rich and corrupt, seen young idealists transformed into bloody dictators, seen the vulgar image of Miami stamped over the soft, grey, baroque elegance of the Havana of their youth.

"Above all, my boy, don't get old," Garcia Velez said. "It imposes an excess of reflection. I do practically nothing these days but read and think. See that pile of *Edinburgh Journals.* I've every number since 1764, and I've read them all. Mostly I read history with the inner reservation that it's largely romance and lies. At least nearly everything that I can check on from my own personal experience is. Did you ever see the film *A Message to Garcia,* for example? The Garcia in the film was my father."

"Calixto Garcia—the liberator of our country," General Loynaz explained.

"I didn't see it myself," General Velez said. "As a matter of principle I've never been to the cinema. Nor have I even seen the television. I've always believed in living my life, not watching how other people are supposed to live theirs. But from what they tell me about this film, and the book it was based on, it was pure rubbish."

"The actress was Barbara Stanwyck," General Loynaz said. "A very pretty girl. I much regret never having met her."

"You cannot awaken the interest of Americans without a big fraud," General Velez said. "It was supposed to be some secret mission to my father, shown as carried through in the face of all kinds of nonsensical adventures. My father was depicted as a sort of romantic bandit hiding in the mountains. How they managed to bring Barbara Stanwyck into it, don't ask me. The real truth is there was no adventure. The American agent met my father in a hotel in the town of Bayamo. I don't think the message was particularly important either, whatever it was. My father certainly never bothered to mention it to me."

"Our old friend's a sceptic," Loynaz said. "He's lost the power of passionate conviction."

"A circumstance in which I rejoice," Garcia Velez said. "Our war was terrible enough, but when I say that it was conducted with the utmost brutality, I say this of both sides. Thousands of our people died of starvation and disease in the concentration camps the Spanish set up. Their *guerrilleros* didn't spare our women and children. But let's at least admit we weren't much better."

He knocked the ash from the end of his cigar into a tin which had held herrings.

"Mind you, it wasn't particularly comfortable to be a general in those days. If you got into a mix-up in a battle they always went for the uniform. I can't remember how many times I was wounded. General Maceo collected 27 wounds. We seemed to be indestructible. When they took my father prisoner, he shot himself in the head. The bullet came out of his mouth. He still lived for seventeen years. Tell us about that famous wound of yours, Enrique."

General Loynaz said: "Those were the days when generals died with their boots on. I was in 107 combats. The 107th was at Babinay in '98—the last stages of the war, when our American deliverers had belatedly decided to come in. I was in command of an infantry brigade."

"He was a real general, I might say," Garcia Velez said. "He was always at the head of his troops on a white horse. An admirable spectacle, but not for me. Not for my father, either."

"On this occasion there was no white horse," Loynaz said. "I'd been on one earlier in the battle, but it had been shot under me. I can't remember the colour of the second horse, but it certainly wasn't white. Anyway, there I was on the horse, as usual, with a cavalry escort, and the Spanish *guerrilleros* were waiting for us behind a stockade. We were undergoing heavy rifle fire and a moderate artillery barrage. I gave the order to charge."

"In true Cuban style," Garcia Velez said. "Light Brigade stuff. Into the Valley of Death. The kind of thing they love. I shudder at the thought of it."

"When you run up against cannon fire at point blank range, it's the only way," Loynaz said. "Above all things, you want to get it over with. I was the first over the stockade. Unfortunately I was never much good at jumping, and this time I landed on the horse's neck. A Spanish *guerillero* brought his machete down on top of my head."

"You should have led your charges from the rear," Garcia Velez said.

General Loynaz took my hand and placed it on his scalp. I felt a shallow trough in the skull, about six inches long.

"Three American Presidents have asked to touch that wound," Loynaz said; "Teddy Roosevelt, Hoover, and I can't remember the name of the third. I managed to scramble back into the saddle holding in the few brains I possess with one hand, and I sat there not able to contribute much to the course of the battle, until it was over.

"They took me to a hut where a honeymoon couple had installed themselves, and I commandeered their bed. The effects of this wound by the way, after the initial pain quietened down, were wholly beneficial. Up till that time I was a martyr to headaches, but I've never had one since. It probably made more space for my brains. That was pretty well the end of the war so far as I was concerned. The Americans decided to come in after that. They were just about a year too late. We should have welcomed them in '97."

"Friends are always welcome," Garcia Velez said.

"We had won the war," Loynaz said. "The whole country was in our hands."

"But not the towns," Garcia Velez said. "The Spanish still held the towns. You speak as a patriot, not a historian."

"For six years the foreigners ran our country," Loynaz said. "They bought up the best land in the island. Do you know how much they paid? Ten cents a *caballeriá* of 33 acres. The price of two bottles of Coca Cola."

Garcia Velez shook his head at him. When Loynaz had gone, he said: "My old friend has always remained a Cuban, whereas the twelve years I spent in London has wrought a profound change in my character. I see things calmly now; almost I believe, through Anglo-Saxon eyes. Moreover, living abroad, I became wholly a pacifist. Had my twelve years in England come before the war, I don't believe I'd have fought in it. The things I was forced as a patriot to do, now seem to me to be hateful—against nature."

It was within weeks of Fidel Castro's capture of the capital, and from where I sat I could see through the window a squad of feminine militia come marching down the road. Half of them were in uniform, the rest in pretty dresses. A sergeant marching beside them called out the time. With them came a blare of martial music from the speakers of an escorting van.

"Please close the window," General Velez said. "The noise oppresses me. What do their banners say?"

I read: "Fatherland or Death. We will fight to the last drop of our blood against foreign aggressors."

"And they will," the general said. "And they will if necessary. Alas, haven't I seen it all before."

The Silent Season of a Hero

GAY TALESE

❧

Gay Talese's portrayal of Joe DiMaggio illustrates his artistry with a resistant subject. The opening vignette, where Talese casts himself as "the man from New York," establishes DiMaggio's demand for privacy. Yet even though Talese eventually gained access and trust, his portrayal remains resolutely dramatic: instead of hearing DiMaggio being interviewed, we overhear him conversing with others in a series of intriguing scenes. Talese's profile becomes a short story, borrowing—as he often does—the tone of favorite fiction writers like John O'Hara or Irwin Shaw.

"I try to follow my subjects unobtrusively while observing them in revealing situations," Talese has said. "I attempt to absorb the whole scene, the dialogue and mood, the tension, drama, conflict, and then I usually write it from the point of view of the subject, sometimes revealing what these individuals are thinking during those moments I am describing."

Talese takes us into Joe DiMaggio's mind by means of specific objects, what Tom Wolfe has called the "status details" of everyday life. A painting of Marilyn Monroe, a tobacco humidor, a newspaper at the breakfast table: each triggers a memory that opens up a new section of the story.

Talese served a ten-year apprenticeship as a reporter for the *New York Times*. By the time he left in 1965, he was already a regular contributor to *Esquire,* whose editor, Harold Hayes, sponsored some of the most innovative magazine journalism of the era. The DiMaggio story appeared in July of 1966.

Fame and Obscurity (1970) includes "The Silent Season of a Hero" and much of Talese's other *Esquire* writing as well as the full text of *The Bridge,* a classic nonfiction novella about the construction of the Verrazano Narrows span.

—K. K.

❧

"I would like to take the great DiMaggio fishing," the old man said. "They say his father was a fisherman. Maybe he was as poor as we are and would understand."

—ERNEST HEMINGWAY,
The Old Man and the Sea

It was not quite spring, the silent season before the search for salmon, and the old fishermen of San Francisco were either painting their boats or repairing their nets along the pier or sitting in the sun talking quietly among themselves, watching the tourists come and go, and smiling, now, as a pretty girl paused to take their picture. She was about twenty-five, healthy and blue-eyed and wearing a red turtle-neck sweater, and she had long, flowing blonde hair that she brushed back a few times before clicking her camera. The fishermen, looking at her, made admiring comments but she did not understand because they spoke a Sicilian dialect; nor did she notice the tall grey-haired man in a dark suit who stood watching her from behind a big bay window on the second floor of DiMaggio's Restaurant that overlooks the pier.

He watched until she left, lost in the crowd of newly arrived tourists that had just come down the hill by cable car. Then he sat down again at the table in the restaurant, finishing his tea and lighting another cigarette, his fifth in the last half hour. It was eleven-thirty in the morning. None of the other tables was occupied, and the only sounds came from the bar where a liquor salesman was laughing at something the headwaiter had said. But then the salesman, his briefcase under his arm, headed for the door, stopping briefly to peek into the dining room and call out, "See you later, Joe." Joe DiMaggio turned and waved at the salesman. Then the room was quiet again.

At fifty-one, DiMaggio was a most distinguished-looking man, aging as gracefully as he had played on the ball field, impeccable in his tailoring, his nails manicured, his six-foot two-inch body seeming as lean and capable as when he posed for the portrait that hangs in the restaurant and shows him in Yankee Stadium swinging from the heels at a pitch thrown twenty years ago. His grey hair was thinning at the crown, but just barely, and his face was lined in the right places, and his expression, once as sad and haunted as a matador's, was more in repose these days, though, as now, tension had returned and he chain-smoked and occasionally paced the floor and looked out the window at the people below. In the crowd was a man he did not wish to see.

The man had met DiMaggio in New York. This week he had come to San Francisco and had telephoned several times but none of the calls had been returned because DiMaggio suspected that the man, who had said he was doing research on some vague sociological project, really wanted to delve into DiMaggio's private life and that of DiMaggio's former wife, Marilyn Monroe. DiMaggio would never tolerate this. The memory of her death is still very painful to him, and yet, because he keeps it to himself, some people are not sensitive to it. One night in a supper club a woman who had been drinking approached his table, and when he did not ask her to join him, she snapped:

"All right, I guess I'm *not* Marilyn Monroe."

He ignored her remark, but when she repeated it, he replied, barely controlling his anger, "No—I wish you were, but you're not."

The tone of his voice softened her, and she asked, "Am I saying something wrong?"

"You already have," he said. "Now will you please leave me alone?"

His friends on the wharf, understanding him as they do, are very careful when discussing him with strangers, knowing that should they inadvertently betray a confidence he will not denounce them but rather will never speak to them again; this comes from a sense of propriety not inconsistent in the man who also, after Marilyn Monroe's death, directed that fresh flowers be placed on her grave "forever."

Some of the older fishermen who have known DiMaggio all his life remember him as a small boy who helped clean his father's boat, and as a young man who sneaked away and used a broken oar as a bat on the sandlots nearby. His father, a small mustachioed man known as Zio Pepe, would become infuriated and call him *lagnuso*, lazy, *meschino*, good-for-nothing, but in 1936 Zio Pepe was among those who cheered when Joe DiMaggio returned to San Francisco after his first season with the New York Yankees and was carried along the wharf on the shoulders of the fishermen.

The fishermen also remember how, after his retirement in 1951, DiMaggio brought his second wife, Marilyn, to live near the wharf, and sometimes they would be seen early in the morning fishing off DiMaggio's boat, the *Yankee Clipper*, now docked quietly in the marina, and in the evening they would be sitting and talking on the pier. They had arguments, too, the fishermen knew, and one night Marilyn was seen running hysterically, crying as she ran, along the road away from the pier, with Joe following. But the fishermen pretended they did not see this; it was none of their affair. They knew that Joe wanted her to stay in San Francisco and avoid the sharks in Hollywood, but she was confused and torn then—"She was a child," they said—and even today DiMaggio loathes Los Angeles and many of the people in it. He no longer speaks to his onetime friend, Frank Sinatra, who had befriended Marilyn in her final years, and he also is cool to Dean Martin and Peter Lawford and Lawford's former wife, Pat, who once gave a party at which she introduced Marilyn Monroe to Robert Kennedy, and the two of them danced often that night, Joe heard, and he did not take it well. He was very possessive of her that year, his close friends say, because Marilyn and he had planned to remarry; but before they could she was dead, and DiMaggio banned the Lawfords and Sinatra and many Hollywood people from her funeral. When Marilyn Monroe's attorney complained that DiMaggio was keeping her friends away, DiMaggio answered coldly, "If it weren't for those friends persuading her to stay in Hollywood she would still be alive."

Joe DiMaggio now spends most of the year in San Francisco, and each day tourists, noticing the name on the restaurant, ask the men on the wharf if they ever see him. Oh yes, the men say, they see him nearly every day; they have not seen him yet this morning, they add, but he should be arriving shortly. So the tourists continue to walk along the piers past the crab vendors, under the circling sea gulls, past the fish 'n' chip stands, sometimes stopping to watch a large vessel steaming toward the Golden Gate Bridge which, to their dismay, is painted red. Then they visit the Wax Museum, where there is a life-size figure of DiMaggio in uniform, and walk across the street and spend a quarter to peer through the silver telescopes focused on the island of Alcatraz, which is no longer a Federal prison. Then they return to ask the men if DiMaggio has been seen. Not yet, the men say, although they notice his blue Impala parked in the lot next to the restaurant. Sometimes tourists will walk into the restaurant and have lunch and will see him sitting calmly in a corner signing autographs and being extremely gracious with everyone. At other times, as on this particular morning when the man from New York chose to visit, DiMaggio was tense and suspicious.

When the man entered the restaurant from the side steps leading to the dining room he saw DiMaggio standing near the window talking with an elderly maître d' named Charles Friscia. Not wanting to walk in and risk intrusion, the man asked one of DiMaggio's nephews to inform Joe of his presence. When DiMaggio got the message he quickly turned and left Friscia and disappeared through an exit leading down to the kitchen.

Astonished and confused, the visitor stood in the hall. A moment later Friscia appeared and the man asked, "Did Joe leave?"

"Joe who?" Friscia replied.

"Joe DiMaggio!"

"Haven't seen him," Friscia said.

"You haven't *seen* him! He was standing right next to you a second ago!"

"It wasn't me," Friscia said.

"You were standing next to him. I saw you. In the dining room."

"You must be mistaken," Friscia said, softly, seriously. "It wasn't me."

"You *must* be kidding," the man said, angrily, turning and leaving the restaurant. Before he could get to his car, however, DiMaggio's nephew came running after him and said, "Joe wants to see you."

He returned expecting to see DiMaggio waiting for him. Instead he was handed a telephone. The voice was powerful and deep and so tense that the quick sentences ran together.

"You are invading my rights, I did not ask you to come, I assume you have a lawyer, you must have a lawyer, get your lawyer!"

"I came as a friend," the man interrupted.

"That's beside the point," DiMaggio said. "I have my privacy, I do not want it violated, you'd better get a lawyer. . . ." Then, pausing, DiMaggio asked, "Is my nephew there?"

He was not.

"Then wait where you are."

A moment later DiMaggio appeared, tall and red-faced, erect and beautifully dressed in his dark suit and white shirt with the grey silk tie and the gleaming silver cuff links. He moved with big steps toward the man and handed him an airmail envelope, unopened, that the man had written from New York.

"Here," DiMaggio said. "This is yours."

Then DiMaggio sat down at a small table. He said nothing, just lit a cigarette and waited, legs crossed, his head held high and back so as to reveal the intricate construction of his nose, a fine sharp tip above the big nostrils and tiny bones built out from the bridge, a great nose.

"Look," DiMaggio said, more calmly. "I do not interfere with other people's lives. And I do not expect them to interfere with mine. There are things about my life, personal things, that I refuse to talk about. And even if you asked my brothers they would be unable to tell you about them because they do not know. There are things about me, so many things, that they simply do not know. . . ."

"I don't want to cause trouble," the man said. "I think you're a great man, and. . . ."

"I'm not great," DiMaggio cut in. "I'm not great," he repeated, softly. "I'm just a man trying to get along."

Then DiMaggio, as if realizing that he was intruding upon his own privacy, abruptly stood up. He looked at his watch.

"I'm late," he said, very formal again. "I'm ten minutes late. *You're* making me later."

The man left the restaurant. He crossed the street and wandered over to the pier, briefly watching the fishermen hauling their nets and talking in the sun, seeming very calm and contented. Then, after he had turned and was headed back toward the parking lot, a blue Impala stopped in front of him and Joe DiMaggio leaned out the window and asked, "Do you have a car?" His voice was very gentle.

"Yes," the man said.

"Oh," DiMaggio said. "I would have given you a ride."

Joe DiMaggio was not born in San Francisco but in Martinez, a small fishing village twenty-five miles northeast of the Golden Gate. Zio Pepe had settled there after leaving Isola delle Femmine, an islet off Palermo where the DiMaggios had been fishermen for generations. But in 1915, hearing of the luckier waters off San Francisco's wharf, Zio Pepe left Martinez, packing his boat with furniture and family, including Joe who was one year old.

San Francisco was placid and picturesque when the DiMaggios arrived, but there was a competitive undercurrent and struggle for power along the pier. At dawn the boats would sail out to where the bay meets the ocean and the sea is rough, and later the men would race back with their hauls, hoping to beat their fellow fishermen to shore and sell it while they could. Twenty or thirty boats would sometimes be trying to gain the channel shoreward at the same time, and a fisherman had to know every rock in the water, and later know every bargaining trick along the shore, because the dealers and restaurateurs would play one fisherman off against the other, keeping the prices down. Later the fishermen became wiser and organized, predetermining the maximum amount each fisherman would catch, but there were always some men who, like the fish, never learned, and so heads would sometimes be broken, nets slashed, gasoline poured onto their fish, flowers of warning placed outside their doors.

But these days were ending when Zio Pepe arrived, and he expected his five sons to succeed him as fishermen, and the first two, Tom and Michael, did; but a third, Vincent, wanted to sing. He sang with such magnificent power as a young man that he came to the attention of the great banker, A. P. Giannini, and there were plans to send him to Italy for tutoring and the opera. But there was hesitation around the DiMaggio household and Vince never went; instead he played ball with the San Francisco Seals and sportswriters misspelled his name.

It was DeMaggio until Joe, at Vince's recommendation, joined the team and became a sensation, being followed later by the youngest brother, Dominic, who was also outstanding. All three later played in the big leagues and some writers like to say that Joe was the best hitter, Dom the best fielder, Vince the best singer, and Casey Stengel once said: "Vince is the only player I ever saw who could strike out three times in one game and not be embarrassed. He'd walk into the clubhouse whistling. Everybody would be feeling sorry for him, but Vince always thought he was doing good."

After he retired from baseball Vince became a bartender, then a milkman, now a carpenter. He lives forty miles north of San Francisco in a house he partly built, has been happily married for thirty-four years, has four grandchildren, has in the closet one of Joe's tailor-made suits that he has never had altered to fit, and when people ask if he envies Joe he always says, "No, maybe Joe would like to have what I have. He won't admit it, but he just might like to have what I have." The brother Vince most admired was Michael, "a big earthy man, a dreamer, a fisherman who wanted things but didn't want to take from Joe, or to work in the restaurant. He wanted a bigger boat, but wanted to earn it on his own. He never got it." In 1953, at the age of forty-four, Michael fell from his boat and drowned.

Since Zio Pepe's death at seventy-seven in 1949, Tom, at sixty-two the oldest brother—two of his four sisters are older—has become nominal head of the family and manages the restaurant that was opened in 1937 as Joe DiMaggio's Grotto. Later Joe sold out his share and now Tom is the co-owner of it with Dominic. Of all the brothers, Dominic, who was known as the "Little Professor" when he played with the Boston Red Sox, is the most successful in business. He lives in a fashionable Boston suburb with his wife and three children and is president of a firm that manufactures fiber-cushion materials and grossed more than $3,500,000 last year.

Joe DiMaggio lives with his widowed sister, Marie, in a tan stone house on a quiet residential street not far from Fisherman's Wharf. He bought the house almost thirty years ago for his parents, and after their death he lived there with Marilyn Monroe; now it is cared for by Marie, a slim and handsome dark-eyed woman who has an apartment on the second floor, Joe on the third. There are some baseball trophies and plaques in the small room off DiMaggio's bedroom, and on his dresser are photographs of Marilyn Monroe, and in the living room downstairs is a small painting of her that DiMaggio likes very much: it reveals only her face and shoulders and she is wearing a very wide-brimmed sun hat, and there is a soft sweet smile on her lips, an innocent curiosity about her that is the way he saw her and the way he wanted her to be seen by others—a simple girl, "a warm bighearted girl," he once described her, "that everybody took advantage of."

The publicity photographs emphasizing her sex appeal often offended him, and a memorable moment for Billy Wilder, who directed her in *The Seven Year Itch*, occurred when he spotted DiMaggio in a large crowd of people gathered on Lexington Avenue in New York to watch a scene in which Marilyn, standing over a subway grating to cool herself, had her skirts blown high by a sudden wind below. "What the hell is going on here?" DiMaggio was overheard to have said in the crowd, and Wilder recalled, "I shall never forget the look of death on Joe's face."

He was then thirty-nine, she was twenty-seven. They had been married in January of that year, 1954, despite disharmony in temperament and time: he was tired of publicity, she was thriving on it; he was intolerant of tardiness, she was always late. During their honeymoon in Tokyo an American general had introduced himself and asked if, as a patriotic gesture, she would visit the troops in Korea. She looked at Joe. "It's your honeymoon," he said, shrugging, "go ahead if you want to."

She appeared on ten occasions before 100,000 servicemen, and when she returned she said, "It was so wonderful, Joe. You never heard such cheering."

"Yes I have," he said.

Across from her portrait in the living room, on a coffee table in front of a sofa, is a sterling-silver humidor that was presented to him by his Yankee teammates at a time when he was the most talked-about man in America, and when Les Brown's band had recorded a hit that was heard day and night on the radio:

> . . . From Coast to Coast, that's all you hear
> Of Joe the One-Man Show

He's glorified the horsehide sphere,
Jolting Joe DiMaggio . . .
Joe . . . Joe . . . DiMaggio . . . we
want you on our side. . . .

The year was 1941, and it began for DiMaggio in the middle of May after the Yankees had lost four games in a row, seven of their last nine, and were in fourth place, five-and-a-half games behind the leading Cleveland Indians. On May 15th, DiMaggio hit only a first-inning single in a game that New York lost to Chicago, 13–1; he was barely hitting .300, and had greatly disappointed the crowds that had seen him finish with a .352 average the year before and .381 in 1939.

He got a hit in the next game, and the next, and the next. On May 24th, with the Yankees losing 6–5 to Boston, DiMaggio came up with runners on second and third and singled them home, winning the game, extending his streak to ten games. But it went largely unnoticed. Even DiMaggio was not conscious of it until it had reached twenty-nine games in mid-June. Then the newspapers began to dramatize it, the public became aroused, they sent him good-luck charms of every description, and DiMaggio kept hitting, and radio announcers would interrupt programs to announce the news, and then the song again: *"Joe . . . Joe . . . DiMaggio . . . we want you on our side . . ."*

Sometimes DiMaggio would be hitless his first three times up, the tension would build, it would appear that the game would end without his getting another chance—but he always would, and then he would hit the ball against the left-field wall, or through the pitcher's legs, or between two leaping infielders. In the forty-first game, the first of a double-header in Washington, DiMaggio tied an American League record that George Sisler had set in 1922. But before the second game began a spectator sneaked onto the field and into the Yankees' dugout and stole DiMaggio's favorite bat. In the second game, using another of his bats, DiMaggio lined out twice and flied out. But in the seventh inning, borrowing one of his old bats that a teammate was using, he singled and broke Sisler's record, and he was only three games away from surpassing the major-league record of forty-four set in 1897 by Willie Keeler while playing for Baltimore when it was a National League franchise.

An appeal for the missing bat was made through the newspapers. A man from Newark admitted the crime and returned it with regrets. And on July 2, at Yankee Stadium, DiMaggio hit a home run into the left-field stands. The record was broken.

He also got hits in the next eleven games, but on July 17th in Cleveland, at a night game attended by 67,468, he failed against two pitchers, Al Smith and Jim Bagby, Jr., although Cleveland's hero was really its third baseman, Ken Keltner, who in the first inning lunged to his right to make a spectacular backhanded stop of a drive and, from the foul line behind third base, he threw DiMaggio out. DiMaggio received a walk in the fourth inning. But in the seventh he again hit a hard shot at Keltner, who again stopped it and threw him out. DiMaggio hit sharply toward the shortstop in the eighth inning, the ball taking a bad hop, but Lou Boudreau speared it off his shoulder and threw to the second baseman to start a double play and DiMaggio's streak was stopped at fifty-six games. But the New York Yankees were on their way to winning the pennant by seventeen games, and the World Series too, and so in August, in a hotel suite in Washington, the players threw a surprise party for DiMaggio and toasted him with champagne and presented him with this Tiffany silver humidor that is now in San Francisco in his living room. . . .

Marie was in the kitchen making toast and tea when DiMaggio came down for breakfast; his grey hair was uncombed but, since he wears it short, it was not untidy. He said good-morning to Marie, sat down and yawned. He lit a cigarette. He wore a blue wool bathrobe over his pajamas. It was eight A.M. He had many things to do today and he seemed cheerful. He had a conference with the president of Continental Television, Inc., a large retail chain in California of which he is a partner and vice-president; later he had a golf date, and then a big banquet to attend, and, if that did not go on too long and he were not too tired afterward, he might have a date.

Picking up the morning paper, not rushing to the sports page, DiMaggio read the front-page news, the people-problems of '66: Kwame Nkrumah was overthrown in Ghana, students were burning their draft cards (DiMaggio shook his head), the flu epidemic was spreading through the whole state of California. Then he flipped inside through the gossip columns, thankful they did not have him in there today—they had printed an item about his dating "an electrifying airline hostess" not long ago, and they also spotted him at dinner with Dori Lane, "the frantic frugger" in Whiskey à Go Go's glass cage—and then he turned to the sports page and read a story about how the injured Mickey Mantle may never regain his form.

It had all happened so quickly, the passing of Mantle, or so it seemed; he had succeeded DiMaggio as DiMaggio had succeeded Ruth, but now there was no great young power hitter coming up and the Yankee management, almost desperate, had talked Mantle out of retirement; and on September 18, 1965, they gave him a "day" in New York during which he received several thousand dollars' worth of gifts—an automobile, two quarter horses, free vacation trips to Rome, Nassau, Puerto Rico—and DiMaggio had flown to New York to make the introduction before 50,000: it had been a dramatic day, an almost holy day for the believers who had jammed the grandstands early to witness the canonization of a new stadium saint. Cardinal Spellman was on the committee, President Johnson sent a telegram, the day was officially proclaimed by the Mayor of New York, an orchestra assembled in center field in front of the trinity of monuments to Ruth, Gehrig, Huggins; and high in the grandstands, billowing in the breeze of early autumn, were white banners that read: "Don't Quit Mick," "We Love the Mick."

The banners had been held by hundreds of young boys whose dreams had been fulfilled so often by Mantle, but also seated in the grandstands were older men, paunchy and balding, in whose middle-aged minds DiMaggio was still vivid and invincible, and some of them remembered how one month before, during a pre-game exhibition at Old-timers' Day in Yankee Stadium, DiMaggio had hit a pitch into the left-field seats, and suddenly thousands of people had jumped wildly to their feet, joyously screaming— the great DiMaggio had returned, they were young again, it was yesterday.

But on this sunny September day at the Stadium, the feast day of Mickey Mantle, DiMaggio was not wearing No. 5 on his back nor a black cap to cover his greying hair; he was wearing a black suit and white shirt and blue tie, and he stood in one corner of the Yankees' dugout waiting to be introduced by Red Barber, who was standing near home plate behind a silver microphone. In the outfield Guy Lombardo's Royal Canadians were playing soothing soft music; and moving slowly back and forth over the sprawling green grass between the left-field bullpen and the infield were two carts driven by groundskeepers and containing dozens and dozens of large gifts for Mantle—a six-foot, one-hundred-pound Hebrew National salami, a Winchester rifle, a mink coat for Mrs. Mantle, a set of Wilson golf clubs, a Mercury 95-horsepower outboard motor, a Necchi portable, a year's supply of Chunky Candy. DiMaggio smoked a cigarette, but cupped it in his hands as if not wanting to be caught in the act by teen-aged boys near enough to peek down into the dugout. Then, edging forward a step, DiMaggio poked his head out and looked up. He could see nothing above except the packed towering green grandstands that seemed a mile high and moving, and he could see no clouds or blue sky, only a sky of faces. Then the announcer called out his name—*"Joe DiMaggio!"*—and sud-denly there was a blast of cheering that grew louder and louder, echoing and reechoing within the big steel canyon, and DiMaggio stomped out his cigarette and climbed up the dugout steps and onto the soft green grass, the noise resounding in his ears, he could almost feel the breeze, the breath of 50,000 lungs upon him, 100,000 eyes watching his every move and for the briefest instant as he walked he closed his eyes.

Then in his path he saw Mickey Mantle's mother, a smiling elderly woman wearing an orchid, and he gently reached out for her elbow, holding it as he led her toward the microphone next to the other dignitaries lined up on the infield. Then he stood, very erect and without expression, as the cheers softened and the Stadium settled down.

Mantle was still in the dugout, in uniform, standing with one leg on the top step, and lined on both sides of him were the other Yankees who, when the ceremony was over, would play the Detroit Tigers. Then into the dugout, smiling, came Senator Robert Kennedy, accompanied by two tall curly-haired young assistants with blue eyes, Fordham freckles. Jim Farley was the first on the field to notice the Senator, and Farley muttered, loud enough for others to hear, "Who the hell invited *him?*"

Toots Shor and some of the other committeemen standing near Farley looked into the dugout, and so did DiMaggio, his glance seeming cold, but he remaining silent. Kennedy walked up and down within the dugout shaking hands with the Yankees, but he did not walk onto the field.

"Senator," said the Yankees' manager, Johnny Keane, "why don't you sit down?" Kennedy quickly shook his head, smiled. He remained standing, and then one Yankee came over and asked him about getting relatives out of Cuba, and Kennedy called over one of his aides to take down the details in a notebook.

On the infield the ceremony went on, Mantle's gifts continued to pile up—a Mobilette motor bike, a Sooner Schooner wagon barbecue, a year's supply of Chock Full O'Nuts coffee, a year's supply of Topps Chewing Gum—and the Yankee players watched, and Maris seemed glum.

"Hey, Rog," yelled a man with a tape recorder, Murray Olderman, "I want to do a thirty-second tape with you."

Maris swore angrily, shook his head.

"It'll only take a second," Olderman said.

"Why don't you ask Richardson? He's a better talker than me."

"Yes, but the fact that it comes from you. . . ."

Maris swore again. But finally he went over and said in an interview that Mantle was the finest player of his era, a great competitor, a great hitter.

Fifteen minutes later, standing behind the microphone at home plate, DiMaggio was telling the crowd, "I'm proud to introduce the man who succeeded me in center field in 1951," and from every corner of the Stadium the cheering, whistling, clapping came down. Mantle stepped forward. He stood with his wife and children, posed for the photographers kneeling in front. Then he thanked the crowd in a short speech, and, turning, shook hands with the dignitaries standing nearby. Among them now was Senator Kennedy, who had been spotted in the dugout five minutes before by Red Barber, and been called out and introduced. Kennedy posed with Mantle for a photographer, then shook hands with the Mantle children, and with Toots Shor and James Farley and others. DiMaggio saw him coming down the line and at the last second he backed away, casually, hardly anybody noticing it, and Kennedy seemed not to notice it either, just swept past shaking more hands. . . .

Finishing his tea, putting aside the newspaper, DiMaggio went upstairs to dress, and soon he was waving good-bye to Marie and driving toward his business appointment in downtown San Francisco with his partners in the retail television business. DiMaggio, while not a millionaire, has invested wisely and has always had, since his retirement from baseball, executive positions with big companies that have paid him well. He also was among the organizers of the Fisherman's National Bank of San Francisco last year, and, though it never came about, he demonstrated an acuteness that impressed those businessmen who had thought of him only in terms of base-ball. He has had offers to manage big-league baseball teams but always has rejected them, saying, "I have enough trouble taking care of my own prob-lems without taking on the responsibilities of twenty-five ballplayers."

So his only contact with baseball these days, excluding public appear-ances, is his unsalaried job as a batting coach each spring in Florida with the New York Yankees, a trip he would make once again on the following Sunday, three days away, if he could accomplish what for him is always the dreaded responsibility of packing, a task made no easier by the fact that he lately has fallen into the habit of keeping his clothes in two places—some hang in his closet at home, some hang in the back room of a saloon called Reno's.

Reno's is a dimly-lit bar in the center of San Francisco. A portrait of DiMaggio swinging a bat hangs on the wall, in addition to portraits of other star athletes, and the clientele consists mainly of the sporting crowd and newspapermen, people who know DiMaggio quite well and around whom he speaks freely on a number of subjects and relaxes as he can in few other places. The owner of the bar is Reno Barsocchini, a broad-shouldered and handsome man of fifty-one with greying wavy hair who began as a fiddler in Dago Mary's tavern thirty-five years ago. He later became a bartender there and elsewhere, including DiMaggio's Restaurant, and now he is probably DiMaggio's closest friend. He was the best man at the DiMaggio-Monroe wedding in 1954, and when they separated nine months later in Los Ange-les, Reno rushed down to help DiMaggio with the packing and drive him back to San Francisco. Reno will never forget the day.

Hundreds of people were gathered around the Beverly Hills home that DiMaggio and Marilyn had rented, and photographers were perched in the trees watching the windows, and others stood on the lawn and behind the rose bushes waiting to snap pictures of anybody who walked out of the house. The newspapers that day played all the puns—"Joe Fanned on Jealousy"; "Marilyn and Joe—Out at Home"—and the Hollywood columnists, to whom DiMag-gio was never an idol, never a gracious host, recounted instances of incom-patibility, and Oscar Levant said it all proved that no man could be a success in two national pastimes. When Reno Barsocchini arrived he had to push his way through the mob, then bang on the door for several minutes before being admitted. Marilyn Monroe was upstairs in bed, Joe DiMaggio was downstairs with his suitcases, tense and pale, his eyes bloodshot.

Reno took the suitcases and golf clubs out to DiMaggio's car, and then DiMaggio came out of the house, the reporters moving toward him, the lights flashing.

"Where are you going?" they yelled. "I'm driving to San Francisco," he said, walking quickly.

"Is that going to be your home?"

"That *is* my home and always has been."

"Are you coming back?"

DiMaggio turned for a moment, looking up at the house.

"No," he said, "I'll never be back."

Reno Barsocchini, except for a brief falling out over something he will not discuss, has been DiMaggio's trusted companion ever since, joining him whenever he can on the golf course or on the town, otherwise waiting for him in the bar with other middle-aged men. They may wait for hours sometimes, waiting and knowing that when he arrives he may wish to be alone; but it does not seem to matter, they are endlessly awed by him, moved by the mystique, he is a kind of male Garbo. They know that he can be warm and loyal if they are sensitive to his wishes, but they must never be late for an appointment to meet him. One man, unable to find a parking place, arrived a half-hour late once and DiMaggio did not talk to him again for three months. They know, too, when dining at night with DiMaggio, that he generally prefers male companions and occasionally one or two young women, but never wives; wives gossip, wives complain, wives are trouble, and men wishing to remain close to DiMaggio must keep their wives at home.

When DiMaggio strolls into Reno's bar the men wave and call out his name, and Reno Barsocchini smiles and announces, "Here's the Clipper!", the "Yankee Clipper" being a nickname from his baseball days.

"Hey, Clipper, Clipper," Reno had said two nights before, "where you been, Clipper? . . . Clipper, how 'bout a belt?"

DiMaggio refused the offer of a drink, ordering instead a pot of tea, which he prefers to all other beverages except before a date, when he will switch to vodka.

"Hey, Joe," a sportswriter asked, a man researching a magazine piece on golf, "why is it that a golfer, when he starts getting older, loses his putting touch first? Like Snead and Hogan, they can still hit a ball well off the tee, but on the greens they lose the strokes. . . ."

"It's the pressure of age," DiMaggio said, turning around on his bar stool. "With age you get jittery. It's true of golfers, it's true of any man when he gets into his fifties. He doesn't take chances like he used to. The younger golfer, on the greens, he'll stroke his putts better. The older man, he becomes hesitant. A little uncertain. Shaky. When it comes to taking chances the younger man, even when driving a car, will take chances that the older man won't."

"Speaking of chances," another man said, one of the group that had gathered around DiMaggio, "did you see that guy on crutches in here last night?"

"Yeah, had his leg in a cast," a third said. "Skiing."

"I would never ski," DiMaggio said. "Men who ski must be doing it to impress a broad. You see these men, some of them forty, fifty, getting onto skis. And later you see them all bandaged up, broken legs. . . ."

"But skiing's a very sexy sport, Joe. All the clothes, the tight pants, the fireplace in the ski lodge, the bear rug—Christ, nobody goes to ski. They just go out there to get it cold so they can warm it up. . . ."

"Maybe you're right," DiMaggio said. "I might be persuaded."

"Want a belt, Clipper?" Reno asked.

DiMaggio thought for a second, then said, "All right—first belt tonight."

Now it was noon, a warm sunny day. DiMaggio's business meeting with the television retailers had gone well; he had made a strong appeal to George Shahood, president of Continental Television, Inc., which has eight retail outlets in Northern California, to cut prices on color television sets and increase the sales volume, and Shahood had conceded it was worth a try. Then DiMaggio called Reno's bar to see if there were any messages, and now he was in Lefty O'Doul's car being driven along Fisherman's Wharf toward the Golden Gate Bridge en route to a golf course thirty miles upstate. Lefty O'Doul was one of the great hitters in the National League in the early Thirties, and later he managed the San Francisco Seals when DiMaggio was the shining star. Though O'Doul is now sixty-nine, eighteen years older than DiMaggio, he nevertheless possesses great energy and spirit, is a hard-drinking, boisterous man with a big belly and roving eye; and when DiMaggio, as they drove along the highway toward the golf club, noticed a lovely blonde at the wheel of a car nearby and exclaimed, "Look at *that* tomato!" O'Doul's head suddenly spun around, he took his eyes off the road, and yelled, "Where, *where?*" O'Doul's golf game is less than what it was—he used to have a two-handicap—but he still shoots in the 80's, as does DiMaggio.

DiMaggio's drives range between 250 and 280 yards when he doesn't sky them, and his putting is good, but he is distracted by a bad back that both pains him and hinders the fullness of his swing. On the first hole, waiting to tee off, DiMaggio sat back watching a foursome of college boys ahead swinging with such freedom. "Oh," he said with a sigh, "to have *their* backs."

DiMaggio and O'Doul were accompanied around the golf course by Ernie Nevers, the former football star, and two brothers who are in the hotel and movie-distribution business. They moved quickly up and down the green hills in electric golf carts, and DiMaggio's game was exceptionally good for the first nine holes. But then he seemed distracted, perhaps tired, perhaps even reacting to a conversation of a few minutes before. One of the movie men was praising the film *Boeing, Boeing,* starring Tony Curtis and Jerry Lewis, and the man asked DiMaggio if he had seen it.

"No," DiMaggio said. Then he added swiftly, "I haven't seen a film in eight years."

DiMaggio hooked a few shots, was in the woods. He took a No. 9 iron and tried to chip out. But O'Doul interrupted DiMaggio's concentration to remind him to keep the face of the club closed. DiMaggio hit the ball. It caromed off the side of his club, went skipping like a rabbit through the high grass down toward a pond. DiMaggio rarely displays any emotion on a golf course, but now, without saying a word, he took his No. 9 iron and flung it into the air. The club landed in a tree and stayed up there.

"Well," O'Doul said, casually, "there goes *that* set of clubs."

DiMaggio walked to the tree. Fortunately the club had slipped to the lower branch and DiMaggio could stretch up on the cart and get it back.

"Every time I get advice," DiMaggio muttered to himself, shaking his head slowly and walking toward the pond, "I shank it."

Later, showered and dressed, DiMaggio and the others drove to a banquet about ten miles from the golf course. Somebody had said it was going to be an elegant dinner, but when they arrived they could see it was more like a county fair; farmers were gathered outside a big barnlike building, a candidate for sheriff was distributing leaflets at the front door, and a chorus of homely ladies were inside singing *You Are My Sunshine.*

"How did we get sucked into this?" DiMaggio asked, talking out of the side of his mouth, as they approached the building.

"O'Doul," one of the men said. "It's his fault. Damned O'Doul can't turn *anything* down."

"Go to hell," O'Doul said.

Soon DiMaggio and O'Doul and Ernie Nevers were surrounded by the crowd, and the woman who had been leading the chorus came rushing over and said, "Oh, Mr. DiMaggio, it certainly is a pleasure having you."

"It's a pleasure being here, ma'am," he said, forcing a smile.

"It's too bad you didn't arrive a moment sooner, you'd have heard our singing."

"Oh, I heard it," he said, "and I enjoyed it very much."

"Good, good," she said. "And how are your brothers Dom and Vic?"

"Fine. Dom lives near Boston. Vince is in Pittsburgh."

"Why, *hello* there, Joe," interrupted a man with wine on his breath, patting DiMaggio on the back, feeling his arm. "Who's gonna take it this year, Joe?"

"Well, I have no idea," DiMaggio said.

"What about the Giants?"

"Your guess is as good as mine."

"Well, you can't count the Dodgers out," the man said.

"You sure can't," DiMaggio said.

"Not with all that pitching."

"Pitching is certainly important," DiMaggio said.

Everywhere he goes the questions seem the same, as if he has some special vision into the future of new heroes, and everywhere he goes, too, older men grab his hand and feel his arm and predict that he could still go out there and hit one, and the smile on DiMaggio's face is genuine. He tries hard to remain as he was—he diets, he takes steam baths, he is careful; and flabby men in the locker rooms of golf clubs sometimes steal peeks at him when he steps out of the shower, observing the tight muscles across his chest, the flat stomach, the long sinewy legs. He has a young man's body, very pale and little hair; his face is dark and lined, however, parched by the sun of several seasons. Still he is always an impressive figure at banquets such as this—an *immortal,* sportswriters called him, and that is how they have written about him and others like him, rarely suggesting that such heroes might ever be prone to the ills of mortal men, carousing, drinking, scheming; to suggest this would destroy the myth, would disillusion small boys, would infuriate rich men who own ball clubs and to whom baseball is a business dedicated to profit and in pursuit of which they trade mediocre players' flesh as casually as boys trade players' pictures on bubble-gum cards. And so the baseball hero must always act the part, must preserve the myth, and none does it better than DiMaggio, none is more patient when drunken old men grab an arm and ask, "Who's gonna take it this year, Joe?"

Two hours later, dinner and the speeches over, DiMaggio is slumped in O'Doul's car headed back to San Francisco. He edged himself up, however, when O'Doul pulled into a gas station in which a pretty red-haired girl sat on a stool, legs crossed, filing her fingernails. She was about twenty-two, wore a tight black skirt and tighter white blouse.

"Look at *that*," DiMaggio said.

"Yeah," O'Doul said.

O'Doul turned away when a young man approached, opened the gas tank, began wiping the windshield. The young man wore a greasy white uniform on the front of which was printed the name "Burt." DiMaggio kept looking at the girl, but she was not distracted from her fingernails. Then he looked at Burt, who did not recognize him. When the tank was full, O'Doul paid and drove off. Burt returned to his girl; DiMaggio slumped down in the front seat and did not open his eyes again until they'd arrived in San Francisco.

"Let's go see Reno," DiMaggio said.

"No, I gotta go see my old lady," O'Doul said. So he dropped DiMaggio off in front of the bar, and a moment later Reno's voice was announcing in the smoky room, "Hey, here's the Clipper!" The men waved and offered to buy him a drink. DiMaggio ordered a vodka and sat for an hour at the bar talking to a half dozen men around him. Then a blonde girl who had been with friends at the other end of the bar came over, and somebody introduced her to DiMaggio. He bought her a drink, offered her a cigarette. Then he struck a match and held it. His hand was unsteady.

"Is that me that's shaking?" he asked.

"It must be," said the blonde. "I'm calm."

Two nights later, having collected his clothes out of Reno's back room, DiMaggio boarded a jet; he slept crossways on three seats, then came down the steps as the sun began to rise in Miami. He claimed his luggage and golf clubs, put them into the trunk of a waiting automobile, and less than an hour later he was being driven into Fort Lauderdale, past palm-lined streets, toward the Yankee Clipper Hotel.

"All my life it seems I've been on the road traveling," he said, squinting through the windshield into the sun. "I never get a sense of being in any one place."

Arriving at the Yankee Clipper Hotel, DiMaggio checked into the largest suite. People rushed through the lobby to shake hands with him, to ask for his autograph, to say, "Joe, you look great." And early the next morning, and for the next thirty mornings, DiMaggio arrived punctually at the baseball park and wore his uniform with the famous No. 5, and the tourists seated in the sunny grandstands clapped when he first appeared on the field each time, and then they watched with nostalgia as he picked up a bat and played "pepper" with the younger Yankees, some of whom were not even born when, twenty-five years ago this summer, he hit in fifty-six straight games and became the most celebrated man in America.

But the younger spectators in the Fort Lauderdale park, and the sportswriters, too, were more interested in Mantle and Maris, and nearly every day there were news dispatches reporting how Mantle and Maris felt, what they did, what they said, even though they said and did very little except for walk around the field frowning when photographers asked for another picture and when sportswriters asked how they felt.

After seven days of this, the big day arrived—Mantle and Maris would swing a bat—and a dozen sportswriters were gathered around the big batting cage that was situated beyond the left-field fence; it was completely enclosed in wire, meaning that no baseball could travel more than thirty or forty feet before being trapped in rope; still Mantle and Maris would be swinging, and this, in spring, makes news.

Mantle stepped in first. He wore black gloves to help prevent blisters. He hit right-handed against the pitching of a coach named Vern Benson, and soon Mantle was swinging hard, smashing line drives against the nets, going *ahhh ahhh* as he followed through with his mouth open.

Then Mantle, not wanting to overdo it on his first day, dropped his bat in the dirt and walked out of the batting cage. Roger Maris stepped in. He picked up Mantle's bat.

"This damn thing must be thirty-eight ounces," Maris said. He threw the bat down into the dirt, left the cage and walked toward the dugout on the other side of the field to get a lighter bat.

DiMaggio stood among the sportswriters behind the cage, then turned when Vern Benson, inside the cage, yelled, "Joe, wanna hit some?"

"No chance," DiMaggio said.

"Com'on, Joe," Benson said.

The reporters waited silently. Then DiMaggio walked slowly into the cage and picked up Mantle's bat. He took his position at the plate but obviously it was not the classic DiMaggio stance; he was holding the bat about two inches from the knob, his feet were not so far apart, and, when DiMaggio took a cut at Benson's first pitch, fouling it, there was none of that ferocious follow through, the blurred bat did not come whipping all the way around, the No. 5 was not stretched full across his broad back.

DiMaggio fouled Benson's second pitch, then he connected solidly with the third, the fourth, the fifth. He was just meeting the ball easily, however, not smashing it, and Benson called out, "I didn't know you were a choke hitter, Joe."

"I am now," DiMaggio said, getting ready for another pitch.

He hit three more squarely enough, and then he swung again and there was a hollow sound.

"Ohhh," DiMaggio yelled, dropping his bat, his fingers stung, "I was waiting for that one." He left the batting cage rubbing his hands together. The reporters watched him. Nobody said anything. Then DiMaggio said to one of them, not in anger nor in sadness, but merely as a simply stated fact, "There was a time when you couldn't get me out of there."

From *In Cold Blood*

TRUMAN CAPOTE

It took two decades for another author to apply, on a broad scale, the innovations of John Hersey's *Hiroshima*—that is, to write a book of journalism in the form of a novel. The writer was Truman Capote (1924–1984), who in 1959 read a short newspaper story about a brutal murder in Kansas and decided to investigate. The result was *In Cold Blood*. Like *Hiroshima*, it was first published in *The New Yorker;* if anything, it made even more of an impact.

The long middle section of the book is cinematic as well as novelistic, as the narrative cuts back and forth between the killers—a pair of drifters named Dick Hickock and Perry Smith—and their pursuers, agents Alvin Dewey and Harold Nye of the Kansas Bureau of Investigation. In the following selection, with the agents closing in, Capote builds tension by making the scenes shorter and shorter.

Capote's signal achievement in the book may be his portrayal of Perry and Dick and their flight. For a journalist to re-create events he did not witness requires a prodigious amount of reporting, and Capote could not have written *In Cold Blood* had he not met the two men after their capture, obtained their sympathy and cooperation, and interviewed them for hour after hour. Even so, novelistic re-creation raises new issues of accuracy. In traditional journalism, unless an event is witnessed by a reporter, every fact is reflexively attributed to a source. Here, Capote implicitly pledges, for example, that Dick told a particular joke in certain particular words. It is a pledge he cannot back up.

Re-creating events is now a journalistic convention, sometimes practiced very honorably, sometimes less so. Dialogue remains sticky for all: how can *any* witness remember exactly what was said years, months, or even days before? The questions and concerns surrounding the technique will not be soon resolved, but it is undisputable that Capote, with his novelist's ear, heard what his characters *could* have said and transcribed it more faithfully than any journalist before or since.

—B. Y.

❧

It was late afternoon, and the driver of the car, a middle-aged traveling sales-man who shall here be known as Mr. Bell, was tired. He longed to stop for a short nap. However, he was only a hundred miles from his destination—Omaha, Nebraska, the headquarters of the large meat packing company for which he worked. A company rule forbade its salesmen to pick up hitchhik-ers, but Mr. Bell often disobeyed it, particularly if he was bored and drowsy, so when he saw the two young men standing by the side of the road, he immediately braked his car.

They looked to him like "O.K. boys." The taller of the two, a wiry type with dirty-blond, crew-cut hair, had an engaging grin and a polite manner, and his partner, the "runty" one, holding a harmonica in his right hand and, in his left, a swollen straw suitcase, seemed "nice enough," shy but amiable. In any event, Mr. Bell, entirely unaware of his guests' intentions, which included throttling him with a belt and leaving him, robbed of his car, his money, and his life, concealed in a prairie grave, was glad to have company, somebody to talk to and keep him awake until he arrived at Omaha.

He introduced himself, then asked them their names. The affable young man with whom he was sharing the front seat said his name was Dick. "And that's Perry," he said, winking at Perry, who was seated directly behind the driver.

"I can ride you boys as far as Omaha."

Dick said, "Thank you, sir. Omaha's where we were headed. Hoped we might find some work."

What kind of work were they hunting? The salesman thought perhaps he could help.

Dick said, "I'm a first-class car painter. Mechanic, too. I'm used to making real money. My buddy and me, we just been down in Old Mexico. Our idea was, we wanted to live there. But hell, they don't pay any wages. Nothing a white man could live off."

Ah, Mexico. Mr. Bell explained that he had honeymooned in Cuernavaca. "We always wanted to go back. But it's hard to move around when you've got five kids."

Perry, as he later recalled, thought, Five kids—well, too bad. And listen-ing to Dick's conceited chatter, hearing him start to describe his Mexican "amorous conquests," he thought how "queer" it was, "egomaniacal." Imag-ine going all out to impress a man you were going to kill, a man who wouldn't be alive ten minutes from now—not if the plan he and Dick had devised went smoothly. And why shouldn't it? The setup was ideal—exactly what they had been looking for during the three days it had taken them to hitchhike from California to Nevada and across Nevada and Wyoming into Nebraska. Until now, however, a suitable victim had eluded them. Mr. Bell was the first prosperous-seeming solitary traveler to offer them a lift. Their other hosts had been either truck drivers or soldiers—and, once, a pair of Negro prizefighters driving a lavender Cadillac. But Mr. Bell was perfect. Perry felt inside a pocket of the leather windbreaker he was wearing. The pocket bulged with a bottle of Bayer aspirin and with a jagged, fist-size rock wrapped in a yellow cotton cowboy handkerchief. He unfastened his belt, a Navajo belt, silver-buckled and studded with turquoise beads; he took it off, flexed it, placed it across his knees. He waited. He watched the Nebraska prairie rolling by, and fooled with his harmonica—made up a tune and played it and waited for Dick to pronounce the agreed-upon signal: "Hey, Perry, pass me a match." Whereupon Dick was supposed to seize the steering wheel, while Perry, wielding his handkerchief-wrapped rock, belabored the salesman's head—"opened it up." Later, along some quiet side road, use would be made of the belt with the sky-blue beads.

Meanwhile, Dick and the condemned man were trading dirty jokes. Their laughter irritated Perry; he especially disliked Mr. Bell's outbursts—hearty barks that sounded very much like the laughter of Tex John Smith, Perry's father. The memory of his father's laughter increased his tension; his head hurt, his knees ached. He chewed three aspirin and swallowed them dry. Jesus! He thought he might vomit, or faint; he felt certain he would if Dick delayed "the party" much longer. The light was dimming, the road was straight, with neither house nor human being in view—nothing but land winter-stripped and as somber as sheet iron. Now was the time, *now*. He stared at Dick, as though to communicate this realization, and a few small signs—a twitching eyelid, a mustache of sweat drops—told him that Dick had already reached the same conclusion.

And yet when Dick next spoke, it was only to launch another joke. "Here's a riddle. The riddle is: What's the similarity between a trip to the bathroom and a trip to the cemetery?" He grinned. "Give up?"

"Give up."

"When you gotta go, you gotta go!"

Mr. Bell barked.

"Hey, Perry, pass me a match."

But just as Perry raised his hand, and the rock was on the verge of descent, something extraordinary occurred—what Perry later called "a goddam miracle." The miracle was the sudden appearance of a third hitchhiker, a Negro soldier, for whom the charitable salesman stopped. "Say, that's pretty cute," he said as his savior ran toward the car. "When you gotta go, you gotta go!"

December 16, 1959, Las Vegas, Nevada. Age and weather had removed the first letter and the last—an R and an S—thereby coining a somewhat ominous word: OOM. The word, faintly present upon a sun-warped sign, seemed appropriate to the place it publicized, which was, as Harold Nye wrote in his official K.B.I. report, "run-down and shabby, the lowest type of hotel or rooming house." The report continued: "Until a few years ago (according to information supplied by the Las Vegas police), it was one of the biggest cathouses in the West. Then fire destroyed the main building, and the remaining portion was converted into a cheap-rent rooming house." The "lobby" was unfurnished except for a cactus plant six feet tall and a makeshift reception desk; it was also uninhabited. The detective clapped his hands. Eventually, a voice, female, but not very feminine, shouted, "I'm coming," but it was five minutes before the woman appeared. She wore a soiled housecoat and high-heeled gold leather sandals. Curlers pinioned her thinning yellowish hair. Her face was broad, muscular, rouged, powdered. She was carrying a can of Miller High Life beer; she smelled of beer and tobacco and recently applied nail varnish. She was seventy-four years old, but in Nye's opinion, "looked younger—maybe ten minutes younger." She stared at him, his trim brown suit, his brown snapbrim hat. When he displayed his badge, she was amused; her lips parted, and Nye glimpsed two rows of fake teeth. "Uh-huh. That's what I figured," she said. "O.K. Let's hear it."

He handed her a photograph of Richard Hickock. "Know him?"

A negative grunt.

"Or him?"

She said, "Uh-huh. He's stayed here a coupla times. But he's not here now. Checked out over a month ago. You wanna see the register?"

Nye leaned against the desk and watched the landlady's long and lacquered fingernails search a page of pencil-scribbled names. Las Vegas was the first of three places that his employers wished him to visit. Each had been chosen because of its connection with the history of Perry Smith. The two others were Reno, where it was thought that Smith's father lived, and San Francisco, the home of Smith's sister, who shall here be known as Mrs. Frederic Johnson. Though Nye planned to interview these relatives, and anyone else who might have knowledge of the suspect's whereabouts, his main objective was to obtain the aid of the local law agencies. On arriving in Las Vegas, for example, he had discussed the Clutter case with Lieutenant B. J. Handlon, Chief of the Detective Division of the Las Vegas Police Department. The lieutenant had then written a memorandum ordering all police personnel to be on the alert for Hickock and Smith: "Wanted in Kansas for parole violation, and said to be driving a 1949 Chevrolet bearing Kansas license JO-58269. These men are probably armed and should be considered dangerous." Also, Handlon had assigned a detective to help Nye "case the pawnbrokers"; as he said, there was "always a pack of them in any gambling town." Together, Nye and the Las Vegas detective had checked every pawn ticket issued during the past month. Specifically, Nye hoped to find a Zenith portable radio believed to have been stolen from the Clutter house on the night of the crime, but he had no luck with that. One broker, though, remembered Smith ("He's been in and out of here going on a good ten years"), and was able to produce a ticket for a bearskin rug pawned during the first week in November. It was from this ticket that Nye had obtained the address of the rooming house.

"Registered October thirtieth," the landlady said. "Pulled out November eleventh." Nye glanced at Smith's signature. The ornateness of it, the mannered swoops and swirls, surprised him—a reaction that the landlady apparently divined, for she said, "Uh-huh. And you oughta hear him talk. Big, long words coming at you in this kinda lispy, whispery voice. Quite a personality. What you got against him—a nice little punk like that?"

"Parole violation."

"Uh-huh. Came all the way from Kansas on a parole case. Well, I'm just a dizzy blonde. I believe you. But I wouldn't tell that tale to any brunettes." She raised the beer can, emptied it, then thoughtfully rolled the empty can between her veined and freckled hands. "Whatever it is, it ain't nothing big-big. Couldn't be. I never saw the man yet I couldn't gauge his shoe size. This one, he's only a punk. Little punk tried to sweet-talk me out of paying rent the last week he was here." She chuckled, presumably at the absurdity of such an ambition.

The detective asked how much Smith's room had cost.

"Regular rate. Nine bucks a week. Plus a fifty-cent key deposit. Strictly cash. Strictly in advance."

"While he was here, what did he do with himself? Does he have any friends?"

"You think I keep an eye on every crawly that comes in here?" the landlady retorted. "Bums. Punks. I'm not interested. I got a daughter married big-big." Then she said, "No, he doesn't have any friends. Least, I never noticed him run around with anybody special. This last time he was here, he spent most every day tinkering with his car. Had it parked out front there. An old Ford. Looked like it was made before he was born. He gave it a paint job. Painted the top part black and the rest silver. Then he wrote 'For Sale' on the windshield. One day I heard a sucker stop and offer him forty bucks—that's forty more than it was worth. But he allowed he couldn't take less than ninety. Said he needed the money for a bus ticket. Just before he left I heard some colored man bought it."

"He said he needed the money for a bus ticket. But you don't know where it was he wanted to go?"

She pursed her lips, hung a cigarette between them, but her eyes stayed on Nye. "Play fair. Any money on the table? A reward?" She waited for an answer; when none arrived, she seemed to weigh the probabilities and decided in favor of proceeding. "Because I got the impression wherever he was going he didn't mean to stay long. That he meant to cut back here. Sorta been expecting him to turn up any day." She nodded toward the interior of the establishment. "Come along, and I'll show you why."

Stairs. Gray halls. Nye sniffed the odors, separating one from another: lavatory disinfectant, alcohol, dead cigars. Beyond one door, a drunken tenant wailed and sang in the firm grip of either gladness or grief. "Boil down, Dutch! Turn it off or out you go!" the woman yelled. "Here," she said to Nye, leading him into a darkened storage room. She switched on a light. "Over there. That box. He asked would I keep it till he came back."

It was a cardboard box, unwrapped but tied with cord. A declaration, a warning somewhat in the spirit of an Egyptian curse, was crayoned across the top: "*Beware!* Property of Perry E. Smith! *Beware!*" Nye undid the cord; the knot, he was unhappy to see, was not the same as the half hitch that the killers had used when binding the Clutter family. He parted the flaps. A cockroach emerged, and the landlady stepped on it, squashing it under the heel of her gold leather sandal. "Hey!" she said as he carefully extracted and slowly examined Smith's possessions. "The sneak. That's *my* towel." In addition to the towel, the meticulous Nye listed in his notebook: "One dirty pillow, 'Souvenir of Honolulu'; one pink baby blanket; one pair khaki trousers; one aluminum pan with pancake turner." Other oddments included a scrapbook thick with photographs clipped from physical-culture magazines (sweaty studies of weight-lifting weight-lifters) and, inside a shoebox, a collection of medicines: rinses and powders employed to combat trench mouth, and also a mystifying amount of aspirin—at least a dozen containers, several of them empty.

"Junk," the landlady said. "Nothing but trash."

True, it was valueless stuff even to a clue-hungry detective. Still Nye was glad to have seen it; each item—the palliatives for sore gums, the greasy Honolulu pillow—gave him a clearer impression of the owner and his lonely, mean life.

The next day in Reno, preparing his official notes, Nye wrote: "At 9:00 A.M. the reporting agent contacted Mr. Bill Driscoll, chief criminal investigator, Sheriff's Office, Washoe County, Reno, Nevada. After being briefed on the circumstances of this case, Mr. Driscoll was supplied with photographs, fingerprints and warrants for Hickock and Smith. Stops were placed in the files on both these individuals as well as the automobile. At 10:30 A.M. the reporting agent contacted Sgt. Abe Feroah, Detective Division, Police Department, Reno, Nevada. Sgt. Feroah and the reporting agent checked the police files. Neither the name of Smith or Hickock was reflected in the felon registration file. A check of the pawnshop-ticket files failed to reflect any information about the missing radio. A permanent stop was placed in these files in the event the radio is pawned in Reno. The detective handling the pawnshop detail took photographs of Smith and Hickock to each of the pawnshops in town and also made a personal check of each shop for the radio. These pawnshops made an identification of Smith as being familiar, but were unable to furnish any further information."

Thus the morning. That afternoon Nye set forth in search of Tex John Smith. But at his first stop, the post office, a clerk at the General Delivery window told him he need look no farther—not in Nevada—for "the individual" had left there the previous August and now lived in the vicinity of Circle City, Alaska. That, anyway, was where his mail was being forwarded.

"Gosh! Now, there's a tall order," said the clerk in response to Nye's request for a description of the elder Smith. "The guy's out of a book. He calls himself the Lone Wolf. A lot of his mail comes addressed that way—the Lone Wolf. He doesn't receive many letters, no, but bales of catalogues and advertising pamphlets. You'd be surprised the number of people send away for that stuff—just to get some mail, must be. How old? I'd say sixty. Dresses Western—cowboy boots and a big ten-gallon hat. He told me he used to be with the rodeo. I've talked to him quite a bit. He's been in here almost every day the last few years. Once in a while he'd disappear, stay away a month or so—always claimed he'd been off prospecting. One day last August a young man came here to the window. He said he was looking for his father, Tex John Smith, and did I know where he could find him. He didn't look much like his dad; the Wolf is so thin-lipped and Irish, and this boy looked almost pure Indian—hair black as boot polish, with eyes to match. But next morning in walks the Wolf and confirms it; he told me his son had just got out of the Army and that they were going to Alaska. He's an old Alaska hand. I think he once owned a hotel there, or some kind of hunting lodge. He said he expected to be gone about two years. Nope, never seen him since, him or his boy." . . .

A cloudburst. Rain. Buckets of it. Dick ran. Perry ran too, but he could not run as fast; his legs were shorter, and he was lugging the suitcase. Dick reached shelter—a barn near the highway—long before him. On leaving Omaha, after a night spent in a Salvation Army dormitory, a truck driver had given them a ride across the Nebraska border into Iowa. The past several hours, however, had found them afoot. The rain came when they were sixteen miles north of an Iowa settlement called Tenville Junction.

The barn was dark.

"Dick?" Perry said.

"Over-here," Dick said. He was sprawled on a bed of hay.

Perry, drenched and shaking, dropped beside him. "I'm so cold," he said, burrowing in the hay, "I'm so cold I wouldn't give a damn if this caught fire and burned me alive." He was hungry, too. Starved. Last night they had dined on bowls of Salvation Army soup, and today the only nourishment they'd had was some chocolate bars and chewing gum that Dick had stolen from a drugstore candy counter. "Any more Hershey?" Perry asked.

No, but there was still a pack of chewing gum. They divided it, then settled down to chewing it, each chomping on two and a half sticks of Doublemint, Dick's favorite flavor (Perry preferred Juicy Fruit). Money was the problem. Their utter lack of it had led Dick to decide that their next move should be what Perry considered "a crazy-man stunt"—a return to Kansas City. When Dick had first urged the return, Perry said, "You ought to see a doctor." Now, huddled together in the cold darkness, listening to the dark, cold rain, they resumed the argument, Perry once more listing the dangers of such a move, for surely by this time Dick was wanted for parole violation—"*if* nothing more." But Dick was not to be dissuaded. Kansas City, he again insisted, was the one place he was certain he could successfully "hang a lot of hot paper. Hell, I know we've got to be careful. I know they've got a warrant out. Because of the paper we hung before. But we'll move fast. One day—that'll do it. If we grab enough, maybe we ought to try Florida. Spend Christmas in Miami—stay the winter if it looks good." But Perry chewed his gum and shivered and sulked. Dick said, "What is it, honey? That other deal? Why the hell can't you forget it? They never made any connection. They never will."

Perry said, "You could be wrong. And if you are, it means The Corner." Neither one had ever before referred to the ultimate penalty in the State of Kansas—the gallows, or death in The Corner, as the inmates of Kansas State Penitentiary have named the shed that houses the equipment required to hang a man.

Dick said, "The comedian. You kill me." He struck a match, intending to smoke a cigarette, but something seen by the light of the flaring match brought him to his feet and carried him across the barn to a cow stall. A car was parked inside the stall, a black-and-white two-door 1956 Chevrolet. The key was in the ignition.

From *The Electric Kool-Aid Acid Test*

TOM WOLFE

❈

Among his many areas of literary and ideological influence, Tom Wolfe will probably always be best known for pumping up the volume and vastly broadening the range of the journalistic voice. "The Girl of the Year" (page 469) showcases his pipes well. But Wolfe, who was born in 1931 and received a doctorate in American Studies from Yale, also deserves credit for substantial achievement in narrative. *The Electric Kool-Aid Acid Test* (1968), published three years after *In Cold Blood*, builds on that book's innovations with distinctly Wolfean architecture.

The first difference is weight. *In Cold Blood* was about crime and punishment, *Acid Test* about the drug-addled cross-country bus trip of a group of proto-hippies revolving around the novelist Ken Kesey. (One of them is Neal Cassady, famous as the prototype for Dean Moriarity in Jack Kerouac's *On the Road*.) Even more striking is how much more comfortable and adventurous Wolfe is with the notion of the nonfiction novel. Where Capote's prose was formal, sometimes almost stilted, Wolfe's is conversational and kaleidoscopic, its pyrotechnics almost always solidly reported and in service of the story it is telling.

Two particular innovations bear mention. One is the use of phrases that become capitalized thematic leitmotifs over the course of an article or book ("On the Bus" here; "The Right Stuff" in the work of that name). The second is Wolfe's appropriation of point of view—long a fictional technique but rarely used by journalists. From the values and perceptions he sees in his subjects, he constructs a kind of community narrative voice, capable of modulating from fairly straight exposition to out-there stream of consciousness. This became a well-established convention; Wolfe did it first and best.

—B. Y.

❈

I couldn't tell you for sure which of the Merry Pranksters got the idea for the bus, but it had the Babbs touch. It was a superprank, in any case. The original fantasy, here in the spring of 1964, had been that Kesey and four or five others would get a station wagon and drive to New York for the New York World's Fair. On the way they could shoot some film, make some tapes, freak out on the Fair and see what happened. They would also be on hand, in New York, for the publication of Kesey's second novel, *Sometimes a Great Notion*, early in July. So went the original fantasy.

Then somebody—Babbs?—saw a classified ad for a 1939 International Harvester school bus. The bus belonged to a man in Menlo Park. He had a big house and a lot of grounds and a nice set of tweeds and flannels and eleven children. He had rigged out the bus for the children. It had bunks and benches and a refrigerator and a sink for washing dishes and cabinets and shelves and a lot of other nice features for living on the road. Kesey bought it for $1,500—in the name of Intrepid Trips, Inc.

Kesey gave the word and the Pranksters set upon it one afternoon. They started painting it and wiring it for sound and cutting a hole in the roof and fixing up the top of the bus so you could sit up there in the open air and play music, even a set of drums and electric guitars and electric bass and so forth, or just ride. Sandy went to work on the wiring and rigged up a system with which they could broadcast from inside the bus, with tapes or over microphones, and it would blast outside over powerful speakers on top of the bus. There were also microphones outside that would pick up sounds along the road and broadcast them inside the bus. There was also a sound system inside the bus so you could broadcast to one another over the roar of the engine and the road. You could also broadcast over a tape mechanism so that you said something, then heard your own voice a second later in variable lag and could rap off of that if you wanted to. Or you could put on earphones and rap simultaneously off sounds from outside, coming in one ear, and sounds from inside, your own sounds, coming in the other ear. There was going to be no goddamn sound on that whole trip, outside the bus, inside the bus, or inside your own freaking larynx, that you couldn't tune in on and rap off of.

The painting job, meanwhile, with everybody pitching in in a frenzy of primary colors, yellows, oranges, blues, reds, was sloppy as hell, except for the parts Roy Seburn did, which were nice manic mandalas. Well, it was sloppy, but one thing you had to say for it; it was freaking lurid. The manifest, the destination sign in the front, read: "Furthur," with two *u*'s.

They took a test run up into northern California and right away this wild-looking thing with wild-looking people was great for stirring up consternation and vague befuddling resentment among the citizens. The Pranksters were now out among them, and it was exhilarating—look at the mothers staring!—and there was going to be holy terror in the land. But there would also be people who would look up out of their poor work-a-daddy lives in some town, some old guy, somebody's stenographer, and see this bus and register . . . delight, or just pure open-invitation wonder. Either way, the Intrepid Travelers figured, there was hope for these people. They weren't totally turned off. The bus also had great possibilities for altering the usual order of things. For example, there were the cops.

One afternoon the Pranksters were on a test run in the bus going through the woods up north and a forest fire had started. There was smoke beginning to pour out of the woods and everything. Everybody on the bus had taken acid and they were zonked. The acid was in some orange juice in the refrigerator and you drank a paper cup full of it and you were zonked. Cassady was driving and barreling through the burning woods wrenching the steering wheel this way and that way to his inner-wired beat, with a siren wailing and sailing through the rhythm.

A *siren?* It's a highway patrolman, which immediately seems like the funniest thing in the history of the world. Smoke is pouring out of the woods and they are all sailing through leaf explosions in the sky, but the cop is bugged about this freaking bus. The cop yanks the bus over to the side and he starts going through a kind of traffic-safety inspection of the big gross bus, while more and more of the smoke is billowing out of the woods. Man, the license plate is on wrong and there's no light over the license plate and this turn signal looks bad and how about the brakes, let's see that hand brake there. Cassady, the driver, is already into a long monologue for the guy, only he is throwing in all kinds of sirs: "Well, yes sir, this is a Hammond bi-valve serrated brake, you understand, sir, had it put on in a truck ro-de-o in Springfield, Oregon, had to back through a slalom course of baby's bottles and yellow nappies, in the existential culmination of Oregon, lots of outhouse freaks up there, you understand, sir, a punctual sort of a state, sir, yes, sir, holds to 28,000 pounds, 28,000 pounds, you just look right here, sir, tested by a pure-blooded Shell Station attendant in Springfield, Oregon, winter of '62, his gumball boots never froze, you understand, sir, 28,000 pounds hold, right here—" Whereupon he yanks back on the hand-brake handle as if it's attached to something, which it isn't, it is just dangling there, and jams his foot on the regular brake, and the bus shudders as if the hand brake has a hell of a bite, but the cop is thoroughly befuddled now, anyway, because Cassady's monologue has confused him, for one thing, and what the hell are these . . . *people* doing. By this time everybody is off the bus rolling in the brown grass by the shoulder, laughing, giggling, yahooing, zonked to the skies on acid, because, mon, the woods are burning, the whole world is on fire, and a Cassady monologue on automotive safety is rising up from out of his throat like weenie smoke, as if the great god Speed were frying in his innards, and the cop, representative of the people of California in this total freaking situation, is all hung up on a hand brake that doesn't exist in the first place. And the cop, all he can see is a bunch of crazies in screaming orange and green costumes, masks, boys and girls, men and women, twelve or fourteen of them, lying in the grass and making hideously crazy sounds—christ almighty, why the hell does he have to contend with . . . So he wheels around and says, "What are you, uh—show people?"

"That's right, officer," Kesey says. "We're show people. It's been a long row to hoe, I can tell you, and it's *gonna* be a long row to hoe, but that's the business."

"Well," says the cop, "you fix up those things and . . ." He starts backing off toward his car, cutting one last look at the crazies. ". . . And watch it next time . . ." And he guns on off.

That was it! How can you give a traffic ticket to a bunch of people rolling in the brown grass wearing Day-Glo masks, practically Greek masques, only with Rat phosphorescent *élan*, giggling, keening in their costumes and private world while the god Speed sizzles like a short-order French fry in the gut of some guy who doesn't even stop talking to breathe. A traffic ticket? The Pranksters felt more immune than ever. There was no more reason for them to remain in isolation while the ovoid eyes of La Honda suppurated. They could go through the face of America muddling people's minds, but it's a momentary high, and the bus would be gone, and all the Fab foam in their heads would settle back down into their brain pans.

So the Hieronymus Bosch bus headed out of Kesey's place with the destination sign in front reading "Furthur" and a sign in the back saying "Caution: Weird Load." It was weird, all right, but it was euphoria on board, barreling through all that warm California sun in July, on the road, and everything they had been working on at Kesey's was on board and heading on Furthur. Besides, the joints were going around, and it was nice and high out here on the road in America. As they headed out, Cassady was at the wheel, and there was Kesey, Babbs, Page Browning, George Walker, Sandy, Jane Burton, Mike Hagen, Hassler, Kesey's brother Chuck and his cousin Dale, a guy known as Brother John, and three newcomers who were just along for the ride or just wanted to go to New York.

One of them was a young, quite handsome kid—looked sort of like the early, thin Michael Caine in *Zulu*—named Steve Lambrecht. He was the brother-in-law of Kesey's lawyer, Paul Robertson, and he was just riding to New York to see a girl he knew named Kathy. Another was a girl named Paula Sundsten. She was young, plump, ebullient, and very sexy. Kesey knew her from Oregon. Another one was some girl Hagen of the Screw Shack had picked up in San Francisco, on North Beach. She was the opposite of Paula Sundsten. She was thin, had long dark hair, and would be moody and silent one minute and nervous and carrying on the next. She was good-looking like a TV witch.

By the time they hit San Jose, barely 30 miles down the road, a lot of the atmosphere of the trip was already established. It was nighttime and many souls were high and the bus had broken down. They pulled into a service station and pretty soon one of the help has his nose down in under the hood looking at the engine while Cassady races the motor and the fluorescent stan-chion lights around the station hit the bus in weird phosphorescent splashes, the car lights stream by on the highway, Cassady guns the engine some more, and from out of the bus comes a lot of weird wailing, over the speak-ers or just out the windows. Paula Sundsten has gotten hold of a microphone with the variable-lag setup and has found out she can make weird radio-spook laughing ghoul sounds with it, wailing like a banshee and screaming "How was your stay-ay-ay-ay . . . in San Ho-zay-ay-ay-ay-ay," with the variable lag picking up the ay-ay-ay-ays and doubling them, quadrupling them, octu-pling them. An endless ricocheting echo—and all the while this weird, slightly hysterical laugh and a desperate little plunking mandolin sail through it all, coming from Hagen's girl friend, who is lying back on a bench inside, plunking a mandolin and laughing—in what way . . .

Outside, some character, some local, has come over to the bus, but the trouble is, he is not at all impressed with the bus, he just has to do the Amer-ican Man thing of when somebody's car is broken down you got to come over and make your diagnosis.

And he is saying to Kesey and Cassady, "You know what I'd say you need? I'd say you need a good mechanic. Now, I'm not a good mechanic, but I—" And naturally he proceeds to give his diagnosis, while Paula wails, making spook-house effects, and the Beauty Witch keens and goons—and—

"—like I say, what you need is a good mechanic, and I'm not a good mechanic, but—"

And—of course!—the Non-people. The whole freaking world was full of people who were bound to tell you they weren't qualified to do this or that but they were determined to go ahead and do just that thing anyway. Kesey decided he was the Non-navigator. Babbs was the Non-doctor. The bus trip was already becoming an allegory of life.

Before heading east, out across the country, they stopped at Babbs's place in San Juan Capistrano, down below Los Angeles. Babbs and his wife Anita had a place down there. They pulled the bus into Babbs's garage and sat around for one final big briefing before taking off to the east.

Kesey starts talking in the old soft Oregon drawl and everybody is quiet.

"Here's what I hope will happen on this trip," he says. "What I hope will continue to happen, because it's already starting to happen. All of us are beginning to do our thing, and we're going to keep doing it, right out front, and none of us are going to deny what other people are doing."

"Bullshit," says Jane Burton.

This brings Kesey up short for a moment, but he just rolls with it.

"That's Jane," he says. "And she's doing her thing. Bullshit. That's her thing and she's doing it.

"None of us are going to deny what other people are doing. If saying bull-shit is somebody's thing, then he says bullshit. If somebody is an ass-kicker, then that's what he's going to do on this trip, kick asses. He's going to do it right out front and nobody is going to have anything to get pissed off about. He can just say, 'I'm sorry I kicked you in the ass, but I'm not sorry I'm an ass-kicker. That's what I do, I kick people in the ass.' Everybody is going to be what they are, and whatever they are, there's not going to be anything to apologize about. What we are, we're going to wail with on this whole trip."

Haul ass, and what we are, out across the Southwest, and all of it on film and on tape. Refrigerator, stove, a sink, bunk racks, blankets, acid, speed, grass— with Hagen handling the movie camera and everybody on microphones and the music blaring out over the roar of the bus, rock 'n' roll, Jimmy Smith. Cassady is revved up like they've never seen him before, with his shirt off, a straw version of a cowboy hat on his head, bouncing up and down on the driver's seat, shifting gears—doubledy-clutch, doubledy-clutch, blamming on the steering wheel and the gearshift box, rapping over the microphone rigged up by his seat like a manic tour guide, describing every car going by,

"—there's a barber going down the highway cutting his hair at 500 miles an hour, you understand—"

"So remember those expressions, sacrifice, glorious and in vain!" Babbs says.

"Food! Food! Food!" Hagen says.

"Get out the de-glom ointment, sergeant!" says Babbs, rapping at Steve Lambrecht. "The only cure for joint glom, gets the joint off the lip in instant De-Glom—"

—and so on, because Steve always has a joint glommed onto his lip and, in fact, gets higher than any man alive, on any and all things one throws his way, and picks up the name Zonker on this trip—

"—De-Glom for the Zonker!—"

—and then Babbs parodies Cassady—

"—and there's a Cadillac with Marie Antoinette—"

—and the speakers wail, and the mandolin wails and the weird laugh wails, and the variable lag wails-ails-ails-ails-ails-ails, and somebody— who?—hell, *every*body wails.

"—we're finally beginning to move, after three fucking days!"

On the second day they reached Wikieup, an old Wild West oasis out in the Arizona desert along Route 60. It was all gray-brown desert and sun and this lake, which was like a huge slimy kelpy pond, but the air was fantastic. Sandy felt great. Then Kesey held the second briefing. They were going to take their first acid of the trip here and have their first major movie production. He and Babbs and the gorgeous sexy Paula Sundsten were going to take acid— *Wikieup!*—and the others were going to record what happened. Hagen and Walker were going to film it, Sandy was going to handle the sound, and Ron Bevirt was going to take photographs.

174

Sandy feels his first twinge of—what? Like . . . there is going to be Authorized Acid only. And like . . . they are going to be separated into performers and workers, stars and backstage. Like . . . there is an inner circle and an outer circle. This was illogical, because Hagen and Walker, certainly, were closer to Kesey than any other Pranksters besides Babbs, and they were "workers," too, but that was the way he feels. But he doesn't say anything. Not . . . out front.

Kesey and Babbs and Paula hook down some acid orange juice from the refrigerator and wait for the vibrations. Paula is in a hell of a great mood. She has never taken LSD before, but she looks fearless and immune and ready for all, and she hooks down a good slug of it. They wait for the vibrations . . . and here they come.

Babbs has a big cane, a walking stick, and he is waving it around in the air, and the three of them, Babbs, Kesey and Paula, go running and kicking and screaming toward the lake and she dives in—and comes up with her head covered in muck and great kelpy strands of green pond slime—and beaming in a way that practically radiates out over the face of the lake and the desert. She has surfaced euphoric—

"Oooooh! It sparkles!"

—pulling her long strands of slime-slithering hair outward with her hands and grokking and freaking over it—

"Ooooooooh! It sparkles!"

—the beads of water on her slime strands are like diamonds to her, and everybody feels her feeling at once, even Sandy—

"Ooooooooooh! It sparkles!"

—surfaced euphoric! euphorically garlanded in long greasy garlands of pond slime, the happiest slime freak in the West—

—and Babbs is euphoric for her—

"Gretchen Fetchin the Slime Queen!" he yells and waves his cane at the sky.

"Ooooooooh! It sparkles!"

"Gretchen Fetchin the Slime Queen!"

"It sparkles!"

"Gretchen Fetchin!"

And it is beautiful. Everybody goes manic and euphoric like a vast contact high, like they have all suddenly taken acid themselves. Kesey is in an athletic romp, tackling the ferns and other slimy greenery in the lake. Babbs and Paula—Gretchen Fetchin!—are yahooing at the sky. Hagen is feverishly filming it all, Sandy has a set of huge cables stretched out to the very edge of the lake, picking up the sound, Ron Bevirt is banging away with his camera. Babbs and Paula—Gretchen Fetchin!—and Kesey keep plunging out into the mucky innards of the lake.

"Come back!" Hagen the cameraman starts yelling. "You're out of range!"

But Babbs and Paula and Kesey can't hear him. They are cartwheeling further and further out into the paradise muck—

"It sparkles!"

"Gretchen Fetchin—Queen of the Slime!"

But meanwhile Hagen's Beauty Witch, in the contagion of the moment, has slipped to the refrigerator and taken some acid, and now she is outside the bus on the desert sand wearing a black snakeskin blouse and a black mantle, with her long black hair coming down over it like a pre-Raphaelite painting and a cosmic grin on her witch-white face, lying down on the desert, striking poses and declaiming in couplets. She's zonked out of her nut, but it's all in wild manic Elizabethan couplets:

> "Methinks you need a gulp of grass
> And so it quickly came to pass
> You fell to earth with eely shrieking,
> Wooing my heart, freely freaking!"

—and so forth. Well, she wins Hagen's manic heart right away, and soon he has wandered off from the Lake of the Slime Euphoria and is in a wide-legged stance over her with the camera as she lies declaiming on the desert floor, camera zeroed in on her like she is Maria Montez in a love scene—and now the Beauty Witch is off on her trip for good . . .

Back on the bus and off for Phoenix in the slime-euphoric certitude that they and the movie—The Movie!—many allegories of life—that they could not miss now. Hagen pressed on with the film, hour after hour in the bouncing innards of the bus. There were moments in the History of Film that broke everybody up. One was when they reached Phoenix. This was during the 1964 election excitement and they were in Barry Goldwater's home town, so they put a streamer on the bus reading: "A Vote for Barry is a Vote for Fun." And they put American flags up on the bus and Cassady drove the bus backward down the main drag of Phoenix while Hagen recorded it on film and the flags flew backward in the windstream. The citizens were suitably startled, outraged, delighted, nonplused, and would wheel around and stare or else try to keep their cool by sidling glances like they weren't going to be impressed by any *weird shit*—and a few smiled in a frank way as if to say, I am with you—if only I could be with you!

The fact that they were all high on speed or grass, or so many combinations thereof that they couldn't keep track, made it seem like a great secret life. It was a great secret life. The befuddled citizens could only see the outward manifestations of the incredible stuff going on inside their skulls. They were all now characters in their own movies or the Big Movie. They took on new names and used them.

Steve Lambrecht was Zonker. Cassady was Speed Limit. Kesey was Swashbuckler. Babbs was Intrepid Traveler. Hagen, bouncing along with the big camera, soaring even while the bus roared, was Mal Function. Ron

Bevirt had charge of all the equipment, the tools, wires, jacks, and stuff, and became known as Equipment Hassler, and then just Hassler. George Walker was Hardly Visible. And Paula Sundsten became . . . Gretchen Fetchin the Slime Queen, of course . . .

A notebook!—for each of the new characters in The Movie, a plain child's notebook, and each character in this here movie can write in his notebook himself or other people can pick up the notebook and write in it—who knows who wrote what?—and in Gretchen Fetchin's it says:

> Bury them in slime!
> She cried, flailing about the garden—
> With a sprig of parsley clutched in
> her hands—which had always been
> clamped in her hands.
>   This is strange business,
> Gets weirder all the time,
> She said, wrapping some around
> her finger, for we are always
> moist in her hand . . . "Naturally," she
> said, "The roots are deep."
>   That was no surprise, but she
> was mildly curious to
> know what the hell is
>
>   THAT
>   Whereupon he got very
> clumsy, giggled confidentially,
> and tripped over her shadow,
> carrying them both into
> an unaccountable adventure.

Barely a week out and already beautiful ebullient sexy Gretchen Fetchin the Slime Queen, Gretch, is *synched* in. Kesey, the very Swashbuckler himself, makes a play for her, and that should be that, but she looks at—Babbs—who tripped over her shadow?—Hmmmmmmmm? So many shadows and shafts of Southwest sun bouncing in through the windows and all over the floor, over the benches over the bunk uprights bouncing out of the freaking roar of the engine bouncing two sets of Gretch eyes two sets of Babbs eyes, four sets of Gretch eyes four sets of Babbs eyes eight sets of Gretch eyes eight sets of Babbs eyes all grinning vibrating bouncing in among one another carrying them both into an unaccountable adventure, you understand. Kesey sulks a bit—Kesey himself—but the sulk bounces and breaks up into Southwestern sunballs. *Drivin' on dirt in Utah, a '46 Plymouth with an overhead cam,* says Cassady. The refrigerator door squeaks open, gurgle gurgle, this acid O.J. makes a body plumb smack his lips, Hagen and his Black Witch girl friend hook down a cup of acid orange juice apiece and Hagen's sweet face spirals, turning sweet Christian boy clockwise and sweet sly Screw Shack counterclockwise, back and forth, and they disappear, bouncing, up the ladder, up through the turret hole and onto the roof where, under the mightily hulking sun of the Southwest and 70 miles an hour—Pretty soon Hagen is climbing back down the ladder and heading for the refrigerator and hooking down another cup of orange juice and smiling for all, Christian boy and Screw Shack sly, spiraling this way and that way—and climbing back up top the bus in order to—

MAL FUNCTION!
If only I had $10, then we
could split 1/2 a Ritalin order
with Margo—I eat
Ritalin like aspirin
Now, let's charm Brooks Brothers—
impressed?

At night the goddamn bus still bouncing and the Southwest silvery blue coming in not exactly bouncing but slipping and sliding in shafts, sickly shit, and car beams and long crazy shadows from car beams sliding in weird bends over the inside, over the love bunk. The love bunk'll get you if you don't wash out. One shelf on the bunk has a sleeping bag on it and into this sleeping bag crawl whoever wants to make it, do your thing, bub, and right out front, and wail with it, and Sandy looks over and he can see a human . . . bobbing up and down in the sleeping bag with the car beams sliding over it and the motor roaring, the fabulous love bunk, and everyone—*synch*—can see that sleeping bag veritably filling up with sperm, the little devils swimming like mad in there in the muck, oozing into the cheap hairy shit they quilt the bag with, millions billions trillions of them, darting around, crafty little flagellants, looking to *score*, which is natural, and if any certified virgin on the face of the earth crawled into that sleeping bag for a nap after lunch she would be a hulking knocked-up miracle inside of three minutes—but won't this goddamn *bouncing* ever stop—

This being a school bus, and not a Greyhound, the springs and the shock absorbers are terrible and the freaking grinding straining motor shakes it to pieces and hulking vibrations synched in to no creature on earth keep batting everybody around on the benches and the bunks. It is almost impossible to sleep and the days and nights have their own sickly cycle, blinding sun all day and the weird car beams and shadows sliding sick and slow at night and all the time the noise. Jane Burton is nauseous practically the whole time. Nobody can sleep so they keep taking more speed to keep going, psychic energizers like Ritalin, anything, and then smoke more grass to take the god-damn tachycardiac edge off the speed, and acid to make the whole thing turn into something else. Then it all starts swinging back and forth between grueling battering lurching flogging along the highway—and unaccountable delays, stopped, unendurable frustration by the side of the road in the middle of nowhere while the feeling of no-sleep starts turning the body and the skull into a dried-out husk inside with a sour greasy smoke like a tenement fire curdling in the brainpan. They have to pull into gasoline stations to go to the bathroom, cop a urination or an egestion—keep regular, friends—but 12—how many, 14?—did we lose somebody—did we pick up somebody—climbing out of this bus, which is weird-looking for a start, but all these weird people are too much, clambering out—the service station attendant and his Number One Boy stare at this—Negro music is blaring out of the speakers and these weird people clamber out, half of them in costume, lurid shirts with red and white stripes, some of them with weird paint on their faces, like comic-book Indians, with huge circles under their eyes, eyes red, noses not blue, not nearly blue enough, but eyes red—all trooping out toward the Clean Rest Rooms, already queuing up, practically—

"Wait a minute," the guy says. "What do you think you're doing?"

"Fill 'er up!" says Kesey, very soft and pleasant. "Yes, sir, she's a big bus and she takes a lotta gas. Yep."

"I mean what are *they* doing?"

"Them? I 'spect they're going to the bathroom. Ay-yuh, that big old thing's the worst gas-eater you ever saw"—all the time motioning to Hagen to go get the movie camera and the microphone.

"Well, can't all those people use the bathrooms."

"All they want to do is go to the bathroom"—and now Kesey takes the microphone and Hagen starts shooting the film—*whirrrrrrrrrrrrrrrrrrr*—but all very casual as if, well, sure, don't *you* record it all, every last morsel of friendly confrontation whenever you stop on the great American highway to cop a urination or two? or a dozen?

"Well, now, listen! You ain't using the bathrooms! You hear me, now! You see that motel back there? I own that motel, too, and we got one septic tank here, for here and there, and you're not gonna overflow it for me. Now git that thing out of my face!"

—Kesey has the microphone in the guy's face, like this is all for the six o'clock news, and then he brings the microphone back to his face, just like the TV interview shows, and says,

"You see that bus out there? Every time we stop to fill 'er up we have to lay a *whole lot* of money on somebody, and we'd like it to be you, on account of your hospitality."

"It's an unaccountable adventure in consumer spending," says Babbs.

"Get those cameras and microphones out of here," the guy says. "I'm not afraid of you!"

"I should hope not," says Kesey, still talking soft and down-home. "All that money that big baby's gonna drink up. Whew!"

Sheerooooooo—all this time the toilets are flushing, this side and that side and the noise of it roars and gurgles right through the cinder block walls until it sounds like there's nothing in the whole wide open U. S. of A. except for Clean Rest Room toilets and Day-Glo crazies and cameras and microphones from out of nowhere, and the guy just caves in under it. He can't fit it into his movie of Doughty American Entrepreneur—*not no kind of way*—

"Well, they better make it fast or there's going to be trouble around here." And he goes out to fill 'er up, this goddamn country is going down the drain.

But they don't speed it up. Walker is over to the coin telephone putting in a call to Faye back in La Honda. Babbs is clowning around out on the concrete apron of the gas station with Gretchen Fetchin. Jane Burton feels bilious—the idea is to go to New York, isn't it? even on a 1939 school bus it could be done better than this. What are we waiting, waiting, waiting, waiting for, playing games with old crocks at gas stations. Well, we're waiting for Sandy, for one thing. Where in the hell is Sandy. But Sandy—he hasn't slept in days and he has an unspecific urge to *get off the bus*—but not to sleep, just to get off—for—what?—before:::::what? And Sandy is back over at the motel, inspecting this electro-pink slab out in the middle of nowhere—somebody finally finds him and brings him back. Sandy is given the name Dis-mount in the great movie.

"There are going to be times," says Kesey, "when we can't wait for somebody. Now, you're either on the bus or off the bus. If you're on the bus, and you get left behind, then you'll find it again. If you're off the bus in the first place—then it won't make a damn." And nobody had to have it spelled out for them. Everything was becoming allegorical, understood by the group mind, and especially this: "You're either on the bus . . . or off the bus."

Except for Hagen's girl, the Beauty Witch. It seems like she never even gets off the bus to cop a urination. She's sitting back in the back of the bus with nothing on, just a blanket over her lap and her legs wedged back into the corner, her and her little bare breasts, silent, looking exceedingly witch-like. Is she on the bus or off the bus? She has taken to wearing nothing but the blanket and she sheds that when she feels like it. Maybe that is her thing and she is doing her thing and *wailing with it* and the bus barrels on off, heading for Houston, Texas, and she becomes Stark Naked in the great movie, one moment all conked out, but with her eyes open, staring, the next laughing and coming on, a lively Stark Naked, and they are all trying to just snap their fingers to it but now she is getting looks that have nothing to do with the fact that she has not a thing on, hell, big deal, but she is now waxing extremely freaking ESP. She keeps coming up to somebody who isn't saying a goddamn thing and looking into his eyes with the all-embracing look of total acid understanding, our brains are one brain, so let's *visit*, you and I, and she says: "Oooooooooh, you really *think* that, *I* know what you mean, but do you-u-u-u-u-u-u-ueeeeeeeeeeeeeeeeeeeeeeeeee"—finishing off in a sailing tremolo laugh as if she has just read your brain and it is the weirdest of the weird shit ever, your brain eeeeeeeeeeeeeeeeeeeeeeeeeeeeeeeeeeeeee—

> STARK NAKED!
>
> in a black blanket—
> > Reaching out for herself,
> she woke up one morning to
> find herself accosted on all
> sides by   LARGE
>   MEN
> surrounding her threatening her
> with their voices, their presence, their always
> desire reaching inside herself
> and touching her obscenely upon her
> desire and causing her to laugh
> and
> LAUGH
> > with the utter
> > ridiculousness
> > of it . . .

—but no one denied her a moment of it, neither the conked-out bug-eyed paranoia nor the manic keening coming on, nobody denied her, and she could wail, nobody tried to cool that inflamed brain that was now seeping out Stark Naked into the bouncing goddamn—*stop it!*—currents of the bus throgging and roaring 70 miles an hour into Texas, for it was like it had been ordained, by Kesey himself, back in San Juan Capistrano, like there was to be a reaction scale in here, from negative to positive, and no one was to rise up negative about anything, one was to go positive with everything—*go with the flow*—everyone's cool was to be tested, and to shout No, no matter what happened, was to fail. And hadn't Kesey passed the test first of all? Hadn't Babbs taken Gretchen Fetchin, and did he come back at either one of them uptight over that? And wasn't it Walker who was calling La Honda from the Servicenters of America? All true, and go with the flow. And they went with the flow, the whole goddamn flow of America. The bus barrels into the superhighway toll stations and the microphones on top of the bus pick up all the clacking and ringing and the mumbling by the toll-station attendant and the brakes squeaking and the gears shifting, all the sounds of the true America that are screened out everywhere else, it all came amplified back inside the bus, while Hagen's camera picked up the faces, the faces in Phoenix, the cops, the service-station owners, the stragglers and the strugglers of America, all laboring in their movie, and it was all captured and kept, piling up, inside the bus. Barreling across America with the microphones picking it all up, the whole roar, and microphone up top gets eerie in a great rush and then *skakkkkkkkkkkkkkk* it is ripping and roaring over asphalt and *thok* it's gone, no sound at all. The microphone has somehow ripped loose on top of the bus and hit the roadway and dragged along until it snapped off entirely—and Sandy can't believe it. He keeps waiting for somebody to tell Cassady to stop and go back and get the microphone, because this was something Sandy had rigged up with great love and time, it was his *thing*, his part of the power—but instead they are all rapping and grokking over the sound it made—"Wowwwwwwwwww! Did you—wowwwwwwww"—as if they had synched into a never-before-heard thing, a unique thing, the sound of an object, a microphone, hitting the American asphalt, the open road at 70 miles an hour, like if it was all there on tape they would have the instant, the moment, of anything, *anyone* ripped out of the flow and hitting the Great Superhighway at 70 miles an hour—and they *had* it on tape—and played it back in variable lag skakkkkkk-akkk-akkkk-akkkooooooooooooo.

ooooooooooooooooooooooooo—Stark Naked waxing weirder and weirder, huddled in the black blanket shivering, then out, bobbing wraith, her little deep red areolae bobbing in the crazed vibrations—finally they pull into Houston and head for Larry McMurtry's house. They pull up to McMurtry's house, in the suburbs, and the door of the house opens and out comes McMurtry, a slight, slightly wan, kindly-looking shy-looking guy, ambling out, with his little boy, his son, and Cassady opens the door of the bus so everybody can get off, and suddenly Stark Naked shrieks out: "Frankie! Frankie! Frankie! Frankie!"—this being the name of her own divorced-off little boy—and she whips off the blanket and leaps off the bus and out into the suburbs of Houston, Texas, stark naked, and rushes up to McMurtry's little boy and scoops him up and presses him to her skinny breast, crying and shrieking, "Frankie! oh Frankie! my little Frankie! oh! oh! oh!"—while McMurtry doesn't know what in the name of hell to do, reaching tentatively toward her stark-naked shoulder and saying, "Ma'am! Ma'am! Just a minute, ma'am"—

—while the Pranksters, spilling out of the bus—stop. The bus is stopped. No roar, no crazed bounce or vibrations, no crazed car beams, no tapes, no microphones. Only Stark Naked, with somebody else's little boy in her arms, is bouncing and vibrating.

And there, amid the peaceful Houston elms on Quenby Road, it dawned on them all that this woman—which one of us even knows her?—had completed her trip. She had gone with the flow. She had gone stark raving mad.

From *Alive*

PIERS PAUL READ

∞

In October 1972, an airplane carrying fifteen members of a Uruguayan rugby team and an additional thirty friends, relatives, and crew members crash-landed in the Andes on its way to Chile, where the team was to play a game. Remarkably, twenty-seven survived the crash; even more remarkably, sixteen of these survived ten weeks in the snow-covered mountains before two of their number trekked across the mountains and literally stumbled on a Chilean peasant tending his cattle.

In *Alive*, British writer Piers Paul Read reconstructed this ordeal with the aid of extensive interviews with all of the survivors. Although he is a novelist, Read was scrupulous about the facts, and our sense of this gives the book some of its power. This is not to say that he hides his novelistic gifts; *Alive* stands apart from countless other works of narrative journalism in its characterization, description, dialogue, pacing, and structure (the chapter excerpted here revolves tightly and artfully around the issue of food).

What finally makes *Alive* such an extraordinary document is that Read, in his calmly straightforward yet riveting prose, does what the great works of literature have always done. He provides a singular look at the workings of the human spirit, and an illuminated path to the great questions—in this case, what does it mean to be alive?

—B. Y.

∞

1

On the morning of the ninth day, the body of Susana Parrado was dragged out onto the snow. No sound but the wind met the ears of the survivors as they stumbled from the cabin; nothing was to be seen but the same monotonous arena of rock and snow.

As the light changed, the mountains took on different moods and appearances. Early in the morning, they seemed bright and distant. Then, as the day progressed, shadows lengthened and the gray, reddish, and green stone became the features of brooding beasts or disgruntled gods frowning down upon the intruders.

The seats of the plane were laid out on the snow like deck chairs on the veranda of an *estancia*. Here, the first out would sit down to melt snow for drinking water while staring at the horizon. Each could see in the face of his companions the rapid progress of their physical deterioration. The movements of those who busied themselves in the cabin or around the fuselage had grown heavy and slow. They were all exhausted by the slightest exertion. Many remained sitting where they had slept, too listless and depressed even to go out into the fresh air. Irritability was an increasing problem.

Marcelo Pérez, Daniel Fernández, and the older members of the group feared that some of the boys were on the verge of hysteria. The waiting was wearing them down. They had started to squabble among themselves.

Marcelo did what he could to set an example. He was optimistic and he was fair. He talked confidently of rescue and tried to get his team to sing songs. There was one desultory rendering of "Clementine," but no one had the spirit to sing. It was also becoming evident to them all that their captain was not as confident as he seemed. At night he was overtaken by melancholy; his mind turned to his mother and how much she must be suffering, to his brother on a honeymoon in Brazil, and to the rest of his family. He tried to hide his sobs from the others, but if he slept he would dream and wake screaming. His friend Eduardo Strauch did his best to comfort him, but Marcelo felt that as captain of the team —and chief exponent of the trip to Chile—he had been responsible for what had happened.

"Don't be a fool," said Eduardo. "You can't look at things like that. I persuaded Gaston and Daniel Shaw to come, and they're both dead. I even rang Daniel to remind him, but I don't feel responsible for his death."

"If anyone's responsible," said his cousin Fito, "it's God. Why did He let Gaston die?" Fito was referring to the fact that Gaston Costemalle, who had fallen out of the back of the plane, was not the first of his family to die; his mother had already lost her husband and other son. "Why does God let us suffer like this? What have we done?"

"It's not as simple as that," said Daniel Fernández, the third of the Strauch cousins.

There were two or three among the twenty-seven whose courage and example acted as pillars to their morale. Echavarren, in considerable pain from his smashed leg, remained cheerful and outgoing, screaming and cursing at anyone who stepped on him but always making up for it afterward with a courteous apology or a joke. Enrique Platero was energetic and brave, despite the wound in his stomach. And Gustavo Nicolich made his "gang" get up in the morning, tidy the cabin, and then play such games as charades, while at night he persuaded them to say the rosary with Carlitos Páez.

Liliana Methol, the one woman among them, was a unique source of solace. Though younger, at thirty-five, than their mothers, she became for them all an object of filial affection. Gustavo Zerbino, who was only nineteen, called her his godmother, and she responded to him and to the others with comforting words and gentle optimism. She too realized that the boys' morale was in danger of collapse and thought of ways to distract them from their predicament. On the evening of that ninth day, she gathered them around her and suggested that each tell an anecdote from his past life. Few of them could think of anything to say. Then Pancho Delgado volunteered to tell three stories, all about his future father-in-law.

When he had first met his *novia,* he told them, she was only fifteen, while he was three or four years older. He was not at all sure whether her parents would welcome him, and he was anxious about the impression he would create. Within a short time, Delgado reported, he had accidentally pushed her father into a swimming pool, injuring his leg; he had discharged a shotgun into the roof of their family car, a brand-new BMW 2002, leaving an enormous hole with pieces of metal bent back like the petals of a flower; and he had very nearly electrocuted her father while helping him prepare for a party in the garden of their house in Carrasco.

His anecdotes were like a tonic to the boys sitting in the dank atmosphere of the plane, waiting to feel tired enough to sleep, and for this they felt grateful. Yet when the turn came for other stories, no one spoke, and as the light faded, each returned to his own thoughts.

2

They awoke on the morning of Sunday, October 22, to face their tenth day on the mountain. First to leave the plane were Marcelo Pérez and Roy Harley. Roy had found a transistor radio between two seats and by using a modest knowledge of electronics, acquired when helping a friend construct a hi-fi system, he had been able to make it work. It was difficult to receive signals in the deep cleft between the huge mountains, so Roy made an aerial with strands of wire from the plane's electric circuits. While he turned the dial, Marcelo held the aerial and moved it around. They picked up scraps of broadcasts from Chile but no news of the rescue effort. All that came over the radio waves were the strident voices of Chilean politicians embroiled in the strike by the middle classes against the socialist government of President Allende.

Few of the other boys came out into the snow. Starvation was taking its effect. They were becoming weaker and more listless. When they stood up they felt faint and found it difficult to keep their balance. They felt cold, even when the sun rose to warm them, and their skin started to grow wrinkled like that of old men.

Their food supplies were running out. The daily ration of a scrap of chocolate, a capful of wine, and a teaspoonful of jam or canned fish—eaten slowly to make it last—was more torture than sustenance for these healthy, athletic boys; yet the strong shared it with the weak, the healthy with the injured. It was clear to them all that they could not survive much longer. It was not so much that they were consumed with ravenous hunger as that they felt themselves grow weaker each day, and no knowledge of medicine or nutrition was required to predict how it would end.

Their minds turned to other sources of food. It seemed impossible that there should be nothing whatsoever growing in the Andes, for even the meanest form of plant life might provide some nutrition. In the immediate vicinity of the plane there was only snow. The nearest soil was a hundred feet beneath them. The only ground exposed to sun and air was barren mountain rock on which they found nothing but brittle lichens. They scraped some of it off and mixed it into a paste with melted snow, but the taste was bitter and disgusting, and as food it was worthless. Except for lichens there was nothing. Some thought of the cushions, but even these were not stuffed with straw. Nylon and foam rubber would not help them.

For some days several of the boys had realized that if they were to survive they would have to eat the bodies of those who had died in the crash. It was a ghastly prospect. The corpses lay around the plane in the snow, preserved by the intense cold in the state in which they had died. While the thought of cutting flesh from those who had been their friends was deeply repugnant to them all, a lucid appreciation of their predicament led them to consider it.

Gradually the discussion spread as these boys cautiously mentioned it to their friends or to those they thought would be sympathetic. Finally, Canessa brought it out into the open. He argued forcefully that they were not going to be rescued; that they would have to escape themselves, but that nothing could be done without food; and that the only food was human flesh. He used his knowledge of medicine to describe, in his penetrating, high-pitched voice, how their bodies were using up their reserves. "Every time you move," he said, "you use up part of your own body. Soon we shall be so weak that we won't have the strength even to cut the meat that is lying there before our eyes."

Canessa did not argue just from expediency. He insisted that they had a moral duty to stay alive by any means at their disposal, and because Canessa was earnest about his religious belief, great weight was given to what he said by the more pious among the survivors.

"It is meat," he said. "That's all it is. The souls have left their bodies and are in heaven with God. All that is left here are the carcasses, which are no more human beings than the dead flesh of the cattle we eat at home."

Others joined the discussion. "Didn't you see," said Fito Strauch, "how much energy we needed just to climb a few hundred feet up the mountain? Think how much more we'll need to climb to the top and then down the other side. It can't be done on a sip of wine and a scrap of chocolate."

The truth of what he said was incontestable.

A meeting was called inside the Fairchild, and for the first time all twenty-seven survivors discussed the issue which faced them—whether or not they should eat the bodies of the dead to survive. Canessa, Zerbino, Fernández, and Fito Strauch repeated the arguments they had used before. If they did not they would die. It was their moral obligation to live, for their own sake and for the sake of their families. God wanted them to live, and He had given them the means to do so in the dead bodies of their friends. If God had not wished them to live, they would have been killed in the accident; it would be wrong now to reject this gift of life because they were too squeamish.

"But what have we done," asked Marcelo, "that God now asks us to eat the bodies of our dead friends?"

There was a moment's hesitation. Then Zerbino turned to his captain and said, "But what do you think *they* would have thought?"

Marcelo did not answer.

"I know," Zerbino went on, "that if my dead body could help you to stay alive, then I'd certainly want you to use it. In fact, if I do die and you don't eat me, then I'll come back from wherever I am and give you a good kick in the ass."

This argument allayed many doubts, for however reluctant each boy might be to eat the flesh of a friend, all of them agreed with Zerbino. There and then they made a pact that if any more of them were to die, their bodies were to be used as food.

Marcelo still shrank from a decision. He and his diminishing party of optimists held onto the hope of rescue, but few of the others any longer shared their faith. Indeed, a few of the younger boys went over to the pessimists—or the realists, as they considered themselves—with some resentment against Marcelo Pérez and Pancho Delgado. They felt they had been deceived. The rescue they had been promised had not come.

The latter were not without support, however. Coche Inciarte and Numa Turcatti, both strong, tough boys with an inner gentleness, told their companions that while they did not think it would be wrong, they knew that they themselves could not do it. Liliana Methol agreed with them. Her manner was calm as always but, like the others, she grappled with the emotions the issue aroused. Her instinct to survive was strong, her longing for her children was acute, but the thought of eating human flesh horrified her. She did not think it wrong; she could distinguish between sin and physical revulsion, and a social taboo was not a law of God. "But," she said, "as long as there is a chance of rescue, as long as there is *something* left to eat, even if it is only a morsel of chocolate, then I can't do it."

Javier Methol agreed with his wife but would not deter others from doing what they felt must be done. No one suggested that God might want them to choose to die. They all believed that virtue lay in survival and that eating their dead friends would in no way endanger their souls, but it was one thing to decide and another to act.

Their discussions had continued most of the day, and by midafternoon they knew that they must act now or not at all, yet they sat inside the plane in total silence. At last a group of four—Canessa, Maspons, Zerbino, and Fito Strauch—rose and went out into the snow. Few followed them. No one wished to know who was going to cut the meat or from which body it was to be taken.

Most of the bodies were covered by snow, but the buttocks of one protruded a few yards from the plane. With no exchange of words Canessa knelt, bared the skin, and cut into the flesh with a piece of broken glass. It was frozen hard and difficult to cut, but he persisted until he had cut away twenty slivers the size of matchsticks. He then stood up, went back to the plane, and placed them on the roof.

Inside there was silence. The boys cowered in the Fairchild. Canessa told them that the meat was there on the roof, drying in the sun, and that those who wished to do so should come out and eat it. No one came, and again Canessa took it upon himself to prove his resolution. He prayed to God to help him do what he knew to be right and then took a piece of meat in his hand. He hesitated. Even with his mind so firmly made up, the horror of the act paralyzed him. His hand would neither rise to his mouth nor fall to his side while the revulsion which possessed him struggled with his stubborn will. The will prevailed. The hand rose and pushed the meat into his mouth. He swallowed it.

He felt triumphant. His conscience had overcome a primitive, irrational taboo. He was going to survive.

Later that evening, small groups of boys came out of the plane to follow his example. Zerbino took a strip and swallowed it as Canessa had done, but it stuck in his throat. He scooped a handful of snow into his mouth and managed to wash it down. Fito Strauch followed his example, then Maspons and Vizintín and others.

Meanwhile Gustavo Nicolich, the tall, curly-haired boy, only twenty years old, who had done so much to keep up the morale of his young friends, wrote to his *novia* in Montevideo.

Most dear Rosina:

I am writing to you from inside the plane (our *petit hotel* for the moment). It is sunset and has started to be rather cold and windy which it usually does at this hour of the evening. Today the weather was wonderful—a beautiful sun and very hot. It reminded me of the days on the beach with you—the big difference being that then we would be going to have lunch at your place at midday whereas now I'm stuck outside the plane without any food at all.

Today, on top of everything else, it was rather depressing and a lot of the others began to get discouraged (today is the tenth day we have been here), but luckily this gloom did not spread to me because I get incredible strength just by thinking that I'm going to see you again. Another of the things leading to the general depression is that in a while the food will run out: we have only got two cans of seafood (small), one bottle of white wine, and a little cherry brandy left, which for twenty-six men (well, there are also boys who want to be men) is nothing.

One thing which will seem incredible to you—it seems unbelievable to me—is that today we started to cut up the dead in order to eat them. There is nothing else to do. I prayed to God from the bottom of my heart that this day would never come, but it has and we have to face it with courage and faith. Faith, because I came to the conclusion that the bodies are there because God put them there and, since the only thing that matters is the soul, I don't have to feel great remorse; and if the day came and I could save someone with my body, I would gladly do it.

I don't know how you, Mama, Papa, or the children can be feeling; you don't know how sad it makes me to think that you are suffering, and I constantly ask God to reassure you and give us courage because that is the only way of getting out of this. I think that soon there will be a happy ending for everyone.

You'll get a shock when you see me. I am dirty, with a beard, and a little thinner, with a big gash on my head, another one on my chest which has healed now, and one very small cut which I got today working in the cabin of the plane, besides various small cuts in the legs and on the shoulder; but in spite of it all, I'm all right.

3

Those who first peered through the portholes of the plane the next morning could see that the sky was overcast but that a little sun shone through the clouds onto the snow. Some darted cautious looks toward Canessa, Zerbino, Maspons, Vizintín, and the Strauch cousins. It was not that they thought that God would have struck them down, but they knew from their *estancias* that one should never eat a steer that dies from natural causes, and they wondered if it might not be just as unhealthy to do the same with a man.

The ones who had eaten the meat were quite well. None of them had eaten very much and in fact they felt as enfeebled as the others. As always, Marcelo Pérez was the first to raise himself from the cushions.

"Come on," he said to Roy Harley. "We must set up the radio."

"It's so cold," said Roy. "Can't you get someone else?"

"No," said Marcelo. "It's your job. Come on."

Reluctantly Roy took his shoes down from the hat rack and put them on over his two pairs of socks. He squeezed himself out of the line of dozing figures and climbed over those nearest the entrance to follow Marcelo out of the plane. One or two others followed him out.

Marcelo had already taken hold of the aerial and was waiting while Roy picked up the radio, switched it on, and began to turn the dial. He tuned in to a station in Chile which the day before had broadcast nothing but political propaganda; now, however, as he held the radio to his ear, he heard the last words of a news bulletin. "The SAR has requested all commercial and military aircraft overflying the cordillera to check for any sign of the wreckage of the Fairchild Number Five-seventy-one. This follows the cancellation of the search by the SAR for the Uruguayan aircraft because of negative results."

The newscaster moved on to a different topic. Roy took the radio away from his ear. He looked up at Marcelo and told him what he had heard. Marcelo dropped the aerial, covered his face with his hands, and wept with despair. The others who had clustered around Roy, upon hearing the news, began to sob and pray, all except Parrado, who looked calmly up at the mountains which rose to the west.

Gustavo Nicolich came out of the plane and, seeing their faces, knew what they had heard.

"What shall we tell the others?" he asked.

"We mustn't tell them," said Marcelo. "At least let them go on hoping."

"No," said Nicolich. "We must tell them. They must know the worst."

"I can't, I can't," said Marcelo, still sobbing into his hands.

"I'll tell them," said Nicolich, and he turned back toward the entrance to the plane.

He climbed through the hole in the wall of suitcases and rugby shirts, crouched at the mouth of the dim tunnel, and looked at the mournful faces which were turned toward him.

"Hey, boys," he shouted, "there's some good news! We just heard it on the radio. They've called off the search."

Inside the crowded cabin there was silence. As the hopelessness of their predicament enveloped them, they wept.

"Why the hell is that good news?" Páez shouted angrily at Nicolich.

"Because it means," he said, "that we're going to get out of here on our own."

The courage of this one boy prevented a flood of total despair, but some of the optimists who had counted on rescue were unable to rally. The pessimists, several of them as unhopeful about escape as they had been about rescue, were not shocked; it was what they had expected. But the news broke Marcelo. His role as their leader became empty and automatic, and the life went out of his eyes. Delgado, too, was changed by the news. His eloquent and cheerful optimism evaporated into the thin air of the cordillera. He seemed to have no faith that they would get out by their own efforts and quietly withdrew into the background. Of the old optimists, only Liliana Methol still offered hope and consolation. "Don't worry," she said. "We'll get out of here, all right. They'll find us when the snow melts." Then, as if remembering how little food remained besides the bodies of the dead, she added, "Or we'll walk to the west."

To escape: that was the obsession of the new optimists. It was disconcerting that the valley in which they were trapped ran east, and that to the west there was a solid wall of towering mountains, but this did not deter Parrado. No sooner had he learned of the cancellation of the search than he announced his intention of setting off—on his own, if necessary—to the west. It was only with great difficulty that the others restrained him. Ten days before he had been given up for dead. If anyone was going to climb the mountains, there were others in a much better physical condition to do so. "We must think this out calmly," said Marcelo, "and act together. It's the only way we'll survive."

There was still sufficient respect for Marcelo and enough team discipline in Parrado to accept what the others decided. He was not alone, however, in his insistence that, before they got any weaker, another expedition should set out, either to climb the mountain and see what was on the other side or to find the tail.

It was agreed that a group of the fittest among them should set off at once, and a little more than an hour after they had heard the news on the radio, Zerbino, Turcatti, and Maspons set off up the mountain, watched by their friends.

Canessa and Fito Strauch returned to the corpse they had opened the day before and cut more meat off the bone. The strips they had put on the roof of the plane had now all been eaten. Not only were they easier to swallow when dried in the outside air, but the knowledge that they were not going to be rescued had persuaded many of those who had hesitated the day before. For the first time, Parrado ate human flesh. So, too, did Daniel Fernández, though not without the greatest effort of will to overcome his revulsion. One by one, they forced themselves to take and swallow the flesh of their friends. To some, it was merely an unpleasant necessity; to others, it was a conflict of conscience with reason.

Some could not do it: Liliana and Javier Methol, Coche Inciarte, Pancho Delgado. Marcelo Pérez, having made up his mind that he would take this step, used what authority he still possessed to persuade others to do so, but nothing he said had the effect of a short statement from Pedro Algorta. He was one of the two boys who had been dressed more scruffily at the airport than the others, as if to show that he despised their bourgeois values. In the crash, he had been hit on the head and suffered total amnesia about what had happened the day before. Algorta watched Canessa and Fito Strauch cutting the meat but said nothing until it came to the moment when he was offered a slice of flesh. He took it and swallowed it and then said, "It's like Holy Communion. When Christ died he gave his body to us so that we could have spiritual life. My friend has given us his body so that we can have physical life."

It was with this thought that Coche Inciarte and Pancho Delgado first swallowed their share, and Marcelo grasped it as a concept which would persuade others to follow his example and survive. One by one they did so until only Liliana and Javier Methol remained.

Now that it was established that they were to live off the dead, a group of stronger boys was organized to cover the corpses with snow, while those who were weaker or injured sat on the seats, holding the aluminum water makers toward the sun, catching the drops of water in empty wine bottles. Others tidied the cabin. Canessa, when he had cut enough meat for their immediate needs, made a tour of inspection of the wounded. He was moderately content with what he saw. Almost all the superficial wounds were continuing to heal, and none showed signs of infection. The swelling around broken bones also was subsiding; Alvaro Mangino and Pancho Delgado, for example, both managed, despite considerable pain, to hobble around outside the plane. Arturo Nogueira was worse off; if he went outside the plane he had to crawl, pulling himself forward with his arms. The state of Rafael Echavarren's leg was growing serious; it showed the first indications of gangrene.

Enrique Platero, the boy who had had the tube of steel removed from his stomach, told Canessa that he was feeling perfectly well but that a piece of his insides still protruded from the wound. The doctor carefully unwound the rugby shirt which Platero continued to use as a bandage and confirmed the patient's observation; the wound was healing well but something stuck out from the skin. Part of this projection had gone dry, and Canessa suggested to Platero that if he cut off the dead matter the rest might be more easily pushed back under the skin.

"But what is it sticking out?" asked Platero.

Canessa shrugged his shoulders. "I don't know," he said. "It's probably part of the lining of the stomach, but if it's the intestine and I cut it open, you've had it. You'll get peritonitis."

Platero did not hesitate. "Do what you have to do," he said, and lay back on the door.

Canessa prepared to operate. As scalpel he had a choice between a piece of broken glass or a razor blade. His sterilizer was the subzero air all around them. He disinfected the area of the wound with eau du cologne and then carefully cut away a small slice of the dead skin with the glass. Platero did not feel it, but the protruding gristle still would not go back under the skin. With even greater caution Canessa now cut yet closer to the living tissue, dreading all the time that he might cut into the intestine, but again he seemed to have done no harm and this time, with a prod from the surgeon's finger, the gut retired into Platero's stomach where it belonged.

"Do you want me to stitch you up?" Canessa asked his patient. "I should warn you that we don't have any surgical thread."

"Don't worry," said Platero, rising on his elbows and looking down at his stomach. "This is fine. Just tie it up again and I'll be on my way."

Canessa retied the rugby shirt as tightly as he could, and Platero swung his legs off the door and got to his feet. "Now I'm ready to go on an expedition," he said, "and when we get back to Montevideo I'll take you on as my doctor. I couldn't possibly hope for a better one."

Outside the plane, following the example of Gustavo Nicolich, Carlitos Páez was writing to his father, his mother, and his sisters. He also wrote to his grandmother:

> You can have no idea how much I have thought about you because I love you, I adore you, because you have already received so many blows in your life, because I don't know how you are going to stand this one. You, Buba, taught me many things but the most important one was faith in God. That has increased so much now that you cannot conceive of it. . . . I want you to know that you are the kindest grandmother in the world and I shall remember you each moment I am alive.

4

Zerbino, Turcatti, and Maspons followed the track of the plane up the mountain. Every twenty or twenty-five steps the three were forced to rest, waiting for their hearts to beat normally again. The mountain seemed almost vertical, and they had to clutch at the snow with their bare hands. They had left in such a hurry that they had not thought of how they should equip themselves for the climb. They wore only sneakers or moccasins and shirts, sweaters, and light jackets, with thin trousers covering their legs. All three were strong, for they were players who had been in training, but they had barely eaten for the past eleven days.

The air that afternoon was not so cold. As they climbed, the sun shone on their backs and kept them warm. It was their feet, sodden with freezing snow, which suffered most. In the middle of the afternoon they reached a rock, and Zerbino saw that the snow around it was melting. He threw himself down and sucked at drops of water suspended from the disintegrating crystals. There was also another form of lichen, which he put into his mouth, but it had the taste of soil. They continued to climb but by seven o'clock in the evening found that they were only halfway to the peak. The sun had gone behind the mountain and only a short span of daylight remained. They sat down to discuss what they should do. All agreed that it would get much colder and if they stayed on the mountain the three of them might well die of exposure. On the other hand, if they simply slid back down, the whole climb was for nothing. To get to the top or find the tail with the batteries was the only chance of survival for all twenty-seven. They made up their minds to remain on the mountain for the night and look for an outcrop of rocks which would provide some shelter.

A little farther up they found a small hillock where the snow had been blown away to reveal the rocks underneath. They piled up loose stones to form a windbreak and, as dark was almost upon them, lay down to sleep. With the dark, as always, came the cold, and for all the protection their light clothes afforded them against the subzero wind, they might as well have been naked. There was no question of sleep. They were compelled to hit one another with their fists and feet to keep their circulation going, begging one another to be hit in the face until their mouths were frozen and no words would come from them. Not one of the three thought that he would survive the night. When the sun eventually rose in the east, each one was amazed to see it, and as it climbed in the sky it brought a little warmth back to their chilled bodies. Their clothes were soaked through, so they stood and took off their trousers, shirts, and socks and wrung them out. Then the sun went behind a cloud so they dressed again in their wet clothes and set off up the mountain.

Every now and then they stopped to rest and glance back toward the wreck of the Fairchild. By now it was a tiny dot in the snow, indistinguishable from any of the thousand outcrops of rock unless one knew exactly where to look. The red S which some of the boys had painted on the roof was invisible, and it was clear to the three why they had not been rescued: the plane simply could not be seen from the air. Nor was this all that depressed them. The higher they climbed, the more snow-covered mountains came into view. There was nothing to suggest that they were at the edge of the Andes, but they could only see to the north and the east. The mountain they were climbing still blocked their view to the south and west, and they seemed little nearer its summit. Every time they thought they had reached it, they would find that they were only at the top of a ridge; the mountain itself still towered above them.

At last, at the top of one of these ridges, their efforts were rewarded. They noticed that the rocks of an exposed outcrop had been broken, and then they saw scattered all around them the twisted pieces of metal that had once been part of the wingspan. A little farther up the mountain, where the ground fell into a small plateau, they saw a seat face down in the snow. With some difficulty they pulled it upright and found, still strapped to it, the body of one of their friends. His face was black, and it occurred to them that he might have been burned from the fuel escaping from the engine of the plane.

With great care Zerbino took from the body a wallet and identity card and, from around the neck, a chain and holy medals. He did the same when they came across the bodies of the three other Old Christians and the two members of the crew who had fallen out the back of the plane.

The three now made a count of those who were there and those who were below, and the tally came to forty-four. One body was missing. Then they remembered the floundering figure of Valeta, who had disappeared in the snow beneath them on that first afternoon. The count was now correct: six bodies at the top of the mountain, eleven down below, Valeta, twenty-four alive in the Fairchild, and the three of them there. All were accounted for.

They were still not at the summit, but there was no sign of the tail section or any other wreckage above them. They started back down the mountain, again following the track made by the fuselage, and on another shelf on the steep decline they found one of the plane's engines. The view from where they stood was majestic, and the bright sunlight reflecting off the snow made them squint as they observed the daunting panorama around them. They all had sunglasses, but Zerbino's were broken at the bridge, and as he climbed the mountain they had slipped forward so that he found it easier to peer over them. He did the same as they started to slide down again, using cushions they had taken from the seats at the top as makeshift sleds. They zigzagged, stopping at each piece of metal or debris to see if they could find anything useful. They discovered part of the plane's heating system, the lavatory, and fragments of the tail, but not the tail itself. Coming to a point where the track of the fuselage followed too steep a course, they crossed to the side of the mountain. By this time, Zerbino was so blinded by the snow that he could hardly see. He had to grope his way along, guided at times by the others. "I think," said Maspons, as they approached the plane once again, "that we shouldn't tell the others how hopeless it seems."

"No," said Turcatti. "There's no point in depressing them." Then he said, "By the way, what's happened to your shoe?"

Maspons looked down at his foot and saw that his shoe had come off while he was walking. His feet had become so numb with cold that he had not noticed.

The twenty-four other survivors were delighted to see the three return, but they were bitterly disappointed that they had not found the tail and appalled at their physical condition. All three hobbled on frozen feet and looked dreadful after their night out on the mountainside, and Zerbino was practically blind. They were immediately taken into the fuselage on cushions and brought large pieces of meat, which they gobbled down. Next Canessa treated their eyes, all of which were watering, with some drops called Colirio which he had found in a suitcase and thought might do them good. The drops stung but reassured them that something was being done for their condition. Then Zerbino bandaged his eyes with a rugby shirt, keeping it on for the next two days. When he removed his bandage he could still see only light and shadow, and he kept the rugby shirt as a kind of veil, shielding his eyes from the sun. He ate under the veil, and his blindness made him intolerably aggressive and irritable.

Their feet had also suffered. They were red and swollen with the cold, and their friends massaged them gently. It escaped no one's notice, however, that this expedition of a single day had almost killed three of the strongest among them, and morale once again declined.

5

On one of the days which followed, the sun disappeared behind clouds, rendering the water-making devices useless, so the boys had to return to the old method of putting the snow in bottles and shaking them. Then it occurred to Roy Harley and Carlitos Páez to make a fire with some empty Coca-Cola crates they had found in the luggage compartment of the plane. They held the aluminum sheets over the fire, and water was soon dripping into the bottles. In a short time they had enough.

The embers of the fire were still hot; it seemed sensible to try cooking a piece of meat on the hot foil. They did not leave it on for long, but the slight browning of the flesh gave it an immeasurably better flavor—softer than beef but with much the same taste.

The aroma soon brought other boys around the fire, and Coche Inciarte, who had continued to feel the greatest repugnance for raw flesh, found it quite palatable when cooked. Roy Harley, Numa Turcatti, and Eduardo Strauch also found it easier to overcome their revulsion when the meat was roasted and they could eat it as though it were beef.

Canessa and the Strauch cousins were against the idea of cooking the meat, and since they had gained some authority over the group, their views could not be ignored. "Don't you realize," said Canessa, knowledgeable and assertive as ever, "that proteins begin to die off at temperatures above forty degrees centigrade? If you want to get the most benefit from the meat, you must eat it raw."

"And when you cook it," said Fernández, looking down on the small steaks spitting on the aluminum foil, "the meat shrinks in size. A lot of its food value goes up in smoke or just melts away."

These arguments did not convince Harley or Inciarte, who could hardly derive nutrition from raw meat if they could not bring themselves to eat it, but in any case the limit to cooking was set by the extreme shortage of fuel—there were only three crates—and the high winds which so often made it impossible to light a fire out in the snow.

In the next few days, after Eduardo Strauch became very weak and emaciated, he finally overcame his revulsion to raw meat—forced to by his two cousins. Harley, Inciarte, and Turcatti never did, yet they were committed to survival and managed to consume enough to keep alive. The only ones who still had not eaten human flesh were the two eldest among them, Liliana and Javier Methol, and as the days passed and the twenty-five young men grew stronger on their new diet, the married couple, living on what remained of the wine, chocolate, and jam, grew thinner and more feeble.

The boys watched their growing debility with alarm. Marcelo begged them over and over again to overcome their reluctance and eat the meat. He used every argument, above all those words of Pedro Algorta. "Think of it as Communion. Think of it as the body and blood of Christ, because this is food that God has given us because He wants us to live."

Liliana listened to what he said, but time and again she gently shook her head. "There's nothing wrong with you doing it, Marcelo, but I can't, I just can't." For a time Javier followed her example. He still suffered from the altitude and was cared for by Liliana almost as though he were her child. The days passed slowly and there were moments when they found themselves alone; then they would talk together of their home in Montevideo, wondering what their children were doing at that hour, anxious that little Marie Noel, who was three, might be crying for her mother, or that their ten-year-old daughter, María Laura, might be skipping her homework.

Javier tried to reassure his wife that her parents would have moved into their house and would be looking after the children. They talked about Liliana's mother and father, and Liliana asked whether it would be possible when they returned to have her parents come and live in their house in Carrasco. She looked a little nervously at her husband when she suggested it, knowing that not every husband likes the idea of his parents-in-law living under the same roof, but Javier simply smiled and said, "Of course. Why didn't we think of that before?"

They discussed how they might build an annex onto the house so that Liliana's parents could be more or less independent. Liliana worried that they might not be able to afford it or that an extra wing might spoil the garden, but on every point Javier reassured her. Their conversation, however, weakened his resolution not to eat human meat, and so when Marcelo next offered him a piece of flesh, Javier took it and thrust it down his throat.

There remained only Liliana. Weak though she was, with life ebbing from her body, her mood remained serene. She wrote a short note to her children, saying how dear they were to her. She remained close to her husband, helping him because he was weaker, sometimes even a little irritable with him because the altitude sickness made his movements clumsy and slow, but with death so near, their partnership did not falter. Their life was one, on the mountain as it had been in Montevideo, and in these desperate conditions the bond between them held fast. Even sorrow was a part of that bond, and when they talked together of the four children they might never see again, tears not only of sadness but of joy fell down their cheeks, for what they missed now showed them what they had had.

One evening just before the sun had set, and when the twenty-seven survivors were preparing to take shelter from the cold in the fuselage of the plane, Liliana turned to Javier and told him that when they returned she would like to have another baby. She felt that if she was alive it was because God wanted her to do so.

Javier was delighted. He loved his children and had always wanted to have more, yet when he looked at his wife he could see through the tears in his eyes the poignancy of her suggestion. After more than ten days without food the reserves had been drawn from her body. The bones protruded from her cheeks and her eyes were sunk into their sockets; only her smile was the same as before. He said to her, "Liliana, we must face up to it. None of this will happen if we don't survive."

She nodded. "I know."

"God wants us to survive."

"Yes. He wants us to survive."

"And there's only one way."

"Yes. There's only one way."

Slowly, because of their weakness, Javier and Liliana returned to the group of boys as they lined up to climb into the Fairchild.

"I've changed my mind," Liliana said to Marcelo. "I will eat the meat."

Marcelo went to the roof of the plane and brought down a small portion of human flesh which had been drying in the sun. Liliana took a piece and forced it down into her stomach.

From *House*

TRACY KIDDER

∞

Tracy Kidder likes to write about people at work. His style of reporting—
often in the present tense, with a slow pace and close attention to casual
dialogue—seems ideal for capturing the rhythm of a job, the engagement
of mind and body in a consuming task, the collective intelligence and spe-
cialized slang of a skilled team.

After graduating from Harvard, Kidder served as an army officer in Vietnam, and then studied at the Iowa Writers' Workshop. For ten years he was
on the staff of *The Atlantic,* illuminating technical subjects (nuclear power,
solar energy, American railroads) in lucid and graceful articles. One of his
assignments led to a book about computer designers, *The Soul of a New
Machine* (1982), which won a Pulitzer Prize and National Book Award.

House (1985) is another book about a project. As it chronicles the construction of one dwelling, it raises larger issues about work, wealth, social
class, and personal pride. Kidder presents a triangular narrative, focusing on
the often tense relations among the house's owners, architect, and builders.
He also offers historical perspectives, not only in his expository chapters but
even, as this excerpt shows, in the very heart of a dramatized scene.

—K. K.

∞

Richard sits on a stack of two-by-tens, the one on which Jim presented his
framing plan. The big pile of wood gives off a delicate aroma, like a woods
with a pine-needle carpet. The stack makes a clean, fragrant, somewhat
expensive picnic table for Richard. Sitting on it, feet dangling over the edge,
he shakes his head over that day's Lindy cake, in order to ensure his partners' jealousy, and dislodges the pencil from behind his ear. It vanishes down
a crack between the boards.

"Whoops," says Richard, peering after it. "This pile just ate my pencil."

The next day at lunchtime, Richard finds his pencil, on the ground,
between two twelve-foot-long two-by-tens, which are all that remain of the pile.

Finish work never seems to end, but the frames of houses go up swiftly. And time passes quickly for Apple Corps when they're framing.

Ned stands on soggy, sandy ground and measures the distances between the bolts that protrude, threads up, out of the top of the foundation's gray walls, and Richard bores the necessary holes in a length of the two-by-six, pressure-treated southern pine. The board slips down right over the bolts. "The first piece of wood. Yaaay!" cries Richard. They install another piece of sill, then another, and then Ned says, "Wait a minute." The sills are sticking out over the edges of the foundation a little too far. Ned and Richard investigate. They measure the two-by-six lengths of pine, which are supposed to be five and a half inches wide. These are five and five-eighths. Maybe they were sawn wrong. More likely, they sat outside and absorbed an eighth of an inch of water. Richard pulls the wood off the bolts. "We can't make this house thirty feet and a quarter inches right at the *start,*" he says. They begin again. "It's just work," says Ned.

Observing this scene from the other side of the foundation, Jim nods approval. He says the difference between amateur and professional carpenters lies in the facts that pros make few mistakes and when they err they make corrections at once. Thus they prevent both brooding and remorse. Half an hour later, Jim drives a nail that splits a fresh piece of lumber, one he's spent some time cutting and installing. "This piece of wood just split from end to end," he says. He stares at the ruined board. Then he beats on it with his large framing hammer. But hadn't he said that a pro doesn't brood over an error? "That's right. But I never said you don't let it upset you." He wallops and wallops the board, tearing it along the grain. Jim smiles. He tosses the ruined wood aside. "I never said *that.* Send this back to the factory."

It's clear they do not like to leave mistakes behind. When Ned bends a nail, he withdraws that nail, pounds it straight again, and hammers it back in. Nails are cheap. Time costs the carpenters much more. But Ned seems interested not merely in correcting errors. He wants to erase them.

Each carpenter owns a short-handled crowbar with a rounded claw, known as a cat's paw. There's nothing like a cat's paw for extracting nails from mistakes. "What would a carpenter do without a cat's paw, Ned?"

"Buy one," Ned replies.

None of them carries his cat's paw, but each knows where it is. If he makes a mistake, he has to go and get the tool. They prepare for errors. They don't assume that errors will occur. When one of them does make a mistake, he usually blames it on whichever of the team happens to be absent or out of earshot at the moment.

"Oh, shit."

"Blame it on Jim."

For now, Jim usually gets the blame. Almost hourly it seems, he leaps over the trench near the foundation and trudges off up the hill, briefcase in hand, toward the phone in Jules Wiener's red horse barn, so he can call the lumberyard or a subcontractor or one of the utilities or Jonathan. Jim rarely accepts abuse without retorting, though. He makes a practice of signing his partners' mistakes. "Richard was here," he'll write in pencil on the wood at the site of a withdrawn nail. In Apple Corps parlance, a carpenter gone sloppy is "a beaver," "a jabronie," or "a Hoople," and "thrashing" is the disjointed set of bad procedures that leads to "cobby" work or, worst of all, "a cob job." The last is a very old term. In one of its earliest meanings, *cob* meant a lump of something, and in medieval England to "build in cob" meant to make a house out of lumps of clay, earth, even manure. It was not thought to be a form of high-quality construction. "Cob job" probably came across the ocean with the first New England carpenters and has survived in such sanctuaries of the old-fashioned as the hilltowns. The term is more usual there than in the valley. The carpenters don't remember exactly when they first heard the expression, and they do not know its history, but it has the right pejorative sound for the kind of act that none wishes to be truly guilty of committing. When one of Apple Corps accuses another of thrashing or beavering or cobbing up some piece of work, he usually does so falsely, sometimes even in order to praise, but they also seem to be warning each other and themselves of the nearness of sin.

Usually, if one of them wants praise, he has to administer it himself. When Richard fixes a cobby piece of work, he "tunes it up" or he "fusses with it," and what comes out well is "custom," and for all of them a very good result is "perfect," "perfect enough," or "perfect or equal." And in nearly every case, a satisfactorily completed piece of the job is good enough for whatever town they happen to be working in, in this case, "good enough for Amherst."

"Close enough for Amherst," Ned pauses over his hammer to say. "It's a joke, but it's also a way of keeping perspective. Don't lose the building for the stick. You're always making value judgments, you know, about what's straight or plumb, but sooner or later you gotta nail it. You've got to have confidence it's right enough, or if it's not, that you can fix it."

On the second day of framing, the fourth partner, Alex Ghiselin, joins them. They set up, as they will every morning, a small factory beside the foundation: generator, extension cords, ladders, sawhorses, electric and hand-driven saws. "Tooling up," as they call it, they buckle on belts and make themselves into roving hardware displays, hammers and numerous pouches hanging from their waists, red handkerchiefs in their back pockets, pencils behind their ears. Proper and efficient framing is the art of thinking ahead with clarity, of seeing the end in the beginning, and they have made the exercise of forethought, which is the opposite of thrashing, part of their daily routine in all departments of houseraising.

Alex is their cutter nonpareil. He likes nothing better than to get from Richard an order for thirty two-by-tens, all fifteen feet, five and three-eighths inches long. Alex writes down the numbers. He sets up the company's radial arm saw and the portable bench Jim once built for it. Then Alex measures that prescribed distance down the bench from the saw's blade and nails down a piece of wood at the spot. The end of each successive two-by-ten he'll place against this stop. It takes him a couple of minutes to set up the jig, but once it's done he can cut one board after another and measure only occasionally to make sure that nothing has moved.

Whenever they can, the carpenters assemble a portion of the frame out on the open ground, where they don't have to hang off ladders and there's room to swing their hammers freely. Then, standing on the foundation's walls and on stepladders, they install the construction, a section of floor joists, say, into its place within the frame. Most of the failures of most spare-time carpenters stem from misplaced haste. They haven't got much time. They want to see results at once. Apple Corps spends time now to save time later. It's a form of deferred gratification, which, the psychologists say, is the essence of true adulthood. Apple Corps has acquired the knack for looking calmly on the future. They always pause to remove any nails from boards they cast aside. The practice cuts down on tetanus shots. It was not always this way, but most of them have worked together for ten years now, and they have learned consideration.

Erecting girders, from stepladders set on the basement floor, Richard and Alex struggle to speak geometry. "Move it five-sixteenths that way. No, out that way, toward Pelham. No, up. Whoops. No, down. This sounds like *Sesame Street*," says Richard.

Richard climbs out of the cellar. He studies and restudies Jim's intricate framing plan. He does so out loud: "Oh, I'm being confused right now. That seems rather odd. Unh-hunh. Ohhhh. I see. I see what happened. Oh-*Kay!* Yup, right where it should be. Excellent. Just where it should be. Okay. Good." He adds, addressing Alex, "A *custom*-fit girder." Richard emits a guttural sound, which could imply some twisted pleasure.

"Nicely done," says Alex.

"Custom," says Richard. "I think we're winning."

Not all the two-by-tens they take from that first pile, nor all of the lumber that follows, is of high quality. A few pieces have rotten patches, and a few more than that are twisted. "Goodness gracious, Buffalo Bob, these somebitch she no good. She crooked, like some beetch," says Jim, with a wild look, sighting down a board. Ned says he thinks the lumber grading standards have declined since he started out. "I don't know, Ned," says Richard. "As long as I can remember, everybody's always bitched about it. 'God, the lumber isn't like it used to be.' We're still sayin' that." They find places for the twisty stuff, where nails will straighten it or it can do no harm, and the worst stuff they cut into pieces for blocking between floor joists.

When he is going well, Alex cuts lumber quickly and to within a thirty-second of an inch of the specified lengths. They attempt to keep their frame within about a sixteenth of an inch of perfection, which is about as accurate as their tape measures are and more precise, in fact, than wood and weather allow. They work in sunshine and a few days into the framing, they even get their shirts off for a while. On the next day, a cold drizzle falls. Jim, who is responsible for worrying, measures the first floor's frame at the end of one sunny day and finds it jibes exactly with the numbers on his plan. Two rainy days later, he measures again and finds that the bottom deck has grown a quarter of an inch along one wall and not at all along the others. They can easily rectify the discrepancy in the next level of the frame. Jim expected this to happen. He is not disappointed. He says again, "Perfection is an insult to the gods." They often speak about the fact of imperfection. The words must have a consoling ring for them.

From *Brothers*

SYLVESTER MONROE AND

PETER GOLDMAN

Brothers (1988) began as a special project for *Newsweek:* a group portrait of twelve black men who had grown up in a housing project on Chicago's South Side. One of those twelve men was the story's coauthor, Sylvester ("Vest") Monroe, who had made it out of the street life, all the way to Harvard and a career in magazine journalism. Monroe approached old friends like Edward ("Half Man") Carter, asking them to share the most intimate details of their lives. Until then, Carter noted, "nobody had ever asked me what I thought about *anything*."

Monroe's coauthor was *Newsweek* senior editor Peter Goldman, who assembled and directed a reporting team and edited the final copy to provide a continuous narrative voice. "My work," Goldman says, "was to weave the yard goods into a suit." He had coauthored previous book-length magazine projects—most notably *Charlie Company: What Vietnam Did to Us* (1983)—and had shown special interest and skill in treating racial topics. Both black and white critics had praised *The Death and Life of Malcolm X* (1973), a biography that grew out of many interviews Goldman had conducted with Malcolm X in the 1960s.

"Peter Goldman gave me a model of balance and fairness," Sylvester Monroe says. "And by 1987 *Newsweek* had evolved to the point where you could write a story like *Brothers* without a big sociological overview. You could dispense with that prism, and try to tell about characters' lives in their own voices."

Monroe and his fellow reporters (particularly Terry E. Johnson) used tape recorders to capture those voices but relied on a third-person novelistic style—a kind of streetwise omniscience—rather than conventional oral history. Monroe also wanted to protect his friends from self-incrimination, because over the years several of them had become outlaws.

By contrast, Half Man Carter represented the hidden heroism of the working poor, and his "scuffling" life was essential to the mosaic of *Brothers*. "To meet Half Man unencumbered by numbers and theories," Monroe and Goldman concluded, "is to discover a bright, competent, and likable man who *believes* in the bedrock values of American society and has tried all his life to live by them. He is the work ethic made flesh."

—K. K.

A Blues Life

A friend once asked Half Man Carter to name something, anything, that would make him happy, and his imagination shorted out. He didn't say $4 million or $5 million like Big Honk might, or Billy. He didn't even say hitting the number, or owning a boat or a Cadillac Eldorado. He said he might *pray* for $20,000, but he would settle for $500 and would naturally expect to have to work to get it.

Half Man had never given his dreams much running room; he didn't believe in them, and in his middle thirties, he had drawn, or accepted, a tight line around his existence. It was a boundary inside which he had found a form of contentment, the peace that flows from the absence of hunger or risk. He was not, he thought, where he was supposed to be; he was working two jobs and was still out there dancing a half step ahead of a pack of bill collectors holding IOU's on the free-range days of his past. But he had a decent place to stay and a lady who loved him enough to put up with his moods and attitudes, and if his life was a roller-coaster ride above and below the poverty line, at least he was *working* poor. He didn't have to borrow a dollar or beg for his beer.

Except at love, in fact, he counted himself lucky. He had never *not* worked, not even when he was adrift between steady jobs for eleven or twelve months one time; he did day labor as a temporary for the minimum wage and hustled housepainting gigs on the side. He considered any job better than welfare and two jobs better than one, no matter what kind of work at what kind of money. Sometimes when he was between jobs, he would fill out an application form someplace and scare people off with the sheer length and variety of his past work record. "You're at the wrong place, we're only paying five dollars an hour here," the Man would tell him, to which Half Man would reply, "I'll take it." White people wouldn't work for $5. Half Man would if he had to.

He had lately been doing a good deal better than that. His course, up and down for most of his thirty-six years, seemed to him to be going steady up. He was working days in a paint factory, filling cans on an assembly line that might have been designed by Charlie Chaplin, and moonlighting as a janitor in the three-building apartment complex where he lived. The wage at the plant was as good as he had ever made, nearly $10 an hour, and his basement flat was rent-free. If he had managed his finances better, he thought, he could have been living pretty medium, the only phrase he could think of to describe his minimalist hopes. He could have had steak any day he felt like it, he thought. He didn't need or want caviar every night.

But he had handled his money about as carelessly as he ran his life. His days had been spent hopscotching from moment to moment without much regard for the lessons of the past, which seemed best forgotten, or the needs of the future, which was a blank. He could not in fact be sure there *was* a future. Sudden death is a sad commonplace in the ghetto, and two of his own brothers had died young. One, Wilbert, had had a stroke at nineteen. The other, Waddell, had come home from Vietnam at twenty-four with his mind all messed up by the war. Waddell was dealing drugs on Thirty-ninth Street, in partnership with Moose Harper, except some of Waddell's heroin was going into his own arm. No one in the family knew it or wanted to confront it, not till he shot up in the bathroom at the Carters' house one night and hit the floor with a loud thud. Moose and one of the Carter brothers splintered the door. Waddell was lying on the tile, the needle still stuck in his arm.

They hauled him to his feet and walked him out of trouble, that time. A sister, trying to save him, set him up with a job, an apartment, and a car in Milwaukee. But he was still doing H, and one day he just disappeared. The mail was overflowing his mailbox and parking tickets were wadding up on his windshield when the police finally got curious. They checked out his place and found him, alone this time and dead of an overdose at twenty-five.

Half Man's parents sought solace in religion, as Jehovah's Witnesses. Half Man found his in motion, the aimless journey of a rolling stone. He seemed to have a hard time making lasting connections; he had about him the air of a man constantly reckoning the odds on the profitability of human relationships. Twenty years after the collapse of his first marriage, he was still haunted by the feeling that he had blown it all emotionally then and there—that his life had been damaged beyond repair. He drifted from bed to bed for years thereafter, his attachments as impermanent as his jobs and his bankroll. He liked women but felt he could not love them anymore, not in the old way. Instead, he used them; he had a power over them, a promise in his deep-set eyes and his awkward smile, and they came easily under his spell. He fathered a daughter by one lady and a son by another, five months apart, and moved on. The mothers got to be friends with one another; the well-known unreliability of men was something they had vividly in common.

Half Man did try marriage a second time, fourteen years after the first. He was working part-time as an attendant in a launderette, trying to pay the bills during the winter-layoff season in the construction trade. She was a customer, a lady named Barbara with two kids of her own. He was attentive. She responded; she began bringing in her wash three times a week, and lunch for Half Man besides. He shut down early one day and met her at the lakefront. Lights flashed. They started seeing each other. He was broke;

he had a place on South Shore Drive, a nice place in a middle-class neighborhood, but he was having a hard time keeping up with the bills. His phone had been disconnected. He couldn't even buy groceries.

She was sympathetic. "You payin' that high rent and tryin' to make it, too," she said. "Whyn't you give up South Shore, honey, and come live with me?"

He did, and for a time he didn't *need* money. She paid the rent, stocked the kitchen, and put some coin in his pockets for walking-around expenses; she even bought the sticker for his car. But when they married after three or four years together, she changed her ways and wanted him to change his. He was suddenly the man of the house, the breadwinner for her and her children, responsible for this and that. She was piling on the burdens, more than he could handle right then. He had been fired from one job as a tool salesman. Another, as a carpenter, folded under him. The mother of one of his own kids had the law on him for child support. He couldn't produce what Barbara was demanding, and she wouldn't ease off. She picked fights with him, loud battles with a lot of broken china and torn sateen, and then called the police on *him*, telling them *he* gone crazy.

The time finally came when Half Man could no longer live with her nagging and his own failure as provider. He moved out, and the marriage split, one more casualty of the oppressive home economics of the ghetto. They stayed man and wife, nominally, and saw each other sometimes, until the Saturday morning Half Man came by in his father's pickup truck to collect his painting gear for a job. He walked in the back door and found her with another man. Her children—his stepchildren—were in the house. She should have went out to a hotel, he thought. She should have had more respect.

He walked out hurt and angry, gathered up his gear, and left.

"What you do then?" his parents asked when he told them the story.

"Went on and finished paintin'," he said. "Made that money and kept on pushin'."

He might have been summing up his life. He had spent it at a succession of unskilled and semiskilled jobs, most of them vulnerable to the cycles of the seasons and the economy and none very rewarding except for the money. It struck him that there were guys out there who had been working their way up, while he had just been working. His job at the paint company, for example, filling those cans and smashing on the lids at about two seconds per can—it was nothing but elbow-and-ass work, he thought, like most of the jobs he had had.

He owned a mind, too, and wished he could use it, but they didn't pay him for that. They didn't pay *blacks* for that, he told himself, 'cause white folks always think they smarter; they never think you got any sense, and they hate for you to show them you do. He didn't even like to give them suggestions, 'cause if you give them a suggestion and it *work*, they ain't even gonna act like they appreciate it. You would see them do something wrong around the plant, try to put a part on backwards or some such foolishness, and you couldn't say anything—you just had to sit there, even though it hurt you, and wait until they figured it out. So Half Man eased silently on through his days, doing what he got paid for, smiling all the time. They thought he was dumb, he guessed, but they were going to think that any damn way. He knew what time it was, and what color he was. He knew how far he could go.

It wasn't that he didn't like white people, or couldn't get along with them. He could; he wasn't prejudiced. You could come around to his crib and check out his record collection, just for instance; he could throw on a couple of Elvises, or some Elton Johns, or a Cyndi Lauper, or even an old Walter Brennan side, "Mama Sang a Song." He sometimes thought that he disliked more black people than white. Blacks on the job would get on him for talking to white folks, and he would answer, "Man, these white folks speak to me, I speak to them. What you all want to be—ignorant?" He didn't even care if they spoke back or not. It was about him being a man, too, just like them, and if they wanted to be ignorant, it didn't mean he had to be.

It was whites who had helped him at work, he mused, and blacks who had tried to hold him back; one of them almost slit his damn throat. He had been assistant foreman on one of his early jobs and had had a hard time getting his way with his black workers. When the white man came around and told them to do something, they grinned and smiled and did it, but when he tried, they wanted to act the fool and call him an Uncle Tom. He shrugged it off as jealousy; didn't nobody like to see nobody else black get ahead. He got in a fight at a company picnic with a guy who had been hard-timing him on the job. They were both drunk, and when the guy came around looking for trouble, Half Man didn't give him no play; he was still a hot-tempered kid then, and he just went off on the guy, started in whupping his tail without a word of warning. The dude came back on him with a knife, going for the throat. Half Man jumped back. The flick missed his neck, narrowly, and laid open his face instead. It was a black guy tried to kill him and a white guy who drove him to the hospital to get sewn up. The repair took thirty-five stitches.

Half Man had grown up in the ghetto, and he remained in some measure prey to its deep, wounding undercurrents of self-doubt, the suspicion that if white people owned the world, there must be a reason. He was pleased when a black man, Harold Washington, became mayor of Chicago in the 1980's, but it did not seem to improve the conditions of life materially down in the street, where the brothers were, and he guessed that the entire city, *the whole MF,* would burn down if black people were put all the way in charge. Sometimes he thought the white man *should* go on ahead and run things, 'cause they the ones trained, he said. It was a lot of things black people had accomplished that they don't put in the books, he believed, but everybody know who made the electricity and the telephone; it was the white man.

Half Man wasn't the kind, in any case, to blame white people alone for the way his life had got dead-ended. It was true, he thought, that white folks run things and that they don't cut black folks no breaks. But he saw his own complicity in what had become of him. He regretted that he hadn't stayed in school and that he had thrown away his money on the pleasures of the moment instead of making it work for him, buying a little piece of real estate or something. He had got caught in a trap, he knew that, and it was at least partly of his own making. He and Vest Monroe had been best friends at Trey-nine, but he had chosen one course and Vest had taken another when they were still boys. It was Vest who got over; he had gone away to college and *Newsweek,* and when he came home sharp in his downtown clothes, the brothers weren't calling him Brainiac anymore; they were calling him Big-Time Vest Monroe.

"I was very lucky," Vest told Half Man one day twenty years later, when their separate paths crossed again.

"Well, you wasn't *lucky,* you know," Half Man said. "You worked for it, you went to school for it. That ain't lucky."

"You've been working all your life," Vest said.

"But see, that's different," Half Man said. "That's *all* I've been doing is working."

Working, he added, and partying; the money had disappeared, and the years, and he wasn't much ahead of where he had been when Vest went away. He wasn't faulting the Man for that, not entirely. Opportunities had begun opening up a little bit for black people back when he was still young enough to seize them; things weren't all the way straightened out yet, he thought, but at least you didn't have to sit in the back of the bus no more. He realized that life was inherently hard for a man living on the margin as he did. You caught so much hell just surviving that you couldn't tell where it was coming from. Is it racist or is it straight up? Is it BS or not? You could never know for sure; if some honky ain't hiring you, Half Man thought, you don't know whether it's because you black or because he don't need help.

So he lived inside his personal age of limits, seeing no way out and no higher destiny to pursue even if he could. It was still a blues life, still strait-ened by short money and demanding women. His wages were garnisheed in the winter of 1985–86 to satisfy a bad note he had co-signed, and he had had to pawn his color TV to get his car repaired. The paint plant shut down for part of the winter season, and except for his janitoring, he had no work at all. His three children were all in their teens. He provided what he could for them and tried to show a fatherly interest in what they were doing—more interest, anyway, than he remembered his parents having shown in him. But he was an absentee daddy to his two thirteen-year-olds living in town, Muneerah and Edward, and his first and favorite child, Sherri, at seventeen was in St. Louis somewhere with her mother or her grandmother; he had lost track of which. She was never far from Half Man's mind; still, he reck-oned he hadn't seen her more than once in two years.

What had changed in his life was its tempo; inside its narrow ambit, he felt nearer than he had ever been to repose. The anchor of his days was his third wife, Matilda, a quiet woman with a lot of gold on her fingers and in her smile. It was like she *colored* gold, he thought, she was that cute. She was nice, too, real nice by his revised criteria. In his rambling days, he had had ladies with two or three children, raising them as his own as long as he was around, but no more. He wanted his woman working, not sitting at home with a bunch of kids and a jealous attitude, and Matilda fit the specifications. She had a job and didn't mind going every day, earning her own money instead of constantly wanting his; he couldn't get her to stay home even when she was sick. She had no kids, no extravagances, no obvious desire in life except to please him. He gave her a hundred-dollar bill once and asked about it several days later. "I ain't cashed it yet," she told him. She was saving up to buy him a diamond watch for his birthday, which was the way she was; give the woman money and she spend it back on you.

The day they met was like a smile from Lady Luck, the first Half Man had known since his teenage marriage broke up. He was seeing someone else then, and so was she; her old man in those days was a guy Half Man drank beer with, and for a time the two couples went out together. But Half Man and his woman got in a fight one night, a spasm of rage that began with him calling her bitch and ended with her throwing his belongings out the window into the street. Matilda's old man happened by, wandering into the hailstorm of clothes and shoes flying out the house. He helped pick up afterward and hauled Half Man's gear, along with Half Man, to his own place.

"Man, you can let your stuff stay here," he said. "If you don't have nowhere to go, you can spend the night. Sleep on the couch."

The overnight guest became a boarder, at $40 a week. The arrangement suited Matilda's old man just fine at first. He was skin-popping heroin in those days, injecting it under the skin instead of into the vein, and he needed the money to support his habit; he had just come out of prison and didn't have a job. The longer Half Man stayed, the better that $40 looked to the dude. He would take it and vanish for a night or a weekend, disappearing into his drugs and sometimes into the arms of another woman who lived just down the street.

Matilda barely saw him anymore; she would be off to work when he slipped in in the morning to change his clothes, and he was frequently gone when she got back at night. In his lengthening absences, she got lonely. She began wanting Half Man to sit up nights talking with her, and some of the things she was saying were a little—he searched for the word—aggressive. He felt caught in the middle, and he held back at first, wondering what was with this chick; *she* was cutting in on *him* instead of the other way around, which was the way it usually worked. And then one day her old man was gone; there had been an angry last scene, and she had kicked him out of the house.

"Well, I guess I ought to leave," Half Man told her. He had been her old man's guest.

"This *my* house," she said, and she invited Half Man to share it.

Half Man insisted on going to her old man first and telling him what time it was, up front, before he found them together.

"Don't do *that*," Matilda pleaded. The guy was bigger than Half Man. She was scared.

"Yeah, but I gotta do it," Half Man said, " 'cause he gonna be crazy as a dog if he walk up and catch us. I think we might have a chance if I break it to him."

He did lay in a pint of brand-name gin and a six-pack of Coors as a precaution, and he kept it flowing while he was running it down to the dude about him and Matilda. The guy wasn't used to nothing but cheap wine, and the good stuff seemed to ease whatever pain he felt, if any. They both got high, and everything was cool between them. They stayed friends, and when Half Man and Matilda found their new apartment, her old old man helped them move in.

Half Man felt settled there, the underground man, living in his basement flat out of sight of the larger world. He didn't like *outside* too much; there was too much happening out there, he thought, and nothing much he felt he needed anymore—nothing, that is, except work. He began his days at four in the morning, cleaning his buildings for his keep, and when the paint plant was open, he had to be out the door by 6:15 to get there in time. His evenings were mostly spent at home. He almost never went downtown and only infrequently visited his old friends on Thirty-ninth Street. He and Matilda had married in the winter of 1986–87, and the street had lost a lot of its appeal for him. He much preferred the safety of his place, Half Man sitting in the half light with a cold beer and a warm smoke and the glow of the TV playing over the bare wood floor.

There remained trace elements of regret in his life, but he wasn't crying. There were, he thought, a lot of people worse off than he was. He had learned, in his thirty-six years, that you can't have everything you want; he had learned not to mistake his dreams for anything *but* dreams that vanish in the first light of day. If the impossible happened, he thought, it was going to have to come to him; he was too busy getting by to go chasing after it. He had made his choices and was making the best of them, and while he couldn't honestly say he was happy, he thought he might be, sometime soon.

So . . . We Meet at Last, Mr. Bond

BOB GREENE

"I'm not a pundit and I'm not a political philosopher," Bob Greene says. "I really see myself as a storyteller." Greene has been telling stories for twenty-five years as a columnist for the Chicago *Sun Times,* the Chicago *Tribune,* and *Esquire.*

His human interest stories can be tragic, sweet, or simply bizarre. Green writes of a paralyzed youth summoning all his strength to testify in court against another youth who shot him; of a hardworking adult finally learning to read; of a group of teens entering a contest to meet the band Motley Crüe on the strength of an extreme proposal. (One boy offered his mother to the band.)

"Usually I'm telling other people's stories," Greene has said. "When I use myself in them, it's a device to tell a story about something else." He delves into buried feelings about being cut from his seventh-grade basketball team, and then expands the story to encompass the adolescent trauma of countless American males. More typically, Greene's first-person writing begins with nostalgia, as when he searches for the real meaning of the song "Louie Louie," or when he tracks down the Doublemint twins.

His profile of Sean Connery also begins with nostalgia, but it provides a clever twist on standard celebrity journalism. Greene's conversations with Connery, and his lingering awe for the he-man icon, tie together a series of vignettes about frailty and phobia. Greene shows how the elements of literary journalism, especially dialogue and scenic construction, can illuminate the human comedy.

—K. K.

Sometimes when I think back to the Sixties, and the heroes I grew up with, it seems that no one is left.

President Kennedy is dead. The Beatles can never sing together again. Martin Luther King is dead.

But then it occurs to me: one man remains. James Bond is still alive.

He is still alive in the person of Sean Connery. Connery no longer portrays Bond in the movies, but to a generation of Americans he was, and is, the only James Bond. His successors were merely imitations.

Connery made seven James Bond movies, beginning with *Doctor No* in 1962, and in so doing set the standard for everything that was daring and thrilling and cool. Was there an American boy who did not secretly want to grow up to be James Bond? Apparently, though, Connery himself wanted to grow out of being James Bond; he made it clear that he was tired of playing the role.

But Connery is still walking around, acting in other movies and living his life. The man who is James Bond remains among us.

"My knee had been hurting me for three or four years," Sean Connery said. "I hadn't been able to kneel on it. Then, whenever I had to do some running, it began to ache. Finally I had to do something about it."

We were in a car headed for Downers Grove, Illinois, where Connery had an appointment with the orthopedic surgeons who had recently operated on his knee. He was going in for a checkup.

"The doctors frightened me to death by asking me to watch a television tape of the operation," Connery said. "They used an instrument with a little camera attached when they went into my knee, and they made a tape of the whole thing.

"I have such an aversion to needles. That's putting it mildly. When I was a child in Scotland, all of the school pupils had to be inoculated because there was a diphtheria epidemic going around. We all had to stand in line. Standing right in front of me was this big, fat girl with great big arms. Her arm was directly at my eye level. They stuck her with the hypodermic needle, and I saw the whole thing. The fear of needles has been with me ever since."

The voice was hypnotic. The reality of the situation was that a fifty-six-year-old man was sitting in a car telling a story about something that had happened to him at the beginning of his life. But it was James Bond talking; whether Connery prefers it to be that way or not, it was James Bond talking.

"Do you want a piece of gum?" he said, offering me a stick of Juicy Fruit.

Thirty minutes before, we had been on Michigan Avenue in Chicago, where Connery had been rehearsing a scene for the movie *The Untouchables*. In the movie, Kevin Costner plays Eliot Ness, Robert De Niro plays Al Capone, and Connery plays Jimmy Malone, an old Chicago cop who shows Ness the way that the city operates.

The lobby of Roosevelt University had been turned into a replica of a

Thirties hotel. Costner, De Niro, and Connery were supposed to run through their lines, but everything was behind schedule.

Connery had been wearing a blue hooded parka, a thick sweater, and running shoes. A production assistant had come up to him and said, "There's something on your face."

"What?" Connery had said.

"Something sparkling," the production assistant had said.

"Must have been from the tiara I was wearing," Connery had said.

He had stood there studying his script. I had made idle conversation with him, all the while doing my best to hide the fact that there was no one in the world that I had ever wanted to meet more.

Now we were in the car heading for the doctors' offices in Downers Grove. I asked him how he would rate Ian Fleming's original James Bond novels.

"To tell you the truth, I never read them all," Connery said. "I read *Thunderball,* because initially that was supposed to be the first movie. But I was never all that crazy about the books.

"I liked Fleming. He was erudite—and a real snob. Being a genuine snob can be quite healthy. At least you know who you're dealing with.

"Fleming had approval over the casting of James Bond. He had wanted Cary Grant to play the role. But there was no money. The whole budget for *Doctor No* was $1 million. By the time we had had all the success with the movies and were shooting *You Only Live Twice,* one set alone cost more than the entirety of *Doctor No* had cost to film."

I asked if there had been any suppressed rivalry between Fleming and Connery. After all, Fleming had created James Bond. Until the novels were turned into movies, Fleming could pretty much pretend that he *was* James Bond. As soon as the movies came out, though, Connery was Bond forever.

"We got along rather well, surprisingly," Connery said. "We had both been in the Royal Navy—although he was a commander and I was an able-bodied seaman."

He said that he had no particular opinion about the news that Timothy Dalton will be the latest actor to portray Bond. "The guy should be young," Connery said. "Or at least under fifty."

Connery said that he had seen very few of the Roger Moore James Bond movies—"I think I saw two of them. I don't remember the one I saw first. I think it took place in New Orleans, with some black guys in a jazz band.

"I didn't particularly like what the movies had become. All the hardware, and people falling through the Eiffel Tower or something, and then getting up and walking away."

We pulled into the parking lot of the doctors' offices. Connery walked into the reception area and was immediately escorted back to an examining room.

Jo Ann Ready, a nurse, said, "You look like you're walking okay."

"It doesn't feel too bad," Connery said.

Dr. E. Thomas Marquardt and Dr. Timothy C. Payne came into the room. "Take off your pants and lie down," Dr. Marquardt said.

Connery removed his trousers and reclined on a couch that was in the room. Dr. Marquardt took one of Connery's legs and began to bend it.

"No pain here at all?" Dr. Marquardt said.

"Not really," Connery said.

"No catching sensation?" Dr. Marquardt said.

"I haven't really been trying anything fancy," Connery said. "I've been playing some golf. And I've been doing this business in the swimming pool." He lifted his leg several times to show the doctors what he meant.

"Well, you're coming along remarkably well," Dr. Marquardt said.

"But my shoulder has started to hurt," Connery said. "And my arm gets a little sore when I'm playing golf."

Dr. Marquardt laughed. "That's what usually happens," he said. "We alleviate one thing, and then the other parts of the body start acting up. Let me take a look at the shoulder."

Connery stood up and stripped off his shirt. "You won't need a needle to look at this, will you?" he said.

"No," Dr. Marquardt said. "Let's get some X rays taken, though."

Connery walked down a short hallway and then lay down on an X-ray table in a narrow room.

Vicki Kybartas, an X-ray technologist, said, "Do you want a lead shield?"

"What?" Connery said.

"Do you want an apron over you?" Kybartas said.

"Why?" Connery said.

"Some people prefer it when they're being X-rayed," Kybartas said.

So Connery let her put the apron over his chest.

"Roll over on your right side," Kybartas said. "And hold on to the table with both hands. I don't want to have to pick you up off the floor."

She took the X-ray.

"Now flat on your back," she said.

The X-ray machine hovered over Connery, pointing down at him. He seemed trapped, covered by the heavy apron, and the machine seemed somehow menacing. I was watching, and suddenly I realized what it reminded me of: a moment from a movie.

"The laser scene," I said to Connery.

"I know, I know," he said. *Goldfinger*."

Back in the examining room, Dr. Marquardt and Dr. Payne took a look at the X rays.

"You've got a little arthritis in the shoulder joint, and a little rotator-cuff tear," Dr. Marquardt said.

"Can you fix it?" Connery said.

"It's a little bigger job than the knee," Dr. Marquardt said.

"I thought the knee was more serious," Connery said.

"On a scale of one to ten, the knee operation was a two," Dr. Marquardt said. "The shoulder would be a seven."

Connery, still in his shorts, went into a golf stance.

"If I swing correctly, the ball just flies," he said.

In the car on the way back downtown, Connery said, "I don't want you to think I go to doctors all the time, but if we've got some time before I'm due back on the set, there's a dermatologist I'd like to see. I've been having some trouble with my scalp."

I was already thinking about how I was going to bring up what I had in mind. It was totally immature, and I knew I would regret it, but I had to do it.

I took a deep breath.

"In every movie, there was sort of a signature line," I said. "There was a line you said every time."

"Yes, I know it," Connery said.

"I was just wondering . . . was there a certain way you said it?" I said.

"The reading of the line?" Connery said. "I suppose there was a way that I delivered it."

"There was a pause in it," I said.

"Yes," Connery said. "There was a pause in it."

"Was the pause built in?" I said.

"I don't know," Connery said. "I just put the pause there whenever I said it."

"So how did you say it?" I said.

He began to get what I was driving at. "I just said it," he said.

I had to go for it.

"Would you mind saying it?" I said.

Connery exhaled. He seemed to think about it for a moment.

Then, in the middle of traffic, he said:

"My name is Bond . . . James Bond."

"Thank you," I said.

In the waiting room of Dr. Keith M. Kozeny's office, the receptionist asked Connery to fill out a new-patient form.

He did, and in a moment Dr. Kozeny, the dermatologist, called Connery back to his examining room.

"I have these little pinpoints on my head that itch a little," Connery said. "I think I got them from being out in the sun."

Dr. Kozeny looked at Connery's scalp under a light. "I have a little cream

I can give you," he said. "It should provide some relief. I've got some sample bottles in the back."

"Another thing," Connery said. "There's this little growth." He indicated a spot between his neck and his shoulder.

"That's nothing," Dr. Kozeny said. "We can take that right off. Let me give you a little novocain."

"Novocain?" Connery said. "Does that mean a needle?"

Shadow of a Nation

GARY SMITH

❈

Now that journalists have been given license to write like novelists, it is curious how many of them turn out to write like *bad* novelists. There is too much dialogue, and it doesn't ring true. Characters are "ruggedly handsome" or "slim." Doors are always being slammed, grins grinned, and coffee sipped.

Gary Smith is one journalist who writes like a very *good* novelist. A former sports reporter for the Philadelphia *Daily News* and a special contributor for *Sports Illustrated* since the early 1980s, Smith is the master of the nonfiction short story, the article that eloquently and dramatically inhabits the consciousness of its subject and whose momentum takes us toward the kind of artistic and emotional payoff we expect from the best literary art. "Shadow of a Nation," first published in *Sports Illustrated* in 1991, is typical. A product of estimable reporting, literary skill, and psychological and cultural understanding, the piece has the feel of a tale told, or at some moments chanted, around an Indian campfire. It effortlessly moves back and forth across time, which is appropriate, since the story of Jonathan Takes Enemy, the great Crow basketball player, simply cannot be understood without understanding the history into which Jonathan was born. He lives among ghosts; only a writer of the caliber of Gary Smith could bring those ghosts to life.

—B. Y.

❈

> I have not told you half that happened when I was young. I can think back and tell you much more of war and horse stealing. But when the buffalo went away the hearts of my people fell to the ground, and they could not lift them up again. After this nothing happened. There was little singing anywhere.
>
> —PLENTY COUPS,
> Chief of the Crows, 1930

Singing. Did you hear it? There was singing in the land once more that day. How could you not call the Crows a still-mighty tribe if you saw them on the move that afternoon? How could your heart not leave the ground if you were one of those Indian boys leading them across the valley of the Big Horn?

It was March 24, 1983, a day of thin clouds and pale sun in southern Montana. A bus slowed as it reached the crest of a hill, and from there, for the first time, the boys inside it could see everything. Fender to fender stretched the caravan of cars behind them, seven miles, eight—they had made the asphalt go away! Through the sage and the buffalo grass they swept, over buttes and boulder-filled gullies, as in the long-ago days when their scouts had spotted buffalo and their village had packed up its lodge poles and tepee skins, lashed them to the dogs and migrated in pursuit of the herd.

But what they pursued now was a high school basketball team, twelve teenagers on their way to Billings to play in a state tournament. The boys stared through their windows at the caravan. There was bone quiet in the bus. It was as if, all at once, the boys had sensed the size of this moment . . . and what awaited each of them once this moment was done.

In one seat, his nose pressed to the window was one of Hardin High's starting guards, Everette Walks, a boy with unnaturally large hands who had never known his father. In a few weeks he would drop out of school, then cirrhosis would begin to lay waste his mother. He would wind up pushing a mop at 2 A.M. in a restaurant on the Crow reservation.

In another seat sat one of the forwards, an astounding leaper named Miles Fighter. He too had grown up with no father, and recently his mother had died of cirrhosis. In just a few years, he would be unemployed and drinking heavily.

Not far away sat the other starting guard, Jo Jo Pretty Paint, a brilliant long-range shooter, a dedicated kid—just a few minutes before a game at Miles City, his coach had found him alone, crouched, shuffling, covering an invisible opponent in the locker room shower. In two years Pretty Paint would go out drinking one evening, get into a car and career over an embankment. He would go to his grave with a photograph of himself in his uniform, clutching a basketball.

Hunched nearby, all knees and elbows and shoulders, was Darren Big Medicine, the easygoing center. Sixteen months after Pretty Paint's death, he would leave a party after a night of drinking, fall asleep as he sped along a reservation road, drive into a ditch and die.

And then there was Takes Enemy . . .

Weeping. Did you hear it? There was weeping in the land that day. Sobs for those missing from that glorious caravan, those decaying in the reservation dust, for Dale Spotted and Star Not Afraid and Darrell Hill and Tim Falls Down, Crow stars of the past dead of cirrhosis and suicide and knife-stabbing and a liquor-fogged car wreck. Sobs for the slow deaths occurring every night a mile from Jonathan Takes Enemy's high school, where an entire squad of jump shooters and dunkers and power forwards from the past could be found huddling against the chill and sprawled upon the sidewalks outside the bars on the south side of Hardin. Jonathan's predecessors. Jonathan's path-beaters. "Good Lord!" cries Mickey Kern, the computer-science teacher and former basketball scorekeeper at Hardin High. "How many have we lost? How *many*?"

But Takes Enemy—he would be the one who escaped, wouldn't he? That was what the white coaches and teachers and administrators at his school kept telling him. His mind was sharp, his skill immense; the destiny of all those others needn't be his. Brigham Young wanted him. Oregon State and Arizona State had sent letters. O.J. Simpson would shake his hand in New York City and present him with a crystal cup for being named Montana's Outstanding Athlete of 1984. He was six foot two, he could twirl 360 degrees in the air and dunk the ball, he could shoot from distance. He loved to take a rebound with one hand and bring it to his other palm with a resounding *slap*, make a right-angle cut on the dribble at a velocity that ripped the court wide open, then thread it with a blind running pass, an orange blur straight from the unconscious. "Watching him play," says Janine Pease–Windy Boy, the president of Little Big Horn College, the junior college on the Crow reservation, "was like watching clean water flow across rocks."

Young Indian boys formed trails behind him, wearing big buttons with his picture on their little chests. They ran onto the court and formed a corridor for him and his teammates to trot through during pregame introductions, they touched his hands and arms, they pretended to *be* him. The coaches had to lock the gym doors to start practice. Girls lifted their pens to the bathroom walls: "I was with Jonathan Takes Enemy last night," they wrote. "I'm going to have Jonathan Takes Enemy's baby." He was a junior in high school. Already he was the father of two. Already he drank too much. Already his sister Sharolyn was dead of cirrhosis. Sometimes he walked alone in the night, shaking and sobbing. He was the newest hero of the tribe that loved basketball too much.

Takes Enemy felt the bus wheels rolling beneath him. The sun arced through the Montana sky. The circle was the symbol of never-ending life to the Crows—they saw it revealed in the shape and movement of the sun and moon, in the path of the eagle, in the contours of their tepees and the whorl of their dances. As long as the people kept faith with the circle, they believed, their tribe would endure. Jonathan settled back in his seat. Sometimes it seemed as if his life were handcuffed to a wheel, fated to take him up . . . and over . . . and down . . .

Somewhere behind him on the highway, his first cousin would soon be getting off his job on the reservation's road crew and joining the exodus to the ball game in Billings—*the* legendary Crow player, some people said; the best player, *period*, in Montana high school history, said others; the one who ignited his tribe's passion for high school basketball back in the 1950s and seemed to start this dark cycle of great players arising and vanishing: Larry Pretty Weasel. The one whose drinking helped drive him out of Rocky Mountain College in Billings and back to the reservation in 1958, just a few days before the NAIA's weekly bulletin arrived proclaiming him the best field-goal percentage shooter in the country.

Horns honked in the caravan behind Takes Enemy, passengers waved. In the long-ago days before white men had brought their horses or guns or cars or liquor, his people had chased buffalo in this same direction, across these same valleys, stampeding them over cliffs near the land where Billings would one day arise. This same creature whose skull the Crows would mount on a pole and make the centerpiece of their religious Sun Dance . . . they would drive over the edge of the cliff and then scramble down to devour.

The bus ascended another hill. Takes Enemy looked back at his people one more time.

One winter night in 1989, the custodian at Lodge Grass High on the Crow reservation forgot to flick off a switch. When the team bus pulled into the parking lot after a road game nearly four hours away, the lights above six of the seventeen outdoor baskets that surround the school were still burning. It was 2 A.M. It was snowing. Two games of five-on-five were being played.

Somehow, in the mindless way that rivers sculpt valleys and shame shapes history, the Montana Indians' purest howl against a hundred years of repression and pain had become . . . high school basketball. Yes, the Crows' eighty-three hundred people were racked by alcoholism and poverty, 75 percent of them were unemployed, the attrition rate for those who went to college was 95 percent, and their homeland, through cheating, broken treaties and sell-outs, had dwindled from the 38.8 million acres guaranteed them by the U.S. government in 1851 to the present-day 1.1 million—*however,* just let them lace on sneakers and lay their hands on a basketball. Though Indians constituted but 7 percent of Montana's population, their schools would win ten Class A, B and C state high school basketball titles between 1980 and 1990.

To the north and northwest of the Crow reservation lay the reservations of the Blackfeet, Sioux, Flathead, Assiniboine, Gros Ventre, Chippewa, Cree, Salish, Kootenai and Pen D'Oreilles; to the east lay the Cheyenne. These tribes too loved to run and shoot and jump. At tournament time in Montana, Indian teams were known to streak onto the floor for lay-up drills in war headdress, their fans to shake arenas with chants and war cries and pounding drums as their boys raced up and down the floor at speeds few white teams could sustain. Old women wrapped in blankets were known to pound the bleachers in unison with their canes, to lose their cool and swing the canes at the calves of enemy players; a few, back in the 1940s, even jabbed opponents with hat pins as the boys ran up the sidelines.

Their children spent their days shooting at crooked rims and rotting wooden backboards. Their young men drove for days to reach Indian tournaments all across America and came home to strut the dusty streets in the sheeny jackets they had won there.

Of all the perplexing games that the white man had brought with him—frantic races for diplomas and dollar bills and development—here was the one that the lean, quick men on the reservations could instinctively play. Here was a way to bring pride back to their hollow chests and vacant eyes, some physical means, at last, for poor and undereducated men to reattain the status they once had gained through hunting and battle. Crow men had never taken up the craftwork, weaving or metallurgy that males in other tribes had. They were warriors, meat eaters, nomads whose prestige and self-esteem had come almost entirely from fulfilling an intricate set of requirements—called "counting coup"—while capturing enemy horses or waging battle. A man could count coup by touching an enemy, by seizing a bow or a gun in a hand-to-hand encounter, by capturing a horse in a hostile camp or by being the pipe carrier (which signified leadership) on a successful raid. Only by counting coup, some say, could a man marry before the age of twenty-five; only by counting coup in all four categories could he become a chief. Children were named after the exploits of warriors; men starved themselves for days and slept alone in the mountains to invite dreams that would guide them on raids; a woman attained honor by the number of scalps and the war booty captured by her man, tokens of which she brandished when she danced.

And then the white men hunted the buffalo nearly to extinction and banned intertribal warfare. "It castrated the Crow male," says Ben Pease, a tribal elder who played basketball for Hardin High in the 1940s. "It created a vacuum. During World War I we still weren't citizens, so our men couldn't gain prestige from that war. People began living off the war deeds of their ancestors, depending on them for their status. Some Crows fought in World War II, and for a while these men, especially those who came back with wounds or proof of bravery, became our leaders, and our ceremonies often revolved around them. But time passed, and there weren't enough wars or war heroes; there was a void that needed to be filled. In the late fifties Larry Pretty Weasel emerged at Hardin High, and our basketball players began to be noticed in the newspapers. That continued through the sixties and seventies; more and more of our children began to play. Something had to take war's place, some way had to be found to count coups. It was basketball."

Old Crow rituals had warm blood and fresh drama again. Some players tucked tiny medicine bundles—little pouches that might contain tobacco seeds or small pieces of bone or feather—inside their socks or tied them to their jerseys, the way warriors once had tied them to their braids before entering battle. Some burned cedar and prayed before big games. The same drum cadence and honor songs used two hundred years ago to celebrate the seizing of a dozen horses or the killing of three Sioux now reverberated through gymnasiums and community halls at the capture of a basketball trophy.

"For us, a victory in a high school basketball game is a victory over everyday misery and poverty and racism," says Dale Old Horn, who heads the Department of Crow Studies and Social Sciences at Little Big Horn College. "But it's not a *real* victory. It doesn't decrease bigotry. It doesn't lessen alcoholism. It doesn't remove one Indian from the welfare rolls or return a single acre of our land. It gives us pseudo-pride. It hasn't led us on to greater things."

No Indian has ever played in the NBA. Only one, Don Wetzel of the Blackfeet, ever came off a Montana reservation to play for an NCAA Division I team (the University of Montana, 1967–71). Trophy cases in the lobbies of Indian schools throughout the state are filled with gleaming silver . . . and with black-bordered dedications to the dead. This is not just the Crow's tragedy. Two months after graduating from Browning High on the Blackfeet reservation in 1987, six-foot-three All-Stater Gary Cross Guns packed his car to go to a junior college in Kansas. One last night out was all he wanted. The next morning his sister went for a horseback ride. She found her brother's car and his body in Cut Bank Creek.

Wetzel, who once coached basketball at Browning and is now superintendent of schools in Harlem, Montana, could bear it no longer. In the three years since Cross Guns's death, he has traveled fourteen thousand miles and talked to twelve thousand kids, "trying," he says, "to make people see how scary this whole situation has become."

Every now and then, a lesser player left the Crow reservation and quietly, with no scholarship or fanfare, got his degree. But as best as anyone can figure, since 1970 only one prominent Crow player, Luke Spotted Bear, has received a college scholarship and graduated (from Mary College in Bismarck, North Dakota)—and Spotted Bear often felt that his people held this *against* him. "Some of them say I'm too good for them now," he says. "If possible, they don't want to be around me."

College recruiters stopped coming to the reservation, opportunities disappeared. Sean Fritzler, who averaged 29.8 points a game as a senior in 1989, shot 68 percent from the field and was valedictorian of his class at Plenty Coups High School, did not receive a letter of interest from a single university.

"Well, I tried to work with Indians," says Herb Klindt, coach at Rocky Mountain College for thirty-seven years. "I tried to keep them in college. But I got to a point where I just threw up my hands in disgust and gave up, and most of the other coaches did too."

The game that was a highway into mainstream America for black men . . . was a cul-de-sac for red ones. Something happened to their heroes when the drumbeats died, when the war whoops faded, when the faces in the audience were not like theirs. Something in the Crows' love for basketball was toxic.

And along came a boy who was asked to change all that. Along came a nice, shy kid—Jonathan Takes Enemy.

*　　　　*　　　　*

His people understood his significance. They sent him off to do battle with all the spiritual might they could muster. Before big games a medicine man would receive a cigarette from the Takes Enemy family, take it outside their house just in front of the Little Big Horn River in the town of Crow Agency, light it and pray to the Great Spirit for Jonathan.

Once, the medicine man wafted cedar smoke and an eagle feather over the gold chain that Takes Enemy carried with him to games for good luck. He warned Takes Enemy not to shake his opponents' hands before a game, so they could not drain away his power. All these steps were meant to protect Jonathan from harm, but he couldn't quite trust them. How could he escape the reservation and take up the solitary quest for success in the white world if he let himself think in the old way? How could he escape the dark fate of Spotted and Not Afraid and Falls Down if he believed that a man's destiny hung upon a puff of smoke in the wind?

When members of the tribe invited players on Jonathan's team to join them in sweat baths before the division and state tournaments, in order to purify their bodies and spirits in the ritual way their ancestors had before battle, Jonathan had refused; it was simply too hot in the sweat lodge. Jonathan's coach at Hardin, George Pfeifer—in his first year of coaching Indians and curious about their rituals—consented to do it. On a 20-degree day on the banks of the Little Big Horn, a powdery snow falling from the sky, the short, stout white man followed the example of eight Crow men and stripped off his clothes. "Go in, Brother George," directed one of them. Brother George got on his knees and crawled behind them into a low, dome-shaped shelter made of bent willows and covered by blankets. Inside, it was so dark that Brother George could not see the hand he held up in front of his face.

Someone poured a dipper of water over sandstones that had been heated in a bonfire for hours. Steam erupted from the rocks, hissed up and filled the sweat lodge with heat more intense than any sauna's. Sitting cheek to cheek, the men put a switch in Brother George's hand, expecting him to beat himself upon the back and legs to make it even hotter. In the darkness, he heard the others thwacking themselves, groaning and praying for his team in the Crow tongue. He gave up all pretense, flopped onto the floor and cupped his hands around his mouth to find a gulp of cooler air.

A half hour passed like this. A couple of dozen more dippers of water were poured onto the scalded rocks. At last the sweat-soaked men crawled out into the frigid daylight and promptly leapt into the icy river. Brother George's legs refused. He stood there, trembling with cold, about to be sick for three days.

"You're not going to dive in the river, Brother George?" one cried.

"No way."

"That's all right, Brother George. No goddamn magic in that."

*   *   *

But here was the difference: in a few weeks Pfeifer would laugh and tell anecdotes about the day that he left his world and entered another. Jonathan could not. Sometimes he felt the suspicious eyes of whites upon him, felt his tongue turn to stone, his English jumble, when he tried to express to them his feelings. He had but to utter that name to white ears—Takes Enemy—to feel his own ears begin to turn red.

All day and night as he grew up, the television had been on in his home, floating images into his head of white men who drove long cars and lived in wide houses, of Indians who were slow-witted and savage and usually, by the movie's end, dead. One day when he was in junior high, he saw a movie about Custer's Last Stand. He couldn't help himself; in his stomach he felt thrilled when the Indians rolled over the hills and slaughtered every white man. It bewildered him, a few years later, to learn that it was the Sioux and Cheyenne who had slain Custer's troops—that several Crow scouts had ridden *with* Custer. Everything was muddy, nothing ran clean. It was whites who made him speak English most of the day when he entered first grade, rather than the Crow language he had grown up speaking; whites who hung a dead coyote from the outside mirror of Plenty Coups High School's team bus; whites who sang "One little, two little, three little Indians" at his brothers when they played away games in high school. And yet it was Hardin's white athletic director and assistant principal, Kim Anderson, who sometimes drove far out of his way to make sure Jonathan made it to school in the morning; white teachers who offered him encouragement and hope when he passed them in the halls.

Sometimes he would bicycle up the steep incline to the Custer Battlefield, a mile and a half from his home, to sit alone near the markers that showed where each of the white men had fallen, and to stare off into the distance. From here the world stretched out and waited for him to touch it; from here he could see land and a life beyond the reservation. In the daydream he often had here, it would be *he* who was walking from the wide house to the long car, *he* waving a cheery goodbye to his wife and kids, *he* driving off down the well-paved road to the well-paid job, *he* acting out the clichéd American dream he saw on the TV screen. What choice had he? There no longer existed an Indian success cliché to dream of.

An hour or two later he would fly back down the hillside from the battlefield, barely needing to touch his pedals, determined to make the dream come true. It was only when the long hill ran out, when he labored back into his town, that the heaviness returned to his legs.

One evening a few months after his senior season, in which he averaged 28 points a game and shattered a Montana record by scoring 123 points in three state tournament games, his mother, Dorothy, held a "giveaway" in his honor. She was suffering from diabetes, which in a few years would force the amputation of her right leg below the knee and lash her to a kidney dialysis machine three days each week, yet she was determined to thank God and her tribe for the greatness of her son. Jonathan, her seventh surviving child (two had died shortly after birth), had been born with a crooked face and a too large nose, and so in her hospital bed Dorothy had lifted the infant above her eyes and turned all her fears for him over to God. "Here, Lord," she whispered, "raise him up, he's all yours." The Lord's day-care center turned out to be a basketball court; from the age of three, all Jonathan did was dribble and shoot. On dry, frigid days he would play for so long that the ball would chafe away his skin, and he would come home at dusk with bloody fingers for his mother to bandage. Dorothy's eyes still shone when she stared at the Mother's Day card he had drawn in crayon for her in second grade: three yellow flowers in a blue vase, a snow-capped mountain beneath the sun—and a man slam-dunking a basketball. And just look how the boy had turned out, with a face straight and well proportioned, a body long and strong, a name that the wind had carried across the Big Horn and Wolf Mountains, had whispered into the ears of the Cheyenne and Sioux, even laid upon the tongues of the paleskins. If only the boy's eyes would leave his shoes. If only the boy would stop stumbling home at 4 A.M. with the same stink on his breath as her husband, Lacey . . .

In the giveaway ceremony, Jonathan's exploits were to be celebrated in the same manner in which Crows once commemorated a successful raid. Besides all the cousins and uncles and aunts and nephews and nieces who gathered, Jonathan's other "family," his clan, was there. (There are ten clans in the Crow tribe, some consisting of as many as a thousand members; at birth one automatically becomes a member of the same clan as one's mother.) First Jonathan was to dance in a circle as singers sang his honor song, then he was to stand to the side as an "announcer" gave an account of his deeds, and finally he was to give away packages that consisted of four gifts to his clan uncles and aunts. It is a lovely ritual, one in which the hero, in a reversal of the white man's custom, showers his community with gifts in gratitude for the support and prayers that enabled him to succeed. Jonathan's family, just barely getting by on his father's meager salary as a custodian in the reservation hospital, couldn't possibly afford all these gifts, but in keeping with tradition his relatives had contributed so that the giveaway could take place.

Jonathan dreaded the stares that would be drawn to him if he wore the ritual Indian clothing, but he couldn't bear to disappoint his people. Slowly he pulled on the ribbon shirt, the buckskin vest, the colorful beaded armband and the war bonnet. They felt so odd upon him; he felt like no warrior at all. The first horse he had ever ridden had flung him from its back; the first bullet he had ever fired at an animal had slain a dirt clod far from its target. One of his great-great grandfathers, known simply as Fly, had been a powerful warrior, a possessor of six wives. Another, Red Bear, had been a medicine man so potent that he simply had to fill his peace pipe and hold it toward the sun and all the tobacco in it would burn. Their home had been the river-fed valleys and shimmering plains, their roof the sky, their walls the snow-topped mountains a week's walk away. Jonathan? His home was a cramped three-bedroom box in which as many as fifteen siblings and cousins often vied for sleeping space, sometimes on the floor beneath the kitchen table or even in the driveway, in the backseat of a car. Jonathan's bed, until he was seven, was a mattress jammed between the beds of his mom and dad.

With his family and his clan trailing behind him, he lowered his eyes and led them into the Little Big Horn College building for the giveaway. Rather than tokens of scalps or war booty captured from the enemy, Dorothy wore a huge orange shawl with large black letters stitched upon it that listed his coups: JONATHAN TAKES ENEMY, STATE CLASS A MVP, ALL-STATE 1ST TEAM, ALL-CONFERENCE 1984, CONVERSE BASKETBALL ALL-AMERICA HONORABLE MENTION, HERTZ AWARD, ATHLETE OF THE YEAR. Beneath were sewn four white stars; four is the Crows' sacred number. Jonathan was supposed to lead the assembly in a dance, but his feet could not quite bring themselves to do it. Almost imperceptibly he shifted his weight from one foot to the other, leading everyone around the room again and again in a plodding circle as the big drum pounded and the eleven singers in the center lifted their voices to his glory—and reminded him of his obligation to those around him.

> Outstanding man
> Look all around you
> Nothing lasts forever
> Look all around you
> Share your talent and knowledge

Share what? All he had to divvy up, it sometimes seemed, were self-doubt and pain. One day in ninth grade, at the end of basketball practice, his family had come to the school and told him that his sister had died at the age of twenty-four, after years of hard drinking. He turned to the wall and broke down. Just a few weeks later his girlfriend told him she was pregnant. Terrified, he dropped out of school for the rest of the year, hid from his teachers on the streets, sometimes even hid from his own family—and reached for the same poison as his sister had.

He knew the danger he was wooing. The night he learned he had made the varsity, a rare honor for a freshman, he and a few friends went out in a pickup truck to drink beer. A tribal police car pulled up to the truck. Alcohol was banned on the reservation, but Crow policemen sometimes looked the other way. "Go home," this cop ordered the teenagers, but the kid at the wheel panicked, jammed the accelerator and roared away. Suddenly, Takes Enemy, a boy who was afraid even on a sled, found himself hurtling down a curving country road at 100 mph, four police cars with flashing lights and howling sirens just behind him. One came screaming up beside the truck, trying to slip by and box the teenagers in. Instead of letting it pass,

Jonathan's friend lurched into the other lane to cut the car off. The pickup truck skidded off the road, toppled onto its roof and into a ditch. Takes Enemy limped out, somehow with just a badly bruised hip.

He vowed not to drink again. He remembered how uneasy he had been as a child, awakening on the mattress between his parents' beds to see the silhouette of his father stagger into the room. Even in an alcoholic haze his father was a gentle man, but still, that silhouette was not Dad—it was a *stranger*. Then, too, there was what alcohol had done to his cousin the legend, Pretty Weasel. So many fans thronged gymnasiums to watch Pretty Weasel play for Hardin High that his team had to crawl through windows to get to its locker room. He could shoot jump shots with either hand, fake so deftly that he put defenders on their pants and, at five-ten, outjump players a half foot taller. It was almost, an opponent would muse years later, "as if you were playing against a kind of enchanted person." Pretty Weasel's younger brother Lamonte got drunk and died in a car accident. Then Pretty Weasel partied his way out of a four-year college scholarship and onto a reservation road crew.

But Jonathan couldn't keep his vow. He felt as if he were locked up in a tiny room inside his body, and it was only when he was playing basketball or drinking that he could break out of it. The first time he was drunk had been in seventh grade at Crow Fair, the week-long celebration every August when the field on the edge of his town became the tepee capital of the world. Hundreds of tepees were erected, and Indians from far away came to dance and drink and sing with his people deep into the night. Jonathan slipped the bootlegger four dollars for a half pint of whiskey, poured it down—and out poured the talking, laughing Jonathan he had always yearned to be. His mother came and found him at the fair at 3 A.M. Dorothy, a sweet, passive woman dedicated to the Pentecostal Church, began yelling that he would end up just like his father . . . but that was all. In many homes across the reservation . . . that was all.

His sophomore year he moved in with his girlfriend and her parents, to help her bring up their baby daughter. Four months after his girlfriend delivered, she had news for him. She was pregnant again. His whole life seemed hopeless, his daydream of escaping snuffed out. Was it his fault? No matter how hard Jonathan thought about it, he could never be sure. So many things had happened to his people that *were* beyond their control, it had become almost impossible to identify those that were *not*. He watched three brothers go to college and quickly drop out. He watched all three of them take turns with the bottle.

There were no movie theaters or bowling alleys or malls on the reservation. When it became too dark to see the rim on the courts behind the elementary school, Jonathan and his friends would drive up and down the main street of Crow Agency—from JR's Smokehouse to the irrigation supply yard and back again—seeing the same people, the same mange-eaten dogs and rust-eaten cars, until the monotony numbed them. Then someone would say, "Let's go drinking." It was a ritual that had become a display of solidarity and shared values among his tribe, so much so that to say no was to mark oneself as an alien. None of the teenagers had enough money to buy liquor, but all of them had Indian wealth—relatives. Uncles and aunts, cousins and grandparents are as close to most Crows as parents and siblings are to a white child; a boy can walk into five or six houses without knocking, open the refrigerator without asking, eat without cleaning up the crumbs. Jonathan and his friends would each ask a relative or two for a buck, and all of the sharing and family closeness in which the Crows pride themselves would boomerang. Each kid would come up with three or four dollars to pitch into the pot, and off they'd go to the liquor stores that waited for them half a hiccup past the reservation borders. It wouldn't take long to see someone they knew who was of drinking age—the boys were related by blood or clan, it seemed, to *everyone*. They whisked their beer or whiskey back onto the reservation, where the statutes against juveniles drinking were less severe, and began gulping it as if they were racing to see who could sledgehammer reality quickest, who could forget his life first.

Jonathan's absences from school mounted. That was how he responded to trouble. He disappeared. His parents wanted him to get an education, but to make the house quiet for two hours each night and insist that he study, to pull him out of his bed when the school bus was rolling up the road—no, they couldn't quite do that. Each of them had dropped out after the ninth grade, but there was more to it than that. Almost every Crow parent had a close relative who had been forcibly taken from his home by white government agents in the early 1900s and sent off to a faraway boarding school, where his hair was shorn, his Indian clothes and name were taken away, and he was beaten for speaking his own language. How many Indians could chase an education without feeling an old pang in their bones?

On intelligence alone, Takes Enemy had made the honor roll in junior high, but now he fell behind in class and was too ashamed to ask the white teachers for help. He lost his eligibility for the first half-dozen games of both his sophomore and junior seasons, regained it after each Christmas and started dropping in 25 or 30 points with a dozen assists a game, leading his teammates flying up and down the floor. His coaches called it Blur Ball. His people called it Indian Ball. And his brothers, three of whom had also been stars at Hardin High, would whip the crowd to wildness, reaching back into imaginary quivers on their backs, loading their make-believe bows and zinging invisible arrows at the other teams; vibrating their hands over their mouths to make the high, shrill *wooo-wooo* battle cry that once froze frontiersmen's hearts; shouting themselves hoarse, making Takes Enemy feel as if he could simply lift up his legs and let his people's ecstasy wash him up and down the hardwood.

He scored 49 points in a state tournament game his senior year and was named the tournament's MVP. The outside walls of his house literally vanished, swathed in posters of congratulation from his fans. "A great major college prospect," said then BYU coach Ladell Andersen.

Do it, teachers urged him. Do it so *they* could once more believe in what they were doing, do it so *all* the Crow children whose eyes were on him could see how it was done. "Just *one*," they kept saying to him. "If just one great basketball player from here could make the break and succeed, it could change *everything*. College recruiters would start coming here, other kids would follow your example. You can be the one, Jonathan. You can be the breakthrough."

He was flown to BYU. He stared at the twenty-six thousand white faces strolling across campus. He stood at the top of the basketball arena and looked down, his eyes growing wider and wider, the court growing tinier and farther away. He had never heard of anyone like himself playing in a place like this; he couldn't even fathom it. "He said almost nothing the whole time," recalls Andersen. "I asked him a few questions. He was nodding his head yes when he should have been shaking it no."

The stack of letters from universities grew at his home. Jonathan never replied. His senior year was ending, his sun descending toward the hills. In the long-ago days a Crow hero could go on doing what he did until an arrow or a bullet found him, then let the breeze carry off his soul to the Other Side Camp. But in the twentieth century the hero's bullet was high school graduation—and then he had to go on living. "Where are you going to college?" people asked Jonathan everywhere he went. "He'll be home by Thanksgiving," they told each other. "Like crabs in a bucket, that's how we are," says Dell Fritzler, the coach at Plenty Coups High. "Whoever tries to get out, we yank him back down." Even Jonathan's own Indian name—bestowed upon him during his senior season after it had come to the medicine man in a dream—tugged downward at the boy. Iiwaaialetasaask, he was called. Does Not Put Himself Above Others. Go off to college? That would Definitely Put Himself Above Others. No, white people couldn't understand this; Jonathan himself could barely grasp the code: it was O.K. for an Indian to clench his teeth and compete as part of a team, especially an Indian team. But to do it alone, to remove yourself from the dozen people in your living room at midnight and go sit over a chemistry or algebra book—in many families, that tainted you. "We want our young people to go off and show the world how great a Crow can be," says Fritzler, "but as soon as someone does, as soon as anyone starts trying or studying too hard, a lot of us say, 'Look at him. He's trying to be a white man.' "

Takes Enemy's head spun. There were just too many mixed signals, too many invisible arrows from the audience whizzing by. Like most Crows, he'd been brought up not to make autonomous decisions but to take his cues from his immediate family, his extended family, his clan and his tribe. If *they* hadn't decided whether to assimilate into the white man's world or to recoil from it, how could he? And then, his two little children—he couldn't just walk away from them. The small living room he grew up in, with its sixty-five photographs of family members on the wall—a warm, happy place that the people in those pictures would flow into with no invitation, sit around sipping coffee and exchanging the sly puns and double entendres that his people excelled at, talking until there was nothing left to talk about and then talking some more—he couldn't just leave that behind. "Why?" he remembers wondering. "Why do I have to do it the white man's way to be a success in this world?" Why did all the human wealth he had gathered in his life, all the close friends and relatives, count for nothing when he crossed the reservation borders; why did material wealth seem to be the only gauge? And then his eyes and whys would turn the other way: "Why am I so important to my people? Why do *I* have to carry the hopes of the Crows?" All he had really wanted to do, ever since taking apart a stereo in the tenth grade and staring in wonder at all the whatchamacallits inside, was to go to a vocational school and learn electronics. But no, the herd was rolling, the people were waving and shouting him on, his legs were pulling him closer and closer to the ledge. He drank to close his eyes to it. One night at a school dance an administrator found out he was drunk. The next day he was ordered to take a chemical-dependency class.

Where were the people in his tribe who had lived through this? Why weren't they at Takes Enemy's door? Myron Falls Down, a prolific scorer for a Crow independent team in the 1970s, heard the rumors and wondered if he should do something. Six years earlier it had come to Falls Down like thunder through a hangover: that the addiction sucking the life from him and his people went beyond the beer they drank at night after playing ball, beyond the pills some ingested and the weed they puffed, beyond the Aqua Velva and Lysol and fingernail-polish remover some of them swilled; that *basketball,* the way the Crows were using it, had become a drug too. One morning in 1979, at the age of twenty-seven, he stood up from the bed where he slept every night with his ball. He went to the two glass-enclosed cases in the living room where his fifty trophies were displayed, and he began throwing them into cardboard boxes. "What are you doing?" cried his mother. She and Myron's nieces raced to unscrew the little figurines from their wooden bases before he could sweep all of them away. He grabbed the five jackets he had won in tournaments, loaded them and his trophies into his car, drove to the dumpster on the edge of Lodge Grass and heaved them all in. He would never take another drink or drug after that day. He would never play, or go to see, another basketball game—not even, ten years later, the junior high school games of his thirteen-year-old son. "If there was a connection between education and basketball on this reservation, there would be nothing wrong with basketball," says Falls Down, now a tribal health administrator. "But right now there is none. Basketball is an escape from reality for us. But I never did speak to Jonathan. I felt he or his family would have approached me if they wanted to hear my message."

Pretty Weasel—where was he? The man named Montana's Outstanding Athlete twenty-seven years before Takes Enemy, the one recruited by the University of Utah, Texas A&M and Seattle University, the cousin caught in this same crossfire eight years before Jonathan was born. Relatives and friends had sat at Takes Enemy's dinner table to spill their guts and offer counsel, but the man who with one look or word might have given Jonathan a glimpse at the ledger, at the remorse and relief in the soul of a man who has walked away from his greatness, had signaled nothing. Pretty Weasel stood in the shadows at basketball games, refused invitations to giveaways, belittled his own legend. "Never saw myself play," he said. "Can't picture myself being able to play with those black boys." Years later, at the age of fifty-one and no longer a drinker, he would wish that he had gotten his degree, explored the borders of his talent. "But I don't give advice," he says. "I guess I feel more like the whites do. That every man can be as good as he wants to. That every man does it on his own."

Graduation day came. Jonathan still hadn't decided. Barely, just barely, he got his diploma. As the teachers watched him carry it across the stage, Anderson, the assistant principal, turned and said, "I hope we're not looking at the first day of the end of his life."

> When the dance is over, sweetheart,
> I will take you home in my one-eyed Ford.

That sloppy man with the red-rimmed eyes and the puffy face, taller than the others . . .

That whiskered man with the slurred speech and the thick belly and the slumped shoulders, standing on the riverbank near Two Leggins Bridge . . . that's him. That's Jonathan Takes Enemy.

It's 1989. It's 3 A.M. When the bars close in Hardin, Jonathan and his friends often come here to sing and laugh and drink and dance until the sun comes up. At dawn somebody often hits somebody, and somebody's brother or cousin jumps in to help, and there's a whole pile of them in the dirt. And then they go home to sleep. There's no work for most of them to do.

But the sky's still dark, they all still feel good. They're singing "49" songs, native chants interspersed with English lyrics, sad-happy tunes to the beat of a drum. Takes Enemy still can't bring himself to dance or sing, but he's thumping out the drumbeat on a car hood. "Way-la-hey-ley, way-la-hey-ley . . . ya-hey-oh-way-la-hey. . . ," his companions croon. "When the dance is over, sweetheart, I will take you home in my one-eyed Ford."

The dance is over. It ended four years ago, as soon as it began. Six games into Jonathan's freshman season at Sheridan College, the Wyoming school whose scholarship offer he grabbed at the last minute because it was just an hour's drive from home, he quit. It's all still a blur to him: Hiding from everyone when it was time to leave home. Reporting to college two days late and

only because Anderson found him and took him there. Being stopped in the
yard as he left, asked by his teary-eyed mother, "Are you *sure* you want to go,
Jonathan? They aren't *forcing* you?" Trying to go from a world where it's disrespectful to look someone in the eye into one where it's disrespectful *not* to.
Sitting alone in his dorm room for days, walking alone to the cafeteria, eating alone. Telling none of the white people about his fear and loneliness.
Being guided by no one through the bewildering transition from reservation
to white world. Knowing before his first game that something was wrong,
because he had done something he could never do the night before a high
school game—sleep. Knowing that the feeling he had had at Hardin—that
he was on a mission, playing for his people—was gone. Returning to the
reservation three straight weekends and not coming back in time for Monday practice. Two weekends later not coming back at all. Walking away from
the number one–ranked junior college team in the nation . . . but whose
nation, *whose?*

"Crawled back under the blanket," said the whites. They've seen Indians
do it so often that they have a cliché for it. "Every Indian that leaves has a
rubber band attached to his back," says Jonathan's brother James. The
Crows have seen their people do it so often that they only shrug. In some
strange way, by going away to college and then by quitting, too, Takes Enemy
has managed to fulfill *everyone's* expectations.

Somewhere, perhaps upon the hilltop at Custer Battlefield, his daydream
still exists. More and more, he bicycles back there as if in search of it. After
all, he is only twenty-four, he tells himself, his life is just beginning—or
already half over, according to Crow life-expectancy charts.

His pockets are empty. He bums beer money from his dad, who has
stayed clean since entering an alcohol rehabilitation program recently. No
one will hire Jonathan. No one will buy him drinks at the bars in Hardin the
way they did when he was in high school. Sometimes he walks out of the
bars and onto the streets, sees a teacher from the school driving by and
slinks into the shadows. He's not a bum, he's *not*. Twice he has been thrown
into the reservation jail for drinking, lain on the floor all night in a cell with
thirty other drunk men, listened to them moan and retch.

He has gained more than twenty pounds. He still plays ball, lumbering up
the floor in Indian tournaments held across the state and the country. After
games the team goes drinking—and sometimes even right before them. He
signs up for courses at the reservation's junior college; some he completes,
some he doesn't. He has a new girlfriend, Trudi Big Hair, and two more children, Jonathan and Tashina. The four of them sleep in a small room at his
parents' house, and no one ever hints that it's time he moved out. Sometimes in the morning the children jump on him in bed and shout, exploding
his hangovers. He drifts back to sleep until noon, goes to a class or two, kills
a few hours staring at the TV or picking up his welfare check, plays pickup
basketball with his friends until dark . . . and then often starts all over again.

Each time he drinks, Trudi etches an X on the calendar. Day by day, Jonathan watches his life get crossed out.

Once or twice he has gone to see his old school play. He doesn't go inside. He watches from a half-open door. It's not his court anymore, not his domain. A new hero has arisen, a boy at Lodge Grass High named Elvis Old Bull. Old Bull took his team to state titles in 1988 and 1989, was named tournament MVP both years, noticed kids beginning to dress and cut their hair like he does, heard himself called a major college prospect. He has a child, but isn't married; he skips school too much; he drinks too much; his eyes are haunted. Sometimes Jonathan feels as if there is something he could tell the boy—but no, he can't, he *can't*. Old Bull enters a rehabilitation center just after his junior season. The treatment fails. He misses far too many days of school to remain eligible for his final season, but the people need that third straight title too much, and school administrators can't quite bring themselves to sit him down. "You're going to end up just like Jonathan Takes Enemy," people in the tribe keep telling him. He leads his team to the third state title, wins his third tournament MVP trophy, then simply stops going to school. He watches his classmates graduate through eyes swollen from a car wreck from another night's drinking. And the sun arcs across the Montana sky, and the eagle wheels, and the circle remains unbroken.

Autumn 1990. The sun drops behind the Big Horn Mountains. An orange 1980 Mustang turns onto the highway and bears north across the reservation, toward Billings. There is no caravan behind him. Takes Enemy goes alone.

His face is clean-shaven, his clothes are neat, his cheekbones have bloomed again. He is twenty-five, but he looks like that boy in those high school pictures once more. All summer he has jumped rope, slipping into his back yard to do it at midnight when no one on the reservation could see.

He presses the accelerator. Just a short visit home today; he cannot dally. He needs to get off the reservation by nightfall and back to his apartment in Billings, to Trudi and little Jonathan and Tashina, back to his new life as a student and a basketball player at Rocky Mountain College. Because when the darkness comes and his friends come . . . "To do this," he says, "I can't be near them. I *miss* them. But I have to be alone." He hasn't had a drink in months. He hears that Old Bull has made a change too, moving to Bozeman with hopes of fulfilling his high school requirements and getting a shot at college ball.

"It's *my* decision to go to college this time," Jonathan says. "I finally realized that I was running out of time. It's not that the reservation is a bad place. There are many good people there. But it's just not a place where you can become what you want to become. It's not a place where you can achieve your dreams."

Last spring he convinced Luke Gerber, the coach at Hardin High, that he was serious. Gerber called Jeff Malby, the coach at Rocky Mountain College, and Malby remembered how the clean water had once flowed across the rocks. He offered Takes Enemy a scholarship to the liberal arts college in Billings, with 810 students. So far, it fits Jonathan just right.

He passed the reservation border, glances into his rearview mirror. He knows that some people back there are now calling him an "apple"—red on the outside, white on the inside. He knows what he is leaving behind, what he is losing. Knows it in the morning when he passes his new neighbors in Billings and they just barely nod. Knows it when it's midnight and he and Trudi are buried in textbooks, and the apartment is silent. "It's just too quiet here," he'll say. "We're so isolated." And when he lies in bed at night and thinks of his sick mother, he knows it then, too.

His eyes move back to the windshield. Ahead of him, over the rolling hills, across the sage and buffalo grass, he can just make out the soft electric glow of Billings. He's starting to get an idea of what lies this way. He's passing all four of his classes. He's averaging 19.8 points and 4.6 assists for his new team. He's just getting his bearings, but his coaches say that he'll soon establish himself as the best player in Montana and that he's destined to be an NAIA All-America before he's done.

Everything's still so new to him. Paying his own rent each month from the grant money allotted to him by the tribe and the Bureau of Indian Affairs, paying electric bills, buying his own food. Studying until 1 A.M., making sure that Trudi gets off to Eastern Montana College in the morning, that his kids get off to day care and preschool, living in the white man's world, in a hurry, on a schedule.

He wants to go back to the reservation someday and help kids to take the risk, to see both the beauty and the danger of the circle. But he may never live there again. He rolls down his car window. He listens to the air. There is no singing in the land. There is only a quiet, sad-happy song inside a young man's heart.

From *What It Takes: The Way to the White House*

RICHARD BEN CRAMER

∞

As a newspaper journalist, Richard Ben Cramer won a 1979 Pulitzer Prize for his dispatches from the Middle East. His stories, published in the Philadelphia *Inquirer,* portrayed individuals on all sides caught in the maelstrom of politics and war. As a magazine journalist, Cramer has contributed stories to *Rolling Stone* and *Esquire* on such American icons as Jerry Lee Lewis and Ted Williams.

When Cramer received a $500,000 advance for a book on the 1988 presidential election, he spent it all on research. In the year leading up to the national party conventions, he crisscrossed the United States to cover the preliminary skirmishes, and family stories, of six candidates. The result, published in 1992 during another presidential campaign, was *What It Takes: The Way to the White House,* a thousand pages of intimate reporting on the psychology of political ambition.

Cramer's revelations rarely dealt with the candidates' secret peccadilloes. He focused on each man's childhood dreams, the origins of his gigantic self-confidence, and his tireless (and often shameless) political drive. To tell these stories, Cramer wrote in the voice of an insider—slangy, exclamatory, and freely associative—as if the narrator were within each candidate's inner circle. At times the voice is even within the candidate's mind.

Cramer's chapters on the 1988 New Hampshire primary were especially provocative. In the final days of the Republican race, George Bush overtook Bob Dole on the strength of a TV blitz focusing on a pledge never to raise taxes. As Cramer showed, New Hampshire offered a preview of the fall campaign, a microcosm of modern presidential politics, and a glimpse of each candidate's essential self.

—K. K.

∾

That weekend, Dole felt it slipping away. Before he ever saw the Straddle Ad . . . before network numbers showed his curve topping out and Bush on the way up again . . . even with Wirthlin still telling him, "You're going to win— three or four points, at least . . . maybe big—ten or better."

"No, I'm not," Dole said. "I'm going to lose by five or six."

What Dole felt was the heat slipping from his own events. What disappeared was that feeling of history pushing with him. He could still go out and say (as he did) that momentum was his: five days ago, Bush had led in New Hampshire by twenty points—now Bush's lead was *nothing* . . . but the reason for that momentum was back in Iowa—there was nothing new bringing voters to Dole.

What Dole saw on TV were pictures of Bush—Bush touring with Ted Williams, Bush throwing snowballs, Bush at McDonald's . . . on a forklift . . . driving a plow. The guy was showing he wasn't going to curl up and die. There was news tape of busloads of college volunteers for Bush, arriving in state, met by Atwater. Each kid got a map and a kit and an area to cover. They were organized—twenty colleges! (Dole was lucky to have people who'd been to college.) The Bush operation put out tens of thousands of fliers and made twenty thousand calls, reminding voters to watch "Ask George Bush." It was an obvious phony, a "town meeting" of Ailes-town . . . but by the time the Bushies had thumped the tub so hard, the TV ran snips of the thing like it was news!

Dole did his events—schools, old-age homes, town halls—remembering to say, at almost every stop, that Bob Dole was not going to raise taxes. He'd look for revenue—anyone facing a deficit had to look everywhere he could— but Dole would not raise the rates in the new income-tax law. The crowds applauded—good crowds—hundreds of people in a little town! But, as Dole muttered in the car, he was "dipping the ocean with a spoon." At that moment, Bush might be reaching a hundred thousand viewers with the message that Dole could not wait to get at their wallets.

By that weekend, even Rudman's people were bitching: their plan had been ignored—they were sold out! Where was Dole's tax ad? Rudman himself came at Dole to complain about Brock. "Even a half-baked Senate campaign can turn an ad around in two days!" Dole just said: "What can I do now?" . . . In fact, he *had* an attack ad on Bush—the Footprints Ad: boots crunching through snow while a narrator ran through Bush's résumé . . . the last shot showing the snow—undisturbed. (Bush never left any footprints, despite all those Important Jobs.) The ad was ready before the week began, but Rudman said it was too negative. (They were winning! Bob had to Be Nice!) . . . Now it was too late. Dole hadn't bought airtime.

There was one chance to send a message, statewide: a televised debate at

St. Anselm College. Dole spent most of ninety minutes trying to Be Nice . . . and angling for a chance to answer Bush on taxes. But all of a sudden, from Dole's other side, Pete du Pont pulled out a copy of the standard New Hampshire no-tax pledge—and poked it at Dole.

"Sign it," du Pont said.

Dole wasn't going to sign anything—couldn't hold it down to sign it, couldn't read it without his glasses! (If Dole were the kind to sign whatever they handed him, he could have saved himself a huge headache on the INF treaty—he could have signed on, like Bush, before he'd even seen the thing.)

But now he was squinting at this paper, on stage, on TV—with du Pont and everyone else staring at him . . . what was he supposed to do? This kind of stunt was fine for du Pont. But if Dole got to be President, he was going to have to close a gap of $200 billion a year.

Dole let the paper drop from his gaze. "Give it to George," he said. "I'd have to read it first."

Good line. Got a laugh. And Dole lost his chance to make his point on taxes.

Dole would replay that scene in his head for years afterward. Sometimes he'd lie awake at night, thinking what he could have said. Maybe he should have signed the damn thing.

It was certainly bad politics to refuse—his supporters said it killed his chances in New Hampshire. They said it was the only time in '88 that anyone lost on a matter of public policy.

He did lose, decisively. By Tuesday, it wasn't close, though Dole kept hoping it wasn't true—maybe the feeling in his belly was wrong, things had changed, or . . . maybe his Big Guys were right! There were Wirthlin's numbers in the paper, again: Dole was going to win!

By Tuesday, it came clear with a sickening lurch that the big mistake was saying—ever—Dole was going to win. If Dole could have set his goal for the week to cutting into Bush's lead, he might have looked terrific. But it wasn't Dole who said—aloud—he was going to win. That's what he had Big Guys for. That's what people told Dole to do: find some guys and turn the campaign over. Well, he did that! . . . What'd it get him?

They'd sat there all weekend and done *nothing* . . . while Bush killed him! Seemed like every ten minutes on TV: Bob Dole was gonna raise your taxes! Bob Dole wouldn't back Reagan on the INF! Bob Dole would raise the price of *heating oil* . . . for God's sake, in the middle of winter! Bush might as well have said that Dole liked to bury children in ice! . . . Bush and Ailes . . . *killed him* . . . while Dole and his Big Guys sat in their hotel.

Dole did his events that Tuesday morning—enough to get on TV . . . then it was lunch, and back to the hotel for a meeting with the savants. Bill Brock was there, along with the Political Director he'd hired (another twelve grand a month), Bernie Windon. There were a couple of true Dole-folk who shrank into the woodwork, as they did whenever high Klingons were present.

Rudman's smart guys were in and out, with news from local polling places. Wirthlin was there, of course, as was Dole's old pollster, Tully Plesser—both calling friends at the networks for news of the exit polls. David Keene, Dole's right-winger consultant, flew up from D.C. He was drafting a statement ("We've come a long way . . . proud of our volunteers . . .") for Dole to use if the news was true—if he had fallen short.

Keene detested Brock and disrespected Windon—not just as ideological sellouts, but incompetents, wastrels, and failures. Rudman's people were furious at Wirthlin, contemptuous of the Dole command that pissed away this chance in New Hampshire. The true and humble Dole-folk reviled all Klingons and regarded the New Hampshire ops with secret but satisfying sneers of comeuppance—those were the know-it-alls who tried to tell *Bob Dole* what to do! . . . That evening, CNN reported "a high official in the Dole campaign said this election was kicked away by people who didn't know what they were doing." The source might have been any man in that room. (The sad fact—Riker breathed the word amid the faithful: the "high official" was Dole.)

Dole was sitting on the luggage bench at the foot of his bed while this gaggle of helpers discussed his prospects. That meant he had his back to half of them. That was okay. They tell you, you've got to hand the campaign over . . . till you lose—then it's your fault.

He thought it was his fault—he could have signed that paper from du Pont. He could have insisted they make the ad about taxes. He could have ordered them to run the ad about Bush. They tell you, people don't like that kind of ad—maybe they don't. But they watch it. Bush knew that—his people did. Dole thought it would have been different if he'd had an Atwater, someone to carry the attack. Dole couldn't get Brock to *answer* Atwater—Brock thought it was beneath him. Dole said, "I'll do it myself." Then everybody's wringing their hands: *Oh, no! Senator's got to Be Nice!* He was nice. No one answered Atwater.

But nobody's got to be nice when they're kickin' you in the face! A *President's* got to be tough. People didn't know Dole was tough. People knew what they saw on TV—they thought Bob Dole was a liar. *Bush made him a liar.* All the while, they told Bob Dole he was winning—so he sat on his hands and took it.

"Look," Keene was saying, "we get through Super Tuesday if we target right, we got four million for media, if you target that, we get back to the Midwest with a spending edge, and then . . ."

Brock said: "We've got eight hundred thousand."

Dole looked up, his eyes on the wall opposite. He didn't speak. He looked like he'd frozen.

"Eight hundred thousand for Super Tuesday?" Keene was humphing—he wanted it clear whose doing this was. "Well, if I were *you*, I'd start cannibalizing everything I could get my hands on. We gotta have at least . . ."

Brock said, "Eight hundred thousand for the campaign."

"Total?"

"There's four million budget!"

"Things have changed."

Dole knew things changed last fall, when he handed it over . . . changed at L Street—had to rent another floor of that building, glass walls. You walked in, there were glass walls, two or three layers, you could look through, past the valets and flunkies, to Bill Brock. Cars waiting downstairs—limos, drivers, guys standing around . . . staff, consultants. Clink said it cost a hundred thousand a day just to keep the doors open. Hands off! . . . Dole was hands off—and they spent his money.

He turned it over and they cut his throat!

He would *never* do that again.

When would he ever have the chance again?

It was over. The Big Guys were talking about the South, Super Tuesday, Illinois. But Dole knew it was over. The way Bush was organized down South, Dole's only chance was to win New Hampshire, to win everything on the way to Super Tuesday. Dole didn't speak again in that meeting. Didn't talk to Brock that afternoon.

That night, George Bush won New Hampshire by nine points. Dole spent the night trying to be gracious: he hit his marks, he made his statement, he thanked his volunteers and supporters, he vowed to go on. He smiled ruefully and told the cameras: he'd made up a lot of ground in a week—he never expected things to be easy.

At the end of the night, the very end . . . he was on live remote with NBC . . . and who was next to Brokaw—beaming like the cohost of the big election special? George Bush! . . . But Dole didn't know that. He had no monitor . . . no one warned him. He was sandbagged.

Brokaw said to Bush: Any message for Dole?

"Naw, just wish him well," Bush said. "And meet him in the South."

Then, Brokaw and Bush, both smiling, turned toward the monitors—to see Dole . . . but he couldn't see them. He was sitting in a hotel room, looking at a camera lens. The talk in his earpiece sounded like the chatter before any interview:

Senator, can we get a mike check? . . .

Senator, can you hear Tom? . . .

And then Brokaw's voice:

Senator? Any message for the Vice President?

It was Dole's face on the air—but he didn't know that. . . . The camera caught the dark flash in Dole's eyes, as he said:

"Yeah. Stop lying about my record."

Dole said later, he deserved one chance to tell the truth.

Elizabeth said later, Bob was *so* tired . . . he was not himself.

Of course, the wise-guy community said right away, Dole was a hatchet man. New Hampshire proved, the voters *saw*, Dole could never learn to Be Nice.

What did it prove? What did any of it prove? All the work, all the people who helped him—little people who never took a dime, didn't want anything—they're the ones who got shafted for trying, against the odds. Dole thought he should have known. He blamed himself. There were a hundred things he could have done, could have *tried*. God knows, he tried, but . . .

He couldn't sleep—couldn't sleep at all, lay there all night, tried to lie still . . . until he couldn't try anymore and it was five o'clock and there was no reason to lie in bed. That's when Dole came down to the lobby of the hotel and sat—no one around, he just sat. Pen in his hand. Careful suit. Perfect shirt, tie. And no one around. What would he have said, anyway? He was sorry? . . . He *was* sorry. He didn't say that often . . . but that's what it was, this time.

This was his time. And now, it was over.

He'd lost it, lost the feeling—and the hope. It was always going to be tough in the South, even if he'd won New Hampshire. Bush had been making friends in the South for . . . well, ten years, probably more. People would say to Dole: "Well, we like you, Bob. But this is George's time . . ."

When was Bob Dole's time?

This was his time. And they took it away! . . . He'd lost before. He wasn't going to whine. But this time was different. This time, he couldn't sleep at all, couldn't stop his head: things that could have been different . . . all the things he'd done . . . probably wrong—half the things, anyway.

But the worst part wasn't things he'd done. It was the pictures of Bush—that's what he couldn't stop—*pictures of Bush!* In his head! Bush throwing snowballs, driving trucks, forklifts . . . unwrapping his Big Mac. Dole never wanted to see that in his head. And he never wanted to say—even in his head . . .

It would not leave him alone . . . five in the morning! Had to come down to the lobby . . . but he couldn't get away from it. For the first time in his career—first time in thirty years, anyway—Bob Dole said to himself:

"Maybe I could have done that . . . if I was whole."

THE REPORTER
TAKES THE STAGE

The Spike

GEORGE ORWELL

∞

George Orwell (1903–1950) was still using his real name, Eric Blair, in 1931 when he published "The Spike" in *Adelphi* magazine. By the time it reappeared in 1933, cut and reshaped into two discrete chapters of *Down and Out in Paris and London*, he had found not only a pen name but an identity as a writer. (The original version appears here.)

As the son of a colonial civil servant, Eric Blair described his class status as "lower-upper-middle." At eighteen he graduated from Eton. But after five years in Burma as a colonial policeman, and another in Paris as a menial worker, he returned to England with no gentlemanly ambitions. Instead, he explored slum life in London, traveled with tramps, and occasionally stayed in workhouse wards known as "spikes." In France his poverty had been involuntary; in England it was a role, a disguise that enabled him to update a favorite book: Jack London's *The People of the Abyss.*

In London's account, the chapter titled "The Spike" dwells on disgusting sights, smells, and sensations, and ends on a Darwinian note: the men of the spike, quintessential losers in the economic struggle for existence, "clutter the earth with their presence, and are better out of the way." By contrast, Blair focuses on the petty indignities that accompany public charity, and on the ever-present consciousness of class—surfacing as snobbery even among the down and out. His report, in the form of a sketch, dramatizes more than London's and editorializes less.

In *Down and Out in Paris and London,* George Orwell wove this material into a continuous narrative about poverty. In the process, he found his vocation as a politically engaged reporter: an idiosyncratic socialist with conservative tastes and a passion for honesty transcending party affiliation. Orwell later became famous for novels about totalitarianism (*Animal Farm* and *Nineteen Eighty-four*), but his reputation as a novelist has been outstripped by his achievement and influence as a journalist. After reading through Orwell's collected nonfiction, the critic Irving Howe observed: "In his readiness to stand alone and take on all comers, Orwell was a model for every writer of our age."

—K. K.

∞

It was late afternoon. Forty-nine of us, forty-eight men and one woman, lay on the green waiting for the spike to open. We were too tired to talk much. We just sprawled about exhaustedly, with homemade cigarettes sticking out of our scrubby faces. Overhead the chestnut branches were covered with blossom, and beyond that great woolly clouds floated almost motionless in a clear sky. Littered on the grass, we seemed dingy, urban riff-raff. We defiled the scene, like sardine-tins and paper bags on the seashore.

What talk there was ran on the Tramp Major of this spike. He was a devil, everyone agreed, a tartar, a tyrant, a bawling, blasphemous, uncharitable dog. You couldn't call your soul your own when he was about, and many a tramp had he kicked out in the middle of the night for giving a back answer. When you came to be searched he fair held you upside down and shook you. If you were caught with tobacco there was hell to pay, and if you went in with money (which is against the law) God help you.

I had eightpence on me. "For the love of Christ, mate," the old hands advised me, "don't you take it in. You'd get seven days for going into the spike with eightpence!"

So I buried my money in a hole under the hedge, marking the spot with a lump of flint. Then we set about smuggling our matches and tobacco, for it is forbidden to take these into nearly all spikes, and one is supposed to sur- render them at the gate. We hid them in our socks, except for the twenty or so per cent who had no socks, and had to carry the tobacco in their boots, even under their very toes. We stuffed our ankles with contraband until any- one seeing us might have imagined an outbreak of elephantiasis. But it is an unwritten law that even the sternest Tramp Majors do not search below the knee, and in the end only one man was caught. This was Scotty, a little hairy tramp with a bastard accent sired by cockney out of Glasgow. His tin of cig- arette ends fell out of his sock at the wrong moment, and was impounded.

At six the gates swung open and we shuffled in. An official at the gate entered our names and other particulars in the register and took our bun- dles away from us. The woman was sent off to the workhouse, and we others into the spike. It was a gloomy, chilly, lime-washed place, consisting only of a bathroom and dining-room and about a hundred narrow stone cells. The terrible Tramp Major met us at the door and herded us into the bathroom to be stripped and searched. He was a gruff, soldierly man of forty, who gave the tramps no more ceremony than sheep at the dipping-pond, shoving them this way and that and shouting oaths in their faces. But when he came to myself, he looked hard at me, and said:

"You are a gentleman?"

"I suppose so," I said.

He gave me another long look. "Well, that's bloody bad luck, guv'nor," he said, "that's bloody bad luck, that is." And thereafter he took it into his head to treat me with compassion, even with a kind of respect.

It was a disgusting sight, that bathroom. All the indecent secrets of our underwear were exposed; the grime, the rents and patches, the bits of string doing duty for buttons, the layers upon layers of fragmentary garments, some of them mere collections of holes held together by dirt. The room became a press of steaming nudity, the sweaty odours of the tramps competing with the sickly, sub-faecal stench native to the spike. Some of the men refused the bath, and washed only their "toe-rags," the horrid, greasy little clouts which tramps bind round their feet. Each of us had three minutes in which to bathe himself. Six greasy, slippery roller towels had to serve for the lot of us.

When we had bathed our own clothes were taken away from us, and we were dressed in the workhouse shirts, grey cotton things like nightshirts, reaching to the middle of the thigh. Then we were sent into the dining-room, where supper was set out on the deal tables. It was the invariable spike meal, always the same, whether breakfast, dinner or supper—half a pound of bread, a bit of margarine, and a pint of so-called tea. It took us five minutes to gulp down the cheap, noxious food. Then the Tramp Major served us with three cotton blankets each, and drove us off to our cells for the night. The doors were locked on the outside a little before seven in the evening, and would stay locked for the next twelve hours.

The cells measured eight feet by five, and had no lighting apparatus except a tiny, barred window high up in the wall, and a spyhole in the door. There were no bugs, and we had bedsteads and straw palliasses, rare luxuries both. In many spikes one sleeps on a wooden shelf, and in some on the bare floor, with a rolled-up coat for pillow. With a cell to myself, and a bed, I was hoping for a sound night's rest. But I did not get it, for there is always something wrong in the spike, and the peculiar shortcoming here, as I discovered immediately, was the cold. May had begun, and in honour of the season—a little sacrifice to the gods of spring, perhaps—the authorities had cut off the steam from the hot pipes. The cotton blankets were almost useless. One spent the night in turning from side to side, falling asleep for ten minutes and waking half frozen, and watching for dawn.

As always happens in the spike, I had at last managed to fall comfortably asleep when it was time to get up. The Tramp Major came marching down the passage with his heavy tread, unlocking the doors and yelling to us to show a leg. Promptly the passage was full of squalid shirt-clad figures rushing for the bathroom, for there was only one tub full of water between us all in the morning, and it was first come first served. When I arrived twenty tramps had already washed their faces. I gave one glance at the black scum on top of the water, and decided to go dirty for the day.

We hurried into our clothes, and then went to the dining-room to bolt our breakfast. The bread was much worse than usual, because the military-minded idiot of a Tramp Major had cut it into slices overnight, so that it was as hard as ship's biscuit. But we were glad of our tea after the cold, restless night. I do not know what tramps would do without tea, or rather the stuff they miscall tea. It is their food, their medicine, their panacea for all evils. Without the half gallon or so of it that they suck down a day, I truly believe they could not face their existence.

After breakfast we had to undress again for the medical inspection, which is a precaution against smallpox. It was three-quarters of an hour before the doctor arrived, and one had time now to look about him and see what manner of men we were. It was an instructive sight. We stood shivering naked to the waist in two long ranks in the passage. The filtered light, bluish and cold, lighted us up with unmerciful clarity. No one can imagine, unless he has seen such a thing, what pot-bellied, degenerate curs we looked. Shock heads, hairy, crumpled faces, hollow chests, flat feet, sagging muscles—every kind of malformation and physical rottenness were there. All were flabby and discoloured, as all tramps are under their deceptive sunburn. Two or three figures seen there stay ineradicably in my mind. Old "Daddy," aged seventy-four, with his truss, and his red, watering eyes: a herring-gutted starveling, with sparse beard and sunken cheeks, looking like the corpse of Lazarus in some primitive picture: an imbecile, wandering hither and thither with vague giggles, coyly pleased because his trousers constantly slipped down and left him nude. But few of us were greatly better than these; there were not ten decently built men among us, and half, I believe, should have been in hospital.

This being Sunday, we were to be kept in the spike over the weekend. As soon as the doctor had gone we were herded back to the dining-room, and its door shut upon us. It was a lime-washed, stone-floored room, unspeakably dreary with its furniture of deal boards and benches, and its prison smell. The windows were so high up that one could not look outside, and the sole ornament was a set of Rules threatening dire penalties to any casual who misconducted himself. We packed the room so tight that one could not move an elbow without jostling somebody. Already, at eight o'clock in the morning, we were bored with our captivity. There was nothing to talk about except the petty gossip of the road, the good and bad spikes, the charitable and uncharitable counties, the iniquities of the police and the Salvation Army. Tramps hardly ever get away from these subjects; they talk, as it were, nothing but shop. They have nothing worthy to be called conversation, because emptiness of belly leaves no speculation in their souls. The world is too much with them. Their next meal is never quite secure, and so they cannot think of anything except the next meal.

Two hours dragged by. Old Daddy, witless with age, sat silent, his back bent like a bow and his inflamed eyes dripping slowly on to the floor. George, a dirty old tramp notorious for the queer habit of sleeping in his hat, grumbled about a parcel of tommy that he had lost on the road. Bill the moocher, the best built man of us all, a Herculean sturdy beggar who smelt of beer even after twelve hours in the spike, told tales of mooching, of pints stood him in the boozers, and of a parson who had peached to the police and got him seven days. William and Fred, two young ex-fishermen from Norfolk, sang a sad song about Unhappy Bella, who was betrayed and died in the snow. The imbecile drivelled about an imaginary toff who had once given him two hundred and fifty-seven golden sovereigns. So the time passed, with dull talk and dull obscenities. Everyone was smoking, except Scotty, whose tobacco had been seized, and he was so miserable in his smokeless state that I stood him the makings of a cigarette. We smoked furtively, hiding our cigarettes like schoolboys when we heard the Tramp Major's step, for smoking, though connived at, was officially forbidden.

Most of the tramps spent ten consecutive hours in this dreary room. It is hard to imagine how they put up with it. I have come to think that boredom is the worst of all a tramp's evils, worse than hunger and discomfort, worse even than the constant feeling of being socially disgraced. It is a silly piece of cruelty to confine an ignorant man all day with nothing to do; it is like chaining a dog in a barrel. Only an educated man, who has consolations within himself, can endure confinement. Tramps, unlettered types as nearly all of them are, face their poverty with blank, resourceless minds. Fixed for ten hours on a comfortless bench, they know no way of occupying themselves, and if they think at all it is to whimper about hard luck and pine for work. They have not the stuff in them to endure the horrors of idleness. And so, since so much of their lives is spent in doing nothing, they suffer agonies from boredom.

I was much luckier than the others, because at ten o'clock the Tramp Major picked me out for the most coveted of all jobs in the spike, the job of helping in the workhouse kitchen. There was not really any work to be done there, and I was able to make off and hide in a shed used for storing potatoes, together with some workhouse paupers who were skulking to avoid the Sunday morning service. There was a stove burning there, and comfortable packing cases to sit on, and back numbers of the *Family Herald,* and even a copy of *Raffles* from the workhouse library. It was paradise after the spike.

Also, I had my dinner from the workhouse table, and it was one of the biggest meals I have ever eaten. A tramp does not see such a meal twice in the year, in the spike or out of it. The paupers told me that they always gorged to the bursting point on Sundays, and went hungry six days of the week. When the meal was over the cook set me to do the washing-up, and told me to throw away the food that remained. The wastage was astonishing; great dishes of beef, and bucketfuls of bread and vegetables, were pitched away like rubbish, and then defiled with tea-leaves. I filled five dustbins to overflowing with good food. And while I did so my fellow tramps were sitting two hundred yards away in the spike, their bellies half filled with the spike

dinner of the everlasting bread and tea, and perhaps two cold boiled potatoes each in honour of Sunday. It appeared that the food was thrown away
from deliberate policy, rather than that it should be given to the tramps.

At three I left the workhouse kitchen and went back to the spike. The
boredom in that crowded, comfortless room was now unbearable. Even
smoking had ceased, for a tramp's only tobacco is picked-up cigarette ends,
and, like a browsing beast, he starves if he is long away from the pavement-
pasture. To occupy the time I talked with a rather superior tramp, a young
carpenter who wore a collar and tie, and was on the road, he said, for lack of
a set of tools. He kept a little aloof from the other tramps, and held himself
more like a free man than a casual. He had literary tastes, too, and carried
one of Scott's novels on all his wanderings. He told me he never entered a
spike unless driven there by hunger, sleeping under hedges and behind ricks
in preference. Along the south coast he had begged by day and slept in
bathing-machines for weeks at a time.

We talked of life on the road. He criticised the system which makes a
tramp spend fourteen hours a day in the spike, and the other ten in walking
and dodging the police. He spoke of his own case—six months at the public
charge for want of three pounds' worth of tools. It was idiotic, he said.

Then I told him about the wastage of food in the workhouse kitchen, and
what I thought of it. And at that he changed his tune immediately. I saw that
I had awakened the pew-renter who sleeps in every English workman.
Though he had been famished along with the rest, he at once saw reasons
why the food should have been thrown away rather than given to the tramps.
He admonished me quite severely.

"They have to do it," he said. "If they made these places too pleasant
you'd have all the scum of the country flocking into them. It's only the bad
food as keeps all that scum away. These tramps are too lazy to work, that's all
that's wrong with them. You don't want to go encouraging of them. They're
scum."

I produced arguments to prove him wrong, but he would not listen. He
kept repeating:

"You don't want to have any pity on these tramps—scum, they are. You
don't want to judge them by the same standards as men like you and me.
They're scum, just scum."

It was interesting to see how subtly he dissociated himself from his fellow
tramps. He has been on the road six months, but in the sight of God, he
seemed to imply, he was not a tramp. His body might be in the spike, but his
spirit soared far away, in the pure aether of the middle classes.

The clock's hands crept round with excruciating slowness. We were too
bored even to talk now, the only sound was of oaths and reverberating
yawns. One would force his eyes away from the clock for what seemed an
age, and then look back again to see that the hands had advanced three
minutes. Ennui clogged our souls like cold mutton fat. Our bones ached

because of it. The clock's hands stood at four, and supper was not till six, and there was nothing left remarkable beneath the visiting moon.

At last six o'clock did come, and the Tramp Major and his assistant arrived with supper. The yawning tramps brisked up like lions at feeding-time. But the meal was a dismal disappointment. The bread, bad enough in the morning, was now positively uneatable; it was so hard that even the strongest jaws could make little impression on it. The older men went almost supperless, and not a man could finish his portion, hungry though most of us were. When we had finished, the blankets were served out immediately, and we were hustled off once more to the bare, chilly cells.

Thirteen hours went by. At seven we were awakened, and rushed forth to squabble over the water in the bathroom, and bolt our ration of bread and tea. Our time in the spike was up, but we could not go until the doctor had examined us again, for the authorities have a terror of smallpox and its distribution by tramps. The doctor kept us waiting two hours this time, and it was ten o'clock before we finally escaped.

At last it was time to go, and we were let out into the yard. How bright everything looked, and how sweet the winds did blow, after the gloomy, reeking spike! The Tramp Major handed each man his bundle of confiscated possessions, and a hunk of bread and cheese for midday dinner, and then we took the road, hastening to get out of sight of the spike and its discipline. This was our interim of freedom. After a day and two nights of wasted time we had eight hours or so to take our recreation, to scour the roads for cigarette ends, to beg, and to look for work. Also, we had to make our ten, fifteen, or it might be twenty miles to the next spike, where the game would begin anew.

I disinterred my eightpence and took the road with Nobby, a respectable, downhearted tramp who carried a spare pair of boots and visited all the Labour Exchanges. Our late companions were scattering north, south, east and west, like bugs into a mattress. Only the imbecile loitered at the spike gates, until the Tramp Major had to chase him away.

Nobby and I set out for Croydon. It was a quiet road, there were no cars passing, the blossom covered the chestnut trees like great wax candles. Everything was so quiet and smelt so clean, it was hard to realise that only a few minutes ago we had been packed with that band of prisoners in a stench of drains and soft soap. The others had all disappeared; we two seemed to be the only tramps on the road.

Then I heard a hurried step behind me, and felt a tap on my arm. It was little Scotty, who had run panting after us. He pulled a rusty tin box from his pocket. He wore a friendly smile, like a man who is repaying an obligation.

"Here y'are, mate," he said cordially. "I owe you some fag ends. You stood me a smoke yesterday. The Tramp Major give me back my box of fag ends when we come out this morning. One good turn deserves another—here y'are."

And he put four sodden, debauched, loathly cigarette ends into my hand.

From "The Bronx Slave Market"

MARVEL COOKE

∞

The impulse to go undercover, so common among reporters in the late nineteenth century, waned thereafter, partly because society became less interested in the downtrodden and partly because journalistic fashions come and go. But putting on unfamiliar clothing—literally and figuratively—and passing unnoticed through an exotic realm has remained a powerful tool, both for pure fact-gathering and for the implications it raises about social and literary identity. Orwell's "The Spike" proves this proposition; so does Marvel Cooke's "The Bronx Slave Market."

Cooke has been a witness to the century. Born in Minnesota in 1903, she came to New York after college to work as an assistant to the legendary social critic, editor, and activist W. E. B. Du Bois, and was party to the last years of the Harlem Renaissance. In 1950, after two decades of working on black newspapers in New York, she became the only black and the only woman reporter on *The Daily Compass,* a generally circulated paper descended from Marshall Field's *PM.* Cooke had become a member of the Communist party in 1935, and in the years after *The Daily Compass* folded in 1952, she worked for various left-wing organizations, including the Angela Davis Defense Committee. Now retired from writing and activism, she lives in the same Harlem apartment building that has been her home since 1933.

"The Bronx Slave Market," which appeared as a five-part series in *The Daily Compass* in 1950, concerns one of several New York street corners where, in the years following World War II, black women would gather every day in hopes of being hired as domestic day laborers. The women, Cooke wrote in the first installment, "are most easily identified . . . by the paper bag in which they invariably carry their work clothes. It is a sort of badge of their profession."

—B. Y.

∞

I took up my stand in front of Woolworth's in the early chill of a December morning. Other women began to gather shortly afterwards. Backs pressed to the store window, paper bags clutched in their hands, they stared bleakly, blankly into the street. I lost my identity entirely. I was a member of the "paper bag brigade."

Local housewives stalked the line we had unconsciously formed, picked out the most likely "slaves," bargained with them and led them off down the street. Finally I was alone. I was about to give up, when a short, stout, elderly woman approached. She looked me over carefully before asking if I wanted a day's work. I said I did.

"How much do you want?"

"A dollar." (I knew that $1 an hour is the rate the Domestic Workers Union, the New York State Employment Service and other bona fide agencies ask for work by the hour.)

"A dollar an hour!" she exclaimed. "That's too much. I pay seventy cents."

The bargaining began. We finally compromised on eighty cents. I wanted the job.

"This way." My "madam" pointed up Townsend Ave. Silently we trudged up the street. My mind was filled with questions, but I kept my mouth shut. At 171st St., she spoke one of my unasked questions.

"You wash windows?"

I wasn't keen on washing windows. Noting my hesitation, she said: "It isn't dangerous. I live on the ground floor."

I didn't think I'd be likely to die from a fall out a first-floor window, so I continued on with her.

She watched me while I changed into my work clothes in the kitchen of her dark three-room, ground-floor apartment. Then she handed me a pail of water and a bottle of ammonia and ordered me to follow her into the bedroom.

"First you are to wash this window," she ordered.

Each half of the window had six panes. I sat on the window ledge, pulled the top section down to my lap and began washing. The old woman glanced into the room several times during the 20 minutes it took me to finish the job. The window was shining.

I carried my work paraphernalia into the living room, where I was ordered to wash the two windows and the venetian blinds.

As I set about my work again, I saw my employer go into the bedroom. She came back into the living room, picked up a rag and disappeared again. When she returned a few moments later, I pulled up the window and asked if everything was all right.

"You didn't do the corners and you missed two panes." Her tone was accusing.

I intended to be ingratiating because I wanted to finish this job. I started to answer her meekly and offer to go back over the work. I started to explain that the windows were difficult because the corners were caked with paint. I started to tell her that I hadn't missed a single pane. Of this I was certain. I had checked them off as I did them, with great precision—one, two, three—

Then I remembered a discussion I'd heard that very morning among members of the "paper bag brigade." I learned that it is a common device of Slave Market employers to criticize work as a build-up for not paying the worker the full amount of money agreed on. . . .

Suddenly I was angry—angry at this slave boss—angry for all workers everywhere who are treated like a commodity. I slipped under the window and faced the old woman. The moment my feet hit the floor and I dropped the rag into the pail of water, I was no longer a slave.

My voice shaking with anger, I exclaimed: "I washed every single pane and you know it."

Her face showed surprise. Such defiance was something new in her experience. Before she could answer, I had left the pail of dirty water on the living room floor, marched into the kitchen and put on my clothes. My ex–slave boss watched me while I dressed.

"I'll pay you for the time you put in," she offered. I had only worked 40 minutes. I could afford to be magnanimous.

"Never mind. Keep it as a Christmas present from me."

With that, I marched out of the house. It was early. With luck, I could pick up another job.

Again I took my stand in front of Woolworth's. . . . I found five members of the "paper bag brigade" still waiting to be "bought" by housewives looking for cheap household labor.

One of the waiting "slaves" glanced at me. I hoped she would be friendly enough to talk.

"Tough out here on the street," I remarked. She nodded.

"I had one job this morning, but I quit," I went on. She seemed interested.

"I washed windows for a lady, but I fired myself when she told me that my work was no good."

It was as though she hadn't heard a thing I said. She was looking me over appraisingly.

"I ain't seen you here before," she said. "You're new, ain't you?"

I was discovering that you just can't turn up cold on the market. The "paper bag brigade" is like a fraternity. You must be tried and found true before you are accepted. Until then, you are on the outside, looking in.

Many of the "new" women are fresh from the South, one worker told me, and they don't know how to bargain.

"They'll work for next to nothing," she said, "and that makes it hard for all of us." . . .

There seemed little likelihood of another job that morning. I decided to call it a day. As I turned to leave, I saw a woman coming down the street with the inevitable bag under her arm. She looked as if she knew her way around.

"Beg your pardon," I said as I came abreast of her. "Are you looking for work, too?"

"What's it to you?" Her voice was brash and her eyes were hard as steel. She obviously knew her way around and how to protect herself. No foolishness about her.

"Nothing," I answered. I felt crushed.

"I'm new up here. Thought you might give me some pointers," I went on.

"I'm sorry, honey," she said. "Don't mind me. I ain't had no work for so long, I just get cross. What you want to know?"

When I told her about my morning's experience, she said that "they [the employers] are all bitches." She said it without emotion. It was spoken as a fact, as if she had remarked, "The sun is shining."

"They all get as much as they can out of your hide and try not to pay you if they can get away with it." . . .

I asked if she had ever tried the State Employment Service.

"I can't," she answered candidly. "I'm on relief and if the relief folks ever find out I'm working another job, they'll take it off my check. Lord knows, it's little enough now, and it's going to be next to nothing when they start cutting in January."

She went on down the street. I watched her for a moment before I turned toward the subway. I was half conscious that I was being followed. At the corner of 170th St. and Walton Ave., I stopped a moment to look at the Christmas finery in Jack Fine's window. A man passed me, walked around the corner a few yards on Walton Ave., retraced his steps and stopped by my side.

I crossed Walton Avenue. The man was so close at my heels that when I stopped suddenly on the far corner, he couldn't break his stride. I went back to Jack Fine's corner. When the man passed me again, he made a lewd, suggestive gesture, winked and motioned me to follow him up Walton Ave.

I was sick to my stomach. I had had enough for one day.

Woolworth's on 170th Street was beginning to feel like home to me. It seemed natural to be standing there with my sister slaves, all of us with paper bags, containing our work clothes, under our arms.

I recognized many of the people who passed. I no longer felt "new."

But I was not at peace. Hundreds of years of history weighed upon me.

I was the slave traded for two truck horses on a Memphis street corner in 1849.

I was the slave trading my brawn for a pittance on a Bronx street corner in 1949.

As I stood there waiting to be bought, I lived through a century of indignity.

It was that rainy, muggy day after the two-day Christmas holiday, but there was no holiday cheer in the air. The "paper bag brigade" assembled unwillingly—slowly. These women knew, even better than I, that there would be little trading on the market that day.

I waited with six others one hour—two. Four gave up and left. Then a young couple approached, looked us over, and bargained with the woman next to me. I didn't blame them for not choosing me. She was younger, obviously more fit. She went off trailing behind them.

I was alone. I was drenched and my feet were wet. I was about to give up when a little old woman with a bird-like face asked if I wanted a few hours' work.

I let my fellow workers down, for I went off with my new "madam" with a bad verbal contract—75 cents an hour for an undetermined amount of work, knowing only vaguely that there was general cleaning and ironing to do. What that meant in detail, I didn't know.

By the end of the day I knew very well. Every muscle in my body ached.

On the way back to her home on Morris Ave., the little old woman informed me that she had been hiring girls off the street for 20 years and that she'd never been disappointed.

"I've always picked nice girls," she said. "I knew you were nice the minute I laid eyes on you."

That pat on the back was worse in a way than a kick in the teeth.

"I was almost afraid to ask you to work," she went on. "You look like you belong in an office."

I glanced down at her. Was it in her mind that the old clothing I was wearing was too good for a Negro? I couldn't interpret her expression. She had none.

'What's your name?" she asked.

"Margo," I answered, quickly selecting a name near enough my own not to be confusing. However, five minutes later, she was calling me Margie. By the end of the day I was Mary, a name that to her mind, I suppose, was more befitting my station.

Her apartment had two rooms and a bath, with the kitchen unit in one end of the large living room.

She watched while I changed into my work clothes. She seemed to be taking stock of my strength. Without turning, I could almost see her licking her lips. She had bought a strapping, big animal.

"First, rinse those clothes and hang them on the drier in the bathroom," she said, pointing to the tub. "And then you can dust the walls down all over the house." She handed me a makeshift wall mop.

There were endless chores. I ironed a man's shirt, four full-length ruffled curtains and a tablecloth. I took the stove apart and gave it a thorough cleaning. I cleaned and scrubbed the refrigerator, a cabinet, the sink and tub and shelves above the sink. I rubbed all of the furniture in the apartment with furniture oil.

Through it all, my employer sat unperturbed, watching my every move. Once or twice she arose from her chair to flick imaginary dust from an area I had already been over. Then she'd sit down again to watch me.

She was gentle, and persistent, and cruel. She had bought her pound of flesh and she was going to get every ounce of work out of it.

The pay-off came when she asked me to get down on my hands and knees to scrub all the floors, which were covered with linoleum. I just couldn't do it. I realized with some surprise that the ache in my chest I had been feeling all day was old-fashioned anger. Suddenly it flared. I stood up and faced her.

"I can't do it."

"Can't do what, Mary?"

"I can't scrub all of these floors on my hands and knees. This method of scrubbing went out with the Civil War. There are all sorts of modern methods to make floor washing easier. And if they must be scrubbed that way, why don't you provide a knee pad?"

My words tumbled over each other. But she caught their meaning all right.

"All of my girls clean the floors this way, Mary," she said gently. "This is the way I like them done. Well, finish this one and I'll call it a day."

I gathered strength as I scrubbed the floor. I cleaned with the strength of all slaves everywhere who feel the whip.

I finished the job. After I had changed into my street clothes, this gentle Mrs. Legree counted $3.40 into my hands—exactly what she owed me (by the hands of the clock, at least) minus my car fare.

I was too exhausted to argue about 20 cents.

From *The Earl of Louisiana*

A. J. LIEBLING

❧

Along with Joseph Mitchell, Alva Johnston, Morris Markey, St. Clair Mc-
Kelway, and a few others, Abbott Joseph Liebling (1904–1963) helped
make *The New Yorker* the premier showcase for literary journalism in mid-
century America. A native Manhattanite, Liebling wrote about prizefighters, reporters, Broadway lowlife; during World War II, he filed memorable
dispatches from France. What united his disparate subjects was that they
were always viewed through the prism of A. J. Liebling. Although his
early training was as a newspaperman, Liebling quickly, and thankfully,
unlearned the trade's rules about impersonal objectivity: his best pieces are
so delightful *because* of the digressions on arcane racetrack lore or Moroccan cuisine, the unexpected similes, the editorial asides.

    In 1959, Liebling went down to Louisiana to cover the reelection cam-
paign of Governor Earl "Uncle Earl" Long, the late Huey's brother and an
eccentric of estimable proportions. Shortly before Liebling's arrival, Long
had been institutionalized by his wife, Blanche. Theo Cangelosi, a Baton
Rouge attorney, had also made allegations of financial impropriety. Now he
was trying simultaneously to clear his name and win an election. As with
Boswell and Johnson, Liebling's dispatches (collected in the book *The Earl
of Louisiana*) are at least as much about the genially misanthropic reporter
as about the governor. So, in this excerpt, we hear about Liebling's theories
of humor, his "ability to exude sincerity as far as a llama can spit," and—in
the most Boswellian moment of all—the way he cadges a dinner invitation
from Long by seizing an opportune moment to offer him a lemon drop.

—B. Y.

❧

Lunch in the Capitol House confirmed my theory of culture belts. The
Capitol House lies within ninety miles of Galatoire's and Arnaud's in New
Orleans, but its fare bears a closer resemblance to Springfield, Illinois,
where a distinguished hostess once served me a green salad peppered with

marshmallow balls. So Dover, within twenty-three miles of the French coast, eats as un-Frenchly as the farthest side of England.

A statewide convention of high-school football coaches was in session, and there seemed to be hundreds of them—a cross between the plantation overseer and YMCA secretary. In the night they congregated over bottles of bourbon, building character for transfusion to their charges in the fall, and in the day they attended seminars on whipless slave-driving and how to induce adolescents to play on two broken legs.

The Governor's Mansion at Baton Rouge, like the State House, is a monument to the administration of Huey Long. The story goes that the Martyr, when he gave the architect his riding orders, said he wanted a replica of the White House so he would know where the light switches were in the bathrooms when he got to be President. Huey lived in it from 1930 to 1932, and Earl inhabited it briefly for the first time in 1939, when he filled out the term of the unfortunate Mr. Leche. After that he lived in it again as Governor from 1948 to 1952 and began a third tenancy in 1956. When I saw it, Longs had been masters of the house for ten out of the nineteen years of its existence, almost enough to give it status as an elegant old gracious family mansion. Earl and Miz Blanche had built their new house in a newer and more stylish part of Baton Rouge, before the Governor decided against moving.

Tom [Sancton, a local reporter] and I arrived half an hour before the hour appointed for the Governor's press conference. We were in company with Margaret Dixon, editor of the Baton Rouge *Morning Advocate,* one of the few people in Louisiana who could usually get along with Earl. Mrs. Dixon, handsome, stable and strong, has a firm, serene personality. She is the kind of woman motherless drunks turn to instinctively to tell their troubles with their wives.

"Earl is the funniest man in the world," she said over her shoulder as she drove. "Life in the Capitol would be dull without him. Did you hear what he said to Leander Perez, the States'-rights man, the other day? 'What are you going to do now, Leander? Da Feds have got da atom bomb.' And when Blanche went to live in the new house, he said she had 'dis-domiciled' him. He has a style of his own—he's a poet. He said he was so groggy when he got off the plane that took him to Houston that he felt 'like a muley bull coming out of a dipping vat.' I don't know why it should, but the 'muley' makes that line sound a hundred times funnier. It just means without horns."

"It particularizes the image," I suggested. "Bull is a word so general that it blurs: the dumb bulls in Spain, the tight bulls in flytime. 'Muley' makes you see a bull of a peculiarly ineffectual kind."

"You sound more like Huey," Mrs. Dixon said. "Earl says, 'Huey tried that highbrow route and he couldn't carry his home parish. I carry Winn Parish every time.'

"He praises Huey up, but he never misses a chance to mention when he does something better—in 1956, when he won the Governorship on the first primary, without a runoff, the first thing he said was 'Huey never done that.' "

Now we were on the Mansion driveway lined with laurel and packed with press cars.

Inside, the press had taken over, as if the Mansion were the scene of a first-class murder and the cops were still upstairs. Reporters in large groups are ill at ease, and they try to make up for it by acting too easy. Each is preoccupied with his own time situation—his paper's deadlines and the accessibility of telephones. Each, before a public conference, shapes in his mind what would make a good story if the principal said it, and how he can trap him into saying it. If the principal delays his appearance, the reporter begins to wonder whether he will have time to write the story. Then, with further delay, he begins to wonder if he will have time to telephone. Next, he gets angry. He resents his subjection to the whims of his inferiors, and he vents his resentment by a show of elaborate contempt.

We turned left inside the fanlighted door and went down a couple of steps into a great reception room furnished like a suite in a four-star general's house on an army post, where the furniture comes out of the quartermaster's stores. The bleakness of such pieces, all bought on contract sale, increases in proportion to the square of their sum: two hotel sofas are four times as depressing as one; three, nine times. The Governor's drawing room, of good height and proportions, contained at least twenty-six paired pieces, all covered with pink or green brocade chosen for its wearing qualities. The mauve drapes were of the tint and gloss of the kind of spun-sugar candy that is usually filled with rancid peanut paste; the carpets were a flushed beige. There were two wall mirrors reflecting each other, a blackamoor candelabra, three chandeliers, and no pictures. There was not a piece of furniture from before 1930 nor a portrait of a former Governor or his lady. I wondered where the loot from the old Mansion was.

Huey had cleared out the lot, as a link with the hated aristocratic past. As it was, it made a perfect waiting room—a place in which boredom began in the first ten seconds.

At half past four the Governor's press secretary, an intimidated former state senator named Fredericks, appeared at the top of the two steps. He announced that the Governor's party had telephoned from the road: they were still about fifty miles from town, and the Governor had given orders to serve cake and coffee to the reporters and tell them to wait. Negro servants in white jackets served coffee and sponge cake, both good. A couple of the bloods of the press who covered the beat regularly had found their way to some bourbon concealed from the rest of us and came smirking back.

One fellow went about canvassing colleagues to join him in a walkout. He proposed that everybody go off and leave the Governor flat—insult to the press, showing up so late. That would let him see where he stood. His colleagues, knowing where they stood, paid no heed.

An hour passed, and the Governor's party arrived. State troopers shoved us back, and the Governor's party headed straight upstairs, to "wash up and be right back." A minute later, word came down that the Governor was going to shave. The Negroes served more coffee, this time without cake. Nobody talked of leaving now.

A reporter with good connections learned the cause of the long delay from a state cop who had ridden in the convoy. "Governor stopped at a few farms along the way to buy some guinea hens, but he couldn't get the right price on them."

Forty-five minutes more, and the Governor made his entrance. He hadn't shaved but had taken a nap and put in a telephone call to a woman friend in Alick. Fortunately for the press, she had not been at home. Once on the line, he talked for hours.

Mrs. Dixon said that this was his first press conference in the Mansion since deputy sheriffs, whom he called bone crushers, had hustled him down his own steps and into an ambulance on the night of May 30.

He was wearing a black mohair suit even less elegantly adjusted than the one at Alick, and a sober necktie of black with atom-bomb mushrooms of white and magenta. He moved to a seat in the middle of a long sofa with its back to the cold fireplace. There, crossing one leg over the other knee, which exposed his white cotton socks, he faced his familiar persecutors with the air of a country Odysseus home from a rough trip, with no Penelope to greet him.

This Odysseus didn't care if he never set eyes on Penelope again. A woman reporter asked him if he was going to make it up with Mrs. Long, and if he didn't think that would help him get the women's vote in the primary.

He said, "If dat's da price of victory, I'd rather go ahead and be defeated. After all, lots of men have lost elections before."

Somebody asked him if he was set on the special session of the Legislature and he said he was, that the call would go out before five o'clock the next day. That was the latest moment when he could call a session for Monday, August 11. The Governor must include with the call a list of the legislation he means to propose; none other can be voted at the session. He said he was readying his list.

A reporter asked him if he would include any new tax bill, and he said no, if the state won its suit against two oil companies, "we might get by with no taxes at all." But if the money did not come in that way, he would try for some new taxes at the regular session. This was a flat assumption that he would run and be re-elected.

He had already said that, rather than cut state services, he would be in favor of "any kind of a tax but a sales tax, because that falls on the poor devil."

Now he began again to lay into the rich people, who "wanted to cut out the spastic school," but the reporters, who had heard that number in his repertory, managed to get him off on Cangelosi.

"There never has been a man who *misused* and unduly *abused* my confidence like Cangelosi," the Governor said. "If he hadn't a done me like he done, and rubbed it in, I might forgive him, but that long-legged sapsucker made more money than any man I ever knew," he said, adding quickly, "of which I have not participated in any of the profits."

The Governor's moist hazel eyes, filled with sweetness, clouded over at the memory of what he had suffered. His voice, low and hoarse at the beginning of the conference, as it well might be after the weekend of stump-speaking, rose indignantly, like a fighter knocked down by a fluke punch.

"They misled me," he said. "The reason I was feeling so poorly at the last Legislature was I had kept on postponing an operation that I was to have at the Oshner Clinic in New Orleans. When my sweet little wife and my dear little nephew got me to go on that plane, they told me a damn lie that I was going to Oshner for my operation.

"Then when they got me to the plane, the bone crushers strapped me to the stretcher and a doctor stuck me through the britches with a needle. My wife and my nephew promised they would come right down to Oshner next day to see me. But the plane flew me to Galveston, and my sweet little wife hasn't showed up yet, neither my little nephew. When the plane landed me at that airport, there, they told me I was going to a rest house, where I was promised a double bed and quiet. The doctors gave me pills to make me sleep. First I took them one by one, then by the paper cupful. Then I got to chunkin' them in there by the wad. While I was in that condition, they got me to sign a thing that I wouldn't sue them for kidnapping. I went contrary to what my lawyers would have wanted." This, I learned long later, was precisely true. His Texas counsel believed he had his transporters cold under the Lindbergh Act.

Uncle Earl looked out at the reporters with bottomless pity in his eyes, as if he were recounting the ills, not of one storm-tossed traveler, but of all our common kind.

"They snatched me out without even enough clothes on me to cover up a red bug," he said, "and a week after I arrived in Texas I was enjoying the same wardrobe. They put me in a room with the door open and crazy people walking in and out all night; one of them thought it was the toilet."

"Pardon me," said a lady of the press, interrupting, "but what was the operation you were expecting?"

"I guess you can guess," the Governor answered, and he pointed down. "On my lower parts."

He was still intent on his sorrows. "Then, this Corner here," he said. "Wasn't he a nice judge to commit me to Mandeville when I come back? We been on opposite sides in politics as long as I remember, but if the position had been reversed, I might have given him a break. And Bankston, the superintendent, a man I appointed myself, could have left me out, but he wouldn't. But I got out, all right. I put *him* out and *got* out."

"Governor," a reporter queried, "what is your personal opinion of who's going to win this election?"

"I am," the seated orator replied without hesitation. "Uncle Earl. It's going to be a case of Katy bar the door. Little old Dellasoups Morrison will be second."

"And third?" pursued the questioner.

"Jimmie Davis, if he stays in the race," the man who picked himself said. "And little Willie Rainach and Big Bad Bill Dodd a dogfall for fourth." In country wrestling, a dogfall means that the men lose their footing simultaneously and both go down, which makes that fall a draw.

"We going to have a party here tomorrow, a homecoming party for the press," he said, "and you are all invited. Going to have something for everybody—religious music over here on one side of the room and honkytonk on the other. But no Bedbug Blues—that's Jimmie Davis' tune."

There was a good deal of the discourse that I have not recorded. Carried away by the stream of idiom like a drunk on a subway train, I missed a lot of stations.

Somebody asked the Governor what he thought of the Luce publications' having asked for a change of venue to a Federal court in his libel suit for 6 million dollars. He said he didn't care what kind of court the case came up in.

"They going to find themselves lighter and wiser when it's over," he said. "The Luce people been going on too long picking on people too poor to sue them, and now they're going to get it in the neck. Mr. Luce is like a man that owns a shoestore and buys all the shoes to fit himself. Then he expects other people to buy them."

This was the best thing said about publishers, I felt, since I myself wrote thirteen years ago, "To the foundation of a school for publishers, without which no school of journalism can have meaning."

I put all my admiration in my glance and edged my chair up to the end of the Governor's sofa. When I try, I can exude sincerity as far as a llama can spit, and the Governor's gaze, swinging about the room, stopped when it lit on me. My eyes clamped it in an iron grip of approval.

I inched forwarder, trying not to startle him into putting a cop on me, and said, "Governor, I am not a newspaperman. I am with you all the way about publishers. Nor am I primarily interested in politics. I came all the way down here to find out your system for beating the horses."

An expression of modest disclaimer dropped like a curtain in front of the cocky old face.

"I got no particular system," he said. "I think I'm doing good to break even. I think horse betting should be dissected—into them that can afford it and them that can't. I think if you can afford it, it's a good thing to take your mind off your troubles and keep you out in the air."

"Do you play speed ratings?" I asked. The Governor, in his eagerness to talk simultaneously about all phases of handicapping, choked up—it was the bronchiectasis—and began to cough.

Quickly, I offered him a lemon drop and he accepted it. Once it was in his mouth, I knew, from my experience among the Arabs in the opposite end of the interrupted sea, that I had won. He had accepted my salt; now he would reciprocate. The bronchiectasis struggled with the lemon drop for a moment and then yielded.

The Governor's throat cleared, and he said, "Yo'all stay'n' eat."

"Y'all stay, too," the Governor said to Mrs. Dixon and Tom and a couple of the other press people. "There's aplenty." I imagined he must have a great surplus of supermarket bargains in the larder. "Just set here and wait. We got a lot to talk about."

The reporters and television men who had deadlines were already clearing out. Earl shouted after them, "Y'all come back and I'll say this—" But they, who had waited for him so long, had had enough.

There had been so many people in the room, and for so long, that they had taken the snap out of the air conditioning. The men staying on for dinner—about fifteen of us—took off their coats and laid them down on chairs and sofas.

One of the women guests, a Northerner, inadvertently sat on a jacket a political gent had laid aside. It was a silvery Dacron-Acrilan-nylon-airpox miracle-weave nubbled in Danish-blue asterisks. She made one whoop and rose vertically, like a helicopter. She had sat on his gun, an article of apparel that in Louisiana is considered as essential as a zipper. Eyebrows rose about as rapidly as she did, and by the time she came down, she decided that comment would be considered an affectation.

A colored man brought a glass wrapped in a napkin to the Governor— "Something for my throat," the latter explained—and the members of his inner council gathered at his flanks and knees for the powwow on catfish bait. One of the bills Earl had in mind would give individual members of the Legislature scholarship funds to allot personally to young people in their districts. Another would raise the salaries of assistant attorney generals, whose friends in the Legislature might be expected to respond. There were various local baits, funds for construction. The compounders kept their voices low and mysterious, as if saying "One-half pint of fish oil, one ounce of tincture of asafetida, one ounce of oil of rhodium—that will fetch them," or "Mix equal parts of soft Limburger cheese and wallpaper cleaner—never fails." Sometimes a conspirator would be unable to suppress a laugh.

A Mr. Siegelin, a political catfisherman arriving late, brought with him two children, a girl of about ten and a boy of five.

"Give them Cokes," the Governor said, and while a state cop hurried off to fill the order, he said to the little girl, "I hope you ain't going steady yet."

The little girl shook her head, and Uncle Earl said, "That's right. I went with more than a hundred before I made up *my* mind."

Made it up too soon at that, he probably thought, as he wondered about Miz Blanche and the mortgage money.

The children took their Cokes and settled down on facing identical love seats to drink them, while their father, a fair man in shirt-sleeves, sat down to join in the bait suggestions, with his equivalent of "Cut smoked herring into bits. Soak in condensed milk several days." The group was still in the midst of bait-mixing when a plug-ugly, either a state trooper or a bodyguard from civilian life, came to the top of the steps leading to the dining room and shouted, "It's ready!" By his tone I judged him ravenously hungry.

The catfishermen remained engrossed in their concoctive deliberations, and the plug-ugly shouted at Mrs. Dixon, whom he judged less engaged, "C'mawn, *Maggie!*"

Mrs. Dixon rose, and the catfishermen, Southern gentlemen after all, perforce rose too and rushed toward the dining room in her wake, the Governor dragging the two children.

The ballroom smacked of Bachelors' Hall, lacking the touch of a woman's fastidious hand, but the dining end of the Mansion, I was happy to see, was well kept up. The long table under the great chandelier was covered with a mountain range of napkins folded into dunce caps, with streams of table silver in the valleys between them, and the iced tea, Sargassified with mint and topped with cherry, was pretty near *Ladies' Home Journal* color-ad perfection. Negro waiters and waitresses swarmed about, smiling to welcome Odysseus home. None of them, either, seemed to miss Penelope. The wanderer, his heart expanding in this happy atmosphere, propelled me to a seat at the head of the table.

He took his place at my left, with the Northern lady across the table from him. Around the long board crouched plug-uglies in sports shirts, alternating with the guests: Tom, Mrs. Dixon, Senator Fredericks, Siegelin, the two Siegelin children clutching Coca-Cola bottles, and half a dozen politicians I hadn't met. The colossal figure of Mr. Joe Arthur Sims, the Governor's personal counsel, dominated the other end of the table. Mr. Sims had his right arm in a plaster cast that kept his hand above his head, as if perpetually voting Aye. He had sustained an odd sort of fracture on July 4, he explained. It had followed hard on his stump speech for the Governor, a great oratorical effort, but he denied that he had thrown the arm out of joint. He said he was in an auto crash.

The Governor said, "We don't serve hard liquor here. Da church people wouldn't like it. But I'll get you some beer. Bob," he called to one of the somber seneschals, "get da man some beer." Quickly, the waiter fetched a can, two holes newly punched in the top, ready for drinking, and set it down on the table.

The beer bore an unfamiliar label, and the Governor said, "Dat looks like some of dat ten-cent beer from Schwegmann's." (He had probably bought it himself, on one of his raids for bargains.) "Dat looks like some of da stuff dat when da brewers got an overstock, dey sell it to da supermarkets. Get da man some *good* beer. And bring a glass—hear?"

He looked so healthy now that I ventured a compliment. "You fooled those doctors, all right," I said. "You're like that Swede Johansson—you have your own way of training."

"You see dat fight?" the Governor asked, suspending his attack on the salad, which he was tossing between his dentures with the steady motion of a hay forker. I said I had.

"I didn't see it, but I would have if I thought da fellow had a chance to lick Patterson," the Governor said. "Patterson's pretty good." (If he looked at the return fight, he was let down again.)

"I hear they've got a law here in Louisiana that a white boy can't even box on the same card with colored boys," I said.

"Yeah," said the Governor, "but dat kind of stuff is foolish. If dere's enough money in it, dey're bound to get together."

I recognized the theory of an economic resolution of the race conflict.

He sat there like a feudal lord, and his *maisnie,* the men of his household, leaned toward him like Indians around a fire. The trenchers went around, great platters of country ham and fried steak, in the hands of the black serv-ingmen, and sable damsels toted the grits and gravy. There was no court musician, possibly because he would have reminded the Earl of Jimmie Davis, but there was a court jester, and now the master called for a jape.

"Laura, Laura," he called out to one of the waitresses, "set your tray down—dere, hand it to Bob. Tell us what your husband does for a living."

"Prizefighter, sir," the girl said.

"Show us how he does when he goes in da ring," the Governor ordered.

The girl, long, thin and whippy, was instantly a-grin. This was evidently a standard turn, and she loved the spotlight. She got rid of the tray and showed how her husband climbed through the ropes, lifting her right knee high to get over the imaginary strand, and holding the hem of her short skirt against the knee as a boxer sometimes holds his robe to keep it from getting in his way. Once inside, she danced about the ring, waving her clasped hands at friends in the imaginary crowd. Then she retired to a corner and crouched on an imaginary stool until the Governor hit the rim of a glass with a gravy spoon.

The girl came out, sparring fast, dancing around the ring and mugging for friends at ringside, with an occasional wink. The opposition didn't amount to much, I could see. Laura's husband, impersonated by Laura, was jabbing him silly. Then her expression changed; the other man was begin-ning to hit her husband where he didn't like it. Her head waggled. She began to stagger. Even the bodyguards, who must have seen the act often, were howling.

"Show us how your husband does when he gets tagged," the Governor ordered, and Laura fell forward, her arms hanging over the invisible ropes, her head outside the ring, her eyes bulged and senseless.

The feudal faces were red with mirth. I applauded as hard as I could. Laura stood up and curtsied.

"You gonna let him keep on fightin'?" the Governor asked.

"I don't want him to," Laura said, "don't want him get hurt. But I don't know if he'll quit."

"Is he easier to live with when he loses?" a State Senator asked.

"Yes, sir, he is," the jester said, and took her tray back from the colleague who had been holding it.

The meal went on.

"Dat's da way some a dese stump-wormers going to be when dis primary is over," Uncle Earl said. "Hanging on da ropes. If it's a pretty day for the primary, I'll win it all. I'll denude dem all, da *Times-Picayune* included."

Outside the air-conditioned keep, the enemy might howl, but inside, the old vavasor held his court without worrying.

"Da voting machines won't hold me up," he said. "If I have da raight commissioners, I can make dem machines play 'Home Sweet Home.'" He laughed confidingly. "Da goody-goodies brought in dose machines to put a crimp in da Longs," he said. "Da first time dey was used, in 1956, I won on da first primary. Not even my brother Huey ever did dat.

"Da machines is less important dan who's allowed to vote," he said. "I appointed a man State Custodian of Voting Machines here dat run up a bill of a hundred and sixty-three thousand dollars for airplane hire in one year, just flying around da state, inspecting da machines. Good man, Southern gentleman—da *Times-Picayune* recommended him and I thought I'd satisfy dem for once. Den he got an appropriation from da Legislature to keep da machines in repair, but it said in da contract with da voting-machine company dat da company had to keep dem in repair for one year for free. So he split da money wit da company—dey sent him six thousand dollars, and den another six thousand, but I grabbed half of da second six thousand for my campaign fund. Should have took it all."

The cellarer he had sent for the name-brand beer returned with a report that none except the supermarket kind was cold.

"Dey keeping da good beer for demself," the Governor said indulgently. "You drink dis." It tasted fine.

The Northern woman, who had listened with awe to the career of the voting-machine man, asked, "What happened to him?"

"I denuded him," the Governor said. "It's an electoral office now."

"And where is he now?" the woman asked, expecting, perhaps, to hear that he was confined in a *cachot* beneath the Mansion.

"He's hypnotizing people and telling fortunes and locating oil wells," the Governor said, "and he got himself a fine blonde and built her a big house and quit home."

Outside of the *Lives of the Troubadours*, which was compiled in the thirteenth century, I had never known a better-compressed biography. I felt that I knew the denuded hypnotist well. I remembered the comparable beauty of the Governor's account of the last day of a beloved uncle in Winnfield: "He got drunk and pulled a man out of bed and got into bed with the man's wife, and the man got mad and shot my poor uncle, and he died."

I asked him what he thought of Governor Faubus of north-neighboring Arkansas, who had won a third term by closing the schools, and he said Faubus was a fine man, but nobody had told him about the Civil War.

"Fellas like Faubus and Rainach and Leander Perez and da rest of da White Citizens and Southern Gentlemen in dis state want to go back behind Lincoln," he said. "And between us, gentlemen, as we sit here among ourselves," he said, arresting a chunk of fried steak in midair and leaning forward to give his statement more impetus, "we got to admit dat Lincoln was a fine man and dat he was right."

Then, as he turned back to the steak, skewering it against a piece of ham before swallowing both, he caught my look of astonishment and cried, too late, "But don't quote me on dat!"

Since he has won his last primary, I disregard his instructions. It was a brave thing for a Governor of Louisiana to say and would have made a lethal headline in his enemies' hands: LONG ENDORSES LINCOLN; HINTS WAR BETWEEN STATES ENDED.

We had up another can of beer, and the Governor and I shared it with a sense of double complicity.

"Laura, Laura," the Governor called to his jester, "get rid of dat tray."

"Yes, sir, Mr. Governor," and the star turn passed the grits to a coworker.

"Now, Laura," the Governor said, "can you make a speech like Mr. McLemore?" (McLemore had been the White Citizens' candidate in '56.)

This was plainly another well-used bit of repertory. The Prizefighter and Mr. McLemore may be Laura's *Cavalleria* and *Pagliacci*, always done as a double bill. But I'd love to hear her sing Jimmie Davis.

She took a stance, feet wide apart and body stick-straight, looking as foolish as she could.

"Ladies and gentlemen," she said, "do not vote for Mr. Earl Long, because he has permitted da Supreme Court of da United States to make a decision by which, by which, Little White Johnny will have to attend da same school with Little Black Mary. If you wish to prevent dis, vote for, vote for—" and she hesitated, like a man fumbling in his mind for his own name. Then, running her hands over her body, she located, after some trouble, a white card in her breast pocket. The card, a planted prop, showed she had expected to perform. She took the card, peered at it, turned it around and finally read, "McLemore. Dat's it. Vote for McLemore."

The Earl howled, and so did all his guests and men-at-arms. I do not imagine that Penelope would have found it all that funny. She probably cramped his style.

The meal ended with a great volume of ice cream. The Governor, in high humor and perhaps still thinking of the frustrated voting machines, said to the lady across from him, "Would you mind if I told you a semi-bad story?"

She said she would not mind, and the Governor began: "There was an important man once who had a portable mechanical-brain thinking machine that he carried everywhere with him. Da machine was about as big as a small model of one of dose fruit machines dey have in a Elks clubhouse. When he wanted a answer—How many square feet in a room by so and so much? or, Has dat blonde a husband and is he home?—he submitted his question and da machine answered it correctly. He would write out da question on a piece of paper and put it in a slot, da machine would read it, and pretty soon it would go blam, blam, blam—blam, blam, blam—dat was da brain working, and it would give him a printed slip with da correct answer. Well, finally da man got jealous of dis machine, it was such a Jim-cracker, and he thought he take it down a little for its own good.

"So he wrote out a message: 'Where is my dear father at this minute, and what is he doing?' He put it in da slot, and da machine says, 'Blam, blam, blam,' very calm, like he had asked it something easy, and it write out da answer: 'Your dear father is in a pool hall in Philadelphia, *Penn*sylvania, at dis moment, shooting a game of one hundred points against a man named Phil Brown. Your dear father is setting down watching, and Phil Brown has da cue stick and is about to break."

"Philadelphia, *Penn*sylvania" had the romantic sound in the Governor's mouth of Coromandel in Sinbad's.

The Governor's manner changed, and his voice became indignant. " 'Why,' da man says, 'dat's da most unmitigated libelous slander I ever heard of. My dear father is sleeping in da Baptist cemetery on da side of da hill in *Pitt*sburgh, Pennsylvania, and has been for da last five years. I am sure of da dates because my dear mother who is still living reminded me of da anniversary of his death and I telegraphed ten dollars worth of flowers to place on his grave. I demand a *re*investigation and an *apology.*'

"And he writes it out and puts it in da slot. 'Dis time I got you,' he says. 'You ain't nothing but a machine anyway.'

"Da machine reads da message and gets all excited. It says, 'Blam, *Blam*' and 'Blam, *blam*,' like it was scratching its head, and den 'Blam, blam, blam, blam . . . blam, blam, blam, blam,' like it was running its thoughts through again, and den 'BLAM!' like it was mad, and out comes da message."

All eyes were on the Governor now, as if the ladies and men-at-arms half expected him to materialize the ticker tape.

"Da message said 'REPEAT,' " the Governor said, "It said 'REPEAT' and den, 'RE-REPEAT. Your dear father is in a pool hall at Philadelphia, *Penn*sylvania, playing a game with a man named Phil Brown. YOUR MOTHER'S LEGALLY WEDDED HUSBAND is in the Baptist cemetery on the side of the hill in *Pitt*sburgh, *Penn*sylvania, and has been there these last five years, you BASTARD. The only change in the situation is that Phil Brown has run fourteen and missed, and your old man now has the cue stick. I predict he will win by a few points.' "

It broke everybody up, and soon the Governor said to the outsiders politely, "Y'all go home. We got a lot to do tonight." But he said he might be able to see me at nine next morning.

I arose at that hour and got over there, but there were already so many cars on the driveway that if it hadn't been morning I would have guessed there was a cockfight in the basement. Inside the Mansion, the nearly book-less library on the right of the door that serves as a waiting room was full of politicians, all wearing nubbly suits and buckskin shoes, and each sporting the regulation enlargement of the left breast beneath the handkerchief pocket. (This group included no left-handed pistol shot.) The length of the queue demonstrated that the public reaction to the speeches had been favorable, and that the sheiks who had raided the herds in Earl's absence were there to restore the stolen camels.

A Negro in a white jacket came in and asked the ritual "Y'all have coffee?" Since I had no deal to offer, I just had coffee and went.

Odysseus ruled in Ithaca again.

The Fight to Live

AL STUMP

∞

Tom Wolfe has cited this "extraordinary chronicle" of Ty Cobb's last days as a direct predecessor of new journalism. Al Stump published the story in *True* magazine 1961, a year after ghostwriting Cobb's sanitized and self-serving memoir, *My Life in Baseball*. In "The Fight to Live" the ghostwriter materializes as nursemaid, enabler, and ambivalent judge. Stump dramatizes the psychopathic ferocity that made the young Cobb such a great individual performer, while evoking the universal struggle of an old man raging against the dying of the light.

After graduating from the University of Washington and apprenticing at the Portland *Oregonian,* Stump built a successful freelance career. In the 1950s and '60s he was a mainstay at *True,* a magazine memorable for innovative nonfiction. (Among its frequent contributors were Jimmy Breslin, W. C. Heinz, and Mackinlay Kantor.)

"The Fight to Live" follows *True* style in its rapid narrative pace. The opening episode, a terrifying trek down a snowy mountain, is the first of several journeys that connect the story, and Cobb's restless energy is conveyed in the very tempo of Stump's writing. The scenes are constructed around dialogue that continually deepens our interest in both characters.

In 1994 Cobb and Stump were portrayed by Tommy Lee Jones and Robert Wuhl in the movie *Cobb,* loosely based on "The Fight to Live." That same year Stump tried to set the whole record straight with a new biography, *Cobb: The Life and Times of the Meanest Man Who Ever Played Baseball.*

—K. K.

∞

Ever since sundown the Nevada intermountain radio had been crackling warnings: "Route 50 now highly dangerous. Motorists stay off. Repeat: AVOID ROUTE 50."

By one in the morning the 21-mile, steep-pitched passage from Lake Tahoe's 7,000 feet in Carson City, a snaky grade most of the way, was snow-

271

struck, ice-sheeted, thick with rock slides, and declared unfit for all transport vehicles by the State Highway Patrol.

Such news was right down Ty Cobb's alley. Anything that smacked of the impossible brought an unholy gleam to his eye. The gleam had been there in 1959 when a series of lawyers advised Cobb that he stood no chance against the Sovereign State of California in a dispute over income taxes, whereupon he bellowed defiance and sued the commonwealth for $60,000 and damages. It had been there more recently when doctors warned that liquor would kill him. From a pint of whiskey per day he upped his consumption to a quart and more.

Sticking out his chin, he told me, "I think we'll take a little run into town tonight."

A blizzard rattled the windows of Cobb's luxurious hunting lodge on the crest of Lake Tahoe, but to forbid him anything—even at the age of 73—was to tell an ancient tiger not to snarl. Cobb was both the greatest of all ball players and a multimillionaire whose monthly income from stock dividends, rents, and interests ran to $12,000. And he was a man contemptuous, all his life, of any law other than his own.

"We'll drive in," he announced, "and shoot some craps, see a show and say hello to Joe DiMaggio—he's in Reno at the Riverside Hotel."

I looked at him and felt a chill. Cobb, sitting there haggard and unshaven in his pajamas and a fuzzy old green bathrobe at one o'clock in the morning, wasn't fooling.

"Let's not," I said. "You shouldn't be anywhere tonight but in bed."

"Don't argue with me!" he barked. "There are fee-simple sonofbitches all over the country who've tried it and wish they hadn't." He glared at me, flaring the whites of his eyes the way he'd done for 24 years to quaking pitchers, basemen, umpires, and fans.

"If you and I are going to get along," he went on ominously, *"don't increase my tension."*

We were alone in his isolated ten-room $75,000 lodge, having arrived six days earlier, loaded with a large smoked ham, a 20-pound turkey, a case of Scotch and another of champagne, for purposes of collaborating on Ty's book-length autobiography—a book which he'd refused to write for 30 years, but then suddenly decided to place on record before he died. In almost a week's time we hadn't accomplished 30 minutes of work.

The reason: Cobb didn't need a risky auto trip into Reno, but immediate hospitalization, and by the emergency-door entrance. He was desperately ill and had been even before we'd left California.

We had traveled 250 miles to Tahoe in Cobb's black Imperial limousine, carrying with us a virtual drugstore of medicines. These included Digoxin (for his leaky heart), Darvon (for his aching back), Tace (for a recently operated-upon malignancy of the pelvic area), Fleet's compound (for his infected bowels), Librium (for his "tension"—that is, his violent rages), codeine (for his pain), and an insulin needle-and-syringe kit (for his diabetes), among a dozen other panaceas which he'd substituted for doctors. Cobb despised the medical profession.

At the same time, his sense of balance was almost gone. He tottered about the lodge, moving from place to place by grasping the furniture. On any public street, he couldn't navigate 20 feet without clutching my shoulder, leaning most of his 208 pounds upon me and shuffling along at a spraddle-legged gait. His bowels wouldn't work: they impacted, repeatedly, an almost total stoppage which brought moans of agony from Cobb when he sought relief. He was feverish, with no one at his Tahoe hideaway but the two of us to treat this dangerous condition.

Everything that hurts had caught up with his big, gaunt body at once and he stuffed himself with pink, green, orange, yellow, and purple pills—guessing at the amounts, often, since labels had peeled off many of the bottles. But he wouldn't hear of hospitalizing himself.

"The hacksaw artists have taken $50,000 from me," he said, "and they'll get no more." He spoke of "a quack" who'd treated him a few years earlier. "The joker got funny and said he found urine in my whiskey. I fired him."

His diabetes required a precise food-insulin balance. Cobb's needle wouldn't work. He'd misplaced the directions for the needed daily insulin dosage and his hands shook uncontrollably when he went to plunge the needle into a stomach vein. He spilled more of the stuff than he injected.

He'd been warned by experts—from Johns Hopkins to California's Scripps Clinic—that liquor was deadly. Tyrus snorted and began each day with several gin-and-orange-juices, then switched to Old Rarity Scotch, which held him until night hours, when sleep was impossible, and he tossed down cognac, champagne, or "Cobb Cocktails"—Southern Comfort stirred into hot water and honey.

A careful diet was essential. Cobb wouldn't eat. The lodge was without a cook or manservant—since, in the previous six months, he had fired two cooks, a male nurse, and a handyman in fits of anger—and any food I prepared for him he pushed away. As of the night of the blizzard, the failing, splenetic old king of ball players hadn't touched food in three days, existing solely on quarts of booze and booze mixtures.

My reluctance to prepare the car for the Reno trip burned him up. He beat his fists on the arms of his easy chair. "I'll go alone!" he threatened.

It was certain he'd try it. The storm had worsened, but once Cobb set his mind on an idea, nothing could change it. Beyond that, I'd already found that to oppose or annoy him was to risk a violent explosion. An event of a week earlier had proved *that* point. It was then I discovered that he carried a loaded Luger wherever he went and looked for opportunities to use it.

En route to Lake Tahoe, we'd stopped overnight at a motel near Hangtown, California. During the night a party of drunks made a loud commotion in the parking lot. In my room next to Cobb's, I heard him cursing and then his voice, booming out the window.

"Get out of here, you ———— heads!"

The drunks replied in kind. Then everyone in the motel had his teeth jolted.

Groping his way to the door, Tyrus the Terrible fired three shots into the dark that resounded like cannon claps. There were screams and yells. Reaching my door, I saw the drunks climbing each other's backs in their rush to flee. Before anyone could think of calling the police, the manager was cut down by the most caustic tongue ever heard in a baseball clubhouse.

"What kind of a pest house is this?" roared Cobb. "Who gave you a license, you mugwump? Get the hell out of here and see that I'm not disturbed! I'm a sick man and I want it quiet!"

"B-b-beg your pardon, Mr. Cobb," the manager said feebly. He apparently felt so honored to have baseball's greatest figure as a customer that no police were called. When we drove away the next morning, a crowd gathered and stood gawking with open mouths.

Down the highway, with me driving, Cobb checked the Luger and reloaded its nine-shell clip. "Two of those shots were in the air," he remarked. "The *third* kicked up gravel. I've got permits for this gun from governors of three states. I'm an honorary deputy sheriff of California and a Texas Ranger. So we won't be getting any complaints."

He saw nothing strange in his behavior. Ty Cobb's rest had been disturbed—therefore he had every right to shoot up the neighborhood.

About then I began to develop a twitch of the nerves, which grew worse with time. In past years, I'd heard reports of Cobb's weird and violent ways, without giving them much credence. But until early 1960 my own experience with the legendary Georgian had been slight, amounting only to meetings in Scottsdale, Arizona, and New York to discuss book-writing arrangements and to sign the contract.

Locker-room stories of Ty's eccentricities, wild temper, ego, and miserliness sounded like the usual scandalmongering you get in sports. I'd heard that Cobb had flattened a heckler in San Francisco's Domino Club with one punch; had been sued by Elbie Felts, an ex–Coast League player, after assaulting Felts; that he booby-trapped his Spanish villa at Atherton, California, with high-voltage wires; that he'd walloped one of his ex-wives; that he'd been jailed in Placerville, California, at the age of 68 for speeding, abusing a traffic cop, and even inviting the judge to return to law school at his, Cobb's, expense.

I passed these things off. The one and only Ty Cobb was to write his memoirs and I felt highly honored to be named his collaborator.

As the poet Cowper reflected, "The innocents are gay." I was eager to start. Then—a few weeks before book work began—I was taken aside and tipped off by an in-law of Cobb's and one of Cobb's former teammates with the Detroit Tigers that I hadn't heard the half of it. "Back out of this book deal," they urged. "You'll never finish it and you might get hurt."

They went on: "Nobody can live with Ty. Nobody ever has. That includes two wives, who left him, butlers, housekeepers, chauffeurs, nurses, and a few mistresses. He drove off all his friends long ago. Max Fleischmann, the yeast-cake heir, was a pal of Ty's until the night a house guest of Fleischmann's made a remark about Cobb spiking other players when he ran the bases. The man only asked if it was true. Cobb knocked the guy into a fish pond and after that Max never spoke to him again. Another time, a member of Cobb's family crossed him—a woman, mind you. He broke her nose with a ball bat.

"Do you know about the butcher? Ty didn't like some meat he bought. In the fight, he broke up the butcher shop. Had to settle $1,500 on the butcher out of court."

"But I'm dealing with him strictly on business," I said.

"So was the butcher," replied my informants. "In baseball, a few of us who really knew him well realized that he was wrong in the head—unbalanced. He played like a demon and had everybody hating him because he *was* a demon. That's how he set all those records that nobody has come close to since 1928. It's why he was always in a brawl, on the field, in the clubhouse, behind the stands and in the stands. The public's never known it, but Cobb's always been off the beam where other people are concerned. Sure, he made millions in the stock market—but that's only cold business. He carried a gun in the big league and scared hell out of us. He's mean, tricky, and dangerous. Look out he doesn't blow up some night and clip you with a bottle. He specializes in throwing bottles.

"Now that he's sick he's worse than ever. And you've signed up to stay with him for months. You poor sap."

Taken aback, but still skeptical, I launched the job—with my first task to drive Cobb to his Lake Tahoe retreat, where, he declared, we could work uninterrupted.

As indicated, nothing went right from the start. The Hangtown gunplay incident was an eye-opener. Next came a series of events, such as Cobb's determination to set forth in a blizzard to Reno, which were too strange to explain away. Everything had to suit his pleasure or he had a tantrum. He prowled about the lodge at night, suspecting trespassers, with the Luger in hand. I slept with one eye open, ready to move fast if necessary.

At one o'clock of the morning of the storm, full of pain and 90-proof, he took out the Luger, letting it rest casually between his knees. I had continued to object to a Reno excursion in such weather.

He looked at me with tight fury and said, biting out the words:

"In 1912—and you can write this down—I killed a man in Detroit. He and two other hoodlums jumped me on the street early one morning with a knife. I was carrying something that came in handy in my early days—a Belgian-made pistol with a heavy raised sight at the barrel end.

"Well, the damned gun wouldn't fire and they cut me up the back."

Making notes as fast as he talked, I asked, "Where in the back?"

"WELL, DAMMIT ALL TO HELL, IF YOU DON'T BELIEVE ME, COME AND LOOK!" Cobb flared, jerking up his shirt. When I protested that I believed him implicitly, only wanted a story detail, he picked up a half-full whiskey glass and smashed it against the brick fireplace. So I gingerly took a look. A faint whitish scar ran about five inches up the lower left back.

"Satisfied?" jeered Cobb.

He described how, after a battle, the men fled before his fists.

"What with you wounded and the odds 3–1," I said, "that must have been a relief."

"Relief? Do you think they could pull that on *me*? I WENT AFTER THEM!"

Where anyone else would have felt lucky to be out of it, Cobb chased one of the mugs into a dead-end alley. "I used that gun-sight to rip and slash and tear him for about ten minutes until he had no face left," related Ty, with relish. "Left him there, not breathing, in his own rotten blood."

"What was the situation—where were you going when it happened?"

"To catch a train to a ball game."

"You saw a doctor, instead?"

"I DID NOTHING OF THE SORT, DAMMIT! I PLAYED THE NEXT DAY AND GOT TWO HITS IN THREE TIMES UP!"

Records I later inspected bore out every word of it: on June 3, 1912, in a blood-soaked, makeshift bandage, Ty Cobb hit a double and triple for Detroit, and only then was treated for the knife wound. He was that kind of ball player through a record 3,033 games. No other player burned with Cobb's flame. Boze Bulger, a great old-time baseball critic, said, "He was possessed by the Furies."

Finishing his tale, Cobb looked me straight in the eye.

"You're driving me to Reno tonight," he said softly. The Luger was in his hand.

Even before I opened my mouth, Cobb knew he'd won. He had a sixth sense about the emotions he produced in others: in this case, fear. As far as I could see (lacking expert diagnosis and as a layman understands the symptoms), he wasn't merely erratic and trigger-tempered, but suffering from megalomania, or acute self-worship; delusions of persecution; and more than a touch of dipsomania.

Although I'm not proud of it, he scared hell out of me most of the time I was around him.

And now he gave me the first smile of our association. "As long as you don't aggravate my tension," he said, "we'll get along."

Before describing the Reno expedition, I would like to say in this frank view of a mighty man that the greatest, and strangest, of all American sport figures had his good side, which he tried to conceal. During the final ten months of his life I was his one constant companion. Eventually, I put him to bed, prepared his insulin, picked him up when he fell down, warded off irate taxi drivers, bartenders, waiters, clerks, and private citizens whom Cobb was inclined to punch, cooked what food he could digest, drew his bath, got drunk with him, and knelt with him in prayer on black nights when he knew death was near. I ducked a few bottles he threw, too.

I think, because he forced upon me a confession of his most private thoughts, that I know the answer to the central, overriding secret of his life: was Ty Cobb psychotic throughout his baseball career?

Kids, dogs, and sick people flocked to him and he returned their instinctive liking. Money was his idol, but from his $4 million fortune he assigned large sums to create the Cobb Educational Foundation, which financed hundreds of needy youngsters through college. He built and endowed a first-class hospital for the poor of his backwater home town, Royston, Georgia. When Ty's spinster sister, Florence, was crippled, he tenderly cared for her until her last days. The widow of a onetime American League batting champion would have lived in want but for Ty's steady money support. A Hall of Fame member, beaned by a pitched ball and enfeebled, came under Cobb's wing for years. Regularly he mailed dozens of anonymous checks to indigent old ball players (relayed by a third party)—a rare act among retired tycoons in other lines of business.

If you believe such acts didn't come hard for Cobb, guess again: he was the world's champion pinchpenny.

Some 150 fan letters reached him each month, requesting his autograph. Many letters enclosed return-mail stamps. Cobb used the stamps for his own outgoing mail. The fan letters he burned.

"Saves on firewood," he'd mutter.

In December of 1960, Ty hired a one-armed "gentleman's gentleman" named Brownie. Although constantly criticized, poor Brownie worked hard as cook and butler. But when he mixed up the grocery order one day, he was fired with a check for a week's pay—$45—and sent packing.

Came the middle of that night and Cobb awakened me.

"We're driving into town *right now*," he stated, "to stop payment on Brownie's check. The bastard talked back to me when I discharged him. He'll get no more of my money."

All remonstrations were futile. There was no phone, so we had to drive 20 miles from Cobb's Tahoe lodge into Carson City, where he woke up the president of the First National Bank of Nevada and arranged for a stop-pay on the piddling check. The president tried to conceal his anger—Cobb was a big depositor in his bank.

"Yes, sir, Ty," he said. "I'll take care of it first thing in the morning."

"You goddamn well better," snorted Cobb. And then we drove through the 3 A.M. darkness back to the lake.

But this trip was a light workout compared to that Reno trip.

Two cars were available at the lodge. Cobb's 1956 Imperial had no tire chains, but the other car did.

"We'll need both for this operation," he ordered. "One car might get stuck or break down. I'll drive mine and you take the one with chains. You go first. I'll follow your chain marks."

For Cobb to tackle precipitous Route 50 was unthinkable in every way. The Tahoe road, with 200 foot drop-offs, has killed a recorded 80 motorists. Along with his illness, his drunkenness, and no chains, he had bad eyes and was without a driver's license. California had turned him down at his last test; he hadn't bothered to apply in Nevada.

Urging him to ride with me was a waste of breath.

A howling wind hit my car a solid blow as we shoved off. Sleet stuck to the windshield faster than the wipers could work. For the first three miles, snowplows had been active, and at 15 mph, in second gear, I managed to hold the road. But then came Spooner's Summit, 7,000 feet high, and then a steep descent of nine miles. Behind me, headlamps blinking, Cobb honked his horn, demanding more speed. Chainless, he wasn't getting traction. *The hell with him,* I thought. Slowing to third gear, fighting to hold a roadbed I couldn't see even with my head stuck out the window, I skidded along. No other traffic moved as we did our crazy tandem around icy curves, at times brushing the guard rails. Cobb was blaring his horn steadily now.

And then here came Cobb.

Tiring of my creeping pace, he gunned the Imperial around me in one big skid. I caught a glimpse of an angry face under a big Stetson hat and a waving fist. He was doing a good 3 mph when he'd gained 25 yards on me, fishtailing right and left, but straightening as he slid out of sight in the thick sleet.

I let him go. Suicide wasn't in my contract.

The next six miles was a matter of feeling my way and praying. Near a curve, I saw tail lights to the left. Pulling up, I found Ty swung sideways and buried, nose down, in a snow bank, his hind wheels two feet in the air. Twenty yards away was a sheer drop-off into a canyon.

"You hurt?" I asked.

"Bumped my ——— head," he muttered. He lit a cigar and gave four-letter regards to the Highway Department for not illuminating the "danger" spot. His forehead was bruised and he'd broken his glasses.

In my car, we groped our way down-mountain, a nightmare ride, with Cobb alternately taking in Scotch from a thermos jug and telling me to step on it. At 3 A.M. in Carson City, an all-night garage man used a broom to clean the car of snow and agreed to pick up the Imperial—"when the road's passable." With dawn breaking, we reached Reno. All I wanted was a bed and all Cobb wanted was a craps table.

He was rolling now, pretending he wasn't ill, and with the Scotch bracing him, Ty was able to walk into the Riverside Hotel casino with a hand on my shoulder and without staggering so obviously as usual. Everybody present wanted to meet him. Starlets from a film unit on location in Reno flocked

278

around and comedian Joe E. Lewis had the band play "Sweet Georgia Brown"—Ty's favorite tune.

"Hope your dice are still honest," he told Riverside co-owner Bill Miller. "Last time I was here I won $12,000 in three hours."

"How I remember, Ty," said Miller. "How I remember."

A scientific craps player who'd won and lost huge sums in Nevada in the past, Cobb bet $100 chips, his eyes alert, not missing a play around the board. He soon decided that the table was "cold" and we moved to another casino, then a third. At this last stop, Cobb's legs began to grow shaky. Holding himself up by leaning on the table edge with forearms, he dropped $300, then had a hot streak in which he won over $800. His voice was a croak as he told the other players, "Watch 'em and weep."

But then suddenly his voice came back. When the stickman raked the dice his way, Cobb loudly said, "You touched the dice with your hand."

"No, sir," said the stickman. "I did *not*."

"I don't lie!" snarled Cobb.

"I don't lie either," insisted the stickman.

"Nobody touches my dice!" Cobb, swaying on his feet, eyes blazing, worked his way around the table toward the croupier. It was a weird tableau. In his crumpled Stetson and expensive camel's-hair coat, stained and charred with cigarette burns, a three-day beard grizzling his face, the gaunt old giant of baseball towered over the dapper gambler.

"You fouled the dice. I saw you," growled Cobb, and then he swung.

The blow missed, as the stickman dodged, but, cursing and almost falling, Cobb seized the wooden rake and smashed it over the table. I jumped in and caught him under the arms as he sagged.

And then, as quickly as possible, we were put into the street by two large uniformed guards. "Sorry, Mr. Cobb," they said, unhappily, "but we can't have this."

A crowd had gathered and as we started down the street, Cobb swearing and stumbling and clinging to me, I couldn't have felt more conspicuous if I'd been strung naked from the neon arch across Reno's main drag, Virginia Street. At the street corner, Ty was struck by an attack of breathlessness. "Got to stop," he gasped. Feeling him going limp on me, I turned his six-foot body against a lamppost, braced my legs, and with an underarm grip held him there until he caught his breath. He panted and gulped for air.

His face gray, he murmured, "Reach into my left-hand coat pocket." Thinking he wanted his bottle of heart pills, I did. But instead pulled out a six-inch-thick wad of currency, secured by a rubber band. "Couple of thousand there," he said weakly. "Don't let it out of sight."

At the nearest motel, where I hired a single, twin-bed room, he collapsed on the bed in his coat and hat and slept. After finding myself some breakfast, I turned in. Hours later I heard him stirring. "What's this place?" he muttered.

I told him the name of the motel—Travelodge.

"Where's the bankroll?"

"In your coat. You're wearing it."

Then he was quiet.

After a night's sleep, Cobb felt well enough to resume his gambling. In the next few days, he won more than $3,000 at the tables, and then we went sight-seeing in historic Virginia City. There as in all places, he stopped traffic. And had the usual altercation. This one was at the Bucket of Blood, where Cobb accused the bartender of serving watered Scotch. The bartender denied it. Crash! Another drink went flying.

Back at the lodge a week later, looking like the wrath of John Barleycorn and having refused medical aid in Reno, he began to suffer new and excruciating pains—in his hips and lower back. But between groans he forced himself to work an hour a day on his autobiography. He told inside baseball tales never published:

". . . Frank Navin, who owned the Detroit club for years, faked his turnstile count to cheat the visiting team and Uncle Sam. So did Big Bill Devery and Frank Farrell, who owned the New York Highlanders—later called the Yankees.

". . . Walter Johnson, the Big Train, tried to kill himself when his wife died.

". . . Grover Cleveland Alexander wasn't drunk out there on the mound, the way people thought—he was an epileptic. Old Pete would fall down with a seizure between innings, then go back and pitch another shutout.

". . . John McGraw hated me because I tweaked his nose in broad daylight in the lobby of the Oriental Hotel, in Dallas, after earlier beating the hell out of his second baseman, Buck Herzog, upstairs in my room."

But before we were well started, Cobb suddenly announced we'd go riding in his 23-foot Chris-Craft speedboat tied up in a boathouse below the lodge. When I went down to warm it up, I found the boat sunk to the bottom of Lake Tahoe in 15 feet of water.

My host broke all records for blowing his stack when he heard the news. He saw in this a sinister plot. "I told you I've got enemies all around here! It's sabotage as sure as I'm alive!"

A sheriff's investigation turned up no clues. Cobb sat up all night for three nights with his Luger. "I'll salivate the first dirty skunk who steps foot around here after dark," he swore.

Parenthetically, Cobb had a vocabulary all his own. To "salivate" something meant to destroy it. Anything easy was "soft-boiled," to outsmart someone was to "slip him the oskafagus," and all doctors were "truss-fixers." People who displeased him—and this included almost everyone he met— were "fee-simple sonsofbitches," "mugwumps," or (if female) "lousy slits."

Lake Tahoe friends of Cobb's had stopped visiting him long before, but one morning an attractive blonde of about 50 came calling. She was an old chum—in a romantic way, I was given to understand, of bygone years—but

Ty greeted her coldly. "Lost my sexual powers when I was 69," he said, when she was out of the room. "What the hell use to me is a woman?"

The lady had brought along a three-section electric vibrator bed, which she claimed would relieve Ty's back pains. We helped him mount it. He took a 20-minute treatment. Attempting to dismount, he lost balance, fell backward, the contraption jackknifed, and Cobb was pinned, yelling and swearing, under a pile of machinery.

When I freed him and helped him to a chair, he told the lady—in the choicest gutter language—where she could put her bed. She left, sobbing.

"That's no way to talk to an old friend, Ty," I said. "She was trying to do you a favor."

"And you're a hell of a poor guest around here, too!" he thundered. "You can leave any old time!" He quickly grabbed a bottle and heaved it in my direction.

"Thought you could throw straighter than that!" I yelled back. Cobb broke out a bottle of vintage Scotch, said I was "damned sensitive," half-apologized, and the matter was forgotten.

While working one morning on an outside observation deck, I heard a thud inside. On his bedroom floor, sprawled on his back, lay Ty. He was unconscious, his eyes rolled back, breathing shallowly. I thought he was dying.

There was no telephone. "Eavesdropping on the line," Cobb had told me. "I had it cut off." I ran down the road to a neighboring lodge and phoned a Carson City doctor, who promised to come immediately.

Back at the lodge, Ty remained stiff and stark on the floor, little bubbles escaping his lips. His face was bluish-white. With much straining, I lifted him halfway to the bed and by shifting holds finally rolled him onto it, and covered him with a blanket. Twenty minutes passed. No doctor.

Ten minutes later, I was at the front door, watching for the doctor's car, when I heard a sound. There stood Ty, swaying on his feet. "You want to do some work on the book?" he said.

His recovery didn't seem possible. "But you were out cold a minute ago," I said.

"Just a dizzy spell. Have 'em all the time. Must have hit my head on the bedpost when I fell."

The doctor, arriving, found Cobb's blood pressure standing at a grim 210 on the gauge. His temperature was 101 degrees and, from gross neglect of his diabetes, he was in a state of insulin shock, often fatal if not quickly treated. "I'll have to hospitalize you, Mr. Cobb," said the doctor.

Weaving his way to a chair, Cobb angrily waved him away. "Just send me your bill," he grunted. "I'm going home."

"Home" was the multimillionaire's main residence at Atherton, California, on the San Francisco Peninsula, 250 miles away, and it was there he headed later that night. With some hot soup and insulin in him, Cobb recovered with the same unbelievable speed he'd shown in baseball. In his heyday, trainers often sewed up deep spike cuts in his knees, shins, and thighs, on a clubhouse bench, without anesthetic, and he didn't lose an inning. Grantland Rice one 1920 day sat beside a bedridden, feverish Cobb, whose thighs, from sliding, were a mass of raw flesh. Sixteen hours later, he hit a triple, double, three singles, and stole two bases to beat the Yankees. On the Atherton ride, he yelled insults at several motorists who moved too slowly to suit him. Reaching Atherton, Ty said he felt ready for another drink.

My latest surprise was Cobb's 18-room, two-story, richly landscaped Spanish-California villa at 48 Spencer Lane, an exclusive neighborhood. You could have held a ball game on the grounds.

But the $90,000 mansion had no lights, no heat, no hot water.

"I'm suing the Pacific Gas & Electric Company," he explained, "for overcharging me on the service. Those rinky-dinks tacked an extra $16 on my bill. Bunch of crooks. When I wouldn't pay, they cut off my utilities. Okay—I'll see them in court."

For months previously, Ty Cobb had lived in a totally dark house. The only illumination was candlelight. The only cooking facility was a portable Coleman stove, such as campers use. Bathing was impossible, unless you could take it cold. The electric refrigerator, stove, deep-freeze, radio, and television, of course, didn't work. Cobb had vowed to "hold the fort" until his trial of the P. G. & E. was settled. Simultaneously, he had filed a $60,000 suit in San Francisco Superior Court against the State of California to recover state income taxes already collected—on the argument that he wasn't a permanent resident of California, but of Nevada, Georgia, Arizona, and other waypoints. State's attorneys claimed he spent at least six months per year in Atherton, thus had no case.

"I'm gone so much from here," he claimed, "that I'll win hands-down." All legal opinion, I later learned, held just the opposite view, but Cobb ignored their advice.

Next morning, I arranged with Ty's gardener, Hank, to turn on the lawn sprinklers. In the outdoor sunshine, a cold-water shower was easier to take. From then on, the back yard became my regular washroom.

The problem of lighting a desk so that we could work on the book was solved by stringing 200 feet of cord, plugged into an outlet of a neighboring house, through hedges and flower gardens and into the window of Cobb's study, where a single naked bulb, hung over the chandelier, provided illumination.

The flickering shadows cast by the single light made the vast old house seem haunted. No "ghost" writer ever had more ironical surroundings.

At various points around the premises, Ty showed me where he'd once installed high-voltage wires to stop trespassers. "Curiosity-seekers?" I asked. "Hell, no," he said. "Detectives broke in here once looking for evidence against me in a divorce suit. After a couple of them got burned, they stopped coming."

To reach our bedrooms, Cobb and I groped our way down long, black corridors. Twice he fell in the dark. And then, collapsing completely, he became so ill that he was forced to check in at Stanford Hospital in nearby Palo Alto. Here another shock was in store.

One of the physicians treating Ty's case, a Dr. E. R. Brown, said, "Do you mean to say that this man has traveled 700 miles in the last month without medical care?"

"Doctor," I said, "I've hauled him in and out of saloons, motels, gambling joints, steam baths, and snow banks. There's no holding him."

"It's a miracle he's alive. He has almost every major ailment I know about."

Dr. Brown didn't reveal to me Ty's main ailment, which news Cobb, himself, broke late one night from his hospital bed. "It's cancer," he said, bluntly. "About a year ago I had most of my prostate gland removed when they found it was malignant. Now it's spread up into the backbones. These pill-peddlers here won't admit it, but I haven't got a chance."

Cobb made me swear I'd never divulge the fact before he died. "If it gets in the papers, the sob sisters will have a field day. I don't want sympathy from anybody."

At Stanford, where he absorbed seven massive doses of cobalt radiation, the ultimate cancer treatment, he didn't act like a man on his last legs. Even before his strength returned, he was in the usual form.

"They won't let me have a drink," he said, indignantly. "I want you to get me a bottle. Smuggle it in your tape-recorder case."

I tried, telling myself that no man with terminal cancer deserves to be dried up, but sharp-eyed nurses and orderlies were watching. They searched Ty's closet, found the bottle, and over his roars of protest appropriated it.

"We'll have to slip them the oskefagus," said Ty.

Thereafter, a drink of Scotch-and-water sat in plain view in his room, on his bedside table, under the very noses of his physicians—and nobody suspected a thing. The whiskey was in an ordinary water glass, and in the liquid reposed Ty's false teeth.

There were no dull moments while Cobb was at the hospital. He was critical of everything. He told one doctor that he was not even qualified to be an intern, and told the hospital dietician—at the top of his voice—that she and the kitchen workers were in a conspiracy to poison him with their "foul" dishes. To a nurse he snapped, "If Florence Nightingale knew about you, she'd spin in her grave."

(Stanford Hospital, incidentally, is one of the largest and top-rated medical plants in the United States.)

But between blasts he did manage to buckle down to work on the book, dictating long into the night into a microphone suspended over his bed. Slowly the stormy details of his professional life came out. He spoke often of having "forgiven" his many baseball enemies, then lashed out at them with such passionate phrases that it was clear he'd done no such thing. High on his "hate" list were McGraw; New York sports writers; Hub Leonard, a pitcher who in 1926 accused Cobb and Tris Speaker of "fixing" a Detroit-Cleveland game; American League President Ban Johnson; onetime Detroit owner Frank Navin; former Baseball Commissioner Kenesaw Mountain Landis; and all those who intimated that Cobb ever used his spikes on another player without justification.

After a night when he slipped out of the hospital, against all orders, and we drove to a San Francisco Giants–Cincinnati Reds game at Candlestick Park, 30 miles away, Stanford Hospital decided it couldn't help Tyrus R. Cobb, and he was discharged. For extensive treatment his bill ran to more than $1,200.

"That's a nice racket you boys have here," he told the discharging doctors. "You clip the customers and then every time you pass an undertaker, you wink at him."

"Good-by, Mr. Cobb," snapped the medical men.

Soon after this Ty caught a plane to his native Georgia and I went along. "I want to see some of the old places again before I die," he said.

It now was Christmas eve of 1960 and I'd been with him for three months and completed but four chapters. The project had begun to look hopeless. In Royston, a village of 1,200, Cobb headed for the town cemetery. I drove him there, we parked, and I helped him climb a windswept hill through the growing dusk. Light snow fell. Faintly, yule chimes could be heard.

Amongst the many headstones, Ty looked for the plot he'd reserved for himself while in California and couldn't locate it. His temper began to boil. "Dammit, I ordered the biggest damn mausoleum in the graveyard! I know it's around here somewhere." On the next hill, we found it: a large marble, walk-in-size structure with "Cobb" engraved over the entrance.

"You want to pray with me?" he said, gruffly. We knelt and tears came to his eyes.

Within the tomb, he pointed to crypts occupied by the bodies of his father, Professor William Herschel Cobb, his mother, Amanda (Chitwood) Cobb, and his sister, Florence, whom he'd had disinterred and placed here. "My father," he said reverently, "was the greatest man I ever knew. He was a scholar, state senator, editor, and philosopher. I worshipped him. So did all the people around here. He was the only man who ever made me do his bidding."

Arising painfully, Ty braced himself against the marble crypt that soon would hold his body. There was an eerie silence in the tomb. He said deliberately:

"My father had his head blown off with a shotgun when I was 18 years old—*by a member of my own family*. I didn't get over that. I've never gotten over it."

We went back down the hill to the car. I asked no questions that day.

Later, from family sources and old Georgia friends of the baseball idol, I learned about the killing. One night in August of 1905, they related, Professor Cobb announced that he was driving from Royston to a neighboring village and left home by buggy. But, later that night, he doubled back and crept into his wife's bedroom by the way of the window. "He suspected her of being unfaithful to him," said these sources. "He thought he'd catch her in the act. But Amanda Cobb was a good woman. She was all alone when she saw a menacing figure climb through her window and approach her bed. In the dark, she assumed it to be a robber. She kept a shotgun handy by her bed and she used it. Everybody around here knows the story, but it was hushed up when Ty became famous."

News of the killing reached Ty in Augusta, where he was playing minor-league ball, on August 9. A few days later he was told that he'd been purchased by the Detroit Tigers, and was to report immediately. "In my grief," Cobb says in the book, "it didn't matter much. . . ."

Came March of 1961 and I remained stuck to the Georgia Peach like court plaster. He'd decided that we were born pals, meant for each other, that we'd complete a baseball book beating anything ever published. He had astonished doctors by rallying from the spreading cancer and, between bouts of transmitting his life and times to a tape recorder, was raising more whoopee than he had at Lake Tahoe and Reno.

Spring-training time for the big leagues had arrived and we were ensconced in a $30-a-day suite at the Ramada Inn at Scottsdale, Arizona, close by the practice parks of the Red Sox, Indians, Giants, and Cubs. Here, each year, Cobb held court. He didn't go to see anybody; Ford Frick, Joe Cronin, Ted Williams, and other diamond notables came to him. While explaining to sports writers why modern stars couldn't compare to the Wagners, Lajoies, Speakers, Jacksons, Mathewsons, and Planks of his day, Ty did other things.

For one, he commissioned a noted Arizona artist to paint him in oils. He was emaciated, having dropped from 208 pounds to 176. The preliminary sketches showed up his sagging cheeks and thin neck.

"I wouldn't let you kalsomine my toilet," ripped out Ty, and fired the artist.

But at analyzing the Dow-Jones averages and playing the stock market, he was anything but eccentric. Twice a week he phoned experts around the country, determined good buys, and bought in blocks of 500 to 1,500 shares. He made money consistently, even when bedridden, with a mind that read behind the fluctuations of a dozen different issues. "The State of Georgia," Ty remarked, "will realize about one million dollars from inheritance taxes when I'm dead. But there isn't a man alive who knows what I'm worth." According to the *Sporting News,* there was evidence upon Cobb's death that his worth approximated $12 million. Whatever the true figure, he did not confide the amount to me—or, most probably, to anyone except attorneys who drafted his last will and testament. And Cobb fought off making his will until the last moment.

His fortune began in 1908, when he bought into United (later General) Motors; as of 1961, he was "Mr. Coca-Cola," holding more than 20,000 shares of stock, valued at $85 per share. Wherever we traveled, he carried with him, stuffed into an old brown bag, more than $1 million in stock certificates and negotiable government bonds. The bag never was locked up. Cobb assumed nobody would dare rob him. He tossed the bag into any handy corner of a room, inviting theft. And in Scottsdale it turned up missing.

Playing Sherlock, he narrowed the suspects to a room maid and a man he'd hired to cook meals. When questioned, the maid broke into tears and the cook quit (fired, said Cobb). Hours later, I discovered the bag under a pile of dirty laundry.

Major-league owners and league officials hated to see him coming, for he thought their product was putrid and said so, incessantly. "Today they hit for ridiculous averages, can't bunt, can't steal, can't hit-and-run, can't place-hit to the opposite field, and you can't call them ball players." He told sports writers, "I blame Frick, Cronin, Bill Harridge, Horace Stoneham, Dan Topping, and others for wrecking baseball's traditional league lines. These days, any tax-dodging mugwump with a bankroll can buy a franchise, field some semi-pros, and get away with it. Where's our integrity? Where's *baseball*?"

No one could quiet Cobb. Who else had a lifetime average of .367, made 4,191 hits, scored 2,244 runs, won 12 batting titles, stole 892 bases, repeatedly beat whole teams single-handedly? Who was first into the Hall of Fame? Not Babe Ruth—but Cobb, by a landslide vote.

By early April, he could barely make it up the ramp of the Scottsdale Stadium, even hanging onto me. He had to stop, gasping for breath, every few steps. But he kept coming to games—loving the sounds of the ball park. His courage was tremendous. "Always be ready to catch me if I start to fall," he said. "I'd hate to go down in front of the fans."

People of all ages were overcome with emotion upon meeting him; no sports figure I've known produced such an effect upon the public.

We went to buy a cane. At a surgical supply house, Cobb inspected a dozen $25 malacca sticks, bought the cheapest, $4, white-ash cane they had. "I'm a plain man," he informed the clerk, the $7,500 diamond ring on his finger glittering.

But pride kept the old tiger from ever using the cane, any more than he'd wear the $600 hearing aid built into the bow of his glasses.

One day a Mexican taxi driver aggravated Cobb with his driving. Throwing the fare on the ground, he waited until the cabbie had bent to retrieve it, then tried to punt him like a football.

"What's your sideline," he inquired, "selling opium?"

It was all I could do to keep the driver from swinging on him. Later, a lawyer called on Cobb, threatening a damage suit. "Get in line, there's 500 ahead of you," said Tyrus, waving him away.

Every day was a new adventure. He was fighting back against the pain that engulfed him again—cobalt treatments no longer helped—and I could count on trouble anywhere we went. He threw a salt shaker at a Phoenix waiter, narrowly missing. One of his most treasured friendships—with Ted Williams—came to an end.

From the early 1940's, Williams had sat at Ty Cobb's feet. They often met, exchanged long letters on the art of batting. At Scottsdale one day, Williams dropped by Ty's rooms. He hugged Ty, fondly rumpled his hair, and accepted a drink. Presently the two greatest hitters of past and present fell into an argument over what players should comprise the all-time, all-star team. Williams declared, "I want DiMaggio and Hornsby on my team over anybody you can mention."

Cobb's face grew dark. "Don't give me that! Hornsby couldn't go back for a pop fly and he lacked smartness. DiMaggio couldn't hit with Speaker or Joe Jackson."

"The hell you say!" came back Williams, jauntily. "Hornsby out-hit *you* a couple of years."

Almost leaping from his chair, Cobb shook a fist. He'd been given the insult supreme—for Cobb always resented, and finally hated, Rogers Hornsby. Not until Cobb was in his sixteenth season did Hornsby top him in the batting averages. "Get . . . away from me!" choked Cobb. "Don't come back!"

Williams left with a quizzical expression, not sure how much Cobb meant it. The old man meant it all the way. He never invited Williams back, nor talked to him, nor spoke his name again. "I cross him off," he told me.

We left Arizona shortly thereafter for my home in Santa Barbara, California. Now failing fast, Tyrus had accepted my invitation to be my guest. Two doctors inspected him at my beach house by the Pacific and gave their opinions: he had a few months of life left, no more. The cancer had invaded the bones of his skull. His pain was intense, unrelenting—requiring heavy sedation—yet with teeth bared and sweat pouring down his face, he fought off medical science. "They'll never get me on their damn hypnotics," he swore. "I'll never die an addict . . . an idiot. . . ."

He shouted, "Where's anybody who cares about me? Where are they? The world's lousy . . . no good."

One night later, on May 1, Cobb sat propped up in bed, overlooking a starlit ocean. He had a habit, each night, of rolling up his trousers and placing them under his pillows—an early-century ball player's trick, dating from the time when Ty slept in strange places and might be robbed. I knew that his ever-present Luger was tucked into that pants-roll.

I'd never seen him so sunk in despair. At last the fire was going out. "Do we die a little at a time, or all at once?" he wondered aloud. "I think Max had the right idea."

The reference was to his onetime friend, multimillionaire Max Fleischmann, who'd cheated lingering death by cancer some years earlier by putting a bullet through his brain. Ty spoke of Babe Ruth, another cancer victim. "If Babe had been told what he had in time, he could've got it over with."

Had I left Ty that night, I believe he would have pulled the trigger. His three living children (two were dead) had withdrawn from him. In the wide world that had sung his fame, he had not one intimate friend remaining.

But we talked, and prayed, until dawn, and then sleep came; in the morning, aided by friends, I put him into a car and drove him home, to the big, gloomy house in Atherton. He spoke only twice during the six-hour ride.

"Have you got enough to finish the book?" he asked.

"More than enough."

"Give 'em the word then. I had to fight all my life to survive. They all were against me . . . tried every dirty trick to cut me down. But I beat the bastards and left them in the ditch. Make sure the book says that. . . ."

I was leaving him now, permanently, and I had to ask one question I'd never put to him before.

"Why did you fight so hard in baseball, Ty?"

He'd never looked fiercer than then, when he answered. "I did it for my father, who was an exalted man. They killed him when he was still young. They blew his head off the same week I became a major leaguer. He never got to see me play. But I knew he was watching me and I never let him down."

You can make what you want of that. Keep in mind what Casey Stengel said, later: "I never saw anyone like Cobb. No one even close to him. When he wiggled those wild eyes at a pitcher, you knew you were looking at the one bird nobody could beat. It was like he was superhuman."

To me it seems that the violent death of a father whom a sensitive, highly talented boy loved deeply, and feared, engendered, through some strangely supreme desire to vindicate that father, the most violent, successful, thoroughly maladjusted personality ever to pass across American sports. The shock tipped the 18-year-old mind, making him capable of incredible feats.

Off the field, he was still at war with the world. For the emotionally disturbed individual, in most cases, does not change his pattern. To reinforce that pattern, he was viciously hazed by Detroit Tiger veterans when he was a rookie. He was bullied, ostracized, and beaten up—in one instance, a 210-pound catcher named Charlie Schmidt broke the 165-pound Ty Cobb's nose. It was persecution immediately heaped upon the deepest desolation a young man can experience.

Yes, Ty Cobb was a badly disturbed personality. It is not hard to understand why he spent his entire life in deep conflict. Nor why a member of his family, in the winter of 1960, told me, "I've spent a lot of time terrified of him . . . I think he was psychotic from the time that he left Georgia to play in the big league."

"Psychotic" is not a word I'd care to use. I believe that he was far more than the fiercest of all competitors. He was a vindicator who believed that "father was watching" and who could not put that father's terrible fate out of his mind. The memory of it threatened his sanity.

The fact that he recognized and feared this is revealed in a tape recording he made, in which he describes his own view of himself: "I was like a steel spring with a growing and dangerous flaw in it. If it is wound too tight or has the slightest weak point, the spring will fly apart and then it is done for. . . ."

The last time I saw him, he was sitting in his armchair in the Atherton mansion. The place still was without lights or heat. I shook his hand in farewell, and he held it a moment longer.

"What about it? Do you think they'll remember me?" He tried to say it as if it didn't matter.

"They'll always remember you," I said.

On July 8, I received in the mail a photograph of Ty's mausoleum on the hillside in the Royston cemetery with the words scribbled on the back: "*Any time now.*" Nine days later he died in an Atlanta hospital. Before going, he opened the brown bag, piled $1 million in negotiable securities beside his bed, and placed the Luger atop them.

From all of major-league baseball, three men and three only appeared for his funeral.

From *The Armies of the Night*

NORMAN MAILER

∞

First famous as a novelist, then as an essayist-celebrity-provocateur, Norman Mailer became a journalist in 1964, when he was assigned by *Esquire* to cover the national political conventions. His choice to refer to himself in the third person in those articles and most of his subsequent journalistic works—including *Of a Fire on the Moon, Miami and the Siege of Chicago,* and *The Armies of the Night,* from which the following excerpt is taken—is commonly compared to Henry Adams's similar narrative strategy in his classic *The Education of Henry Adams:* that is, undertaken in order to present himself as a figure representative of his times. Another reason was suggested by Tom Wolfe: The volume of Mailer's egocentrism would probably become unbearable had he referred to himself as "I." "Instead," wrote Wolfe, "one finds 'Mailer' quite lovable."

The Armies of the Night, Mailer's participant-observation of the 1967 march on the Pentagon to protest the Vietnam War, calls to mind another canonical Henry—James, that is. In the following excerpt, which takes place at a cocktail party the night before the march, there is roughly half a [pa]ge of action and ten pages of introspection. Mailer carries it off splen[didl]y, in part because admitted self-obsession literately carried to these [limi]ts really can be rather charming. But part of it stems from the validity of Mailer's implicit themes in the book: the political is the personal, and [to rep]ort the great events of the time in purely objective terms is to miss[an ess]ential part of the story.

—B. Y.

∞

There was a[...]
Mailer's heart, first, however, given by an attractive liberal couple. "sodden" by a [...] buoyant at best, and in fact once with justice called his feet but his s[...]w collected into a leaden little ball and sank, not to desire to have a [...] He was aware for the first time this day of a healthy [...] the party gave every promise of being dreadful.

290

Mailer was a snob of the worst sort. New York had not spoiled him, because it had not chosen to, but New York had certainly wrecked his tolerance for any party but a very good one. Like most snobs he professed to believe in the aristocracy of achieved quality—"Just give me a hovel with a few young artists, bright-eyed and bold"—in fact, a party lacked flavor for him unless someone very rich or social was present. An evening without a wicked lady in the room was like an opera company without a large voice. Of course there were no wicked ladies when he entered this room. Some reasonably attractive wives to be certain, and a couple of young girls, too young for him, they were still in the late stages of some sort of extraordinary progressive school, and were innocent, decent-spirited, merry, red-cheeked, idealistic, and utterly lobotomized away from the sense of sin. Mailer would not have known what to do with such young ladies—he had spent the first forty-four years of his life in an intimate dialogue, a veritable dialectic with the swoops, spooks, starts, the masks and snarls, the calm lucid abilities of sin, sin was his favorite fellow, his tonic, his jailer, his horse, his sword, say he was not inclined to flirt for an hour with one bright seventeen-year-old or another when they conceived of lust as no more than the gymnasium of love. Mailer had a diatribe against LSD, hippies, and the generation of love, but he was keeping it to himself. . . .

But we are back with the wives, and the room has not yet been described. It was the sort of room one can see at many a faculty party in places like Berkeley, the University of Chicago, Columbia—the ground of common being is that the faculty man is a liberal. Conservative professors tend to have a private income, so their homes show the flowering of their taste, the articulation of their hobbies, collections adhere to their cabinets and odd statements of whim stand up in the nooks; but liberal instructors, liberal assistant professors, and liberal associate professors are usually poor and programmatic, so secretly they despise the arts of home adornment. Their houses look one like the other, for the wives gave up herculean careers as doctors, analysts, sociologists, anthropologists, labor relations experts— great servants of the Social Program were lost when the women got married and relinquished all for hubber and kids. So the furnishings are functional, the prevailing hues of wall and carpet and cloth are institutional brown and library gray, the paintings and sculpture are stylized abstract hopeless imitation I. Rice Pereira, Leonard Baskin, Ben Shahn, but bet your twenty-five dollars to win an assured ten dollars that the artist on the wall is a friend of the host, has the right political ideas, and will talk about literature so well, you might think you were being addressed by Maxim Gorky.

Such were the sour and near to unprintable views of the semi-distinguished and semi-notorious author as he entered the room. His deepest detestation was often reserved for the nicest of liberal academics, as if their lives were his own life but a step escaped. Like the scent of the void which comes off the pages of a Xerox copy, so was he always depressed in such homes by their hint of oversecurity. If the republic was now managing to convert the citizenry to a plastic mass, ready to be attached to any manipulative gung ho, the author was ready to cast much of the blame for such success into the undernourished lap, the overpsychologized loins, of the liberal academic intelligentsia. They were of course politically opposed to the present programs and movements of the republic in Asian foreign policy, but this political difference seemed no more than a quarrel among engineers. Liberal academics had no root of a real war with technology land itself, no, in all likelihood, they were the natural managers of that future air-conditioned vault where the last of human life would still exist. Their only quarrel with the Great Society was that they thought it temporarily deranged, since the Great Society seemed to be serving as instrument to the Goldwater wing of the Republican party, a course of action so very irrational to these liberal technologues that they were faced with bitter necessity to desert all their hard-earned positions of leverage on real power in the Democratic party, a considerable loss to suffer merely because of an irrational development in the design of the Great Society's supermachine. Well, the liberal technologues were not without character or principle. If their living rooms had little to keep them apart from the look of waiting rooms of doctors with a modern practice, it was exactly because the private loves of the ideologues were attached to no gold standard of the psyche. Those true powers of interior decoration—greed, guilt, compassion and trust—were hardly the cornerstones of their family furnishings. No, just as money was a concept, no more, to the liberal academic, and needed no ballast of gold to be considered real, for nothing is more real to the intellectual than a concept! so position or power in society was, to the liberal technologue, also a concept, desirable, but always to be relinquished for a better concept. They were servants of that social machine of the future in which all irrational human conflict would be resolved, all conflict of interest negotiated, and nature's resonance condensed into frequencies which could comfortably phase nature in or out as you please. So they were servants of the moon. Their living rooms looked like offices precisely because they were ready to move to the moon and build Utope cities there—Utope being, one may well suppose, the only appropriate name for pilot models of Utopia in Non-Terrestrial Ecologically Sub-Dependent Non-Charged Staging Areas, that's to say dead planets where the food must be flown in, but the chances for good civil rights and all-out social engineering are one hundred percent zap!

As is invariably the case with sociological ruminations the individual guests at this party disproved the general thesis, at least in part. The hostess was small, for example, almost tiny, but vivid, bright-eyed, suggestive of a fiery temper and a childlike glee. It was to pain Mailer later to refuse her cooking (she had prepared a buffet to be eaten before the move to the theater) but he was drinking with some devotion by then, and mixing seemed fair neither to the food nor the bourbon. It was of course directly unfair to the hostess: Mailer priding himself on his good manners precisely because the legend of his bad manners was so prevalent, hated to cause pain to a hostess, but he had learned from years of speaking in public that an entertainer's first duty was to deliver himself to the stage with the maximum of energy, high focus, and wit—a good heavy dinner on half a pint of bourbon was likely to produce torpor, undue search for the functional phrase, and dry-mouthed maunderings after a little spit. So he apologized to the lady, dared the look of rejection in her eye which was almost balanced on a tear— she was indeed surprisingly adorable and childlike to be found in such a liberal academic coven—tried to cover the general sense of loss by marshaling what he assumed his most radiant look, next assuring her that he would take a rain check on the meal.

"Promise?"

"Next time I'm in Washington," he lied like a psychopath. The arbiter of nicety in him had observed with horror over many a similar occasion that he was absolutely without character for any social situation in which a pause could become the mood's abyss, and so he always filled the moment with the most extravagant amalgams of possibility. Particularly he did this at the home of liberal academics. They were brusque to the world of manners, they had built their hope of heaven on the binary system and the computer, 1 and 0, Yes and No—they had little to do therefore with the spectrum of grace in acceptance and refusal; if you did not do what they wished, you had simply denied them. Now Mailer was often brusque himself, famous for that, but the architecture of his personality bore resemblance to some provincial cathedral which warring orders of the church might have designed separately over several centuries, the particular cathedral falling into the hands of one architect, then his enemy. (Mailer had not been married four times for nothing.) If he was on many an occasion brusque, he was also to himself at least so supersensitive to nuances of manner he sometimes suspected when in no modest mood that Proust had lost a cell mate the day they were born in different bags. (Bag is of course used here to specify milieu and not the exceptional character of the mothers, Mme. Proust and Mrs. I. B. Mailer.) At any rate, boldness, attacks of shyness, rude assertion, and circumlocutions tortured as arthritic fingers working at lace, all took their turn with him, and these shuttlings of mood became most pronounced in their resemblance to the banging and shunting of freight cars when he was with liberal academics. Since he—you are in on the secret—disapproved of them far more than he could afford to reveal (their enmity could be venomous) he therefore exerted himself to push up a synthetic exaggerated sweetness of manner, and his conversations with liberal ideologues on the consequence consisted almost entirely of overcorrections of the previous error.

"I know a friend of yours," says the ideologue. A nervous voice from the novelist for answer. "Yes? Who?" Now the name is given: it is X.

Mailer: I don't know X.

The ideologue proceeds to specify a conversation which M held with X. M recollects. "Oh, yes!" he says; "of course! X!" Burbles of conversation about the merits of X, and his great ebullience. Actually X is close to flat seltzer.

There had been just this sort of dialogue with a stranger at the beginning of the party. So Mailer gave up quickly any thought of circulation. Rather, he huddled first with Dwight Macdonald, but Macdonald was the operative definition of the gregarious and could talk with equal facility and equal lack of personal observation to an Eskimo, a collector from the New York Department of Sanitation, or a UN diplomat—therefore was chatting happily with the world fifteen minutes after his entrance. Hence Mailer and Robert Lowell got into what was by all appearances a deep conversation at the dinner table sometime before food was laid out, Mailer thus doubly wounding the hostess with his later refusal.

We find, therefore, Lowell and Mailer ostensibly locked in converse. In fact, out of the thousand separate enclaves of their very separate personalities, they sensed quickly that they now shared one enclave to the hilt: their secret detestation of liberal academic parties to accompany worthy causes. Yes, their snobbery was on this mountainous face close to identical—each had a delight in exactly the other kind of party, a posh evil social affair, they even supported a similar vein of vanity (Lowell with considerably more justice) that if they were doomed to be revolutionaries, rebels, dissenters, anarchists, protesters, and general champions of one Left cause or another, they were also, in private, *grands conservateurs,* and if the truth be told, poor damn émigré princes. They were willing if necessary (probably) to die for the cause—one could hope the cause might finally at the end have an unexpected hint of wit, a touch of the Lord's last grace—but wit or no, grace or grace failing, it was bitter rue to have to root up one's occupations of the day, the week, and the weekend and trot down to Washington for idiot mass manifestations which could only drench one in the most ineradicable kind of mucked-up publicity and have for compensation nothing at this party which might be representative for some of the Devil's better creations. So Robert Lowell and Norman Mailer feigned deep conversation. They turned their heads to one another at the empty table, ignoring the potentially acolytic drinkers at either elbow, they projected their elbows out in fact like flying buttresses or old Republicans, they exuded waves of Interruption Repellent from the posture of their backs, and concentrated on their conversation, for indeed they were the only two men of remotely similar status in the room. (Explanations about the position of Paul Goodman will follow later.)

Lowell, whose personal attractiveness was immense (since his features were at once virile and patrician and his characteristic manner turned up facets of the grim, the gallant, the tender and the solicitous as if he were the nicest Boston banker one had ever hoped to meet) was not concerned too much about the evening at the theater. "I'm just going to read some poems," he said. "I suppose you're going to speak, Norman."

"Well, I will."

"Yes, you're awfully good at that."

"Not really." Harumphs, modifications, protestations and denials of the virtue of the ability to speak.

"I'm no good at all at public speaking," said Lowell in the kindest voice. He had indisputably won the first round. Mailer the younger, presumptive, and self-elected prince was left to his great surprise—for he had been exercised this way many times before—with the unmistakable feeling that there was some faint strain of the second-rate in this ability to speak on your feet.

Then they moved on to talk of what concerned them more. It was the subject first introduced to Mailer by Mitch Goodman. Tomorrow, a group of draft resisters, led by William Sloane Coffin, Jr., Chaplain at Yale, were going to march from their meeting place at a church basement, to the Department of Justice, and there a considerable number of draft cards would be deposited in a bag by individual students representing themselves, or their groups at different colleges, at which point Coffin and a selected few would walk into the Department of Justice, turn the cards over to the Attorney General, and await his reply.

"I don't think there'll be much trouble at this, do you?" asked Lowell.

"No, I think it'll be dull, and there'll be a lot of speeches."

"Oh, no," said Lowell with genuine pain, "Coffin's not that kind of fool."

"It's hard to keep people from making speeches."

"Well, you know what they want us to do?" Lowell explained. He had been asked to accompany a draft resister up to the bag in which the draft cards were being dropped. "It seems," said Lowell, with a glint of the oldest Yankee light winging off like a mad laser from his eye, "that they want us to be *big buddy*."

It was agreed this was unsuitable. No, Lowell suggested, it would be better if they each just made a few remarks. "I mean," said Lowell, beginning to stammer a little, "we could just get up and say we respect their action and support it, just to establish, I suppose, that we're there and behind them and so forth."

Mailer nodded. He felt no ease for any of these suggestions. He did not even know if he truly supported the turning in of draft cards. It seemed to him at times that the students who disliked the war most should perhaps be the first to volunteer for the Army in order that their ideas have currency in the Army as well. Without them, the armed forces could more easily become Glamour State for the more mindless regions of the proletariat if indeed the proletariat was not halfway to Storm Troop Junction already. The military could make an elite corps best when the troops were homogenized. On the other hand, no soldier could go into combat with the secret idea that he would not fire a gun. If nothing else, it was unfair to friends in his outfit; besides it suggested the suicidal. No, the iron of the logic doubtless demanded that if you disapproved of the war too much to shoot Vietcong, then your draft card was for burning. But Mailer arrived at this conclusion somewhat used up as we have learned from the number of decisions he had to make at various moral crossroads en route and so felt no enthusiasm whatsoever for the preliminary demonstration at the Department of Justice tomorrow in which he would take part. To the contrary, he wondered if he would burn or surrender his own draft card if he were young enough to own one, and he did not really know the answer. How then could he advise others to take the action, or even associate his name? Still, he was going to be there.

He started to talk of these doubts with Lowell, but he could hear the sound of his own voice, and it offended him. It seemed weak, plaintive, as if his case were—no less incriminating word—phony, he did not quite know why. So he shut up.

A silence.

"You know, Norman," said Lowell in his fondest voice, "Elizabeth and I really think you're the finest journalist in America."

Mailer knew Lowell thought this—Lowell had even sent him a postcard once to state the enthusiasm. But the novelist had been shrewd enough to judge that Lowell sent many postcards to many people—it did not matter that Lowell was by overwhelming consensus judged to be the best, most talented, and most distinguished poet in America—it was still necessary to keep the defense lines in good working order. A good word on a card could keep many a dangerous recalcitrant in the ranks.

Therefore, this practice annoyed Mailer. The first card he'd ever received from Lowell was on a book of poems, *Deaths for the Ladies and other disasters* it had been called, and many people had thought the book a joke which whatever its endless demerits, it was not. Not to the novice poet at least. When Lowell had written that he liked the book, Mailer next waited for some word in print to canonize his thin tome; of course it never came. If Lowell were to begin to award living American poets in critical print, two hundred starving worthies could with fairness hold out their bowl before the escaped Novelist would deserve his turn. Still Mailer was irked. He felt he had been part of a literary game. When the second card came a few years later telling him he was the best journalist in America, he did not answer. Elizabeth Hardwick, Lowell's wife, had just published a review of *An American Dream* in *Partisan Review* which had done its best to disembowel the novel. Lowell's card might have arrived with the best of motives, but its timing suggested to Mailer an exercise in neutralsmanship—neutralize the maximum of possible future risks. Mailer was not critically equipped for the task, but there was always the distant danger that some bright and not unauthoritative voice, irked at Lowell's enduring hegemony, might come along with a long lance and presume to tell America that posterity would judge Allen Ginsberg the greater poet.

This was all doubtless desperately unfair to Lowell who, on the basis of two kind cards, was now judged by Mailer to possess an undue unchristian talent for literary logrolling. But then Mailer was prickly. Let us hope it was not because he had been beaten a little too often by book reviewers, since the fruit of specific brutality is general suspicion.

Still Lowell now made the mistake of repeating his remark. "Yes, Norman, I really think you are the best journalist in America."

The pen may be mightier than the sword, yet at their best, each belong to extravagant men. "Well, Cal," said Mailer, using Lowell's nickname for the first time, "there are days when I think of myself as being the best writer in America."

The effect was equal to walloping a roundhouse right into the heart of an English boxer who has been hitherto right up on his toes. Consternation, not Britannia, now ruled the waves. Perhaps Lowell had a moment when he wondered who was guilty of declaring war on the minuet. "Oh, Norman, oh, certainly," he said, "I didn't mean to imply, heavens no, it's just I have such *respect* for good journalism."

"Well, I don't know that I do," said Mailer. "It's much harder to write"— the next said with great and false graciousness—"a good poem."

"Yes, of course."

Chuckles. Headmastermanship.

Chuckles. Fellow headmastermanship.

They were both now somewhat spoiled for each other. Mailer got up abruptly to get a drink. He was shrewd enough to know that Lowell, like many another aristocrat before him, respected abrupt departures. The pain of unexpected rejection is the last sweet vice left to an aristocrat (unless they should happen to be not aristocrats, but secret monarchs—then watch for your head!).

Next, Mailer ran into Paul Goodman at the bar—a short sentence which contains two errors and a misrepresentation. The assumption is that Goodman was drinking alcohol but he was not; by report, Goodman never took a drink. The bar, so-called, was a table with a white tablecloth, set up near the archway between the dining room where Lowell and Mailer had been talking and the living room where most of the party was being enacted—to the tune of ten couples perhaps—so the bar did not qualify as a bar, just a poor table with a cloth to support Mailer's irritated eye. Finally he did not run into Goodman. Goodman and Mailer had no particular love for one another—they tended to slide about each other at a party. In fact, they hardly knew each other.

Their lack of cordiality had begun on the occasion of a piece written by Goodman for *Dissent* which had discussed Washington in the early days of the Kennedy Administration. Goodman had found much to displease him then, and kept referring to the "wargasms" of this Kennedy Administration which wargasms he attached with no excessive intellectual jugglery to the existential and Reichian notions of the orgasm which Mailer had promulgated in his piece *The White Negro*. (Goodman was a sexologue—that is, an ideologue about sex—Mailer was then also a sexologue; no war so rich without quarter as the war between two sexologues.) Goodman, at any rate, had scored off Mailer almost at will, something to the general effect that the false prophet of the orgasm was naturally attached to the false hero of Washington who went in for wargasms. Writing for a scholarly Socialist quarterly like *Dissent,* it was hard to miss. The magnetic field of *Dissent*—hostile to Kennedy at the time—bent every wild shot to the target. So Mailer wrote a letter in reply. It was short, sought to be urbane, and was delivered exactly to the jugular, for it began by asserting that he could not judge the merits of Goodman's intellectual points since the other had made a cardinal point of emphasizing Mailer's own incapacity to reason and Goodman was doubtless correct, but Mailer did nonetheless feel competent to comment on the literary experience of encountering Goodman's style and that was not unrelated to the journeys one undertook in the company of a laundry bag . . . Great ferment in scholarly Socialist quarters! A small delegation of the Editors assured Mailer they would print his letter if he insisted, but the hope was that he would not. Mailer had always thought it senseless to undertake an attack unless you made certain it was printed, for otherwise you were left with a determined enemy who was an unmarked man, and therefore able to repay you at leisure and by the lift of an eyebrow. Mailer acceded however. He was fond of the Editors of *Dissent,* although his private mixture of Marxism, conservatism, nihilism, and large parts of existentialism could no longer produce any polemical gravies for the digestive apparatus of scholarly Socialist minds; nonetheless Mailer had never been asked to leave the Board, and would not have resigned on his own since that would have suggested a public attack on the ideas of people with whom he had no intellectual accord but of whom he was personally fond.

Nonetheless, from that day, Mailer and Goodman slid around one another at parties and waved languid hands in greeting. It was just as well. Each seemed to have the instinct a discussion would use up intellectual ordnance best reserved for articles. Besides, they had each doubtless read very little of the other.

Mailer, of course, was not without respect for Goodman. He thought Goodman had had an enormous influence in the colleges and much of it had been, from his own point of view, very much to the good. Paul Goodman had been the first to talk of the absurd and empty nature of work and education in America, and a generation of college students had formed around the core of his militancy. But, oh, the style! It set Mailer's teeth on edge to read it; he was inclined to think that the body of students who followed Goodman must have something de-animalized to put up with the style or at least such was Mailer's bigoted view. His fundamental animus to Goodman was still, unhappily, on sex. Goodman's ideas tended to declare in rough that heterosexuality, homosexuality, and onanism were equal valid forms of activity, best denuded of guilt. Mailer, with his neo-Victorianism, thought that if there was anything worse than homosexuality and masturbation, it was putting the two together. The super-hygiene of all this mental prophylaxis offended him profoundly. Super-hygiene impregnated the air with medicated Vaseline—there was nothing dirty in the damn stuff; and sex to Mailer's idea of it was better off dirty, damned, even slavish! than clean, and without guilt. For guilt was the existential edge of sex. Without guilt, sex was meaningless. One advanced into sex against one's sense of guilt, and each time guilt was successfully defied, one had learned a little more about the contractual relation of one's own existence to the unheard thunders of the deep—each time guilt herded one back with its authority, some primitive awe—hence some creative clue to the rages of the deep—was left to brood about. Onanism and homosexuality were not, to Mailer, light vices—to him it sometimes seemed that much of life and most of society were designed precisely to drive men deep into onanism and homosexuality; one defied such a fate by sweeping up the psychic profit which derived from the existential assertion of yourself—which was a way of saying that nobody was born a man; you earned manhood provided you were good enough, bold enough.

This most conservative and warlike credo could hardly have meaning to a scientific humanist like Goodman for whom all obstacles to the good life derived precisely from guilt: guilt which was invariably so irrational—for it derived from the warped burden of the past. Goodman therefore said hello mildly to Mailer, who answered in as mild a voice, and that was all they had to say. Lowell, following, expressed his condolences to Goodman on the recent death of his son, and Mailer after depressing the hostess by his refusal to eat, went on to talk to Macdonald.

That was most brief. They were old friends, who had a somewhat comic relation, for Macdonald—at least as Mailer saw it—was forever disapproving of the younger author until the moment they came together at one or another party or meeting. Then Macdonald would discover he was glad to see Mailer. In fact, Macdonald could hardly help himself. Of all the younger American writers, Mailer was the one who had probably been influenced most by Macdonald, not so much from the contents of Macdonald's ideas which were always going in and out of phase with Mailer's, but rather by the style of Macdonald's attack. Macdonald was forever referring the act of writing to his sense of personal standards which demanded craft, care, devotion, lack of humbug, and simple *a fortiori* honesty of sentiment. All this was a little too simple for Mailer's temper. Nonetheless, Macdonald had given him an essential clue which was: look to the feel of the phenomenon. If it feels bad, it *is* bad. Mailer could have learned this as easily from Hemingway, as many another novelist had, but he had begun as a young ideologue—his mind had been militant with positions fixed in concrete, and Macdonald's method had worked like Zen for him—at the least it had helped to get his guns loose. Macdonald had given the hint that the clue to discovery was not in the substance of one's idea, but in what was learned from the style of one's attack. (Which was one reason Mailer's style changed for every project.) So, the younger author was unquenchably fond of Macdonald, and it showed. Not a minute would go by before he would be poking Macdonald's massive belly with a finger.

But for now, they were ill at ease. Macdonald was in the process of reviewing Mailer's new novel *Why Are We In Vietnam?* for *The New Yorker,* and there was an empty space in the presence of the mood. Mailer was certain Macdonald did not like the new novel, and was going to do a negative review. He had seemed professionally unfriendly these past few weeks. The Novelist would have liked to assure the Critic that the review could not possibly affect their good feeling for one another, but he did not dare, for such a remark would break a rule, since it would encourage Macdonald to talk about what was in his review, or at worst trick him into an unwilling but revealing reply. Besides, Mailer did not trust himself to speak calmly about the matter. Although Macdonald would not admit it, he was in secret carrying on a passionate love affair with *The New Yorker*—Disraeli on his knees before Victoria. But the Novelist did not share Macdonald's infatuation at all—*The New Yorker* had not printed a line in review of *The Presidential Papers, An American Dream,* or *Cannibals and Christians,* and *that,* Mailer had long ago decided, was an indication of some of the worst things to be said about the magazine. He had once had a correspondence with Lillian Ross who asked him why he did not do a piece for *The New Yorker.* "Because they would not let me use the word 'shit,' " he had written back. Miss Ross suggested that all liberty was his if only he understood where liberty resided. True liberty, Mailer had responded, consisted of his right to say shit in *The New Yorker.* So there was old rage behind the arms-length bantering about Dwight's review of Norman's book, and Mailer finally left the conversation. Macdonald was beginning to like him again, and that was dangerous. Macdonald was so full of the very beans of that old-time Wasp integrity, that he would certainly bend over much too far backward if for a moment while reviewing the book he might have the thought he was sufficiently fond of Norman to conceivably be giving him too-gentle treatment. "No," thought the Novelist, "let him keep thinking he disapproves of me until the review is written."

Among his acquaintances at the party, this now left de Grazia. As has been indicated, they were old friends of the most superficial sort, which is to say that they hardly knew each other, and yet always felt like old friends when they met. Perhaps it was no more than the ability of each man to inspire an odd sense of intimacy. At any rate they never wasted time in needless conversation, since they were each too clever about the other to be penned in position by an evasion.

"How would you like to be the first speaker of the evening?" de Grazia asked.

"There'll be nothing interesting to follow me."

De Grazia's eyes showed pleasure. "Then I thought of starting with Macdonald."

300

"Dwight is conceivably the world's worst speaker." It was true. Macdonald's authority left him at the entrance to the aura of the podium. In that light he gesticulated awkwardly, squinted at his text, laughed at his own jokes, looked like a giant stork, whinnied, shrilled, and was often inaudible. When he spoke extempore, he was sometimes better, often worse.

"Well," said de Grazia, "I can't start with Lowell."

"No, no, no, you must save him."

"That leaves Goodman."

They nodded wisely. "Yes, let's get rid of Goodman first," said Mailer. But then the thought of that captive audience tuned to their first awareness of the evening by the pious drone of Goodman's voice injured every showman's instinct for the opening. "Who is going to be M.C.?" Mailer asked.

"Unless you want to, I thought I might be."

"I've never been an M.C." said Mailer, "but maybe I should be. I could warm the audience up before Goodman drops them." De Grazia looked uneasily at Mailer's bourbon. "For Christ's sakes, Ed," said Mailer.

"Well, all right," said de Grazia.

Mailer was already composing his introductory remarks, percolating along on thoughts of the subtle annoyance his role as Master of Ceremonies would cause the other speakers.

From "The Scum Also Rises"

HUNTER S. THOMPSON

∞

Hunter S. Thompson is to post-1960s American journalism what Ernest Hemingway was to post-1920s American fiction: the innovator whose estimable contributions have proved irresistible to a legion of less talented imitators. The self-styled "Gonzo journalism" (part of the Thompson package is a strong tendency toward self-mythologizing) that he began writing for *Rolling Stone* and *Scanlan's* in the late sixties gleefully defenestrated all the traditional rules of journalism: conciseness, sobriety, objectivity, even accuracy, and especially unobtrusiveness. Generations of reporters had been indoctrinated never to write "I"; Thompson *reveled* in "I."

Besides the sheer audacity of Gonzo, the amazing thing was how well it worked. In 1971 Thompson published *Fear and Loathing in Las Vegas,* a grossly hyperbolic, frequently purple-prosed recounting of a stoned road trip—and, it has been persuasively argued, a book that revealed more about contemporary America than any number of traditional objective dispatches. Pulling something like this off is harder than it looks, as Thompson's merely sulf-indulgent heirs have abundantly proved.

Gonzo met politics in *Fear and Loathing on the Campaign Trail,* about the 1972 presidential campaign, and subsequently in Thompson's Watergate coverage for *Rolling Stone.* The following is excerpted from his 1974 piece on Richard Nixon's resignation, and it displays all the usual Gonzo attributes. One of them, generally overlooked amidst Thompson's general iconoclasm, is a curiously old-fashioned diction and affect. Thus he sets the opening scene in a driving summer rainstorm that sentimentally mirrors his own foul mood: a textbook use of the pathetic fallacy that would have done a Victorian novelist—or a pulp detective-story writer—proud.

—B. Y.

∞

HONKY TONK TUNES AND A LONG-REMEMBERED DREAM . . . CONSTANT
HAGGLING, USELESS BRIEFINGS AND A HOWLING VOICE AT THE DOOR

American politics will never be the same again.
—Senator George McGovern,
Acceptance Speech,
July 13th, 1972, Miami, Florida

Another hot, heavy rain in Washington, at 4:33 on a wet Wednesday morning, falling like balls of sweat against my window. . . . Twelve feet wide and
six feet tall, the high yellow eye of the National Affairs Suite looking out
across the rotting roofs of our nation's capital at least a mile away through
the haze and the rain to the fine white marble spire of the Washington Monument and the dark dome of the Capitol. . . . Hillbilly music howling out of
the radio across the room from the typewriter.

. . . And when it's midnight in Dallas, I'll be somewhere on a big jet plane.
. . . If I could only understand you, maybe I could cope with the loneliness
I feel. . . .

Honky-tonk tunes and a quart of Wild Turkey on the sideboard, ripped to
the tits on whatever it was in that bag I bought tonight from the bull fruit in
Georgetown, looking down from the desk at yesterday's huge *Washington
Post* headline:

PRESIDENT ADMITS WITHHOLDING DATA
TAPES SHOW HE APPROVED COVER-UP

Every half-hour on the half-hour, WXRA—the truckers' station over in
Alexandria—keeps babbling more and more hideous news of "rapidly dissolving" support in the House and the Senate. All ten members of the House
Judiciary Committee who voted *against* the articles of impeachment on
national TV last week have now reversed themselves, for the record, and
said they plan to vote *for* impeachment when—or if—it comes to a vote in
the House on August 19th. Even Barry Goldwater has leaked (and then
denied) a UPI report that he thinks Nixon should resign, for the good of the
country . . . and also for the good of Goldwater and everybody else in the
Republican party, such as it is.
    Indeed. The rats are deserting the ship at high speed. Even the dingbat
senator from Colorado, Peter Dominick—the GOP claghorn who nomi-
nated Nixon for the Nobel Peace Prize less than two years ago—has called
the president's 11th-hour admission of complicity in the Watergate cover-up
"sorrowful news."
    We will not have Richard Nixon to kick around much longer—which is
not especially "sorrowful news" to a lot of people, except that the purging of

the cheap little bastard is going to have to take place here in Washington and will take up the rest of our summer.

One day at a time, Sweet Jesus. . . . That's all I'm askin' from you. . . .

And now the Compton Brothers with a song about ". . . when the wine ran out and the jukebox ran out of tunes . . ."

Jesus, we need more ice and whiskey here. Fill the bag with water and suck down the dregs. The rain is still lashing my window, the dawn sky is still black and this room is damp and cold. Where is the goddamn heat switch? Why is my bed covered with newspaper clips and U.S. Government Printing Office evidence books from the Nixon impeachment hearings?

Ah . . . madness, madness. On a day like this, not even the prospect of Richard Nixon's downfall can work up the blood. This is stone, flat-out fucking weather.

On another day like this, a long time ago, I was humming across the bridge out of Louisville, Kentucky, in an old Chevy with three or four good ole boys who worked with me at a furniture factory in Jeffersonville, Indiana. . . . The tires were hissing on the wet asphalt, the windshield wipers were lashing back and forth in the early morning rain and we were hunkered down in the car with our lunch bags and moaning along with a mean country tune on the radio when somebody said:

"Jesus Christ: Why are we going to *work* on a day like this? We must be *goddamn crazy.* This is the kind of day when you want to be belly-to-belly with a good woman, in a warm bed under a tin roof with the rain beating down and a bottle of good whiskey right next to the bed."

Let me be there in your mornin', let me be there in your night. . . . Let me be there when you need me . . . and make it right.

Ah, this haunting, honky music. . . . I am running a serious out-of-control fever for that long-remembered dream of a tin-roof, hard-rain, belly-to-belly day with a big iron bolt on the door and locked away in a deep warm bed from every connection to the outside world except a $14.95 tin radio wailing tunes like "I Smell a Rat" and "The Wild Side of Life."

This is not your ideal flying weather. Both National and Dulles airports are "closed for the rest of the morning," they say. . . . But despite all that I find myself on the phone demanding plane reservations back to Colorado. Fuck the weather . . .

Whoever answered the phone at United Airlines said the weather was "expected to be clear" by early afternoon and there were plenty of seats open for the 4:40 flight to Denver.

"Wonderful," I said, "but I want a first-class seat in the *smokers'* section."

"I'll check," she said, and moments later she was back with bad news: "The smoking seats are all taken, sir, but if it makes no difference to you—"

304

"It does," I said. "I *must* smoke. I insist on it."

She checked again and this time the news was better: "I think we can open a smoking seat for you, sir. Could I have your name?"

"Nader," I said. "R. Nader."

"How do you spell that?"

I spelled it for her, then set my alarm for two and fell asleep on the couch, still wearing my wet swimming trunks. After two months on the Nixon Impeachment Trail, my nerves were worn raw from the constant haggling and frustrated hostility of all those useless, early morning White House press briefings and long, sweaty afternoons pacing aimlessly around the corridors of the Rayburn Office Building on Capitol Hill, waiting for crumbs of wisdom from any two or three of those 38 luckless congressmen on the House Judiciary Committee hearing evidence on the possible impeachment of Richard Nixon.

It was an eerie spectacle: The whole Nixonian empire—seemingly invincible less than two years ago—was falling apart of its own foul weight right in front of our eyes. There was no denying the vast and historic proportions of the story, but covering it on a day-to-day basis was such a dull and degrading experience that it was hard to keep a focus on what was really happening. It was essentially a lawyer's story, not a journalist's.

I never made that plane. Sometime around noon I was jolted awake by a pounding on my door and a voice shouting, "Wake up, goddamnit, the whole town's gone crazy—the sonofabitch has caved in—he's quitting."

"No!" I thought. "Not now! I'm too weak to handle it." These goddamn rumors had kept me racing frantically around Washington day and night for almost a week—and when the shitrain finally began, I was helpless. My eyes were swollen shut with chlorine poisoning and when I tried to get out of bed to open the door, I almost snapped both ankles. I had fallen asleep wearing rubber-soled basketball shoes, which had wedged themselves between the sheets at the foot of the bed so firmly that my first thought was that somebody had strapped me down on the bed.

The howling voice at my door was Craig Vetter, another *Rolling Stone* writer who had been in town for two weeks trying to make some kind of connection with Nixon's priest. . . . But the priest was finished now and the town was going wild. A *Washington Post* reporter said he had never seen the newsroom so frantic—not even when John Kennedy was murdered or during the Cuban missile crisis. The prevailing rumors on Capitol Hill had Nixon either addressing a joint session of Congress at 4:30 that afternoon or preparing a final statement for delivery at 7:00 on all three networks . . . but a call to the White House pressroom spiked both these rumors, although the place was filling up with reporters who'd picked up an entirely different rumor: That either Ziegler or Nixon himself would soon appear in the pressroom to make a statement of some kind.

Six more calls from the National Affairs Suite churned up at least six more impossible rumors. Every switchboard in town that had any connection with either journalism or politics was jammed and useless. Later that night, even the main White House switchboard jammed up for the first time most reporters could remember, and for the next two days almost everybody who worked in the White House—even private secretaries—kept their home phones off the hook because of the chaos.

It was about 1:30 on Wednesday afternoon when I got through to Marty Nolan in the White House pressroom. We compared rumors and killed both lists very quickly. "This is all crazy bullshit," said Nolan. "We're just being jerked around. He's not going to do anything serious today, but just on the chance that he might, I don't dare leave this goddamn dungeon."

I had been on the verge of going down there, but after arranging with Nolan and about six other people in strategic positions in different parts of town to call me instantly if anything started to happen, I decided that the best thing to do was to take both the TV set and the FM radio down to a table by the pool and have all my calls transferred down to the lifeguard's telephone. . . . Which turned out to be the best of all possible solutions: Vetter and I set up a totally efficient communications post beside the pool, and for the next 48 hours we were able to monitor the whole craziness from our table beside the pool.

THE SUCK-TIDE REACHES SAN CLEMENTE . . . ZIEGLER BRINGS THE NEWS TO THE BOSS . . . GENERAL HAIG AND THE BAG OF DIMES . . . THE SYBARITIC PRIEST AND THE MENTALLY RETARDED RABBI . . . MORE TALK OF THE 'SUICIDE OPTION'

Well . . . the goddamn thing is over now; it ended on Thursday afternoon with all the grace and meaning of a Coke bottle thrown off a third-floor fire escape on the Bowery—exploding on the sidewalk and scaring the shit out of everybody in range, from the ones who got righteously ripped full of glass splinters to the swarm of "innocent bystanders" who still don't know what happened. . . .

. . . And probably never will; there is a weird, unsettled, painfully incomplete quality about the whole thing. All over Washington tonight is the stench of a massive psychic battle that *nobody* really won. Richard Nixon has been broken, whipped and castrated all at once, but even for me there is no real crank or elation in having been a front-row spectator at the final scenes, the Deathwatch, the first time in American history that a president has been chased out of the White House and cast down in the ditch with all the other geeks and common criminals. . . .

Looking back on the final few months of his presidency, it is easy to see that Nixon was doomed all along—or at least from that moment when

Archibald Cox first decided to force a showdown on the "executive privilege" question by sending a U.S. marshal over to the White House with a subpoena for some of the Oval Office tapes.

Nixon naturally defied that subpoena, but not even the crazed firing of Cox, Richardson and Ruckelshaus could make it go away. And when Jaworski challenged Nixon's right to defy that subpoena in the U.S. Supreme Court, the wheels of doom began rolling. And from that point on, it was clear to all the principals except Nixon himself that the Unthinkable was suddenly inevitable; it was only a matter of time. . . . And it was just about then that Richard Nixon began losing his grip on reality.

Within hours after Jaworski and Nixon's "Watergate lawyer" James St. Clair had argued the case in a special session of the Court, I talked to Pat Buchanan and was surprised to hear that Nixon and his wizards in the White House were confident that the verdict would be 5–3 in their favor. Even Buchanan, who thinks rationally about 79% of the time, apparently believed—less than two weeks before the Court ruled unanimously *against* Nixon—that five of the eight justices who would have to rule on that question would see no legal objection to ratifying Nixon's demented idea that anything discussed in the president's official office—even a patently criminal conspiracy—was the president's personal property, if he chose to have it recorded on his personal tape-recording machinery.

The possibility that even some of the justices The Boss himself had appointed to the Court might not cheerfully endorse a concept of presidential immunity that mocked both the U.S. Constitution and the Magna Carta had apparently been considered for a moment and then written off as too far-fetched and crazy even to worry about by all of Nixon's personal strategists.

It is still a little difficult to believe, in fact, that some of the closest advisers to the president of a constitutional democracy in the year nineteen hundred and seventy-four might actually expect the highest court in *any* constitutional democracy to crank up what is probably the most discredited precedent in the history of Anglo-American jurisprudence—the "divine right of kings"—in order to legalize the notion that a president of the United States or any other would-be democracy is above and beyond "the law."

That Nixon and his personal Gestapo actually believed this could happen is a measure of the insanity quotient of the people Nixon took down in the bunker with him when he knew the time had come to get serious.

But even as they raved, you could hear a hollow kind of paranoid uncertainty in their voices, as if they could already feel the ebb tide sucking around their ankles—just as Nixon must have felt it when he walked alone on the beach at San Clemente a few weeks earlier, trudging slowly along in the surf with his pantlegs rolled up while he waited in angry solitude for the results of the Supreme Court vote on his claim of "executive privilege." That rush of sucking water around his ankles must have almost pulled him out to sea when

307

Ziegler called down from the big dune in front of La Casa Pacifica: "Mister President! Mister President! We just got the news! The vote was unanimous—eight to zero."

Nixon whoops with delight: He stops in his waterfilled tracks and hurls out both arms in the twin-victory sign. "Wonderful!" he shouts. "I *knew* we'd win it, Ron! Even without that clown Renchburg. It wasn't for nothing that I appointed those other dumb farts to the Court!"

Ziegler stares down at him, at this doomed scarecrow of a president down there on the edge of the surf. Why is he grinning? Why does he seem so happy at this terrible news?

"No!" Ziegler shouts. "That is not what I meant. That is not what I meant at all!" He hesitates, choking back a sob. "The vote was eight to zero, Mister President—*against* you."

"What?" The scarecrow on the beach goes limp. His arms collapse, his hands flap crazily around the pockets of his wet pants. "Those dirty bastards!" he screams. "We'll break their balls!"

"Yes *sir!*" Ziegler shouts. "They'll wish they'd never been born!" He jerks a notebook out of his inside coat pocket and jots: "Break their balls."

By this time the wet president is climbing the dune in front of him. "What happened?" Nixon snarls. "Did somebody get to Burger?"

Ziegler nods. "What else? Probably it was Edward Bennet Williams."

"Of course," says Nixon. "We should never have left that dumb sonofabitch back there in Washington by himself. We know he'll do business: That's why we put him there." He kicks savagely at a lone ice plant in the sand. "Goddamnit! Where was Colson? Burger was *his* assignment, right?"

Ziegler winces. "Colson's in jail, sir. Don't you remember?"

Nixon stares blankly, then recovers. "Colson? In jail? What did he do?" He picks up a kelp head and lashes it against his shin. "Never mind, I remember now—but what about Ehrlichman? He can jerk Burger and those other clowns around like a goddamn Punch and Judy show!"

Ziegler stares out to sea for a moment, his eyes cloud over. "Well, sir . . . John's not much good to us anymore. He's going to prison."

Nixon stiffens, dropping the kelp head in the sand. "Holy shit, Ron! Why should John go to prison? He's one of the finest public servants I've ever had the privilege of knowing!"

Ziegler is weeping openly now, his emaciated body is wracked by deep sobs. "I *don't know*, sir. I can't explain it." He stares out to sea again, fighting to gain control of himself. "These are terrible times, Mister President. Our enemies are closing in. While you were out there on the beach, the Avis agency in Laguna called and canceled our credit. *They took my car*, Mister President! My gold Cadillac convertible! I was on the phone with Buzhardt—about the Supreme Court business, you know—when I looked out the window and saw this little nigger in an Avis uniform driving my car out the gate. The guards said he had a writ of seizure, signed by the local sheriff."

"My God!" Nixon exclaims. "We'll break his balls! Where's a telephone? I'll call Haldeman."

"It's no use, sir," Ziegler replies. "We can't make any outgoing calls until we pay the phone company $33,000. They sent a man down to fix the lines so we can only take incoming calls—for the next 86 hours, and then we'll be cut off entirely. If you want to call Washington, we'll have to walk to the San Clemente Inn and use a pay phone. I think General Haig has a bag of dimes in his room."

Nixon stiffens again; his brain is mired in deep thought. Then his eyes light up and he grabs Ziegler by the arm, dragging him toward the house. "Come on, Ron," he snaps, "I have an idea."

Ziegler stumbles along behind the president: He feels the energy flowing into him—The Boss is on the move.

Nixon is talking as he runs: "I think I've isolated our problem, Ron. We need credit, right? OK, where's that Jew?"

"Jew?"

"You know who I mean, goddamnit—that rabbi. They can always get credit, can't they? A rabbi? We'll send some of the Secret Service boys up there to Laguna to round him up. He's probably in the bar up there on top of the Surf and Sand; that's where he hangs out." Nixon laughs wildly now. "Shit, *nobody* questions a rabbi's credit! You tell the SS boys to pick him up and throw a real scare into him, then bring him down here and I'll *stroke* him."

Now Ziegler is laughing. His eyes are bright and he is writing fast in his notebook. "It's a wonderful idea, sir, just wonderful! First we stonewall the bastards, then we outflank them with a Jew!"

Nixon nods happily. "They'll never know what hit 'em, Ron. You know what I've always said: 'When the going gets tough, the tough get going.' "

"That's right, sir. I remember when Coach Lombardi—"

Nixon cuts him off with a sudden clap of his wet hands; the sound causes two Secret Service agents in the nearby shrubbery to go for their guns. "Hold on, Ron! Just hold it right there! You know who taught Coach Lombardi everything he knew?" He smiles deeply. "Me! The President!"

Ziegler wrings his hands, his eyeballs bulge, his face is twisted with reverence. "I *remember* that, sir—I remember!"

"*Good*, Ron, good! Only losers forget. . . . And you know what Coach Lombardi said about *that*." Nixon seizes his press secretary by both elbows and comes up close to his face: His breath is foul, his eyeballs are bloodshot, his pupils are dangerously dilated, his words come in short, high-pitched barks like a rabid hyena: "You show me a good loser, Ron—and I'll show you a *loser*."

Ziegler is overwhelmed: His eyes are so wide that he can't even blink; his body is rigid but his soul is on fire. His face is a mask of pure zeal: Ron Ziegler—left-hand man to a doomed and criminal president, the political flip side of every burned-out acid freak who voted for Goldwater and then switched to Tim Leary until the pain got too bad and the divine light of either Jesus or Maharaj Ji lured him off in the wake of another Perfect Master.

Ah, poor Ron. I knew him well enough. It was Ziegler, in fact, who tipped me off many months ago that Nixon was finished. This was back in July, in that lull before the storm when the wizards in Washington were beginning to nod glumly at each other whenever somebody suggested that the impeachment drive seemed to be faltering and that maybe Nixon was bottoming out, that in fact he had already bounced off the bottom and was preparing to take the offensive once again.

These were the salad days of early summer, before the fateful Supreme Court decision, when Nixon's Goebbels—ex–White House "communications director" Ken Clawson—was creating a false dawn over the White House by momentarily halting Nixon's year-long slide in the public opinion polls with a daily drumbeat of heavy, headline-grabbing attacks on "professional Nixon-haters" in the press, and "unprincipled, knee-jerk liberals in Congress." At that point in time, most of Nixon's traditional allies were beginning to hear the death shrieks of the banshee floating over the White House lawns at night, and even Billy Graham had deserted him. So Clawson, in a stroke of cheap genius, put a sybaritic Jesuit priest and a mentally retarded rabbi on the payroll and sent them forth to do battle with the forces of Evil.

Father John McLaughlin, the Jesuit, wallowed joyfully in his role as "Nixon's priest" for a month or so, but his star faded fast when it was learned he was pulling down more than $25,000 a year for his efforts and living in a luxury apartment at the Watergate. His superiors in the church were horrified, but McLaughlin gave them the back of his hand and, instead, merely cranked up his speechmaking act. In the end, however, not even Clawson could live with the insistent rumor that the Good Jesuit Father was planning to marry his girlfriend. This was too much, they say, for the rigid sensibilities of General Haig, the White House chief of staff, whose brother was a legitimate priest in Baltimore. McLaughlin disappeared very suddenly, after six giddy weeks on the national stage, and nothing has been heard of him since.

But Clawson was ready for that. No sooner had the priest been deep-sixed than he unveiled another holy man—the Rabbi Baruch Korff, a genuine dingbat with barely enough sense to tie his own shoes, but who eagerly lent his name and his flaky presence to anything Clawson aimed him at. Under the banner of something called the "National Citizens' Committee for Fairness to the President," he "organized" rallies, dinner parties and press conferences all over the country. One of his main financial backers was Hamilton Fish Sr., a notorious fascist and the father of New York Congressman Hamilton Fish Jr., one of the Republican swing votes on the House Judiciary Committee who quietly voted for impeachment.

*   *   *

Only a month ago, the storms of destiny seemed to be subsiding for President Nixon. Among the Knowledgeable in Washington, the conviction was growing that the impeachment campaign against him had spent its moment. . . . [But] it is now clear that the Knowledgeable were wrong, that they mistook a break in the clouds for lasting sunshine. . . .

—R. W. APPLE JR.,
The New York Times,
July 28th, 1974

In fact, however, Nixon was already doomed by the time the Rodino committee got around to voting. The unanimous Supreme Court vote on the question of "executive privilege" with regard to the 64 disputed tapes was the beginning of the end. Nixon had known all along that the release of those tapes would finish him—but he had consistently lied about their contents: not only to the press and the public, but also to his wife and his daughters and all the hardcore loyalists on his staff. He lied about the tapes to Barry Goldwater and Gerry Ford, to Hugh Scott and John Rhodes, to Al Haig and Pat Buchanan and even to his own attorney, James St. Clair—who was stupid enough, like the others, to have believed him when he swore that the tapes he refused to let anybody listen to would finally prove his innocence.

Both of his lawyers, in fact, had done everything in their power to *avoid* hearing the goddamn things. It finally required a direct order from Judge Sirica, on two separate occasions, to compel Buzhardt and St. Clair to listen to the tapes. Buzhardt was first, and within hours after hearing the fatal conversation with Haldeman of June 23rd, 1972, he was rushed to the intensive care ward of a private hospital in Virginia with a serious "heart attack" that rendered him incommunicado for almost two months.

I was sitting in a bar called the Class Reunion, about two blocks from the White House, when I heard the tragic news. . . . And I recall saying to *Boston Globe* correspondent Marty Nolan: "We'll never see Buzhardt again. They can't afford to let him live. If he survives whatever Ziegler put in his coffee when he was listening to those tapes, Haldeman will go out there and stick a hatpin up his nose while he's wasted on Demerol, jam it straight into his brain when the nurse gets out of the room. Take my word for it, Marty. I know how these people operate. Buzhardt will never leave that hospital alive."

Nolan nodded, oblivious to Buzhardt's grim fate. At that point, almost every journalist in Washington assigned to the Nixon Deathwatch had been averaging about two hours sleep a night since the beginning of summer. Many were weak and confused, succumbing to drink or drugs whenever possible. Others seemed to hover from day to day on the brink of terminal fatigue. Radio and TV reporters in the White House pressroom were reduced to tearing articles out of the nearest newspaper and reading them verbatim straight over the air—while the newspaper and magazine people would tape the live broadcasts and then transcribe them word for word under their own bylines. By the end of July, the prospect of having to cover an impeachment debate in the House and then a trial in the Senate for three or four months without relief was almost unbearable. As August began and Nixon still showed no signs of giving up, there was more and more talk of "the suicide option."

LAST BREAKFAST AT THE WHITE HOUSE . . . THE SCUMBAG I PASSED
TO A NEW GENERATION . . . COLD TURKEY SWOOPS DOWN & PANIC
FOR WATERGATE JUNKIES

Sometime around dawn on the Friday morning of Richard Milhous Nixon's last breakfast in the White House I put on my swimming trunks and a red rain parka, laced my head with some gray Argentine snuff, and took an elevator down to the big pool below my window in the National Affairs Suite at the Washington Hilton. It was still raining, so I carried my portable TV set, a notebook and four bottles of Bass Ale in a waterproof canvas bag.

The lower lobby was empty, except for the night watchman—a meaty black gentleman whose main duty was to keep people like me out of the pool at night, but we had long since come to a friendly understanding on this subject. It was against the rules to swim when the pool was closed but there was no rule to prevent a Doctor of Divinity from going out there to meditate on the end of the diving board.

"Mornin', Doc," said the watchman. "Up a little early, ain't you? Especially on a nasty day like this."

"Nasty?" I replied. "What are you—some kind of goddamn Uncle Tom Republican? Don't you know who's leaving town today?"

He looked puzzled for a moment, then his face cracked into a grin. "You're right, by god! I almost forgot. We finally got rid of that man, didn't we, Doc?" He nodded happily. "Yes sir, we finally got rid of him."

I reached into my bag and opened two Bass Ales. "This is a time for celebration," I said, handing him one of the bottles. I held mine out in front of me: "To Richard Nixon," I said, "may he choke on the money he stole."

The watchman glanced furtively over his shoulder before lifting his ale for the toast. The clink of the two bottles coming together echoed briefly in the vast, deserted lobby.

"See you later," I said. "I have to meditate for a while, then hustle down to the White House to make sure he really leaves. I won't believe it until I see it with my own eyes."

The flat surface of the pool was pocked with millions of tiny raindrops beating steadily down on the water. There was a chain lock on the gate, so I climbed over the fence and walked down to the deep end, where I located a dry spot under a tree near the diving board. *The CBS Morning News* would be on in about 20 minutes; I turned on the TV set, adjusted the aerial and turned the screen so I could see it from the pool about 20 feet away. It was a system I'd worked out last summer at the Senate Watergate hearings: After every two laps, I could look over the edge of the pool and check the screen to see if Hughes Rudd's face had appeared yet. When it did, I would climb out of the water and lie down on the grass in front of the set—turn up the sound, light a cigarette, open a fresh Bass Ale and take notes while I watched the tiny screen for a general outline of whatever action Sam Ervin's Roman circus might be expected to generate that day.

I stayed out there by the pool for almost two hours, sliding in and out of the water to run a few laps and then back out to stretch out on the grass to make a note now and then on the news. Not much was happening, except for a few kinky interviews down by the White House gate with people who claimed to have been on the Deathwatch for three days and nights without sleeping. . . . But very few of them could even begin to explain why they were doing it. At least half the crowd around the White House during those last few days looked like people who spend every weekend prowling the Demolition Derby circuit.

The only other action on the news that Friday morning was an occasional rerun of Nixon's official resignation speech from the night before. I had watched it with Vetter in the Watergate bar. It seemed like a good place to be on that night, because I had also been there on the night of June 17th, 1972—while the Watergate burglary was happening five floors above my head.

But after I'd watched Nixon's speech for the third time, a strange feeling of nervousness began working on me and I decided to get out of town as soon as possible. The movie was over—or at least it would be over in two or three hours. Nixon was leaving at 10:00, and Ford would be sworn in at noon. I wanted to be there on the White House lawn when Nixon was lifted off. That would be the end of *my* movie.

It was still raining when I left and the pool was still empty. I put the TV set back in the canvas bag and climbed over the gate by the lifeguard shack. Then I stopped and looked back for a moment, knowing I would never come back to this place, and if I did it would not be the same. The pool would be the same, and it would be easy enough to pick up a case of Bass Ale or a battery TV set. . . . And I could even come down here on rainy summer mornings and watch the morning news. . . .

But there would not be this kind of morning anymore, because the main ingredient for that mix was no longer available in Washington; and if you asked any of the people who were known to have a real taste for it, the hardcore Nixon aficionados, they all understood that it would not be available again for a hell of a long time and probably never.

Nobody even talks about substitutes or something almost exactly the same. The mold disappeared about three minutes after they made that evil bastard . . . and although there was never any doubt about who stole it, nobody had any proof.

No . . . even with the pool and the ale and grass and the portable TV set, the morning news will not be the same without the foul specter of Richard Nixon glaring out of the tube. But the war is over now and he lost. . . . Gone but not forgotten, missed but not mourned; we will not see another one like him for quite a while. He was dishonest to a fault, the truth was not in him, and if it can be said that he resembled any other living animal in this world, it could only have been the hyena.

I took a cab down to the White House and pushed through the sullen mob on the sidewalk to the guardhouse window. The cop inside glanced at my card, then looked up—fixing me with a heavy-lidded Quaalude stare for just an instant, then nodded and pushed his buzzer to open the gate. The press-room in the West Wing was empty, so I walked outside to the Rose Garden, where a big olive-drab helicopter was perched on the lawn, about 100 feet out from the stairs. The rain had stopped and a long, red carpet was laid out on the wet grass from the White House door to the helicopter. I eased through the crowd of photographers and walked out, looking back at the White House, where Nixon was giving his final address to a shocked crowd of White House staffers. I examined the aircraft very closely, and I was just about to climb into it when I heard a loud rumbling behind me; I turned around just in time to see Richard and Pat coming toward me, trailing their daughters and followed closely by Gerald Ford and Betty. Their faces were grim and they were walking very slowly; Nixon had a glazed smile on his face, not looking at anybody around him, and walked like a wooden Indian full of Thorazine.

His face was a greasy death mask. I stepped back out of his way and nod-ded hello but he didn't seem to recognize me. I lit a cigarette and watched him climb the steps to the door of the helicopter. . . . Then he spun around very suddenly and threw his arms straight up in the famous twin-victory sig-nal; his eyes were still glazed, but he seemed to be looking over the heads of the crowd at the White House.

Nobody was talking. A swarm of photographers rushed the plane as Nixon raised his arms—but his body had spun around too fast for his feet, and as his arms went up I saw him losing his balance. The grimace on his face went slack, then he bounced off the door and stumbled into the cock-pit. Pat and Ziegler were already inside; Ed Cox and Tricia went in quickly without looking back, and a Marine in dress blues shut the door and jumped away as the big rotor blades began turning and the engine cranked up to a dull, whining roar.

I was so close that the noise hurt my ears. The rotor blades were invisible now, but the wind was getting heavier; I could feel it pressing my eyeballs back into their sockets. For an instant I thought I could see Richard Nixon's face pressed up to the window. Was he smiling? Was it Nixon? I couldn't be sure. And now it made no difference.

The wind blast from the rotors was blowing people off-balance now; photographers were clutching their equipment against their bodies and Gerald Ford was leading his wife back toward the White House with a stony scowl on his face.

I was still very close to the helicopter, watching the tires. As the beast began rising, the tires became suddenly fat; there was no more weight on them. . . . The helicopter went straight up and hovered for a moment, then swooped down toward the Washington Monument and then angled up into the fog. Richard Nixon was gone.

The Last Secrets of Skull and Bones

RON ROSENBAUM

∞

Ron Rosenbaum is America's foremost Gonzo essayist. That is to say, like Hunter Thompson, Gonzo journalism's founder and dean, Rosenbaum is the main character in any story he writes. A significant difference is that Rosenbaum—who began writing for the *Village Voice* in the early 1970s and since then has contributed to nearly every major magazine—concentrates on his thoughts rather than his actions. A typical piece traces his introduction to some unusual idea or subculture (the cancer-cure underground, Kennedy-assassination buffs, conspiracy theorists of various stripes), and then his private-eye-like process of discovery and reflection, resulting ultimately in, if not The Truth, then at least a measure of truth. In a Rosenbaum article, the climactic scene can take place in a dusty archive where an elusive clipping induces epiphany.

"The Last Secrets of Skull and Bones," originally published in *Esquire* in 1977, concerns one of his less momentous topics—a Yale secret society where grown men meet in a windowless clubhouse, share sexual secrets, roll around in the mud, and then go off to assume the nation's leadership positions. (The piece was written a decade before George Bush became the first Bonesman president.) But Rosenbaum, in his characteristically entertaining way, extracts some meaning from his investigation, as well as a hitherto unknown link between Skull and Bones and the nineteenth-century Bavarian Illuminists.

—B. Y.

∞

Take a look at that hulking sepulcher over there. Small wonder they call it a tomb. It's the citadel of Skull and Bones, the most powerful of all secret societies in the strange Yale secret-society system. For nearly a century and a half, Skull and Bones has been the most influential secret society in the nation, and now it is one of the last.

In an age in which it seems that all that could possibly be concealed about anything and anybody has been revealed, those blank tombstone walls could be holding the last secrets left in America.

You could ask Averell Harriman whether there's really a sarcophagus in the basement and whether he and young Henry Stimson and young Henry Luce lay down naked in that coffin and spilled the secrets of their adolescent sex life to fourteen fellow Bonesmen. You could ask Supreme Court Justice Potter Stewart if there came a time in the year 1937 when he dressed up in a skeleton suit and howled wildly at an initiate in a red-velvet room inside the tomb. You could ask McGeorge Bundy if he wrestled naked in a mud pile as part of his initiation and how it compared with a later quagmire into which he so eagerly plunged. You could ask Bill Bundy or Bill Buckley, both of whom went into the C.I.A. after leaving Bones—or George Bush, who *ran* the C.I.A.—whether their Skull and Bones experience was useful training for the clandestine trade. ("Spook," the Yale slang word for secret-society member, is, of course, Agency slang for spy.) You could ask J. Richardson Dilworth, the Bonesman who now manages the Rockefeller fortune, just how wealthy the Bones society is and whether it's true that each new initiate gets a no-strings gift of fifteen thousand dollars cash and guaranteed financial security for life.

You could ask . . . but I think you get the idea. The leading lights of the Eastern establishment—in old-line investment banks (Brown Brothers Harriman pays Bones's tax bill), in blue-blood law firms (Simpson, Thacher & Bartlett, for one), and particularly in the highest councils of the foreign-policy establishment—the people who have shaped America's national character since it ceased being an undergraduate power, had *their* undergraduate character shaped in that crypt over there. Bonesman Henry Stimson, Secretary of War under F.D.R., a man at the heart of the heart of the American ruling class, called his experience in the tomb the most profound one in his entire education.

But none of them will tell you a thing about it. They've sworn an oath never to reveal what goes on inside and they're legendary for the lengths to which they'll go to avoid prying interrogation. The mere mention of the words "skull and bones" in the presence of a true-blue Bonesman, such as Blackford Oakes, the fictional hero of Bill Buckley's spy thriller, *Saving the Queen,* will cause him to "dutifully leave the room, as tradition prescribed."

I can trace my personal fascination with the mysterious goings-on in the sepulcher across the street to a spooky scene I witnessed on its shadowy steps late one April night eleven years ago. I was then a sophomore at Yale, living in Jonathan Edwards, the residential college (anglophile Yale name for dorm) built next to the Bones tomb. It was part of Jonathan Edwards' folklore that on the April evening following "tap night" at Bones, if one could climb to the tower of Weir Hall, the odd castle that overlooks the Bones courtyard, one could hear strange cries and moans coming from the bowels of the tomb as the fifteen newly "tapped" members were put through what sounded like a harrowing ordeal. Returning alone to my room late at night, I would always cross the street rather than walk the sidewalk that passed right in front of Bones. Even at that safe distance, something about it made my skin crawl.

But that night in April I wasn't alone; a classmate and I were coming back from an all-night diner at about two in the morning. At the time, I knew little about the mysteries of Bones or any of the other huge windowless secret-society tombs that dominated with dark authority certain key corners of the campus. They were nothing like conventional fraternities. No one lived in the tombs. Instead, every Thursday and Sunday night, the best and the brightest on campus, the fifteen seniors in Skull and Bones and in Scroll and Key, Book and Snake, Wolf's Head, Berzelius, in all the seven secret societies, disappeared into their respective tombs and spent hours doing *something*—something they were sworn to secrecy about. And Bones, it was said, was the most ritualistic and secretive of all. Even the very door to the Bones tomb, that huge triple-padlocked iron door, was never permitted to open in the presence of an outsider.

All this was floating through my impressionable sophomore mind that night as my friend Mike and I approached the stone pylons guarding the entrance to Bones. Suddenly we froze at the sight of a strange thing lying on the steps. There in the gloom of the doorway on the top step was a long white object that looked like the thighbone of a large mammal. I remained frozen. Mike was more venturesome: he walked right up the steps and picked up the bone. I wanted to get out of there fast; I was certain we were being spied upon from a concealed window. Mike couldn't decide what to do with the bone. He went up to the door and began examining the array of padlocks. Suddenly a bolt shot. The massive door began to swing open and something reached out at him from within. He gasped, terrified, and jumped back, but not before something clutched the bone, yanked it out of his hand and back into the darkness within. The door slammed shut with a clang that rang in our ears as we ran away.

Recollected in tranquillity, that dreamlike gothic moment seems to me an emblem of the strangeness I felt at being at Yale, at being given a brief glimpse of the mysterious workings of the inner temples of privilege but feeling emphatically shut out of the secret ceremonies within. I always felt irrelevant to the real purpose of the institution, which was from its missionary beginnings devoted to converting the idle progeny of the ruling class into morally serious leaders of the establishment. It is frequently in the tombs that the conversions take place.

NOVEMBER, 1976: SECURITY MEASURES

It's night and we're back in front of the tomb, Mike and I, reinforced by nine years in the outside world, two skeptical women friends and a big dinner at

Mory's. And yet once again there is an odd, chilling encounter. We're re-creating that first spooky moment. I'm standing in front of the stone pylons and Mike has walked up to stand against the door so we can estimate its height by his. Then we notice we're being watched. A small red foreign car has pulled up on the sidewalk a few yards away from us. The driver has been sitting with the engine running and has been watching us for some time. Then he gets out. He's a tall, athletic-looking guy, fairly young. He shuts the car door behind him and stands leaning against it, continuing to observe us. We try to act oblivious, continuing to sketch and measure.

The guy finally walks over to us. "You seen Miles?" he asks.

We look at each other. Could he think we're actually Bones alumni, or is he testing us? Could "You seen Miles?" be some sort of password?

"No," we reply. "Haven't seen Miles."

He nods and remains there. We decide we've done enough sketching and measuring and stroll off.

"Look!" one of the women says as she turns and points back. "He just ran down the side steps to check the basement-door locks. He probably thought he caught us planning a break-in."

I found the episode intriguing. What it said to me was that Bones still cared about the security of its secrets. Trying to find out what goes on inside could be a challenge.

And so it was that I set out this April to see just how secure those last secrets are. It was a task I took on not out of malice or sour grapes. I was not tapped for a secret society so I'm open to the latter charge, but I plead guilty only to the voyeurism of a mystery lover. I'd been working on a novel, a psychological thriller of sorts that involved the rites of Bones, and I thought it wouldn't hurt to spend some time in New Haven during the week of tap night and initiation night, poking around and asking questions.

You could call it espionage if you were so inclined, but I tried to play the game in a gentlemanly fashion: I would not directly ask a Bonesman to violate his sacred oath of secrecy. If, however, one of them happened to have fudged on the oath to some other party and that other party were to convey the gist of the information to me, I would rule it fair game. And if any Bonesman wants to step forward and add something, I'll be happy to listen.

What follows is an account of my search for the meaning behind the mysterious Bones rituals. Only information that might be too easily traced to its source has been left out, because certain sources expressed fear of reprisals against themselves. Yes, reprisals. One of them even insisted, with what seemed like deadly seriousness, that reprisals would be taken against me.

"What bank do you have your checking account at?" this party asked me in the middle of a discussion of the Mithraic aspects of the Bones ritual.

I named the bank.

"Aha," said the party. "There are three Bonesmen on the board. You'll never have a line of credit again. They'll tap your phone. They'll . . ."

THE ART OF FACT

Before I could say, "A line of *what*?" the source continued: "The alumni still care. Don't laugh. They don't like people tampering and prying. The power of Bones is incredible. They've got their hands on every lever of power in the country. You'll see—it's like trying to look into the Mafia. Remember, they're a secret society, too."

WEDNESDAY NIGHT, APRIL 14: THE DOSSIER

Already I have in my possession a set of annotated floor plans of the interior of the tomb, giving the location of the sanctum sanctorum, the room called 322. And tonight I received a dossier on Bones ritual secrets that was compiled from the archives of another secret society. (It seems that one abiding preoccupation of many Yale secret societies is keeping files on the secrets of other secret societies, particularly Bones.)

This dossier on Bones is a particularly sophisticated one, featuring "reliability ratings" in percentiles for each chunk of information. It was obtained for me by an enterprising researcher on the condition that I keep secret the name of the secret society that supplied it. Okay. I will say, though, that it's not the secret society that is rumored to have Hitler's silverware in its archives. That's Scroll and Key, chief rival of Bones for the elite of Yale— Dean Acheson and Cy Vance's society—and the source of most of the rest of the American foreign-policy establishment.

But to return to the dossier. Let me tell you what it says about the initiation, the center of some of the most lurid apocryphal rumors about Bones. According to the dossier, the Bones initiation ritual of 1940 went like this: "New man placed in coffin—carried into central part of building. New man chanted over and 'reborn' into society. Removed from coffin and given robes with symbols on it [*sic*]. A bone with his name on it is tossed into bone heap at start of every meeting. Initiates plunged naked into mud pile."

THURSDAY EVENING: THE FILE AND CLAW SOLUTION
TO THE MYSTERY OF 322

I'm standing in the shadows across the street from the tomb, ready to tail the first person to come out. Tonight is tap night, the night fifteen juniors will be chosen to receive the one-hundred-forty-five-year-old secrets of Bones. Tonight the fifteen seniors in Bones and the fifteen in each of the other societies will arrive outside the rooms of the prospective tappees. They'll pound loudly on the doors. When the chosen junior opens up, a Bonesman will slam him on the shoulder and thunder: "Skull and Bones: Do you accept?"

At that point, according to my dossier, if the candidate accepts, he will be handed a message wrapped with a black ribbon sealed in black wax with the skull-and-crossbones emblem and the mystic Bones number, 322. The message appoints a time and a place for the candidate to appear on initiation night—next Tuesday—the first time the newly tapped candidate will be permitted inside the tomb. Candidates are "instructed to wear no metal" to the initiation, the dossier notes ominously. (Reliability rating for this stated to be one hundred percent.)

Not long before eight tonight, the door to Bones swings open. Two dark-suited young men emerge. One of them carries a slim black attaché case. Obviously they're on their way to tap someone. I decide to follow them. I want to check out a story I heard that Bones initiates are taken to a ceremony somewhere near the campus before the big initiation inside the tomb. The Bonesmen head up High Street and pass the library, then make a right.

Passing the library, I can't help but recoil when I think of the embarrassing discovery I made in the manuscript room this afternoon. The last thing I wanted to do was reduce the subtleties of the social function of Bones to some simpleminded conspiracy theory. And yet I do seem to have come across definite, if skeletal, links between the origins of Bones rituals and those of the notorious Bavarian Illuminists. For me, an interested but skeptical student of the conspiracy world, the introduction of the Illuminists, or Illuminati, into certain discussions (say, for instance, of events in Dallas in 1963) has become the same thing that the mention of Bones is to a Bonesman—a signal to leave the room. Because although the Bavarian Illuminists did have a real historical existence (from 1776 to 1785 they were an esoteric secret society within the more mystical freethinking lodges of German Freemasonry), they have also had a paranoid fantasy existence throughout two centuries of conspiracy literature. They are *the* imagined megacabal that manipulated such alleged plots as the French and Russian revolutions, the elders of Zion, the rise of Hitler and the house of Morgan. Yes, the Bilderbergers and George De Mohrenschildt, too. Silly as it may sound, there are suggestive links between the historical, if not mythoconspiratorial, Illuminists and Bones.

First consider the account of the origins of Bones to be found in a century-old pamphlet published by an anonymous group that called itself File and Claw after the tools they used to pry their way inside Bones late one night. I came upon the File and Claw break-in pamphlet in a box of disintegrating documents filed in the library's manuscript room under Skull and Bones's corporate name, Russell Trust Association. The foundation was named for William H. (later General) Russell, the man who founded Bones in 1832. I was trying to figure out what mission Russell had for the secret order he founded and why he had chosen that particular death's-head brand of mumbo jumbo to embody his vision. Well, according to the File and Claw break-in crew, "Bones is a chapter of a corps of a German university. It should properly be called the Skull and Bones chapter. General Russell, its founder, was in Germany before his senior year and formed a warm friendship with a leading member of a German society. The meaning of the permanent number '322' in all Bones literature is that it was founded in '32 as the second chapter of the German society. But the Bonesman has a pleasing fiction that his fraternity is a descendant of an old Greek patriot society founded by Demosthenes, who died in 322 B.C."

They go on to describe a German slogan painted "on the arched walls above the vault" of the sacred room, 322. The slogan appears above a painting of skulls surrounded by Masonic symbols, a picture said to be "a gift of the German chapter." *"Wer war der Thor, wer Weiser, Bettler oder Kaiser? Ob Arm, ob Reich, im Tode gleich,"* the slogan reads, or, "Who was the fool, who the wise man, beggar or king? Whether poor or rich, all's the same in death."

Imagine my surprise when I ran into that very slogan in a 1798 Scottish anti-Illuminist tract reprinted in 1967 by the John Birch Society. The tract (*Proofs of a Conspiracy* by John Robison) prints alleged excerpts from Illuminist ritual manuals supposedly confiscated by the Bavarian police when the secret order was banned in 1785. Toward the end of the ceremony of initiation into the "Regent degree" of Illuminism, according to the tract, "a skeleton is pointed out to him [the initiate], at the feet of which are laid a crown and a sword. He is asked *whether that is the skeleton of a king, nobleman or a beggar.* As he cannot decide, the president of the meeting says to him, 'The character of being a man is the only one that is of importance' " (my italics).

Doesn't that sound similar to the German slogan the File and Claw team claims to have found inside Bones? Now consider a haunting photograph of the altar room of one of the Masonic lodges at Nuremberg that is closely associated with Illuminism. Haunting because at the altar room's center, approached through an aisle of hanging human skeletons, is a coffin surmounted by—you guessed it—a skull and crossed bones that look exactly like the particular arrangement of jawbones and thighbones in the official Bones emblem. The skull and crossbones was the official crest of another key Illuminist lodge, one right-wing Illuminist theoretician told me.

Now you can look at this three ways. One possibility is that the Bircher right—and the conspiracy-minded left—are correct: the Eastern establishment is the demonic creation of a clandestine elite manipulating history, and Skull and Bones is one of its recruiting centers. A more plausible explanation is that the death's-head symbolism was so prevalent in Germany when the impressionable young Russell visited that he just stumbled on the same mother lode of pseudo-Masonic mummery as the Illuminists. The third possibility is that the break-in pamphlets are an elaborate fraud designed by the File and Claw crew to pin the taint of Illuminism on Bones and that the rituals of Bones have innocent Athenian themes, 322 being *only* the date of the death of Demosthenes. (In fact, some Bones literature I've seen in the archives does express the year as if 322 B.C. were the year one, making 1977 anno Demostheni 2299.)

*　　*　　*

I am still following the dark-suited Bonesmen at a discreet distance as they make their way along Prospect Street and into a narrow alley, which, to my dismay, turns into a parking lot. They get into a car and drive off, obviously to tap an off-campus prospect. So much for tonight's clandestine work. I'd never get to my car in time to follow them. My heart isn't in it, anyway. I am due to head off to the graveyard to watch the initiation ceremony of Book and Snake, the secret society of Deep Throat's friend Bob Woodward (several Deep Throat theories have postulated Yale secret-society ties as the origin of Woodward's underground-garage connection, and two Bonesmen, Ray Price and Richard Moore, who were high Nixon aides, have been mentioned as suspects—perhaps because of their experience at clandestine underground truth telling). And later tonight I hope to make the first of my contacts with persons who have been inside—not just inside the tomb, but inside the skulls of some of the Bonesmen.

LATER THURSDAY NIGHT: TURNING THE TABLES ON THE SEXUAL AUTOBIOGRAPHIES

In his senior year, each member of Bones goes through an intense two-part confessional experience in the Bones crypt. One Thursday night, he tells his life story, giving what is meant to be a painfully forthright autobiography that exposes his traumas, shames and dreams. (Tom Wolfe calls this Bones practice a forerunner of The Me Decade's fascination with self.) The following Sunday-night session is devoted exclusively to sexual histories. They don't leave out anything these days. I don't know what it was like in General Russell's day, maybe there was less to talk about, but these days the sexual stuff is totally explicit and there's less need for fabricating exploits to fill up the allotted time. Most Sunday-night sessions start with talk of prep-school masturbation and don't stop until the intimate details of Saturday night's delights have come to light early Monday morning.

This has begun to cause some disruptions in relationships. The women the Bonesmen talk about in the crypt are often Yale co-eds and frequently feminists. None of these women is too pleased at having the most intimate secrets of her relationship made the subject of an all-night symposium consecrating her lover's brotherhood with fourteen males she hardly knows. As one woman put it, "I objected to fourteen guys knowing whether I was a good lay. . . . It was like after that each of them thought I was his woman in some way."

Some women have discovered that their lovers take their vows to Bones more solemnly than their commitments to women. There is the case of the woman who revealed something very personal—not embarrassing, just private—to her lover and made him swear never to repeat it to another human. When he came back from the Bones crypt after his Sunday-night sex session, he couldn't meet her eyes. He'd told his brothers in Bones.

It seems that the whole secret-society system at Yale is in the terminal stages of a sexual crisis. By the time I arrived this April, all but three of the formerly all-male societies had gone co-ed, and two of the remaining holdouts—Scroll and Key and Wolf's Head—were embroiled in bitter battles over certain members' attempts to have them follow the trend. The popular quarterback of the football team had resigned from Scroll and Key because its alumni would not even let him make a pro-coeducation plea to their convocation. When one prominent alumnus of Wolf's Head was told the current members had plans to tap women, he threatened to "raze the building" before permitting it. Nevertheless, it seemed as though it wouldn't be long before those two holdouts went co-ed. But not Bones. Both alumni and outsiders see the essence of the Bones experience as some kind of male bonding, a Victorian, muscular, Christian-missionary view of manliness and public service.

While changing the least of all the societies over its one hundred forty-five years, Bones did begin admitting Jews in the early Fifties and tapping blacks in 1949. It offered membership to some of the most outspoken rebels of the late Sixties and, more recently, added gay and bisexual members, including the president of the militant Gay Activist Alliance, a man by the name of Miles.

But women, the Bones alumni have strenuously insisted, are different. When a rambunctious Seventies class of Bones proposed tapping the best and brightest of the new Yale women, the officers of the Russell Trust Association threatened to bar that class from the tomb and change the locks if they dared. They didn't.

That sort of thing is what persuaded the person I am meeting with late tonight—and a number of other persons—to talk about what goes on inside: after all, isn't the core of the Bones group experience the betrayal of their loved ones' secrets? Measure for measure.

TUESDAY, APRIL 20: INITIATION NIGHT—
TALES OF THE TOMB AND DEER ISLAND

When I return to New Haven on initiation night to stand again in the shadows across the street from Bones in the hope of glimpsing an initiate enter, it is, thanks to my sources (who insist on anonymity), with a greater sense of just what it means for the initiate to be swallowed up by the tomb for the first time.

The first initiate arrives shortly before eight p.m., proceeds up the steps and halts at attention in front of the great door. I don't see him ring a bell; I don't think he has to. They are expecting him. The doors open. I can't make out who or what is inside, but the initiate's reaction is unmistakable: he puts his hands up as if a gun has been pointed at him. He walks into the gloom and the door closes behind him.

Earlier, according to my source, before the initiate was allowed to approach that door, he was led blindfolded to a Bones house somewhere on Orange Street and conducted to the basement. There two older Bonesmen dressed in skeleton suits had him swear solemn oaths to keep secret whatever he was to experience in the tomb during the initiation rite and forever after.

Now I am trying to piece together what I know about what is happening to that initiate tonight and, more generally, how his life will change now that he has been admitted inside. Tonight he will die to the world and be born again into the Order, as he will thenceforth refer to it. The Order is a world unto itself in which he will have a new name and fourteen new blood brothers, also with new names.

The "death" of the initiate will be as frightful as the liberal use of human skeletons and ritual psychology can make it. Whether it's accompanied by physical beatings or wrestling or a plunge into a mud or dung pile I have not been able to verify, but I'd give a marginally higher reliability rating to the mud-pile plunge. Then it's into the coffin and off on a symbolic journey through the underworld to rebirth, which takes place in room number 322. There the Order clothes the newborn knight in its own special garments, implying that henceforth he will tailor himself to the Order's mission.

Which is—if you take it at face value—to produce an alliance of good men. The Latin for "good men" is *"boni,"* of course, and each piece of Bones literature sports a Latin maxim making use of *"boni."* "Good men are rare," is the way one maxim translates. "Of all societies none is more glorious nor of greater strength than when good men of similar morals are joined in intimacy," proclaims another.

The intimacy doesn't really begin to get going until the autobiographical sessions start in September. But first there are some tangible rewards. In the months that follow tonight's initiation, the born-again Bonesmen will begin to experience the wonderful felicity of the Protestant ethic: secular rewards just happen to accrue to the elect as external tokens of their inner blessedness.

Fifteen thousand dollars, for instance. According to one source, each initiate gets a no-strings, tax-free gift of fifteen thousand dollars from the Russell Trust Association just for having been selected by Bones. I'd heard rumors that Bonesmen were guaranteed a secure income for life in some way—if only to prevent a downtrodden alcoholic brother from selling the secrets for a few bucks. When I put this question to my source, the reply was that of course the society would always help a downtrodden member with interest-free loans, if necessary, but, he added, the only outright contribution was a flat fifteen-thousand-dollar payment.

When I mentioned the fifteen-thousand-dollar figure to writer Tom Powers, a member of a secret society called Elihu, he, like members of other secret societies, professed incredulity. But the day after I spoke to him I received this interesting communication from Powers:

"I have checked with a Bones penetration and am now inclined to think you have got the goods where the fifteen thousand dollars is concerned. A sort of passive or negative confirmation. I put the question to him and he declined to comment in a tone of voice that might have been, but was not, derisory. Given an ideal opportunity to say, 'That's bullshit!' he did not.

"The interesting question now is what effect the fifteen-thousand-dollar report is going to have on next tap day. The whole Bones mystique will take on a mercenary air, sort of like a television game show. If there is no fifteen thousand, the next lineup of tappees will be plenty pissed. I can hear the conversations now: outgoing Bones members telling prospects there is one thing they've got to understand, really and truly—*there is no fifteen thousand!!!* While the prospects will be winking and nudging and saying, 'I understand. Ha-ha! You've got to say that, but just between us. . . .'

"If Bones has got a cell in C.I.A.," Powers concluded his letter, "you could be in big trouble."

Ah, yes. The Bones cell in the Central Intelligence Agency. Powers had called my attention to a passage in Aaron Latham's new novel, *Orchids for Mother,* in which the thinly veiled version of C.I.A. master spy James Angleton recalls that the Agency is "Langley's New Haven all over again. . . . Secret society'd be closer, like Skull and Bones."

"There are a lot of Bonesmen around, aren't there?" asks a young C.I.A. recruit.

Indeed, says the master spy, with all the Bones spooks it's "a regular haunted house."

If you were a supersecret spy agency seeking to recruit the most trustworthy and able men for dangerous missionary work against the barbarian threat wouldn't you want someone whose life story, character and secrets were already known to you? You'd certainly want to know if there were any sexual proclivities that might make the future spy open to temptation or blackmail.

Now, I'm not saying the C.I.A. has bugged the Bones crypt (although who could rule it out with certainty?). But couldn't the Agency use old Bonesmen to recruit new ones, or might they not have a trusted descendant of a Bonesman—just one in each fifteen would be enough—advise them on the suitability of the other fourteen for initiation into postgraduate secrets?

Consider the case of once gung-ho-C.I.A. Bonesman William Sloane Coffin, who later became a leader of the antiwar movement. A descendant of an aptly named family with three generations of Bonesmen, Coffin headed for the C.I.A. not long after graduation from Bones. And the man Coffin tapped for Bones, William F. Buckley Jr., was himself tapped by the C.I.A. the following year.

When I tried to reach Coffin to ask him about C.I.A. recruiting in Bones, I was told that he was "in seclusion," writing his memoirs. (Okay, Chaplain, but I want to let you know that I'll be looking in your memoirs to see just how much you tell about the secrets of Bones and the C.I.A., how loyal you still are to their secrets. Which side are you on?)

*   *   *

In the late summer following his initiation, right before he begins his senior year, the initiate is given a gift of greater value than any putative fifteen-thousand-dollar recruitment fee: his first visit to the private resort island owned and maintained by the Russell Trust Association in the St. Lawrence River. There, hidden among the Thousand Islands, the reborn initiate truly finds himself on an isle of the blessed. For there, on this place called Deer Island, are assembled the active Bones alumni and their families, and there he gets a sense of how many powerful establishment institutions are run by wonderful, civilized, silver-haired Bonesmen eager to help the initiate's establishment dreams come true. He can also meet the wives of Bonesmen of all ages and get a sense of what kind of woman is most acceptable and appropriate in Bones society and perhaps even meet that most acceptable of all types of women—the daughter of a Bonesman.

A reading of the lists of Bonesmen selected over the past one hundred forty-five years suggests that like the secret society of another ethnic group, certain powerful families dominate: the Tafts, the Whitneys, the Thachers, the Lords, for instance. You also get the feeling there's a lot of intermarriage among these Bones families. Year after year there will be a Whitney Townsend Phelps in the same Bones class as a Phelps Townsend Whitney. It's only natural, considering the way they grow up together with Bones picnics, Bones outings and a whole quiet panoply of Bones social events outside the campus and the tomb. Particularly on the island.

Of course, if the initiate has grown up in a Bones family and gone to picnics on the island all his life, the vision—the introduction to powerful people, the fine manners, the strong bonds—is less awesome. But to the nonhereditary slots in a Bones class of fifteen, the outsiders—frequently the football captain, the editor of the *Yale Daily News,* a brilliant scholar, a charismatic student politician—the island experience comes as a seductive revelation: these powerful people want me, want my talents, my services; perhaps they even want my genes. Play along with their rules and I can become one of them. They *want* me to become one of them.

In fact, one could make a half-serious case that functionally Bones serves as a kind of ongoing informal establishment eugenics project bringing vigorous new genes into the bloodlines of the Stimsonian elite. Perhaps that explains the origin of the sexual autobiography. It may have served some eugenic purpose in General Russell's vision: a sharing of birth-control and self-control methods to minimize the chance of a good man and future steward of the ruling class being trapped into marriage by a fortune hunter or a working-class girl—the way the grand tour for an upper-class American youth always included an initiation into the secrets of Parisian courtesans so that once back home the young man wouldn't elope with the first girl who let him get past second base.

However, certain of the more provincial Bones families do not welcome *all* genes into the pool. There is a story about two very well-known members of a Bones class who haven't spoken to each other for more than two decades. One of them was an early Jewish token member of Bones who began to date the sister of a fellow Bonesman. Apparently the Christian family made its frosty reaction to this development very plain. The Christian Bonesman did not convince his Jewish blood brother he was entirely on his side in the matter. The dating stopped and so did the speaking. It's an isolated incident, and I wouldn't have brought it up had I not been told of the "Jew-canoe" incident, which happened relatively recently.

There's a big book located just inside the main entrance to Bones. In it are some of the real secrets. Not the initiation rites or the grip, but reactions to, comments on and mementos of certain things that went on in the tomb, personal revelations, interpersonal encounters. The good stuff. I don't know if the tale of the brokenhearted token gay and the rotting-paella story are in there, but they should be. I'm almost sure the mysterious "Phil" incident *isn't* there. (According to one source, the very mention of the name "Phil" is enough to drive certain Bonesmen up the wall.) But the unfortunate "Jew-canoe" incident *is* in that book.

It seems that not too long ago the boys in a recent Bones class were sitting around the tomb making some wisecracks that involved Jewish stereotypes. "He drives a Cadillac—you know, the Jew canoe." Things like that. Well, one Jewish token member that year happened to be present, but his blood brothers apparently didn't think he'd mind—it being only in fun and all that. Then it got more intense, as it can in groups when a wound is suddenly opened in one of their number. The Jewish member stalked out of the tomb, tears in his eyes, feeling betrayed by his brothers and thinking of resigning forthwith. But he didn't. He went back and inscribed a protest in the big book, at which time his brothers, suitably repentant, persuaded him not to abandon the tomb.

Outsiders often do have trouble with the Bones style of intimacy. There was, for instance, the story of one of the several token bisexuals and gays that Bones has tapped in recent years. He had the misfortune to develop, during the long Thursday and Sunday nights of shared intimacy, a deep affection for a member of his fifteen-man coven who declared himself irrevocably heterosexual. The intimacy of the tomb experience became heartbreaking and frustrating for the gay member. When the year came to a close and it came time to pick the next group of fifteen from among the junior class, he announced that he was not going to tap another token gay and recommended against gay membership because he felt the experience was too intense to keep from becoming sexual.

There's a kind of backhanded tribute to something genuine there. The Bones experience can be intense enough to work real transformations. Idle, preppie Prince Hals suddenly become serious students of society and themselves, as if acceptance into the tomb were a signal to leave the tavern and prepare to rule the land. Those embarrassed at introspection and afraid of trusting other men are given the mandate and the confidence to do so.

"Why," said one source, "do old men—seventy and over—travel thousands of miles for Bones reunions? Why do they sing the songs with such gusto? Where else can you hear Archibald MacLeish take on Henry Luce in a soul-versus-capital debate with no holds barred? Bones survives because the old men who are successful need to convince themselves that not luck or wealth put them where they are, but raw talent, and a talent that was recognized in their youth. Bones, because of its elitism, connects their past to their present. It is more sustaining, for some, than marriage."

Certainly the leaders that Bones has turned out are among the more humane and civilized of the old Yankee establishment. In addition to cold warriors, Viet warriors and spies, there are as many or more missionaries, surgeons, writers (John Hersey, Archibald MacLeish) and great teachers (William Graham Sumner, F.O. Matthiessen) as there are investment bankers. There is, in the past of Bones, at least, a genuine missionary zeal for moral, and not merely surplus, value.

It's now a century since the break-in pamphlet of the File and Claw crew announced "the decline and fall of Skull and Bones," so it would be premature for me to announce the imminence of such an event, but almost everyone I spoke to at Yale thought that Bones was in headlong decline. There have been unprecedented resignations. There have been an increasing number of rejections—people Bones wants who don't want Bones. Or who don't care enough to give up two nights a week for the kind of marathon encounter any Esalen graduate can put on in the Bougainvillea Room of the local Holiday Inn. Intimacy is cheap and zeal is rare these days. The word is out that Bones no longer gets the leaders of the class but lately has taken on a more lackadaisical, hedonist, comfortable—even, said some, decadent—group. (I was fascinated to learn from my source that some Bones members still partake in certain sacraments of the Sixties. Could it be that the old black magic of Bones ritual has kind of lost its spell and needs a psychedelic dramatizing these days?)

And the reasons people give now for joining Bones are often more foreboding than the rejections. They talk about the security of a guaranteed job with one of the Bones-dominated investment banks or law firms. They talk about the contacts and the connections and maybe in private they talk about the fifteen thousand dollars (regardless of whether Bones actually delivers the money, it may deliberately plant the story to lure apathetic but mercenary recruits). Bones still has the power to corrupt, but does it have the power to inspire? The recent classes of Bones just do not, it seems, take themselves as seriously as General Russell or Henry Stimson or Blackford Oakes might want them to.

The rotting-paella story seems a perfect emblem of the decay. The story goes that a recent class of Bones decided they would try to cook a meal in the basement kitchen of the tomb. It was vacation time and the servants were not on call to do it for them. They produced a passable paella, but left the remains of the meal there in the basement kitchen, presuming that someone would be in to clean up after them. Nobody came in for two weeks. When they returned, they found the interior of the tomb smelling worse than if there actually *had* been dead bodies there. The servants refused to cook the meal for the next autobiographical session unless the Bonesmen cleaned up the putrefying paella themselves. The Bonesmen went without food. I don't know who finally cleaned up, but there's a sense that like the paella, the original mission of Bones has suffered from neglect and apathy and that the gene pool, like the stew, is becoming stagnant.

I began to feel sorry for the old Bonesmen: after a few days of asking around, I found the going too easy; almost too many people were willing to spill their secrets. I had to call a halt. In the spirit of Bonesman Gifford Pinchot, godfather of the conservation movement, I'm protecting some of the last secrets—they're an endangered species. I have to save some for my novel. And besides, I like mumbo jumbo.

It's strange: I didn't exactly set out to write an exposé of Skull and Bones, but neither did I think I'd end up with an elegy.

From *Coyotes*

TED CONOVER

❧

Ted Conover writes as a participant observer. While a student at Amherst, he decided that his experience had been limited by his middle-class upbringing. He took a year off and rode freight trains as a hobo, crisscrossing the western states among the down-and-out. He chronicled that year in *Rolling Nowhere* (1984). For his second book, *Coyotes* (1987), Conover traveled and worked with Mexicans on both sides of the border. And for *Whiteout* (1991), he viewed the culture of Aspen, Colorado, from multiple perspectives, working as a taxi driver, a ski instructor, and an extra in a John Denver TV Christmas show. "I am a great believer," Conover has said, "in the value of a writer witnessing something firsthand, of putting himself in others' shoes, be they huaraches or ski boots. Of writing from other than a sitting position, you might say."

In researching *Coyotes,* Conover toiled alongside Mexican immigrants and picked fruit for as many as seventy hours a week. He speaks fluent Spanish and, at the climax of the story, was able to melt in with illegals being guided across the border by a hired smuggler *(coyote)*. His narrative uses italicized English to represent dialogue in Spanish.

Conover's social analyses are embedded in storytelling and in an open-hearted approach to his subjects. This excerpt, set in Los Angeles, shows his rapport with Mexican friends and his understanding—delayed but powerful—of one more reality of life among illegals.

—K. K.

❧

. . . It was Friday, and that night Martín said he'd take us out. The five of us, his old friend Dogie, and one-armed Luis, all piled into his '69 Chevrolet Impala, four in front and four in back. This particular evening, desiring some personal space in the way Americans do, I was a little exasperated to see that, even though there was no need for it—Martín had another vehicle, the truck—we were going the sardine route again. I made some jokes, dropped some hints, about the difficulty of breathing or something, but got no response. Deciding to be more blunt, I inquired: "Doesn't this make the police suspicious, an older car like this filled with so many people?" Dogie answered no, that in L.A. you don't worry about things like that—in a way that made me wish I had never asked. To the Mexicans, there simply was nothing out of the ordinary about this sort of travel.

We pulled into a McDonald's drive-in lane and up to the menu board. Martín did all the talking; he was no foreigner here. "Eight Big Mac, eight larch french fry, eight Coke, big." After a few moments the order taker repeated Martín's request, but it was all for naught: Martín was already pulling around to the pickup window.

Martín insisted on paying for everything; I was the only one to protest, perhaps because I was the only one with money, perhaps because I just did not understand. "Ted," said Martín in English, "my life is good now. I have lots of money, I have lots of work. Sometime, maybe I don't have money. Then, you buy the Big Mac!" The others laughed as they heard a phrase they recognized, and Martín smiled. "Lots of money," to Martín, was more like poverty level where I came from. His cash flow might be okay, but Martín couldn't have much to fall back on if problems arose. Certainly he didn't have health insurance; probably he would lose everything if the INS were to find out about him. And yet Martín was more generous—generosity considered in relative terms, the most meaningful—than 99 percent of the people I had ever known.

We drove a couple of miles down the boulevard to a crowded parking lot, where we parked and Dogie distributed the food. If you think a sedan filled with eight people feels crowded, try one filled with eight people eating McDonald's hamburgers, trying to balance their Cokes, trying to find a place for all the used wrappers. I experienced a small wave of claustrophobia, but it subsided. Perhaps it was Martín's jokes, or the bright *ranchera* music on the AM radio; but probably it was all these guys with uncertain futures, at the mercy of any powers that be, having such an unabashed great time, enjoying each other's company, possessed of nothing in the world but their hope and their friends, led by one of their own who had made it in this big foreign city. There was a lot to make you feel good in that old car.

Dinner finished, we climbed out of the Impala—not to take a pee, I realized, but because we were at our destination. I was a bit alarmed as we walked toward the squat little bar, with the old neon sign on top advertising "Rita's Elbow Rest"—there were a couple of pickup trucks in the parking lot, and it looked like a real redneck hangout.

"I thought we were going to the 'El Paso,' " I said to Martín.

"This is the 'El Paso,' " he said. *"They just changed the name. Didn't bother to get a new sign."*

As we entered, I realized that the era of *gringos* in Rita's Elbow Rest had come to an end. It was rednecks now, not Hispanics, who would be worried upon walking into the dimly lit bar. There was not a blue eye in sight. A full-size pool table dominated the floor, illuminated by a light hanging directly overhead; everything else lay in its shadow: the bar itself, at the end of the room, the assorted stools along the walls, the doorway leading to the rest rooms. With our arrival, the place was very nearly filled.

"*Puros mexicanos?*" I asked Martín, who was at the bar, ordering eight beers.

"*Mexicanos y salvadoreños,*" he answered. *"The owners are from El Salvador, and there are a lot of Salvadorans in Los Angeles. But we're closer to a Mexican neighborhood."*

Besides no *gringos*, there were virtually no women. Two waitresses helped to take beer orders and collect the empty bottles, but bars, for Mexicans, were places that men gathered, not women. Unless you were looking for a hooker, you met women somewhere else, someplace less sinful.

Carlos and I, leaning by the pool cue rack, assessed the female situation. One waitress was rather heavy, wearing vast synthetic slacks and a blouse of the sort once known as a muumuu. Because of the limited space, she brushed against almost everyone as she parted the sea of men, taking orders. She piqued a certain sort of interest. *"Mucho jamón por dos huevos,"* was all Carlos had to say—lots of ham for two eggs. The other waitress was slender, dressed in jeans and a soft blouse, with a pretty face and hair that looked authentically auburn. Probably, I thought, she was Salvadoran—there were fewer mestizos there and more direct descendants of Europeans, especially among those from the professional classes who had had the wherewithal to escape the civil war. She looked up and saw me watching her.

My friends were my passport, and I had no trouble with other patrons of the bar, though a couple came up just to chat and see what I was all about. Dogie challenged me to a game of pool. I beat him but then lost the next game to Martín. All the while, every time I looked up, it seemed I was meeting the glance of the pretty waitress. This was more than chance, as no one on earth seemed more adept at avoiding men's eyes than the Mexican and Central American women I had been around in the past few months—and with the men as aggressive as they were, it was a necessary survival skill.

But it presented a problem. The better looking of the two lone women in the crowded bar seemed to find me—an outsider—attractive, and the feeling was mutual. For months I had been walking a sort of sexual tightrope with my Mexican friends. I didn't want to show undue interest in females they had designs on for fear of awakening macho rivalry. And yet at the same time it was important to show some sort of interest—some wolfish hunger—to reassure them of my heterosexuality. The unaggressive man was likely to be the butt of the next Mexican faggot joke.

The kind of outsider I was—an American—complicated matters too. A Mexican man could be charismatic, physically attractive, influential, and even rich, but still he couldn't be as powerful—and, therefore, as attractive on the macho scale—as an American with the same qualities. Machismo is obsessed with rivalry, and to a citizen of that proud but very poor country to the south, northern neighbors could be powerful rivals indeed. I enjoyed a degree of acceptance at the bar—but I was worried, just the same, about the insecurities that might be simmering just under the surface of the cama- raderie, awaiting a crisis to bring them out. As always, I had to watch my step.

And, of course, the final complication was that, after so many weeks of fraternal living, this woman looked very pretty. I swallowed hard when she came up and asked me if I wanted another beer, but managed a smile and a "*Sí.*" The next time I looked up she was behind the bar, looking at me again and pointing to a bottle she had placed in front of an empty stool. I took a deep breath, moved to the bar, and took a seat. She had green eyes, wet- looking lips, a nice voice. She asked where I was from.

"*Denver—do you know where that is?*"

"*No, but it must be nicer than here. Any place would be nicer than here.*"

"*You mean Los Angeles?*"

"*Yeah, Los Angeles, the bar . . . I'm so tired of it.*"

"*Are you salvadoreña?*" She nodded. "*From the capital?*" She couldn't have been from the countryside. I had read much about El Salvador, and was eager to learn more. But she didn't want to talk about El Salvador. She wanted to talk about me.

"*Where did you learn Spanish? You speak it perfectly!*"

That was a lie. "*Here and there. In school and in some other countries.*"

"*I'd love to go to some other countries! But, oh—my situation . . . I can't travel anywhere.*"

"*Why not?*"

"*Well, uhh, you know—documents.*"

"*Uhh.*" I looked around the bar to size up the reaction to our little chat. My eyes caught Martín's as he bent over the pool table to line up a shot. The quick wink and lifting of the eyebrows a couple times quickly was his equiv- alent of a thumbs-up, a "go for it."

"*What's your name?*"

"*Ted. It's short for* Theodore*—'Teodoro,' in Spanish.*"

"*Teodoro, te adoro,*" she said. This was a timeworn pun among Spanish speakers.

"*I adore you, too,*" I said, laughing with the joke. "*What's your name?*"

"*I'm Marisol.*"

"*That's a lovely name.*"

"*Are you American?*"

The question caught me off guard; of course I was. "*What do you mean?*"

"*Nothing. Oh, you know, a citizen.*"

"*Oh, yeah, sure. Born and raised. Though, actually, I was born outside the country on a military base . . .*" But something had caught her attention. It was Martín, holding up two fingers and pointing at his beer bottle and then at the two of us. She blushed slightly; it was becoming on her.

334

"*What's he saying?*"

"*He is buying two beers for you and me,*" she said. I winked facetiously at Martín. Marisol opened two more beers and drank hers from the bottle.

"*Do you have wishes?*" she asked.

"*What do you mean?*"

"*You know, things you wish would come true?*"

"*Well, sure I do.*" I take such questions too literally; I started giving it some thought, but she interrupted.

"*I'll tell you what my wishes are. . . . You know what I would like? What I would prize most of all? A green card!*" She beamed at me, at the thought.

But my bubble suddenly burst. Why had she said that? She had tipped her hand much, much too soon. I was disheartened, deflated. Instead of seeing in me the things I thought she had, she had seen in me a ticket. I wasn't a sex object, but something sexier: a green-card object, a hollow marriage object, a means to an end. I took another swallow of beer, and it tasted bad.

"*Ted—isn't that your name? What is it you do?*"

"*I'm a writer.*"

"*Ooh, a writer! You don't say! Someday, will you write me a poem?*"

Someday, I said, I would do that. She would want a love poem, and that's what I would write. A sonnet, maybe, or something shorter, of an unexpected love in an unlikely place, of a poisoned circumstance.

From "The Snap Revolution"

JAMES FENTON

∞

The English poet James Fenton was pursuing the traditional literary pursuit of travel writing when he found himself in a place (Southeast Asia) and a time (the late seventies and the eighties) of historic political change. So he became a reporter. He uses that term intentionally, he writes in the introduction to his collected pieces, *All the Wrong Places: Adrift in the Politics of Asia:* "By reporting I mean something that predates journalism—the fundamental activity.

"Journalism becomes unnatural when it strays too far from [its] origins," he goes on. "It is quite astonishing to me how much interesting material is jettisoned by newspaper reporters because they know they will not be able to write it up, *because to do so would imply they had been present at the events they are describing.* And not only present—alive, conscious, and with a point of view" [italics Fenton's].

The following is excerpted from Fenton's account of the 1987 deposing of Philippine president Ferdinand Marcos. Like much of his work, it was first published in the British quarterly *Granta,* which was started in 1979 by the American expatriate Bill Buford and, like *The New Yorker, True, Esquire,* and *Rolling Stone* in earlier periods, has been a catalyst and congenial home for much distinguished literary journalism. Typically, Fenton foregrounds himself, telling us almost too much about his movements, his reactions, his thought processes. We sense, of course, that his volubility is a reaction against turning into that classically anonymous "journalist" who cancels himself out of his account. Typically, too, Fenton and his Philippine journalist friends, Fred, Bing, and Jojo, are not on the scene when rebels finally take over the presidential palace, Malacañang. For most journalists, missing the moment would be a disaster. For Fenton, it only supports his underlying notion that life is conducted, and history made, not in the middle ground but on the edges.

—B.Y.

∞

Back at J. P. Laurel Street, the road one normally took to Malacañang, the marines were under orders not to let any journalists into the palace. A crowd of street urchins had gathered to taunt the "sip-sip" brigade (the ass lickers or cocksuckers—translations were various) who were being brought in by jeepney for the inauguration. The limousines were arriving as well, ferrying in the loyal elements of the upper military echelons.

The journalists were disconsolate. We pleaded with the commanding officer to let us through. Around us the crowd was managing to turn away several of the vans full of Marcos supporters, and when anyone came out from the direction of the palace they were jostled and jeered at mercilessly. This was not a nice sort of crowd to be on the wrong side of.

A few moments later we were let through. Along J. P. Laurel Street, there were dumpy ladies with Marcos badges, who were saying things like: "No one paid us to come. We are real Marcos supporters. It's you foreign press who have ruined everything, meddling in our country." People were in tears and very angry.

Then someone with a radio said: "Imelda's started to speak." And we ran, as somebody shouted from the pavement: "CIA."

When I got through the palace gates I saw that the new-laid lawn was already dry and shriveled. Lunch boxes were being unloaded from trucks. People had planted their Marcos flags in the lawn in festive clusters. We ran down past the sculpture garden, which had been almost completely dismantled, and through the gates to where the crowd had assembled.

As I moved among them, people nudged each other and pointed to the fact that I was carrying the radical opposition paper, *Malaya*. It was one of a bundle, but there was no way of concealing it now. If I was seen concealing it, that would make matters worse. I could hear the scandalized reaction of the crowd. Many people came up to me, saying that no one had paid them to attend—this was for real. I suppose there were 5,000 of them, and where there was not anger there was a frightening mixture of levity and menace. People offered me flags to wave or badges to wear. I couldn't stand the thought of taking them. So I kept laughing back at them, as if the occasion was indeed all part of a great joke.

On the platform stood a very fat, short fellow with a loud-hailer. He was singing snatches of song, apparently anything that occurred to him, and then shouting a few slogans or making jokes, whipping up the crowd. For his rally Marcos could still get a small crowd of T-shirted supporters, but he couldn't lay his hands on any pop stars. Instead there was simply this grotesque, possibly mad, individual, trying to raise a good noise for the aging dictator, whipping through "My Way" at triple speed. Who was he? The palace cook? A torturer? An expert ballot stuffer?

I and the other journalists had made our way to the platform, and now we were ordered to sit on one side. Great, I thought, I can sit on *Malaya* and somehow lose it. Then we were told to move further back, and as soon as we had done so they made us get up and move to the other side. Back and forth, up and down we went, obeying the insane instructions with as much good humor as we could manage to feign. A friend said to me: "It feels like being a hostage in Iran." I wished he hadn't said it. We were issued with Marcos badges in a very meaningful way. I thought: If I throw *Malaya* away, they'll see that I read the *Inquirer*. If I throw the *Inquirer* away, they'll see that I read the *Manila Times*. I hadn't got a single crony newspaper.

The people in the crowd had been at pains to point out that no one had paid them to attend, and yet, when they saw the chicken dinners being handed out at the other end of the grounds, whole sections of them detached themselves and ran off. Maybe they were not all such convinced fascists.

"Martial law!" they shouted, when Marcos appeared on the balcony with Imelda and Bongbong and the rest. "Martial law!" "Catch the snakes!" was another slogan, meaning, Get Enrile and Ramos. But the strangest of their cries, to English ears, repeated over and over, was "Give us back Channel Four!" We didn't then know that, while the Marcos inauguration was just beginning to be broadcast and as the commentator from inside Malacañang was saying, "And now ladies and gentlemen, the moment you have all been waiting for," the rebels had knocked them off the one remaining television channel available. Marcos had no broadcasting facility left. He had only the balcony and the crowd. And he must have known this as he came out to us. We were his last audience.

He looked somewhat puffy and less unactual than the day before, less like the Mighty Mekon. He could still rant—and he did so—but there was less power in the baritone voice. You felt that the members of the audience were carrying him along, rather than he exerting his power over them, and this sense of a man faltering in his performance was underlined by Imelda at his side. She was acting out her emotions again, as she had done the first time I saw her, and today's emotion seemed to be: Look what they've done to him, the dear, great old man. Had they no pity? Had they no loyalty? Had they no memory of his greatness?

Marcos's idea had apparently been that this would be his answer to People's Power. People's Power, he said, was for the rich, but he had always been the champion of the poor. Imelda's idea was much the same. It was said that one of the forbidden topics in Malacañang was *Evita*. To William Deedes, who had once made the comparison, she had said: "Well at least I was never a prostitute." But here she was in her long white dress, the figure of glamour, the focus, she always felt, of the aspirations of the poor. And when she gave her speech, and the audience began to sing her song, she languidly took the microphone off the stand and led the final encore. The song was called "Because of You." For the Marcoses and their faction it was the second national anthem.

When they came to the final bars, Marcos himself joined in, froglike, for a few notes. The conjugal dictatorship embraced before the crowd.

Imelda's dress had a slit up the back, and, somewhat inelegantly from our point of view, she reached into this slit for a handkerchief. She dabbed her eyes. She blew her nose (rather too loudly). She looked again at the crowd with a look that said: My *people*, oh my *people*, you are the ones who have always supported us, you are the ones who have always understood. Marcos was gently helped from the balcony, but Imelda gave a version of not being able to bear the thought of leaving the crowd. She came back to the microphone and said words to the effect that at least there was still some spirit among the Filipino people and she would never forget them.

People had indeed been weeping. Valediction was in the air. As for the press, I think we all thought the sooner we got out of this place, the better. We were the enemy as much as Ramos and Enrile, the CIA, the NPA and the rest. As we walked back to the barricades along J. P. Laurel Street, the limousines and jeepneys were leaving the palace, and when we reached the crowd outside it had grown appreciably nastier. Before, they had banged the cars with their hands. Now they began stoning them. Those who left Malacañang on foot were really made to run the gauntlet, which they did defiantly and in a furious temper. The dumpy, angry ladies; the aged goons; the young bloods—they were all in for a bad time. But they kept their badges on and they were ready for a fistfight if provoked.

In the crowd, people seemed to be working themselves up to that point where they could kill a Marcos supporter. There was much the same mad jocularity as there had been at the inauguration.

A boy who had been threatening one of the departing goons turned to me and said: "He—he—he very very bad man."

"Who is he?" I said.

"I don't know. Just very very very bad." As he said this, a shiver ran down his body that was so strong it lifted him in the air. I'd never seen anything quite like it. He took off from the pavement on a little rocket of disgust.

"WE'VE BEATEN POLAND!"

Fred and I were trying to think what the next thing would be. As far as we could tell, the only thing left was Malacañang. The rebels were going to have to move in and take it at some stage, and it seemed extraordinary that nothing had been done about it so far. We were in my studio at Boulevard Mansion, not far from the U.S. embassy. It was dark. Helicopters came over. "That's the Americans taking Marcos," said Fred. I didn't think so. A kind of slack wisdom told me to say: "Have a look if they're twin-bladed. If they're Jolly Green Giants, it's the Americans." (I was back in Saigon.)

So Fred ran to the end of the corridor to look from the fire escape, and then I thought I'd better do the same, and the fire door swung shut behind me and we were trapped on the stairs. By now I was beginning to think Fred might be right again. The helicopters were definitely coming from the direction of the U.S. embassy. But it took a few minutes to get us back into the building.

Jojo was on the phone from nearby. He had heard that the marines at Malacañang had suddenly said there was no point hanging around any more and they were going back to barracks. We'd better get round there quickly, before the crowd moved in. I phoned Helen at home in Quezon City. It would take her half an hour to get down, and I told her we'd meet her in J. P. Laurel Street.

The noise barrage was on again. Everyone must have suspected that this time Marcos was really gone. We cursed the taxi driver for his slowness and argued about the best way to the palace. There were two ways of approaching J. P. Laurel Street, and Jojo had chosen the nearer end. Then as we crossed the river, Fred saw a helicopter coming from the palace toward the embassy, and he wanted to photograph it. "Oh Fred it's not a photograph. It's just a tiny fucking helicopter in the moonlight." I doubt if Fred will ever forgive me for losing him that shot.

Jojo led us down some darkened streets, past a few youths with sticks on their way to the palace. He was right. We got right to the gates very quickly, but we soon realized that we were in the wrong crowd. It was the Marcos crowd. The remainder of the thugs who had attended the inauguration were now, in the absence of soldiers, manning the gates. We knew that some of them had guns. Others were carrying great lengths of wood for clubs. A journalist at the gate asked to be let in and was told fiercely, No, that it was foreign press who were to blame. Nobody knew what was happening. We explained to the bystanders that Marcos had left by helicopter and the marines had gone home. "Let's get into the palace," said one youth, "there might be some money."

The thugs were panicking. I could see it in their eyes, and I could see Jojo seeing it as well. These people were angry and scared and they were very likely to take it out on us. Some of them thought they were going to be killed, and indeed as we stood there a horribly battered body was brought through the gates. Others apparently believed that Marcos had left the palace and its treasure for them, and their job was to defend it. Others no doubt just could not believe that Marcos had walked out on them, and I feared their disappointment very much. I knew from what I had seen earlier that day that the Cory crowd fighting their way along J. P. Laurel Street were not pacifists of EDSA and Camp Aguinaldo, but street urchins, the rabble. If we were to go in with the rabble, I wanted to be with the friendly, not the hostile rabble.

Jojo agreed, but it was very hard to convince Fred. His courage and his guts were on the line. To go away now, even in order to come back right away, seemed unthinkable. "Listen Robert Capa," I said furiously, "if you want to take great photographs you've got to stay alive. Just for a bit." He smiled.

There was a terrified young man who said: "Look, I'm neutral. I don't support either side. Can you get me out of here? I only came today because they said there was going to be food." He'd been after those chicken dinners.

"Come with me," I said.

"And my friends? Can they come?"

"How many friends do you have?" I said, drawing a breath.

His friends emerged from the shadows, boys and girls, five or six of them. We agreed to stick together. We walked down the middle of the road toward Mendiola Bridge, where a large crowd was waiting but was held in check by the nuns and seminarians praying at the front. I could see the barricades were by now almost denuded of their barbed wire. No one was manning them. We slipped down a side street and ushered the chicken-dinner brigade to safety.

By now Fred was going wild with frustration, but we finally made our way to the other end of J. P. Laurel Street, which the marines had indeed abandoned. And now the crowd was moving down toward Malacañang. Here too people were carrying sticks, and some of them held bits of plywood over their heads. You could see the stones flying at the front of the crowd. Fred made a bee-line for the action. Jojo told me, if we were pushed back, to jump into a front yard and stay out of the way. Then he too was off.

I had no interest in being stoned. There were gunshots too, and plenty of firecrackers. The eerie thing about the front of the crowd was the way it was marked by flashing lights. It took me some time to realize that this was where the photographers were concentrated with their flashes. It looked like an electric storm, but with the wrong soundtrack. After a while we were halted. The Marcos men were holding their ground very well. Indeed we were being forced slightly back.

I took shelter in a side street with a few others. As I did so, I heard a voice in my skull saying: *He made the classic mistake, during a street fight, of taking refuge in a cul-de-sac; then he was cut off and hacked to death by enraged thugs.* Where had this belated wisdom come from? People leaned out of an upstairs window and shouted to us to wait. The rebel army was sending some soldiers to establish order. I examined the gates in the street for one I might climb in a hurry. The crowd on J. P. Laurel Street were still being pushed back. The side street had a left turn, but when I investigated it people said: "It's a dead end." They didn't want me to go down near their houses.

Then a man who lived at the dead end told me there was a wounded KBL supporter who needed help. We went down together. The street ended at a small canal, pretty much a sewer. The man showed me where he had seen the KBL guy being beaten up by the crowd. He had called out to him to wade across the canal, which he had done with difficulty. The man had helped wash him and had put alcohol on his wounds, but he had nasty gashes on his head and back.

I told the KBL guy that I would try to get him out. He emerged with difficulty from the house, saying "No ID," by which I presumed he meant that he was not wearing any Marcos paraphernalia. His possessions were in a plastic bag, which I took. He was clutching a walkie-talkie and holding his head with his other hand. He had obviously been very badly mauled.

We walked to the turning, where I immediately saw that what I had feared had happened. The Marcos thugs had beaten back the crowd, and we were cut off. We could see them throwing stones and wielding their clubs. I was back on the wrong side of the action.

A gate opened to my left and someone stepped out for a look. I pushed the wounded guy into the front garden, and followed him, to hear a voice saying: "Close the gate. Oh, you stupid! Look! You, get out!"

"This man is badly wounded," I said. "He needs help."

The man resisted for a moment, and then said crossly: "All right, it's a humanitarian act." So we got indoors, which was nice.

Nicer still, there was a doctor in the house. Nicer than that, there was a beer for me. We sat in a hall at the foot of the stairs, while the doctor gave first aid, tying the man's hair in little knots over the wounds so that they would close up. I was impressed by the determination with which the man held onto his walkie-talkie. The owner of the house said: "Hmm, a Motorola, the most expensive. What do you need that for?"

"To talk to my friends," said the wounded man. We gradually realized that what we had here was a goon, but a goon in such sorry shape that it seemed unfair to ask him point-blank: Are you a goon?

Then the houseowner saw the plastic bag and said: "Who brought that in?"

"I did," I said, "It's his possessions." He looked at the bag as if it was about to explode.

"It's probably loot," he said.

"I think it's just his clothes." It was only then I wondered whether the bag contained a gun.

Shots were fired outside, then the battle had subsided. It was obvious the soldiers had arrived and taken control. I thought: And now I *have* missed it. Fred would be in the palace with Jojo and Helen and all the gang, and I'd miss it. And when they said: But what *happened* to you? I'd have to say I was looking after a goon.

The houseowner and I went out into the street. All was quiet again. He had a glass of whiskey in his hand. He had been celebrating. "You don't realize," he said, "how deep this goes. Nobody will call us cowards again. We've done it. We've had a peaceful revolution. We've beaten Poland."

I thought at first he was talking about football. Then I realized he was the first guy who had drawn the comparison which had been regularly in my mind for the last few days. The nationalism, the Catholicism, the spontaneous organization, the sheer power of aspiration—that's what Poland must have been like.

The goon was all patched up and the houseowner gave him his taxi fare. When we got back onto J. P. Laurel Street we found the statue of the Virgin in place in the road, and a barricade of praying nuns. I tapped a nun on the shoulder and handed over the goon. As we said goodbye he smiled for the first time.

BACK TO MALACAÑANG

Well, I thought, if I've missed it all, I've missed it. That's that.

I turned back and walked down the center of the road to Malacañang, my feet crunching broken glass and stones. I asked a policeman whether he thought it safe to proceed. Yes, he said, there were a few Marcos men hiding in the side streets, but the fighting had all stopped. A child came running past me and called out, "Hey Joe, what's the problem?" but didn't wait for an answer.

As I came within view of the palace I saw that people were climbing over the railings, and just as I caught up with them a gate flew open. Everyone was pouring in and making straight for the old Budget Office. It suddenly occurred to me that very few of them knew where the palace itself was. Documents were flying out of the office and the crowd was making whoopee. I began to run.

One of the columnists had written a couple of days before that he had once asked his grandmother about the Revolution of 1896. What had it been like? She had replied: "A lot of running." So in his family they had always referred to those days as the Time of Running. It seemed only appropriate that, for the second time that day, I should be running through Imelda's old vegetable patch. The turf looked sorrier than ever. We ran over the polystyrene boxes that had once contained the chicken dinners, past the sculpture garden, past where people were jumping up and down on the armored cars, and up onto the platform from where we had watched Marcos on the balcony. Everyone stamped on the planks and I was amazed the whole structure didn't collapse.

We came to a side entrance and as we crowded in I felt a hand reach into my back pocket. I pulled the hand out and slapped it. The thief scurried away.

Bing was just behind me, looking seraphically happy, with his cameras bobbing around his neck. We pushed our way through to a kind of hall, where an armed civilian told us we could go no further. The journalists crowded around him, pleading to be allowed a look. The man had been sent by the rebel troops. He had given his word of honor, he said. He couldn't let anybody past. But it was all, I'm afraid, too exciting. One of the Filipino photographers just walked past the guard, then another followed, then Bing went past; and finally I was the only one left.

I thought: Oh well, he hasn't shot them, he won't shoot me. I scuttled past him in that way people do when they expect to be kicked up the backside. "Hey, man, stop," said the guard, but as he followed me around the corner we both saw he had been standing in the wrong place: The people in the crowd had come around another way and were now going through boxes and packing cases to see what they could find. There were no takers for the Evian water. But everything else was disappearing. I caught up with Bing, who was looking through the remains of a box of monogrammed towels. We realized they had Imelda's initials. There were a couple left. They were irresistible.

I couldn't believe I would be able to find the actual Marcos apartments, and I knew there was no point in asking. We went up some servants' stairs, at the foot of which I remember seeing an opened crate with two large green jade plates. They were so large as to be vulgar. On the first floor a door opened, and we found ourselves in the great hall where the press conferences had been held. This was the one bit of the palace the crowd would recognize, as it had so often watched Marcos being televised from here. People ran and sat on his throne and began giving mock press conferences, issuing orders in his deep voice, falling about with laughter or just gaping at the splendor of the room. It was fully lit. Nobody had bothered, as they left, to turn out the lights.

I remembered that the first time I had been here, the day after the election, Imelda had slipped in and sat at the side. She must have come from that direction. I went to investigate.

And now, for a short while, I was away from the crowd with just one other person, a shy and absolutely thunderstruck Filipino. We had found our way, we realized, into the Marcoses' private rooms. There was a library, and my companion gazed in wonder at the leather-bound volumes while I admired the collection of art books all carefully catalogued and with their numbers on the spines. This was the reference library for Imelda's world-wide collection of treasures. She must have thumbed through them thinking: *I'd like one of them,* or *I've got a couple of them in New York,* or *That's in our London House.* And then there was the blue drawing room with its twin portraits of the Marcoses, where I simply remember standing with my companion and saying, "It's beautiful, isn't it." It wasn't that it *was* beautiful. It looked as if it had been purchased at Harrods. It was just that, after all the crowds and the riots, we had landed up in this peaceful, luxurious den. My companion had never seen anything like it. He didn't take anything. He hardly dared touch the furnishings and trinkets. We both simply could not believe that we were there and the Marcoses weren't.

I wish I could remember it all better. For instance, it seemed to me that in every room I saw, practically on every available surface, there was a signed photograph of Nancy Reagan. But this can hardly be literally true. It just felt as if there was a lot of Nancy in evidence.

Another of the rooms had a grand piano. I sat down.

"Can you play?" said my companion.

"A little," I exaggerated. I can play Bach's Prelude in C, and this is what I proceeded to do, but my companion had obviously hoped for something more racy. Beside the piano stood a framed photograph of Pham Van Dong, and beside the photograph lay a letter. It was a petition from members of a village, asking for property rights to the land they lived on. It was dated well before the Snap Election. Someone (Marcos himself? the letter was addressed to him) must have opened it, seen it was a petition, popped it back in the envelope and sat down to play a tune. The keys were stiff. I wondered if the piano was brand new.

A soldier came in, carrying a rifle. "Please cooperate," he said. The soldier looked just as overawed by the place as we were. We cooperated.

When I returned down the service stairs, I noticed that the green jade plates had gone, but there was still some Evian water to be had. I was very thirsty, as it happened. But the revolution has asked me to cooperate. So I did.

Outside, the awe had communicated itself to several members of the crowd. They stood by the fountain looking down at the colored lights beneath the water, not saying anything. I went to the parapet and looked across the river. I thought Somebody's still fighting; there are still some loyal troops. Then I thought That's crazy—they can't have started fighting now. I realized that I was back in Saigon yet again. *There,* indeed, there had been fighting on the other side of the river. But here it was fireworks. The whole city was celebrating.

Bing emerged from the palace. We decided we must see the crowds coming over the Mendiola Bridge. The experience would not be complete without that. And besides, we were both hungry. Somewhere must still be open.

We had grown used to the sight of millions of people on the streets, but there was something wonderful about this crowd, noisy but not mad, pouring across the forbidden bridge. Imelda's soothsayer had got it slightly wrong. He should have said: When the crowds pour over the Mendiola Bridge, that will mean the regime *has already* fallen, not that it is about to fall. Still, that error was minor. The man had been right in broad outline. Many members of the crowd were wearing crowns of barbed wire. Bing snapped out of his dream. "And now," he said, "now they will begin to crack down on the communists. Now there'll be a real crackdown."

We went down a dark, quiet street in the university area, found some food and started chatting to others who had been at the palace. They had taken boxes and boxes of ammunition. We sat out on the pavement. I said to one guy: "Congratulations. You've just had a real bourgeois revolution. They don't happen very often nowadays. You should be pleased."

He said: "If it's a bourgeois revolution, it's supposed to bring in socialism."

I said: "You read Marx?"

He said: "No! I read Lenin!" Then he laughed, and said he was only joking. But I didn't think he was joking, actually. He said: "Cory's a rich woman and a landowner. These people aren't the good guys. You come back for the next revolution. The next revolution it'll be the NPA. The next revolution it'll be the Reds!"

Bing took me to find a taxi, and we said goodbye. He couldn't resist it: He had to go back to the palace. The taxi driver had a linguistic habit I had never come across before. He could survive without any personal pronouns except I, me, and my. "Well James," he said, as I got in, "have I been to Malacañang?"

I thought for a moment.

"Have I been to Malacañang, James?" he repeated.

"Yes," I said. "I have been to Malacañang."

"Has Marcos gone?"

Yes, this time he really had gone.

"Marcos is a good man, James," said the driver, "but my wife is very bad. Yes, James. Marcos is a good man. But my wife is very bad."

"Yes," I said, finally understanding the rules, "my wife is very bad indeed."

Tiananmen Square

JOHN SIMPSON

∞

John Simpson is a familiar presence on British television, usually reporting from abroad. As a BBC correspondent, he has covered the revolution in Iran, the fall of the Berlin Wall, the violent overthrow of Nicolae Ceauşescu in Romania, and the election of Nelson Mandela in South Africa. He spent six months in Baghdad before, during, and after the Gulf War, and four months reporting on the siege of Sarajevo.

Unlike his counterparts on American television, Simpson is a serious and prolific writer. His books include studies of military rule in Argentina, the cocaine industry in Peru, and social life in revolutionary Iran. Often he turns to print journalism when his film plans are thwarted, as when Iraqi officials seized all his footage on the eve of the Gulf War. But his writing has its own strength and artistry. In telegrammatic sentences Simpson piles up small details—the smells, the sounds, the look on someone's face—and thus grounds big historical events in an immediate present. His reportage, like George Orwell's, conveys a fundamental decency and political balance through the very directness of its style. In his dispatch from Tiananmen Square, Simpson juggles the roles of film and print reporter, and at a climactic moment abandons journalistic detachment in order to save a life.

Simpson is now foreign affairs editor at the BBC.

—K. K.

∞

It was humid and airless, and the streets around our hotel were empty. We had set out for Tiananmen Square: a big, conspicuous European television team—reporter, producer, cameraman, sound-recordist, translator, lighting man, complete with gear. A cyclist rode past, shouting and pointing. What it meant we couldn't tell. Then we came upon a line of soldiers. Some of them had bleeding faces; one cradled a broken arm. They were walking slowly, limping. There had been a battle somewhere, but we couldn't tell where.

When we reached Changan Avenue, the main east-west thoroughfare, it was as full of people as in the days of the great demonstrations—a human river. We followed the flow of it to the Gate of Heavenly Peace, under the bland, moonlike portrait of Chairman Mao. There were hundreds of small groups, each concentrated around someone who was haranguing or lecturing the others, using the familiar, heavy public gestures of the Chinese. Other groups had formed around radios tuned to foreign stations. People were moving from group to group, pushing in, crushing round a speaker, arguing, moving on, passing along any new information.

For the most part these were not students. They were from the factories, and the red cloths tied around their heads made them look aggressive, even piratical. Trucks started arriving from the outskirts of the city, full of more young workers, waving the banners of their factories, singing, chanting, looking forward to trouble.

People were shouting: there was a battle going on between tanks and the crowd, somewhere to the east of the city centre. Details differed, and I had trouble finding out what was being said: I watched the animated faces, everyone pushing closer to each new source of information, pulling at each other's sleeves or shoulders. Tanks and armoured personnel carriers, they were saying, were heading towards the Square. They were coming from two directions, east and west. The crowds that gathered couldn't stop them.

"It's a different army. It's not the Thirty-eighth!" The man who said this was screaming it, clutching at our translator, holding on to him, trying to make him understand the significance of it. "It is *not* the Thirty-eighth!" It had been the Thirty-eighth Army that had tried to recapture the city twice before. The soldiers had been unarmed: the commander, the father of a student in the Square, had ordered that operations be carried out peacefully.

We pushed our way towards the Square where, despite the rumours and the panic, we saw something very different: several thousand people standing in silence, motionless, listening to a large loudspeaker, bolted to a street lamp:

> Go home and save your life. You will fail. You are not behaving in the correct
> Chinese manner. This is not the West, it is China. You should behave like
> a good Chinese. Go home and save your life. Go home and save your life.

The voice was expressionless, epicene, metallic, like that of a hypnotist. I looked at these silent, serious faces, illuminated by the orange light of the street lamps, studying the loudspeaker. Even the small children, brought there with the rest of the family, stared intently. The order was repeated again and again. It was a voice the people of China had been listening to for forty years, and continued listening to even now. But now no one did what the hypnotist said. No one moved.

And then, suddenly, everything changed: the loudspeaker's spell was broken by shouts that the army was coming. There was the sound of a violent scraping, and across the Avenue I saw people pulling at the railings that ran along the roadway and dragging them across the pavement to build a barricade. Everyone moved quickly, a crowd suddenly animated, its actions fast and decisive, sometimes brutal. They blocked off Changan Avenue and the Square itself, and we began filming—flooding the sweating enthusiasts with our camera-light. People danced around us, flaunting their weaponry: coshes, knives, crude spears, bricks. A boy rushed up to our camera and opened his shabby green windcheater like a black marketeer to reveal a row of Coca-Cola bottles strapped to his waist, filled with petrol and plugged with rags. He laughed, and mimed the action of pulling out each bottle and throwing it. I asked him his age. He was sixteen. Why was he against the government? He couldn't answer. He gripped another of his Molotov cocktails, laughing all the time.

That the army was coming was no longer rumour but fact and our translator heard that it would move in at one o'clock. It was half-past midnight. In the distance, above the noise of the crowd, I thought I could hear the sound of guns. I wanted to find a vantage point from which we could film, without being spotted by the army. But the tension that was bonding members of the crowd together did not have the same effect on the members of our small team. It was hot and noisy. We argued. We started shouting, and I headed off on my own.

I pushed through the crowds, immediately feeling better for being on my own. There were very few foreign journalists left in the Square by now, and I felt especially conspicuous. But I also felt good. People grabbed my hand, thanking me for being with them. I gave them a V for Victory sign and was applauded by everyone around me. It was hard to define the mood. There was still a spirit of celebration, that they were out on the streets, defying the government, but the spirit was also giving way to a terrible foreboding. There was also something else. Something I hadn't seen before: a reckless ferocity of purpose.

I crossed back into the main part of Tiananmen Square, the village of student tents. There were sticks and cardboard and broken glass underfoot. The smells were familiar and strong—wood-smoke, urine and heavy disinfectant. A couple clung to each other, her head on his shoulder. I passed in front of them, but they didn't raise their eyes. A student asked me to sign his T-shirt, a craze from earlier days. He had thick glasses and a bad complexion, and he spoke English. "It will be dangerous tonight," he said. "We are all very afraid here."

I finished signing his shirt, at the back below the collar. He grabbed my hand and shook it excitedly. His grip was bony and clammy. I asked him what he thought would happen.

"We will all die."

He straightened up and shook my hand again, and slipped away between the tents.

The camp was dark. There were a few students left; most of them had gathered in the centre of the Square, around the Monument to the People's Heroes. I could hear their speeches and the occasional burst of singing—the Internationale, as always. Here, though, it was quiet. This was where the students had chosen to build their statue of the Goddess of Democracy, with her sightless eyes, her torch held in both hands. The symbol of all our aspirations, one of the student leaders called her: the fruit of our struggle. To me, she looked very fragile.

The speeches and the songs continued in the distance. Then suddenly they stopped. There was a violent grinding and a squealing sound—the familiar sound of an armoured personnel carrier. I heard screaming, and behind me, in the Avenue, everyone started running. When I finally spotted the vehicle, I could see that it was making its way with speed down the side of the Square. It seemed uncertain of its direction—one moment driving straight for the Square, and then stopping, turning, stopping again, as if looking for a way to escape. There was a sudden angry roar, and I know it was because the vehicle had crushed someone under its tracks. It then turned in my direction—it was pointed at me—and I felt a different kind of panic. The action was starting and I was separated from my colleagues: it is an article of faith to stay with your camera crew in times of danger.

The vehicle carried on, careering back and forth. It must have knocked down six or seven people. By now it was on fire, having been hit repeatedly by Molotov cocktails. Somehow, though, it escaped and headed off to the west.

Then a second armoured personnel carrier came along Changan Avenue, alone and unsupported like the first. This time everyone turned and ran hard towards the vehicle, knowing that they, with their numbers and their petrol bombs, had the power to knock it out. They screamed with anger and hate as the vehicle swung randomly in different directions, threatening to knock people down as it made its way through the Square. The Molotov cocktails arched above our heads, spinning over and over, exploding on the thin shell of armour that protected the men inside. Still the vehicle carried on, zigzagging, crossing the Avenue, trying to find a way through the barricade. A pause, and it charged, head-on, straight into a block of concrete—and then stuck, its engine whirring wildly. A terrible shout of triumph came from the crowd: primitive and dark, its prey finally caught. The smell of petrol and burning metal and sweat was in the air, intoxicating and violent. Everyone around me was pushing and fighting to get to the vehicle. At first I resisted; then, close beside it, I saw the light of a camera, just where the crowd was starting to swarm. There were only three cameramen still filming in the entire Square, and I knew that my colleague was the only one crazy enough to be that close. Now I was the one fighting, struggling to get through the crowd, pulling people back, pushing them out of my path, swearing, a big brutal Englishman stronger than any of them. I tore one man's shirt and punched another in the back. All around me the men

seemed to be yelling at the sky, their faces lit up; the vehicle had caught fire.
A man—his torso bare—climbed up the side of the vehicle and stood on top
of it, his arms raised in victory, the noise of the mob welling up around him.
They knew they had the vehicle's crew trapped inside. Someone started
beating at the armoured glass with an iron bar.

I reached the cameraman and pulled hard at his arm to get his attention.
He scarcely noticed me, amid the buffeting and the noise and the violence,
and carried on filming. He and his sound recordist and the Chinese lighting
man were a few feet from the vehicle: close enough to be killed if it exploded
or if the soldiers came out shooting. But I couldn't make them step back, and
so we stayed there, the four of us, the heat beating against our faces as people continued to pour petrol on the bonnet and roof and smashed at the
doors and the armoured glass. What was it like inside? I imagined the soldiers
half-crazed with the noise and the heat and the fear of being burned alive.

The screaming around me rose even louder: the handle of the door at the
rear of the vehicle had turned a little, and the door began to open. A soldier
pushed the barrel of a gun out, but it was snatched from his hands, and then
everyone started grabbing his arms, pulling and wrenching until finally he came
free, and then he was gone: I saw the arms of the mob, flailing, raised above
their heads as they fought to get their blows in. He was dead within seconds,
and his body was dragged away in triumph. A second soldier showed his head
through the door and was then immediately pulled out by his hair and ears and
the skin on his face. This soldier I could see: his eyes were rolling, and his
mouth was open, and he was covered with blood where the skin had been
ripped off. Only his eyes remained—white and clear—but then someone was
trying to get them as well, and someone else began beating his skull until the
skull came apart, and there was blood all over the ground, and his brains, and
still they kept on beating and beating what was left.

Then the horrible sight passed away, and the ground was wet where he
had been.

There was a third soldier inside. I could see his face in the light of the
flames, and some of the crowd could too. They pulled him out, screaming,
wild at having missed killing the other soldiers. It was his blood they wanted,
I was certain, it was to feel the blood running over their hands. Their
mouths were open and panting, like dogs, and their eyes were expressionless. They were shouting, the Chinese lighting man told me afterwards, that
the soldier they were about to kill wasn't human, that he was just a thing, an
object, which had to be destroyed. And all the time the noise and the heat
and the stench of oil burning on hot metal beat at us, overwhelming our
senses, deadening them.

Just as the third soldier was lifted out of the vehicle, almost fainting, an
articulated bus rushed towards us stopping, with great skill, so that its rear
door opened just beside the group with the soldier. The students had heard
what was happening, and a group had raced the bus over to save whomever

they could. The mob did not want to give up its prize. The students tried to drag the soldier on board, and the crowd held on to him, pulling him back. By some mischance the bus door started closing and it seemed that he must be killed.

I had seen people die in front of me before. But I had never seen three people die, one after the other, in this way. Once again the members of the crowd closed around the soldier, their arms raised over their heads to beat him to death. The bus and the safety it promised were so close. It seemed to me then that I couldn't look on any longer, a passive observer, watching another man's skin torn away or his head broken open, and do nothing. I saw the soldier's face, expressing only horror and pain as he sank under the blows of the people around him, and I started to move forward. The ferocity of the crowd had entered me, but I felt it was the crowd that was the animal, that it wasn't properly human. The soldier had sunk down to the ground, and a man was trying to break his skull with a half-brick, bringing it down with full force. I screamed obscenities at the man—stupid obscenities, as no one except my colleagues could have understood them—and threw myself at him, catching him with his arm up, poised for another blow. He looked at me blankly, and his thin arm went limp in my grasp. I stopped shouting. He relaxed his grip on the brick, and I threw it under the bus. It felt wet. A little room had been created around the soldier, and the student who had tried to rescue him before could now get to him. The rest of the mob hadn't given up, but the students were able to pull the soldier away and get him on to the bus by the other door. He was safe.

The vehicle burned for a long time, its driver and the man beside him burning with it. The flames lit up the Square and reflected on the face of the Monument where the students had taken their stand. The crowd in Changan Avenue had been sated. The loudspeakers had stopped telling people to save their lives. There was silence.

The students sang the Internationale. It would be for the last time, and it sounded weak and faint in the vastness of the Square. Many were crying. No doubt some students joined in the attacks on the army, but those in the Square kept to their principle of nonviolence. Although the army suffered the first casualties, it was the students who would be the martyrs that night.

My colleagues and I wanted to save our pictures in case we were arrested, and I told the others that we should go back to the Beijing Hotel and come out again later. I now feel guilty about the decision; it was wrong: we ought to have stayed in the Square, even though the other camera crews had already left and it might have cost us our lives. Someone should have been there when the massacre took place, filming what happened, showing the courage of the students as they were surrounded by tanks and the army advancing, firing as it went.

Instead, we took up our position on the fourteenth floor of the Beijing

Hotel. From there, everything seemed grey and distant. We saw most of what happened, but we were separated from the fear and the noise and the stench of it. We saw the troops pouring out of the Gate of Heavenly Peace, bayonets fixed, shooting first into the air and then straight ahead of them. They looked like automata, with their rounded dark helmets. We filmed them charging across and clearing the northern end of the Square, where I had signed the student's T-shirt. We filmed the tanks as they drove over the tents where some of the students had taken refuge, among them, perhaps, the young couple I had seen sitting silently, their arms around each other. Dozens of people seem to have died in that way, and those who saw it said they could hear the screams of the people inside the tents over the noise of the tanks. We filmed as the lights in the Square were switched off at four a.m. They were switched on again forty minutes later, when the troops and the tanks moved towards the Monument itself, shooting first in the air and then, again, directly at the students themselves, so that the steps of the Monument and the heroic reliefs which decorated it were smashed by bullets.

Once or twice, we were ourselves shot at, and during the night the security police sent men to our room to arrest us: but I shouted at them in English, and they went away, uncertain of the extent of their powers. Below us, people still gathered in the Avenue, shouting their defiance at the troops who were massed at the farther end. Every now and then the crack of a rifle would bring down another demonstrator, and the body would be rescued by a trishaw driver or the crew of an ambulance. Below us, the best and noblest political protest since Czechoslovakia in 1968 was being crushed as we watched. I knelt on the balcony, beside the cameraman and a Chinese woman, one of the student leaders.

She had taken refuge in our room because we were foreigners. I shouted at her to go back inside, but she refused, turning her head from me so that I wouldn't see she was crying, her hands clenched tight enough to hurt, intent on watching the rape of her country and the movement she and her friends had built up in the course of twenty-two days. I had seen the river of protest running along Changan Avenue in that time; I had seen a million people in the streets, demanding a way of life that was better than rule by corruption and secret police. I recalled the lines of the T'ang dynasty poet Li Po, that if you cut water with a sword you merely made it run faster. But the river of change had been dammed, and below me, in the Avenue where it had run, people were dying. Beside me, the cameraman spotted something and started filming. Down in the Square, in the early light, the soldiers were busy unrolling something and lifting it up. Soon a great curtain of black cloth covered the entrance to Tiananmen Square. What was happening there was hidden from us.

From *Among the Thugs*

BILL BUFORD

∞

Born in Louisiana in 1954, Bill Buford went to England to study at Cambridge and stayed. Along the way he founded the journal *Granta* and developed an interest in the phenomenon of football hooligans, the young men whose devotion to particular soccer teams led them to riot on an amazingly violent and destructive level. Buford called his 1991 book about the hooligans *Among the Thugs,* and the preposition is telling: he quickly concluded that in order to understand this subculture, one could not simply study it from afar but had in some way to *join* it.

Anthropologists have always been aware of the dangers of "going native." For Buford, it is not a danger at all, rather a way to begin to understand how human beings can engage in inhuman behavior. One of the things that gives *Among the Thugs* its great power is the way Buford monitors his own reactions, flinching a little each time the thug worldview becomes less bizarre and more understandable. In this excerpt, Buford, who has ventured to Turin with a group of Manchester United supporters to see the team play the Italian club Juventus, is swept along with a group of supporters as they leave the stadium and stream out into the city.

—B. Y.

∞

Somehow the match started, was played, ended. And, while it could be said that there was no single serious incident, it could also be said that there was no moment without one. Several people were hurt, and one supporter was taken away to the hospital. During half time, when yet another Manchester lad was felled by a beer bottle, the English supporters, with a sudden roar, rushed to the top of the terraces, trying to climb the wall that separated them from the Italians. The wall was too high to scale, and the supporters ended up jumping up and down, trying to grab the Italians by their shoes until the police arrived to pull them away.

Police kept pouring through the tunnel, now wearing riot gear—moon helmets and blue uniforms instead of green—with obvious instructions to place themselves between each English supporter and everybody else. It was evident that the police continued to regard the English supporters as the problem, and they probably were the problem simply because they were there. But they were not the only problem, which the police discovered after surrounding every English supporter and ignoring the Italians above them, who, in that uninhibited way that has come to characterize the Mediterranean temperament, continued to express their strong feelings. By the end it appeared to me that the police were being struck down more frequently than the English.

It was a peculiar setting for watching a sporting event, although, oddly, it didn't seem so at the time. The day had consisted of such a strange succession of events that, by this point in the evening, it was the most natural thing in the world to be watching a football game surrounded by policemen: there was one on my left, another on my right, two directly behind me, and five in front. It didn't bother me; it certainly didn't bother the supporters, who, despite the distractions, were watching the match with complete attentiveness. And when Manchester United tied, the goal was witnessed, as it unfolded, by everyone there (except me; I was looking over my shoulder for missiles), and jubilation shot through them, their cheers and songs suddenly tinny and small in that great cavity of the Juventus football ground, its seventy thousand Italians now comprehensively silent. The United supporters jumped up and down, fell over each other, embraced.

But the euphoria was brief. In the final two minutes Juventus scored again. The exhilaration felt but minutes before by that small band of United supporters was now felt—magnified many times—by the seventy thousand Italian fans who, previously humiliated, directed their powerful glee into our corner. The roar was deafening, invading the senses like a bomb.

And with that explosive roar, the mood changed.

What happened next is confusing to recall. Everything started moving at great speed. Everything would continue to move at great speed for many hours. I remember that riot police started kicking one of the supporters who had fallen down. I remember hearing that Sammy had arrived and then coming upon him. He was big, well-dressed, with heavy horn-rimmed glasses that made him look like a physics student, standing underneath the bleachers, his back to the match, an expensive leather bag and camera hanging over his shoulder, having (like Robert) just come from France by taxi. I remember watching Ricky and Micky, the improbable pair I had met on my early morning minibus in London, scooting underneath the stands, exploiting the moment in which the Italians were embracing, crushed together in their celebrations, to come away with a handful of wallets, three purses, and a watch, got by reaching up from below the seats. And I remember some screaming: there had been a stabbing (I didn't see it) and, with the screaming, everyone bolted—animal speed, instinct speed—and pushed past the police and rushed for the exit. But the gate into the tunnel was locked, and the United supporters slammed into it.

It was impossible to get out.

Throughout this last period of the match, I had been hearing a new phrase: "It's going to go off."

It's going to go off, someone said, and his eyes were glassy, as though he had taken a drug.

If this keeps up, I heard another say, then it's going to go off. And the phrase recurred—it's going to go off, it's going to go off—spoken softly, but each time it was repeated it gained authority.

Everyone was pressed against the locked gate, and the police arrived moments later. The police pulled and pushed in one direction, and the supporters pushed in another, wanting to get out. It was shove and counter shove. It was crushing, uncomfortable. The supporters were humorless and determined.

It's going to go off.

People were whispering.

I heard: "Watch out for knives. Zip up your coat."

I heard: "Fill up your pockets."

I heard: "It's going to go off. Stay together. It's going to go off."

I was growing nervous and slipped my notebook into my shirt, up against my chest, and buttoned up my jacket. A chant had started: "United. United. United." The chant was clipped and sure. "United. United. United." The word was repeated, *United,* and, through the repetition, its meaning started changing, pertaining less to a sporting event or a football club and sounding instead like a chant of unity—something political. It had become the chant of a mob.

"United. United. United. United. United. United . . ."

And then it stopped.

There was a terrible screaming, a loud screaming, loud enough to have risen above the chant. The sound was out of place; it was a woman's screaming.

Someone said that it was the mother of the stabbed boy.

Someone said that it was no such thing, just a "fucking Eyetie."

The screaming went on. It appeared that a woman had been caught by the rush to get away and swept along by it. I spotted her: she was hemmed in and thrashing about, trying to find some space, some air. She couldn't move towards the exit and couldn't move away from it, and she wasn't going to be able to: the crush was too great, and it wouldn't stay still, surging back and forth by its own volition, beyond the control of anyone in it. She was very frightened. Her scream, piercing and high-pitched, wouldn't stop. She started hyperventilating, taking in giant gulps of air, and her screams undulated with the relentless rhythm of her over-breathing. It was as if she were drowning in her own high-pitched oxygen, swinging her head from side to side, her eyes wild. I thought: Why hasn't she passed out? I was waiting for her to lose consciousness, for her muscles to give up, but she didn't pass out. The scream went on. Nobody around me was saying a word. I could tell that they were thinking what I was thinking, that she was going to have a fit, that she was going to die, there, now, pressed up against them. It went on, desperate and unintelligible and urgent.

And then someone had the sense to lift her up and raise her above his shoulders—it was so obvious—and he passed her to the person in front of him. And he passed her to the person in front of him. And in this way, she was passed, hand to hand, above everyone's heads, still screaming, still flailing, slowly making her way to the exit, and then, once there, the gate was opened to let her out.

And it was all that was needed. Once the gate had been opened, the English supporters surged forwards, pushing her heavily to one side.

I was familiar with the practice of keeping visiting supporters locked inside at the end of a match until everyone had left and of using long lines of police, with horses and dogs, to direct the visitors to their buses. The plan in Turin had been the same, and the police were there, outside the gate, in full riot regalia, waiting for the United supporters. But they weren't ready for what came charging out of the tunnel.

For a start, owing to the trapped woman, the supporters came out earlier than expected—the streets were filled with Juventus supporters—and when they emerged, they came out very fast, with police trailing behind, trying to keep up. They came as a mob, with everyone pressed together, hands on the shoulders of the person in front, moving quickly, almost at a sprint, racing down the line of police, helmets and shields and truncheons a peripheral blur. The line of police led to the buses, but just before the bus door someone in the front veered sharply and the mob followed. The police had anticipated this and were waiting. The group turned again, veering in another direction, and rushed out into the space between two of the buses. It came to a sudden stop, and I slammed into the person in front of me, and people slammed into me from behind: the police had been there as well. Everyone turned around. I don't know who was in front—I was trying only to keep up—and nothing was being said. There were about two hundred people crushed together, but they seemed able to move in unison, like some giant, strangely coordinated insect. A third direction was tried. The police were not there. I looked behind: the police were not there. I looked to the left and the right: there were no police anywhere.

What was the duration of what followed? It might have been twenty minutes; it seemed longer. It was windy and dark, and the trees, blowing back and forth in front of the street lamps, cast long, moving shadows. I was never able to see clearly.

I knew to follow Sammy. The moment the group broke free, he had handed his bag and camera to someone, telling him to give them back later at the hotel. Sammy then turned and started running backwards. He appeared to be measuring the group, taking in its size.

The energy, he said, still running backwards, speaking to no one in particular, the energy is very high. He was alert, vital, moving constantly, looking in all directions. He was holding out his hands, with his fingers outstretched.

Feel the energy, he said.

There were six or seven younger supporters jogging beside him, and it would be some time before I realized that there were always six or seven younger supporters jogging beside him. When he turned in one direction, they turned with him. When he ran backwards, they ran backwards. No doubt if Sammy had suddenly become airborne there would have been the sight of six or seven younger supporters desperately flapping their arms trying to do the same. The younger supporters were in fact very young. At first I put their age at around sixteen, but they might have been younger. They might have been fourteen. They might have been nine: I take pleasure, even now, in thinking of them as nothing more than overgrown nine-year-olds. They were nasty little nine-year-olds who, in some kind of prepubescent confusion, regarded Sammy as their dad. The one nearest me had a raw, skinny face with a greasy texture that suggested an order of fish'n'chips. He was the one who turned on me.

Who the fuck are you?

I said nothing, and Fish'n'chips repeated his question—Who the fuck are you?—and then Sammy said something, and Fish'n'chips forgot about me. But it was a warning: the nine-year-old didn't like me.

Sammy had stopped running backwards and had developed a kind of walk-run, which involved moving as quickly as possible without breaking into an outright sprint. Everybody else did the same. The idea, it seemed, was to be inconspicuous—not to be seen to be actually running, thus attracting the attention of the police—but nevertheless to jet along as fast as you could. The effect was ridiculous: two hundred English supporters, tattooed torsos tilted slightly forwards, arms straight, hurtling stiffly down the sidewalk, believing that nobody was noticing them.

Everyone crossed the street, decisively, without a word spoken. A chant broke out—"United, United, United"—and Sammy waved his hands up and down, as if trying to bat down the flames of a fire, urging people to be quiet. A little later there was another one-word chant. This time it was "England." They couldn't help themselves. They wanted so badly to act like normal football supporters—they wanted to sing and behave drunkenly and carry on doing the same rude things that they had been doing all day long—and they had to be reminded that they couldn't. Why this pretense of being invisible? There was Sammy again, whispering, insistent: no singing, no singing, waving his hands up and down. The nine-year-olds made a shushing sound to enforce the message.

Sammy said to cross the street again—he had seen something—and his greasy little companions went off in different directions, fanning out, as if to hold the group in place, and then returned to their positions beside him. It was only then that I appreciated fully what I was witnessing: Sammy had taken charge of the group—moment by moment giving it specific instructions—and was using his obsequious little lads to ensure that his commands were being carried out.

I remembered, on my first night with Mick, hearing that leaders had their little lieutenants and sergeants. I had heard this and I had noted it, but I hadn't thought much of it. It sounded too much like toyland, like a war game played by schoolboys. But here, now, I could see that everything Sammy said was being enforced by his entourage of little supporters. Fish'n'chips and the other nine-year-olds made sure that no one ran, that no one sang, that no one strayed far from the group, that everyone stayed together. At one moment, a cluster of police came rushing towards us, and Sammy, having spotted them, whispered a new command, hissing that we were to disperse, and the members of the group split up—some crossing the street, some carrying on down the center of it, some falling behind—until they had got past the policemen, whereupon Sammy turned around, running backwards again, and ordered everyone to regroup: and the little ones, like trained dogs, herded the members of the group back together.

I trotted along. Everyone was moving at such a speed that, to ensure I didn't miss anything, I concentrated on keeping up with Sammy. I could see that this was starting to irritate him. He kept having to notice me.

What are you doing here? he asked me, after he had turned around again, running backwards, doing a quick head count after everyone had regrouped.

He knew precisely what I was doing there, and he had made a point of asking his question loudly enough that the others had to hear it as well.

Just the thing, I thought.

Fuck off, one of his runts said suddenly, peering into my face. He had a knife.

Didja hear what he said, mate? Fish'n'chips had joined the interrogation. He said fuck off. What the fuck are you doing here anyway, eh? Fuck off.

It was not the time or the occasion to explain to Fish'n'chips why I was there, and, having got this far, I wasn't about to turn around now.

I dropped back a bit, just outside of striking range. I looked about me. I didn't recognize anyone. I was surrounded by people I hadn't met; worse, I was surrounded by people I hadn't met who kept telling me to fuck off. I felt I had understood the drunkenness I had seen earlier in the day. But this was different. If anyone here was drunk, he was not acting as if he was. Everyone was purposeful and precise, and there was a strong quality of aggression about them, like some kind of animal scent. Nobody was saying a word. There was a muted grunting and the sound of their feet on the pavement; every now and then, Sammy would whisper one of his commands. In fact the loudest sound had been Sammy's asking me what I was doing there, and the words of the exchange rang round in my head.

What the fuck are you doing here anyway, eh? Fuck off.
What the fuck are you doing here anyway, eh? Fuck off.

I remember thinking in the clearest possible terms: I don't want to get beaten up.

I had no idea where we were, but, thinking about it now, I see that Sammy must have been leading his group around the stadium, hoping to find Italian supporters along the way. When he turned to run backwards, he must have been watching the effect his group of two hundred walk-running Frankensteins was having on the Italian lads, who spotted the English rushing by and started following them, curious, attracted by the prospect of a fight or simply by the charisma of the group itself, unable to resist tagging along to see what might happen.

And then Sammy, having judged the moment to be right, suddenly stopped, and, abandoning all pretence of invisibility, shouted: "Stop."

Everyone stopped.

"Turn."

Everyone turned. They knew what to expect. I didn't. It was only then that I saw the Italians who had been following us. In the half-light, streetlight darkness I couldn't tell how many there were, but there were enough for me to realize—holy shit!—that I was now unexpectedly in the middle of a very big fight: having dropped back to get out of the reach of Sammy and his lieutenants I was in the rear, which, as the group turned, had suddenly become the front.

Adrenaline is one of the body's more powerful chemicals. Seeing the English on one side of me and the Italians on the other, I remember seeming quickly to take on the properties of a small helicopter, rising several feet in the air and moving out of everybody's way. There was a roar, everybody roaring, and the English supporters charged into the Italians.

In the next second I went down. A dark blur and then smack: I got hit on the side of the head by a beer can—a full one—thrown powerfully enough to knock me over. As I got up, two policemen, the only two I saw, came rushing past, and one of them clubbed me on the back of the head. Back down I went. I got up again, and most of the Italians had already run off, scattering in all directions. But many had been tripped up before they got away.

Directly in front of me—so close I could almost reach out to touch his face—a young Italian, a boy really, had been knocked down. As he was getting up, an English supporter pushed the boy down again, ramming his flat hand against the boy's face. He fell back and his head hit the pavement, the back of it bouncing slightly.

Two other Manchester United supporters appeared. One kicked the boy in the ribs. It was a soft sound, which surprised me. You could hear the impact of the shoe on the fabric of the boy's clothing. He was kicked again—this time very hard—and the sound was still soft, muted. The boy reached down to protect himself, to guard his ribs, and the other English supporter then kicked him in the face. This was a soft sound as well, but it was different: you could tell that it was his face that had been kicked and not his body and not something protected by clothing. It sounded gritty. The boy tried to get up and he was pushed back down—sloppily, without much force. Another Manchester United supporter appeared and another and then a third. There were now six, and they all started kicking the boy on the ground. The boy covered his face. I was surprised that I could tell, from the sound, when someone's shoe missed or when it struck the fingers and not the forehead or the nose.

I was transfixed. I suppose, thinking about this incident now, I was close enough to have stopped the kicking. Everyone there was off-balance—with one leg swinging back and forth—and it wouldn't have taken much to have saved the boy. But I didn't. I don't think the thought occurred to me. It was as if time had dramatically slowed down, and each second had a distinct beginning and end, like a sequence of images on a roll of film, and I was mesmerized by each image I saw. Two more Manchester United supporters appeared—there must have been eight by now. It was getting crowded and difficult to get at the boy: they were bumping into each other, tussling slightly. It was hard for me to get a clear view or to say where exactly the boy was now being kicked, but it looked like there were three people kicking him in the head, and the others were kicking him in the body—mainly the ribs but I couldn't be sure. I am astonished by the detail I can recall. For instance, there was no speech, only that soft, yielding sound—although sometimes it was a gravelly, scraping one—of the blows, one after another. The moments between the kicks seemed to increase in duration, to stretch elastically, as each person's leg was retracted and then released for another blow.

The thought of it: eight people kicking the boy at once. At what point is the job completed?

It went on.

The boy continued to try to cushion the blows, moving his hands around to cover the spot where he had just been struck, but he was being hit in too many places to be able to protect himself. His face was now covered with blood, which came from his nose and his mouth, and his hair was matted and wet. Blood was all over his clothing. The kicking went on. On and on and on, that terrible soft sound, with the boy saying nothing, only wriggling on the ground.

A policeman appeared, but only one. Where were the other police? There had been so many before. The policeman came running hard and knocked over two of the supporters, and the others fled, and then time accelerated, no longer slow motion time, but time moving very fast.

We ran off. I don't know what happened to the boy. I then noticed that all around me there were others like him, others who had been tripped up and had their faces kicked; I had to side step a body on the ground to avoid running on top of it.

In the vernacular of the supporters, it had now "gone off." With that first violent exchange, some kind of threshold had been crossed, some notional boundary: on one side of that boundary had been a sense of limits, an ordinary understanding—even among this lot—of what you didn't do; we were now someplace where there would be few limits, where the sense that there were things you didn't do had ceased to exist. It became very violent.

A boy came rushing towards me, holding his head, bleeding badly from somewhere on his face, watching the ground, not knowing where he was going, and looked up just before he would have run into me. The fact of me frightened him. He thought I was English. He thought I was going to hit him. He screamed, pleading, and spun round backwards to get away and ran off in another direction.

I caught up with Sammy. Sammy was transported. He was snapping his fingers and jogging in place, his legs pumping up and down, and he was repeating the phrase, It's going off, it's going off. Everyone around him was excited. It was an excitement that verged on being something greater, an emotion more transcendent—joy at the very least, but more like ecstasy. There was an intense energy about it; it was impossible not to feel some of the thrill. Somebody near me said that he was happy. He said that he was very, very happy, that he could not remember ever being so happy, and I looked hard at him, wanting to memorize his face so that I might find him later and ask him what it was that made for this happiness, what it was like. It was a strange thought: here was someone who believed that, at this precise moment, following a street scuffle, he had succeeded in capturing one of life's most elusive qualities. But then he, dazed, babbling away about his happiness, disappeared into the crowd and the darkness.

There was more going on than I could assimilate: there were violent noises constantly—something breaking or crashing—and I could never tell where they were coming from. In every direction something was happening. I have no sense of sequence.

I remember the man with his family. Everyone had regrouped, brought together by the little lieutenants, and was jogging along in that peculiar walk-run, and I noticed that in front of us was a man with his family, a wife and two sons. He was shooing them along, trying to make them hurry, while looking repeatedly over his shoulder at us. He was anxious, but no one seemed to notice him: everyone just carried on, trotting at the same speed, following him not because they wanted to follow him but only because he happened to be running in front of us. When the man reached his car, a little off to the side of the path we were following, he threw open the door and shoved the members of his family inside, panicking slightly and badly bumping the head of one of his sons. And then, just as he was about to get inside himself, he looked back over his shoulder—just as the group was catching up to him—and he was struck flatly across the face with a heavy metal bar. He was struck with such force that he was lifted into the air and carried over his car door on to the ground on the other side. Why him, I thought? What had he done except make himself conspicuous by trying to get his family out of the way? I turned, as we jogged past him, and the supporters behind me had rammed into the open car door, bending it backwards on its hinges. The others followed, running on top of the man on the ground, sometimes slowing down to kick him—the head, the spine, the ass, the ribs, anywhere. I couldn't see his wife and children, but knew they were inside, watching from the back seat.

There was an Italian boy, eleven or twelve years old, alone, who had got confused and ran straight into the middle of the group and past me. I looked behind me and saw that the boy was already on the ground. I couldn't tell who had knocked him down, because by the time I looked back six or seven English supporters had already set upon him, swarming over his body, frenzied.

There was a row of tables where programs were sold, along with flags, T-shirts, souvenirs, and as the group went by each table was lifted up and overturned. There were scuffles. Two English supporters grabbed an Italian and smashed his face into one of the tables. They grabbed him by the hair on the back of his head and slammed his face into the table again. They lifted his head up a third time, pulling it higher, holding it there—his face was messy and crushed—and slammed it into the table again. Once again the terrible slow motion of it all, the time, not clock time, that elapsed between one moment of violence and the next one, as they lifted his head up—were they really going to do it again?—and smashed it into the table. The English supporters were methodical and serious; no one spoke.

An ambulance drove past. Its siren made me realize that there were still no police.

The group crossed a street, a major intersection. It had long abandoned the pretense of invisibility and had reverted to the arrogant identity of the violent crowd, walking, without hesitation, straight into the congested traffic, across the hoods of the cars, knowing that they would stop. At the head of the traffic was a bus, and one of the supporters stepped up to the front of it, and from about six feet, hurled something with great force—it wasn't a stone; it was big and made of a metal, like the manifold of a car engine—straight into the driver's windshield. I was just behind the one who threw this thing. I don't know where he got it from, because it was too heavy to have been carried for any distance, but no one had helped him with it; he had stepped out of the flow of the group, and in those moments between throwing his heavy object and turning back to his mates, he had a peculiar look on his face. He knew he had done something that no one else had done yet, that it had escalated the violence, that the act had crossed another boundary of what was permissible. He had thrown a missile that was certain to cause serious physical injury. He had done something bad—extremely bad—and his face, while acknowledging the badness of it, was actually saying something more complex. It was saying that what he had done wasn't all that bad, really; in the context of the day, it wasn't that extreme, was it? What his face expressed, I realized—his eyes seemed to twinkle—was no more than this: I have just been naughty.

He had been naughty and he knew it and was pleased about it. He was happy. Another happy one. He was a runt, I thought. He was a little shit, I thought. I wanted to hurt him.

The sound of the shattering windshield—I realize now—was a powerful stimulant, physical and intrusive, and it had been the range of sounds, of things breaking and crashing, coming from somewhere in the darkness, unidentifiable, that was increasing steadily the strength of feeling of everyone around me. It was also what was making me so uneasy. The evening had been a series of stimulants, assaults on the senses, that succeeded, each time, in raising the pitch of excitement. And now, crossing this intersection, traffic coming from four directions, supporters trotting on top of cars, the sound of this thing going through the windshield, the crash following its impact, had the effect of increasing the heat of the feeling: I can't describe it any other way; it was almost literally a matter of temperature. There was another moment of disorientation—the milliseconds between the sensation of the sound and knowing what accounted for it, an adrenaline moment, a chemical moment—and then there was the roar again, and someone came rushing at the bus with a pole (taken from one of the souvenir tables?) and smashed a passenger's window. A second crashing sound. Others came running over and started throwing stones and bottles with great ferocity. They were, again, in a frenzy. The stones bounced off the glass with a shuddering thud, but then a window shattered, and another shattered, and there was screaming from inside. The bus was full, and the passengers were not lads like the ones attacking them but ordinary family supporters, dads and sons and wives heading home after the match, on their way to the suburbs or a village outside the city. Everyone inside must have been covered with glass. They were shielding their faces, ducking in their seats. There were glass splinters everywhere: they would cut across your vision suddenly. All around me people were throwing stones and bottles, and I felt afraid for my own eyes.

We moved on.

I felt weightless. I felt nothing would happen to me. I felt that anything might happen to me. I was looking straight ahead, running, trying to keep up, and things were occurring along the dark peripheries of my vision: there would be a bright light and then darkness again and the sound, constantly, of something else breaking, and of movement, of objects being thrown and of people falling.

A group of Italians appeared, suddenly stepping forward into the glare of a street lamp. They were different from the others, clearly intending to fight, full of pride and affronted dignity. They wanted confrontation and stood there waiting for it. Someone came towards us swinging a pool cue or a flag-pole, and then, confounding all sense, it was actually grabbed from out his hands—it was Roy; Roy had appeared out of nowhere and had taken the pole out of the Italian's hands—and broken it over his head. It was flamboyantly timed, and the next moment the other English supporters followed, that roar again, quickly overcoming the Italians, who ran off in different directions. Several, again, were tripped up. There was the sight, again, of Italians on the ground, wriggling helplessly while English supporters rushed up to them, clustering around their heads, kicking them over and over again.

Is it possible that there were simply no police?

Again we moved on. A bin was thrown through a car showroom window, and there was another loud crashing sound. A shop: its door was smashed. A clothing shop: its window was smashed, and one or two English supporters lingered to loot from the display.

I looked behind me and I saw that a large vehicle had been overturned, and that further down the street flames were issuing from a building. I hadn't seen any of that happen: I realized that there had been more than I had been able to take in. There was now the sound of sirens, many sirens, different kinds, coming from several directions.

The city is ours, Sammy said, and he repeated the possessive, each time with greater intensity: It is *ours, ours, ours.*

A police car appeared, its siren on—the first police car I had seen—and it stopped in front of the group, trying to cut it off. There was only one car. The officer threw open his door, but by the time he had got out the group had crossed the street. The officer shouted after us, helpless and angry, and then dropped back inside his car and chased us down, again cutting us off. Once again, the group, in the most civilized manner possible, crossed the street: well-behaved football supporters on their way back to their hotel, flames receding behind us. The officer returned to his car and drove after us, this time accelerating dangerously, once again cutting off the group, trying, it seemed to me, to knock down one of the supporters, who had to jump out of the way and who was then grabbed by the police officer and hurled against the hood, held there by his throat. The officer was very frustrated. He knew that this group was responsible for the damage he had seen; he knew, beyond all reasonable doubt, that the very lad whose throat was now in his grip had been personally responsible for mayhem of some categorically illegal kind, but the officer had not personally seen him do anything. He hadn't personally seen the group do anything. He had not seen anyone commit a crime. He saw only the results. He kept the supporter pinned there, holding him by the throat, and then in disgust he let him go.

A fire engine passed, an ambulance, and finally the police—many police. They came from two directions. And once they started arriving, it seemed that they would never stop. There were vans and cars and motorcycles and paddy wagons. And still they came. The buildings were illuminated by their flashing blue lights. But the group of supporters from Manchester, governed by Sammy's whispered commands, simply kept moving, slipping past the cars, dispersing when needing to disperse and then regrouping, turning this way, that way, crossing the street again, regrouping, reversing, with Sammy's greasy little lieutenants bringing up the rear, keeping everyone together. They were well-behaved fans of the sport of football. They were once again the law-abiding supporters they had always insisted to me that they were. And, thus, they snaked through the streets of the ancient city of Turin, making their orderly way back to their hotels, the police following behind, trying to keep up.

"We did it," Sammy declared, as the group reached the railway station. "We took the city."

From *Whoredom in Kimmage:*
Irish Women Coming of Age

ROSEMARY MAHONEY

Rosemary Mahoney was born in America but holds dual citizenship in the United States and Ireland. Her sense of double identity enlivens *Whoredom in Kimmage: Irish Women Coming of Age* (1993), a social survey that becomes a participant-observer's account of life in Dublin and in a small village, Corofin, in the west of Ireland. She portrays herself as both fearful and bravely curious—and as a feminist ambivalent about the erosion of traditional Irish values. In the chapter reprinted here, Mahoney's sense of doubleness becomes sexual as well.

After earning her M.A. in the writing program at Johns Hopkins in 1985, Mahoney taught English at Hangzhou University. Her 1990 memoir, *The Early Arrival of Dreams: A Year in China,* dramatizes the frustrations of Chinese intellectuals in the months prior to the Tiananmen Square confrontation.

Mahoney has written award-winning short stories. Her nonfiction also has a literary flair, most evident in her ear for dialect, her eye for details of scene, and her evocation of character: the ordinary, and extraordinary, people of Ireland.

—K. K.

J. J. SMYTHE'S

If there was little tolerance for abortion rights in Ireland, there was next to none for the rights of homosexuals. On a trip to the Aran Islands, one of the most secluded places in all Ireland, I fell into conversation with a middle-aged man who, like me, was leaning back against a high stone wall, watching a tiny red fishing boat slide through the flat waters of Kilronan Harbor. We stood with our boots sunk ankle-deep in mud. Though the day was warm, the man wore a wool cap and a heavy overcoat with the collar up, as though against a winter wind. The great wings of the collar hid the lower half of his face—all I could see of him was a black brow, a long, graying sideburn, and an enormous hairy ear.

The man addressed me without introduction or preface and without taking his eyes off the red dot of the fishing boat. I thought he was speaking Irish and stepped closer, the better to hear him, but it was English he was speaking, his second language. Aran Islanders—indeed most native Irish speakers—speak English in a mournful, faintly suspicious way, as though it pains them to be speaking such an unwieldy tongue, but this man's tone was exceptionally gloomy; it made him sound like the spy he resembled. We stared at the sea as he spoke. The water was the same milky color as the sky, and the entire stone-strewn island seemed to have gone pale gray with the weather. The Aran Islands were so bare and wild that even indoors I felt exposed to the elements.

The man was born here on Inis Mor and had spent eight years in New York City working as an elevator operator. He was recently offended by the unflattering things the newspapers had to say about Ted Kennedy in connection with the William Kennedy Smith rape case. He believed the press had been hounding the senator, the press had always hounded the Kennedys, and lately they were dragging the memory of Jack Kennedy through the mud with a lot of clattering chatter about women and the Mafia. What was more, when Ted Kennedy drove off a bridge and plunged into the sea they crucified him and recrucified him.

The fishing boat approached the pier with melancholy reluctance.

"Didn't they?" the man said; he expected an answer.

"Yes," I said, "they did."

"That's right," he said, "they did."

The man's idolatrous feelings about the Kennedys were directly bound up with his feelings about Frank Sinatra. Why was Frank Sinatra never hounded by the press the way Jack Kennedy was hounded by the press? Everyone knew Sinatra was in thick with the Mafia. (He drew his huge hand out of his coat pocket and held it up for me with the middle and index fingers tightly crossed in illustration of how thick.) Turning his head slightly in my direction, he said bitterly, "And everyone knows that animal cannot sing."

I could see the man's dark eyes now over the top of the coat collar—contempt had reduced them to slits. His sinister discontent was puzzling and a little unnerving. In a spitting, petulant, childlike way he proceeded to discuss Frank Sinatra's daughter. "And the little wop always had his vicious daughter up in public, singing that brutal song about her boots. 'Twas an ugly song. Put me off songs altogether. She was a nasty little streel, whatever her effing name was."

A streel, I knew, was a slatternly woman. The man stared at me, waiting. I could think of nothing to say. The fishing boat bumped against the pilings of the pier. "I think her name was Nancy," I said.

"Same as that other vicious voodoo doll."

I moved closer to him, my boots slipping in the mud, sweater snagging on a sharp rock in the wall. "*Voodoo* doll?" I said. He was very hard to understand.

He nodded. "That old cowboy's wife."

I stared at his ear. "You mean Nancy Reagan?"

He made a venomous hissing sound. "Nancy *voodoo*," he said. "And the Sinatra girl was forever in the public eye, but the Sinatra son was never heard about. They kept Sinatra's son's life very quiet. Shall I tell you why? Because Sinatra's son is bent as a hoop."

"Bent as a what?" I said.

"*Hoop*," he said impatiently. "Hoop. Hoop. Bent. *Queer*."

He put a blistering Gaelic spin on the word "queer," heaping it with so much disdain it came creaking out in two long syllables: "*kwee*-yar." He lifted his cap to two men climbing off the now docked fishing boat. "I hate the queers. The goddam bum-blasters. Sinatra is a queer. Both them Sinatras was queers. But the Kennedys was never a queer."

Without excusing himself he wandered off toward the pier, then stopped and turned to look at me. "What are you?" he said.

I studied his long, narrow face, the deep-set eyes, the lantern chin. I wanted to provoke him, to say, Italian, Jewish, *and* queer. Instead I said, "What do you mean?"

"You're American?"

I nodded.

"What kind?"

He had, after all, lived in New York—he knew it never stopped at just plain American.

"Not Italian," he said suspiciously.

"No."

"Irish then."

"I'm not Irish," I said.

"You are Irish," he said smugly, his hatchet face splitting with a smile of derision. "You are Irish. The Yanks never come to this godforsaken place unless they are Irish some way or another." He leaned back contentedly on his muddy heels, sizing me up. "Irish," he said, and before turning away he pointed a finger at me. "You mark me," he said, "the Kennedys was never goddam queers."

Homosexuals were among the people living in Ireland's tiny margins, and the mainstream was so large, so strict, and so unanimous that its margins struck me as particularly cold and lonely. I wanted to talk with Irish homosexuals, to know how they endured. When I returned from Aran to Dublin, I went to the women's bathroom in Trinity College and took down the number of the lesbian hotline written on the back of the door. I called the line and asked where in Dublin gay women congregated. The pleasant, bored voice on the other end said, "J. J. Smythe's Pub."

"Where's that?" I said.

"Aungier Street."

"Every night?"

"Saturday nights."

"Anywhere else?"

"The Parliament Bar on Friday nights."

"Anywhere else?"

"No, love."

"Any other nights?"

"No, love."

"Are you sure?"

"I am, love."

Two pubs, two nights a week.

I went to Aungier Street to look for J. J. Smythe's. It was a dingy place, with little amber windowpanes that were frosted and pimpled and impossible to see through. It looked like a shanty, like any other pub on that street. From the sidewalk I could hear the driving pulse of rock music pressing at the windowpanes.

The following Saturday night I returned to the pub but was too self-conscious to go in. I found it difficult to walk into any city pub alone, let alone a lesbian pub. I stared at the place from across the street. Two women in army jackets went through its doors, and three women in leather followed. My fears were powerful and troubling and annoyingly vague; I couldn't establish exactly what it was that frightened me. I had no idea what to expect, and I feared that I wouldn't fit in, that I might be rejected. Later I realized that this was precisely the feeling the lesbians in Dublin had to live with every day of their lives. I turned from the pub and walked home, disgusted by my failure of courage and resolving to return the following Saturday night.

When that night arrived I walked apprehensively across the city to J. J. Smythe's. I walked the longest route I could think of, and the closer I came to the pub, the weaker I felt my resolve. I stood outside the door, wet-palmed and breathless with anxiety. Several women breezed by me, pausing just long enough to glance quizzically at my face before they swung through the door. I decided it was worse to stand staring in the street than it was to go in. I plunged through the door, and when my eyes adjusted to the near-total darkness I found myself facing a long, narrow staircase. I took the stairs two at a time, my heart pounding stupidly in my throat; I knew that if I slowed down, I would never make it in. At the top of the stairs was another door—I flung myself through it, again into darkness, and music so loud it filled my lungs with a thump, like a gust of wind. I could make out tables and booths here, and people smoking. As I approached the bar I felt a hand fall heavily on my shoulder. I jumped and heard a woman saying sternly behind me, "You're very welcome, of course, but there's a door fee of two pounds." I searched in my pockets and paid the woman, apologizing profusely. She stared impassively at me, jingling in her fist the pound coins I had given her. She had the harried, irritated look of a mother blessed with many children.

"American," she said.

I nodded.

"Welcome to Dublin," she said unconvincingly.

At the bar I was served a drink by a woman I thought was a man, and looking around the very small room I wondered if I had come to the wrong place. This was supposed to be a lesbian pub, but I seemed to be seeing both men and women. After watching the room for several minutes, I decided they were all women; I had been misled not simply because so many were dressed like men, but because some of them had extraordinarily masculine features and mannerisms. I turned from the bar and sat down at the table closest to me. Two powerful, pale-faced young women in jeans and T-shirts sat with their chairs tipped back against the wall and their crew-cut heads— one blond, one red—lolling against the greasy wallpaper. They were both pretty. They held their beer bottles clamped between their thighs. Their posture and their impressive size gave them a faintly challenging air.

The redhead, the larger of the two, scrutinized me as I sat down. I said, "Mind if I sit here?" and without a trace of warmth or encouragement the redhead replied, "Nuh." She and her friend stared stonily at me, and under the crushing pressure of their stares I had no choice but to look away from them. I was stuck. Now that I was seated, with a beer in front of me, it would have been exactly as difficult to stand up and leave as it had been to come in.

I sipped nervously at my beer and looked around the room. It was a dark, hot, smoky place, appointed in the manner of a brothel: the carpet was red, the vinyl booth benches were red, the velvet curtains were red, and there were tiny lamps with little red shades all along the upper half of the wall. The place smelled like boiled peas, the result of years of beer spilled on the carpet. Approximately twenty women were sitting in small groups, most in their mid-twenties and early thirties, a few of them older, and there was a clubbish attitude among them, as though they had all known each other for years. I realized I was probably the only newcomer in the room and probably the only person who wasn't Irish. Several women looked at me critically. One woman whispered something to her friend, who responded to the whisper by twisting around in her chair to peer at me—the pair were so unsubtle that I tossed them a decidedly impertinent wave. Fear can make a person reckless.

At the far end of the room a tiny patch of dance floor and a big, pony-tailed DJ were illuminated by colored lights. Everyone here looked settled and as if they were not going to talk with a stranger. Giddy with unease, I began to gibber at my two tablemates. My hands, gesticulating over the table, looked like someone else's hands. I made comments about the price of the beer I was drinking, how much cheaper it was here than in other pubs I had been to in the city, how you never knew what a pint might cost, how it usually cost around a pound sixty-nine, but a half-pint—which for some odd reason was only ever referred to in this country as "a glass"—cost around one pound five pence, which didn't seem right, if you stopped to think about it, and how a person could become thoroughly confused by pubs and prices in today's world.

The redhead smiled skeptically at me, showing a broken front tooth. She tipped her chair forward and put her big arms squarely on the table. I saw the sleeves of her T-shirt tighten around her biceps. There was a tattoo of an ivy-entwined crucifix on her upper arm. I heard myself saying—unbelievably—*So, what do you girls do?* to which the redhead replied, *Work in a prison,* to which I said, *Prison! Nice!*

The conversation slogged on in that asinine fashion for another five minutes, and it became clear that these women neither trusted nor wanted to talk to me. Eventually the redhead said, "You're not American or something, are you?"

I said, "I am."

"What are you doing here?"

"Visiting."

"Been here long?"

"Pretty long."

"*How* long?" The question was unmistakably threatening.

"Long enough," I said.

"Long enough for what?"

"Who wants to know?"

"Aoife. Aoife wants to know."

"Oh, really?" I said. "Who's Aoife?"

The woman leaned forward. "Bleedin' Aoife is *me!*"

The delicate, ancient name didn't fit this contrary article. "Nice name," I said and was alarmed by the sarcasm in my own voice. The way the woman grabbed her beer bottle, I thought she might hurl it at me. Her thick neck was like a plinth. "Ya like it in Ireland, do ya?" she snarled.

For my own safety I relented. I said, "I like it a lot. I really do. It's interesting."

Aoife softened suddenly. "I like it too," she said sadly, and her wide shoulders collapsed into a slouch over the table. "I live in London. But I come home to visit as often as I can. I go mad missing Ireland. London's a kip."

"Kip" was the Irish term for a dumpster.

"What do you do in the prison?" I said.

"Keep records. It's stupid."

Like every last person in Ireland, Aoife said "schewpid." She told me she was in a bad mood that night because her best friend had just had an abortion. She herself had twenty-one or twenty-two nieces and nephews, and though she would never have children of her own, she loved children and felt abortion was a terrible crime. I was surprised to hear this. I had assumed that the lesbian community would be in favor of the right to choose, but I was learning quickly that in Ireland the strong feeling against abortion was not merely a generational phenomenon; it transected age, class, and gender.

Aoife said, "It was like a slap in the face when my friend told me about the abortion. I took it as a personal insult." She added that she didn't want to go back to London and was hoping to be transferred to a prison in Belfast. "I'd be happier there," she said. "It may be the North, but it's still Ireland."

The blond tipped forward in her chair and pressed her smooth, angular face against Aoife's tattoo. Aoife pointed at her and said, "This is Maggie. She used to be my girlfriend, but we're not together anymore."

Maggie sucked resentfully on the mouth of her empty beer bottle and stared through me.

The room was filling up. Alone at a table to my left sat a short-haired woman in an electric-blue track suit who had picked the labels off four empty beer bottles and was starting in on the fifth. She did not appear drunk, nor did she seem to care that she was alone. She was lost in open-mouthed thought. The lenses of her glasses—the thickness of sliced bread—were like a wall between her and the world. As I stared at her, she leaned across to me, pressing the glasses to her face and grinning with the strain of trying to see me in the dark. Without warning she reached out and struck me on the shoulder, trying to capture the attention she didn't know she already had.

"Mind me seat for me while I go to the loo?" she asked.

Minding her seat was a struggle, as chairs were growing scarce. Women glared and muttered "Shite" when I told them the seat was taken. I threw my jacket over the chair. When the woman returned she thanked me with a nod of her head and went back to clawing at her beer bottle. I turned my chair toward her and, for lack of anything else to say, I said, "How much did that beer cost?" She winced at me; she seemed unnerved by the question, unnerved at having been spoken to. She leaned forward, trying to find my face. "I don't actually know how much it cost, to tell you the truth," she said.

The woman was long-legged and slender, had a sad, spade-shaped face, a pointed chin, and a lipless mouth crowded with sharp little teeth—like a shark's mouth. Her features were bland and blurred, and her pale skin was porous. Her short hair looked laid on in clumps, like sod, and her beautifully soft voice was marred by a heavy Dublin accent, an accent that often sounded leering and defeated. "You're not American, are you?" she said.

We chatted. I said it seemed as though everyone here knew each other. She said, "I been coming here for years and I don't know a soul in the place. I usually come in with a friend, but she's not here tonight." She explained that she and her friend would normally talk only to each other, because they felt excluded by the other women. "I hate coming in here alone," she said, "and I've been coming for years. It's hard. I don't know a soul. They're not friendly here. They exclude you. They judge you."

I was relieved to meet someone who felt as bad as I did, and I told her that I had felt a bit nervous myself coming in here alone.

She listened with her mouth open and her head tilted to one side, as though hearing the miracle of speech for the first time. "But I thought you knew these people," she said. "The way you just came swannin' in and sat straight down with them two things across."

"I forced myself to do that," I said. "I hated doing it. I don't know anybody here."

"Well, you'd want to have a power of confidence to do that. Especially in this place." She shuddered. She said she would have no trouble going alone into a pub full of men, because men didn't judge a person. Men didn't care who you were. Men just talked to you. But Irish women were unfriendly, and they were always judging you and comparing you to themselves, and they wouldn't talk to you. She thought Irish people were secretive and unfriendly because they felt inferior. "I don't know why that is, but I hate it about us," she said. "I think it's because we're an island, and nobody ever comes through here in history. And we never get any sun. Not like in France, where everything's nice. I wish I could go to France or someplace like that. But I could never leave Ireland. I love it too much."

The woman spoke in a softly sorrowing way, and without confusion or irony. She seemed personally pained by her nation's character. There was puzzlement and anxiety in her voice, as though these were thoughts that kept her awake at night. She spoke the way one might speak of a difficult daughter who years ago had run away from home and never returned. She had few physical gestures and sat perfectly still as she spoke, both hands clutching the beer bottle. Her lack of animation was oddly attractive. When I asked her if she had any children, she said, "Where would the likes of myself get children?" I was struck by her gentility and her seriousness. She was forty-two years old. Her name was Freddy. When I asked what Freddy was short for, she lowered her head in a sweet sulk and said, "Never you mind what it's short for."

The name was short for Frederica, which she pronounced "Frej-ri-cah." She said, "'Tis a fuckin' schewpid name," and she peered intently at me, waiting to see whether I would agree.

"I agree," I said. "Frederica is a very stupid name."

She wagged her head at me and grinned, showing her shark's teeth. "Hardy-har-har, very fuckin' funny, Rose." Emboldened by my teasing, Freddy leaned over the table and mooed, "*Stoo-pid.* That's what *you* say."

I laughed, and she persisted. "And Yanks say 'Toosday' and 'noosepaper' as well." She cackled at her own disrespectful approach to me, then said seriously, "Rose, do you not think the women in Dublin are very butch?"

"Straight women or gay women?" I said.

"Gay."

I looked around the room again at the anomalously masculine faces. A tall woman stood near the bar drinking a pint of Guinness—drinking it fast, I could tell by the many white rings the creamy head had left on the near-empty glass. The woman looked for all the world like a fisherman up from the Blasket Islands. She had a jutting chin, a collapsed mouth, a heavy brow, and long flat cheeks like slats. The oversized bones of her face looked battered, as though they had been misshapen and distorted by the trauma of her birth. She stood silently, feet apart, big gentle eyes staring diffidently at the other women, free hand stuffed into the pocket of her baggy mechanic's trousers.

Lamely I said to Freddy that I thought there might be a few mannish women here. She said, "Well, I wouldn't want to judge, because I once asked a friend that same question, and she said to me, 'But sure, aren't you very butch yourself, Freddy?' And I suppose it's true that I am, but I'm not like some of these women here tonight who dress like men and have men's attitudes and are snobby as well."

Freddy had the unmysterious androgyny of a high school basketball coach. She said feminine women occasionally came into this pub dressed in skirts and other pretty clothes, but before many Saturdays had passed they would switch to jeans and leather jackets in order to fit in.

"A woman gets forced to be butch around here," she said. "You don't fit in if you're not butch. I don't like it. They ought to accept you for what you are. These women look like men and they act like men. But if I wanted a man, I'd go out and get one. I like what's soft and gentle about women. That's what makes us special." She lifted her chin and studied me for a moment. "For example," she said, "you seem very feminine to me."

I sipped my beer and smiled.

"These women," she continued, "they should be happy they're women. They go home and get their period anyway"—she uttered the word "period" so forcefully that her breath gently lifted the hair on my forehead—"and no matter how they act in here they still have to be a woman."

Freddy, like so many Dubliners I knew, was not working at the moment. She had recently bought a house with money provided by her mother under the condition that the mother could come and live with her. "I feel sorry for my mother. She's going senile. Every last one of us has to get old, and we should remember that," she said.

I asked Freddy if she had ever considered moving to the country; the idea horrified her. "I've never been out of Dublin," she said.

"You've never been to Mayo?"

"I've never been beyond Rath*mines*. I've never even been to visit my brother in Kerry."

"Where in Kerry does your brother live?"

She tipped her face up toward the ceiling and sneered, "Ballygoback-ward. Who fuckin' knows? Country people are nice to you. Know why? They never see you. They never see you but once a week. You look out the window: grass and a cow. Look out the other window: grass and a cow. And I hate all the shit all over the place. And it's boots all the time. I hate the country. That's all I know."

Freddy spoke of Ireland's rural life with utter contempt. What she wanted more than anything was to be a chef. "A cook, like," she said, "a person cooking food for people. I have heard about this cooking course that would end you up a certified chef. The problem is, and I don't like to make myself fail a thing before I even get started at it, but you see, in this cooking course you would have to cut up animals, and I am a person who is for animal rights. But don't get me wrong. I don't like animals at all. I hate them; it's connected to the country. But I believe they have their rights, so I'd be in a dilemma cutting them up just to get the certificate."

Freddy said she had a dog, but she didn't really like him; he was dirty and busy and a nuisance, but he had his rights, certainly.

Freddy was one of the more judicious people I had met in Dublin. When I told her that, she spun one of her empty bottles on the tabletop and tried to stifle a smile. She said shyly, "I don't actually take compliments very well."

Over the sound system Cher was singing "It's in His Kiss." Two women danced hard into my chair. Freddy was talking eagerly now. She said, "I left school too young, Rose. I was only fifteen. I left because what good is a diploma in this country? How are you going to get any jobs? There's no jobs. Nothing changes."

I admired the nerve—or perhaps it was simply the terrible force of loneliness—that had motivated this woman to come here by herself on a Saturday night when she knew that no one would talk with her.

"I haven't talked like this in ages," she said. "I don't talk much to my mother. She doesn't know I'm gay. She wouldn't agree with it. She wouldn't understand it. She would think I was sick or perverse, or that it was her fault, or maybe my fault. I think my brothers and sisters know about it. They don't like it. I was always on the outside of my family. You're gay yourself, Rose?"

The question startled me. It was the question I'd been dreading. It was put with great eagerness, and I should have been prepared for it but was not. I had thought a great deal about what I would say if asked to define my sexuality that night, and still I had no answer. I looked at Freddy's ingenuous face. If I said I was not gay, would she grow wary of me? If I said I was, would it not be a lie? And between those poles wasn't there the possibility that everyone was capable of homosexual feelings, that there was an element of sexuality in every relationship? If I explained my reason for coming here, would my interest seem clinical and voyeuristic and false? Why did she need to know, and why should I have to define myself? But even as my mind spun down that path I knew my defensiveness was born of the fear that I would be spurned if I revealed that I was not gay. I feared my presence in this pub might be offensive to women for whom it was a haven, that I might seem to be disrespectful of the seriousness of their situation. Trapped by what I did not know, I lied and said yes and felt a muscle in my face twitch with the lie.

The room was dangerously overcrowded now, with many women standing between tables or in the doorway or dancing wildly on the patch of dance floor. Beside me a snappy, big-toothed blond in cutoff shorts that reached to her knees hung drunkenly around the neck of an older woman in a sheepskin coat. The older woman looked depressed. She was overweight, and her fuzzy hair stood on end. The blond released her and began to spin recklessly in place, like a top. A young woman who had been standing with her hip against my shoulder bent over and shouted, "I can hear you're American. What's the gay scene like in America?"

I had no idea what the gay scene was like in America, but I knew I could safely say, "It's bigger than this." My deceit filled me with dread. The girl's name was Siobhan, and she was slight and pretty. She introduced me to her friends: Nora, whom I had seen earlier pretending to dab beer under her ears as if it were cologne, and a woman named Shleen, who looked like a jockey.

"Shleen?" I said. "How do you spell that?"

Siobhan said, "C-e-l-i-n-e. Shleen. I think it might be French. You can pronounce it two ways: Shleen or Shayleen."

Either way it sounded Irish.

"French names always sound better than Irish ones," Siobhan said.

What was this obsession with France? It reminded me of Samuel Beckett saying, "I preferred France in war to Ireland in peace."

I realized I was a little drunk, and I was smoking a cigarette, something I hadn't done in years. I asked Siobhan if she minded the cigarette smoke, and she laughed loudly in my face and said, "Cop yourself on, Rose. You're in Dublin now." Siobhan, with her overfriendliness, had squeezed Freddy out of the conversation.

Two seats opened up at Freddy's table, and a pair of women no older than high school age flung themselves into them. The taller of the two had a pretty, plumpish face. She hugged a paperback book titled *The Pogues!* to her chest. "I love the Pogues to death," she said. She held the book up and kissed its cover. She talked a great deal and happily: she had been to New York with her father, and it was there that she discovered she was gay. "I was never attracted to men," she said. "I only went out with them because when you're just beginning you don't really know what you are. But I just did it because my friends did it." She looked around the pub and said cheerily, "It's always so dykie in here! But if you got these women alone they would be very different. Irish people always get into a rut. They need a good shake."

She said she liked feminine women, and it puzzled her, as it did Freddy, that women would want to dress like men. "Oh, Christ!" she gasped. "There's that creature Aoife home from London. What a piss artist. I s'pose she can't help herself—the women who go to work in London always develop an awful problem with drink. They get lonesome and want to come home. I loved New York because it was exciting, fun, and you could be gay. But I would never ever leave Ireland."

The overhead lights came on in an ugly flash, a message to the patrons that it was 11:30 and time to leave. The DJ shouted, "Go home to yer husbands and yer wives!" in a tone that suggested she would show us all the back of her hand given half an opportunity.

I went into the bathroom, where two middle-aged women were discussing how early they had gotten up that morning—ten and eleven, respectively. "I got up at seven," I said absently and a little drunkenly, and immediately I regretted it, for the women twisted their faces at me and one of them yelped, "Shite! What in the fuck did you do that for?"

I told them I had wanted to hear Mary Robinson speaking at a morning conference in Parnell Square. The women's faces grew suddenly reverent, and the shorter one cried, "Mary Robinson is grand! She is the best president Ireland ever had! She is one of the people!" Her friend supported that proclamation by hollering mawkishly at her own dark-eyed reflection in the mirror, "And you're dead right, Una!"

Una's hem was hanging. She teetered on her high heels and gripped the edge of the sink with both hands. "That woman has brought Ireland into the twentieth century!" she cried, then, frustrated that it was broken, she dealt the chrome hand dryer a savage blow that nearly knocked it off the wall.

Just outside the bathroom door I ran into Freddy, who had been waiting for me. In the bright lights her skin was gray. She was a head taller than I. She held her hands clasped behind her back and stood with one sneakered foot covering the other. She raised a hand at me in a half wave and said softly, "Well, I guess I'll see ya sometime, Rose."

"See ya, Freddy," I said.

Freddy plucked hesitantly at her lower lip. "Can I ask you something, Rose? If you saw me again sometime, would you talk to me?"

"Of course I would," I said, "and I hope I do see you again."

"I hope so too, Rose," she said. She waved again and went forlornly out of the pub with her head down and one hand visoring the side of her face, as though she expected a heavy object to come hurtling through the air and hit her in the glasses.

Siobhan caught my arm as I was going out the door. "Are you coming to Ulysses with us, Rose?" she said. "It's a nightclub. Stays open all night. Gay. Men and women both."

I went down the stairs and out to Aungier Street with Siobhan and her two friends, Nora and Shleen. The streets were crowded with people streaming all at once out of the city's many pubs. It struck me that Dublin's streets at midnight were exactly as crowded as they were at noon, but now, unhindered by automobile traffic, pedestrians strayed off the sidewalks and weaved dreamily down the middle of the wide streets. The relative absence of cars made the familiar streets seem soft and quiet, and comforting as half-lighted rooms in a beloved house; voices and footsteps echoed off the shadowy buildings, and the pavement, studded with chips of glass, glittered brilliantly in the glow of the wrought-iron streetlights. That night the heavy mist that had traveled up from the Liffey hung yellow in the lights of Aungier Street.

Strange events occurred in Dublin when the pubs let out. I had witnessed, at different times, a group of people hoisting a body like a rolled-up carpet into the back of a tiny car; a slack-jawed, glassy-eyed face pressed against the inside of a storefront window; a man in a tuxedo peacefully asleep in the doorway of the Bank of Ireland, head pillowed by a marble step. In groups of three and four, people strolled, arms slung around each other's shoulders. And every night at half past twelve the streets were festooned with empty glasses placed on curbsides, doorsteps, and windowsills. They were placed with great care, as though the people who put them there did not want them to break. The glasses were like mushrooms that had sprung up through the pavement during the night—they made the streets look strange and magical.

A group of men passed by, and Shleen shouted at them, "Hiya, fellas!" An aging bum with pitch-black palms begged us for two pence so he could buy a bed in the shelter that night. When I turned toward him, Siobhan grabbed my arm and pulled me away. The man shouted after me with inspiring clarity, "Fuck you, fuck you, fuck you, ya lousy bleedin' motherfuckin' old hoor! Fuck you! Filthy old filthy old filthy old hoor!" I was spellbound by the rhythm and imagination of his cursing—it had all the musicality of a nursery rhyme—and fascinated at being addressed in this fashion. The invective was like steam spraying out of him. "Filthy old bleedin' hoors the lot of ye!" he shrieked.

Ulysses, the nightclub, was the low-ceilinged stone cellar of a restaurant on Parliament Street. It was half the size of J. J. Smythe's and twice as loud. People were sitting on every inch of the floor, chins on their knees like refugees, or standing two deep along the walls. Siobhan went to the bar and brought me back a tall can of Heineken, which I couldn't drink.

Nora jeered, "Americans don't know how to drink at all. You're always seeing five of them huddled around one glass of Coke in a pub."

Nora's hair was like Spanish moss. She was jocular and coarse and had a barking laugh. She stood swaybacked, with her belly pushed forward. She was forty-four, and she reminded me of working mothers in the streets of South Boston: harassed and slightly overweight. Stress, disappointment, and indomitable humor were evident around her eyes; her fingernails were bitten so close to the root that they were raw and inflamed. "Where's the accent from, Rose?" she said.

I told her where it was from and guessed correctly that hers was from Donegal. "I left Donegal ten years ago. The only way they could get me to go back to that fuckin' place is if they dragged me in a pine box."

I asked her why.

"They couldn't handle my homosexuality. They just couldn't handle it. I made them sick. I was the village monster. I think they wanted to kill me."

Most of the men in the room were dressed neatly in ties and jackets; they looked smooth-faced and well fed. The air was thick with smoke and sex. I watched a couple kissing passionately against a pole that seemed to be holding up the ceiling. Their hair was matted with sweat, their damp shirts clung to their backs. It was minutes before I realized they were women. I saw hands sliding up under blouses, a man standing at the bar with his hand slipped down the front of another man's trousers. The pub's two DJs (female) were locked in an infinite kiss in front of the turntable, the taller of the two running her hand up the inside of the smaller one's thigh. Siobhan hissed in my ear, "I think the tall one is gorgeous, but she never says hello to me."

I sat on a tabletop and listened to Siobhan's vaporing. The room was so loud that she had to speak with her lips half an inch from my ear. She had opinions about every woman who passed by us, and she took great care to point out which women used to be hers. She said, "Nora has it on for you, Rose. Watch out."

"How do you know that?" I said.

"I know Nora. She's a snake. Here she comes. Hi, Nora."

Nora had swaggered over to ask me to dance. I demurred. She grabbed my hand and yanked me off the table and into the middle of the room. The song was deathly slow. Bodies crowded around us. Nora wrapped her arms around me, and I thought to myself, *You deserve this.* Nora's hands traveled slowly up my back. She put her cheek against my sternum and pressed herself into me. Her lips were wet on my collarbone, and surprisingly cold. I couldn't help imagining her family sitting bitterly on the steepest hillside in Donegal, couldn't banish the image from my mind. I had a powerful desire to make a comment about Nora's shortness but checked myself. Nora's exploring hands traveled ever higher up my side, thumbs approaching my breasts. "You're too thin, Rose," she said.

"And you're too short, Nora," I said. Fortunately Nora thought this was funny. She snorted, "Ha!" into my shoulder and stepped on my foot.

When the song was over I went back to sit with Siobhan and met Deirdre, a short blond woman in a skirt. I talked to a young man in a cowboy hat who said, as though this fact haunted him, "I always felt like an outsider in my family, even though they accept my homosexuality. I was always the quiet one. I was always the weird one. I remember looking out the window and thinking: I got born into the wrong family; I got born into the wrong country." As I listened to him, Siobhan kept tapping me on the back and saying, "Don't talk to him. He's an awful bore." When finally I turned from him, she said, "Rose, are you by any chance bisexual?"

"Why are you asking me that, Siobhan? Because I was talking to a man?"

"No. I thought it before, back in J. J.'s. I didn't think you were completely gay."

"How come?" I said.

"It's something about you." She squinted at me. "I don't know what it is."

These questions irritated me. If this were a straight bar, would people be asking me if I was straight? And why did they need to know? I thought it was none of Siobhan's business. But more to the point, I was uncomfortable at having lied.

"You're bisexual, right?" Siobhan said.

"Right," I said, hoping this was the answer.

"I hate bisexuals." She wasn't joking; her harshness puzzled me.

Siobhan's friend Deirdre said, "What do you mean by bisexual, Rose?"

"Boyfriends and girlfriends," I said pathetically.

"Ever had both at once?"

I had an urge to laugh. I said, "Nope," and stared into a corner of the room, where a small man was sitting in a bigger man's lap, crying.

"I'm bi, too, so I can understand you," Deirdre said. "But I could never have a man and a woman at once. Too much hassle."

The snappy blond in the cutoff shorts whom I'd seen spinning in J. J. Smythe's fell against me on her way to the bar. "'S'cuse me, love," she muttered. "I'm a little bit twisted is all, and I'm avoidin' Aoife, if you know what I mean."

I knew what she meant. She said, "Aoife used to be my girlfriend."

Siobhan went off to dance, and Deirdre said, "Watch out, Rose. Your woman's gone off with somebody else."

"My woman?" I said.

"Yours. Siobhan."

I shrugged. "She's not mine. I only met her an hour ago."

Deirdre said, "Did you not come in here with her tonight?"

"Yes, I did."

Deirdre lit her skinny, self-rolled cigarette and killed the match with a ferocious whip of the wrist. She blew smoke into my ear. "Then she's yours, and you're with her."

That was how it worked. Alliances were fierce but lasted all of an evening, and everyone was everyone else's old girlfriend. This was a pickup joint as insidious as any other. I felt a mild panic coming over me.

Deirdre introduced me to Mary, a good-natured, vivacious woman who had spent four years working in Connecticut and Florida. Mary had been arrested in Connecticut. She said, "This little dot of a cop at the side of the highway tried to wave me over for speeding, and I just carried on with me foot to the floor, because it frightened me, you know, the way he pointed his bleedin' finger at me."

Cigarette drooping from her lip, Mary demonstrated the way the cop had pointed his finger: legs apart, arm outstretched, one eye squeezed shut, as if training a pistol on a target. "And didn't the bastard come after me with his siren blowing a bloody blue circle to waken the dead. Pulled me over. Shouted, 'Out of the car!' like in films. Told me to put me cigarette out. I dropped it on the ground. He made me pick it up and put it in the ashtray in the car. Honest to Jesus, I was so nervous I nearly shook the hole off meself."

The hole Mary meant was, to put it plainly, her asshole. Dubliners were always talking about what certain emotions or events had done to their "hole." They were either laughing the hole off themselves, or vomiting the hole off themselves, or shouting their hole off, or having the hole scared off them. I could never get accustomed to this trope; each time I heard it, it was, with all its microscopic precision, newly arresting.

The cop took Mary to jail and handcuffed her to two prostitutes.

"One of the prostitutes had nothing on but a pink shirt down to here"— she pointed to her crotch—"and when I told them what I was arrested for they laughed in my face." Mary slapped the table on behalf of herself. "I'd've thumped the both of 'em if I wasn't chained to the bleedin' bitches." She paused to catch her breath and smooth her wild hair. "And, by the way, what religion are you, Rose? Because I'm supposed to be Catholic. But I guess I'm not Catholic, judging from my lifestyle."

As she talked, Mary kept reaching accidentally for my beer, and when I told her she could have it, she laughed so hysterically I could see her tonsils. "Jays, Rose," she hooted, yanking on my arm, "you're the master of codology!"

Mary expatiated then on Jews and blacks. She said in London blacks would undress you on the street with their eyes. She, for one, had no right to cast stones, being gay as she was, but still she had reservations about blacks and Jews. She interrupted herself to stare at a woman going up to the bar. "Wait a minute," she said furtively, throwing an arm across my shoulders, "d'you see Pat there? That's Pat. Always wears a skirt up to her arse. It's really not a skirt. It's really just a waistband with an inch of fringe, and when she goes up to the bar she still stomps like a fuckin' man anyhow. A leopard cannot change its stripes. Pat is a professional narcissist. Thinks every woman wants to slip between the sheets with her." Mary gave me a hortatory grimace. "Tell me, Rose, would you favor climbing into bed with a person like that?"

When I left Ulysses that night, Siobhan followed me up to the stairs to the door. "You and Deirdre hit it off grand, didn't you, Rose?" she said coyly.

I shrugged. "Deirdre seems nice," I said.

"She's nice, but she's a user. She used to be my girlfriend."

The streets on the west side of the city were bathed in the smell of the Guinness Brewery. The smell was like chicory, like a vat of coffee and chocolate burning slowly over a wood fire. It was kind and inviting and gave me the feeling that something useful was being accomplished while Dublin slept. It accompanied me all the way home, like light.

The bells of three churches struck three o'clock, and the sky was already livid with the approach of the sun. As I turned up Baggot Street I saw a young couple coming out of a basement restaurant, the man blind drunk, the woman in a fury, shouting at him to for fuck's sake come on. She hit him on the chest with both fists and knocked him to the ground. She bent over and shrieked into his face. She grabbed him by the necktie and began to pull him up, as though lifting a bucket of water out of a well. He sat up like a marionette. His head rolled backward, his arms were limp. The woman screamed, "On your feet!" I couldn't stand watching them, but I felt compelled to. The woman's movements, gently lit by a streetlight, were so incongruously careful, so graceful, that it was like watching a ballet or a dance occurring underwater.

From "Harlem on My Mind"

LAWRENCE OTIS GRAHAM

❧

As the writers in this anthology repeatedly show, going undercover is a more complicated endeavor for a journalist than it might first appear. Changing your clothes and your hairstyle isn't always enough; sometimes you have to disguise your soul. in "Harlem on My Mind," Lawrence Otis Graham adds a new wrinkle to the enterprise. Born and raised in an affluent New York suburb, educated at Princeton and Harvard Law School, a practicing attorney and widely published author, Graham took an assignment from *New York* magazine to spend a month in Harlem, living in a one-room apartment and "passing" as a poor black man. (For a similar story the year before, he had taken a job as a busboy in a Greenwich, Connecticutt, country club.)

Reading between the lines of "Harlem on My Mind," which was published in 1993 when Graham was thirty-one, one senses that despite his fade haircut, Malcolm X cap, and Dr. Dre T-shirt, he was never quite able to make the transition from corporate attorney to homeboy from the 'hood. In Harlem, Graham had the worst of both worlds. To a security guard at the Studio Museum, he was black and therefore suspicious; to "Carl," the low-rent gun dealer, he was white in his soul, and therefore a permanent stranger.

—B. Y.

❧

"You want me to give you a *what?*" the hairdresser asked as she reached around my neck to button the bib. Her breasts pressed tightly against her black spandex pullover. I breathed in the aromas of fruity shampoo blends and the burning hair that was being relaxed and straightened throughout Black Hair Is.

"I said give me a cut that will let me fit in with the Harlem scene," I said. "I'm a writer and musician from out of town and I need a hip kind of look that'll get me over."

We confronted each other in the large round mirror. With one hand holding a comb and the other hand on her hips, she launched into a tirade with her cornrows flying at her shoulder.

"What do you mean make you look like everybody else?" she asked. "Ain't nobody getting the same exact haircut."

We settled on giving me a "fade" haircut, and I apologized for not being more decisive. She told me her name was Kelly and that she wanted to be a beautician—but for rich blacks downtown.

"Now if I could get a job down at John Atchison's," she said while shaving strips of my hair into my lap, "or even better, at Joseph's on Park Avenue—now that would be something. They do all the whosits' hair. 'Cause you know this place ain't even *owned* by black people. And in the middle of Harlem, no less."

"Are you serious?"

"Like a heart attack," she said. "Hold it a second while I get my oil."

As Kelly opened up the window and reached out onto the ledge of the building for a small container of hair oil, I looked up into the mirror.

"So tell me, Lekeisha," one of the other stylists said to a coworker nearby while combing gobs of white relaxer onto a client's scalp. "You think we should just go on and burn our own neighborhood down? Just to show the white people that we can't be walked on?" (This was during the second Rodney King trial.)

Lekeisha clipped away at a woman's bangs. "Girl, I don't know. I mean, how are we going to get some justice, some respect?"

"I hear you, Lekeisha," the coworker responded, "but why hurt ourselves all over again?"

"Hey," Lekeisha said while examining the evenness of her client's bangs, "they beat that man on national TV—and still got away with it. If they get away with it in this trial too, then hey, we should at least take the riots to Forty-second Street. That's what I'm saying. How much more can we take—and right when we have proof—on a videotape?"

Both the stylists and their two clients shook their heads in exasperation. I paid my seventeen-dollar bill and left.

Every day I was reminded of how hard it is to find a public phone that works in Harlem, and when I did, it was sometimes impossible to finish a call. I did learn that when you're at a Harlem corner phone booth and someone taps you on the shoulder telling you his beeper just went off, you'd better hang up. Fast.

"Yo, man, I gotta use the phone," a voice called out from behind me as I stood near 137th and Fifth.

I ignored the tap on my shoulder and continued leaving a message on my accountant's answering machine. "If you don't mind," I said without looking back.

Before the words left my mouth, my arm was twisted up behind my back, I was on my knees, and the receiver was dangling like a gray pendulum over my head. I never got a good look at my attacker's face, but I heard him loud and clear.

"You see this fucking beeper?" he asked.

How could I miss it? As I sat facing him at just below waist level, he twisted my arm, harder, up toward the base of my neck.

"When I gotta do business, you better get the fuck off the phone! This is fuckin' *business!*"

"Sorry, I didn't see you," I cried while staring at the beeper. I naively persuaded myself that as long as I didn't look at the man's face, he wouldn't feel compelled to hurt me—particularly since it was only ten o'clock in the morning—broad daylight.

"I can get you a twelve-gauge in an hour, but a thirty-eight may take a little longer. Either way, I want twenty-five bucks up front."

That's what one of the regulars who hung out on Willie's corner told me when I found him sitting on one of the red stools inside the Lenox Avenue bar, John's Recovery Room.

The plan was simple. I was to drive to a phone booth on 125th Street off the West Side Highway. Neither one of us would ever touch the gun during the transaction. He would hand me a steel-belted radial for my Toyota. The gun would be wrapped in a cloth inside the tire.

"I'll be in a green Olds Ninety-Eight," the man said as he pulled down his brown Kangol hat. He took another sip from his glass of apple wine. "Drive up nonchalantlike and talk loud and call me Carl."

I looked around us at the darkened bar and thought this was all a little complicated and ridiculous. I liked the fact that I didn't have to go to his apartment, but this still seemed complicated, just to get a gun in Harlem.

"Is all this really necessary?" I asked the old man. "Can't I just give you the sixty dollars and you give me the gun?"

"Carl" took another sip from his glass. I immediately got the feeling I had said the wrong thing. He was clearly from the old school. Aggressive enough to deal in firearms, but old enough to be self-righteous and paternalistic about it.

"Look," he said with a wrinkled brow. "You and your white boys come in here from your Jersey suburbs to buy stuff all the time. Well, if you're gonna come here, then you're gonna buy it *our way.*"

At first, I thought I didn't hear him correctly. Here I was, a black man, dressed like a Harlemite, and he's comparing me to some white boy from suburban New Jersey? I told myself that dealing with this guy was safer than buying from Jojo or some other young unpredictable hoodlum, even if this was slower and painfully methodical.

"So you want light ammo, right?"

"Yeah, light," I said, not sure of what he was talking about.

"Son, light is what you get if you're shooting inside buildings—unless you don't care about stray bullets going through walls and killing other folks."

I hadn't wanted to buy this gun. After a conversation with a Sergeant Morrissey at the Thirty-second Precinct on 135th Street, I was persuaded not to buy a gun—almost.

But living in a rooming house, where ex-tenants and their former associates have keys to your door, can make you feel uneasy. Uneasy enough to want just the threat of a gun—even if it's not loaded—just so you can wave it at an attacker. (Both Mrs. Jenkins and Willie kept promising me a new lock, which never arrived.) I had witnessed a partially chewed rat left on my bed sheets (presumably a gift from Sadie, the cat) and the slow disappearance of my Pop-Tarts, milk, toilet paper, loose change, a sweater, and several hangers.

What's more, three different people had walked in on me after unlocking my door with their own keys! Each one was looking for some woman who owed them money, but I was quick-witted enough to explain—once at 2:00 A.M. with the lights out—that I was not that woman and had no connection to her, romantically or otherwise.

Then I was a witness to two shootings.

The first was around 8:15 P.M. on a Thursday, just as the sky was getting dark. My plastic blinds were already pulled closed.

"So why the hell didn't you step off like I told you to?"

"Shit—why didn't *you* step off?"

Two young teenagers were shoving each other on the sidewalk. Three others were egging them on and pushing them closer.

"I wouldn't take that."

"Man, you heard what he said?"

Through my blinds, I could just see one of the boys, in a shiny white polyester running suit, push another against a car's front fender. I heard the "ping" of metal hitting metal.

"Yo—look!"

"He got a gun." Someone was wearing a pair of LA Gear Light Gears. I saw the red bulbs on his heels as he ran into the street. I instinctively hit the floor.

"Pop, pop, pop."

"Yo!"

I crawled toward the dresser, reaching for a phone I didn't have. How do you call for help? I stayed down there for almost five minutes—hearing only the sounds of cars and buses going up Lenox Avenue. And down on the sidewalk, there was nothing—no gun, no body, no spectators.

Seconds later, I noticed a thin brown hand pushing a yellow Post-it note through the crack in my door. I recognized Willie's handwriting: "Give me three dollars—need to buy cat food."

There was a second shooting three nights later at around 4:00 A.M. Two men and a woman arguing. Something about who had to ride in the back-seat of the car that the woman was driving. It happened so fast, and the argument—at least from my window—appeared so inconsequential, it made the single "pop" of gunfire seem almost mundane.

And since so many people have guns, the sound of one is just a small part of the Harlem background noise. Noise that you hear right on up to five in the morning. Yelling, crying, screaming kind of noise—some in anger, but most in conversation. A lot of this loud activity is created because people in rooming houses don't have telephones. They also don't have buzzers or door-bells. So the result is a lot of screaming from the street up to a window—any window that will open and receive a message on behalf of an absent neighbor.

With all this noise, one would imagine you'd have residents opening their front windows—Ralph Kramden-like—and telling the screamers to keep it down out there. But this doesn't happen. Either because it's useless or because the noise brings well-awaited drama into the lives of hundreds of bored listeners. For whatever the reason, no one interferes. Tenants either just listen in and get further caught up in the lives of the people who sit out-side their building day after day, or they turn up the television volume and get further caught up in the lives of the soap operas and talk shows they watch from ten in the morning to five in the afternoon.

This was no more apparent to me than on the four days I spent going up and down Lenox Avenue, 135th Street, and 125th Street looking for job openings. I returned each afternoon to my less-commercial neighborhood, passing by windows where people watched well-dressed, well-coiffed soap stars flit through one-dimensional lives of colorful kitchens, picture-perfect patios, obedient children, and thoughtful neighbors who offered fresh flow-ers and small-town gossip.

I saw whole evening conversations revolve around Oprah's latest guest, Erica Kane's newest hairstyle, Arsenio's funniest spoof, or who got taken to the OR at Harlem Hospital that day. One quickly gets a sense of the bore-dom, which soon turns into lethargy and, eventually, hopelessness.

"You can work for me," Jojo offered one evening as we sat on my bed swig-ging from giant cans of Olde English 800 malt liquor and listening to Wendy Williams's "Top 8 at 8" on KISS-FM.

"How can I work for you?" I asked. "You work security."

"Naw, man—I mean *sell* for me." He laughed.

I laughed too. "Thanks," I said, "but I need a *day* job."

I kept plugging on. I started at Frederick Douglass Boulevard and worked my way east on 125th Street. One of the first stops had been the Twin Donuts Shop.

"Is the manager available?" I asked a young Asian woman who stood near the cash register.

"If you want a job, come back in two or three months."

"Can I fill out an application?"

"No applications," she said rather unsympathetically while refilling the coffee machine. "And it probably isn't worth coming back for another three—no, I'd say four—months."

Across the street at Sneaker City, I walked over to the elevated cash register, where there were two men who appeared very distracted.

"What d'ya want?" one asked without looking at me.

"I wanted to apply for a sales or stock boy job."

He finally focused on me. "A what?"

"A job," I repeated.

He waved me away. "No jobs, no jobs—no, no."

I had similar conversations at Popeye's, Martin Paint, Kentucky Fried Chicken, Kids Kingdom, GEM Stores, Key Express Supermarket, and around sixty other markets, bodegas, restaurants, barber shops, liquor stores, and clothing stores. I offered myself as stock boy, hair sweeper, security guard, or anything else that was needed, but there was not a job to be had anywhere.

(But battling unemployment isn't the only fight to be waged. By the time I returned to my room, I resumed the fight that every other Harlem resident faces: the ongoing menace of roaches. They are everywhere you go—a permanent fixture in stores, on sidewalks, on walls, next to refrigerators, everywhere. As I sat at the edge of my bed resting from my job hunt, paying more attention to the *New York Times* crossword puzzle than to my cup of Dannon blueberry yogurt—which I had stirred only five seconds earlier—I take in a second spoonful and realize that one of those crunchy brown critters has already found its way from the ceiling into my breakfast snack.)

And those classifieds don't tell you how to dress once you arrive in Harlem. They don't tell you that to live in a rooming house, you better dress like a hood, but if you want to get into the more respectable Harlem establishments, you better *not* dress like a hood.

One afternoon, after visiting and viewing an exhibit on the history of blacks in film at the Schomburg Center for Research in Black Culture on 135th Street, I strolled down to 125th Street to drop in at the Studio Museum. But when I opened the door, I was met by a security guard. "What can we do for you today?"

The black guard glanced at my clothes with a wary eye. Even though I was now dressed similarly to most other black men my age on this block, he grimaced. "We're about to close."

"I've still got fifteen minutes."

Looking down at my beeper and gold chain, he smiled politely but refused to move. "Negative. We're having a private party. Why don't you call on the phone tomorrow and take a guided tour?"

As I stepped back into the street, I watched two black women hop out of a cab and walk in without being stopped.

My clothes, while ideal for helping me fit in on my block, were a problem in this other world, the one in which blacks wore business suits and carried briefcases. Dressed in dark unlaced work boots, black sweats, a $199 heavy gold chain with an Uzi pendant, beeper, Malcolm X cap, Sony Walkman earphones, black knapsack, dark sunglasses, and a black Dr. Dre T-shirt that said I GOT TO GET FUCKED UP, I was screaming adolescent ghetto defiance—a regular walking ghetto stereotype. It was probably hard for the guard to believe I was interested in surrealist paintings by early-twentieth-century Cuban-African artists.

Back in my room that evening, I figured out a solution to the clothing problem. I developed a quick-change strategy that allowed me to strip and redress myself while walking along the sidewalk day or night between appointments.

Walking out of my building in full ghetto gear and heading to a 7:45 dinner appointment at Sylvia's, I removed my dark sunglasses and Malcolm X cap. My oversized black Dr. Dre T-shirt came off to reveal a light blue buttondown oxford shirt. My gold chain with Uzi machine gun pendant goes underneath the oxford. Beeper and Sony earphones go into the knapsack and out comes my horn-rimmed reading glasses and a fresh copy of the yuppie business magazine *Black Enterprise* to hold underneath my arm. A few blocks later, my shoes are tied, college signet ring is back on my finger, and I am led by Melba, Sylvia's niece, over to a table near a photo of talk-show host Kathie Lee Gifford. I sit down at my place in the green dining room, just underneath one of the small crystal chandeliers. I am ready to be served.

From "Snake Handling
and Redemption"

DENNIS COVINGTON

Like George Orwell or Ted Conover or Bill Buford, Dennis Covington believes that *participating* in your journalistic object of study—in Covington's case, some fundamentalist Christians' practice of handling poisonous snakes in the course of their worship—can provide a better understanding than merely observing and interviewing. Covington differs from the other authors in having a deep personal stake in the subject. As he explains elsewhere in his 1995 book *Salvation on Sand Mountain* (from which the following is taken), he was drawn to snake handling because of questions he was starting to ask himself over his own roots.

Covington's ancestors had lived near rural Sand Mountain, Alabama, before moving to Birmingham, where he was born and bred. He was still living there in the early 1990s, teaching college and writing short stories "about urban couples, with or without children, and the minor perplexities they faced," that might as well have been set in Portland or Des Moines: "I started to wonder if I was still a southern writer. I started to wonder if there was still a South at all."

It took a trip to Sand Mountain to discover that there indeed persisted "a South that resided in the blood, a region of the heart." But the question remained: was he a part of it?

—B. Y.

When I was a kid, the best snakes—the absolutely best snakes of all—came from Ruffner Mountain, a foothill of the Appalachians that overlooked East Lake. It was just out of walking distance from my house. We only tried walking it once. Other times, my father drove and dropped us off. We said we were hiking to the fire tower at the top of the mountain, but I always had my eyes peeled for snakes.

391

The first one I caught on Ruffner Mountain was a corn snake I saw wrapped around the trunk of a pine tree. Docile and graceful, it had scarlet blotches and an intricately patterned head, as surprising as if it were a piece of Arabian carpet dangling in the Alabama woods. The corn snake ate mice, but I couldn't bear to keep it long, even though my father had made me a first-rate snake cage with the power tools he'd bought after someone told him he needed a hobby. I let that corn snake go one day in our neighbors' cauliflower field and always hoped that I would see it again. I never did.

My friend Bert Butts gave me my second Ruffner Mountain snake. It was a speckled king, big and black, freshly shed, with yellow speckles from head to tail, as though a paintbrush had been shaken lightly over it. King snakes are famous for their placid dispositions. Like marine mammals, they seem to wear a perpetual smile, and they happen to eat rattlesnakes. I named this king snake Kuebert Wood, after a track star at a local high school. He would sunbathe on my stomach. I swore I'd never let him go. But then I caught a gigantic five-and-a-half-foot gray rat snake—a record, I thought. I gave that snake the cage my father had built and relegated Kuebert Wood to a number ten washtub with a screen on top, held down by rocks. During the night, Kuebert escaped—or, I prefer to think, wandered off. I have hated the memory of that rat snake ever since.

A final gift came from a friend named Galen Bailey, who lived closer to the mountain than I did. This snake was very delicate and rare, a scarlet snake, with alternating rings of red, black, and yellow. Except for the broken rings and the order of the colors, it looked exactly like a coral snake: quite perfect, but it wouldn't eat. I kept it longer than I should have, because of its beauty. I hope it survived after I released it in the cauliflower field. With snakes, you never know.

The poisonous snakes came later, when I was an adult. I have caught only three, and I did not keep any of them overnight. The first was a pygmy rattlesnake I found sunning on a grave in a cemetery in southwest Louisiana, where I was stationed while in the Army in the early seventies. The pygmy is a small, stout species, rarely over two feet in length. It is ill-tempered and can deliver a painful bite. Its venom is as powerful as that of larger rattlesnakes, but since less venom is injected at a time, the bites of pygmy rattlers are rarely life threatening.

This particular snake looked plenty dangerous to me, though. I was hung over. My first wife Susan and I had taken a Sunday drive to visit old cemeteries. It was springtime, and tarantulas were crossing the road in droves. When I saw the pygmy rattlesnake on the grave, it seemed to be a sign: I had to conquer my fear of it. My heart beat faster. My palms ached. I found a stick, pinned the snake behind the head, and picked it up. Susan was horrified when I told her what it was. She'd hunted nonpoisonous snakes with me, but this was a little much.

The problem, I discovered, was not in catching the snake, but in releasing it. How do you let a rattlesnake go without risking a bite? I wound up taking the steps in nearly reverse order: putting it on the ground, pinning it with the stick, and only then releasing my grip. It worked. I had accomplished something.

The second poisonous snake I found was a copperhead, the last of the summer, stretched out on a road on Red Mountain in Birmingham. I was married to Vicki by then and teaching at the university. Again, I was hung over. I brought the snake home, stretched between my hands, and told Vicki to find an empty ice chest to put it in. She, too, was horrified, but she drove with me into the country to let it go away from houses. I wrote a short story that talked about the way it looked coming out of the ice chest and disappearing into the dark woods.

In the years following, I sobered up. We had our girls and built a house in the woods on the side of Sand Mountain. The last poisonous snake I caught was a canebrake rattlesnake crossing the pavement at the bottom of our driveway. I brought it up to the house so the girls could get a good look and know what kind of snake to avoid. Then I said I was going to let it go in the woods—but I killed it instead. I do not believe it is necessary for a man to allow a poisonous snake to cross his property while his children are young. The canebrake is the only snake I have ever killed like that. It still bothers me some.

Around eight thousand people in the United States are bitten each year by poisonous snakes, but only a dozen or so die. There are two families of poisonous snakes in this country, both of them native to our part of the South. The first, Elapidae, which includes cobras, mambas, and other deadly Old World snakes, is represented in the New World by Eastern and Western coral snakes—shy, beautiful, and extremely dangerous. Their venom is a neurotoxin which attacks the central nervous system, particularly such autonomic functions as breathing and heartbeat. Fortunately, coral snakes are reclusive by nature. They seldom bite, and when they do, their small mouths and fixed fangs make it difficult for them to successfully latch on to humans.

The second family of poisonous snakes, the Crotalidae, contains the pit vipers—rattlesnakes, copperheads, and cottonmouths. The pits for which these snakes are named are infrared heat sensing organs which lie between the nostrils and eyes. With them, the snakes hunt their warm-blooded prey by seeking out body heat. The pit vipers are efficient killers with large, flexible mouths, long retractable fangs, and venom that attacks and destroys cells and tissue. Victims die of internal hemorrhaging, cardiovascular shock, or kidney and respiratory failure.

The least dangerous of the pit vipers to man is the copperhead, although its bite can kill children. The *most* dangerous is the Eastern diamondback rattlesnake, which can grow to a length of eight feet and has a combative temperament and a large reservoir of venom. Somewhere in between lies the timber rattler, often called the canebrake in our part of the country. Herpetologists disagree about whether the canebrake is a color variation or a distinct subspecies. The timber rattler is often seen in serpent-handling churches, because it is the poisonous snake most readily available on the rocky hillsides and grassy valleys of the Appalachians. It shares its range with the copperhead but appears to be more sociable, often found in large numbers in dens or burrows. The timber is somewhat smaller and less aggressive than the diamondback, but it is still a dangerous snake, unpredictable and with venom that can easily kill an adult.

The timber rattler is also, to me, the loveliest of the rattlesnakes, varying in color from pink to straw to nearly uniform black, with sharp, dark chevrons on its back. Its neck is narrow, and its head is as finely defined as an arrow. Oftentimes the tail is velvety in appearance; in such cases, the handlers will call the snake a "satinback." Encountered in the wild, a large timber rattler, *Crotalus horridus,* is an impressive and frightening sight. When cornered, it rattles energetically and coils to strike. But its first impulse is to flee, and perhaps that too is a source of its beauty: a dangerous animal, exquisitely made, turning away from a fight.

In captivity, timber rattlers can live up to thirty years. Their tenure among the handlers is much shorter, rarely exceeding a season. I have seen timber rattlers die while being handled; they are not made to be jerked around. On the other hand, some of the snakes are well cared for, and simply released back into the wild after a few months. Handlers are always in search of new snakes, always trading specimens back and forth. It appears to be a ritual after services for handlers to give snakes to one another, like an offering of brandy or after-dinner mints or hand-rolled cigars in other circles. Some of the handlers regularly catch their own snakes, most of the time in conventional ways, with a snake stick and a burlap bag or pillowcase. Others buy snakes from professional exhibitors at prices the handlers complain are getting more outrageous every year, as much as forty-five dollars at last reckoning.

However the snakes are obtained, they often become objects of affection in the homes of the handlers and their families. The first rattlesnake that Charles McGlocklin's wife Aline took up, for instance, was called Old Crooked Neck, because of the injury it had received during capture. The big copperhead in the terrarium on the McGlocklins' kitchen counter used to be called Mr. Hog, Charles said, until it had eight babies and they had to start calling it Miss Piggy instead. But no amount of affection or care can ensure that a rattlesnake or copperhead won't bite when handled. They do not tame in a conventional sense. No one can predict what will happen when a handler reaches into the serpent box. And contrary to popular misconception, multiple bites do not result in immunity to snake venom, but may even increase the risk of death because of allergic reaction.

I came to know snake handlers in February of 1992, when I covered the trial of Reverend Glenn Summerford for the *New York Times.* Summerford, the pastor of The Church of Jesus with Signs Following in Scottsboro, Alabama, was convicted and sentenced to ninety-nine years in prison for attempting to murder his wife Darlene with rattlesnakes. The trial had echoed themes from a troubled secular society—marital infidelity, spousal abuse, and alcoholism—but it also raised questions about faith, forgiveness, redemption, and of course, snakes. The Church of Jesus with Signs Following, a converted service station on Wood's Cove Road, seemed to me to be the emblem of a submerged and disappearing population. I wasn't content just to report the outcome of its preacher's trial. I had to find out more about the handlers themselves—who they were and why they did what they did.

After Summerford's conviction, his church in Scottsboro split. Some members of the congregation began meeting outdoors on top of Sand Mountain. They invited me to worship with them, and we entered that unspoken conspiracy between journalist and subject. The handlers had something they wanted to show me, and I was willing to be shown. I went to scores of services in Alabama, Georgia, Tennessee, Kentucky, and West Virginia. I wanted something more than a story, but I didn't know exactly what it was.

The handlers eventually taught me there were two kinds of handling, one done as a simple demonstration of faith and the other as the result of a specific anointing by the Holy Ghost. During an anointing, the Holy Ghost would descend on them, they said, and give them power to take up serpents without fear. They described this altered state as "joy unspeakable . . . perfect love." I handled a rattlesnake myself once in Georgia on faith, but I did not experience an anointing until the summer of 1993.

That spring, Charles McGlocklin told me that Glenn Summerford's cousins, Billy and Jimmy, had started a new church on top of Sand Mountain, near a place called Macedonia. Charles didn't worship with them, though.

"Why not?" I asked.

Brother Charles was a big man with hands the size of waffle irons. He took a deep breath and surveyed the land around him, yellow and gray in the afternoon light. We were on the deck behind his and Aline's trailer in New Hope, Alabama. Beside the trailer was a doghouse for their bluetick hound named Smokey, and behind it was a corral for their horse, a buckskin mare named Dixie Honeydew.

"I know enough about some of those people to know I ought not to worship anymore with them," Charles said. As a snake handler, he had set himself apart from the world, and sometimes he even set himself apart from other snake handlers. It was part of the Southern character, I thought, to be always turning away like that toward some secret part of oneself.

"You know how much I love you," Charles said. He put one of his big hands on my shoulder and shook it. "You're my brother. But anytime you go up there on Sand Mountain, you be careful."

We could hear the sound of the wind through trees, a soughing, dry and hesitant, and then Dixie Honeydew neighed.

"You might be anointed when you take up a serpent," Charles continued, "but if there's a witchcraft spirit in the church, it could zap your anointing and you'd be left cold turkey with a serpent in your hand and the spirit of God gone off of you. That's when you'll get bit."

We walked around the corner of the trailer, where photographer and friend Jim Neel was waiting for me in his pickup truck.

"So you really watch and remember what Brother Charles tells you," Charles whispered. "Always be careful who you take a rattlesnake from."

This sounded like solid advice.

I got into Jim's truck, and Charles motioned for us to roll a window down. "Y'all come back any time," he yelled.

So my journey had come back around to the congregation on Sand Mountain, the remnant of Glenn Summerford's flock that had left the converted service station on Wood's Cove Road in Scottsboro and then met under a brush arbor in back of J. L. Dyal's house until the weather got too cold. After worshiping for a while in the basement of an old motel, they finally found a church for sale on the mountain. It was miles from nowhere, in the middle of a hay field south of Section, Alabama—home of Tammy Little, Miss Alabama of 1984. The nearest dot on the map, though, was Macedonia, a crossroads consisting of a filling station, a country store, and a junk emporium. It was not the kind of place you'd visit of your own accord. You'd have to be led there. In fact, Macedonia had gotten its name from the place in the Bible that Paul had been called to go to in a dream. Paul's first European converts to Christianity had been in Macedonia. But that was, you know, a long time ago and in another place.

Glenn's cousins negotiated the deal for the church. Billy was friendly and loose-limbed, with a narrow red face and buck teeth. He'd worked mostly as a carpenter, but he'd also sold coon dogs. Jimmy was less amiable and more compact. Between them, they must have been persuasive. They got the church for $2,000. A guy down the road had offered $5,000, Billy said, but the owner had decided to sell it to them. "God was working in that one," he concluded.

It was called the Old Rock House Holiness Church, in spite of the fact that it wasn't made of rock. But it was old in contrast to the brick veneer churches out on Highway 35, the ones with green indoor/outdoor carpet in the vestibules and blinking U-HAUL IT signs out front.

The Old Rock House Holiness Church had been built in 1916, a few years before Dozier Edmonds first saw people take up serpents in Jackson County at a church in Sauty Bottom, down by Saltpeter Cave. I'd met Dozier during the brush arbor meetings, outdoor revivals held under temporary shelters framed with timbers and topped with brush. A rail-thin old man with thick glasses and overalls, Dozier was the father-in-law of J. L. Dyal and the husband of Burma, the snake handling twin. (Burma's sister, Erma, was always in attendance at the services, but didn't handle serpents herself.) Dozier said he'd seen men get bit in that church in Sauty Bottom more than seventy years ago. They didn't go to a doctor, just swelled up a little bit. He also remembered a Holiness boy at the nearby one-room school who would fall into a trance, reach into the pot-bellied stove, and get himself a whole handful of hot coals. The teacher would have to tell the boy to put them back.

There was also a Baptist church in that area called Hell's Half Acre, Dozier said. They didn't take up serpents, but they'd do just about anything else. They were called Buckeye Baptists. They'd preach and pray till midnight, then gamble and fight till dawn. One time a man rode a horse into the church, right up to the pulpit. Out of meanness, Dozier said. Everything was different then. "They used to tie the mules up to a white mulberry bush in the square," he said. Why, he remembered when Scottsboro itself was nothing but a mudhole. When the carnival came through, the elephants were up to their bellies in mud. There wasn't even a road up Sand Mountain until Dozier helped build one.

Dozier came from a family of sharecroppers who lived on the property of a Confederate veteran, Colonel Mance, who had a bullet hole through his neck. He'd built his own casket. Every Easter, Colonel Mance invited the children of the families who lived on his property to come to the big house for an egg hunt. One Easter, he wanted the children to see what he'd look like when he was dead, so he lay down in the casket and made the children march around it. Some of the grown-ups had to help get him out. "It was a pine casket with metal handles on it," Dozier said. Colonel Mance eventually died, but he wasn't buried in the casket he'd made. He'd taken it apart years before and given the handles to the families who lived on his property, to use as knockers on the doors of their shacks.

That was the kind of place Sand Mountain had been when the Old Rock House Holiness Church was in its heyday. By the time the Summerford brothers bought it in the winter of 1993, it had fallen onto hard times. It didn't even have a back door. Paper wasps had built nests in the eaves. The green shingles on the outside were cracked, and the paint on the window frames had just about peeled off. Billy Summerford and some of the other men from the congregation repaired and restored the church as best they could. It'd be another year, though, before they could get around to putting in a bathroom. In the meantime, there would be an outhouse for the women and a bunch of trees for the men. The church happened to be sited in the very center of a grove of old oaks. Fields of hay surrounded the grove and stretched to the horizon. As you approached the church along a dirt road during summer heat, the oak grove looked like a dark island in the middle of a shimmering sea of gold and green.

That's the way it looked to me, anyway, on a bright Sunday morning in late June, six months after the Summerfords had bought the church, when Jim Neel and I left the McGlocklins' place and drove up for the first annual homecoming. Brother Carl Porter from Georgia had invited us by phone and given us directions; he was scheduled to preach at the homecoming. Other handlers were coming from all over—from east Tennessee and south Georgia, from the mountains of Kentucky and the scrublands of the Florida panhandle. If we hadn't had Carl's directions, we'd never have found the place, though. The right turn off the paved road from Macedonia was unmarked, one of several gravel roads that angled off into the distance. Where it crossed another paved road there finally was a sign, made of cardboard and mounted at waist level on a wooden stake. After that, the gravel turned to dirt. Dust coated the jimsonweed. The passionflowers were in bloom, and the blackberries had begun to ripen in the heat. There were no houses on this road, and no sound except for the cicadas' steady din, like approaching rain.

Jim and I were early. We stepped up on a cement block to get through the back doorway of the church. The door itself was off its hinges, and none of the windows in the church had screens. There were no bathrooms, no cushions on the pews, no ornaments of any kind except a portrait of Jesus etched into a mirror behind the pulpit and a vase of plastic flowers on the edge of the piano bench, where a boy with a withered hand sat staring at the keys. We took our places on a back pew and watched the handlers arrive. They greeted each other with the holy kiss, women with women, men with men, as prescribed by Paul in Romans 16. Among them was the legendary Punkin Brown, the evangelist who I'd been told would wipe the sweat off his brow with rattlesnakes. Jamie Coots from Kentucky and Allen Williams from Tennessee were also there; they sat beside Punkin on the deacons' bench. All three were young and heavyset, the sons of preachers, and childhood friends. Punkin and Jamie both wore scowls, as though they were waiting for somebody to cross their paths in an unhappy way. Allen Williams, though, looked serene. His father had died drinking strychnine in 1973, and his brother had died of snake bite in 1991. Maybe he thought he didn't have anything more to lose. Or maybe he was just reconciled to losing everything he had. Within six months of sitting together on that deacons' bench at the Old Rock House Church, Jamie, Allen, and Punkin would all be bit.

The church continued to fill with familiar faces, many from what used to be The Church of Jesus With Signs Following (over in Scottsboro), and as is customary in spirit-led churches, the music began without an introduction of any kind. It sounded like a cross between Salvation Army and acid rock: tambourines, an electric guitar, drums, cymbals, and voices that careened from one note to the next as though they were being sawn in half. James Hatfield of Old Straight Creek, a Trinitarian church on the mountain, was on drums. My red-haired friend Cecil Esslinder from Scottsboro was on guitar, grinning and tapping his feet. Cecil's wife Carolyn stood in the very middle of the congregation; as was her habit, she faced backwards to see who might come in the rear door. Also in the congregation were Bobbie Sue Thompson, the twins Burma and Erma, J. L. Dyal and his wife and in-laws, and just about the whole Summerford clan. The only ones missing were Charles and Aline McGlocklin. Charles was still recovering from neck surgery on an old injury, but I knew from the conversation we'd had in New Hope that even if he'd been well, he wouldn't have come.

One woman I didn't recognize told me she was originally from Detroit. This came as some surprise, and her story seemed equally improbable. She said her husband used to work in the casinos in Las Vegas, and when he died she moved to Alabama and started handling rattlesnakes at the same church on Lookout Mountain where the lead singer of the group Alabama used to handle. "Didn't you see the photo?" she asked. "It was in *The National Enquirer.*"

I told her I'd missed that one.

Children were racing down the aisles. With high foreheads, eyes far apart, and gaps between their front teeth, they all looked like miniature Glenn Summerfords. Maybe they were. He had at least seven children by his first wife, and all of them were old enough to have children of their own.

About that time, Brother Carl Porter walked in with a serpent box which would prove to contain the biggest rattlesnake I'd ever seen. Carl smelled of Old Spice and rattlesnake and something else underneath: a pleasant smell, like warm bread and cider. I associated it with the Holy Ghost. The handlers had told me that the Holy Ghost had a smell, a "sweet savor," and I had begun to think I could detect it on people and in churches—even in staid, respectable churches like the one I went to in Birmingham. Anyway, that was what I smelled on Brother Carl that day as he talked about the snake in the box. "I just got him today," he said. "He's never been in church before." Carl looked over his glasses at me and smiled. He held the serpent box up to my face and tapped the screen until the snake started rattling good.

"Got your name on him," he said to me.

A shiver went up my spine, but I just shook my head and grinned.

"Come on up to the front," he said. I followed him and sat on the first pew next to J. L. Dyal, but I made a mental note to avoid Carl's eyes during the service and to stay away from that snake of his.

Billy Summerford's wife Joyce led the singing. She was a big woman with a voice that wouldn't quit. *Re-member how it felt, when you, walked out of the wilderness, walked out of the wilderness, walked out of the wilderness. Re-member how it felt, when you, walked out of the wilderness . . .* This was one of my favorite songs because it had multiple meanings now. There was the actual wilderness in the Old Testament that the Israelites were led out of, and there was the spiritual wilderness that was its referent, the condition of being lost. But there was also the wilderness that the New World became for my father's people, the Scotch-Irish immigrants who settled the Appalachians. When I say wilderness, I don't mean the mountains, though. I mean the America that grew up around them, that tangled thicket of the heart.

Re-member how it felt, when you, walked out of the wilderness . . . My throat tightened as I sang and remembered how it had felt when I'd sobered up in 1983. It's not often you get a second chance at life like that. And I remembered the births of my girls, the children Vicki and I had thought we'd never be able to have. Looking around at the familiar faces in the congregation, I figured they were thinking about their own wildernesses and how they'd been delivered out of them. I knew I was still coming out of mine. It was a measure of how far I'd come, that I'd be moved nearly to tears in a run-down Holiness church on Sand Mountain, but my restless and stubborn intellect was still intact. It didn't like what it saw—a crowd of men dancing up to the serpent boxes, unclasping the lids, and taking out the poisonous snakes. Reason told me it was too early in the service. The snakes hadn't been prayed over enough. There hadn't even been any preaching yet, just Billy Summerford screaming into a microphone while the music swirled around us like a fog. But the boys from Tennessee and Kentucky had been hungry to get into the boxes. Soon, Punkin Brown was shouting at his snake, a big black-phase timber rattler that he had draped around his neck. Allen Williams was offering up his copperhead like a sacrifice, hands outstretched. But Brother Carl had the prize, and everyone seemed to know it. It was a yellow-phase timber as big as they ever come. Carl glanced at me, but I wouldn't make eye contact with him. I turned away. I walked to the back of the church and took a long drink of water from the bright yellow cooler propped up against a portrait of Jesus with his head on fire.

"Who knows what this snake is thinking?" Carl shouted. "God knows! God understands the mind of this snake!" And when I turned back around, Carl had laid the snake down and was treading barefoot on it from tail to head, as though he were walking a tightrope. Still, the snake didn't bite. I had heard about this, but never seen it before. The passage was from Luke: *Behold, I give unto you the power to tread on serpents and scorpions, and over all the power of the enemy; and nothing shall by any means hurt you.* Then Carl picked the snake back up and draped it around his neck. The snake seemed to be looking for a way out of its predicament. Carl let it nuzzle into his shirt. Then the snake pulled back and cocked its head, as if in preparation to strike Carl's chest. Its head was as big as a child's hand.

"Help him, Jesus!" someone yelled above the din. Instead of striking, the snake started to climb Carl's sternum toward his collarbone. It went up the side of his neck but then lost interest and fell back against his chest.

The congregation was divided into two camps now, the men to the left with the snakes, the women to the right with each other. In front of Carl, one of the men suddenly began jumping straight up and down, as though he were on a pogo stick. Down the aisle he went and around the sanctuary. When he returned, he collapsed at Carl's feet. One of the Summerford brothers attended to him there by soaking a handkerchief with olive oil and dabbing it against the man's forehead until he sat up and yelled, "Thank God!"

In the meantime, in the corner where the women had gathered, Joyce Summerford's sister Donna was laboring in the spirit with a cataleptic friend. She circled the friend, eying her contortions carefully, and then, as if fitting her into an imaginary dress, she clothed her in the spirit with her hands: an invisible tuck here, an invisible pin there, making sure the spirit draped well over the flailing arms. It took her a while. Both of the women were drenched in sweat and stuttering in tongues by the time they finished.

"They say we've gone crazy!" Brother Carl shouted above the chaos. He was pacing in front of the pulpit, the enormous rattlesnake balanced now across his shoulder. "Well, they're right!" he cried. "I've gone crazy! I've gone Bible crazy! I've got the papers here to prove it!" And he waved his dogeared Bible in the air. "Some people say we're just a bunch of fanatics!"

"Amen. Thank God."

"Well, we are! *Hai-i-salemos-ah-cahn-ne-hi-yee!* Whew! That last one nearly took me out of here!"

It's not true that you become used to the noise and confusion of a snake-handling Holiness service. On the contrary, you become enmeshed in it. It is theater at its most intricate and improvisational—a spiritual jazz. The more you experience it, the more attentive you are to the shifts on the surface and in the dark shoals underneath. For every outward sign, there is a spiritual equivalent. When somebody falls to his knees, a specific problem presents itself, and the others know exactly what to do, whether it's oil for a healing, or a prayer cloth thrown over the shoulders, or a devil that needs to be cast out.

The best, of course, the simplest and cleanest, is when someone gets the Holy Ghost for the first time. The younger the worshiper, the easier it seems to be for the Holy Ghost to descend and speak—lips loosened, tongue flapping, eyes rolling backward in the head. When a thirteen-year-old girl gets the Holy Ghost, the moment transcends the erotic. The older ones often take time. I once saw an old man whose wife had gotten the Holy Ghost at a previous service. He wanted it bad for himself, he said. Brother Charles McGlocklin started praying with him before the service even started, and all through it, the man was in one attitude or another at the front of the church—now lying spread-eagle on the floor while a half-dozen men prayed over him and laid on hands, now up and running from one end of the sanctuary to the other, now twirling, now swooning, now collapsing once again on the floor with his eyes like those of a horse who smells smoke and with the unknown tongue spewing from his mouth. "He got the Holy Ghost at last! He got the Holy Ghost!" you think—until you see him after the service eating a pimento cheese sandwich downstairs. His legs are crossed. He's brushing the crumbs from his lap. He agrees it was a good service all right, but it sure would have been better if he'd only gotten the Holy Ghost.

Maybe he means you can never get enough of the Holy Ghost. You can never exhaust the power when the Spirit comes down, not even when you take up a snake, not even when you take up a dozen of them. The more faith you expend, the more power is released. It's an inexhaustible, eternally renewable resource. It's the only power some of these people have.

The longer you witness such a service, unless you just aren't able to respond to the spontaneous and unexpected, the more you become a part of it. *I* did, and the handlers could tell. They knew before I did what was going to happen. They saw me angling in, and they were already making room for me in front of the deacons' bench. I'd always been drawn to danger. Alcohol. Psychedelics. War. If it made me feel good, I'd do it. I was always up for a little trip. I figured that if I could trust my guide, I'd be all right. I'd come back to earth in one piece. I wouldn't really lose my mind. That's what I thought, anyway. I couldn't be an astronaut, but there were other things I could do and be.

So I got up there in the middle of the handlers. J. L. Dyal, dark and wiry, was standing on my right; a clean-cut boy named Steve Frazier was on my left. Who would it be? Carl's eyes were saying, *You*. And yes, it was the big rattler, the one with my name on it, acrid-smelling, carnal, alive. And the look in Carl's eyes seemed to change as he approached me. He appeared embarrassed. The snake was all he had, his eyes seemed to say. But as low as it was, as repulsive, if I took it I'd be possessing the sacred. Nothing was required except obedience. Nothing had to be given up except my own will. This was the moment.

I didn't stop to think about it. I just gave in. I stepped forward and took the snake with both hands. Carl released it to me. I turned to face the congregation and lifted the rattlesnake up toward the light. It was moving like it wanted to get up even higher, to climb out of that church and into the air. And the experience was exactly as the handlers had told me. I felt no fear. The snake seemed to be an extension of myself. And suddenly there seemed to be nothing in the room but me and the snake. Everything else had disappeared. Carl, the congregation, Jim—all gone, all faded to white. I could not even hear the earsplitting music. The air was silent and still and filled with that strong, even light. And I realized that I, too, was fading into the white. I was losing myself by degrees, like the incredible shrinking man. The snake would be the last to go, and all I could see was the way its scales shimmered one last time in the light, and the way its head moved from side to side, searching for a way out. I knew then why the handlers took up serpents. There is power in the act of disappearing; there is victory in the loss of self. It must be close to our conception of paradise, what it's like before you're born or after you die.

I came back in stages, first with the recognition that the shouting I had begun to hear was coming from my own mouth. Then I realized I was holding a rattlesnake, and the church rushed back with all its clamor, heat, and smell. I remembered Carl and turned toward where I thought he might be. I lowered the snake to waist level. It was an enormous animal, heavy and firm. The scales on its side were as rough as calluses. I could feel its muscles rippling beneath the skin. I was aware it was not a part of me now and that I couldn't predict what it might do. I extended it toward Carl. He took it from me, stepped to the side, and gave it in turn to J.L.

"Jesus," J.L. said. "Oh, Jesus." His knees bent, his head went back. I knew it was happening to him, too.

Then I looked around and saw that I was in a semicircle of handlers by the deacons' bench. Most had returned their snakes to the boxes, but Billy Summerford, Glenn's bucktoothed cousin, still had one, and he offered it to me—a medium-sized canebrake that was rattling violently. I took the snake in one hand without thinking. It was smaller than the first, but angrier, and I realized circumstances were different now. I couldn't seem to steer it away from my belt line. Fear had started to come back to me. I remembered with sudden clarity what Brother Charles had said about being careful who you took a snake from. I studied the canebrake as if I were seeing it for the first time and then gave it back to Billy. He passed it to Steve Frazier, the young man on my left. I watched Steve cradle it, curled and rattling furiously in his hands, and then I walked out the side door of the church and onto the steps, where Bobbie Sue Thompson was clutching her throat and leaning against the green shingles of the church.

"Jesus," she said. "Jesus, Jesus."

It was a sunny, fragrant day, with high-blown clouds. I looked into Bobbie Sue's face. Her eyes were wide and her mouth hooked at the corner. "Jesus," she said again.

I thought at first she was in terrible pain, but then I realized she wasn't. "Yes. I know. Jesus," I said.

STYLE AS SUBSTANCE

The Pig

BEN HECHT

❧

Ben Hecht (1894–1964) not only cowrote *The Front Page*; he lived it. He went to work for the Chicago *Daily Journal* in 1910, at the age of sixteen, moved on to the Chicago *Daily News* four years later, and developed a reputation as one of the greatest reporters in one of the greatest eras of American newspaper history.

In 1921, Hecht inaugurated a *Daily News* column called "One Thousand and One Afternoons." It didn't quite fulfill its title's promise. Shortly before the column's second anniversary, Hecht was brought to trial by the U.S. Postal Service for sending obscene materials (his novel *Fantazius Mallare*) through the mails and was fired by the *Daily News*.

But while it lasted, the column was enormously influential. His editor, Henry Justin Smith, later said it represented "the idea that just under the edge of the news as commonly understood, the news often flatly and unimaginatively told, lay life; that in this urban life there dwelt the stuff of literature, not hidden in remote places, either, but walking the downtown streets, peering from the windows of sky scrapers, sunning itself in parks and boulevards. He was going to be its interpreter. His was to be the lens throwing city life into new colors, his the microscope revealing its contortions in life and death."

"The Pig" is suggestive of a classic Russian short story, and not only because of its protagonists' ethnicity. In a Gogol story, you might find the same uncanny blend of the ridiculous and the pathetic, the same cosmic irony dripping from the narrative voice; you might also find a central narrative place held by a barnyard animal. After concluding "One Thousand and One Afternoons," Hecht went on to produce novels, plays, screenplays, and memoirs, but none of these eclipsed his early success in finding the stuff of literature in city life.

—B. Y.

❧

"Sofie Popapovitch versus Anton Popapovitch," cries the clerk. A number of broken-hearted matrons awaiting their turn before the bar of justice

407

in the Domestic Relations Court find time to giggle at the name Popapovitch.

"Silence," cries the clerk. Very well, silence. Anton steps out. What's the matter with Anton? An indignant face, its chin raised, its eyes marching defiantly to the bar of justice. Sofie too, but weeping. And a lawyer, Sofie's lawyer.

Well, what's up? Why should the Popapovitches take up valuable time. Think of the taxpayers supporting this court and two Popapovitches marching up to have an argument on the taxpayers' money. Well, that's civilization.

Ah, ah! It appears that Anton, the rogue, went to a grand ball and raffle given by his lodge. What's wrong with that? Why must Sofie weep over that? Women are incredible. He went to the grand ball with his wife, as a man should. A very fine citizen, Anton. He belongs to a lodge that gives grand balls and he takes his wife.

Go on, says the judge, what happened? What's the complaint? Time is precious. Let's have it in a nutshell.

This is a good idea. People spend a frightful lot of unnecessary time weeping and mumbling in the courts. Mrs. Popapovitch will please stop weeping and get down to brass tacks. Very well, the complaint is, your honor, that Mr. Popapovitch got drunk at the grand ball. But that wasn't the end of it. There's some more. A paragraph of tears and then, your honor, listen to this: Mr. Popapovitch not only got drunk but he took a chance on the raffle which cost one dollar and he won.

But what did he win! Oh, oh! He won a pig. A live pig. That was the prize. A small, live pig with a ribbon round its neck. And, says Mrs. Popapovitch (there's humor in a long foreign-sounding name because it conjures up visions of bewildered, flat-faced people and bewildered, flat-faced people are always humorous), and, says she, they had been married ten years. Happily married. She washed, scrubbed, tended house. There were no children. Well, what of that? Lots of people had no children.

Anyway, Anton worked, brought home his pay envelope O. K. And then he wins this pig. And what does he do? He takes it home. He won't leave it anywhere.

"What!" he says, "I leave this pig anywhere? Are you crazy? It's my pig. I win him. I take him home with me."

And then? Well, it's midnight, your honor. And Anton carries the pig upstairs into the flat. But there's no place to put him. Where can one put a pig in a flat, your honor? No place. The pig don't like to stand on carpets. And what pig likes to sleep on hard wood floors? A pig's a pig. And what's good for a pig? Aha! a pig pen.

So, your honor, Anton puts him in the bathtub. And he starts down stairs with a basket and all night long he keeps bringing up basketfuls of dirt dug up from the alley. Dirt, cinders, more dirt. And he puts it in the bathtub. And what does the pig do? He squeals, grunts and wants to go home. He fights to get out of the bathtub. There's such a noise nobody can sleep. But Anton says, "Nice little pig. I fix you up fine. Nice little pig."

And so he fills the bathtub up with dirt. Then he turns on the water. And what does he say? He says, "Now, little pig, we have fine mud for you. Nice fine mud." Yes, your honor, a whole bathtub full of mud. And when the pig sees this he gets happy and lies down and goes to sleep. And Anton sits in the bathroom and looks at the pig all night and says, "See. He's asleep. It's like home for him."

But the next day Anton must go to work. All right, he'll go to work. But first, understand everybody, he don't want this pig touched. The pig stays in the bathtub and he must be there when he comes home.

All right. The pig stays in the bathtub, your honor. Anton wants it. Tomorrow the pig will be killed and that'll be an end for the pig.

Anton comes home and he goes in the bathroom and he sits and looks at the pig and complains the mud is dried up and why don't somebody take care of his pig. His damn pig. He brings up more dirt and makes more mud. And the pig tries to climb out and throws mud all over the bathroom.

That's one day. And then there's another day. And finally a third day. Will Anton let anybody kill his pig? Aha! He'll break somebody's neck if he does. But, your honor, Mrs. Popapovitch killed the pig. A terrible thing, isn't it, to kill a pig that keeps squealing in the bathtub and splashing mud all day?

But what does Anton do when he comes home and finds his pig killed? My God! He hits her, your honor. He hits her on the head. His own wife whom he loves and lives with for ten years. He throws her down and hollers, "You killed my little pig! You good for nothing. I'll show you."

What a disgrace for the neighbors! Lucky there are no children, your honor. Married ten years but no children. And it's lucky now. Because the disgrace would have been worse. The neighbors come. They pull him away from his wife. Her eye is black and blue. Her nose is bleeding. That's all, your honor.

A very bad case for Anton Popapovitch. A decidedly bad case. Step forward, Anton Popapovitch, and explain it, if you can. Did you beat her up? Did you do this thing? And are you ashamed and willing to apologize and kiss and make up?

Anton, step forward and tell his honor. But be careful. Mrs. Popapovitch has a lawyer and it will go bad with you if you don't talk carefully.

All right. Here's Anton. He nods and keeps on nodding. What is this? What's he nodding about? Did this happen as your wife says, Anton? Anton blows out his cheeks and rubs his workingman's hand over his mouth. To think that you should beat your wife who has always been good to you, Anton. Who has cooked and been true to you! And there are no children to worry you. Not one. And you beat her. Bah, is that a man? Don't you love your wife? Yes. All right, then why did you do it?

Anton looks up surprised. "Because," says Anton, still surprised, "like she say. She kill my pig. You hear yourself, your honor. She say she kill him. And I put him in the bathtub and give him mud. And she kill him."

But is that a reason to beat your wife and nearly kill her? It is, says Anton. Well, then, why? Tell the judge, why you were so fond of this pig, Anton.

Ah, yes, Anton Popapovitch, tell the judge why you loved this little pig so much and made a home for him with mud in the bathtub. Why you dreamed of him as you stood working in the factory? Why you ran home to him and fed him and sat and looked at him and whispered "Nice little pig?" Why?

God knows. But Anton Popapovitch can't explain it. It must remain one of the mysteries of our city, your honor. Call the next case. Put Anton Popapovitch on parole. Perhaps it was because . . . , well, the matter is ended. Anton Popapovitch sighs and looks with accusing eyes at his wife Sofie, with accusing eyes that hint at evidence unheard.

Japanese Earthquake

ERNEST HEMINGWAY

❧

Living in Paris in the years after World War I, Ernest Hemingway (1899–1961) wrote dispatches for the *Toronto Daily Star* that kept his family solvent while he worked on the short stories eventually published as *In Our Time*. Hemingway later expressed disdain for this work-for-hire, remarking in 1931, "No one has the right to dig this stuff up and use it against the stuff you have written to write the best you can."

Fair enough. But many of his *Star* dispatches are quite striking, and they unquestionably show a writer trying out attitudes and techniques that would be used to brilliant and enormously influential effect in his fiction. "Japanese Earthquake," published in the fall of 1923, has numerous literary elements that set it far apart from a standard newspaper feature: the playlike structure, the interplay between "the reporter" and his colleague, the access to the reporter's thoughts, the throwaway ending, the leitmotif of the kimono. Then there is the unmistakable Hemingway diction, which forces its way even into the quotations of the woman who had witnessed the earthquake: "All the walls were down and we could look through the front of the building to the open compound at the back. Then there was another shock and we knew it wasn't any use going on or trying to get up to our house." She may well have said precisely those words. But Hemingway wrote them down without any commas—part of his process of fashioning a new voice that would change the literary world.

—B. Y.

❧

There are no names in this story.

The characters in it are a reporter, a girl reporter, a quite beautiful daughter in a Japanese kimono, and a mother. There is a small chorus of friends who spend some time talking in the next room, and get up as the reporter and the girl reporter go through the room and out of the door.

411

At four o'clock in the afternoon the reporter and the girl reporter stood on the front porch. The front doorbell had just rung.

"They'll never let us in," said the girl reporter.

Inside the house they heard someone moving around and then a voice said, "I'll go down. I'll attend to them, Mother."

The door opened one narrow crack. The crack ran from the top of the door to the bottom, and about halfway up it was a very dark, very beautiful face, the hair soft and parted in the middle.

"She is beautiful, after all," thought the reporter. He had been sent on so many assignments in which beautiful girls figured, and so few of the girls had ever turned out to be beautiful.

"Who do you want?" said the girl at the door.

"We're from the *Star*," the reporter said. "This is Miss So-and-So."

"We don't want to have anything to do with you. You can't come in," the girl said.

"But—" said the reporter and commenced to talk. He had a very strong feeling that if he stopped talking at any time, the door would slam. So he kept on talking. Finally the girl opened the door. "Well, I'll let you in," she said. "I'll go upstairs and ask my mother."

She went upstairs, quick and lithe, wearing a Japanese kimono. It ought to have some other name. Kimono has a messy, early-morning sound. There was nothing kimonoey about this kimono. The colors were vivid and the stuff had body to it, and it was cut. It looked almost as though it might be worn with two swords to the belt.

The girl reporter and the reporter sat on a couch in the parlor. "I'm sorry to have done all the talking," whispered the reporter.

"No. Go on. Keep it up. I never thought we'd get in at all," said the girl reporter. "She is good-looking, isn't she?" The reporter had thought she was beautiful. "And didn't she know what she was doing when she got that kimono!"

"Sh—. Here they come."

Down the stairs came the girl in the Japanese kimono. With her was her mother. Her mother's face was very firm.

"What I want to know," she said, "is where you got those pictures?"

"They were lovely pictures, weren't they?" said the girl reporter.

Both the girl reporter and the reporter denied any knowledge of the pictures. They didn't know. Really, they didn't know. It was a fact. Eventually they were believed.

"We won't say anything. We don't want to be in the newspapers. We've had too much already. There are plenty of people that suffered much worse than we did in the earthquake. We don't want to talk about it at all."

"But I let them in, Mother," said the daughter. She turned to the reporter. "Just exactly what is it you want to know from us?"

"We just want you to tell us as you remember it just what happened," the reporter said.

"If we talk to you and tell you what you want to know will you promise that you won't use our names?" asked the daughter.

"Why not just use the names," suggested the reporter.

"We don't say a word unless you promise not to use the names," said the daughter.

"Oh, you know newspaper reporters," the mother said. "They'll promise it and then they'll use them anyway." It looked as though there wasn't going to be any story. The remark had made the reporter violently angry. It is the one unmerited insult. There are enough merited ones.

"Mrs. So-and-So," he said, "the president of the United States tells reporters things in confidence which if known would cost him his job. Every week in Paris the prime minister of France tells fifteen newspaper reporters facts that if they were quoted again would overthrow the French government. I'm talking about newspaper reporters, not cheap news tipsters."

"All right," said the mother. "Yes, I guess it's true about newspaper reporters."

The daughter began the story and the mother took it up.

"The boat [the Canadian Pacific's *Empress of Australia*] was all ready to sail," said the daughter. "If Mother and Father hadn't been down at the dock, I don't believe they would have escaped!"

"The *Empress* boats always sail at noon on Saturday," said the mother.

"Just before twelve o'clock, there was a great rumbling sound and then everything commenced to rock back and forth. The dock rolled and bucked. My brother and I were on board the boat leaning against the rail. Everybody had been throwing streamers. It only lasted about thirty seconds," said the daughter.

"We were thrown flat on the dock," said the mother. "It was a big concrete dock and it rolled back and forth. My husband and I hung on to each other and were thrown around by it. Many people were thrown off. I remember seeing a rickshaw driver clambering back up out of the water. Cars and everything else went in, except our car. It stayed on the dock right alongside the Prince de Bearn's, the French consul's car, until the fire came."

"What did you do when the shock was over?" asked the reporter.

"We went ashore. We had to climb. The dock was crumbled in places and great chunks of concrete broken off. We started off up the Bund along the shore and could see that the big go-downs, the storage houses, were all caved in. You know the Bund. The driveway straight along the waterfront. We got as far as the British consulate and it was all caved in. Just fallen in on itself like a funnel. Just crumbled. All the walls were down and we could look through the front of the building to the open compound at the back. Then there was another shock and we knew it wasn't any use going on or trying to get up to our house. My husband heard that the people had been out of the office and there was nothing you could do about the men who had been working in the go-downs. There was a big cloud of dust all over everything from the buildings that had caved in. You couldn't hardly see through it, and fires were breaking out all over."

"What were the people doing? How were they acting?" asked the reporter.

"There wasn't any panic. That was the strange thing. I didn't see anyone even hysterical. There was one woman at the Russian consulate though. It stood right next to the British consulate and it hadn't fallen in yet but was badly shaken. She came out to the front gate crying and there were a bunch of coolies sitting against the iron fence in front of the consulate yard. She begged them to help her get her daughter out of the building. "She's just a little fellow," she said in Japanese. But they just sat there. They wouldn't move. It seemed as though they couldn't move. Of course nobody was going around helping anybody else then. Everybody had themselves to look after."

"How did you get back to the boat?" asked the girl reporter.

"There were some sampans, native boats, and finally my husband found one and we started back. But the fire was going so badly then and the wind was offshore. There was an awful wind for a while. We got to the dock finally and, of course, they couldn't get a gangplank out, but they put out a rope for us and we got on board."

The mother didn't need any prompting or questions now. That day and the following days and nights in Yokohama harbor had her in their grip again. Now the reporter saw why she didn't want to be interviewed and why no one had any right to interview her and stir it all up afresh. Her hands were very quietly nervous.

"The Prince's boy [son of the Prince de Bearn, French consul] was left in their house. He had been sick. They had just come down to the dock to see the boat off. The foreign quarter is up on a bluff where we all lived, and the bluff just slid down into town. The Prince got ashore and made his way up to the wreck of his house. They got the boy out but his back was hurt. They worked hours getting him out. But they couldn't get the French butler out. They had to go away and leave him in there because the fire got too close."

"They had to leave him in there alive with the fire coming on?" asked the girl reporter.

"Yes, they had to leave the French butler in there," said the mother. "He was married to the housemaid so they had to tell her they had gotten him out."

The mother went on in a dull, tired voice.

"There was a woman on the [liner] *Jefferson* coming home that had lost her husband. I didn't recognize her. There was a young couple, too, that had been only out a short time. They'd just been married. His wife was down in the town shopping when it happened. He couldn't get to where she was on account of the fire. They got the head doctor out all right from the American Hospital. They couldn't get out the assistant doctor and his wife though. The fire came so quick. The whole town was solid fire.

"We were on the boat of course. Part of the time you couldn't see the shore on account of the smoke. When it was bad was when the submarine oil tanks burst and the oil caught on fire. It moved down the harbor and toward the dock. When it got to the dock we wondered if we'd been saved on board the *Empress* just to get burned. The captain had all the boats launched on the far side away from the fire and was all ready to put us into them. We couldn't go on the side toward the fire of course. It was too hot. They were playing the hoses on it to drive it away. It kept coming on though.

"All the time they were working to cut through the anchor chain that had fouled in the propeller. Just to cut it away from the boat. Finally they got the *Empress* away from the dock. It was wonderful the way they got her away without any tug. It was something you wouldn't have believed it was possible to do in Yokohama harbor. It was wonderful.

"Of course they were bringing wounded people and refugees on all day and all night. They came out in sampans or anything. They took them all on. We slept on the deck.

"My husband said he was relieved when we'd got outside the breakwater," the mother said. "There're supposed to be two old craters in the harbor itself, and he was worried that something was going to happen from them."

"Was there no tidal wave?" asked the reporter.

"No. There wasn't any at all. When we were on our way to Kobe, after we had left Yokohama finally, there were three or four small shocks that you could feel in the boat. But there weren't any tidal waves."

Her mind was going back to Yokohama harbor. "Some of the people that had stood up all night in the water were very tired," she offered.

"Oh, the people that had stood up all night in the water," said the reporter softly.

"Yes, to keep out of the fire. There was one old woman who must have been seventy-six years old. She was in the water all night. There were lots of people in the canals, too. Yokohama's all cut up with canals, you know."

"Didn't that make it more confused in the earthquake?" asked the girl reporter.

"Oh, no. They were very good things to have in a fire," said the mother quite serenely.

"What did you think when it started?" asked the reporter.

"Oh, we knew it was an earthquake," said the mother. "It was just that nobody knew it was going to be so bad. There's been lots of earthquakes there. Once, nine years ago, we'd had five shocks in one day. We just wanted to get into the town to see if everything was all right. But when we saw it was so bad, we knew then it didn't matter about things. I hadn't intended to come home. Just my daughter and son were sailing. My husband is still in Kobe. He has a lot of work to do now reorganizing."

Just then the telephone rang. "My mother is busy just now interviewing the reporters," the daughter said in the next room. She was talking with some friends that had come in. It was something about music. The reporter listened with his odd ear for a moment to see if it was anything about the earthquake. But it wasn't.

The mother was very tired. The girl reporter stood up. The reporter got up.

"You understand. No names," said the mother.

"You're sure? They wouldn't do any harm, you know."

"You said you wouldn't use the names," the mother said wearily. The reporters went out. The friends stood up as they went through the room.

The reporter took a look at the Japanese kimono as the door was shut.

"Who's going to write the story. You or me?" asked the girl reporter.

"I don't know," said the reporter.

From *Let Us Now Praise Famous Men*

JAMES AGEE

James Agee (1909–1955) spent most of his career as a staff writer in the Luce magazine empire. In 1936 he and photographer Walker Evans were assigned by *Fortune* to create a documentary feature about southern tenant farmers. For about six weeks they lived with three Alabama tenant families, renamed in Agee's text as Gudger, Ricketts, and Woods.

Agee was a southerner, born and raised in Knoxville, and had already written on such regional topics as TVA electrification. But he did not want to use the individuals he had befriended to illustrate a social problem. Instead, he emphasized their dignity in the midst of privation, and the complex actuality of their daily lives. These themes led to experiments in style: passages of prose poetry, self-conscious meditations, and long descriptions simulating the exactitude of Evans's photographs. "Shoes," for example, is based on Evans's still life of a pair of work boots, which in turn is based on Vincent van Gogh's painting *Les Souliers*.

Agee's original article was rejected by *Fortune,* and he spent five years revising and expanding it into *Let Us Now Praise Famous Men.* When the book was published in 1941, it sold fewer than 600 copies, and Agee turned to fiction writing and to new assignments at *Time.* He became a film reviewer and later a film writer, scripting *The African Queen* and *Night of the Hunter.* He died of a heart attack at age forty-six.

When Agee's novel *A Death in the Family* was published posthumously in 1957, it won a Pulitzer Prize and sparked new interest in his work. A 1960 reprinting of *Let Us Now Praise Famous Men* finally found an enthusiastic audience. John Hersey called it "a classic work of metajournalism."

Agee's descriptions of the tenant farmers' clothing reflect his deep religious sensibility. The overalls are almost sacramental: outward and visible signs of a blessedness among the poor in spirit. Walker Evans once said that Agee's prose "was hardly a twentieth-century style; it had Elizabethan colors." As this excerpt suggests, the colors included the King James Bible and The Book of Common Prayer.

—K. K.

∞

OVERALLS

They are pronounced overhauls.

Try—I cannot write of it here—to imagine and to know, as against other garments, the difference of their feeling against your body; drawn-on, and bibbed on the whole belly and chest, naked from the kidneys up behind, save for broad crossed straps, and slung by these straps from the shoulders; the slanted pockets on each thigh, the deep square pockets on each buttock; the complex and slanted structures, on the chest, of the pockets shaped for pencils, rulers, and watches; the coldness of sweat when they are young, and their stiffness; their sweetness to the skin and pleasure of sweating when they are old; the thin metal buttons of the fly; the lifting aside of the straps and the deep slipping downward in defecation; the belt some men use with them to steady their middles; the swift, simple, and inevitably supine gestures of dressing and of undressing, which, as is less true of any other garment, are those of harnessing and of unharnessing the shoulders of a tired and hard-used animal.

They are round as stovepipes in the legs (though some wives, told to, crease them).

In the strapping across the kidneys they again resemble work harness, and in their crossed straps and tin buttons.

And in the functional pocketing of their bib, a harness modified to the convenience of a used animal of such high intelligence that he has use for tools.

And in their whole stature: full covering of the cloven strength of the legs and thighs and of the loins; then nakedness and harnessing behind, naked along the flanks; and in front, the short, squarely tapered, powerful towers of the belly and chest to above the nipples.

And on this façade, the cloven halls for the legs, the strong-seamed, structured opening for the genitals, the broad horizontal at the waist, the slant thigh pockets, the buttons at the point of each hip and on the breast, the geometric structures of the usages of the simpler trades—the complexed seams of utilitarian pockets which are so brightly picked out against darkness when the seam-threadings, double and triple stitched, are still white, so that a new suit of overalls has among its beauties those of a blueprint: and they are a map of a working man.

The shirts too; squarely cut, and strongly seamed; with big square pockets and with metal buttons: the cloth stiff, the sweat cold when it is new, the

418

collar large in newness and standing out in angles under the ears; so that in these new workclothes a man has the shy and silly formal charm of a mail-order-catalogue engraving.

The changes that age, use, weather, work upon these.

They have begun with the massive yet delicate beauty of most things which are turned out most cheaply in great tribes by machines: and on this basis of structure they are changed into images and marvels of nature.

The structures sag, and take on the look, some of use; some, the pencil pockets, the pretty atrophies of what is never used; the edges of the thigh pockets become stretched and lie open, fluted, like the gills of a fish. The bright seams lose their whiteness and are lines and ridges. The whole fabric is shrunken to size, which was bought large. The whole shape, texture, color, finally substance, all are changed. The shape, particularly along the urgent frontage of the thighs, so that the whole structure of the knee and muscula-ture of the thigh is sculptured there; each man's garment wearing the shape and beauty of his induplicable body. The texture and the color change in union, by sweat, sun, laundering, between the steady pressures of its use and age: both, at length, into realms of fine softness and marvel of draping and velvet plays of light which chamois and silk can only suggest, not touch;* and into a region and scale of blues, subtle, delicious, and deft beyond what I have ever seen elsewhere approached except in rare skies, the smoky light some days are filmed with, and some of the blues of Cézanne: one could watch and touch even one such garment, study it, with the eyes, the fingers, and the subtlest lips, almost illimitably long, and never fully learn it; and I saw no two which did not hold some world of exquisiteness of its own. Finally, too; particularly athwart the crest and swing of the shoud-ers, of the shirts: this fabric breaks like snow, and is stitched and patched: these break, and again are stitched and patched and ruptured, and stitches and patches are manifolded upon the stitches and patches, and more on these, so that at length, at the shoulders, the shirt contains virtually nothing of the original fabric and a man, George Gudger, I remember so well, and many hundreds of others like him, wears in his work on the power of his shoulders a fabric as intricate and fragile, and as deeply in honor of the reigning sun, as the feather mantle of a Toltec prince.

Gudger has three; it is perhaps four changes of overalls and workshirts. They are, set by set, in stages of age, and of beauty, distinctly apart from one another; and of the three I remember, each should at best be considered sep-arately and at full length. I have room here to say only that they represent medium-early, middle, and medium-late stages, and to suggest a little more about these. The youngest are still dark; their seams are still visible; the cloth has not yet lost all of its hardness, nor the buttons their brightness. They have taken the shape of the leg, yet they are still the doing as much of machinery

*The textures of old paper money.

as of nature. The middle-aged are fully soft and elegantly textured, and are lost out of all machinery into a full prime of nature. The mold of the body is fully taken, the seams are those of a living plant or animal, the cloth's grain is almost invisible, the buttons are rubbed and mild, the blue is at the full silent, greatly restrained strength of its range; the patches in the overalls are few and strategic, the right* knee, the two bones of the rump, the elbows, the shoulders are quietly fledged: the garments are still wholly competent and at their fullness of comfort. The old: the cloth sleeps against all salients of the body in complete peace, and in its loose hangings, from the knee downward, is fallen and wandered in the first loss of form into foldings I believe no sculptor has ever touched. The blue is so vastly fainted and withdrawn it is discernible scarcely more as blue than as that most pacific silver which the bone wood of the houses and the visage of genius seem to shed, and is a color and cloth seeming ancient, veteran, composed, and patient to the source of being, as too the sleepings and the drifts of form. The shoulders are that full net of sewn snowflakes of which I spoke. The buttons are blind as cataracts, and slip their soft holes. The whole of the seat and of the knees and elbows† are broken and patched, the patches subdued in age almost with the original cloth, drawn far forward toward the feathering of the shoulders. There is a more youthful stage than the youngest of these; Ricketts, in his photograph here, wears such overalls; there are many median modulations; and there is a stage later than the latest here, as I saw in the legs of Woods' overalls, which had so entirely lost one kind of tendency to form that they had gained another, and were wrinkled minutely and innumerably as may best be paralleled by old thin oilskin crumpled, and by the skin of some aged faces.

SHOES

They are one of the most ordinary types of working shoe: the blucher design, and soft in the prow, lacking the seam across the root of the big toe: covering the ankles: looped straps at the heels: blunt, broad, and rounded at the toe: broad-heeled: made up of most simple roundnesses and squarings and flats, of dark brown raw thick leathers nailed, and sewn coarsely to one another in courses and patterns of doubled and tripled seams, and such throughout that like many other small objects they have great massiveness and repose and are, as the houses and overalls are, and the feet and legs of the women, who go barefooted so much, fine pieces of architecture.

*The left knee is rubbed thin and has absorbed irreducibly the gold shadow of the blended colors of the clays of that neighborhood.

†Much of the time the sleeves are rolled high and tight at the height of the biceps; but not always. Enough that these patchings are by other comparisons slight, but not so little but that there are large and manifold patches.

They are softened, in the uppers, with use, and the soles are rubbed thin enough, I estimate, that the ticklish grain of the ground can be felt through at the center of the forward sole. The heels are deeply biased. Clay is worked into the substance of the uppers and a loose dust of clay lies over them. They have visibly though to the eye subtly taken the mold of the foot, and structures of the foot are printed through them in dark sweat at the ankles, and at the roots of the toes. They are worn without socks, and by experience of similar shoes I know that each man's shoe, in long enough course of wear, takes as his clothing does the form of his own flesh and bones, and would feel as uneasy to any other as if A, glancing into the mirror, were met by B's eyes, and to their owner, a natural part though enforcement of the foot, which may be used or shed at will. There is great pleasure in a sockless and sweated foot in the fitted leathers of a shoe.

The shoes are worn for work. At home, resting, men always go barefooted. This is no symptom of discomfort, though: it is, insofar as it is conscious, merely an exchange of mutually enhancing pleasures, and is at least as natural as the habituated use and laying by of hats or of "reading-glasses."

So far as I could see, shoes are never mended. They are worn out like animals to a certain ancient stage and chance of money at which a man buys a new pair; then, just as old sunday shoes do, they become the inheritance of a wife.

Ricketts' shoes are boldly slashed open to accommodate as they scarcely can the years of pain in his feet. The worst of this pain is in stirrup corns, a solid stripe of stony and excruciating pearls across the ball of each foot; for two years, years ago, he rode mules all of each day. Recognizing my own tendency half-consciously to alter my walk or even to limp under certain conditions of mental insecurity, and believing Ricketts to be one of the most piteously insecure men I have ever known, I suspect, too, that nervous modifications in his walking have had much to do with destroying his feet.

The Third Winter

MARTHA GELLHORN

❧

The great British journalist James Cameron said that he admired Martha Gellhorn above all reporters "because she combines a cold eye with a warm heart." Gellhorn's powers of observation and compassion are evident in a lifetime of socially engaged writing, from early sketches of Depression-era America to a 1996 essay on the plight of street children in Brazil.

Born in St. Louis, the daughter of a suffragette, Gellhorn became a citizen of the world. She has traveled to fifty-three countries, lived in seven of them, and chronicled wars in every part of the globe. The title of her collected dispatches—*The Face of War*—indicates her unrelenting focus on the suffering of innocent civilians. As a correspondent for *Collier's*, Gellhorn covered World War II from Finland to China, and entered Dachau just after its liberation by American troops. She later reported on wars in Java, Vietnam, the Middle East, and Central America. "I wrote very fast, as I had to," she says, "and I was always afraid that I would forget the exact sound, smell, words, gestures which were special to this moment and this place."

Gellhorn began her career as a foreign correspondent during the Spanish Civil War—a conflict she understood, even then, as the preliminary action of a second World War. Her rapport with ordinary Spanish citizens illuminated such dispatches as "The Third Winter" (1938), in which a visit with one family in Barcelona provides the structure for narrative flashbacks and personal commentary. Gellhorn alternates between small vignettes in the present and scenes of sacrifice and pathos in the larger arena of war. Underlying everything is her deep respect for the Spanish people, "who are among the noblest and unluckiest on earth."

—K. K.

❧

In Barcelona, it was perfect bombing weather. The cafés along the Ramblas were crowded. There was nothing much to drink; a sweet fizzy poison called orangeade and a horrible liquid supposed to be sherry. There was, of course,

422

nothing to eat. Everyone was out enjoying the cold afternoon sunlight. No bombers had come over for at least two hours.

The flower stalls looked bright and pretty along the promenade. "The flowers are all sold, Señores. For the funerals of those who were killed in the eleven o'clock bombing, poor souls."

It had been clear and cold all day and all day yesterday and probably would be fair from now on. "What beautiful weather," a woman said, and she stood, holding her shawl around her, staring at the sky. "And the nights are as fine as the days. A catastrophe," she said, and walked with her husband toward a café.

It was cold but really too lovely and everyone listened for the sirens all the time, and when we saw the bombers they were like tiny silver bullets moving forever up, across the sky.

It gets dark suddenly and no street lights are allowed in Barcelona, and at night the old town is rough going. It would be a silly end, I thought, to fall into a bomb hole, like the one I saw yesterday, that opens right down to the sewers. Everything you do in war is odd, I thought; why should I be plowing around after dark, looking for a carpenter in order to call for a picture frame for a friend? I found Hernández' house in a back street and I held my cigarette lighter above my head to see my way down the hall and up the stairs and then I was knocking on a door and old Mrs. Hernández opened the door and asked me to come in, to be welcome, her house was mine.

"How are you?" I said.

"As you see," old Hernández said, and he pushed his cap back on his forehead and smiled, "alive."

It wasn't much of a home but they looked very handsome in it. A wick floating in a cup of oil lighted the place. There were four chairs and a big table and some shelves tacked on the wall. The ten-year-old grandson was reading close to the burning wick. The daughter-in-law, the wife of their youngest son, played quietly with her baby in a corner. Old Mrs. Hernández had been working over the stove, and the room was smoky. What they would have to eat would be greens, a mound of cabbage leaves the size of your fist, and some dry bread. The women start cooking greens long in advance because they want to get them soft at least. Boiled flavorless greens go down better if they are soft.

The picture frame was not ready, Hernández could not get the wood. Wood is for dugouts and trenches, bridges, railroad ties, to prop up bombed houses, to make artificial arms and legs, for coffins. He used to collect the fragments from destroyed houses, he said, not to work with, but for firewood, but now that is all saved for the hospitals. It was hard to be a carpenter, there wasn't much wood or much work any more.

"Not that it matters about me," Hernández said, "I am very old."

The little boy had been listening. His grandmother kept looking at him, ready to silence him if he interrupted while his elders spoke.

"What do you do all day?" I said.

"I stand in the food line."

"Miguel is a good boy," Mrs. Hernández said. "He does what he can to help his old grandmother."

"Do you like doing that?" I said.

"When they fight," he said, laughing to himself, "it is fun."

His grandmother looked shocked. "He does not understand," she said. "He is only ten. The poor people—they are so hungry, sometimes they quarrel among themselves, not knowing what they do."

(They put up a sign on the shop door, and word flies through the neighbourhood that you can get food today. Then the lines form. Sometimes they are five blocks long. Sometimes you wait all that time but just before your turn comes the shop closes. There is no more food. The women wait in line and talk or knit, the children invent games that they can play standing in one place. Everyone is very thin. They know perfectly, by the sound of the first explosion, where the bombs are falling. If the first bomb sounds hollow and muffled, they do not move from their places, because they know there is no immediate danger. If they can hear the drone of the planes too clearly or the first explosion is jagged and harsh, they scatter for doorways or refuges. They do this professionally, like soldiers.

The pinched women file into the shop and hand their food cards over the high bare counter. The girls behind the counter look healthy because they are wearing rouge. Then the food is doled out in little grey paper sacks. A sack the size of a cigarette package, full of rice: that will have to do two people for two weeks. A sack half that big, full of dried peas: for one person for two weeks. Wait, there's some codfish too. The girl behind the counter pulls out a slab of the gray-white flat fish and cuts off a little piece with a pair of scissors. She cuts it with scissors, not a knife, because scissors are more accurate. A piece as long as your finger and twice as thick is the ration for one person for two weeks. The woman with gray hair and a gray frozen face and exhausted eyes reaches out to get her piece of fish. She holds it a minute in her hand, looking at it. They all look at it, and say nothing. Then she turns and pushes her way through the crowd and out the door.

Now she will wait every day to hear whether the store in her neighbourhood is open again, whether you can trade anything, whether a farmer she knows is coming to town with a dozen eggs and four cabbages and some potatoes. Whether somewhere, somehow, she can get food for her family. Sometimes when the shop runs out of food before everyone is served, the women are wild with grief, afraid to go home with nothing. Then there's trouble. The little boys don't understand the trouble, all they know is that a quarrel brightens the long hours of waiting.)

"You don't go to school?" I said.

"Not now."

"He did very well at school," his grandmother said.

"I want to be a mechanic," the child said, in a voice that was almost weeping. "I want to be a mechanic."

"We do not let him go to school," Mrs. Hernández said, stroking the child's black head. "Because of the bombs. We cannot have him walking about alone."

"The bombs," I said, and smiled at the boy. "What do you do about the bombs?"

"I hide," he said, and he was shy about it, telling me a secret. "I hide so they won't kill me."

"Where do you hide?"

"Under the bed," he said.

The daughter-in-law, who is very young, laughed at this, but the old people treated the child seriously. They know that you must have safety in something; if the child believes he is safe under the bed it is better for him.

"When will the war end?" the daughter-in-law asked suddenly.

"Now, now," said the old man. "It will end when we have won it. You know that, Lola. Have patience and do not be silly."

"I have not seen my husband for five months," the girl explained, as if this were the very worst thing that could ever happen to anyone. Old Mrs. Hernández nodded her head, which was like a fine worn wood carving, and made a little sympathetic noise.

"You understand, Señora," Mr. Hernández said to me, "I am so old that perhaps I shall not live to see the end of the war. Things do not make any difference to me any longer. But it will be better for the children afterward. That is what I tell Lola. Spain will be better for her and Federico afterward. Besides," he said, "Federico is learning a great deal in the Army."

(The Internationals had left the lines and were waiting to go home, or were already gone. There was a parade for them, down the Diagonal, and women threw flowers and wept, and all the Spanish people thanked them somehow, sometimes only by the way they watched the parade passing. The Internationals looked very dirty and weary and young, and many of them had no country to go back to. The German and Italian anti-Fascists were already refugees; the Hungarians had no home either. Leaving Spain, for most of the European volunteers, was to go into exile. I wonder what happened to the German who was the best man for night patrols in the 11th International Brigade. He was a somber man, whose teeth were irregularly broken, whose fingertips were nailless pulp; the first graduate of Gestapo torture I had known.

The Spanish Republican Army, which had been growing and shaping itself through two winters, now dug in for the third winter of war. They were proud and self-confident soldiers. They had started out as militia companies, citizens carrying any sort of rifle, and had become an army and looked like an army and acted like one.

They were always a pleasure to see and often a surprise. On a clear night, coming back very tired from the Segre front, we stopped at divisional headquarters to look at maps and get some dinner too, if lucky. We were received by the Lieutenant Colonel, who commanded ten thousand men. He was twenty-six years old and had been an electrician at Lerida. He was blond and looked American and he had grown up with the war. The chief of operations was twenty-three and a former medical student from Galicia. The chief of staff was twenty-seven, a lawyer, a Madrid aristocrat who spoke good French and English. Modesto, commanding the Army of the Ebro and a great soldier, was thirty-five. All the new corps commanders were in their late twenties and early thirties. Everybody you saw knew what he was doing and why; it was a cheerful army. The winter is the worst time of all in war and the third winter is long, cold and desperate; but you couldn't feel sorry for that army.)

"Both my boys are soldiers," Mrs. Hernández said. "Miguel's father is the oldest, Tomás, he is at Tortosa; and Federico is up toward Lerida somewhere. Tomás was here only last week."

"What did he say of the war?" I asked.

"We do not speak of the war," she said. "He says to me, 'You are like all the other mothers in Spain. You must be brave like all the others.' And sometimes he speaks of the dead."

"Yes?"

"He said, 'I have seen many dead.' He says that so I will understand, but we do not speak of the war. My sons are always close to the bombs," she said in her blurred old voice. "If my children are in danger, it is not well that I should be safe."

The girl Lola had started to sing to her child, to keep it quiet, and now she brought the baby over near the lighted wick, for me to see. She turned down a grayish blanket showing the child's head and sang, "Pretty little child, my pretty little girl."

The face seemed shrunken and faded, and bluish eyelids rested lightly shut on the eyes. The child was too weak to cry. It fretted softly, with closed eyes, and we all watched it, and suddenly Lola pulled the cover back over the bundle in her arms and said, coldly and proudly, "She does not have the right food to eat and therefore she is not well. But she is a fine child."

(The hospital was huge and ornate, the way all modern buildings are in Catalonia. This one was built of orange bricks and was a real horror to look at. It was new and well equipped and had a garden. The buildings, called pavilions, were placed around this garden. The children's pavilion was off to the right and we followed a lanky, quiet boy who was showing us the way. I did not want to come, really. I knew the statistics, the statistics were enough for me. In Catalonia alone, there were approximately 870,000 children up to school age. Of these, the statistics announced, more than 100,000 suffered from bad nutrition, more than 200,000 suffered from under-nourishment, more than 100,000 were in a state of pre-famine. I thought the statistics were no doubt mild, and I did not want to think at all about Madrid, about the swift dark laughing children in Madrid. I did not want to imagine how hunger had deformed them.

There were two great wards, the surgical ward and the medical ward, and it was almost suppertime and the surgical ward was brightly lit. Small beds lined the walls. It was very cold, between the stone floors and the plaster walls; there is no heat anywhere. The children looked like toys until you came closer—tiny white figures propped up with pillows, swathed in bandages, the little pale faces showing, the great black eyes staring at you, the small hands playing over the sheets. There was not one child in the hospital for any peace-time reason, tonsils or adenoids or mastoid or appendicitis. These children were all wounded.

A little boy named Paco sat up in his bed with great dignity. He was four and beautiful and had a bad head wound. He had been crossing a square to meet a little girl on the other side—he played with her in the afternoons. Then a bomb fell. Many people were killed and he was wounded in the head. He had gone through his pain quietly, the nurse said. The wound was five months old. He had always been patient with it, and as the months wore on he grew solemner and more elderly every day. Sometimes he cried to himself, but without making a sound, and if anyone noticed he tried to stop. We stood by his bed and he watched us gravely but he did not want to talk.

I asked if they had anything to play with and the nurse said, Well, little things, not much. No, not really, she said. Just once in a while someone brings a present for one of them. A jolly little girl, with pigtails and only one leg, was having a nice time making paper balls out of an old newspaper.

There were three little boys with shaved heads and various splints on them; one of them had his leg held up on a rope from the ceiling. They lived in a corner by themselves; they were not only wounded, but they had tuberculosis. The nurse said they had fever and that made them gay, particularly at this hour. They would not live, she didn't think they would live even if there was food to give them, or a sanatorium to send them to. The sanatoriums were all full. Anyhow, they were too far gone. It works very fast on them, the nurse said. The little boys had a sort of Meccano toy, it was on the bed of the boy who had a broken arm. A bomb fragment broke his arm, the nurse said; he did not suffer as much as some but he used to scream at night. The other two were now shouting instructions to their friend, how to play with the toy. They were building a bridge. When we stopped beside them, they grew shy and gave up their game. All the children were the color of their pillows except the little ones with t.b., who looked quite rosy. They were unbelievably thin.

"No," the nurse said, almost impatiently, as if it hurt and angered her to talk about it. "Of course we haven't enough food to give them. What do you think? If only they didn't bomb all the time," she said, "it would help. When the children hear the siren they go crazy, they try to get out of their beds and run. We are only four nurses in these two rooms and we have a hard time with them. At night it is worse. They all remember what happened to them and they go crazy."

We went into the second room. A little boy was crying noisily and the other children were listening to him, frightened by his grief. The nurse explained that he had been wounded today, in one of the morning raids, and of course he was in pain but mainly he was homesick. He wanted his mother. He was also hungry. We stood by his bed helplessly and promised to bring him some food tomorrow if only he would stop crying and we promised that his mother would come right away, only please stop crying. He twisted on the bed and sobbed for his mother. Then she came. She was a dark witch of a woman, outdone by life. Her hair straggled from a knot on top of her head, and her bedroom slippers were worn through and her coat was pinned together with two safety pins. She looked gaunt and a little mad and her voice was as harsh as stone scraping on stone. She sat on the bed [we had been careful not to touch the bed, not to move or shake the small aching wounded child] and talked to him in her shrill voice, telling him of the family's catastrophes.

Their house had been destroyed by the bomb that wounded him, though he was the only one hurt. But now they had no home, no furniture, nothing to cook with, no blankets, no place to go. She told the round-eyed child the story of woe and he listened with interest and sympathy and wasn't homesick any more. Then she took a pot from some pocket, it materialized like a rabbit from a hat, and gave it to the child, and said, "Here, eat." He began to scoop up cold rice from the pot, just cold rice boiled in water. He ate it, his face close to the pot, spilling a little on the bedclothes and stopping only to collect the grayish rice grains with his fingers. He seemed happy then and at home. His mother was now talking with another woman, in her hard tormented voice, and presently the little boy went to sleep.

"Would you like to see the medical ward?" the tall lanky boy said.

"Well," I said. Well, no, I thought.

"I like the children."

So we went.

Three blue lights were burning and the ward was in shadow. The children sat up in bed, silent and waiting. We stepped aside to let the dinner wagon pass. It made a metal clanking sound on the floor, and I watched their eyes follow the wagon down the ward. There was the seven-months-old baby with tuberculosis who did not notice and there was another child, like an old-faced doll against the pillows, who turned away her head. On the wagon were four lumps of something green and cooked, four shrunken lettuces, I think, and a great cauldron of soup. The nurse went over to the cauldron and lifted a ladleful and let it spill back into the pot. It was clear pale-beige water. That was supper. "The children cry for food most of the time," she said, looking at the thin soup with hate.

"What is the matter with them?" I asked. She evidently thought I was not very sound in the head.

"There are only two things the matter with them. Tuberculosis and rickets."

The old-faced doll reached out a tiny white hand. I walked over to her and her hand curled around my fingers and she smiled. She was, the nurse said, seventeen months old and her name was Manuela.

Manuela let go my fingers and began to cry. Had I done something bad? "Only hungry," the nurse said. She picked the child up, lightly and gently, and tossed it in her arms. The child laughed aloud with pleasure at this lovely game. As the nurse held her you saw the rope-thin legs and the swollen stomach of rickets.

"Will she be all right?" I said.

"Certainly," the nurse said and she was lying, you could see that in her face. "Certainly she'll get well. She has to. Somehow.")

"Yes, she's a fine child," I said to Lola Hernández, but I thought, Maybe we can stop looking at the child, when we all know she's sick with hunger and probably will not live until summer. Let's talk about something else, now, just for a change.

"Have you been to the opera?" I said to Lola.

"I went once," she said, "but I do not like to go. All the time I was there, I kept thinking, What if this minute my husband is wounded, or what if he is coming home on leave. I almost thought he had come home and then I would have missed an hour with him. So now I stay home."

"We all stay home," the old man said, "I like the house. We have been here for twenty-five years."

"Do you go often?" Lola asked.

"I've been," I said. "It's wonderful."

(The opera is not as funny as the movies, though the people of Barcelona don't think the movies are funny. But you can't help laughing when you go to see *Jane Eyre*, and it is all about a life none of the audience ever knew or imagined, and then in the middle the film flickers off and you hear the bombs falling somewhere, while the audience groans with irritation, knowing it will take half an hour before the current comes on again, and they are dying to see what happens to Jane and her handsome gentleman friend, and they are fascinated by the madwoman and the burning house. I particularly liked the Westerns, and seeing the horse stopped in midleap for an air alarm, knowing that the dangerous activities of the hero and his horse were much more thrilling to the audience than a mere covey of bombers flying at a great safe height and sending down indiscriminate, expensive steel-encased death and destruction.

It costs about two pesetas for the best seats at any show, and nobody earns less than ten pesetas a day. The only thing you want to spend money on is food, and there is no food, so you might as well go to the opera or to the movies. It would be very stupid to save up to buy furniture, the way the city gets bombed. Besides, it's warm inside the big overdecorated theaters, because there are so many people, and it's friendly, and sitting there with something to look at on the stage you forget for a while that you aren't really safe, you aren't really safe at all. And also you might even forget how hungry you are.

But the opera was a wonder. Some afternoons there was opera and some afternoons there was the symphony orchestra. The people of Barcelona crowded to both. The opera house was far too near the port for comfort, and bombs had ruined much of the neighbourhood. It was surprising that the singers had energy to sing, considering how little they eat. It was surprising to see such thin singers. The women were any age at all, wearing the prewar costumes, a little mussed now but still brilliant and romantic. All the men were old. The young men were at the war. The opera house was full every day and everyone enjoyed the music immensely, and roared with laughter at the stale formal opera jokes, and sighed audibly at the amorous moments and shouted *"Olé!"* at each curtain. We used to sit and scratch, because everyone had fleas this winter, there was no soap any more and everyone was very dirty and malodorous indeed. But we loved the music and loved not thinking about the war.)

The Hernández' only daughter now came home from her job, and there was much loud gay talk as if they had not seen each other for weeks, with everyone reporting on the day's air raids. She wore her dark hair in braids around her head and was glowing with rouge, and quite well dressed. She earned plenty of money because she worked in a munitions factory.

(You never know exactly where the munitions factories are, and are not intended to know. We drove over many streets I had not seen before and stopped before a great grille gateway, somewhere at the edge of town. The factory looked like a series of cement barns, not connected particularly, and shining and clean and cheerful in the winter sun. We walked across the courtyard and into the first open door. The woman in charge of this room came forward; she had a nice smile and was timid and behaved as if I had come to tea unexpectedly.

The women were working at long tables, heaped with shining black squares and oblongs, they looked like trays full of sequins. There were other trays full of shining little leads, like short fillers for an automatic pencil. The woman picked up a handful of the sequins and let them slip through her hands. "They're pretty, aren't they?" she said.

"Very pretty," I said, mystified. "What are they?"

"Powder," she said, "explosive. What makes the shells go off."

At the other end of the room women worked at sewing machines, the old-fashioned kind that you pump with your feet. There was cloth for summer dresses, a lovely pink linen, a nice gray-and-white stripe that would have made handsome shirts, a thick white silk for a bridal gown. They were sewing little bags, and bigger bags, like sacks for sachet. A girl came around and collected them and took them to the front of the room where they were filled with the explosive that looked like sequins. Then the little pink sachet bag of sequins was dropped into a shell base.

Other women carefully and daintily glued together tiny cellophane horseshoes; in these horseshoes was black powder, and this skilled elegant work served to make a mortar the thing it is.

Two barns farther down were the great guns, home for repair. The place looked like a museum full of prehistoric animals, huge gray strangely shaped animals come to rest in this smoky room. Men worked beside each gun, with a little fire to heat the tools and for keeping warm. The room twinkled with light from the charcoal burners. The guns all wore their small name tags: Vickers Armstrong, Schneider, Skoda. We had seen them and watched them being fired day after day and month after month at the front. The grooved rifling inside the barrels had been worn smooth from the many thousand rounds they had fired, and the barrels were being rebored. There were few guns in Republican Spain now that had the same caliber they started with, and with each reboring the size of the shells had to be changed.

"Would you like to see the shells?" the foreman asked. He was obviously proud of them.

He led me out in the sun and around two buildings and then into a vast storeroom. Used shell cases the color of old gold were stacked neatly against one wall; they would be hammered into shape and used again. In the center of the building and against the right wall the new shells were piled in squares and oblongs and pyramids; they were painted black and yellow. There were 75s looking neat and not really harmful at all. And there were the tall shells, the 155s, that frighten one more when they are coming in.

We admired the shells and at this moment, like a dream or a nightmare or a joke, the siren whined out over Barcelona. I think that one of the worst features of an air raid is the siren. The howling whining whistle rises and screams and wails over the city, and almost at once you hear, somewhere, the deep *hud-boom* of the bombs. I looked at my companion and he looked at me and smiled (I thinking, foolishly, never forget your manners, walk do not run) and we sauntered out of doors. I could not see the planes but I heard them; on a clear day they fly high for safety, so you rarely see them. I thought, anyhow, in case a bomb falls around here we won't even know it.

"What do the workers do?" I said.

"Nothing," he said. "They wait."

431

The planes now showed themselves clear and silver just a little way down the sky, the sky dotted with a few small white smoke bubbles from anti-aircraft shells. The men came out of the factory and walked across the courtyard and leaned against a wall where they could get a better view, and smoked. Some played an innocent game, pitching a coin. The women dragged out empty packing cases, in which bullets would be shipped later, and sat down in the sunshine and started knitting. They did not bother to look up. Everyone knew that the electricity was turned off for half an hour, so there would be no more work for a time. They knitted and gossiped, and watching the sky I saw the silver planes wheel and circle and fly back out to sea.

They all like working in a munitions factory because they get two rolls of bread each day as a bonus.)

"I must leave," I said. "Please forgive me for staying so long. Goodbye, Miguel, after the war you'll be a mechanic."

"After we have won the war," old Mrs. Hernández corrected me. "We will invite you to come here and eat a big supper with us."

They were all delighted, delighted with winning the war and delighted with eating a big supper.

"You will see Federico too," Lola said.

"Yes," I said, "that will be a great pleasure. Goodbye, goodbye," I said, shaking hands all around, "and many thanks."

We were standing up now, and looking at them I suddenly said, "The third winter is the hardest."

Then I felt ashamed. They were strong brave people and didn't need me to say cheering words for them.

"We are all right, Señora," Mrs. Hernández said, making it clear at once, saying the last word in her home about her family. "We are Spaniards and we have faith in our Republic."

Marrakech

GEORGE ORWELL

∾

George Orwell's upbringing helped make him an astute critic of imperialism. He was born in India, where his father was stationed as a colonial officer, and as an officer himself, he served in Burma from 1922 to 1927. His revulsion against empire was dramatized in his first novel, *Burmese Days* (1934). In the personal essay "Shooting an Elephant" (1936), Orwell examined the colonial experience from the inside, concluding that "when the white man turns tyrant, it is his own freedom that he destroys."

Because of ill health, Orwell had to spend the winter of 1938–39 in a warm climate. In French Morocco, after observing another colonial regime from the outside, he created a series of vignettes—five "postcards" from sunny Marrakech—as meditations on the natives' invisibility to whites, and on the likely demise of empire in the aftermath of the coming European war.

"Marrakech" is a political essay without an introduction or conclusion: it opens in medias res and ends with a suggestive poetic image. Nor does Orwell provide transitions along the way. The article is linked by common themes, and by an editorial view that includes Orwell himself as representative of colonial consciousness. This commentary is balanced by dramatic understatement and powerful description, as when Orwell views an old man with one leg "warped out of shape" by his work at a primitive lathe. The passage concludes with a simple charged sentence: "At his side his grandson, aged six, is already starting on the simpler parts of the job."

—K. K.

∾

As the corpse went past the flies left the restaurant table in a cloud and rushed after it, but they came back a few minutes later.

The little crowd of mourners—all men and boys, no women—threaded their way across the market-place between the piles of pomegranates and the taxis and the camels, wailing a short chant over and over again. What really

433

appeals to the flies is that the corpses here are never put into coffins, they are merely wrapped in a piece of rag and carried on a rough wooden bier on the shoulders of four friends. When the friends get to the burying-ground they hack an oblong hole a foot or two deep, dump the body in it and fling over it a little of the dried-up, lumpy earth, which is like broken brick. No grave-stone, no name, no identifying mark of any kind. The burying-ground is merely a huge waste of hummocky earth, like a derelict building-lot. After a month or two no one can even be certain where his own relatives are buried.

When you walk through a town like this—two hundred thousand inhab-itants, of whom at least twenty thousand own literally nothing except the rags they stand up in—when you see how the people live, and still more how eas-ily they die, it is always difficult to believe that you are walking among human beings. All colonial empires are in reality founded upon that fact. The people have brown faces—besides, there are so many of them! Are they really the same flesh as yourself? Do they even have names? Or are they merely a kind of undifferentiated brown stuff, about as individual as bees or coral insects? They rise out of the earth, they sweat and starve for a few years, and then they sink back into the nameless mounds of the graveyard and nobody notices that they are gone. And even the graves themselves soon fade back into the soil. Sometimes, out for a walk, as you break your way through the prickly pear, you notice that it is rather bumpy underfoot, and only a cer-tain regularity in the bumps tells you that you are walking over skeletons.

I was feeding one of the gazelles in the public gardens.

Gazelles are almost the only animals that look good to eat when they are still alive, in fact, one can hardly look at their hindquarters without thinking of mint sauce. The gazelle I was feeding seemed to know that this thought was in my mind, for though it took the piece of bread I was holding out it obviously did not like me. It nibbled rapidly at the bread, then lowered its head and tried to butt me, then took another nibble and then butted again. Probably its idea was that if it could drive me away the bread would some-how remain hanging in mid-air.

An Arab navvy working on the path nearby lowered his heavy hoe and sidled slowly towards us. He looked from the gazelle to the bread and from the bread to the gazelle, with a sort of quiet amazement, as though he had never seen anything quite like this before. Finally he said shyly in French:

"I could eat some of that bread."

I tore off a piece and he stowed it gratefully in some secret place under his rags. This man is an employee of the Municipality.

When you go through the Jewish quarters you gather some idea of what the medieval ghettoes were probably like. Under their Moorish rulers the Jews were only allowed to own land in certain restricted areas, and after centuries of this kind of treatment they have ceased to bother about overcrowding.

Many of the streets are a good deal less than six feet wide, the houses are completely windowless, and sore-eyed children cluster everywhere in unbelievable numbers, like clouds of flies. Down the centre of the street there is generally running a little river of urine.

In the bazaar huge families of Jews, all dressed in the long black robe and little black skull-cap, are working in dark fly-infested booths that look like caves. A carpenter sits crosslegged at a prehistoric lathe, turning chair-legs at lightning speed. He works the lathe with a bow in his right hand and guides the chisel with his left foot, and thanks to a lifetime of sitting in this position his left leg is warped out of shape. At his side his grandson, aged six, is already starting on the simpler parts of the job.

I was just passing the coppersmiths' booths when somebody noticed that I was lighting a cigarette. Instantly, from the dark holes all round, there was a frenzied rush of Jews, many of them old grandfathers with flowing grey beards, all clamouring for a cigarette. Even a blind man somewhere at the back of one of the booths heard a rumour of cigarettes and came crawling out, groping in the air with his hand. In about a minute I had used up the whole packet. None of these people, I suppose, works less than twelve hours a day, and every one of them looks on a cigarette as a more or less impossible luxury.

As the Jews live in self-contained communities they follow the same trades as the Arabs, except for agriculture. Fruit-sellers, potters, silversmiths, blacksmiths, butchers, leatherworkers, tailors, water-carriers, beggars, porters—whichever way you look you see nothing but Jews. As a matter of fact there are thirteen thousand of them, all living in the space of a few acres. A good job Hitler wasn't here. Perhaps he was on his way, however. You hear the usual dark rumours about the Jews, not only from the Arabs but from the poorer Europeans.

"Yes, mon vieux, they took my job away from me and gave it to a Jew. The Jews! They're the real rulers of this country, you know. They've got all the money. They control the banks, finance—everything."

"But," I said, "isn't it a fact that the average Jew is a labourer working for about a penny an hour?"

"Ah, that's only for show! They're all moneylenders really. They're cunning, the Jews."

In just the same way, a couple of hundred years ago, poor old women used to be burned for witchcraft when they could not even work enough magic to get themselves a square meal.

All people who work with their hands are partly invisible, and the more important the work they do, the less visible they are. Still, a white skin is always fairly conspicuous. In northern Europe, when you see a labourer ploughing a field, you probably give him a second glance. In a hot country, anywhere south of Gibraltar or east of Suez, the chances are that you don't even see him. I have noticed this again and again. In a tropical landscape one's eye takes in everything except the human beings. It takes in the dried-up soil, the prickly pear, the palm tree and the distant mountain, but it always misses the peasant hoeing at his patch. He is the same colour as the earth, and a great deal less interesting to look at.

It is only because of this that the starved countries of Asia and Africa are accepted as tourist resorts. No one would think of running cheap trips to the Distressed Areas. But where the human beings have brown skins their poverty is simply not noticed. What does Morocco mean to a Frenchman? An orange-grove or a job in Government service. Or to an Englishman? Camels, castles, palm trees, Foreign Legionnaires, brass trays, and bandits. One could probably live there for years without noticing that for nine-tenths of the people the reality of life is an endless, back-breaking struggle to wring a little food out of an eroded soil.

Most of Morocco is so desolate that no wild animal bigger than a hare can live on it. Huge areas which were once covered with forest have turned into a treeless waste where the soil is exactly like broken-up brick. Nevertheless a good deal of it is cultivated, with frightful labour. Everything is done by hand. Long lines of women, bent double like inverted capital L's, work their way slowly across the fields, tearing up the prickly weeds with their hands, and the peasant gathering lucerne for fodder pulls it up stalk by stalk instead of reaping it, thus saving an inch or two on each stalk. The plough is a wretched wooden thing, so frail that one can easily carry it on one's shoulder, and fitted underneath with a rough iron spike which stirs the soil to a depth of about four inches. This is as much as the strength of the animals is equal to. It is usual to plough with a cow and a donkey yoked together. Two donkeys would not be quite strong enough, but on the other hand two cows would cost a little more to feed. The peasants possess no harrows, they merely plough the soil several times over in different directions, finally leaving it in rough furrows, after which the whole field has to be shaped with hoes into small oblong patches to conserve water. Except for a day or two after the rare rainstorms there is never enough water. Along the edges of the fields channels are hacked out to a depth of thirty or forty feet to get at the tiny trickles which run through the subsoil.

Every afternoon a file of very old women passes down the road outside my house, each carrying a load of firewood. All of them are mummified with age and the sun, and all of them are tiny. It seems to be generally the case in primitive communities that the women, when they get beyond a certain age, shrink to the size of children. One day a poor old creature who could not have been more than four feet tall crept past me under a vast load of wood. I stopped her and put a five-sou piece (a little more than a farthing) into her hand. She answered with a shrill wail, almost a scream, which was partly gratitude but mainly surprise. I suppose that from her point of view, by taking any notice of her, I seemed almost to be violating a law of nature. She accepted her status as an old woman, that is to say as a beast of burden. When a family is travelling it is quite usual to see a father and a grown-up son riding ahead on donkeys, and an old woman following on foot, carrying the baggage.

But what is strange about these people is their invisibility. For several weeks, always at about the same time of day, the file of old women had hobbled past the house with their firewood, and though they had registered themselves on my eyeballs I cannot truly say that I had seen them. Firewood was passing—that was how I saw it. It was only that one day I happened to be walking behind them, and the curious up-and-down motion of a load of wood drew my attention to the human being beneath it. Then for the first time I noticed the poor old earth-coloured bodies, bodies reduced to bones and leathery skin, bent double under the crushing weight. Yet I suppose I had not been five minutes on Moroccan soil before I noticed the overloading of the donkeys and was infuriated by it. There is no question that the donkeys are damnably treated. The Moroccan donkey is hardly bigger than a St. Bernard dog, it carries a load which in the British Army would be considered too much for a fifteen-hands mule, and very often its pack-saddle is not taken off its back for weeks together. But what is peculiarly pitiful is that it is the most willing creature on earth, it follows its master like a dog and does not need either bridle or halter. After a dozen years of devoted work it suddenly drops dead, whereupon its master tips it into the ditch and the village dogs have torn its guts out before it is cold.

This kind of thing makes one's blood boil, whereas—on the whole—the plight of the human beings does not. I am not commenting, merely pointing to a fact. People with brown skins are next door to invisible. Anyone can be sorry for the donkey with its galled back, but it is generally owing to some kind of accident if one even notices the old woman under her load of sticks.

As the storks flew northward the Negroes were marching southward—a long, dusty column, infantry, screw-gun batteries, and then more infantry, four or five thousand men in all, winding up the road with a clumping of boots and a clatter of iron wheels.

They were Senegalese, the blackest Negroes in Africa, so black that sometimes it is difficult to see whereabouts on their necks the hair begins. Their splendid bodies were hidden in reach-me-down khaki uniforms, their feet squashed into boots that looked like blocks of wood, and every tin hat seemed to be a couple of sizes too small. It was very hot and the men had marched a long way. They slumped under the weight of their packs and the curiously sensitive black faces were glistening with sweat.

As they went past a tall, very young Negro turned and caught my eye. But the look he gave me was not in the least the kind of look you might expect. Not hostile, not contemptuous, not sullen, not even inquisitive. It was the shy, wide-eyed Negro look, which actually is a look of profound respect. I saw how it was. This wretched boy, who is a French citizen and has therefore been dragged from the forest to scrub floors and catch syphilis in garrison towns, actually has feelings of reverence before a white skin. He has been taught that the white race are his masters, and he still believes it.

But there is one thought which every white man (and in this connection it doesn't matter twopence if he calls himself a socialist) thinks when he sees a black army marching past. "How much longer can we go on kidding these people? How long before they turn their guns in the other direction?"

It was curious, really. Every white man there had this thought stowed somewhere or other in his mind. I had it, so had the other onlookers, so had the officers on their sweating chargers and the white N.C.O.'s marching in the ranks. It was a kind of secret which we all knew and were too clever to tell; only the Negroes didn't know it. And really it was like watching a flock of cattle to see the long column, a mile or two miles of armed men, flowing peacefully up the road, while the great white birds drifted over them in the opposite direction, glittering like scraps of paper.

Lady Olga

JOSEPH MITCHELL

❧

Joseph Mitchell (1908–1996) was the dean of American literary journalism. A native North Carolinian, he came to New York in 1929, worked for several newspapers, and joined the staff of *The New Yorker* in 1938. His gems of reportage regularly appeared there until 1964, the date of his masterwork, *Joe Gould's Secret*. Mitchell thereupon contracted what must have been a wrenching case of writer's block and never published another word. But he had a great popular success with the 1992 publication of his collected writings, *Up in the Old Hotel*. And his colleagues held him in such exalted personal and professional esteem that he remained a *New Yorker* staffer until his death, with no suggestion that he should ever step down.

"Lady Olga" (1940) takes the subject of a typical offbeat newspaper feature story—a bearded lady at the circus—and gives her the full *New Yorker* Profile treatment: a respectfully high number of long paragraphs containing a great many facts and sober declarative sentences. What unmistakably marks the piece as Mitchell's work is its mixture of humor and profound sadness, with a subtle but insistent suggestion that we consider the particular facts under discussion insofar as they relate to the human condition. The suggestion becomes more forceful as "Lady Olga" proceeds, and by the time we get to the bearded lady's stunning last quotation, we have been prepared to accept it as categorically true: "If the truth was known, we're all freaks together."

—B. Y.

∞

Jane Barnell occasionally considers herself an outcast and feels that there is something vaguely shameful about the way she makes a living. When she is in this mood, she takes no pride in the fact that she has had a longer career as a sideshow performer than any other American woman and wishes she had never left the drudgery of her grandmother's cotton farm in North Carolina. Miss Barnell is a bearded lady. Her thick, curly beard measures thirteen and a half inches, which is the longest it has ever been. When she was young and more entranced by life under canvas, she wore it differently every year; in those days there was a variety of styles in beards—she remembers the Icicle, the Indian Fighter, the Whisk Broom, and the Billy Goat—and at the beginning of a season she would ask the circus barber to trim hers in the style most popular at the moment. Since it became gray, she has worn it in the untrimmed, House of David fashion.

The business of exhibiting her beard has taken her into every state in the Union. In fact, she has undoubtedly travelled as widely in the United States as any other person, but she has always been too bored to take much notice of her surroundings and probably would not do well with a grammar-school geography quiz. "I been all over everywhere, up, down, and sideways," she says. "I've hit thousands of towns, but I don't remember much about any of them. Half the time I didn't even know what state I was in. Didn't know or care." Miss Barnell is sixty-nine years old and was first put on exhibition shortly after her fourth birthday; she claims she has been bearded since infancy. As Princess Olga, Madame Olga, or Lady Olga, she has worked in the sideshows of at least twenty-five circuses and carnivals for wages ranging between twenty and a hundred dollars a week. She has forgotten the names of some of these outfits; one circus she remembers only as "that ten-car mess on the West Coast where I and my third husband had to knock the sideshow manager on the noggin with a tent stake to get my pay." She started out with a tramp circus, or "mud show," whose rickety, louse-infested wagons were pulled by oxen, and worked her way up to Ringling Brothers and Barnum & Bailey.

She spent six years in the Ringling circus. She was with it last in 1938, when its season was cut short by a strike in Scranton, an occurrence which made her hysterical. Ringling's sideshow, the Congress of Strange People, is as highly esteemed by freaks as the Palace used to be by vaudeville actors, but she would not sign a contract for the 1939 season. It pained her to make this decision; for six consecutive seasons she had occupied the same berth in Old Ninety-six, the Ringling sleeping car for sideshow people, and had grown attached to it. "Once I heard about a man in the penitentiary who broke down and cried when he finished his term and had to leave his cell for the last time," she says. "It had got to be a home to him. That's how I felt about my berth." She turned down the 1939 contract because she had become obsessed with a notion that out on the road she would somehow be forced to join the circus union. Unions frighten her. Although she has never voted, she is a violently opinionated Republican. Also, she is a veteran reader of Hearst newspapers and believes everything she reads in them. She thinks the average union organizer carries a gun and will shoot to kill. When she sees pickets, she immediately crosses to the other side of the street. "Just as sure as I go back to Ringling's, that union will get me," she told a circus official who tried for hours to reason with her, and added, "To tell you the truth, I think that old union is a corporation, like everything else these days." She also has a fear of corporations; to her, they are as sinister as unions. Since she left, Ringling's has been without a bearded lady. Fred Smythe, manager of the Congress, offers her a contract every spring, but she always tells him that she will never again work for the Big Show. This never surprises Smythe. "Short of blasting," he says, "there's no way of getting a fool notion out of the head of a freak. I'd sure like to get her back. She's the only real, old-fashioned bearded lady left in the country. Most bearded ladies are men. Even when they're women, they look like men. Lady Olga is a woman, and she looks like a woman." Smythe says that bearded ladies are not particularly sensational but they are traditional in sideshows, like clowns in the circus itself. "People don't laugh at clowns any more but they want to see them around," he says. "Likewise, if there isn't a bearded lady in a sideshow, people feel there's something lacking."

Miss Barnell has not been on the road since leaving the Big Show but has stuck pretty close to New York City, which, as much as any other place, she considers home. In the winter she works intermittently in the basement sideshow of Hubert's Museum on West Forty-second Street. She has shown her beard in practically every dime museum in the country and likes Hubert's best of all; she has come to look upon it as her winter headquarters. Professor Le Roy Heckler, who operates the Flea Circus concession in Hubert's, is an old friend of hers. They once lived in the same farming community in Mecklenburg County, North Carolina, and she worked in circuses long ago with his father, the late Professor William Heckler, who was a sideshow strong man before he developed a method of educating fleas and established the family business. She has great respect for Le Roy; she calls him "the young Professor" and says she has known him since he was "diaper size." In the summer she divides her time between Hubert's and Professor Sam Wagner's World Circus Side Show, also a dime museum, in Coney Island. She likes Coney because she feels that salt air is good for her asthma; also, she has a high regard for the buttered roasting-ear corn that is sold in stands down there.

On the dime museum circuit she does not work steadily; she works two or three weeks in a row and then lays off for a week. "I don't want to go nuts," she says. In museums, her hours are from 11 A.M. to 11 P.M. There is an average of two shows an hour and during a show she is on the platform from five to ten minutes. Between appearances, she is free. At Hubert's she kills most of this time dozing in a rocking chair in her dressing room. Sometimes she visits with other performers, usually with Albert-Alberta, the half-man-half-woman. Twice a week she goes into Professor Heckler's booth and watches him feed his fleas. This spectacle always amazes her, although she has seen it scores of times. The Professor rolls up one sleeve, picks the fleas out of their mother-of-pearl boxes with tweezers, and drops them, one by one, on a forearm, where they browse for fifteen minutes. While the fleas are feeding, the Professor reads a newspaper and she smokes a cigarette. They seldom say anything to each other. Taciturn herself, Miss Barnell does not care for talkative people. At least once an afternoon she wraps a scarf around her beard and goes out for coffee or a mug of root beer. She usually goes to the lunchroom in the American Bus Depot, a few doors west of Hubert's. She finds the atmosphere of a bus terminal soothing to her nerves. When showing in Coney Island, she takes brisk turns on the boardwalk between appearances.

In the past, while filling engagements in and around the city, Miss Barnell always lived in small Broadway hotels. A year or so ago she gave up hotel life. One Saturday night, after working late in Hubert's, she walked into a hotel off Times Square in which she had been living since the Ringling strike and a drunk in the lobby saw her and said, "By God, it's the bearded lady!" He followed her to the elevator, shouting, "Beaver! Beaver!" Next day she moved out and took a furnished apartment in a theatrical rooming house on Eighth Avenue, not far from the Garden. The house was recommended by a colleague, a man who eats electric-light bulbs. Among the other tenants are a magician, an old burlesque comedian, a tattooed woman, and a retired circus cook. Surrounded by such people, she feels at ease; when she meets them on the stairs they simply take her for granted and do not look startled. "If an old baboon was to walk down the hall tooting on a cornet, nobody in my house would give him a second look," she says.

Miss Barnell would like to spend the rest of her life in the city, but she knows that sooner or later she will become a stale attraction in the dime museums and will have to run an "At Liberty" notice in *Billboard* and get a job with a circus or carnival again. She wants to put this off as long as possible because she has grown to like apartment life; it has given her a chance, she says, really to get acquainted with Thomas O'Boyle, her fourth husband, and with Edelweiss, her cat. O'Boyle is a veteran Joey, or clown, but recently he has been employed as a talker—the sideshow term for barker—on the box at the gate at Hubert's. He is nineteen years younger than Miss Barnell and, unlike her, is enthralled by sideshow life. He wears dark-blue shirts, lemon-yellow neckties, and Broadway suits. He believes Miss Barnell is one of the great women of all time and treats her accordingly. When she comes into a room he leaps to his feet, and when she takes out a cigarette he hurriedly strikes a match for her. They were married after working together during the season of 1931 in the Johnny J. Jones Exposition, a carnival. Both are short-wave-radio fans, and O'Boyle says that this mutual interest is what brought them together. "Since our marriage, I and Mr. O'Boyle have travelled with the same outfits," Miss Barnell said recently, "but I never felt like I really knew him until we settled in an apartment. In a sleeping car you just don't feel married. To get to know a husband, you have to cook and wash for him." Next to O'Boyle, Edelweiss is her chief concern. Edelweiss is a sullen, overfed, snow-white Persian, for which she paid twenty-five dollars when it was a kitten and which now weighs sixteen pounds. She has nicknamed it Edie, and when she speaks to it she uses baby talk. She owns a comfortable old canvas chair—it came out of a circus dressing tent—and she likes to loll in this chair, hold the cat in her lap, and sing to it. Interminably, one after the other, she sings "Eadie Was a Lady" and "Root, Hog, or Die," an old circus song. Cats and dogs are not permitted in the sleeping cars of most circuses, so when she is on the road she usually has to board Edie in a pet store. "Sometimes out in the sticks," she says, "I get so lonesome for Edie I feel like I just can't bear it." She thinks Hubert's is much nicer than other museums because the manager there understands how she feels about the cat and lets her bring it with her to work. While she is on the platform, Edie sits beside her, purring. After cats, Miss Barnell likes horses best. She is one of those women who cannot pass a horse standing at a curb without trying to stroke its head; she keeps a handful of wrapped cube sugar in her bag for horses. Once a month, no matter how lean the season, she sends a contribution to the A.S.P.C.A. "To an animal, if you're bearded, it don't make no difference," she says.

Miss Barnell has not only a beard but side whiskers and a droopy mustache. In a white, loose-fitting house dress, she looks like an Old Testament prophet. Her appearance is more worldly when she dresses for a party; on such occasion she uses lipstick and rouge. Monty Woolley saw her once when she was dressed for the evening and said she looked like Elsa Maxwell in a property beard. Someone repeated Woolley's remark to her and she snorted with indignation. "Mr. Woolley must not have good eyesight," she said. She is not as plump as Miss Maxwell. She is five feet five and weighs a hundred and eighty-three pounds. She does not look her age; she has few wrinkles and she walks with a firm step. Her face is round and gloomy. Her bobbed gray hair is brushed pompadour style, and on the platform she wears a Spanish comb and two side combs. Once a year she gets a permanent wave. Before going on the street, she always covers her face with a veil and wraps a Paisley scarf around her neck, hiding her beard. To keep it curly, she sleeps with her beard in a pigtail plait; on days off she does not unplait it. She wears a thick gold wedding ring. Her voice is low and feminine.

Years of listening to barkers has had an effect on her speech; she makes long words longer. To her, a monstrosity is a "monsterosity." She uses some circus slang. The men who haunt the pinball machines on the first floor of Hubert's and never spend a dime to visit the sideshow in the basement are "lot lice" to her; in circuses, this term is applied to townspeople who do not buy tickets but stand around the lot, gaping at everything and getting in the way. She uses the word "old" to express contempt. She once said, "If that old Mayor they have here can't think up anything better than that old sales tax, he ought to lay down and quit." She consistently says "taken" for "took." This is a sample of her conversation: "When I was a young'un I taken the name Princess Olga. After I first got married I changed to Madame, but

443

when every confounded swami-woman and mitt-reader in the nation taken to calling herself Madame So-and-So, I decided Lady was more ree-fined." She has a dim but unmistakable Southern accent, and many of her habits of speech are North Carolinian. She heavily accents the first syllable in words like "hotel" and "police." She uses "one" as a contraction for "one or the other." She says, "I'm going to the movie pitchers this afternoon, or down to Coney Island, one." When she gets ready to do her kitchen shopping, she doesn't say, "I'm going up the street"; she says, "I'm going up street,"or, "I'm going down street." Another heritage from her years in rural North Carolina is a liking for snuff. She and O'Boyle own an automobile, and occasionally they get it out of storage and take a long trip. While riding along with the windows lowered, they both dip snuff. "Out in the country, snuff is better than cigarettes," she says. "Of course, I'd never think of using it indoors." She smokes a pack and a half of cigarettes a day. The use of tobacco is her only bad habit. As a rule, sideshow performers are fond of the bottle, but she is a teetotaler and a believer in prohibition.

On a sideshow platform or stage, Miss Barnell is rather austere. To discourage people from getting familiar, she never smiles. She dresses conservatively, usually wearing a plain black evening gown. "I like nice clothes, but there's no use wasting money," she says. "People don't notice anything but my old beard." She despises pity and avoids looking into the eyes of the people in her audiences; like most freaks, she has cultivated a blank, unseeing stare. When people look as if they feel sorry for her, especially women, it makes her want to throw something. She does not sell photographs of herself as many sideshow performers do and does not welcome questions from spectators. She will answer specific questions about her beard as graciously as possible, but when someone becomes inquisitive about her private life—"You ever been married?" is the most frequent query—she gives the questioner an icy look or says quietly, "None of your business." Audiences seem to think that this is admirable. Now and then, after she has told off a persistent or insulting questioner, people will applaud. Miss Barnell's temper has been a blessing; it has kept her from succumbing to utter apathy, which is the occupational disease of freaks. "I don't take no back talk from nobody," she says. She guards her dignity jealously. Once she slapped an apology out of a carnival owner who had suggested that she dye her beard so he could bill her as "Olga, the Lady Bluebeard." Wisecracking professors, or talkers, annoy her; she prefers to be introduced by one who is deadly serious and able to use long medical words. Except for midgets, the majority of freaks in American sideshows are natives, but talkers hate to admit this. Consequently, at one time or another, Miss Barnell has been introduced as having been born in Budapest, Paris, Moscow, Shanghai, and Potsdam. In one carnival she was "the daughter of a Hungarian general," and in another "the half sister of a French duke." She does not have a high opinion of foreigners and is sorely vexed by such introductions. She was grateful to the late Clyde Ingalls, who was once married to Lillian Leitzel and preceded Smythe as manager of Ringling's Congress, because he never seemed to resent the fact that she was born in North Carolina. Ingalls would bow to her, turn to the audience, click his heels, and say, "It gives me the greatest pleasure at this time to introduce a little woman who comes to us from an aristocratic plantation in the Old South and who is recognized by our finest doctors, physicians, and medical men as the foremost, unquestioned, and authentic fee-male bearded lady in medical history. Ladies and gentlemen, Lay-dee Oolgah!"

Among freaks it is axiomatic that Coney Island audiences are the most inhuman, but Miss Barnell has found that a Surf Avenue dime museum on a Saturday night is peaceful compared with a moving-picture studio at any time. She talks bitterly about her experiences in Hollywood, where she has been used in a number of horror and circus pictures. Her most important role was in "Freaks," a Metro-Goldwyn-Mayer study of sideshow life filmed in 1932. It was probably the most frightening picture ever made. In it, among other things, a beautiful trapeze girl of a European circus permits a dwarf to fall in love with her in order to obtain some money he has inherited. At their wedding feast, with a fantastic group of sideshow people around the table, she gets drunk and lets slip the fact that she despises the dwarf. A few nights later, during a terrible storm when the troupe is on the road, the freaks climb into her private wagon and mutilate her, turning *her* into a freak. Miss Barnell thinks this picture was an insult to all freaks everywhere and is sorry she acted in it. When it was finished, she swore she would never again work in Hollywood.

Her self-esteem suffers least of all when she is working in circuses, where sideshow class distinctions are rigidly observed. She herself divides freaks into three classes: born freaks, made freaks, and two-timers. Born freaks are the aristocrats of the sideshow world. She, of course, is a member of this class. So are Siamese twins, pinheads, fat girls, dwarfs, midgets, giants, living skeletons, and men with skulls on which rocks can be broken. Made freaks include tattooed people, sword-swallowers, snake charmers, and glass-eaters. Normal people who obtain sideshow engagements because of past glory or notoriety are two-timers to her. Examples are reformed criminals, old movie stars, and retired athletes like Jack Johnson, the old prizefighter, and Grover Cleveland Alexander, the old ballplayer, both of whom starred for a while on the dime museum circuit. Because Johnson wears a beret and because she has heard that he sips beer through a straw, she particularly dislikes him. "To the general public, old Jack Johnson may be a freak," she says, "but to a freak, he ain't a freak." Paradoxically, she bears no animosity toward fake bearded ladies. They amuse her. She was greatly amused when Frances Murphy, the Gorilla Lady in the "Strange As It Seems" sideshow at the New York World's Fair in 1940, got into an altercation with a truck-driver and was exposed as a male. "If any man is fool enough to be a bearded lady," she says, "it's all right with me."

Some of Miss Barnell's genuine but less gifted colleagues are inclined to think that she is haughty, but she feels that a woman with a beard more than a foot long has a right to be haughty. She undoubtedly does have the most flamboyant female beard in American sideshow history. The beard of Joséphine Boisdechêne, a native of Switzerland and one of P. T. Barnum's most lucrative freaks, was only eight inches long, and she had no mustache. She did, however, have a bearded son—Albert, billed as "Esau, the Hairy Boy"—who helped make up for this shortcoming. Grace Gilbert, who came from Kalkaska, Michigan, and spent most of her professional life in Barnum & Bailey's Circus, had a lush beard, but it was only six inches long. Miss Gilbert used peroxide and was billed as "Princess Gracie, the Girl with the Golden Whiskers." Records of non-professional female beards are scarce. Margaret of Parma, Regent of the Netherlands from 1559 to 1567, had a "coarse, bushy beard." She was proud of it, believing it gave her a regal appearance, and she required court physicians to mix tonics for it. Charles XII of Sweden had a bearded female grenadier in his army, a reputedly beautiful amazon, who was captured by the Russians in the battle of Poltava in 1709 and subsequently taken to St. Petersburg and presented to the Czar, at whose court she was popular for several years. There was a Spanish nun called St. Paula the Bearded, who grew a miraculous beard, according to sacred history. She was being pursued one night by a man with evil intent when hair suddenly sprouted from her chin. She turned and confronted the man and he fled. No reliable statistics on the length of these beards have come down to us.

Most freaks are miserable in the company of non-freaks, but unless she is sunk in one of the morose spells she suffers from occasionally, Miss Barnell welcomes the opportunity to go out among ordinary people. One morning in the winter of 1940 Cole Porter went to her dressing room at Hubert's and asked her to go with him to a cocktail party Monty Woolley was giving at the Ritz-Carlton. Porter told her that Woolley was a student of beards, that he was known as The Beard by his friends, and that he had always wanted to meet a bearded lady. "I'll have to ask my old man," Miss Barnell said. O'Boyle told her to go ahead and enjoy herself. Porter offered to pay for the time she would lose at the museum. "Well, I tell you," she said, "I and you and Mr. Woolley are all in show business, and if this party is for members of the profession, I won't charge a cent." Porter said non-professionals would be present, so she set a fee of eight dollars. Late that afternoon he picked her up at her house. She had changed into a rhinestone-spangled gown. In the Ritz-Carlton elevator she took off the scarf she was wearing around her beard, astonishing the other passengers. There were more than a hundred stage and society people at the party, and Porter introduced her to most of them. Woolley, who got quite interested in her, asked her to have a drink. She hesitated and then accepted a glass of sherry, remarking that it was her first drink in nine years. "I like to see people enjoying theirselves," she said after finishing the sherry. "There's too confounded much misery in this world." She was at the party an hour and a half and said she wished she could stay longer but she had to go home and cook a duck dinner for her husband. Next day, at Hubert's, she told a colleague she had never had a nicer time. "Some of the better class of the Four Hundred were there," she said, "and when I was introduced around I recognized their names. I guess I was a curiosity to them. Some of them sure were a curiosity to me. I been around peculiar people most of my life, but I never saw no women like them before." She was able to recognize the names of the society people because she is a devoted reader of the Cholly Knickerbocker column in the *Journal & American.* She is, in fact, a student of society scandals. "The Four Hundred sure is one cutting-up set of people," she says.

Several endocrinologists have tried vainly to argue Miss Barnell into letting them examine her. She is afraid of physicians. When sick, she depends on patent medicines. "When they get their hands on a monsterosity the medical profession don't know when to stop," she says. "There's nobody so indecent and snoopy as an old doctor." Her hirsuteness is undoubtedly the result of distorted glandular activity. The abnormal functioning of one of the endocrine, or ductless, glands is most often responsible for excessive facial hair in females. Hypertrichosis and hirsutism are the medical terms for the condition. Miss Barnell once read a book called "The Human Body" and is familiar with the glandular explanation, but does not take much stock in it. She says that her parentage was Jewish, Irish, and American Indian, and she believes vaguely that this mixture of bloods is in some way to blame, although she had three beardless sisters.

Miss Barnell has to be persuaded to talk about her early life. "What's the use?" she tells people. "You won't believe me." She says that her father, George Barnell, an itinerant buggy- and wagon-maker, was a Russian Jew who had Anglicized his name. Around 1868, while wandering through the South, he visited a settlement of Catawba Indians on the Catawba River in York County, South Carolina, and fell in love with and was married to a girl who had a Catawba mother and an Irish father. They settled in Wilmington, the principal port of North Carolina, where Barnell established himself in the business of repairing drays on the docks. Miss Barnell was their second child; she was born in 1871 and named Jane, after her Indian grandmother. At birth her chin and cheeks were covered with down. Before she was two years old she had a beard. Her father was kind to her, but her mother, who was superstitious, believed she was bewitched and took her to a succession of Negro granny-women and conjure doctors. Around her fourth birthday, her father inherited some money from a relative and went up to Baltimore to see about starting a business there. While he was away a dismal little six-wagon circus came to Wilmington. It was called the Great Orient Family Circus and Menagerie, and was operated by a family of small, dark foreigners; Miss Barnell calls them "the Mohammedans." The family was composed of a mother, who was a snake charmer; two daughters, who danced; and three sons, who were jugglers and wire-walkers. The wagons were pulled by oxen, and the show stock consisted of three old lions, a few sluggish snakes, some monkeys, a cage of parrots, an educated goat, and a dancing bear. There were many tramp circuses of this type in the country at that time. On the last day of the Great Orient's stay, Mrs. Barnell sold or gave Jane to the Mohammedan mother. "I never been able to find out if Mamma got any money for me or just gave me away to get rid of me," Miss Barnell says bitterly. "She hated me, I know that. Daddy told me years later that he gave her a good beating when he got home from Baltimore and found out what had happened. He had been in Baltimore two months, and by the time he got home I and the Mohammedans were long gone. He and the sheriff of New Hanover County searched all over the better part of three states for us, but they didn't find hide or hair."

She does not remember much about her life with the Great Orient. "My entire childhood was a bad dream," she says. The Mohammedans exhibited her in a small tent separate from the circus, and people had to pay extra to see her. On the road she slept with the Mohammedan mother in the same wagon in which the snakes were kept. Her pallet on the floor was filthy. She was homesick and cried a lot. The Mohammedans were not intentionally cruel to her. "They did the best they could, I guess," she says. "They were half starved themselves. I didn't understand their talk and their rations made me sick. They put curry in everything. After a while the old Mohammedan mother taken to feeding me on eggs and fruits." The circus wandered through the South for some months, eventually reaching a big city, which she thinks was New Orleans. There the Mohammedans sold their stock and wagons to another small circus and got passage on a boat to Europe, taking her along. In Europe, they joined a German circus. In Berlin, in the summer of 1876, after Jane had been exhibited by the German circus for four or five months, she got sick. She thinks she had typhoid fever. She was placed in a charity hospital. "I was nothing but skin and bones," she says. "The day they put me in the hospital was the last I ever saw of the Mohammedans. They thought I was due to die." She does not remember how long she was in the hospital. After she recovered she was transferred to an institution which she thinks was an orphanage. One morning her father appeared and took her away. "I disremember how Daddy located me," she says, "but I think he said the old Mohammedan mother went to the chief of police in Berlin and told who I was. I guess he somehow got in touch with the chief of police in Wilmington. That must have been the way it happened."

Barnell brought Jane back to North Carolina but did not take her home; she did not want to see her mother. Instead, he put her in the care of her Indian grandmother, who, with other Catawbas, had moved up from the settlement in South Carolina to a farming community in Mecklenburg County, near Charlotte. Jane worked on her grandmother's farm, chopping cotton, milking cows, and tending pigs. She never went to school but was taught to read and write by a Presbyterian woman who did missionary work among the Catawbas. Jane remembers stories this woman told her about Florence Nightingale; they made her long to become a nurse. In her teens she taught herself to shave with an old razor that had belonged to her grandfather. When she was around seventeen she went to Wilmington to visit her father, and a doctor he knew got her a place as a student nurse in the old City Hospital. She worked in the hospital for perhaps a year, and she still thinks of this as the happiest period of her life. Eventually, however, something unpleasant happened which caused her to leave; what it was, she will not tell. "I just figured I could never have a normal life," she says, "so I went back to Grandma's and settled down to be a farmhand the rest of my days." Three or four years later she became acquainted with the senior Professor Heckler, who owned a farm near her grandmother's; he worked in circuses in the summer and lived on the farm in the winter. Heckler convinced her she would be happier in a sideshow than on a farm and helped her get a job with the John Robinson Circus. As well as she can remember, she got this job in the spring of 1892, when she was twenty-one. "Since that time," she says, "my beard has been my meal ticket." Until the death of her grandmother, around 1899, Miss Barnell went back to North Carolina every winter. She had three sisters and two brothers in Wilmington, and she visited them occasionally. "They all thought I was a disgrace and seeing them never gave me much enjoyment," she says. "Every family of a freak I ever heard of was the same. I've known families that lived off a freak's earnings but wouldn't be seen with him. My parents passed on long ago, and I reckon my brothers and sisters are all dead by now. I haven't seen any of them for twenty-two years. I had one sister I liked. I used to send her a present every Christmas, and sometimes she'd drop me a card. She was a nurse. She went to China twenty-some-odd years ago to work in a hospital for blind Chinese children, and that's the last I ever heard of her. I guess she's dead."

Miss Barnell was with the Robinson Circus for fourteen years. While with it, she was married to a German musician in the circus band. By him she had two children, both of whom died in infancy. Soon after the death of her second child, her husband died. "After that," she says, "I never got any more pleasure out of circus life. I had to make a living, so I kept on. It's been root, hog, or die. When I got sick of one outfit, I moved on to another. Circuses are all the same—dull as ditch water." She left Robinson's to go with the Forepaugh–Sells Brothers' Circus and Menagerie, leaving it to marry a balloon ascensionist. He was killed about a year after they were married; how, she will not say. "He was just killed," she says, shrugging her shoulders. Her third marriage also ended unhappily. "That one treated me shamefully," she says. "If he was in a bottle, I wouldn't pull out the stopper to give him air. I taken out a divorce from him the year before I and Mr. O'Boyle got married."

Miss Barnell is disposed to blame circuses for much of the unhappiness in her life. Consequently she does not share her present husband's enthusiasm for them. O'Boyle was an orphan who ran away to work with a circus, and has never become disenchanted. Every week he reads *Billboard* from cover to cover, and he keeps a great stack of back copies of the magazine in their apartment; she rarely reads it. Like most old circus men, he is garrulous about the past. He often tries to get his wife to talk about her circus experiences, but she gives him little satisfaction. O'Boyle is proud of her career. Once he begged her to give him a list of the circuses and carnivals she has worked for; he wanted to send the list to the letters-to-the-editor department of *Billboard*. She mentioned Ringling, Barnum & Bailey, Forepaugh-Sells, Hagenbeck-Wallace, the World of Mirth Carnival, the Royal American Shows, the Rubin & Cherry Exposition, and the Beckmann & Gerety Shows, and then yawned and said, "Mr. O'Boyle, please go turn on the radio." He has never been able to get the full list.

In the last year or so Miss Barnell has become a passionate housekeeper and begrudges every moment spent away from her apartment. About once a week she rearranges the furniture in her two small rooms. On a window sill she keeps two geranium plants in little red pots. On sunny afternoons during her days off she places a pillow on the sill, rests her elbows on it, and stares for hours into Eighth Avenue. People who see her in the window undoubtedly think she is a gray-bearded old man. She spends a lot of time in the kitchen, trying out recipes clipped from newspapers. O'Boyle has gained eleven pounds since they moved into the apartment. Before starting work in the kitchen, she turns on four electric fans in various corners of the apartment and opens all the windows; she does not trust gas and believes that stirring up the air is good for her asthma. While the fans are on, she keeps Edie, the cat, who is susceptible to colds, shut up in a closet. She has developed a phobia about New York City tap water; she is sure there is a strange, lethal acid in it, and boils drinking water for fifteen minutes. She even boils the water in which she gives Edie a bath. In her opinion, the consumption of unboiled water is responsible for most of the sickness in the city. On her bureau she keeps two radios, one of them a short-wave set. On her days off she turns on the short-wave radio right after she gets up and leaves it on until she goes to bed. While in the kitchen, she listens to police calls. The whirring of the fans and the clamor of the radio do not bother her in the least. The walls are thin, however, and once the burlesque comedian who lives in the next apartment rapped on the door and said, "Pardon me, Madam, but it sounds like you're murdering a mule in there, or bringing in an oil well."

Miss Barnell's attitude toward her work is by no means consistent. In an expansive mood, she will brag that she has the longest female beard in history and will give the impression that she feels superior to less spectacular women. Every so often, however, hurt by a snicker or a brutal remark made by someone in an audience, she undergoes a period of depression which may last a few hours or a week. "When I get the blues, I feel like an outcast from society," she once said. "I used to think when I got old my feelings wouldn't get hurt, but I was wrong. I got a tougher hide than I once had, but it ain't tough enough." On the road she has to keep on working, no matter how miserable she gets, but in a museum she simply knocks off and goes home. Until she feels better, she does not go out of her apartment, but passes the time listening to the police calls, playing with Edie, reading the *Journal & American*, and studying an old International Correspondence Schools course in stenography which she bought in a secondhand-bookstore in Chicago years ago. Practicing shorthand takes her mind off herself. She is aware that such a thing is hardly possible, but she daydreams about becoming a stenographer the way some women daydream about Hollywood. She says that long ago she learned there is no place in the world outside of a sideshow for a bearded lady. When she was younger she often thought of joining the Catholic Church and going into a nunnery; she had heard of sideshow women who became nuns, although she had never actually known one. A lack of religious conviction deterred her. Religion has been of little solace to her. "I used to belong to the Presbyterians, but I never did feel at home in church," she says. "Everybody eyed me, including the preacher. I rather get my sermons over the radio."

Most of Miss Barnell's colleagues are touchy about the word "freak," preferring to be called artistes or performers. Years ago, because of this, Ringling had to change the name of its sideshow from the Congress of Freaks to the Congress of Strange People. Miss Barnell would like to be considered hardboiled and claims she does not care what she is called. "No matter how nice a name was put on me," she says, "I would still have a beard." Also, she has a certain professional pride. Sometimes, sitting around with other performers in a dressing room, she will say, with a slight air of defiance, that a freak is just as good as any actor, from the Barrymores on down. "If the truth was known, we're all freaks together," she says.

From *Black Lamb and Grey Falcon*

REBECCA WEST

❦

Rebecca West (1893–1985) is well known as a novelist, critic, and political essayist, but her journalism is equally distinguished. Truman Capote and Jimmy Cannon (who rarely appear in the same sentence) both named her as a progenitor of what came to be called new journalism. The book on which much of her reputation rests, *Black Lamb and Grey Falcon* (1941), was also the culmination of another genre, British travel writing. Based on three trips West took through then-Yugoslavia in the late 1930s, the book, which runs to more than 600 pages, is in the tradition of works by such authors as D. H. Lawrence, Graham Greene, Evelyn Waugh, and Robert Byron. What made it so influential (and so long) was its ambition and scope. To West, Europe as a whole could never have peace until the Balkans were internally and externally at liberty, and that thesis underlies every scene, description, digression, and piece of autobiography in *Black Lamb and Grey Falcon.* (Subsequent events—both the Nazi occupation soon after West's trip and the brutal civil war of the 1990s—have tended to confirm her view, and the book's prescience has only added to its stature.)

In this excerpt West, her husband, and their translator/guide, called Constantine, visit the Bosnian town of Travnik. Not much happens: they have lunch with a local couple, take a stroll, sit in a café. Yet West, with her novelist's sensitivity to nuance and her observational vigor, makes the afternoon into a haunting watercolor of a soon-to-vanish world.

—B. Y.

❦

We had been invited to luncheon with the father and mother of the lovely Jewess in Sarajevo whom we called the Bulbul, and we found their home in an apartment house looking over the blossoming trench of the valley from the main road, under a hill crowned with a fortress built by the old Bosnian kings. We found it, and breathed in our nostrils the odour of another civilization. Our appearance there caused cries of regret. The father stood in the shadow of the doorway, a handsome man in his late fifties, whose likeness I had seen often enough in the Persian miniatures, gazelle-eyed and full-bodied. In the delicious voice of the Sephardim, honey-sweet but not cloying, he told us that he was ashamed to let us in, for we would find nothing worthy of us. He had thought we meant to call at his factory, which was a couple of miles outside the town, so he had ordered a real meal, a meal appropriate to us, to be cooked there, and he had left an explanation that he could not be with us, as his wife had broken her ankle and till she was well he would eat all his meals with her. He bowed with shame that he should have blundered so. But a voice, lovely as his own but a woman's, cried from the darkened room beyond and bade him bring the strangers in. It was at once maternal, warm with the desire to do what could be done to comfort our foreignness, and childlike, breathless with a desire to handle the new toy.

She lay on a sofa, fluttering up against the downward pull of her injury, as hurt birds do; and she was astonishing in the force of her beauty. She was at least in her late forties, and she was not one of those prodigies unmarked by time, but she was as beautiful, to judge by her effect on the beholder, as the Bulbul. That could not really be so, of course. As a general rule Horace must be right, for reasons connected with the fatty deposits under the skin and the working of the ductless glands, when he writes, *"O mater pulchra filia pulchrior."* Yet in this case he would have been wrong. He should have ignored his metre and written of *"mater pulchrior pulcherrimæ filiae,"* for there was the more beautiful mother of the most beautiful daughter. The Bulbul was the most perfect example conceivable of the shining Jewish type, but so long as one looked on this woman she seemed lovelier than all other women. Her age was unimportant because it did not mean to her what it means to most Western women: she had never been frustrated, she had always been rewarded for her beautiful body and her beautiful conduct by beautiful gratitude.

My husband and I sat down beside her, smiling as at an unexpected present; and she apologized to us for the poor meal she would have to improvise, and cried over our heads directions to her cook in a voice that floated rather than carried, and then settled to ask us questions which were by Western standards personal, which were extremely sensible if she wished to be able to like us quickly before we left her house. In a painted cage a canary suddenly raised fine-drawn but frantic cheers for the universe, and they checked it with gentle laughter that could not have hurt its feelings. The canary, it seemed, her husband had brought home to divert her while she must lie on the sofa. The room was littered with gifts he had fetched her for that purpose: a carved flute, a piece of brocade, an eighteenth-century book of Italian travel with coloured illustrations, an amber box—a trifle, I should say, for each day she had been kept in the house. Their household rocked gently on a tide of giving and receiving.

They watched us sadly while we ate, uttering coos of regret for the meal that was really worthy of us, waiting uneaten in the factory. But we were not discontented. We were given home-made spaghetti, those eggs called "Spanish eggs" which are boiled for three days in oil and come out grease-less and silky to the palate, lamb chops from small ethereal lambs who probably had wings, sheep's cheese, pure white and delicately sharp, peaches and quinces foundered in syrup that kept all their summer flavour, and raki, the colourless brandy loved by Slavs. As we ate we told them of our meetings with their daughter in Sarajevo, and they stretched like cats in pride and pleasure, owning that all we said of her was true, and reciting some of her accomplishments that they thought we might not have had the chance to observe. Nothing could have been less like the uneasy smile, the deprecating mumble, which is evoked in an Englishman by praise of his family.

But this was a long way from England. Constantine went on to tell the gossip he had picked up in Sarajevo, and the more ambassadorial gossip he had brought from Belgrade, and while they rewarded his perfect story-telling by perfect listening, I looked about the room. It was certainly provincial; anything that had reached the room from Vienna, Berlin, Paris, or London had taken so long to get there and had been so much modified by the thought of the alien taste for which it was destined that it would be antiquated and bizarre. But built into this room, and inherent in every word and gesture of its owners, was a tradition more limited in its scope than the traditions of Vienna, Berlin, Paris, or London, but within its limits just as ancient and sure and competent. Whatever event these people met they could outface; the witness to that was their deep serenity. They would meet it with a formula compounded of Islam and Judaism. Their whole beings breathed the love of pleasure which is the inspiration of Sarajevo, which was perhaps the great contribution the Turks had to make to culture. But it was stabilized, its object was made other than running water, by the Jewish care for the continuity of the race. It was a fusion that would infuriate the Western moralist, who not only believes but prefers that one should not be able to eat one's cake and have it. I went later to comb my hair and wash my hands in these people's bathroom. A printed frieze of naked nymphs dancing in a forest ran from wall to wall, and several pictures bared the breasts and thighs of obsoletely creamy beauties. Naïvely it was revealed that these people thought of the bath as the uncovering of nakedness, and of nakedness as an instrument of infinite delight. It was the seraglio spirit in its purity; and it was made chaste as snow by the consideration that these people would have offered this flesh of which they so perfectly understood the potentialities to burn like tallow in flame if thereby they might save their dearer flesh, their child.

So one can have it, as the vulgar say, both ways. Indeed one can have a great deal more than one has supposed one could, if only one lives, as these people did, in a constant and loyal state of preference for the agreeable over the disagreeable. It might be thought that nothing could be easier, but that is not the case. We in the West find it almost impossible, and are caught unawares when we meet it in practice. That was brought home to me by this woman's tender gesture of farewell. First she took all the lilacs from a vase beside her sofa and gave them to me, but then felt this was not a sufficient civility. She made me lay down the flowers, and took a scent-bottle from her table and sprinkled my hands with the scent, gently rubbing it into my skin. It was the most gracious farewell imaginable, and the Western world in which I was born would not have approved.

There sounded in my mind's ear the probable comment of a Western woman: "My dear, it was too ghastly, she seized me by the hands and simply drenched them with some most frightful scent. I couldn't get rid of it for days." Their fastidiousness would, of course, have been bogus, for the scent was exquisite, a rich yet light derivative from Bulgarian attar of roses. These people were infallible in their judgment on such matters, having been tutored for centuries by their part in the luxury trade between Bosnia and Tsarigrad, as they named Constantinople; and she had assumed that persons of our kind would have a like education and would recognize that this scent was of the first order. She had also assumed that I would like to receive a gift which showed that somebody who had not known me two hours before now liked me. She assumed, in fact, that I too preferred the agreeable to the disagreeable. Remembering the grey ice that forms on an Englishman's face as he is introduced to a stranger, I reflected that she was too audacious in her assumption.

Before we left the town her husband took us for a stroll. A lane wound among the mosques and villas through gardens that held much plum blossom and lilac and irises and, here and there, among the shrubs, the innocent playfulness of witch-balls. Travnik had changed its aspect now, as a town does after one has eaten salt in one of its houses. It is no longer something painted on one's retina, it is third-dimensional, it is a being and a friend or an enemy. We climbed up to the old castle, which is a fortress now, and were met by very grave young soldiers. Slav soldiers look devout and dedicated even when they are drunk; these sober boys, guarding their white town and pale-green valley, were as nuns. There had been an intention of calling on the commandant, but the young soldiers said he was asleep. They looked at us for some time before they told us this, and spoke sadly and with an air of pronouncing judgment; and I think that perhaps they thought that their commandant was a sacred being, and that it would be a profanation to disturb him for the sake of three men not in uniform and a woman no longer young. They bade us good-bye with a worried air as if they wished they were sure they had done right. All to them was still of great moment.

We followed a little path down a grassy hill, miraculously untainted as glades are on the edge of Moslem towns, to a big pool lying among trees. It was fed by three springs, each bursting from the mauve shelter of a clump of cyclamen. It was dammed by a steep stone wall, broken at one end by a channel through which the waters burst in a grooved sliver that looked to be as solid as crystal. We admired it for a long time as if it were a matter of great importance; and then we went down to the main road and found a café which had settled itself in snug melancholy at the corner of a Moslem graveyard, near by the pompous canopied tombs of a couple of pashas.

There we sat and drank black coffee and ate Turkish delight on toothpicks, while a gentle wind stirred the flowering trees that met above the table, and set the grasses waving round a prostrate pillar which had fallen by one of the pashas' tombs. There strolled up and sat down some of those mysterious impoverished and dignified Moslems who seem to have no visible means of support, but some quite effective invisible means. They watched us without embarrassment; we were unembarrassed; and the men talked of country pastimes. Here, the Bulbul's father said, was real game for shooting in winter.

There is deep snow here in winter-time, it seems; and the beasts come down from the heights and loiter hungrily on the outskirts of the town. A friend of his had sauntered a few yards out of his garden, his gun loaded with pellets. He paused to look at a black bush that had miraculously escaped the snow. It stood up and was a bear, a lurch away. His friend raised his gun and shot. The pellets found the bear's brain through the eye, he staggered, charged blindly, and fell dead. He himself had been driving down to his factory one November afternoon when he saw a pack of wolves rushing down the mountain on a herd of goats. He stopped his car and watched. They came straight down like the water we had seen rushing down by the dam. They leaped on the goats and ate what they wanted. He had heard the goats' bones cracking, as loud, he said, as gunshots. When the wolves had eaten their fill they rushed up the mountain again, dragging what was left of the goats. It took only five minutes, he thought, from the time he first saw them till they passed out of sight.

He pointed up to the mountains. "It is only in winter you see them," he said, "but all the same they are up there, waiting for us and the goats." We looked in wonder at the heights that professed the stark innocence of stone, that was honeycombed with the stumbling weighty hostility of bears, the incorporated rapacity of wolves. And as we lowered our eyes we saw that we were ourselves being regarded with as much wonder by other eyes, which also were speculating what the sterile order of our appearance might conceal. A gaunt peasant woman with hair light and straight and stiff as hay and a mouth wide as a door had stopped in the roadway at the sight of us. She was so grand, so acidulated, so utterly at a disadvantage before almost anyone in the civilized world, and so utterly unaware of being at a disadvantage at all, that I made Constantine ask her to let herself be photographed. She whinnied with delight, and arranged herself before the camera with her chin forward, her arms crossed, her weight on her heels, acting a man's pride; I think nothing in her life had ever suggested to her that there is a woman's kind of pride.

She was poor. Dear God, she was poor. She was poor as the people in Rab.

Her sleeveless white serge coat, her linen blouse, the coarse kerchief she had twisted round her head, were stained with age. The wool of the embroidery on her coat was broken so that here and there the pattern was a mere fuzz. Garments of this sort have a long life. To be in this state they must have been worn by more than one generation. She had probably never had new clothes in all her days. This was not the most important aspect of her. There were others which were triumphant. It could be seen that she was a wit, a stoic, a heroine. But for all that it was painful to look at her, because she was deformed by the slavery of her ancestors as she might have been by rheumatism. The deep pits round her eyes and behind her nostrils, the bluish grooves running down her neck, spoke of an accumulated deprivation, an amassed poverty, handed down like her ruined clothes from those who were called rayas, the ransomed ones, the Christian serfs who had to buy the right to live. To some in Bosnia the East gave, from some it took away.

From *Once There Was a War*

JOHN STEINBECK

∞

John Steinbeck (1902–1968) won a 1962 Nobel Prize for his lifetime achievement in fiction, particularly for such epic novels as *The Grapes of Wrath* and *East of Eden*. Although Steinbeck's nonfiction never received major recognition, it has aged well and still offers crystalline examples of his art.

Steinbeck's naturalistic novels, like Zola's, were rooted in detailed journalistic research. "The Harvest Gypsies," his 1936 series in the San Francisco *News,* dramatized the survival power of migrant workers ("Their Blood Is Strong") and provided a factual base for *The Grapes of Wrath*. Steinbeck studied marine biology in the Gulf of California with a partner, Ed Ricketts, who would become a protagonist in several fictional stories. The nonfiction account of their voyage, *The Sea of Cortez* (1940), aspires to literary journalism and prefigures the first-person nature writing of Peter Matthiessen, Annie Dillard, and Edward Abbey.

In 1943 Steinbeck served as a war correspondent for the New York *Herald Tribune* in England, North Africa, and Italy. His dispatches maintained third-person objectivity, even when the reporter was part of the story. Steinbeck participated in several raids with British commandos, and was recommended for a Silver Star, but he makes himself invisible in his writing. In his report of October 6, 1943, occasioned by an Allied invasion near Salerno, Steinbeck becomes "the correspondent" whose immediate impressions—sights, smells, sensations, tastes—convey a truer sense of battle than any panoramic map or plan or statement from headquarters.

Steinbeck resisted the conventions of Allied reporting: official optimism, stringent censorship, and idealized portraits of brave troops and brilliant commanders. But his writing was even more contrarian than he realized at the time. In 1959, when the World War II dispatches were finally published as a book, *Once There Was a War,* Steinbeck reread them with surprise: "There are many things in them I didn't know I was writing— among others a hatred for war. Hell, I thought I was building the war up!"

—K. K.

MEDITERRANEAN THEATER

October 6, 1943—You can't see much of a battle. Those paintings reproduced in history books which show long lines of advancing troops are either idealized or else times and battles have changed. The account in the morning papers of the battle of yesterday was not seen by the correspondent, but was put together from reports.

What the correspondent really saw was dust and the nasty burst of shells, low bushes and slit trenches. He lay on his stomach, if he had any sense, and watched ants crawling among the little sticks on the sand dune, and his nose was so close to the ants that their progress was interfered with by it.

Then he saw an advance. Not straight lines of men marching into cannon fire, but little groups scuttling like crabs from bits of cover to other cover, while the high chatter of machine guns sounded, and the deep proom of shellfire.

Perhaps the correspondent scuttled with them and hit the ground again. His report will be of battle plan and tactics, of taken ground or lost terrain, of attack and counter-attack. But these are some of the things he probably really saw:

He might have seen the splash of dirt and dust that is a shell burst, and a small Italian girl in the street with her stomach blown out, and he might have seen an American soldier standing over a twitching body, crying. He probably saw many dead mules, lying on their sides, reduced to pulp. He saw the wreckage of houses, with torn beds hanging like shreds out of the spilled hole in a plaster wall. There were red carts and the stalled vehicles of refugees who did not get away.

The stretcher-bearers come back from the lines, walking in off step, so that the burden will not be jounced too much, and the blood dripping from the canvas, brother and enemy in the stretchers, so long as they are hurt. And the walking wounded coming back with shattered arms and bandaged heads, the walking wounded struggling painfully to the rear.

He would have smelled the sharp cordite in the air and the hot reek of blood if the going has been rough. The burning odor of dust will be in his nose and the stench of men and animals killed yesterday and the day before. Then a whole building is blown up and an earthy, sour smell comes from its walls. He will smell his own sweat and the accumulated sweat of an army. When his throat is dry he will drink the warm water from his canteen, which tastes of disinfectant.

While the correspondent is writing for you of advances and retreats, his skin will be raw from the woolen clothes he has not taken off for three days, and his feet will be hot and dirty and swollen from not having taken off his shoes for days. He will itch from last night's mosquito bites and from today's sand-fly bites. Perhaps he will have a little sand-fly fever, so that his head pulses and a red rim comes into his vision. His head may ache from the heat and his eyes burn with the dust. The knee that was sprained when he leaped ashore will grow stiff and painful, but it is no wound and cannot be treated.

"The 5th Army advanced two kilometers," he will write, while the lines of trucks churn the road to deep dust and truck drivers hunch over their wheels. And off to the right the burial squads are scooping slits in the sandy earth. Their charges lie huddled on the ground and before they are laid in the sand, the second of the two dog tags is detached so that you know that that man with that Army serial number is dead and out of it.

These are the things he sees while he writes of tactics and strategy and names generals and in print decorates heroes. He takes a heavily waxed box from his pocket. That is his dinner. Inside there are two little packets of hard cake which have the flavor of dog biscuits. There is a tin can of cheese and a roll of vitamin-charged candy, an envelope of lemon powder to make the canteen water taste less bad, and a tiny package of our cigarettes.

That is dinner, and it will keep him moving for several more hours and keep his stomach working and his heart pumping. And if the line has advanced beyond him while he eats, dirty, buglike children will sidle up to him, cringing and sniffling, their noses ringed with flies, and these children will whine for one of the hard biscuits and some of the vitamin candy. They will cry for candy: "*Caramela—caramela—caramela*—okay, okay, shank you, good-by." And if he gives the candy to one, the ground will spew up more dirty, buglike children, and they will scream shrilly, "*Caramela—caramela.*" The correspondent will get the communiqué and will write your morning dispatch on his creaking, dust-filled portable: "General Clark's 5th Army advanced two kilometers against heavy artillery fire yesterday."

Lethal Lightning

JIMMY CANNON

∞

Jimmy Cannon (1910–1973) dropped out of school at fifteen to work as a
copy boy at the New York *Daily News*. He later wrote about murder trials and
political conventions, and during World War II he became a correspondent
for *Stars and Stripes*. But for most of his career Cannon was the sports voice
of the *Daily News*, the *Journal American*, and New York City itself.

Bill Conlin, a sportswriter who grew up in New York, was inspired by
Cannon: "To read him was to touch a live wire with a wet hand. His prose
crackled with a terse imagery ideal for the space strictures of a game story
or column. Cannon could outrage you one day and have tears rolling down
your cheeks the next." When other writers, like Jack Newfield, praised
Cannon for having founded a "new journalism" in the 1940s, he modestly
passed the credit to social journalists—especially Rebecca West.

Cannon's 1946 account of the second Joe Louis–Billy Conn fight shows
what was new about his work. In order to suggest the groggy nausea of
Conn lying defeated on the canvas, Cannon begins with a stream-of-
consciousness memory. Only gradually, as he turns back to the beginning
of the fight, does the writing coalesce toward clarity. By the time the principals gather in the center of the ring, Cannon offers one precise and
haunting image after another. The story ultimately covers every angle of
the event—the crowd, the managers, the comments of the fighters during
the ring action, and the postfight dialogue in each locker room. Hovering
over all is a sense of each combatant's character and the arc of his career.

—K. K.

∞

Once, dreaming with morphine after an operation, I believed the night
climbed through the window and into my room like a second-story worker. I
thought all the night had forsaken the world, and shaped like a fat man,
walked through my face and up into my mind. The night had the dirty color
of sickness and had no face at all as it strolled in my brain. It gradually lost

461

the identity of a man, blowing apart the way smoke does on a windy day. It became a smelly blackness, shoving itself into the corners of my subconsciousness like a man breaking down a door with his shoulder. It hurt me as I lay there, feeling the brightness of the room. But the filthy night stayed in my mind and I lived in it alone.

I remembered that last night in Yankee Stadium when Joe Louis knocked out Billy Conn in the eighth round of a fight that had been tautly dull, the way the slow hours are for reporters sitting on a stoop and waiting for a man to die. I felt that old dream coming from a long way off and finding not me, but Billy Conn, who lay in the spurious day of the ring lights and had the aching blackness all to himself.

It ceased to be sport when Louis let the big right go, then another cobblestone of a right and then the left hook as Conn fell off the rim of the conscious and crumpled into the dark privacy of the night he alone possessed. It was like watching a friend of yours being run over by a trolley car, watching it coming and knowing what would happen but looking at it quietly, the curiosity dominating the horror and compelling you to be attentively silent. Maybe it was sudden but it was there all the time, the knockout inevitable and sure. It was there all the time like the rain in the night that never fell out of the starless sky.

All the big people waited for this plotted accident to happen and down front in the $100 seats was Bernard Baruch and close to him sat a guy who held up banks and now is a legitimate man because they don't put you in jail for selling whiskey any more. Stand up and look back out of the press row and there they were, all the big people waiting for this controlled violence, licensed and sanctioned by the laws of the state.

Waiting for it to break out as the old man of the council tables where they speak as though the world were Billy Conn, and Joe Louis the atom, stopping the breathing and the living, as the world breaks into nothing. The old man sat there among the thieves and the good people and the truly talented and the Broadway trash and the black-market peerage, the Cabinet member and the Hollywood people. All forgetting what they know, and some what they did, and the world rotting with the hatred of man for himself. So they were there and it was a night out for them at $100 a chair on the grass of the ball park.

So there they were at $100 a look, but back of them were empty places in the cheaper seats when Billy Conn first came into the ring. He wore a white green-bordered satin bathrobe and it gleamed under the lights where a lonely moth flew in circles as though indicating to Conn what he should do. They were with him, those who trained him and live off him, the guy from the corner of Pitt and Dennison in East Liberty, a paid-up member of the Peabody Club, which is a poolroom where horse players come to shoot pool.

Johnny Ray, the manager, aimlessly moved around the ring, the name of his fighter in green-blocked letters on the black half-sleeved jersey. He was white with anxiety and seemed to be weak with nervousness as he laid his flabby white arm along the rope and looked into Conn's face as though he were trying to remember the features before they were destroyed.

Then Louis came in, big in his flashy red-edged blue robe of silk, a towel wrapped loosely around his head and moving in the wind of the night. They sat there, and the 45,266 around them on the plains of the playing field and up in the stands mumbled with impatience and expectancy and now and then a lonely shout, blurred by the distance, came down to the ringside. Now the soles of Conn's shoes were being scraped by Billy Joss, a second with an emaciated face. There was a delay because Manny Seaman was tying the laces of Louis's gloves and Conn was standing up, moving his arms slowly, the bathrobe off and you noticed that there was a thick cord of fat hanging off his belly when he moved.

They came to the center in the old ritual, the microphone dropped so Eddie Joseph, the referee, could be heard telling them in a gruffly self-conscious voice what would happen if a foul were committed. Louis had a white bathrobe under the blue one and he still wore the towel and Seaman pulled that away when they went to their corners.

It was a first round of comedy, but there was no humor in it. In that round Conn flapped his left glove into Louis for the first punch of the fight and when they clinched Conn was talking to the empty-faced champion, whose mouth twitched as he pushed Conn away.

"What's your hurry, Joe?" Conn asked, muttering through the mouthpiece. "We got 15 rounds to go."

As they moved in a polite dance of caution, looking at each other as though they were angry men about to argue instead of punch, I saw the puckers of fat where Louis's arms join his shoulders and his stomach moved when his legs did, as though it were not part of him but a slab of meat tied around his waist.

Conn danced leisurely in the first, the head cocked to the left, the legs pale and frail. Once Conn stomped at him, the way Varsity Drag dancers used to do before the Charleston ran them out of the cafés. Louis jabbed occasionally and Conn poked back at him, going backwards from side to side. Conn's fleet yet apparently unconcerned stroll caused Louis to skip, the way a marching soldier does to fall back into step. Once Conn hit to the belly but they seemed fascinated by each other and appeared to be admiring each other's style instead of going about the job they were paid to do.

As the second round started, Conn lunged out of his scampering retreat and hit Louis with a right and then a mild volley of lefts. Billy bluffed with his hands, making up and down feints as he moved his shoulders in tormenting spasms. Once Joe threw a right that couldn't locate the wet-haired head that was out of range. But his jabs were making Billy's head strain at the cords of his big neck and, at the finish, his face was blotchy and mussed with pain.

Now, in the third, Joe winced, closed his eyes, and turned his head when Conn feinted at him with meaningless gestures, never getting close enough to bang at the blank-faced man who moved after him on the big feet that creaked on the pebbles of resin strewn across the canvas. Once in this round Conn flared with a harmless fury and when it was over Louis was there, waiting and harassing him with a sheep dog's harmless awareness. The jeers, which had risen timidly from the crowd in the first, were growing louder and the people insulted the fighters they had paid $1,925,564 to see.

In the fourth Louis's lance of a jab began to slam into Conn's face and once Joe ambushed Conn into a corner and slammed two powerful short lefts to the body. Billy slipped as he moved backwards and Louis politely waited for him to rise, the way a standing man takes an introduction to someone sitting at a table. They touched gloves and Conn smiled, but it was a grin of sadness. Conn, the flashy and agile scientist of the ring, was moving with the panic of a sensibly fearless boxer. But Louis, who was suspected by many of being an ignoramus of the ring with nothing but strength to lick a man, was out-boxing him. In this round it became obvious that Joe was waiting and Conn was running in a fight that would end in disaster.

The fifth was the big round. It was here that Conn must have known he was scheduled for the oblivion that comes to all of them when they fight Louis. The punch was a right hand and it hit the chin. The hinges of Conn's knees bent and he started to sit down but changed his mind and moved off again after the right. Once Joe pursued him into a corner but Conn fought his way out by moving his hands with futile belligerency. Louis hit him another right and this time the smile was slow and the lips moved more in agony than anything else.

The crowd yelled at them, and it was the same in the sixth, the small man going away and the big man after him. Conn slid on his knees getting away and they touched gloves again in the friendly salute of sportsmen. The seventh was mild but when Louis jabbed it was as though he were prodding Conn with a baseball bat. Everyone in the big stockade realized the big man was coming on and the little man was going. The little man was an authority on that. Conn knew it but his legs wouldn't obey his mind and his flight was slow now and laborious.

Now Conn came to the end of the journey that started back on the street corner in Pittsburgh and ended here in tarnished glory because there was nothing in him but an arrogance that at times was wonderful but always sad. It was a bugle blown, and no one answered, and something incomplete and detached from the kid from Pittsburgh who was stricken with old age at 28 last night.

The right hand was the beginning. It cut Conn's left eye, and a brook of blood dribbled down the cheek and widened like a red stream. Louis pawed at it, and from the press rows you could see the night gathering in Conn's eyes, and the features starting to thicken with the stupidity of punishment.

The finish came, unexpected because it destroyed a man, but suddenly, because Conn was always the hunted, who escaped only temporarily from the trap. The right, the right again, and then the left, against the jaw of the falling man.

He was on his back, the blood running all over him and Joseph was counting and his voice was the timekeeper's hoarse echo. Conn's beaten body moved in his special night, the senses groping for the light and he was rising, boneless and helpless, when the number ten was reached.

There was a tumult of excited men in Louis's dressing room and he sat on a rubbing table, taking slow, small swallows out of a big bottle of mineral water.

"You finally picked the round," he said to me. "It's about time."

The flashlights were going and the reporters pressed in asking questions. Joe answered them, bending over in laughter now and then, calm and dignified and not gloating but trying to tell it the way it happened.

"I'm going out this round and fight," Louis said when someone asked him why he closed in quickly after following Conn with a slow languor. "That's what I told my corner. I wanted to see if he could take it. He was a better fighter the first time. He didn't hurt me."

There was a cut across Conn's nose, which had been broken before, and they were working on his eye. But he was laughing and cynical with a wit that denounced himself. He did not change, Conn. Not even having Louis catch his jabs like snowballs thrown by a child could shut off his humor.

"He fixed me, didn't he?" Conn asked.

"When did he hurt you?" a reporter asked.

"When he hit me," he answered, sneering.

"What are you going to do?" a reporter said.

"He racked up my cue for me," Conn said.

"Are you going to fight again?"

"As lousy as I was," Conn said, "and you're asking that. I should re-enlist in the army I was so lousy tonight."

Over in the corner, Milton Jaffee, his co-manager, pale and trembling with confusion, stood back behind the photographers and watched the fighter talk as though relating something that was comical that had happened to someone else.

"He ain't fighting any more," Milton said. "There's an easier way to make a dollar than this. He had nothing tonight."

It's an Honor

JIMMY BRESLIN

❦

Jimmy Breslin has been a sportswriter, general reporter, and Pulitzer-winning columnist for four New York newspapers, and is still best known for his vignettes of the city. At the *Herald Tribune* in the early 1960s, Breslin was writing daily dispatches, often from barrooms or courtrooms, about big events in the lives of obscure people. According to *Trib* colleague Tom Wolfe, Breslin wrote a daily short story "complete with symbolism, in fact, and yet true to life . . . and you could pick it up on the newsstand by eleven tonight for a dime."

Breslin's literary touches have always been grounded in tireless reporting. His presence behind the scenes, typically just before or after a major event, leads to evocative description and expressive dialogue. This approach is epitomized in "It's an Honor." The idea for the story, Breslin says, came "from nowhere" as he was standing with mourners in the White House lobby on the day before John F. Kennedy's funeral. "There were three thousand reporters in Washington. I knew I could not perform the simplest act of reporting if I had to do it in these crowded circumstances."

Breslin's solution emerges from an authentic feel for his subject, and is grounded in direct details—including a precise chronology. As a result, he evokes emotion through emotional restraint. Breslin links Jacqueline Kennedy, "head held high," with Clifton Pollard, an ordinary citizen—and the powerful dignity of both characters suffuses a national tragedy with special poignancy.

—K. K.

❦

Clifton Pollard was pretty sure he was going to be working on Sunday, so when he woke up at 9 a.m. in his three-room apartment on Corcoran Street, he put on khaki overalls before going into the kitchen for breakfast. His wife, Nettie, made bacon and eggs for him. Pollard was in the middle of eating them when he received the phone call he had been expecting.

It was from Mazo Kawalchik, who is the foreman of the gravediggers at Arlington National Cemetery, which is where Pollard works for a living. "Polly, could you please be here by eleven o'clock this morning?" Kawalchik asked. "I guess you know what it's for."

Pollard did. He hung up the phone, finished breakfast, and left his apartment so he could spend Sunday digging a grave for John Fitzgerald Kennedy.

When Pollard got to the row of yellow wooden garages where the cemetery equipment is stored, Kawalchik and John Metzler, the cemetery superintendent, were waiting for him.

"Sorry to pull you out like this on a Sunday," Metzler said. "Oh, don't say that," Pollard said. "Why, it's an honor for me to be here."

Pollard got behind the wheel of a machine called a reverse hoe. Gravedigging is not done with men and shovels at Arlington. The reverse hoe is a green machine with a yellow bucket which scoops the earth toward the operator, not away from it as a crane does. At the bottom of the hill in front of the Tomb of the Unknown Soldier, Pollard started the digging.

Leaves covered the grass. When the yellow teeth of the reverse hoe first bit into the ground, the leaves made a threshing sound which could be heard above the motor of the machine. When the bucket came up with its first scoop of dirt, Metzler, the cemetery superintendent, walked over and looked at it.

"That's nice soil," Metzler said.

"I'd like to save a little of it," Pollard said. "The machine made some tracks in the grass over here and I'd like to sort of fill them in and get some good grass growing there, I'd like to have everything, you know, nice."

James Winners, another gravedigger, nodded. He said he would fill a couple of carts with this extra-good soil and take it back to the garage and grow good turf on it.

"He was a good man," Pollard said.

"Yes, he was," Metzler said.

"Now they're going to come and put him right here in this grave I'm making up," Pollard said. "You know, it's an honor just for me to do this."

Pollard is forty-two. He is a slim man with a mustache who was born in Pittsburgh and served as a private in the 352d Engineers battalion in Burma in World War II. He is an equipment operator, grade 10, which means he gets $3.01 an hour. One of the last to serve John Fitzgerald Kennedy, who was the thirty-fifth President of this country, was a working man who earns $3.01 an hour and said it was an honor to dig the grave.

Yesterday morning, at 11:15, Jacqueline Kennedy started walking toward the grave. She came out from under the north portico of the White House and slowly followed the body of her husband, which was in a flag-covered coffin that was strapped with two black leather belts to a black caisson that had polished brass axles. She walked straight and her head was high. She walked down the bluestone and blacktop driveway and through shadows thrown by the branches of seven leafless oak trees. She walked slowly past the sailors who held up flags of the states of this country. She walked past silent people who strained to see her and then, seeing her, dropped their heads and put their hands over their eyes. She walked out the northwest gate and into the middle of Pennsylvania Avenue. She walked with tight steps and her head was high and she followed the body of her murdered husband through the streets of Washington.

Everybody watched her while she walked. She is the mother of two fatherless children and she was walking into the history of this country because she was showing everybody who felt old and helpless and without hope that she had this terrible strength that everybody needed so badly. Even though they had killed her husband and his blood ran onto her lap while he died, she could walk through the streets and to his grave and help us all while she walked.

There was mass, and then the procession to Arlington. When she came up to the grave at the cemetery, the casket already was in place. It was set between brass railings and it was ready to be lowered into the ground. This must be the worst time of all, when a woman sees the coffin with her husband inside and it is in place to be buried under the earth. Now she knows that it is forever. Now there is nothing. There is no casket to kiss or hold with your hands. Nothing material to cling to. But she walked up to the burial area and stood in front of a row of six green-covered chairs and she started to sit down, but then she got up quickly and stood straight because she was not going to sit down until the man directing the funeral told her what seat he wanted her to take.

The ceremonies began, with jet planes roaring overhead and leaves falling from the sky. On this hill behind the coffin, people prayed aloud. They were cameramen and writers and soldiers and Secret Service men and they were saying prayers out loud and choking. In front of the grave, Lyndon Johnson kept his head turned to his right. He is President and he had to remain composed. It was better that he did not look at the casket and grave of John Fitzgerald Kennedy too often.

Then it was over and black limousines rushed under the cemetery trees and out onto the boulevard toward the White House.

"What time is it?" a man standing on the hill was asked. He looked at his watch.

"Twenty minutes past three," he said.

Clifton Pollard wasn't at the funeral. He was over behind the hill, digging graves for $3.01 an hour in another section of the cemetery. He didn't know who the graves were for. He was just digging them and then covering them with boards.

"They'll be used," he said. "We just don't know when."

"I tried to go over to see the grave," he said. "But it was so crowded a soldier told me I couldn't get through. So I just stayed here and worked, sir. But I'll get over there later a little bit. Just sort of look around and see how it is, you know. Like I told you, it's an honor."

The Girl of the Year

TOM WOLFE

❦

American journalism has never had a practitioner who combined the attributes of talent, audacity, learning, legwork, and pure observation as well as Tom Wolfe. In the early 1960s, while on the staff of the *New York Herald Tribune,* Wolfe began turning out pieces for the *Herald Tribune's* Sunday supplement, *New York,* that changed the face of journalism. He once described an article he wrote at the time as "a garage sale . . . vignettes, odds and ends of scholarship, bits of memoir, short bursts of sociology, apostrophes, epithets, moans, cackles, anything that came into my head." For decades, journalism's collective voice had been modulated and unobtrusive. Looking back to literary types like Whitman or Dickens, Wolfe was blatantly and sometimes joyfully rhetorical, and his eagerness to give any trope a try energized a generation of nonfiction writers.

"The Girl of the Year" (published in *New York* in 1964) could have been written in the conventional manner—a profile of a successful model, with background, interview, and quotes from friends and colleagues. The breathless run-on alliterative impressionism of Wolfe's first sentence suggests this is not his way. For Wolfe, traditional cadences and structure simply could not do justice to the sheer manic energy of the early- and mid-sixties zeitgeist, and so here he gives us present-tense scenes, over-the-top cinematic lap dissolves, a narrative voice bordering on the hysterical, and high-octane punctuation (dashes, ellipses, exclamation points, and italics) that collectively evoke the era.

This was Wolfe's era, to be sure—his best magazine pieces and his two full-length works of journalism, *The Electric Kool-Aid Acid Test* (1968) and *The Right Stuff* (1979), are all set in it. In the 1980s and '90s he turned exclusively to essays and fiction, having indelibly changed literary journalism: whoever came after would have to come to terms with Tom Wolfe.

—B. Y.

∞

Bangs manes bouffants beehives Beatle caps butter faces brush-on lashes decal eyes puffy sweaters French thrust bras flailing leather blue jeans stretch pants stretch jeans honeydew bottoms eclair shanks elf boots ballerinas Knight slippers, hundreds of them, these flaming little buds, bobbing and screaming, rocketing around inside the Academy of Music Theater underneath that vast old mouldering cherub dome up there—aren't they super-marvelous!

"Aren't they super-marvelous!" says Baby Jane, and then: "Hi, Isabel! Isabel! You want to sit backstage—with the Stones!"

The show hasn't even started yet, the Rolling Stones aren't even on the stage, the place is full of a great shabby mouldering dimness, and these flaming little buds.

Girls are reeling this way and that way in the aisle and through their huge black decal eyes, sagging with Tiger Tongue Lick Me brush-on eyelashes and black appliqués, sagging like display window Christmas trees, they keep staring at—her—Baby Jane—on the aisle. What the hell is this? She is gorgeous in the most outrageous way. Her hair rises up from her head in a huge hairy corona, a huge tan mane around a narrow face and two eyes opened—swock!—like umbrellas, with all that hair flowing down over a coat made of . . . zebra! Those motherless stripes! Oh, damn! Here she is with her friends, looking like some kind of queen bee for all flaming little buds everywhere. She twists around to shout to one of her friends and that incredible mane swings around on her shoulders, over the zebra coat.

"Isabel!" says Baby Jane, "Isabel, hi! I just saw the Stones: They look super-divine!"

That girl on the aisle, Baby Jane, is a fabulous girl. She comprehends what the Rolling Stones *mean*. Any columnist in New York could tell them who she is . . . a celebrity of New York's new era of Wog Hip . . . Baby Jane Holzer. Jane Holzer in *Vogue*, Jane Holzer in *Life*, Jane Holzer in Andy Warhol's underground movies, Jane Holzer in the world of High Camp, Jane Holzer at the rock and roll, Jane Holzer is—well, how can one put it into words? Jane Holzer is This Year's Girl, at least, the New Celebrity, none of your old idea of sexpots, prima donnas, romantic tragediennes, she is the girl who knows . . . The Stones, East End vitality . . .

"Isabel!" says Jane Holzer in the small, high, excited voice of hers, her Baby Jane voice, "Hi, Isabel! Hi!"

Down the row, Isabel, Isabel Eberstadt, the beautiful socialite who is Ogden Nash's daughter, has just come in. She doesn't seem to hear Jane. But she is down the row a ways. Next to Jane is some fellow in a chocolate-colored Borsalino hat, and next there is Andy Warhol, the famous pop artist.

"Isabel!" says Jane.

"What?" says Isabel.

"Hi, Isabel!" says Jane.

"Hello, Jane," says Isabel.

"You want to go backstage?" says Jane, who has to speak across everybody.

"Backstage?" says Isabel.

"With the Stones!" says Jane. "I was backstage with the Stones. They look *divine!* You know what Mick said to me? He said, 'Koom on, love, give us a kiss!' "

But Isabel has turned away to say something to somebody.

"Isabel!" says Jane.

And all around, the little buds are batting around in the rococo gloom of the Academy of Arts Theater, trying to crash into good seats or just sit in the aisle near the stage, shrieking. And in the rear the Voice of Fifteen-year-old America cries out in a post-pubertal contralto, apropos of nothing, into the mouldering void: "Yaaaagh! Yuh dirty fag!"

Well, so what; Jane laughs. Then she leans over and says to the fellow in the Borsalino hat:

"Wait'll you see the Stones! They're so sexy! They're pure sex. They're *divine!* The Beatles, well, you know, Paul McCartney—*sweet* Paul McCartney. You know what I mean. He's such a *sweet person.* I mean, the Stones are *bitter*—" the words seem to spring from her lungs like some kind of wonderful lavender-yellow Charles Kingsley bubbles "—they're all from the working class, you know? the East End. Mick Jagger—well, it's all Mick. You know what they say about his lips? They say his lips are *diabolical.* That was in one of the magazines.

"When Mick comes into the Ad Lib in London—I mean, there's nothing like the Ad Lib in New York. You can go into the Ad Lib and everybody is there. They're all young, and they're taking over, it's like a whole revolution. I mean, it's *exciting,* they're all from the lower classes, East End-sort-of-thing. There's nobody exciting from the upper classes anymore, except for Nicole and Alec Londonderry, Alec is a British marquis, the Marquis of Londonderry, and, O.K., Nicole has to put in an appearance at this country fair or something, well, O.K., she does it, but that doesn't mean—you know what I mean? Alec is so—you should see the way he walks, I could just watch him walk—*Undoes-one-ship!* They're *young.* They're all young, it's a whole new thing. It's not the Beatles. Bailey says the Beatles are *passé,* because now everybody's mum pats the Beatles on the head. The Beatles are getting fat. The Beatles—well, John Lennon's still thin, but Paul McCartney is getting a big bottom. That's all right, but I don't particularly care for that. The Stones are thin. I mean, that's why they're beautiful, they're so thin. Mick Jagger—wait'll you see Mick."

Then the show begins. An electronic blast begins, electric guitars, electric bass, enormous speakers up there on a vast yellow-gray stage. Murray the K, the D. J. and M. C., O.K.?, comes out from the wings, doing a kind of twist soft shoe, wiggling around, a stocky chap, thirty-eight years old, wearing Italian pants and a Sun Valley snow lodge sweater and a Stingy Brim straw hat. Murray the K! Girls throw balls of paper at him, and as they are onto the stage, the stage lights explode off them and they look like falling balls of flame.

And, finally, the Stones, now—how can one express it? the Stones come on stage—

"Oh, God, Andy, aren't they *divine!*"

—and spread out over the stage, the five Rolling Stones, from England, who are modeled after the Beatles, only more lower-class-deformed. One, Brian Jones, has an enormous blonde Beatle bouffant.

"Oh, Andy, look at Mick! Isn't he *beautiful!* Mick! Mick!"

In the center of the stage a short thin boy with a sweat shirt on, the neck of the sweat shirt almost falling over his shoulders, they are so narrow, all surmounted by this . . . enormous head . . . with the hair puffing down over the forehead and ears, this boy has exceptional lips. He has two peculiarly gross and extraordinary red lips. They hang off his face like giblets. Slowly his eyes pour over the flaming bud horde soft as Karo syrup and then close and then the lips start spreading into the most languid, most confidential, the wettest, most labial, most concupiscent grin imaginable. Nirvana! The buds start shrieking, pawing toward the stage.

The girls have Their Experience. They stand up on their seats. They begin to ululate, even between songs. The looks on their faces! Rapturous agony! There, right up there, under the sulphur lights, that is *them.* God, they're right there! Mick Jagger takes the microphone with his tabescent hands and puts his huge head against it, opens his giblet lips and begins to sing . . . with the voice of a bull Negro. Bo Diddley. You movung boo meb bee-uhtul, bah-bee, oh vona breemb you' honey snurks oh crim pulzy yo' mim down, and, camping again, then turning toward the shrieking girls with his wet giblet lips dissolving . . .

And, occasionally, breaking through the ululation:

"Get off the stage, you finks!"

"Maybe we ought to scream," says Jane. Then she says to the fellow in the hat: "Tell me when it's five o'clock, will you, pussycat? I have to get dressed and go see Sam Spiegel." And then Baby Jane goes: "Eeeeeeeeeeeeeeeeeeeeeeee

eeeeeeeeeeeceeeeeeyes!" says Diana Vreeland, the editor of *Vogue.* "Jane Holzer is the most contemporary girl I know."

Jane Holzer at the rock and roll—

Jane Holzer in the underground movies—in Andy's studio, Andy Warhol, the famous Pop artist, experiencing the rare world of Jonas and Adolph Mekas, truth and culture in a new holy medium, underground movie-making on the lower East Side. And Jane is wearing a Jax shirt, strung like a Christmas tree with Diamonds, and they are making *Dracula,* or *Thirteen Beautiful Women* or *Soap Opera* or *Kiss*—in which Jane's lips . . . but how can one describe an underground movie? It *is* . . . avant-garde. "Andy calls everything super," says Jane. "I'm a super star, he's a super-director, we make super epics—and I mean, it's a completely new and natural way of acting. You can't imagine what really beautiful things can happen!"

Jane Holzer—with The New Artists, photographers like Jerry Schatzberg, David Bailey and Brian Duffy, and Nicky Haslam, the art director of *Show*. Bailey, Duffy and Haslam are English. Schatzberg says the photographers are the modern-day equivalents of the Impressionists in Paris around 1910, the men with a sense of New Art, the excitement of the salon, the excitement of the artistic style of life, while all the painters, the old artists, have moved uptown to West End Avenue and live in apartment buildings with Kwik-Fiks parquet floors and run around the corner to get a new cover for the ironing board before the stores close.

Jane in the world of High Camp—a world of thin young men in an environment, a decor, an atmosphere so—how can one say it?—so indefinably Yellow Book. Jane in the world of Teen Savage—Jane modeling here and there—wearing Jean Harlow dresses for *Life* and Italian fashions for *Vogue* and doing the most fabulous cover for Nicky at *Show*. David took the photograph, showing Jane barebacked wearing a little yacht cap and a pair of "World's Fair" sunglasses and holding an American flag in her teeth, so—so Beyond Pop Art, if you comprehend.

Jane Holzer at the LBJ Discotheque—where they were handing out aprons with a target design on them, and Jane Holzer put it on backward so that the target was behind and *then* did The Swim, a new dance.

Jane Holzer—well, there is no easy term available, Baby Jane has appeared constantly this year in just about every society and show business column in New York. The magazines have used her as a kind of combination of model, celebrity and socialite. And yet none of them have been able to do much more than, in effect, set down her name, Baby Jane Holzer, and surround it with a few asterisks and exploding stars, as if to say, well, here we have . . . What's Happening.

She is a socialite in the sense that she lives in a twelve-room apartment on Park Avenue with a wealthy husband, Leonard Holzer, heir to a real estate fortune, amid a lot of old Dutch and Flemish paintings, and she goes to a great many exciting parties. And yet she is not in Society the way the Good Book, the *Social Register*, thinks of Society, and the list of hostesses who have not thought of inviting Jane Holzer would be impressive. Furthermore, her stance is that she doesn't care, and she would rather be known as a friend of the Stones, anyway—and here she is at the April in Paris Ball, $150 per ticket, amid the heaving white and gold swag of the Astor Hotel ballroom, yelling to somebody: "If you aren't nice to me, I'll tell everybody you were here!"

Jane Holzer—the sum of it is glamor, of a sort very specific to New York. With her enormous corona of hair and her long straight nose, Jane Holzer can be quite beautiful, but she never comes on as A Beauty. "Some people look at my pictures and say I look very mature and sophisticated," Jane says. "Some people say I look like a child, you know, Baby Jane. And, I mean, I don't know what I look like, I guess it's just 1964 Jewish." She does not attempt to come on sexy. Her excitement is something else. It is almost pure excitement. It is the excitement of the New Style, the New Chic. The press watches Jane Holzer as if she were an exquisite piece of . . . radar. It is as if that entire ciliate corona of hers were spread out as an antenna for new waves of style. To the magazine editors, the newspaper columnists, the photographers and art directors, suddenly here is a single flamboyant girl who sums up everything new and chic in the way of fashion in the Girl of the Year.

How can one explain the Girl of the Year? The Girl of the Year is a symbolic figure the press has looked for annually in New York since World War I because of the breakdown of conventional High Society. The old establishment still holds forth, it still has its clubs, cotillions and coming-out balls, it is still basically Protestant and it still rules two enormously powerful areas of New York, finance and corporate law. But alongside it, all the while, there has existed a large and ever more dazzling society, Café Society it was called in the twenties and thirties, made up of people whose status rests not on property and ancestry but on various brilliant ephemera, show business, advertising, public relations, the arts, journalism or simply new money of various sorts, people with a great deal of ambition who have congregated in New York to satisfy it and who look for styles to symbolize it.

The establishment's own styles—well, for one thing they were too dull. And those understated clothes, dark woods, high ceilings, silver-smithery, respectable nannies, and so forth and so on. For centuries their kind of power created styles—Palladian buildings, starched cravats—but with the thickening democratic façade of American life, it has degenerated to various esoteric understatements, often cryptic—Topsiders instead of tennis sneakers, calling cards with "Mr." preceding the name, the right fork.

The magazines and newspapers began looking for heroines to symbolize the Other Society, Café Society, or whatever it should be called. At first, in the twenties, they chose the more flamboyant debutantes, girls with social credentials who also moved in Café Society. But the Other Society's styles began to shift and change at a madder and madder rate, and the Flaming Deb idea no longer worked. The last of the Flaming Debs, the kind of Deb who made The Cover of *Life*, was Brenda Frazier, and Brenda Frazier and Brenda Frazierism went out with the thirties. More recently the Girl of the Year has had to be more and more exotic . . . and extraordinary. Christina Paolozzi! Her exploits! Christina Paolozzi threw a twenty-first birthday party for herself at a Puerto Rican pachanga palace, the Palladium, and after that the spinning got faster and faster until with one last grand centripetal gesture she appeared in the nude, face on, in *Harper's Bazaar*. Some became Girls of the Year because their fame suddenly shed a light on their style of life, and their style of life could be easily exhibited, such as Jackie Kennedy and Barbra Streisand.

But Baby Jane Holzer is a purer manifestation. Her style of life has created her fame—rock and roll, underground movies, decaying lofts, models, photographers, Living Pop Art, the twist, the frug, the mashed potatoes, stretch pants, pre-Raphaelite hair, Le Style Camp. All of it has a common denominator. Once it was power that created high style. But now high styles come from low places, from people who have no power, who slink away from it, in fact, who are marginal, who carve out worlds for themselves in the nether depths, in tainted "undergrounds." The Rolling Stones, like rock and roll itself and the twist—they come out of the netherworld of modern teenage life, out of what was for years the marginal outcast corner of the world of art, photography, populated by poor boys, pretenders. "Underground" movies—a mixture of camp and Artistic Alienation, with Jonas Mekas crying out like some foggy echo from Harold Stearn's last boat for Le Havre in 1921: "You filthy bourgeois pseudo-culturati! You say you love art—then why don't you give us money to buy the films to make our masterpieces and stop blubbering about the naked asses we show?—you mucky pseuds." Teen-agers, bohos, camp culturati, photographers—they have won by default, because, after all, they *do* create styles. And now the Other Society goes to them for styles, like the decadenti of another age going down to the wharves in Rio to find those raw-vital devils, damn their potent hides, those proles, doing the tango. Yes! Oh my God, those raw-vital proles!

The ice floe is breaking, and can't one see, as Jane Holzer sees, that all these people—well, they *feel,* they are alive, and what does it mean simply to be sitting up in her Park Avenue apartment in the room with two Rubenses on the wall, worth half a million dollars, if they are firmly authenticated? It means almost nothing. One doesn't feel it.

Jane has on a "Poor" sweater, clinging to the ribs, a new fashion, with short sleeves. Her hair is up in rollers. She is wearing tight slacks. Her hips are very small. She has a boyish body. She has thin arms and long, long fingers. She sits twisted about on a couch, up in her apartment on Park Avenue, talking on the telephone.

"Oh, I know what you mean," she says, "but, I mean, couldn't you wait just two weeks? I'm expecting something to jell, it's a movie, and then you'd have a real story. You know what I mean? I mean you would have something to write about and not just Baby Jane sitting up in her Park Avenue apartment with her gotrocks. You know what I mean? . . . well, all right, but I think you'll have more of a story—. . . well, all right . . . bye, pussycat."

Then she hangs up and swings around and says, "That makes me mad. That was————. He wants to do a story about me and do you know what he told me? 'We want to do a story about you,' he told me, 'because you're very big this year.' Do you know what that made me feel like? That made me feel like, All right, Baby Jane, we'll let you play this year, so get out there and dance, but next year, well, it's all over for you next year, Baby Jane. I mean, ————! You know? I mean, I felt like telling him, 'Well, pussycat, you're the Editor of the Minute, and you know what? Your minute's up.' "

The thought leaves Jane looking excited but worried. Usually she looks excited about things but open, happy, her eyes wide open and taking it all in. Now she looks worried, as if the world could be such a simple and exhilarating place if there weren't so many old and arteriosclerotic people around to muck it up. There are two dogs on the floor at her feet, a toy poodle and a Yorkshire terrier, who rise up from time to time in some kind of secret needle-toothed fury, barking coloratura.

"Oh, ————," says Jane, and then, "You know, if you have anything at all, there are so many bitchy people just *waiting* to carve you up. I mean, I went to the opening of the Met and I wore a white mink coat, and do you know what a woman did? A woman called up a columnist and said, 'Ha, ha, Baby Jane rented that coat she went to the Met in. Baby Jane rents her clothes.' That's how bitchy they are. Well, that coat happens to be a coat my mother gave me two years ago when I was married. I mean, I don't care if somebody thinks I rent clothes. O.K. ————! Who cares?"

Inez, the maid, brings in lunch on a tray, one rare hamburger, one cheeseburger and a glass of tomato juice. Jane tastes the tomato juice.

"Oh, ————!" she says. "It's diet."

The Girl of the Year. It is as though nobody wants to give anyone credit for anything. They're only a *phenomenon*. Well, Jane Holzer did a great deal of modeling before she got married and still models, for that matter, and now some very wonderful things may be about to happen in the movies. Some of it, well, she cannot go into it exactly, because it is at that precarious stage— you know? But she has one of the best managers, a woman who manages the McGuire Sisters. And there has been talk about Baby Jane for *Who's Afraid of Virginia Woolf,* the movie, and *Candy*—

"Well, I haven't heard anything about it—but I'd *love* to play Candy."

And this afternoon, later on, she is going over to see Sam Spiegel, the producer.

"He's wonderful. He's, you know, sort of advising me on things at this point."

And somewhere out there in the apartment the dogs are loose in a midget coloratura rage amid patina-green walls and paintings by old Lowland masters. There is a great atmosphere in the apartment, an atmosphere of patina-green, faded plush and the ashy light of Park Avenue reflecting on the great black and umber slicks of the paintings. All that stretches on for twelve rooms. The apartment belongs to the Holzers, who have built a lot of New York's new apartment houses. Jane's husband, Leonard, is a slim, good-looking young man. He went to Princeton. He and Jane were married two years ago. Jane came from Florida, where her father, Carl Brookenfeld, also made a lot of money in real estate. But in a way they were from New York, too, because they were always coming to New York and her father had a place here. There was something so stimulating, so flamboyant, about New York, you know? Fine men with anointed blue jowls combed their hair straight back and had their shirts made at Sulka's or Nica-Rattner's, and their wives had copper-gold hair, real chignons and things, and heavy apricot voices that said the funniest things—"Honey, I've got news for you, you're crazy!"—things like that, and they went to El Morocco. Jane went to Cherry Lawn School in Darien, Connecticut. It was a progressive school.

And then she went to Finch Junior College:

"Oh, that was just ghastly. I wanted to flunk out and go to work. If you miss too many classes, they campus you, if you have a messy room, they campus you, they were always campusing me, and I always sneaked out. The last spring term I didn't spend one night there. I was supposed to be campused and I'd be out dancing at El Morocco. I didn't take my exams because I wanted to flunk out, but do you know what they did? They just said I was out, period. I didn't care about that, because I wanted to flunk out and go to work anyway—but the way they did it. I have a lot of good paintings to give away, and it's too bad, they're not getting any. They were not *educators*. They could have at least kept the door open. They could have said, 'You're not ready to be a serious student, but when you decide to settle down and be a serious student, the door will be open.' I mean, I had already paid for the whole term, they *had* the money. I always wanted to go there and tell them, well, ha ha, too bad, you're not getting any of the paintings. So henceforth, Princeton, which was super-marvelous, will get all the paintings."

Jane's spirits pick up over that. Princeton! Well, Jane left Finch and then she did quite a bit of modeling. Then she married Lennie, and she still did some modeling, but the real break—well the whole *thing* started in summer in London, the summer of 1963.

"Bailey is fantastic," says Jane. "Bailey created four girls that summer. He created Jean Shrimpton, he created me, he created Angela Howard and Susan Murray. There's no photographer like that in America. Avedon hasn't done that for a girl, Penn hasn't, and Bailey created four girls in one summer. He did some pictures of me for the English *Vogue*, and that was all it took."

But how does one really explain about the Stones, about Bailey, Shrimp and Mick—well, it's not so much what they *do*, that's such an old idea, what people *do*—it's what they *are*, it's a revolution, and it's the kids from the East End, Cockneys, if you want, who are making it.

"I mean today Drexel Duke sits next to Weinstein, and why shouldn't he? They both made their money the same way, you know? The furniture king sits next to the catsup king, and why shouldn't he-sort-of-thing. I mean, that's the way it was at the opening of the Met. A friend of mine was going to write an article about it.

"I mean, we don't lie to ourselves. Our mothers taught us to be pure and you'll fall in love and get married and stay in love with one man all your life.

O.K. But we know it doesn't happen that way and we don't lie to ourselves about it. Maybe you won't ever find anybody you love. Or maybe you find somebody you love four minutes, maybe ten minutes. But I mean, why lie to yourself? We know we're not going to love one man all our lives. Maybe it's the Bomb—we know it could all be over tomorrow, so why try to fool yourself today. Shrimp was talking about that last night. She's here now, she'll be at the party tonight—"

The two dogs, the toy poodle and the Yorkshire terrier, are yapping, in the patina-green. Inez is looking for something besides diet. The two Rubenses hang up on the walls. A couple of horns come up through the ashy light of Park Avenue. The high wind of East End London is in the air— whhhooooooooo

oooooooooooooosh! Baby Jane blows out all the candles. It is her twenty-fourth birthday. She and everybody, Shrimp, Nicky, Jerry, everybody but Bailey, who is off in Egypt or something, they are all up in Jerry Schatzberg's . . . *pad* . . . his lavish apartment at 333 Park Avenue South, up above his studio. There is a skylight. The cook brings out the cake and Jane blows out the candles. Twenty-four! Jerry and Nicky are giving a huge party, a dance, in honor of the Stones, and already the people are coming into the studio downstairs. But it is also Jane's birthday. She is wearing a black velvet jump suit by Luis Estevez, the designer. It has huge bell-bottom pants. She puts her legs together . . . it looks like an evening dress. But she can also spread them apart, like so, and strike very Jane-like poses. This is like the Upper Room or something. Downstairs, they'll all coming in for the party, all those people one sees at parties, everybody who goes to the parties in New York, but up here it is like a tableau, like a tableau of . . . Us. Shrimp is sitting there with her glorious pout and her textured white stockings, Barbara Steele, who was so terrific in 8½, with thin black lips and wrought-iron eyelashes. Nicky Haslam is there with his Byron shirt on and his tiger skin vest and blue jeans and boots. Jerry is there with his hair flowing back in curls. Lennie, Jane's husband, is there in a British suit and a dark blue shirt he bought on 42nd Street for this party, because this is a party for the Rolling Stones. The Stones are not here yet, but here in the upper room are Goldie and the Gingerbreads, four girls in gold lamé tights who will play the rock and roll for the party. Nicky discovered them at the Wagon Wheel. Gold lamé, can you imagine? Goldie, the leader, is a young girl with a husky voice and nice kind of slightly thick—you know—glorious sort of *East End* features, only she is from New York—ah, the delicacy of mirror grossness, unabashed. The Stones' music is playing over the hi-fi.

Finally the Stones come in, in blue jeans, sweat shirts, the usual, and people get up and Mick Jagger comes in with his mouth open and his eyes down, faintly weary with success, and everybody goes downstairs to the studio, where people are now piling in, hundreds of them. Goldie and the Gingerbreads are on a stand at one end of the studio, all electric, electric guitars, electric bass, drums, loudspeakers, and a couple of spotlights exploding off the gold lamé. *Baby baby baby where did our love go.* The music suddenly fills up the room like a giant egg slicer. Sally Kirkland, Jr., a young actress, is out on the studio floor in a leopard print dress with her vast mane flying, doing the frug with Jerry Schatzberg. And then the other Girl of the Year, Caterine Milinaire, is out there in a black dress, and then Baby Jane is out there with her incredible mane and her Luis Estevez jump suit, frugging, and then everybody is out there. Suddenly it is very odd. Suddenly everybody is out there in the gloaming, bobbing up and down with the music plugged into *Baby baby baby.* The whole floor of the studio begins to bounce up and down, like a trampoline, the whole floor, some people are afraid and edge off to the side, but most keep bobbing in the gloaming, and—pow!—glasses begin to hit the floor, but every one keeps bouncing up and down, crushing the glass underfoot, while the brown whiskey slicks around. So many heads bobbing, so many bodies jiggling, so many giblets jiggling, so much anointed flesh shaking and jiggling this way and that, so many faces one wanted so desperately to see, and here they are, red the color of dried peppers in the gloaming, bouncing up and down with just a few fights, wrenching in the gloaming, until 5 A.M.—gleeeang—Goldie pulls all the electric cords out and the studio is suddenly just a dim ochre studio with broken glass all over the floor, crushed underfoot, and the sweet high smell of brown whiskey rising from the floor.

Monday's papers will record it as the Mods and Rockers Ball, as the Party of the Year, but that is Monday, a long way off. So they all decide they should go to the Brasserie. It is the only place in town where anybody would still be around. So they all get into cabs and go up to the Brasserie, up on 53rd Street between Park and Lexington. The Brasserie is the right place, all right. The Brasserie has a great entrance, elevated over the tables like a fashion show almost. There are, what?, 35 people in the Brasserie. They all look up, and as the first salmon light of dawn comes through the front window, here come . . . four teen-age girls in gold lamé tights, and a chap in a tiger skin vest and blue jeans and a gentleman in an English suit who seems to be wearing a 42nd Street hood shirt and a fellow in a sweater who has flowing curly hair . . . and then, a girl with an incredible mane, a vast tawny corona, wearing a black velvet jump suit. One never knows who is in the Brasserie at this hour—but are there any so dead in here that they do not get the point? Girl of the Year? Listen, they will *never* forget.

Los Angeles Notebook

JOAN DIDION

∞

One thing—maybe the only thing—Joan Didion and Frank Sinatra have in common is The Voice: you could never hear a phrase of Sinatra's or read a line of Didion's and think it was the creation of anybody else. In Didion's case, her tone is a meticulously crafted irony that suggests a world of significance and hurt below the chiseled surface of her words. In the opinion of many critics, it has always been shown to better effect in her journalism than her novels, in part because irony is less subject to abuse when accompanied by facts rather than by invention.

"Los Angeles Notebook" was published in Didion's 1968 collection, *Slouching Towards Bethlehem*. (Her subsequent nonfiction works have been *The White Album, Salvador* and *After Henry*.) The book's title is a reference to Yeats's "The Second Coming," and almost all the pieces in the book, Didion writes in a preface, were written out of a sense of Yeatsian social disintegration and decay: that "Things fall apart; the center cannot hold." In "Los Angeles Notebook," literary form itself disintegrates. Didion gives us a series of short takes rather than a "well-made" article because the latter would imply a cohesive and meaningful world that no longer seems to exist.

—B. Y.

∞

There is something uneasy in the Los Angeles air this afternoon, some unnatural stillness, some tension. What it means is that tonight a Santa Ana will begin to blow, a hot wind from the northeast whining down through the Cajon and San Gorgonio Passes, blowing up sandstorms out along Route 66, drying the hills and the nerves to the flash point. For a few days now we will see smoke back in the canyons, and hear sirens in the night. I have neither heard nor read that a Santa Ana is due, but I know it, and almost everyone I have seen today knows it too. We know it because we feel it. The baby frets. The maid sulks. I rekindle a waning argument with the telephone company, then cut my losses and lie down, given over to whatever it is in the air. To live with the Santa Ana is to accept, consciously or unconsciously, a deeply mechanistic view of human behavior.

I recall being told, when I first moved to Los Angeles and was living on an isolated beach, that the Indians would throw themselves into the sea when the bad wind blew. I could see why. The Pacific turned ominously glossy during a Santa Ana period, and one woke in the night troubled not only by the peacocks screaming in the olive trees but by the eerie absence of surf. The heat was surreal. The sky had a yellow cast, the kind of light sometimes called "earthquake weather." My only neighbor would not come out of her house for days, and there were no lights at night, and her husband roamed the place with a machete. One day he would tell me that he had heard a trespasser, the next a rattlesnake.

"On nights like that," Raymond Chandler once wrote about the Santa Ana, "every booze party ends in a fight. Meek little wives feel the edge of the carving knife and study their husbands' necks. Anything can happen." That was the kind of wind it was. I did not know then that there was any basis for the effect it had on all of us, but it turns out to be another of those cases in which science bears out folk wisdom. The Santa Ana, which is named for one of the canyons it rushes through, is a *foehn* wind, like the *foehn* of Austria and Switzerland and the *hamsin* of Israel. There are a number of persistent malevolent winds, perhaps the best known of which are the mistral of France and the Mediterranean sirocco, but a *foehn* wind has distinct characteristics: it occurs on the leeward slope of a mountain range and, although the air begins as a cold mass, it is warmed as it comes down the mountain and appears finally as a hot dry wind. Whenever and wherever a *foehn* blows, doctors hear about headaches and nausea and allergies, about "nervousness," about "depression." In Los Angeles some teachers do not attempt to conduct formal classes during a Santa Ana, because the children become unmanageable. In Switzerland the suicide rate goes up during the *foehn,* and in the courts of some Swiss cantons the wind is considered a mitigating circumstance for crime. Surgeons are said to watch the wind, because blood does not clot normally during a *foehn*. A few years ago an Israeli physicist discovered that not only during such winds, but for the ten or twelve hours which precede them, the air carries an unusually high ratio of positive to negative ions. No one seems to know exactly why that should be; some talk about friction and others suggest solar disturbances. In any case the positive ions are there, and what an excess of positive ions does, in the simplest terms, is make people unhappy. One cannot get much more mechanistic than that.

Easterners commonly complain that there is no "weather" at all in Southern California, that the days and the seasons slip by relentlessly, numbingly bland. That is quite misleading. In fact the climate is characterized by infrequent but violent extremes: two periods of torrential subtropical rains which continue for weeks and wash out the hills and send subdivisions sliding toward the sea; about twenty scattered days a year of the Santa Ana, which, with its incendiary dryness, invariably means fire. At the first prediction of a Santa Ana, the Forest Service flies men and equipment from northern California into the southern forests, and the Los Angeles Fire Department cancels its ordinary non-firefighting routines. The Santa Ana caused Malibu to burn the way it did in 1956, and Bel Air in 1961, and Santa Barbara in 1964. In the winter of 1966–67 eleven men were killed fighting a Santa Ana fire that spread through the San Gabriel Mountains.

Just to watch the front-page news out of Los Angeles during a Santa Ana is to get very close to what it is about the place. The longest single Santa Ana period in recent years was in 1957, and it lasted not the usual three or four days but fourteen days, from November 21 until December 4. On the first day 25,000 acres of the San Gabriel Mountains were burning, with gusts reaching 100 miles an hour. In town, the wind reached Force 12, or hurricane force, on the Beaufort Scale; oil derricks were toppled and people ordered off the downtown streets to avoid injury from flying objects. On November 22 the fire in the San Gabriels was out of control. On November 24 six people were killed in automobile accidents, and by the end of the week the Los Angeles *Times* was keeping a box score of traffic deaths. On November 26 a prominent Pasadena attorney, depressed about money, shot and killed his wife, their two sons, and himself. On November 27 a South Gate divorcée, twenty-two, was murdered and thrown from a moving car. On November 30 the San Gabriel fire was still out of control, and the wind in town was blowing eighty miles an hour. On the first day of December four people died violently, and on the third the wind began to break.

It is hard for people who have not lived in Los Angeles to realize how radically the Santa Ana figures in the local imagination. The city burning is Los Angeles's deepest image of itself: Nathanael West perceived that, in *The Day of the Locust*; and at the time of the 1965 Watts riots what struck the imagination most indelibly were the fires. For days one could drive the Harbor Freeway and see the city on fire, just as we had always known it would be in the end. Los Angeles weather is the weather of catastrophe, of apocalypse, and, just as the reliably long and bitter winters of New England determine the way life is lived there, so the violence and the unpredictability of the Santa Ana affect the entire quality of life in Los Angeles, accentuate its impermanence, its unreliability. The wind shows us how close to the edge we are.

2

"Here's why I'm on the beeper, Ron," said the telephone voice on the all-night radio show. "I just want to say that this *Sex for the Secretary* creature—

whatever her name is—certainly isn't contributing anything to the morals in this country. It's pathetic. Statistics *show*."

"It's *Sex and the Office,* honey," the disc jockey said. "That's the title. By Helen Gurley Brown. Statistics show what?"

"I haven't got them right here at my fingertips, naturally. But they *show*."

"I'd be interested in hearing them. Be constructive, you Night Owls."

"All right, let's take *one* statistic," the voice said, truculent now. "Maybe I haven't read the book, but what's this business she recommends about *going out with married men for lunch?*"

So it went, from midnight until 5 A.M., interrupted by records and by occasional calls debating whether or not a rattlesnake can swim. Misinformation about rattlesnakes is a leitmotiv of the insomniac imagination in Los Angeles. Toward 2 A.M. a man from "out Tarzana way" called to protest. "The Night Owls who called earlier must have been thinking about, uh, *The Man in the Gray Flannel Suit* or some other book," he said, "because Helen's one of the few authors trying to tell us what's really going *on*. Hefner's another, and he's also controversial, working in, uh, another area."

An old man, after testifying that he "personally" had seen a swimming rattlesnake, in the Delta-Mendota Canal, urged "moderation" on the Helen Gurley Brown question. "We shouldn't get on the beeper to call things pornographic before we've read them," he complained, pronouncing it porn-ee-oh-graphic. "I say, get the book. Give it a chance." The original *provocateur* called back to agree that she would get the book. "And then I'll burn it," she added.

"Book burner, eh?" laughed the disc jockey good-naturedly.

"I wish they still burned witches," she hissed.

3

It is three o'clock on a Sunday afternoon and 105° and the air so thick with smog that the dusty palm trees loom up with a sudden and rather attractive mystery. I have been playing in the sprinklers with the baby and I get in the car and go to Ralph's Market on the corner of Sunset and Fuller wearing an old bikini bathing suit. That is not a very good thing to wear to the market but neither is it, at Ralph's on the corner of Sunset and Fuller, an unusual costume. Nonetheless a large woman in a cotton muumuu jams her cart into mine at the butcher counter. *"What a thing to wear to the market,"* she says in a loud but strangled voice. Everyone looks the other way and I study a plastic package of rib lamb chops and she repeats it. She follows me all over the store, to the Junior Foods, to the Dairy Products, to the Mexican Delicacies, jamming my cart whenever she can. Her husband plucks at her sleeve. As I leave the check-out counter she raises her voice one last time: *"What a thing to wear to Ralph's,"* she says.

4

A party at someone's house in Beverly Hills: a pink tent, two orchestras, a couple of French Communist directors in Cardin evening jackets, chili and hamburgers from Chasen's. The wife of an English actor sits at a table alone; she visits California rarely although her husband works here a good deal. An American who knows her slightly comes over to the table.

"Marvelous to see you here," he says.

"Is it," she says.

"How long have you been here?"

"Too long."

She takes a fresh drink from a passing waiter and smiles at her husband, who is dancing.

The American tries again. He mentions her husband.

"I hear he's marvelous in this picture."

She looks at the American for the first time. When she finally speaks she enunciates every word very clearly. "He . . . is . . . also . . . a . . . fag," she says pleasantly.

5

The oral history of Los Angeles is written in piano bars. "Moon River," the piano player always plays, and "Mountain Greenery." "There's a Small Hotel" and "This Is Not the First Time." People talk to each other, tell each other about their first wives and last husbands. "Stay funny," they tell each other, and "This is to die over." A construction man talks to an unemployed screenwriter who is celebrating, alone, his tenth wedding anniversary. The construction man is on a job in Montecito: "Up in Montecito," he says, "they got one square mile with 135 millionaires."

"Putrescence," the writer says.

"That's all you got to say about it?"

"Don't read me wrong, I think Santa Barbara's one of the most—Christ, *the* most—beautiful places in the world, but it's a beautiful place that contains a . . . *putrescence*. They just live on their putrescent millions."

"So give me putrescent."

"No, no," the writer says. "I just happen to think millionaires have some sort of lacking in their . . . in their elasticity."

A drunk requests "The Sweetheart of Sigma Chi." The piano player says he doesn't know it. "Where'd you learn to play the piano?" the drunk asks. "I got two degrees," the piano player says. "One in musical education." I go to a coin telephone and call a friend in New York. "Where are you?" he says. "In a piano bar in Encino," I say. "Why?" he says. "Why not," I say.

From *The Pine Barrens*

JOHN MCPHEE

∞

John McPhee's home in Princeton sits only thirty miles from the Pine Barrens, a sandy forest covering much of central and southern New Jersey— "down the coast from the outskirts of Asbury Park to the Cape May peninsula, and inland more than halfway across the state." McPhee's 1968 book about the Barrens, portraying its rough beauty and the distinctive culture of its inhabitants, was the first of his many ventures into environmental journalism. To report about nature, and about human efforts to preserve or control it, McPhee draws on exhaustive research—and on innate powers of description, lucid exposition, and easy rapport with his subjects.

McPhee grew up in Princeton, attended the university, and has been teaching there for over twenty years. His famous course, "The Literature of Fact," is described in the Princeton catalogue as "the application of creative writing techniques to journalism and other forms of nonfiction." Among recent students have been such successful writers as David Remnick (*Lenin's Tomb*) and Richard Preston (*The Hot Zone*). According to Remnick, McPhee "has been for dozens and dozens of nonfiction writers what Robert Lowell used to be for poets and poet wannabes of a certain age: the model."

In 1965 McPhee published a profile of Princeton basketball star Bill Bradley in *The New Yorker*. He has been a staff writer for the magazine ever since, delighting readers with his elegant and playful style, wide curiosity, and storytelling gifts. All are evident in *The Pine Barrens*. McPhee's ear for speech-rhythms and eye for detail imbue this account with a sense of people as well as a sense of place.

—K. K.

∞

Fred Brown's house is on an unpaved road that curves along the edge of a wide cranberry bog. What attracted me to it was the pump that stands in his yard. It was something of a wonder that I noticed the pump, because there were, among other things, eight automobiles in the yard, two of them on their sides and one of them upside down, all ten years old or older. Around the cars were old refrigerators, vacuum cleaners, partly dismantled radios, cathode-ray tubes, a short wooden ski, a large wooden mallet, dozens of cranberry picker's boxes, many tires, an orange crate dated 1946, a cord or so of firewood, mandolins, engine heads, and maybe a thousand other things. The house itself, two stories high, was covered with tarpaper that was peeling away in some places, revealing its original shingles, made of Atlantic white cedar from the stream courses of the surrounding forest. I called out to ask if anyone was home, and a voice inside called back, "Come in. Come in. Come on the hell in."

I walked through a vestibule that had a dirt floor, stepped up into a kitchen, and went on into another room that had several overstuffed chairs in it and a porcelain-topped table, where Fred Brown was seated, eating a pork chop. He was dressed in a white sleeveless shirt, ankle-top shoes, and undershorts. He gave me a cheerful greeting and, without asking why I had come or what I wanted, picked up a pair of khaki trousers that had been tossed onto one of the overstuffed chairs and asked me to sit down. He set the trousers on another chair, and he apologized for being in the middle of his breakfast, explaining that he seldom drank much but the night before he had had a few drinks and this had caused his day to start slowly. "I don't know what's the matter with me, but there's got to be something the matter with me, because drink don't agree with me anymore," he said. He had a raw onion in one hand, and while he talked he shaved slices from the onion and ate them between bites of the chop. He was a muscular and well-built man, with short, bristly white hair, and he had bright, fast-moving eyes in a wide-open face. His legs were trim and strong, with large muscles in the calves. I guessed that he was about sixty, and for a man of sixty he seemed to be in remarkably good shape. He was actually seventy-nine. "My rule is: Never eat except when you're hungry," he said, and he ate another slice of the onion.

In a straight-backed chair near the doorway to the kitchen sat a young man with long black hair, who wore a visored red leather cap that had darkened with age. His shirt was coarse-woven and had eyelets down a V neck that was laced with a thong. His trousers were made of canvas, and he was wearing gum boots. His arms were folded, his legs were stretched out, he had one ankle over the other, and as he sat there he appeared to be sighting carefully past his feet, as if his toes were the outer frame of a gunsight and he could see some sort of target in the floor. When I had entered, I had said hello to him, and he had nodded without looking up. He had a long, straight nose and high cheekbones, in a deeply tanned face that was, somehow, gaunt. I had no idea whether he was shy or hostile. Eventually, when I came to know him, I found him to be as shy a person as I have ever had a chance to know. His name is Bill Wasovwich, and he lives alone in a cabin about half a mile from Fred. First his father, then his mother left him when he was a young boy, and he grew up depending on the help of various people in the pines. One of them, a cranberry grower, employs him and has given him some acreage, in which Bill is building a small cranberry bog of his own, "turfing it out" by hand. When he is not working in the bogs, he goes roaming, as he puts it, setting out cross-country on long, looping journeys, hiking about thirty miles in a typical day, in search of what he calls "events"—surprising a buck, or a gray fox, or perhaps a poacher or a man with a still. Almost no one who is not native to the pines could do this, for the woods have an undulating sameness, and the understory—huckleberries, sheep laurel, sweet fern, high-bush blueberry—is often so dense that a wanderer can walk in a fairly tight circle and think that he is moving in a straight line. State forest rangers spend a good part of their time finding hikers and hunters, some of whom have vanished for days. In his long, pathless journeys, Bill always emerges from the woods near his cabin—and about when he plans to. In the fall, when thousands of hunters come into the pines, he sometimes works as a guide. In the evenings, or in the daytime when he is not working or roaming, he goes to Fred Brown's house and sits there for hours. The old man is a widower whose seven children are long since gone from Hog Wallow, and he is as expansively talkative and worldly as the young one is withdrawn and wild. Although there are fifty-three years between their ages, it is obviously fortunate for each of them to be the other's neighbor.

That first morning, while Bill went on looking at his outstretched toes, Fred got up from the table, put on his pants, and said he was going to cook me a pork chop, because I looked hungry and ought to eat something. It was about noon, and I was even hungrier than I may have looked, so I gratefully accepted his offer, which was a considerable one. There are two or three small general stores in the pines, but for anything as fragile as a fresh pork chop it is necessary to make a round trip from Fred's place of about fifty miles. Fred went into the kitchen and dropped a chop into a frying pan that was crackling with hot grease. He has a fairly new four-burner stove that uses bottled gas. He keeps water in a large bowl on a table in the kitchen and ladles some when he wants it. While he cooked the meat, he looked out a window through a stand of pitch pines and into the cranberry bog. "I saw a big buck out here last night with velvet on his horns," he said. "Them horns is soft when they're in velvet." On a nail high on one wall of the room that Bill and I were sitting in was a large meat cleaver. Next to it was a billy club. The wall itself was papered in a flower pattern, and the wallpaper continued out across the ceiling and down the three other walls, lending the room something of the appearance of the inside of a gift box. In some parts of the ceiling, the paper had come loose. "I didn't paper this year," Fred said. "For the last couple months, I've had sinus." The floor was covered with old rugs. They had been put down in random pieces, and in some places as many as six layers were stacked up. In winter, when the temperature approaches zero, the worst cold comes through the floor. The only source of heat in the house is a wood-burning stove in the main room. There were seven calendars on the walls, all current and none with pictures of nudes. Fading into pastel on one wall was a rotogravure photograph of President and Mrs. Eisenhower. A framed poem read:

> God hath not promised
> Sun without rain
> Joy without sorrow
> Peace without pain.

Noticing my interest in all this, Fred reached into a drawer and showed me what appeared to be a postcard. On it was a photograph of a woman, and Fred said with a straight face that she was his present girl, adding that he meets her regularly under a juniper tree on a road farther south in the pines. The woman, whose appearance suggested strongly that she had never been within a great many miles of the Pine Barrens, was wearing nothing at all.

I asked Fred what all those cars were doing in his yard, and he said that one of them was in running condition and the rest were its predecessors. The working vehicle was a 1956 Mercury. Each of the seven others had at one time or another been his best car, and each, in turn, had lain down like a sick animal and had died right there in the yard, unless it had been towed home after a mishap elsewhere in the pines. Fred recited, with affection, the history of each car. Of one old Ford, for example, he said, "I upset that up to Speedwell in the creek." And of an even older car, a station wagon, he said, "I busted that one up in the snow. I met a car on a little hill, and hit the brake, and hit a tree." One of the cars had met its end at a narrow bridge about four miles from Hog Wallow, where Fred had hit a state trooper, head on.

The pork was delicious and almost crisp. Fred gave me a potato with it, and a pitcher of melted grease from the frying pan to pour over the potato. He also handed me a loaf of bread and a dish of margarine, saying, "Here's your bread. You can have one piece or two. Whatever you want."

Fred apologized for not having a phone, after I asked where I would have to go to make a call, later on. He said, "I don't have no phone because I don't have no electric. If I had electric, I would have had a phone in here a long time ago." He uses a kerosene lamp, a propane lamp, and two flashlights.

He asked where I was going, and I said that I had no particular destination, explaining that I was in the pines because I found it hard to believe that so much unbroken forest could still exist so near the big Eastern cities, and I wanted to see it while it was still there. "Is that so?" he said, three times. Like many people in the pines, he often says things three times. "Is that so? Is *that* so?"

I asked him what he thought of a plan that has been developed by Burlington and Ocean Counties to create a supersonic jetport in the pines, connected by a spur of the Garden State Parkway to a new city of two hundred and fifty thousand people, also in the pines.

"They've been talking about that for three years, and they've never give up," Fred said.

"It'd be the end of these woods," Bill said. This was the first time I heard Bill speak. I had been there for an hour, and he had not said a word. Without looking up, he said again, "It'd be the end of these woods, I can tell you that."

Fred said, "They could build ten jetports around me. I wouldn't give a damn."

"You ain't going to be around very long," Bill said to him. "It would be the end of these woods."

Fred took that as a fact, and not as an insult. "Yes, it would be the end of these woods," he said. "But there'd be people here you could do business with."

Bill said, "There ain't no place like this left in the country, I don't believe—and I travelled around a little bit, too."

Eventually, I made the request I had intended to make when I walked in the door. "Could I have some water?" I said to Fred. "I have a jerry can and I'd like to fill it at the pump."

"Hell, yes," he said. "That isn't my water. That's God's water. That's God's water. That right, Bill?"

"I *guess* so," Bill said, without looking up. "It's good water, I can tell you that."

"That's God's water," Fred said again. "Take all you want."

Outside, on the pump housing, was a bright-blue coffee tin full of priming water. I primed the pump and, before filling the jerry can, cupped my hands and drank. The water of the Pine Barrens is soft and pure, and there is so much of it that, like the forest above it, it is an incongruity in place and time. In the sand under the pines is a natural reservoir of pure water that, in volume, is the equivalent of a lake seventy-five feet deep with a surface of a thousand square miles. If all the impounding reservoirs, storage reservoirs, and distribution reservoirs in the New York City water system were filled to capacity—from Neversink and Schoharie to the Croton basin and Central Park—the Pine Barrens aquifer would still contain thirty times as much water. So little of this water is used that it can be said to be untapped. Its constant temperature is fifty-four degrees, and, in the language of a hydrological report on the Pine Barrens prepared in 1966 for the United States Geological Survey, "it can be expected to be bacterially sterile, odorless, clear; its chemical purity approaches that of uncontaminated rain-water or melted glacier ice."

In the United States as a whole, only about thirty per cent of the rainfall gets into the ground; the rest is lost to surface runoff or to evaporation, transpiration from leaves, and similar interceptors. In the Pine Barrens, fully half of all precipitation makes its way into the great aquifer, for, as the government report put it, "the loose, sandy soil can imbibe as much as six inches of water per hour." The Pine Barrens rank as one of the greatest natural recharging areas in the world. Thus, the City of New York, say, could take all its daily water requirements out of the pines without fear of diminishing the basic supply. New Jersey could sell the Pine Barrens' "annual ground-water discharge"—the part that at the moment is running off into the Atlantic Ocean—for about two hundred million dollars a year. However, New Jersey does not sell a drop, in part because the state has its own future needs to consider. In the eighteen-seventies, Joseph Wharton, the Philadelphia mineralogist and financier for whom the Wharton School of Finance and Commerce of the University of Pennsylvania is named, recognized the enormous potentiality of the Pine Barrens as a source of water for Philadelphia, and between 1876 and 1890 he gradually acquired nearly a hundred thousand contiguous acres of Pine Barrens land. Wharton's plan called for thirty-three shallow reservoirs in the pines, connected by a network of canals to one stupendous reservoir in Camden, from which an aqueduct would go under the Delaware River and into Philadelphia, where the pure waters of New Jersey would emerge from every tap, replacing a water supply that has been described as "dirty, bacterial soup." Wharton's plan was never executed, mainly because the New Jersey legislature drew itself together and passed prohibiting legislation. Wharton died in 1909. The Wharton Tract, as his immense New Jersey landholding was called, has remained undeveloped. It was considered as a site for the United States Air Force Academy. The state was slow in acquiring it in the public interest, but at last did so in 1955, and the whole of it is now Wharton State Forest.

All the major river systems in the United States are polluted, and so are most of the minor ones, but all the small rivers and streams in the Pine Barrens are potable. The pinelands have their own divide. The Pine Barrens rivers rise in the pines. Some flow west to the Delaware; most flow southeast directly into the sea. There are no through-flowing streams in the pines—no waters coming in from cities and towns on higher ground, as is the case almost everywhere else on the Atlantic coastal plain. I have spent many weekends on canoe trips in the Pine Barrens—on the Wading River, the Oswego, the Batsto, the Mullica. There is no white water in any of these rivers, but they move along fairly rapidly; they are so tortuous that every hundred yards or so brings a new scene—often one that is reminiscent of canoeing country in the northern states and in Canada. Even on bright days, the rivers can be dark and almost sunless under stands of white cedar, and then, all in a moment, they run into brilliant sunshine where the banks rise higher and the forest of oak and pine is less dense. One indication of the size of the water resource below the Pine Barrens is that the streams keep flowing without great declines in volume even in prolonged times of drought. When streams in other parts of New Jersey were reduced to near or total dryness in recent years, the rivers in the pines were virtually unaffected. The characteristic color of the water in the streams is the color of tea—a phenomenon, often called "cedar water," that is familiar in the Adirondacks, as in many other places where tannins and other organic waste from riparian cedar trees combine with iron from the ground water to give the rivers a deep color. In summer, the cedar water is ordinarily so dark that the riverbeds are obscured, and while drifting along one has a feeling of being afloat on a river of fast-moving potable ink. For a few days after a long rain, however, the water is almost colorless. At these times, one can look down into it from a canoe and see the white sand bottom, ten or twelve feet below, and it is as clear as an image in the lens of a camera, with sunken timbers now and again coming into view and receding rapidly, at the speed of the river. Every strand of subsurface grass and every contour of the bottom sand is so sharply defined that the deep water above it seems, and is, irresistibly pure. Sea captains once took the cedar water of the Pine Barrens rivers with them on voyages, because cedar water would remain sweet and potable longer than any other water they could find.

According to the government report, "The Pine Barrens have no equal in the northeastern United States not only for magnitude of water in storage and availability of recharge, but also for the ease and economy with which a large volume of water could be withdrawn." Typically, a pipe less than two inches in diameter driven thirty feet into the ground will produce fifty-five gallons a minute, and a twelve-inch pipe could bring up a million gallons a day. But, with all this, the vulnerability of the Pine Barrens aquifer is disturbing to contemplate. The water table is shallow in the pines, and the aquifer is extremely sensitive to contamination. The sand soil, which is so superior as a catcher of rain, is not good at filtering out or immobilizing wastes. Pollutants, if they happen to get into the water, can travel long distances. Industry or even extensive residential development in the central pinelands could spread contaminants widely through the underground reservoir.

When I had finished filling the jerry can from Fred Brown's pump, I took another drink, and I said to him, "You're lucky to live over such good water."

"You're telling me," he said. "You can put this water in a jug and put it away for a year and it will still be the same. Water from outside of these woods would stink. Outside of these woods, some water stinks when you pump it out of the ground. The people that has dug deep around here claims that there are streams of water under this earth that runs all the time."

In the weeks that followed, I stopped in many times to see Fred, and saw nearly as much of Bill. They rode with me through the woods, in my car, for five and six hours at a time. In the evenings, we returned to Fred's place with food from some peripheral town. It is possible to cross the pines on half a dozen state or federal roads, but very little of interest is visible from them. Several county roads—old crown roads with uneven macadam surfaces—connect the pine communities, but it is necessary to get off the paved roads altogether in order to see much of the forest. The areas are spacious—fifty, sixty, and seventy-five thousand acres—through which run no paved roads of any kind. There are many hundreds of miles of unpaved roads through the pines—two tracks in the sand, with underbrush growing up between them. Hunters use them, and foresters, firefighters, and woodcutters. A number of these sand roads have been there, and have remained unchanged, since before the American Revolution. They developed, for the most part, as Colonial stage routes, trails to charcoal pits, pulpwood-and-lumber roads, and connecting roads between communities that have disappeared from the world. In a place called Washington, five of these roads converge in the forest, as if from star points, and they suggest the former importance of Washington, but all that is left of the town is a single fragment of a stone structure. The sand roads are marked on topographic maps with parallel dotted lines, and driving on them can be something of a sport. It is possible to drive all day on the sand roads, and more than halfway across the state, but most people need to stop fairly often to study the topographic maps, for the roads sometimes come together in fantastic ganglia, and even when they are straight and apparently uncomplicated they constantly fork, presenting unclear choices between the main chance and culs-de-sac, of which there are many hundreds. No matter where we were—far up near Mt. Misery, in the northern part of the pines, or over in the western extremities of the Wharton Tract, or down in the southeast, near the Bass River—Fred kept calling out directions. He always knew exactly where he was going. Fred was nearly forty when the first paved roads were built in the pines. Once, not far from the Godfrey Bridge on the Wading River, he said, "Look at these big pines. You would never think that I was as old as these big pines, would you? I seen all of these big pines grow. I remember this when it was all cut down for charcoal." A short distance away, he pointed into a high stand of pitch pines and scarlet oaks, and he said, "That's the old Joe Holloway field. Holloway had a water-powered sawmill." In another part of the woods, we passed a small bald area, and he said, "That's the Dan Dillett field, where Dan made charcoal." As the car kept moving, bouncing in the undulations of the sand and scraping against blueberry bushes and scrub-oak boughs, Fred kept narrating, picking fragments of the past out of the forest, in moments separated by miles: "Right here in this piece of woods is more rattlesnakes than anyplace else in the State of New Jersey. They had a sawmill in there. They used to kill three or four rattlesnakes when they was watering their horses at noon. Rattlesnakes like water. . . . See that fire tower over there? The man in that tower—you take him fifty yards away from that tower and he's lost. He don't know the woods. He don't know the woods. He don't know the woods. He don't know nothing. He can't even fry a hamburger. . . . I've gunned this part of the woods since I was ten years old. I know every foot of it here. . . . Apple Pie Hill is a thunderstriking high hill. You don't realize how high until you get up here. It's the long slope of a hill that makes a high one. . . . See that open spot in there? A group of girls used to keep a house in there. It was called Noah's Ark. . . . I worked this piece of cedar off here. . . . I worked this bog for

Joe Wharton once. My father used to work for Joe Wharton, too. He used to come and stay with my father. Joe Wharton was the nicest man you ever seen. That is, if you didn't lie to him. He was quiet. He didn't smile very often. I don't know as I ever heard him laugh out loud. . . . These are the Hocken Lowlands." The Hocken Lowlands surround the headwaters of Tulpehocken Creek, about five miles northwest of Hog Wallow, and are not identified on maps, not even on the large-scale topographic maps. As we moved along, Fred had a name for almost every rise and dip in the land. "This is Sandy Ridge," he said. "That road once went into a bog. Houses were there. Now there's nothing there. . . . This is Bony's Hole. A man named Bony used to water his horse here." Every so often, Fred would reach into his pocket and touch up his day with a minimal sip from a half pint of whiskey. He merely touched the bottle to his lips, then put it away. He did this at irregular intervals, and one day, when he had a new half pint, he took more than five hours to reduce the level of the whiskey from the neck to the shoulders of the bottle. At an intersection of two sand roads in the Wharton Tract, he pointed to a depression in the ground and said, "That hole in the ground was the cellar of an old jug tavern. That cellar was where they kept the jugs. There was a town here called Mount. That tavern is where my grandpop got drunk the last time he got drunk in his life. Grandmother went up to get him. When she came in, he said, 'Mary, what are you doing here?' He was so ashamed to see her there—and his daughter with her. He left a jug of whiskey right on the table, and his wife took one of his hands and his daughter the other and they led him out of there and past Washington Field and home to Jenkins Neck. He lived fifty years. He lived fifty years, and growed cranberries. He lived fifty years more, and he was never drunk again."

One evening, when it was almost dark and we were about five miles from Fred's place, he told me to stop, and he said, "See that upland red cedar? I helped set that out." Red cedar is not native in the Pine Barrens, and this one stood alone among the taller oaks and pines, in a part of the forest that seemed particularly remote. "I went to school there, by that red cedar," Fred said. "There was twenty-five of us in the school. We all walked. We wore leather boots in the winter that got soaked through and your feet froze. When you got home, you had to pull off your boots on a bootjack. In the summer, when I was a boy, if you wanted to go anywhere you rolled up your pantlegs, put your shoes on your shoulder, and you walked wherever you was going. The pigs and cows was everywhere. There was wild bulls, wild cows, wild boars. That's how Hog Wallow got its name. They call them the good old days. What do you think of that, Bill?"

"I wish I was back there, I can tell you that," Bill said.

From *Dispatches*

MICHAEL HERR

∾

As a twenty-seven-year-old correspondent for *Esquire,* Michael Herr arrived in Vietnam two months before the Viet Cong unleashed the 1968 Tet offensive. He witnessed the devastation of Hue, the once-beautiful Imperial City; the interminable siege of the U.S. air base at Khe Sanh; and the recurring paradox of American technical might and tactical impotence.

"Conventional journalism could no more reveal this war than conventional firepower could win it," Herr decided. The war had no linear "front"; it was everywhere. And official U.S. accounts were essentially disinformation, constructed from misleading numbers (like body counts) and outrageous euphemisms. To convey the surreal quality of Vietnam, and its mind-altering effect on American personnel, Herr created a new style of war correspondence.

His dispatches were fragmentary, nonchronological, and even nondirectional. Accompanied by photographer cronies Tim Page and Sean Flynn, Herr moved freely around Vietnam, hopping one plane or helicopter after another, improvising his assignment. The stories were full of unfinished conversations and unexplained acronyms, bits of song lyrics, and sensory flashes, all held together by Herr's voice—meditative, ironic, compassionate, and often afraid. "You lost your noncombatant status very quickly," Herr told Tom Wolfe, "because nobody thought they were going to get out alive."

Herr used first-person writing for third-person effect. His own feelings of fear, excitement, or disorientation led him to explore the collective mind of the soldiers—their superstitions, bitter jokes, and haunting turns of phrase. When *Dispatches* became a book in 1977, Herr gave it a retrospective structure: a journey of memory, beginning with "Breathing In," back to the scene of a disaster.

Herr later coscripted two movies about the Vietnam War, Francis Ford Coppola's *Apocalypse Now* and Stanley Kubrick's *Full Metal Jacket.* Like *Dispatches,* both are rich in atmosphere and sensibility, tragedy and absurdity, brutal reality and eerie dream.

—K. K.

Breathing In

I

Going out at night the medics gave you pills, Dexedrine breath like dead snakes kept too long in a jar. I never saw the need for them myself, a little contact or anything that even sounded like contact would give me more speed than I could bear. Whenever I heard something outside of our clenched little circle I'd practically flip, hoping to God that I wasn't the only one who'd noticed it. A couple of rounds fired off in the dark a kilometer away and the Elephant would be there kneeling on my chest, sending me down into my boots for a breath. Once I thought I saw a light moving in the jungle and I caught myself just under a whisper saying, "I'm not ready for this, I'm not ready for this." That's when I decided to drop it and do something else with my nights. And I wasn't going out like the night ambushers did, or the Lurps, long-range recon patrollers who did it night after night for weeks and months, creeping up on VC base camps or around moving columns of North Vietnamese. I was living too close to my bones as it was, all I had to do was accept it. Anyway, I'd save the pills for later, for Saigon and the awful depressions I always had there.

I knew one 4th Division Lurp who took his pills by the fistful, downs from the left pocket of his tiger suit and ups from the right, one to cut the trail for him and the other to send him down it. He told me that they cooled things out just right for him, that he could see that old jungle at night like he was looking at it through a starlight scope. "They sure give you the range," he said.

This was his third tour. In 1965 he'd been the only survivor in a platoon of the Cav wiped out going into the Ia Drang Valley. In '66 he'd come back with the Special Forces and one morning after an ambush he'd hidden under the bodies of his team while the VC walked all around them with knives, making sure. They stripped the bodies of their gear, the berets too, and finally went away, laughing. After that, there was nothing left for him in the war except the Lurps.

"I just can't hack it back in the World," he said. He told me that after he'd come back home the last time he would sit in his room all day, and sometimes he'd stick a hunting rifle out the window, leading people and cars as they passed his house until the only feeling he was aware of was all up in the tip of that one finger. "It used to put my folks real uptight," he said. But he put people uptight here too, even here.

"No man, I'm sorry, he's just too crazy for me," one of the men in his team said. "All's you got to do is look in his eyes, that's the whole fucking story right there."

"Yeah, but you better do it quick," someone else said. "I mean, you don't want to let him catch you at it."

But he always seemed to be watching for it, I think he slept with his eyes open, and I was afraid of him anyway. All I ever managed was one quick look in, and that was like looking at the floor of an ocean. He wore a gold earring and a headband torn from a piece of camouflage parachute material, and since nobody was about to tell him to get his hair cut it fell below his shoulders, covering a thick purple scar. Even at division he never went anywhere without at least a .45 and a knife, and he thought I was a freak because I wouldn't carry a weapon.

"Didn't you ever meet a reporter before?" I asked him.

"Tits on a bull," he said. "Nothing personal."

But what a story he told me, as one-pointed and resonant as any war story I ever heard, it took me a year to understand it:

"Patrol went up the mountain. One man came back. He died before he could tell us what happened."

I waited for the rest, but it seemed not to be that kind of story; when I asked him what had happened he just looked like he felt sorry for me, fucked if he'd waste time telling stories to anyone dumb as I was.

His face was all painted up for night walking now like a bad hallucination, not like the painted faces I'd seen in San Francisco only a few weeks before, the other extreme of the same theater. In the coming hours he'd stand as faceless and quiet in the jungle as a fallen tree, and God help his opposite numbers unless they had at least half a squad along, he was a good killer, one of our best. The rest of his team were gathered outside the tent, set a little apart from the other division units, with its own Lurp-designated latrine and its own exclusive freeze-dry rations, three-star war food, the same chop they sold at Abercrombie & Fitch. The regular division troops would almost shy off the path when they passed the area on their way to and from the mess tent. No matter how toughened up they became in the war, they still looked innocent compared to the Lurps. When the team had grouped they walked in a file down the hill to the lz across the strip to the perimeter and into the treeline.

I never spoke to him again, but I saw him. When they came back in the next morning he had a prisoner with him, blindfolded and with his elbows bound sharply behind him. The Lurp area would definitely be off limits during the interrogation, and anyway, I was already down at the strip waiting for a helicopter to come and take me out of there.

"Hey what're you guys, with the USO? Aw, we thought you was with the USO 'cause your hair's so long." Page took the kid's picture, I got the words down and Flynn laughed and told him we were the Rolling Stones. The three of us traveled around together for about a month that summer. At one lz the brigade chopper came in with a real foxtail hanging off the aerial, when the commander walked by us he almost took an infarction.

"Don't you men salute officers?"

"We're not men," Page said. "We're correspondents."

When the commander heard that, he wanted to throw a spontaneous operation for us, crank up his whole brigade and get some people killed. We had to get out on the next chopper to keep him from going ahead with it, amazing what some of them would do for a little ink. Page liked to augment his field gear with freak paraphernalia, scarves and beads, plus he was English, guys would stare at him like he'd just come down off a wall on Mars. Sean Flynn could look more incredibly beautiful than even his father, Errol, had thirty years before as Captain Blood, but sometimes he looked more like Artaud coming out of some heavy heart-of-darkness trip, overloaded on the information, the input! The input! He'd give off a bad sweat and sit for hours, combing his mustache through with the saw blade of his Swiss Army knife. We packed grass and tape: Have You Seen Your Mother Baby Standing in the Shadows, Best of the Animals, Strange Days, Purple Haze, Archie Bell and the Drells, "C'mon now everybody, do the Tighten Up. . . ." Once in a while we'd catch a chopper straight into one of the lower hells, but it was a quiet time in the war, mostly it was lz's and camps, grunts hanging around, faces, stories.

"Best way's to just keep moving," one of them told us. "Just keep moving, stay in motion, you know what I'm saying?"

We knew. He was a moving-target-survivor subscriber, a true child of the war, because except for the rare times when you were pinned or stranded the system was geared to keep you mobile, if that was what you thought you wanted. As a technique for staying alive it seemed to make as much sense as anything, given naturally that you were there to begin with and wanted to see it close; it started out sound and straight but it formed a cone as it progressed, because the more you moved the more you saw, the more you saw the more besides death and mutilation you risked, and the more you risked of that the more you would have to let go of one day as a "survivor." Some of us moved around the war like crazy people until we couldn't see which way the run was even taking us anymore, only the war all over its surface with occasional, unexpected penetration. As long as we could have choppers like taxis it took real exhaustion or depression near shock or a dozen pipes of opium to keep us even apparently quiet, we'd still be running around inside our skins like something was after us, ha ha, La Vida Loca.

In the months after I got back the hundreds of helicopters I'd flown in began to draw together until they'd formed a collective meta-chopper, and in my mind it was the sexiest thing going; saver-destroyer, provider-waster, right hand–left hand, nimble, fluent, canny and human; hot steel, grease, jungle-saturated canvas webbing, sweat cooling and warming up again, cassette rock and roll in one ear and door-gun fire in the other, fuel, heat, vitality and death, death itself, hardly an intruder. Men on the crews would say that once you'd carried a dead person he would always be there, riding with you. Like all combat people they were incredibly superstitious and invariably self-dramatic, but it was (I knew) unbearably true that close exposure to the dead sensitized you to the force of their presence and made for long reverberations; long. Some people were so delicate that one look was enough to wipe them away, but even bone-dumb grunts seemed to feel that something weird and extra was happening to them.

Helicopters and people jumping out of helicopters, people so in love they'd run to get on even when there wasn't any pressure. Choppers rising straight out of small cleared jungle spaces, wobbling down onto city rooftops, cartons of rations and ammunition thrown off, dead and wounded loaded on. Sometimes they were so plentiful and loose that you could touch down at five or six places in a day, look around, hear the talk, catch the next one out. There were installations as big as cities with 30,000 citizens, once we dropped in to feed supply to one man. God knows what kind of Lord Jim phoenix numbers he was doing in there, all he said to me was, "You didn't see a thing, right Chief? You weren't even here." There were posh fat air-conditioned camps like comfortable middle-class scenes with the violence tacit, "far away"; camps named for commanders' wives, LZ Thelma, LZ Betty Lou; number-named hilltops in trouble where I didn't want to stay; trail, paddy, swamp, deep hairy bush, scrub, swale, village, even city, where the ground couldn't drink up what the action spilled, it made you careful where you walked.

Sometimes the chopper you were riding in would top a hill and all the ground in front of you as far as the next hill would be charred and pitted and still smoking, and something between your chest and your stomach would turn over. Frail gray smoke where they'd burned off the rice fields around a free-strike zone, brilliant white smoke from phosphorus ("Willy Peter/Make you a buh liever"), deep black smoke from 'palm, they said that if you stood at the base of a column of napalm smoke it would suck the air right out of your lungs. Once we fanned over a little ville that had just been airstruck and the words of a song by Wingy Manone that I'd heard when I was a few years old snapped into my head, "Stop the War, These Cats Is Killing Themselves." Then we dropped, hovered, settled down into purple lz smoke, dozens of children broke from their hootches to run in toward the focus of our landing, the pilot laughing and saying, "Vietnam, man. Bomb 'em and feed 'em, bomb 'em and feed 'em."

Flying over jungle was almost pure pleasure, doing it on foot was nearly all pain. I never belonged in there. Maybe it really was what its people had always called it, Beyond; at the very least it was serious, I gave up things to it I probably never got back. ("Aw, jungle's okay. If you know her you can live in her real good, if you don't she'll take you down in an hour. Under.") Once in some thick jungle corner with some grunts standing around, a correspondent said, "Gee, you must really see some beautiful sunsets in here," and they almost pissed themselves laughing. But you could fly up and into hot tropic sunsets that would change the way you thought about light forever.

You could also fly out of places that were so grim they turned to black and white in your head five minutes after you'd gone.

That could be the coldest one in the world, standing at the edge of a clearing watching the chopper you'd just come in on taking off again, leaving you there to think about what it was going to be for you now: if this was a bad place, the wrong place, maybe even the last place, and whether you'd made a terrible mistake this time.

There was a camp at Soc Trang where a man at the lz said, "If you come looking for a story this is your lucky day, we got Condition Red here," and before the sound of the chopper had faded out, I knew I had it too.

"That's affirmative," the camp commander said, "we are *definitely* expecting rain. Glad to see you." He was a young captain, he was laughing and taping a bunch of sixteen clips together bottom to bottom for faster reloading, "grease." Everyone there was busy at it, cracking crates, squirreling away grenades, checking mortar pieces, piling rounds, clicking banana clips into automatic weapons that I'd never even seen before. They were wired into their listening posts out around the camp, into each other, into themselves, and when it got dark it got worse. The moon came up nasty and full, a fat moist piece of decadent fruit. It was soft and saffron-misted when you looked up at it, but its light over the sandbags and into the jungle was harsh and bright. We were all rubbing Army-issue nightfighter cosmetic under our eyes to cut the glare and the terrible things it made you see. (Around midnight, just for something to do, I crossed to the other perimeter and looked at the road running engineer-straight toward Route 4 like a yellow frozen ribbon out of sight and I saw it move, the whole road.) There were a few sharp arguments about who the light really favored, attackers or defenders, men were sitting around with Cinemascope eyes and jaws stuck out like they could shoot bullets, moving and antsing and shifting around inside their fatigues. "No sense us getting too relaxed, Charlie don't relax, just when you get good and comfortable is when he comes over and takes a giant shit on you." That was the level until morning, I smoked a pack an hour all night long, and nothing happened. Ten minutes after daybreak I was down at the lz asking about choppers.

A few days later Sean Flynn and I went up to a big firebase in the Americal TAOR that took it all the way over to another extreme, National Guard weekend. The colonel in command was so drunk that day that he could barely get his words out, and when he did, it was to say things like, "We aim to make good and goddammit sure that if *those guys* try *anything cute* they won't catch us with our pants down." The main mission there was to fire H&I, but one man told us that their record was the worst in the whole Corps, probably the whole country, they'd harassed and interdicted a lot of sleeping civilians and Korean Marines, even a couple of American patrols, but hardly any Viet Cong. (The colonel kept calling it "artillerary." The first time he said it Flynn and I looked away from each other, the second time we blew beer through our noses, but the colonel fell in laughing right away and more than covered us.) No sandbags, exposed shells, dirty pieces, guys going around giving us that look, "We're cool, how come you're not?" At the strip Sean was talking to the operator about it and the man got angry. "Oh *yeah*? Well fuck *you*, how tight do you think you want it? There ain't been any veecees around here in three months."

"So far so good," Sean said. "Hear anything on that chopper yet?"

But sometimes everything stopped, nothing flew, you couldn't even find out why. I got stuck for a chopper once in some lost patrol outpost in the Delta where the sergeant chain-ate candy bars and played country-and-western tapes twenty hours a day until I heard it in my sleep, some sleep, *Up on Wolverton Mountain* and *Lonesome as the bats and the bears in Miller's Cave* and *I fell into a burning ring of fire,* surrounded by strungout rednecks who weren't getting much sleep either because they couldn't trust one of their 400 mercenary troopers or their own hand-picked perimeter guards or anybody else except maybe Baby Ruth and Johnny Cash, they'd been waiting for it so long now they were afraid they wouldn't know it when they finally got it, *and it burns burns burns.* . . . Finally on the fourth day a helicopter came in to deliver meat and movies to the camp and I went out on it, so happy to get back to Saigon that I didn't crash for two days.

Airmobility, dig it, you weren't going anywhere. It made you feel safe, it made you feel Omni, but it was only a stunt, technology. Mobility was just mobility, it saved lives or took them all the time (saved mine I don't know how many times, maybe dozens, maybe none), what you really needed was a flexibility far greater than anything the technology could provide, some generous, spontaneous gift for accepting surprises, and I didn't have it. I got to hate surprises, control freak at the crossroads, if you were one of those people who always thought they had to know what was coming next, the war could cream you. It was the same with your ongoing attempts at getting used to the jungle or the blow-you-out climate or the saturating strangeness of the place which didn't lessen with exposure so often as it fattened and darkened in accumulating alienation. It was great if you could adapt, you had to try, but it wasn't the same as making a discipline, going into your own reserves and developing a real war metabolism, slow yourself down when your heart tried to punch its way through your chest, get swift when everything went to stop and all you could feel of your whole life was the entropy whipping through it. Unlovable terms.

The ground was always in play, always being swept. Under the ground was his, above it was ours. We had the air, we could get up in it but not disappear in *to* it, we could run but we couldn't hide, and he could do each so well that sometimes it looked like he was doing them both at once, while our finder just went limp. All the same, one place or another it was always going on, rock around the clock, we had the days and he had the nights. You could be in the most protected space in Vietnam and still know that your safety was provisional, that early death, blindness, loss of legs, arms or balls, major and lasting disfigurement—the whole rotten deal—could come in on the freakyfluky as easily as in the so-called expected ways, you heard so many of those stories it was a wonder anyone was left alive to die in firefights and mortar-rocket attacks. After a few weeks, when the nickel had jarred loose and dropped and I saw that everyone around me was carrying a gun, I also saw that any one of them could go off at any time, putting you where it wouldn't matter whether it had been an accident or not. The roads were mined, the trails booby-trapped, satchel charges and grenades blew up jeeps and movie theaters, the VC got work inside all the camps as shoeshine boys and laundresses and honey-dippers, they'd starch your fatigues and burn your shit and then go home and mortar your area. Saigon and Cholon and Danang held such hostile vibes that you felt you were being dry-sniped every time someone looked at you, and choppers fell out of the sky like fat poisoned birds a hundred times a day. After a while I couldn't get on one without thinking that I must be out of my fucking mind.

Fear and motion, fear and standstill, no preferred cut there, no way even to be clear about which was really worse, the wait or the delivery. Combat spared far more men than it wasted, but everyone suffered the time between contact, especially when they were going out every day looking for it; bad going on foot, terrible in trucks and APC's, awful in helicopters, the worst, traveling so fast toward something so frightening. I can remember times when I went half dead with my fear of the motion, the speed and direction already fixed and pointed one way. It was painful enough just flying "safe" hops between firebases and lz's; if you were ever on a helicopter that had been hit by ground fire your deep, perpetual chopper anxiety was guaranteed. At least actual contact when it was happening would draw long raggedy strands of energy out of you, it was juicy, fast and refining, and traveling toward it was hollow, dry, cold and steady, it never let you alone. All you could do was look around at the other people on board and see if they were as scared and numbed out as you were. If it looked like they weren't you thought they were insane, if it looked like they were it made you feel a lot worse.

I went through that thing a number of times and only got a fast return on my fear once, a too classic hot landing with the heat coming from the trees about 300 yards away, sweeping machine-gun fire that sent men head down into swampy water, running on their hands and knees toward the grass where it wasn't blown flat by the rotor blades, not much to be running for but better than nothing. The helicopter pulled up before we'd all gotten out, leaving the last few men to jump twenty feet down between the guns across the paddy and the gun on the chopper door. When we'd all reached the cover of the wall and the captain had made a check, we were amazed to see that no one had even been hurt, except for one man who'd sprained both his ankles jumping. Afterward, I remembered that I'd been down in the muck worrying about leeches. I guess you could say that I was refusing to accept the situation.

"Boy, you sure get offered some shitty choices," a Marine once said to me, and I couldn't help but feel that what he really meant was that you didn't get offered any at all. Specifically, he was just talking about a couple of C-ration cans, "dinner," but considering his young life you couldn't blame him for thinking that if he knew one thing for sure, it was that there was no one any-where who cared less about what *he* wanted. There wasn't anybody he wanted to thank for his food, but he was grateful that he was still alive to eat it, that the motherfucker hadn't scarfed him up first. He hadn't been any-thing but tired and scared for six months and he'd lost a lot, mostly people, and seen far too much, but he was breathing in and breathing out, some kind of choice all by itself.

He had one of those faces, I saw that face at least a thousand times at a hundred bases and camps, all the youth sucked out of the eyes, the color drawn from the skin, cold white lips, you knew he wouldn't wait for any of it to come back. Life had made him old, he'd live it out old. All those faces, sometimes it was like looking into faces at a rock concert, locked in, the event had them; or like students who were very heavily advanced, serious beyond what you'd call their years if you didn't know for yourself what the minutes and hours of those years were made up of. Not just like all the ones you saw who looked like they couldn't drag their asses through another day of it. (How do you feel when a nineteen-year-old kid tells you from the bottom of his heart that he's gotten too old for this kind of shit?) Not like the faces of the dead or wounded either, they could look more released than overtaken. These were the faces of boys whose whole lives seemed to have backed up on them, they'd be a few feet away but they'd be looking back at you over a dis-tance you knew you'd never really cross. We'd talk, sometimes fly together, guys going out on R&R, guys escorting bodies, guys who'd flipped over into extremes of peace or violence. Once I flew with a kid who was going home, he looked back down once at the ground where he'd spent the year and spilled his whole load of tears. Sometimes you even flew with the dead.

Once I jumped on a chopper that was full of them. The kid in the op shack had said that there would be a body on board, but he'd been given some wrong information. "How bad do you want to get to Danang?" he'd asked me, and I'd said, "Bad."

When I saw what was happening I didn't want to get on, but they'd made a divert and a special landing for me, I had to go with the chopper I'd drawn, I was afraid of looking squeamish. (I remember, too, thinking that a chopper full of dead men was far less likely to get shot down than one full of living.) They weren't even in bags. They'd been on a truck near one of the firebases in the DMZ that was firing support for Khe Sanh, and the truck had hit a Command-detonated mine, then they'd been rocketed. The Marines were always running out of things, even food, ammo and medicine, it wasn't so strange that they'd run out of bags too. The men had been wrapped around in ponchos, some of them carelessly fastened with plastic straps, and loaded on board. There was a small space cleared for me between one of them and the door gunner, who looked pale and so tremendously furious that I thought he was angry with me and I couldn't look at him for a while. When we went up the wind blew through the ship and made the ponchos shake and tremble until the one next to me blew back in a fast brutal flap, uncovering the face. They hadn't even closed his eyes for him.

The gunner started hollering as loud as he could, "Fix it! Fix it!," maybe he thought the eyes were looking at him, but there wasn't anything I could do. My hand went there a couple of times and I couldn't, and then I did. I pulled the poncho tight, lifted his head carefully and tucked the poncho under it, and then I couldn't believe that I'd done it. All during the ride the gunner kept trying to smile, and when we landed at Dong Ha he thanked me and ran off to get a detail. The pilots jumped down and walked away without looking back once, like they'd never seen that chopper before in their lives. I flew the rest of the way to Danang in a general's plane.

II

You know how it is, you want to look and you don't want to look. I can remember the strange feelings I had when I was a kid looking at war photographs in *Life*, the ones that showed dead people or a lot of dead people lying close together in a field or a street, often touching, seeming to hold each other. Even when the picture was sharp and cleanly defined, something wasn't clear at all, something repressed that monitored the images and withheld their essential information. It may have legitimized my fascination, letting me look for as long as I wanted; I didn't have a language for it then, but I remember now the shame I felt, like looking at first porn, all the porn in the world. I could have looked until my lamps went out and I still wouldn't have accepted the connection between a detached leg and the rest of a body, or the poses and positions that always happened (one day I'd hear it called "response-to-impact"), bodies wrenched too fast and violently into unbelievable contortion. Or the total impersonality of group death, making them lie anywhere and any way it left them, hanging over barbed wire or thrown promiscuously on top of other dead, or up into the trees like terminal acrobats, *Look what I can do*.

Supposedly, you weren't going to have that kind of obscuration when you finally started seeing them on real ground in front of you, but you tended to manufacture it anyway because of how often and how badly you needed protection from what you were seeing, had actually come 30,000 miles to see. Once I looked at them strung from the perimeter to the treeline, most of them clumped together nearest the wire, then in smaller numbers but tighter groups midway, fanning out into lots of scattered points nearer the treeline, with one all by himself half into the bush and half out. "Close but no cigar," the captain said, and then a few of his men went out there and kicked them all in the head, thirty-seven of them. Then I heard an M-16 on full automatic starting to go through clips, a second to fire, three to plug in a fresh clip, and I saw a man out there, doing it. Every round was like a tiny concentration of high-velocity wind, making the bodies wince and shiver. When he finished he walked by us on the way back to his hootch, and I knew I hadn't seen anything until I saw his face. It was flushed and mottled and twisted like he had his face skin on inside out, a patch of green that was too dark, a streak of red running into bruise purple, a lot of sick gray white in between, he looked like he'd had a heart attack out there. His eyes were rolled up half into his head, his mouth was sprung open and his tongue was out, but he was smiling. Really a dude who'd shot his wad. The captain wasn't too pleased about my having seen that.

There wasn't a day when someone didn't ask me what I was doing there. Sometimes an especially smart grunt or another correspondent would even ask me what I was *really* doing there, as though I could say anything honest about it except "Blah blah blah cover the war" or "Blah blah blah write a book." Maybe we accepted each other's stories about why we were there at face value: the grunts who "had" to be there, the spooks and civilians whose corporate faith had led them there, the correspondents whose curiosity or ambition drew them over. But somewhere all the mythic tracks intersected, from the lowest John Wayne wetdream to the most aggravated soldier-poet fantasy, and where they did I believe that everyone knew everything about everyone else, every one of us there a true volunteer. Not that you didn't hear some overripe bullshit about it: Hearts and Minds, Peoples of the Republic, tumbling dominoes, maintaining the equilibrium of the Dingdong by containing the ever encroaching Doodah; you could also hear the other, some young soldier speaking in all bloody innocence, saying, "All that's just a *load,* man. We're here to kill gooks. Period." Which wasn't at all true of me. I was there to watch.

Talk about impersonating an identity, about locking into a role, about irony: I went to cover the war and the war covered me; an old story, unless of course you've never heard it. I went there behind the crude but serious belief that you had to be able to look at anything, serious because I acted on it and went, crude because I didn't know, it took the war to teach it, that you were as responsible for everything you saw as you were for everything you did. The problem was that you didn't always know what you were seeing until later, maybe years later, that a lot of it never made it in at all, it just stayed stored there in your eyes. Time and information, rock and roll, life itself, the information isn't frozen, you are.

Sometimes I didn't know if an action took a second or an hour or if I dreamed it or what. In war more than in other life you don't really know what you're doing most of the time, you're just behaving, and afterward you can make up any kind of bullshit you want to about it, say you felt good or bad, loved it or hated it, did this or that, the right thing or the wrong thing; still, what happened happened.

Coming back, telling stories, I'd say, "Oh man I was scared," and, "Oh God I thought it was all over," a long time before I knew how scared I was really supposed to be, or how clear and closed and beyond my control "all over" could become. I wasn't dumb but I sure was raw, certain connections are hard to make when you come from a place where they go around with war in their heads all the time.

"If you get hit," a medic told me, "we can chopper you back to base-camp hospital in like twenty minutes."

"If you get hit real bad," a corpsman said, "they'll get your case to Japan in twelve hours."

"If you get killed," a spec 4 from Graves promised, "we'll have you home in a week."

TIME IS ON MY SIDE, already written there across the first helmet I ever wore there. And underneath it, in smaller lettering that read more like a whispered prayer than an assertion, *No lie, GI.* The rear-hatch gunner on a Chinook threw it to me that first morning at the Kontum airstrip, a few hours after the Dak To fighting had ended, screaming at me through the rotor wind, "You *keep* that, we got *plenty,* good *luck!*" and then flying off. I was so glad to have the equipment that I didn't stop to think where it had to have come from. The sweatband inside was seasoned up black and greasy, it was more alive now than the man who'd worn it, when I got rid of it ten minutes later I didn't just leave it on the ground, I snuck away from it furtive and ashamed, afraid that someone would see it and call after me, "Hey numbnuts, you forgot something. . . ."

That morning when I tried to go out they sent me down the line from a colonel to a major to a captain to a sergeant, who took one look, called me Freshmeat, and told me to go find some other outfit to get myself killed with. I didn't know what was going on, I was so nervous I started to laugh. I told him that nothing was going to happen to me and he gave my shoulder a tender, menacing pat and said, "This ain't the fucking movies over here, you know." I laughed again and said that I knew, but he knew that I didn't.

Day one, if anything could have penetrated that first innocence I might have taken the next plane out. Out absolutely. It was like a walk through a colony of stroke victims, a thousand men on a cold rainy airfield after too much of something I'd never really know, "a way you'll never be," dirt and blood and torn fatigues, eyes that poured out a steady charge of wasted horror. I'd just missed the biggest battle of the war so far, I was telling myself that I was sorry, but it was right there all around me and I didn't even know it. I couldn't look at anyone for more than a second, I didn't want to be caught listening, some war correspondent, I didn't know what to say or do, I didn't like it already. When the rain stopped and the ponchos came off there was a smell that I thought was going to make me sick: rot, sump, tannery, open grave, dump-fire—awful, you'd walk into pockets of Old Spice that made it even worse. I wanted badly to find some place to sit alone and smoke a cigarette, to find a face that would cover my face the way my poncho covered my new fatigues. I'd worn them once before, yesterday morning in Saigon, bringing them out of the black market and back to the hotel, dressing up in front of the mirror, making faces and moves I'd never make again. And loving it. Now, nearby on the ground, there was a man sleeping with a poncho over his head and a radio in his arms, I heard Sam the Sham singing, "Lil' Red Riding Hood, I don't think little big girls should, Go walking in these spooky old woods alone. . . ."

I turned to walk some other way and there was a man standing in front of me. He didn't exactly block me, but he didn't move either. He tottered a little and blinked, he looked at me and through me, no one had ever looked at me like that before. I felt a cold fat drop of sweat start down the middle of my back like a spider, it seemed to take an hour to finish its run. The man lit a cigarette and then sort of slobbered it out, I couldn't imagine what I was seeing. He tried again with a fresh cigarette. I gave him the light for that one, there was a flicker of focus, acknowledgment, but after a few puffs it went out too, and he let it drop to the ground. "I couldn't spit for a week up there," he said, "and now I can't fucking stop."

From *Another Day of Life*

RYSZARD KAPUŚCIŃSKI

∞

Writing for the Polish Press Agency from 1958 to 1980, Ryszard Kapuściński covered twenty-seven revolutions and coups in Africa, the Middle
East, and Latin America. In such books as *The Emperor* (1978), which deals
with the overthrow of Haile Selassie of Ethiopia, Kapuściński evokes psychological atmosphere by blending journalism with autobiography. *Another
Day of Life* (1976) begins with a personal note: "This is a book about being
alone and lost. In summer 1975 my boss . . . said, 'This is your last chance
to get to Angola. How about it?' I always answer yes in such situations."

Earlier that year, a new government in Lisbon had granted independence
to all Portuguese colonies. In Angola a power vacuum led to civil war,
abetted by outside support for various factions. The Soviet Union and
Cuba backed the MPLA; Western powers supported either Holden
Roberto's FLNA or Jonas Savimbi's UNITA. Adding to the chaos in Luanda
were gangs of PIDE, the Portuguese political police.

Kapuściński's account (the first chapter of which follows) focuses less on
factional fighting than on the mind-set of white colonists trying to leave the
country with as many of their possessions as possible. The "city of crates" is
an unforgettable emblem of people owned by things. And around the edges
of the story, as Luanda descends into a "cosmic mess," is the sensibility of
a Kafkaesque journalist, ever attentive to the ironic and the absurd. This
selection is translated from Polish by William R. Brand and Katarzyna
Mroczkowska-Brand.

—K. K.

∞

For three months I lived in Luanda, in the Tivoli Hotel. From my window I had
a view of the bay and the port. Offshore stood several freighters under European flags. Their captains maintained radio contact with Europe and they had
a better idea of what was happening in Angola than we did—we were imprisoned in a besieged city. When the news circulated around the world that the

battle for Luanda was approaching, the ships sailed out to sea and stopped on the edge of the horizon. The last hope of rescue receded with them, since escape by land was impossible, and rumors said that at any moment the enemy would bombard and immobilize the airport. Later it turned out that the date for the attack on Luanda had been changed and the fleet returned to the bay, expecting as always to load cargoes of cotton and coffee.

The movement of these ships was an important source of information for me. When the bay emptied, I began preparing for the worst. I listened, trying to hear if the sound of artillery barrages was approaching. I wondered if there was any truth in what the Portuguese whispered among themselves, that two thousand of Holden Roberto's soldiers were hiding in the city, waiting only for orders to begin the slaughter. But in the middle of these anxieties the ships sailed back into the bay. In my mind I hailed the sailors I had never met as saviors: it would be quiet for a while.

In the next room lived two old people: Don Silva, a diamond merchant, and his wife Dona Esmeralda, who was dying of cancer. She was passing her last days without help or comfort, since the hospitals were closed and the doctors had left. Her body, twisted in pain, was disappearing among a heap of pillows. I was afraid to go into the room. Once I entered to ask if it bothered her when I typed at night. Her thoughts broke free of the pain for a moment, long enough for her to say, "No, Ricardo, I haven't got enough time left to be bothered by anything."

Don Silva paced the corridors for hours. He argued with everyone, cursed the world, carried a chip on his shoulder. He even yelled at blacks, though by this time everybody was treating them politely and one of our neighbors had even got into the habit of stopping Africans he didn't know from Adam, shaking hands, and bowing low. They thought the war had got to him and hurried away. Don Silva was waiting for the arrival of Holden Roberto and kept asking me if I knew anything on that score. The sight of the ships sailing away filled him with the keenest joy. He rubbed his hands, straightened up, and showed his false teeth.

Despite the overwhelming heat, Don Silva always dressed in warm clothes. He had strings of diamonds sewn into the pleats of his suit. Once, in a flush of good humor when it seemed that the FNLA was already at the entrance to the hotel, he showed me a handful of transparent stones that looked like fragments of crushed glass. They were diamonds. Around the hotel it was said that Don Silva carried half a million dollars on his person. The old man's heart was torn. He wanted to escape with his riches, but Dona Esmeralda's illness tied him down. He was afraid that if he didn't leave immediately someone would report him, and his treasure would be taken away. He never went out in the street. He even wanted to install extra locks, but all the locksmiths had left and there wasn't a soul in Luanda who could do the job.

Across from me lived a young couple, Arturo and Maria. He was a colonial official and she was a silent blonde, calm, with misty, carnal eyes. They were waiting to leave, but first they had to exchange their Angolan money for Portuguese, and that took weeks because the lines at the banks stretched endlessly. Our cleaning lady, a warm, alert old woman named Dona Cartagina, reported to me in outraged whispers that Arturo and Maria were living in sin. That meant living like blacks, like those atheists from the MPLA. In her scale of values this was the lowest state of degradation and infamy a white person could reach.

Dona Cartagina was also anticipating Holden Roberto's arrival. She didn't know where his army was and would ask me secretly for news. She also asked if I was writing good things about the FNLA. I told her I was, enthusiastically. In gratitude she always cleaned my room until it shined, and when there was nothing in town to drink she brought me—from where, I don't know—a bottle of mineral water.

Maria treated me like a man who was preparing for suicide after I told her that I'd be staying in Luanda until November 11, when Angola was to become independent. In her opinion there wouldn't be a stone left standing in the city by then. Everyone would die and Luanda would turn into a great burial place inhabited by vultures and hyenas. She urged me to leave quickly. I bet her a bottle of wine that I'd survive and we'd meet in Lisbon, in the elegant Altis Hotel, at five o'clock in the afternoon of November 15. I was late for the rendezvous, but the desk clerk had a note from Maria telling me she had waited, but was leaving for Brazil with Arturo the next day.

The whole Tivoli Hotel was packed to the transoms and resembled our train stations right after the war: jammed with people by turns excited and apathetic, with stacks of shabby bundles tied together with string. It smelled bad everywhere, sour, and a sticky, choking sultriness filled the building. People were sweating from heat and from fear. There was an apocalyptic mood, an expectation of destruction. Somebody brought word that they were going to bomb the city in the night. Somebody else had learned that in their quarters the blacks were sharpening knives and wanted to try them on Portuguese throats. The uprising was to explode at any moment. What uprising? I asked, so I could write it up for Warsaw. Nobody knew exactly. Just an uprising, and we'll find out what kind of uprising when it hits us.

Rumor exhausted everyone, plucked at nerves, took away the capacity to think. The city lived in an atmosphere of hysteria and trembled with dread. People didn't know how to cope with the reality that surrounded them, how to interpret it, get used to it. Men gathered in the hotel corridors to hold councils of war. Uninspired pragmatists favored barricading the Tivoli at night. Those with wider horizons and the ability to see things in a global perspective contended that a telegram appealing for intervention ought to be sent to the UN. But, as is the Latin custom, everything ended in argument.

Every evening a plane flew over the city and dropped leaflets. The plane was painted black, with no lights or markings. The leaflets said that Holden

Roberto's army was outside Luanda and would enter the capital soon, perhaps the next day. To facilitate the conquest, the populace was urged to kill all the Russians, Hungarians, and Poles who commanded the MPLA units and were the cause of the whole war and all the misfortunes that had befallen the distressed nation. This happened in September, when in all Angola there was one person from Eastern Europe—me. Gangs from PIDE were prowling the city; they would come to the hotel and ask who was staying there. They acted with impunity—no authorities existed in Luanda—and they wanted to get even for everything, for the revolution in Portugal, for the loss of Angola, for their shattered careers. Every knock at the door could mean the end for me. I tried not to think about it, which is the only thing to do in such a situation.

The PIDE gangs met in the Adao nightclub next to the hotel. It was always dark there; the waiters carried lanterns. The owner of the club, a fat, ruined playboy with swollen lids veiling his bloodshot eyes, took me into his office once. There were shelves built into the walls from floor to ceiling, and on them stood 226 brands of whisky. He took two pistols from his desk drawer and laid them down in front of him.

"I'm going to kill ten communists with these," he said, "and then I'll be happy."

I looked at him, smiled, and waited to see what he would do. Through the door I could hear music and the thugs having a good time with drunken mulatto girls. The fat man put the pistols back in the drawer and slammed it shut. To this day I don't know why he let me go. He might have been one of those people you meet sometimes who get less of a kick from killing than from knowing that they could have killed but didn't.

All September I went to bed uncertain about what would happen that night and the following day. Several types whose faces I came to know hung about. We kept running into each other but never exchanged a word. I didn't know what to do. I decided right off to stay awake—I didn't want them catching me in my sleep. But in the middle of the night the tension would ease and I'd fall asleep in my clothes, in my shoes, on the big bed that Dona Cartagina had made with such care.

The MPLA couldn't protect me. They were far away in the African quarters, or even farther away at the front. The European quarter in which I was living was not yet theirs. That's why I liked going to the front—it was safer there, more familiar. I could make such journeys only rarely, however. Nobody, not even the people from the staff, could define exactly where the front was. There was neither transport nor communications. Solitary little outfits of greenhorn partisans were lost in enormous, treacherous spaces. They moved here and there without plan or thought. Everybody was fighting a private war, everybody was on his own.

Each evening at nine, Warsaw called. The lights of the telex machine at the hotel reception desk came on and the printer typed out the signal:

814251 PAP PL GOOD EVENING PLEASE SEND

or:

    WE FINALLY GOT THROUGH

or:

    ANYTHING FOR US TODAY? PLS GA GA

I answered:

    OK OK MOM SVP

and turned on the tape with the text of the dispatch.

For me, nine o'clock was the high point of the day—a big event repeated each evening. I wrote daily. I wrote out of the most egocentric of motives: I overcame my inertia and depression in order to produce even the briefest dispatch and so maintain contact with Warsaw, because it rescued me from loneliness and the feeling of abandonment. If there was time, I settled down at the telex long before nine. When the light came on I felt like a wanderer in the desert who catches sight of a spring. I tried every trick I could think of to drag out the length of those séances. I described the details of every battle. I asked what the weather was like at home and complained that I had nothing to eat. But in the end came the moment when Warsaw signed off:

    GOOD RECEPTION CONTACT TOMORROW 20 HRS GMT TKS BY BY

and the light went out and I was left alone again.

Luanda was not dying the way our Polish cities died in the last war. There were no air raids, there was no "pacification," no destruction of district after district. There were no cemeteries in the streets and squares. I don't remember a single fire. The city was dying the way an oasis dies when the well runs dry: it became empty, fell into inanition, passed into oblivion. But that agony would come later; for the moment there was feverish movement everywhere. Everybody was in a hurry, everybody was clearing out. Everyone was trying to catch the next plane to Europe, to America, to anywhere. Portuguese from all over Angola converged on Luanda. Caravans of automobiles loaded down with people and baggage arrived from the most distant corners of the country. The men were unshaven, the woman tousled and rumpled, the children dirty and sleepy. On the way the refugees linked up in long columns and crossed the country that way, since the bigger the group, the safer it was. At first they checked into the Luanda hotels but later, when there were no vacancies, they drove straight to the airport. A nomad city without streets or houses sprang up around the airport. People lived in the open, perpetually soaked because it was always raining. They were living worse now than the blacks in the African quarter that abutted the airport, but they took it apathetically, with dismal resignation, not knowing whom to curse for their fate. Salazar was dead, Caetano had escaped to Brazil, and the government in Lisbon kept changing. The revolution was to blame for everything, they said, because before that it had been peaceful. Now the government had promised the blacks freedom and the blacks had come to blows among themselves, burning and murdering. They aren't capable of governing. Let me tell you what a black is like, they would say: he gets drunk and sleeps all day. If he can hang some beads on himself he walks around happy. Work? Nobody works here. They live like a hundred years ago. A hundred? A thousand! I've seen ones like that, living like a thousand years ago. You ask me who knows what it was like a thousand years ago? Oh, you can tell for sure. Everybody knows what it was like. This country won't last long. Mobutu will take a hunk of it, the ones to the south will take their cut, and that's the end of it. If only I could get out this minute. And never lay eyes on it again. I put in forty years of work here. The sweat of my damn brow. Who will give it back to me now? Do you think anybody can start life all over again?

People are sitting on bundles covered with plastic because it's drizzling. They are meditating, pondering everything. In this abandoned crowd that has been vegetating here for weeks, the spark of revolt sometimes flashes. Women beat up the soldiers designated to maintain order, and men try to hijack a plane to let the world know what despair they've been driven to. Nobody knows when they will fly out or in what direction. A cosmic mess prevails. Organization comes hard to the Portuguese, avowed individualists who by nature cannot live in narrow bounds, in community. Pregnant women have priority. Why them? Am I worse because I gave birth six months ago? All right, pregnant women and those with infants have priority. Why them? Am I worse because my son just turned three? Okay, women with children have priority. Huh? And me? Just because I'm a man, am I to be left here to die? So the strongest board the plane and the women with children throw themselves on the tarmac, under the wheels, so the pilot can't taxi. The army arrives, throws the men off, orders the women aboard, and the women walk up the steps in triumph, like a victorious unit entering a newly conquered city.

Let's say we fly out the ones whose nerves have been shattered. Beautiful, look no further, because if it hadn't been for the war, I'd have been in the lunatic asylum long ago. And us in Carmona, we were raided by a band of wild men who took everything, beat us, wanted to shoot us. I've been nothing but shakes ever since. I'll go nuts if I don't fly out of here at once. My dear fellow, I'll say no more than this: I've lost the fruits of a life's work. Besides, where we lived in Lumbala two UNITA soldiers grabbed me by the hair and a third poked a gun barrel right in my eye. I consider that sufficient reason to take leave of my senses.

No criterion won general approbation. The despondent crowd swarmed around each plane, and hours passed before they could work out who finally got a seat. They have to carry half a million refugees across an air bridge to the other side of the world.

Everybody knows why they want to leave. They know they'll survive September, but October will be very bad and nobody will live through November. How do they know? How can you ask such a question? says one. I've lived here for twenty-eight years and I can tell you something about this country. Do you know what I had to show for it in the end? An old taxi that I left sitting in the street.

Do you believe it? I ask Arturo. Arturo doesn't believe it, but he still wants to leave. And you, Dona Cartagina, do you believe it? Yes, Dona Cartagina is convinced. If we stay till November, that'll be the end of us. The old lady energetically draws a finger across her throat, on which her fingernail leaves a red mark.

People escaped as if from an infectious disease, as if from pestilential air that can't be seen but still inflicts death. Afterward the wind blows and the sand drifts over the traces of the last survivor.

Various things happened before that, before the city was closed and sentenced to death. As a sick person suddenly revives and recovers his strength for a moment in the midst of his agony, so, at the end of September, life in Luanda took on a certain vigor and tempo. The sidewalks were crowded and traffic jams clogged the streets. People ran around nervously, in a hurry, wrapping up thousands of matters. Clear out as quickly as possible, escape in time, before the first wave of deadly air intrudes upon the city.

They didn't want Angola. They had had enough of the country, which was supposed to be the promised land but had brought them disenchantment and abasement. They said farewell to their African homes with mixed despair and rage, sorrow and impotence, with the feeling of leaving forever. All they wanted was to get out with their lives and to take their possessions with them.

Everybody was busy building crates. Mountains of boards and plywood were brought in. The price of hammers and nails soared. Crates were the main topic of conversation—how to build them, what was the best thing to reinforce them with. Self-proclaimed experts, crate specialists, homegrown architects of cratery, masters of crate styles, crate schools, and crate fashions appeared. Inside the Luanda of concrete and bricks a new wooden city began to rise. The streets I walked through resembled a great building site. I stumbled over discarded planks, nails sticking out of beams ripped my shirt. Some crates were as big as vacation cottages, because a hierarchy of crate status had suddenly come into being. The richer the people, the bigger the crates they erected. Crates belonging to millionaires were impressive: beamed and lined with sailcloth, they had solid, elegant walls made of the most expensive grades of tropical wood, with the rings and knots cut and polished like antiques. Into these crates went whole salons and bedrooms, sofas, tables, wardrobes, kitchens and refrigerators, commodes and armchairs, pictures, carpets, chandeliers, porcelain, bedclothes and linen, clothing, tapestries and vases, even artificial flowers (I saw them with my own eyes), all the monstrous and inexhaustible junk that clutters every middle-class home. Into them went figurines, seashells, glass balls, flower bowls, stuffed lizards, a metal miniature of the cathedral of Milan brought back from Italy, letters!—letters and photographs, wedding pictures in gilt frames (Why don't we leave that? the husband asks, and the enraged wife cries, You ought to be ashamed!)—all the pictures of the children, and here's the first time he sat up, and here's the first time he said Give, Give, and here he is with a lollipop, and here with his grandma—everything, and I mean everything, because this case of wine, this supply of macaroni that I laid in as soon as the shooting started, and then the fishing rod, the crochet needles—my yarn!—my rifle, Tutu's colored blocks, birds, peanuts, the vacuum and the nutcracker, have to be squeezed in, too, that's all there is to it, they have to be, and they are, so that all we leave behind are the bare floors, the naked walls, *en déshabille*. The house's striptease goes all the way, right down to the curtain rods—and all that remains is to lock the door and stop along the boulevard en route to the airport and throw the key in the ocean.

The crates of the poor are inferior on several counts. They are smaller, often downright diminutive, and unsightly. They can't compete in quality; their workmanship leaves a great deal to be desired. While the wealthy can employ master cabinetmakers, the poor have to knock their crates together with their own hands. For materials they use odds and ends from the lumber yard, mill ends, warped beams, cracked plywood, all the leftovers you can pick up thirdhand. Many are made of hammered tin, taken from olive-oil cans, old signs, and rusty billboards; they look like the tumbledown slums of the African quarters. It's not worth looking inside—not worth it, and not really the sort of thing one does.

The crates of the wealthy stand in the main downtown streets or in the shadowy byways of exclusive neighborhoods. You can look at them and admire. The crates of the poor, on the other hand, languish in entranceways, in backyards, in sheds. They are hidden for the time being, but in the end they will have to be transported the length of the city to the port, and the thought of that pitiful display is unappetizing.

Thanks to the abundance of wood that has collected here in Luanda, this dusty desert city nearly devoid of trees now smells like a flourishing forest. It's as if the forest had suddenly taken root in the streets, the squares, and the plazas. In the evenings I throw the window open to take a deep breath of it, and the war fades. I no longer hear the moans of Dona Esmeralda, I no longer see the ruined playboy with his two pistols, and I feel just as if I were sleeping it off in a forester's cottage in Bory Tucholski.

The building of the wooden city, the city of crates, goes on day after day, from dawn to twilight. Everyone works, soaked with rain, burned by the sun; even the millionaires, if they are physically fit, turn to the task. The enthusiasm of the adults infects the children. They too build crates, for their dolls and toys. Packing takes place under cover of night. It's better that way, when no one's sticking his nose into other people's business, nobody's keeping track of who puts in how much and what (and everyone knows there are a lot of that sort around, the ones who serve the MPLA and can't wait to inform).

So by night, in the thickest darkness, we transfer the contents of the stone city to the inside of the wooden city. It takes a lot of effort and sweat, lifting and struggling, shoulders sore from stowing it all, knees sore from squeezing it all in because it all has to fit and, after all, the stone city was big and the wooden city is small.

Gradually, from night to night, the stone city lost its value in favor of the wooden city. Gradually too, it changed in people's estimation. People stopped thinking in terms of houses and apartments and discussed only crates. Instead of saying, "I've got to go see what's at home," they said, "I've got to go check my crate." By now that was the only thing that interested them, the only thing they cared about. The Luanda they were leaving had become a stiff and alien stage set, empty, for the show was over.

Nowhere else in the world had I seen such a city, and I may never see anything like it again. It existed for months, and then it suddenly began disappearing. Or rather, quarter after quarter, it was taken on trucks to the port. Now it was spread out at the very edge of the sea, illuminated at night by harbor lanterns and the glare of lights on anchored ships. By day, people wound through its chaotic streets, painting their names and addresses on little plates, just as anyone does anywhere in the world when he builds himself a house. You could convince yourself, therefore, that this is a normal wooden town, except that it's been closed up by its residents who, for unknown reasons, have had to leave it in haste.

But afterward, when things had already turned very bad in the stone city and we, its handful of inhabitants, were waiting like desperadoes for the day of its destruction, the wooden city sailed away on the ocean. It was carried off by a great flotilla with which, after several hours, it disappeared below the horizon. This happened suddenly, as if a pirate fleet had sailed into the port, seized a priceless treasure, and escaped to sea with it.

Even so, I managed to see how the city sailed away. At dawn it was still rocking off the coast, piled up confusedly, uninhabited, lifeless, as if magically transformed into a museum exhibit of an ancient Eastern city and the last tour group had left. At that hour it was foggy and cold. I stood on the shore with some Angolan soldiers and a little crowd of ragtag freezing black children. "They've taken everything from us," one of the soldiers said without malice, and turned to cut a pineapple because that fruit, so overripe that, when it was cut, the juice ran out like water from a cup, was then our only food. "They've taken everything from us," he repeated and buried his face in the golden bowl of the fruit. The homeless harbor children gazed at him with greedy, fascinated eyes. The soldier lifted his juice-smeared face, smiled, and added, "But anyway, we've got a home now. They left us what's ours." He stood and, rejoicing in the thought that Angola was his, shot off a whole round from his automatic rifle into the air. Sirens sounded, seagulls darted and wheeled over the water, and the city stirred and began to sail away.

I don't know if there had ever been an instance of a whole city sailing across the ocean, but that is exactly what happened. The city sailed out into the world, in search of its inhabitants. These were the former residents of Angola, the Portuguese, who had scattered throughout Europe and America. A part of them reached South Africa. All fled Angola in haste, escaping before the conflagration of war, convinced that in this country there would be no more life and only the cemeteries would remain. But before they left they had still managed to build the wooden city in Luanda, into which they packed everything that had been in the stone city. On the streets now there were only thousands of cars, rusting and covered with dust. The walls also remained, the roofs, the asphalt on the roads, and the iron benches along the boulevards.

And now the wooden city was sailing on an Atlantic swept by violent, gale-driven waves. Somewhere on the ocean the partition of the city occurred and one section, the largest, sailed to Lisbon, the second to Rio de Janeiro, and the third to Capetown. Each of these sections reached its haven safely. I know this from various sources. Maria wrote to tell me that her crates ended up in Brazil—crates that had been part of the wooden city. Many newspapers wrote about the fact that one section made it to Capetown. And here's what I saw with my own eyes. After leaving Luanda, I stopped in Lisbon. A friend drove me along a wide street at the mouth of the Tagus, near the port. And there I saw fantastic heaps of crates stacked to perilous heights, unmoved, abandoned, as if they belonged to no one. This was the largest section of the wooden Luanda, which had sailed to the coast of Europe.

Back in the days when the erection of the wooden city had barely begun, the merchants had the biggest headaches. What could they do with the merchandise of all kinds that lay in the shops and filled the warehouses to their cobwebbed ceilings? No one could imagine a crate capable of accommodating the inventory of the leading wholesaler in Luanda, Don Castro Soremenho e Sousa. And the other wholesalers? And the thousand-strong clans of specialist retailers?

In addition, the whole import trade was behaving as if somebody was playing with less than a full deck. European firms—didn't anybody read the newspapers back there?—were shipping back-ordered merchandise to Luanda, oblivious of the fact that flames of armed conflagration were licking at Angola. Who now needed the complete sets of bathroom equipment shipped yesterday by Koenig and Sons GmbH, Hamburg? Who could suppress a chuckle at the arrival from London of an order of tennis balls, rackets, and golf clubs? As if for the sake of irony, a big shipment of insecticide sprayers came in from Marseilles—ordered by the very coffee planters now fighting for seats on flights to Europe.

Don Urbano Tavares, the proprietor of a jewelry shop on the main street, can feel content despite the mad unhappiness everywhere. When he chose his line of work years ago, he hit the bull's-eye. Gold always sells, and what's left fits easily into carry-on luggage. Lively action marks his business now. But not only gold is booming. People are rushing above all to food shops, because there is less and less to eat. Jostling crowds fill clothing and shoe stores. Watches and miniature radios, cosmetics and medicine are selling—small, light items that can be useful in the new life in countries beyond the sea.

A visit to a bookshop on Largo de Portugal leaves a sad impression. It is empty. Dust has settled in a gray layer on the old counter. Not a single customer. Who wants to read books now? The soldiers bought up the last pornographic magazines long ago and took them to the front. What's left— stacks of masterpieces mixed with the most second-rate reading matter— interests no one. Scribblers can draw an important lesson in modesty here. Immortal classics and page-turner romances are equally unattractive to the refugees for a simple reason: Paper is heavy.

A shop bearing the pious name Cruz de Cristo also stands empty. The specialty of the house is selling and renting wedding dresses. The owner, Dona Amanda, sits motionless for hours, unoccupied, among a crowd of similarly unmoving mute mannequins bewitched by some invisible fairy. There are enough dresses to furnish one of those mass weddings still popular in Mexico to this day. All white, right down to the ground, but each one cut differently, each one splendid in its baroque wealth of flounces and lace. What does Dona Amanda look forward to? One need only glance through the display window at her downcast, gloomy face. The time for joy and weddings has passed and left Dona Amanda surrounded by the unneeded props of an extinguished epoch.

Better luck (if that's the right word—I doubt it) attends Don Francisco Amarel Reis, owner of the Caminho ao Ceu (Road to Heaven) firm, concealed discreetly in a side street at the edge of the city center. His specialty: crosses, caskets, foil flowers, funeral accessories. These days there are many deaths, since fear, despair, and frustration lead people to the grave. There is a multitude of tragic automobile accidents here because the general atmosphere of rout, defeat, rage, and entrapment turns every susceptible driver into a beast. So we have funeral after funeral.

I am writing about people to whom Dona Cartagina introduced me. The old lady was the guardian spirit of the hotel and she wanted to arrange everything. She was the only person interested in Dona Amanda's gowns, because she was conjuring up a vision of the wedding of Maria and Arturo. She argued with Don Francisco about the cost of Dona Esmeralda's funeral, because Dona Esmeralda wouldn't come out of her coma. Only to the bookstore did I go alone, because I like to spend time in the company of books.

We buried Dona Esmeralda in a cemetery on a steep slope above the sea. The cemetery is as white as if covered by eternal snow. Needlelike cypresses, almost dark blue in the sunlight, shoot up heavenward out of the snow. The gate is painted blue, a warm and optimistic color in this case, suggesting that those who come here march heavenward like the saints in Louis Armstrong's song.

The next day Don Silva, the crotchety miser with the suit full of diamonds, left. Later I took Maria and Arturo to the airport.

Now several planes a day—French, Portuguese, Russian, and Italian—were flying. The pilots would get out and look around the airport. I watched them, amazed at the thought that only a few hours before they had been in Europe. I looked at them as at people from another planet. Europe—that was a distant, unreal point in a galaxy whose existence could be proved only by complicated deduction. They flew out in the evening. The overloaded machines crept to the runway, gained altitude with difficulty, and disappeared among the stars.

The nomad city without roofs and walls, the city of refugees around the airport, gradually vanished from the earth. At the same time, the wooden city deserted Luanda and waited in the port for its long journey. Of all the cities on the bay, only the stone Luanda, ever more depopulated and superfluous, remained.

That was the beginning of October. The city was becoming more desolate each day. Starting in the morning I wandered the streets without aim, without purpose, until the crushing heat drove me back to the hotel. At noon the sun beat against my head; it became so close and hot that there was nothing to breathe. Summer was beginning and the gates of a tropical hell were opening. Water was running short because the pumping stations were situated on the front lines, and after each repair they were destroyed again in the course of the fighting. I walked around dirty, needing something to drink so badly that I came down with a fever and saw orange spots before my eyes.

More and more merchants closed their shops. Black boys drummed with sticks on the lowered metal shutters. Restaurants and cafés were already out of action; chairs, tables, and folded umbrellas stood around on the sidewalks and afterward disappeared into the African slums. From time to time some car would drive through the empty streets, running the red lights that kept functioning automatically, God knows for whom.

At about this time, someone brought news to the hotel that all the police had left!

Now Luanda, of all the cities in the world, had no police. When you find yourself in such a situation, you feel strange. On the one hand everything seems light, loose, but on the other hand there is a certain uneasiness. The few whites who still wandered the city accepted the development with foreboding. Rumors circulated that the black quarters would descend upon the stone city. Everyone knew that the blacks lived in the most awful conditions, in the worst slums to be seen anywhere in Africa, in clay hovels like heaps of smashed cheap pottery covering the desert around Luanda. And here stood the luxurious stone city of glass and concrete—empty, no one's. If only they would come peacefully, in an orderly way, with their families, and occupy what was abandoned and vacant. But according to the terrified Portuguese who passed themselves off as experts on the native mentality, the blacks would burst in, swept up in a madness of destruction and hatred, drunk, drugged with secret herbs, demanding blood and revenge. Nothing could hold back that invasion. Exhausted people with shattered nerves, unarmed and at bay, talk and dream up the most apocalyptic visions. Everyone is lost and it will be the most hideous death—stabbed to death in the streets, hacked with machetes on their own doorsteps. Those with more presence of mind propose various kinds of self-defense. One says to extinguish all the lights and keep watch in the darkened city. Another says the opposite: Turn on the lights even in empty houses, because only numbers, massed numbers, will be able to scare off the blacks. As usual, no argument prevails and at night the city looks like a curtain full of holes—here a fragment of some scene shines through, then around it nothing can be seen, then there's another fragment, then everything is covered. Dona Cartagina, who more from habit than necessity is cleaning the vacant rooms on my floor (I'm all alone there now), pauses in her sweeping to listen for the sinister rumble of a crowd, the harbinger of our doom, approaching from the black quarters. She freezes just like a village woman in the field listening for thunder. Then she crosses herself solemnly and goes on cleaning.

All the firemen have left! Now no one will save the city from fires. At first, people cannot believe that the firemen have deserted their posts, but to convince themselves they have only to visit the main engine company on the shorefront boulevard. The gates of the station are standing open. Inside sit the big red-and-gold fire engines with ladders and hoses. The firemen's helmets sit on shelves. There isn't a living soul. Of course the FNLA will find out about this, and all it will take is one bomb dropped tomorrow in place of the leaflets. All Luanda will go up like a matchbox. The rains have stopped, the city is sun-baked and dry as sawdust. If only there isn't a short circuit, if only some drunk doesn't get careless. Later the soldiers get one of the pumpers running and use it to carry water to the front. Since it is easy to spot from a distance, it is hit, runs into a ditch, and stays there.

All the garbagemen have left!

At first, nobody noticed. The city was dirty and neglected, so people assumed that the garbagemen had flown to Europe a long time ago. Then it turned out that they had left only the day before. Suddenly, no one knew from where, the garbage started piling up. After all, there was only a handful of residents left and they were so apathetic and inert that no one could accuse them of carrying out such mountains of garbage. Yet mounds of it began piling up on the streets of the abandoned city. It appeared on the sidewalks, in the roads, in the squares, in the entranceways of townhouses, and in the extinct marketplaces. You could walk through some streets only with great effort and disgust. In this climate the excess of sun and moisture accelerate and intensify decay, rot, and fermentation. The whole city began to stink, and anybody who had a long walk through the streets to his hotel picked up that stench, too, and other people spoke to him from a distance. In general, people distanced themselves from each other even though, in the situation to which we were condemned, it should have been the other way around. Dona Cartagina closed all the windows because the putrid air that blew in was unbreathable. The cats started dying. They must have poisoned themselves collectively on some carrion, because one morning dead cats were lying everywhere. After two days they puffed up and swelled to the size of piglets. Black flies swarmed over them. The odor was unbearable. I walked through the city dripping with sweat, holding a handkerchief to my nose. Dona Cartagina said the prayers against pestilence. There were no doctors, and not a single hospital or pharmacy remained open. The garbage grew and multiplied like the rising of a monstrous, disgusting dough expanding in all directions, impelled by a poisonous deadly yeast.

Later, when all the barbers, repairmen, mail carriers, and concierges had left, the stone city lost its reason for existing, its sense. It was like a dry skeleton polished by the wind, a dead bone sticking up out of the ground toward the sun.

The dogs were still alive.

They were pets, abandoned by owners fleeing in panic. You could see dogs of all the most expensive breeds, without masters—boxers, bulldogs, greyhounds, Dobermans, dachshunds, Airedales, spaniels, even Scotch terriers and Great Danes, pugs and poodles. Deserted, stray, they roamed in a great pack looking for food. As long as the Portuguese army was there, the dogs gathered every morning on the square in front of the general headquarters and the sentries fed them canned NATO rations. It was like watching an international pedigreed dog show. Afterward the fed, satisfied pack moved to the soft, juicy mowed grass on the lawn of the Government Palace. An unlikely mass sex orgy began, excited and indefatigable madness, chasing and tumbling to the point of utter abandon. It gave the bored sentries a lot of ribald amusement.

When the army left, the dogs began to go hungry and slim down. For a while they drifted around the city in a desultory mob, looking for a handout. One day they disappeared. I think they followed the human example and left Luanda, since I never came across a dead dog afterward, though hundreds of them had been loitering in front of the general headquarters and frolicking in front of the palace. One could suppose that an energetic leader emerged from the ranks to take the pack out of the dying city. If the dogs went north, they ran into the FNLA. If they went south, they ran into UNITA. On the other hand, if they went east, in the direction of Ndalatando and Saurimo, they might have made it into Zambia, then to Mozambique or even Tanzania.

Perhaps they're still roaming, but I don't know in what direction or in what country.

After the exodus of the dogs, the city fell into rigor mortis. So I decided to go to the front.

From *Homicide*

DAVID SIMON

After joining the Baltimore *Sun* as a police reporter in 1983, David Simon became frustrated by the coverage of local murders (then running about 250 a year). He came to believe that the typical homicide story, brief and formulaic, "anesthetizes readers . . . and simplifies the violence and cruelty of a dirty, complex world."

Simon took a leave of absence in 1988 and spent a year with a Baltimore homicide unit. In his chronicle, *Homicide: A Year on the Killing Streets,* he inhabits the viewpoint of the detectives themselves. "As a result," he says, "the reader travels through a homicide detective's daily routine accompanied by a narrator who is, in effect, the communal voice of the unit rather than an overtly detached reporter."

The communal voice not only connects the subplots; it also makes big blocks of exposition seem dramatic. In set pieces that break up or kick off main story lines, Simon engages the reader through composite conversations and direct address. The excerpt reprinted here turns "you" into both suspect and interrogator.

As a journalist, Simon strenuously avoids the first person. "Instead of my own vision," he says, "I want to convey the reality of those living the event." He now writes scripts for television shows—including *Homicide: Life on the Street,* an adaptation of his book—and has just completed another nonfiction story, *The Corner,* about drugs and crime.

—K. K.

You are a citizen of a free nation, having lived your adult life in a land of guaranteed civil liberties, and you commit a crime of violence, whereupon you are jacked up, hauled down to a police station and deposited in a claustrophobic anteroom with three chairs, a table and no windows. There you sit for a half hour or so until a police detective—a man you have never met before, a man who can in no way be mistaken for a friend—enters the room with a thin stack of lined notepaper and a ball-point pen.

The detective offers a cigarette, not your brand, and begins an uninter-rupted monologue that wanders back and forth for a half hour more, even-tually coming to rest in a familiar place: *"You have the absolute right to remain silent."*

Of course you do. You're a criminal. Criminals always have the right to remain silent. At least once in your miserable life, you spent an hour in front of a television set, listening to this book-'em-Danno routine. You think Joe Friday was lying to you? You think Kojak was making this horseshit up? No way, bunk, we're talking sacred freedoms here, notably your Fifth Fucking Amendment protection against self-incrimination, and hey, it was good enough for Ollie North, so who are you to go incriminating yourself at the first opportunity? Get it straight: A police detective, a man who gets paid government money to put you in prison, is explaining your absolute right to shut up before you say something stupid.

"Anything you say or write may be used against you in a court of law."

Yo, bunky, wake the fuck up. You're now being told that talking to a police detective in an interrogation room can only hurt you. If it could help you, they would probably be pretty quick to say that, wouldn't they? They'd stand up and say you have the right not to worry because what you say or write in this godforsaken cubicle is gonna be used to your benefit in a court of law. No, your best bet is to shut up. Shut up now.

"You have the right to talk with a lawyer at any time—before any question-ing, before answering any questions, or during any questions."

Talk about helpful. Now the man who wants to arrest you for violating the peace and dignity of the state is saying you can talk to a trained profes-sional, an attorney who has read the relevant portions of the Maryland Annotated Code or can at least get his hands on some Cliffs Notes. And let's face it, pal, you just carved up a drunk in a Dundalk Avenue bar, but that don't make you a neurosurgeon. Take whatever help you can get.

"If you want a lawyer and cannot afford to hire one, you will not be asked any questions, and the court will be requested to appoint a lawyer for you."

Translation: You're a derelict. No charge for derelicts.

At this point, if all lobes are working, you ought to have seen enough of this Double Jeopardy category to know that it ain't where you want to be. How about a little something from Criminal Lawyers and Their Clients for $50, Alex?

Whoa, bunk, not so fast.

"Before we get started, lemme just get through the paperwork," says the detective, who now produces an Explanation of Rights sheet, BPD Form 69, and passes it across the table.

"EXPLANATION OF RIGHTS," declares the top line in bold block let-ters. The detective asks you to fill in your name, address, age, and education, then the date and time. That much accomplished, he asks you to read the next section. It begins, "YOU ARE HEREBY ADVISED THAT:"

Read number one, the detective says. Do you understand number one?

"You have the absolute right to remain silent."

Yeah, you understand. We did this already.

"Then write your initials next to number one. Now read number two."

And so forth, until you have initialed each component of the Miranda warning. That done, the detective tells you to write your signature on the next line, the one just below the sentence that says, "I HAVE READ THE ABOVE EXPLANATION OF MY RIGHTS AND FULLY UNDERSTAND IT."

You sign your name and the monologue resumes. The detective assures you that he has informed you of these rights because he wants you to be protected, because there is nothing that concerns him more than giving you every possible assistance in this very confusing and stressful moment in your life. If you don't want to talk, he tells you, that's fine. And if you want a lawyer, that's fine, too, because first of all, he's no relation to the guy you cut up, and second, he's gonna get six hours overtime no matter what you do. But he wants you to know—and he's been doing this a lot longer than you, so take his word for it—that your rights to remain silent and obtain qualified counsel aren't all they're cracked up to be.

Look at it this way, he says, leaning back in his chair. Once you up and call for that lawyer, son, we can't do a damn thing for you. No sir, your friends in the city homicide unit are going to have to leave you locked in this room all alone and the next authority figure to scan your case will be a tie-wearing, three-piece bloodsucker—a no-nonsense prosecutor from the Violent Crimes Unit with the official title of assistant state's attorney for the city of Baltimore. And God help you then, son, because a ruthless fucker like that will have an O'Donnell Heights motorhead like yourself halfway to the gas chamber before you get three words out. Now's the time to speak up, right now when I got my pen and paper here on the table, because once I walk out of this room any chance you have of telling your side of the story is gone and I gotta write it up the way it looks. And the way it looks right now is first-fucking-degree murder. Felony murder, mister, which when shoved up a man's asshole is a helluva lot more painful than second-degree or maybe even manslaughter. What you say right here and now could make the difference, bunk. Did I mention that Maryland has a gas chamber? Big, ugly sumbitch at the penitentiary on Eager Street, not twenty blocks from here. You don't wanna get too close to that bad boy, lemme tell you.

A small, wavering sound of protest passes your lips and the detective leans back in his chair, shaking his head sadly.

What the hell is wrong with you, son? You think I'm fucking with you? Hey, I don't even need to bother with your weak shit. I got three witnesses in three other rooms who say you're my man. I got a knife from the scene that's going downstairs to the lab for latent prints. I got blood spatter on them Air

Jordans we took off you ten minutes ago. Why the fuck do you think we took 'em? Do I look like I wear high-top tennis? Fuck no. You got spatter all over 'em, and I think we both know whose blood type it's gonna be. Hey, bunk, I'm only in here to make sure that there ain't nothing you can say for yourself before I write it all up.

You hesitate.

Oh, says the detective. You want to think about it. Hey, you think about it all you want, pal. My captain's right outside in the hallway, and he already told me to charge your ass in the first fuckin' degree. For once in your beshitted little life someone is giving you a chance and you're too fucking dumb to take it. What the fuck, you go ahead and think about it and I'll tell my captain to cool his heels for ten minutes. I can do that much for you. How 'bout some coffee? Another cigarette?

The detective leaves you alone in that cramped, windowless room. Just you and the blank notepaper and the Form 69 and . . . first-degree murder. First-degree murder with witnesses and fingerprints and blood on your Air Jordans. Christ, you didn't even notice the blood on your own fucking shoes. Felony murder, mister. First-fucking-degree. How many years, you begin to wonder, how many years do I get for involuntary manslaughter?

Whereupon the man who wants to put you in prison, the man who is not your friend, comes back in the room, asking if the coffee's okay.

Yeah, you say, the coffee's fine, but what happens if I want a lawyer?

The detective shrugs. Then we get you a lawyer, he says. And I walk out of the room and type up the charging documents for first-degree murder and you can't say a fucking thing about it. Look, bunk, I'm giving you a chance. He came at you, right? You were scared. It was self-defense.

Your mouth opens to speak.

He came at you, didn't he?

"Yeah," you venture cautiously, "he came at me."

Whoa, says the detective, holding up his hands. Wait a minute. If we're gonna do this, I gotta find your rights form. Where's the fucking form? Damn things are like cops, never around when you need 'em. Here it is, he says, pushing the explanation-of-rights sheet across the table and pointing to the bottom. Read that, he says.

"I am willing to answer questions and I do not want any attorney at this time. My decision to answer questions without having an attorney present is free and voluntary on my part."

As you read, he leaves the room and returns a moment later with a second detective as a witness. You sign the bottom of the form, as do both detectives.

The first detective looks up from the form, his eyes soaked with innocence. "He came at you, huh?"

"Yeah, he came at me."

Get used to small rooms, bunk, because you are about to be dropkicked into the lost land of pretrial detention. Because it's one thing to be a murdering little asshole from Southeast Baltimore, and it's another to be stupid about it, and with five little words you have just elevated yourself to the ranks of the truly witless.

End of the road, pal. It's over. It's history. And if that police detective wasn't so busy committing your weak bullshit to paper, he'd probably look you in the eye and tell you so. He'd give you another cigarette and say, son, you are ignorance personified and you just put yourself in for the fatal stabbing of a human being. He might even tell you that the other witnesses in the other rooms are too drunk to identify their own reflections, much less the kid who had the knife, or that it's always a long shot for the lab to pull a latent off a knife hilt, or that your $95 sneakers are as clean as the day you bought them. If he was feeling particularly expansive, he might tell you that everyone who leaves the homicide unit in handcuffs does so charged with first-degree murder, that it's for the lawyers to decide what kind of deal will be cut. He might go on to say that even after all these years working homicides, there is still a small part of him that finds it completely mystifying that anyone ever utters a single word in a police interrogation. To illustrate the point, he could hold up your Form 69, on which you waived away every last one of your rights, and say, "Lookit here, pistonhead, I told you twice that you were deep in the shit and that whatever you said could put you in deeper." And if his message was still somehow beyond your understanding, he could drag your carcass back down the sixth-floor hallway, back toward the sign that says Homicide Unit in white block letters, the sign you saw when you walked off the elevator.

Now think hard: Who lives in a homicide unit? Yeah, right. And what do homicide detectives do for a living? Yeah, you got it, bunk. And what did you do tonight? You murdered someone.

So when you opened that mouth of yours, what the fuck were you thinking?

Homicide detectives in Baltimore like to imagine a small, open window at the top of the long wall in the large interrogation room. More to the point, they like to imagine their suspects imagining a small, open window at the top of the long wall. The open window is the escape hatch, the Out. It is the perfect representation of what every suspect believes when he opens his mouth during an interrogation. Every last one envisions himself parrying questions with the right combination of alibi and excuse; every last one sees himself coming up with the right words, then crawling out the window to go home and sleep in his own bed. More often than not, a guilty man is looking for the Out from his first moments in the interrogation room; in that sense, the window is as much the suspect's fantasy as the detective's mirage.

The effect of the illusion is profound, distorting as it does the natural hostility between hunter and hunted, transforming it until it resembles a relationship more symbiotic than adversarial. That is the lie, and when the roles are perfectly performed, deceit surpasses itself, becoming manipulation on a grand scale and ultimately an act of betrayal. Because what occurs in an interrogation room is indeed little more than a carefully staged drama, a choreographed performance that allows a detective and his suspect to find common ground where none exists. There, in a carefully controlled purgatory, the guilty proclaim their malefactions, though rarely in any form that allows for contrition or resembles an unequivocal admission.

In truth, catharsis in the interrogation room occurs for only a few rare suspects, usually those in domestic murders or child abuse cases wherein the leaden mass of genuine remorse can crush anyone who is not hardened to his crime. But the greater share of men and women brought downtown take no interest in absolution. Ralph Waldo Emerson rightly noted that for those responsible, the act of murder "is no such ruinous thought as poets and romancers will have it; it does not unsettle him, or frighten him from his ordinary notice of trifles." And while West Baltimore is a universe or two from Emerson's nineteenth-century Massachusetts hamlet, the observation is still useful. Murder often doesn't unsettle a man. In Baltimore, it usually doesn't even ruin his day.

As a result, the majority of those who acknowledge their complicity in a killing must be baited by detectives with something more tempting than penitence. They must be made to believe that their crime is not really murder, that their excuse is both accepted and unique, that they will, with the help of the detective, be judged less evil than they truly are.

Some are brought to that unreasoned conclusion by the suggestion that they acted in self-defense or were provoked to violence. Others fall prey to the notion that they are less culpable than their colleagues—I only drove the car or backed up the robbery, I wasn't the triggerman; or yeah, I raped her, but I stayed out of it when them other guys started strangling her—unaware that Maryland law allows every member of the conspiracy to be charged as a principal. Still others succumb to the belief that they will get a better shake by cooperating with detectives and acknowledging a limited amount of guilt. And many of those who cannot be lured over the precipice of self-incrimination can still be manipulated into providing alibis, denials and explanations—statements that can be checked and rechecked until a suspect's lies are the greatest evidentiary threat to his freedom.

For that reason, the professionals say nothing. No alibis. No explanations. No expressions of polite dismay or blanket denials. In the late 1970s, when men by the names of Dennis Wise and Vernon Collins were matching each other body for body as Baltimore's premier contract killers and no witness could be found to testify against either, things got to the point where both the detectives and their suspects knew the drill:

Enter room.

Miranda.

Anything to say this time, Dennis?

No, sir. Just want to call my lawyer.

Fine, Dennis.

Exit room.

For anyone with experience in the criminal justice machine, the point is driven home by every lawyer worth his fee. Repetition and familiarity with the process soon place the professionals beyond the reach of a police interrogation. Yet more than two decades after the landmark Escobedo and Miranda decisions, the rest of the world remains strangely willing to place itself at risk. As a result, the same law enforcement community that once regarded the 1966 Miranda decision as a death blow to criminal investigation has now come to see the explanation of rights as a routine part of the process—simply a piece of station house furniture, if not a civilizing influence on police work itself.

In an era when beatings and physical intimidation were common tools of an interrogation, the Escobedo and Miranda decisions were sent down by the nation's highest court to ensure that criminal confessions and statements were purely voluntary. The resulting Miranda warning was "a protective device to dispel the compelling atmosphere of the interrogation," as Chief Justice Earl Warren wrote in the majority opinion. Investigators would be required to assure citizens of their rights to silence and counsel, not only at the moment of arrest, but at the moment that they could reasonably be considered suspects under interrogation.

In answer to Miranda, the nation's police officials responded with a veritable jeremiad, wailing in unison that the required warnings would virtually assure that confessions would be impossible to obtain and conviction rates would plummet. Yet the prediction was soon proved false for the simple reason that those law enforcement leaders—and, for that matter, the Supreme Court itself—underestimated a police detective's ingenuity.

Miranda is, on paper, a noble gesture which declares that constitutional rights extend not only to the public forum of the courts, but to the private confines of the police station as well. Miranda and its accompanying decisions established a uniform concept of a criminal defendant's rights and effectively ended the use of violence and the most blatant kind of physical intimidation in interrogations. That, of course, was a blessing. But if the further intent of the Miranda decision was, in fact, an attempt to "dispel the compelling atmosphere" of an interrogation, then it failed miserably.

And thank God. Because by any standards of human discourse, a criminal confession can never truly be called voluntary. With rare exception, a confession is compelled, provoked and manipulated from a suspect by a detective who has been trained in a genuinely deceitful art. That is the essence of interrogation, and those who believe that a straightforward conversation between a cop and a criminal—devoid of any treachery—is going to solve a crime are somewhere beyond naive. If the interrogation process is, from a moral standpoint, contemptible, it is nonetheless essential. Deprived of the ability to question and confront suspects and witnesses, a detective is left with physical evidence and in many cases, precious little of that. Without a chance for a detective to manipulate a suspect's mind, a lot of bad people would simply go free.

Yet every defense attorney knows that there can be no good reason for a guilty man to say anything whatsoever to a police officer, and any suspect who calls an attorney will be told as much, bringing the interrogation to an end. A court opinion that therefore requires a detective—the same detective working hard to dupe a suspect—to stop abruptly and guarantee the man his right to end the process can only be called an act of institutional schizophrenia. The Miranda warning is a little like a referee introducing a barroom brawl: The stern warnings to hit above the waist and take no cheap shots have nothing to do with the mayhem that follows.

Yet how could it be otherwise? It would be easy enough for our judiciary to ensure that no criminal suspect relinquished his rights inside a police station: The courts could simply require the presence of a lawyer at all times. But such a blanket guarantee of individual rights would effectively end the use of interrogation as an investigative weapon, leaving many more crimes unsolved and many more guilty men and women unpunished. Instead, the ideals have been carefully compromised at little cost other than to the integrity of the police investigator.

After all, it's the lawyers, the Great Compromisers of our age, who have struck this bargain, who still manage to keep cuffs clean in the public courts, where rights and process are worshiped faithfully. It is left for the detective to fire this warning shot across a suspect's bow, granting rights to a man who will then be tricked into relinquishing them. In that sense, Miranda is a symbol and little more, a salve for a collective conscience that cannot reconcile libertarian ideals with what must necessarily occur in a police interrogation room. Our judges, our courts, our society as a whole, demand in the same breath that rights be maintained even as crimes are punished. And all of us are bent and determined to preserve the illusion that both can be achieved in the same, small room. It's mournful to think that this hypocrisy is the necessary creation of our best legal minds, who seem to view the interrogation process as the rest of us look upon breakfast sausage: We want it on a plate with eggs and toast; we don't want to know too much about how it comes to be.

Trapped in that contradiction, a detective does his job in the only possible way. He follows the requirements of the law to the letter—or close enough so as not to jeopardize his case. Just as carefully, he ignores that law's spirit and intent. He becomes a salesman, a huckster as thieving and silver-tongued as any man who ever moved used cars or aluminum siding—more so, in fact, when you consider that he's selling long prison terms to customers who have no genuine need for the product.

The fraud that claims it is somehow in a suspect's interest to talk with police will forever be the catalyst in any criminal interrogation. It is a fiction propped up against the greater weight of logic itself, sustained for hours on end through nothing more or less than a detective's ability to control the interrogation room.

A good interrogator controls the physical environment, from the moment a suspect or reluctant witness is dumped in the small cubicle, left alone to stew in soundproof isolation. The law says that a man can't be held against his will unless he's to be charged with a crime, yet the men and women tossed into the interrogation room rarely ponder their legal status. They light cigarettes and wait, staring abstractedly at four yellow cinderblock walls, a dirty tin ashtray on a plain table, a small mirrored window and a series of stained acoustic tiles on the ceiling. Those few with heart enough to ask whether they are under arrest are often answered with a question:

"Why? Do you want to be?"

"No."

"Then sit the fuck down."

Control is the reason a suspect is seated farthest from the interrogation room door, and the reason the room's light switch can only be operated with a key that remains in possession of the detectives. Every time a suspect has to ask for or be offered a cigarette, water, coffee or a trip to the bathroom, he's being reminded that he's lost control.

When the detective arrives with pen and notepaper and begins the initial monologue to which a potential suspect or witness is invariably subjected, he has two goals in mind: first, to emphasize his complete control of the process; second, to stop the suspect from opening his mouth. Because if a suspect or witness manages to blurt out his desire for a lawyer—if he asks for counsel definitively and declines to answer questions until he gets one— it's over.

To prevent that, a detective allows no interruption of his soliloquy. Typically, the speech begins with the detective identifying himself and confiding that this is some serious shit that the two of you have to sort out. In your favor, however, is the fact that he, the detective, is a fair and reasonable man. A great guy, in fact—just ask anyone he works with.

If, at this moment, you try to speak, the detective will cut you off, saying your chance will come in a little while. Right now, he will invariably say, you need to know where I'm coming from. Then he'll inform you that he happens to be very good at what he does, that he's had very few open cases in his long, storied career, and a whole busload of people who lied to him in this very room are now on Death Row.

Control. To keep it, you say whatever you have to. Then you say it over and over until it's safe to stop, because if your suspect thinks for one moment that he can influence events, he may just demand an attorney.

As a result, the Miranda warning becomes a psychological hurdle, a pregnant moment that must be slipped carefully into the back-and-forth of the interrogation. For witnesses, the warning is not required and a detective can question those knowledgeable about a crime for hours without ever advising them of their rights. But should a witness suddenly say something that indicates involvement in a criminal act, he becomes—by the Supreme Court's definition—a suspect, at which point he must be advised of his rights. In practice, the line between a potential suspect and a suspect can be thin, and a common sight in any American homicide unit is a handful of detectives standing outside an interrogation room, debating whether or not a Miranda warning is yet necessary.

The Baltimore department, like many others, uses a written form to confirm a suspect's acknowledgment of Miranda. In a city where nine out of ten suspects would otherwise claim they were never informed of their rights, the forms have proven essential. Moreover, the detectives have found that rather than drawing attention to the Miranda, the written form diffuses the impact of the warning. Even as it alerts a suspect to the dangers of an interrogation, the form co-opts the suspect, making him part of the process. It is the suspect who wields the pen, initialing each component of the warning and then signing the form; it is the suspect who is being asked to help with the paperwork. With witnesses, the detectives achieve the same effect with an information sheet that asks three dozen questions in rapid-fire succession. Not only does the form include information of value to the investigators—name, nickname, height, weight, complexion, employer, description of clothing at time of interview, relatives living in Baltimore, names of parents, spouse, boyfriend or girlfriend—but it acclimates the witness to the idea of answering questions before the direct interview begins.

Even if a suspect does indeed ask for a lawyer, he must—at least according to the most aggressive interpretation of Miranda—ask definitively: "I want to talk to a lawyer and I don't want to answer questions until I do."

Anything less leaves room for a good detective to maneuver. The distinctions are subtle and semantic:

"Maybe I should get a lawyer."

"Maybe you should. But why would you need a lawyer if you don't have anything to do with this?"

Or: "I think I should talk to a lawyer."

"You better be sure. Because if you want a lawyer then I'm not going to be able to do anything for you."

Likewise, if a suspect calls a lawyer and continues to answer questions until the lawyer arrives, his rights have not been violated. If the lawyer arrives, the suspect must be told that an attorney is in the building, but if he still wishes to continue the interrogation, nothing requires that the police allow the attorney to speak with his client. In short, the suspect can demand an attorney; a lawyer can't demand a suspect.

Once the minefield that is Miranda has been successfully negotiated, the detective must let the suspect know that his guilt is certain and easily established by the existing evidence. He must then offer the Out.

This, too, is role playing, and it requires a seasoned actor. If a witness or suspect is belligerent, you wear him down with greater belligerence. If the man shows fear, you offer calm and comfort. When he looks weak, you appear strong. When he wants a friend, you crack a joke and offer to buy him a soda. If he's confident, you are more so, assuring him that you are certain of his guilt and are curious only about a few select details of the crime. And if he's arrogant, if he wants nothing to do with the process, you intimidate him, threaten him, make him believe that making you happy may be the only thing between his ass and the Baltimore City Jail.

Kill your woman and a good detective will come close to real tears as he touches your shoulder and tells you how he knows that you must have loved her, that it wouldn't be so hard for you to talk about if you didn't. Beat your child to death and a police detective will wrap his arm around you in the interrogation room, telling you about how he beats his own children all the time, how it wasn't your fault if the kid up and died on you. Shoot a friend over a poker hand and that same detective will lie about your dead buddy's condition, telling you that the victim is in stable condition at Hopkins and probably won't press charges, which wouldn't amount to more than assault with intent even if he does. Murder a man with an accomplice and the detective will walk your co-conspirator past the open door of your interrogation room, then say your bunky's going home tonight because he gave a statement making you the triggerman. And if that same detective thinks you can be bluffed, he might tell you that they've got your prints on the weapon, or that there are two eyewitnesses who have picked your photo from an array, or that the victim made a dying declaration in which he named you as his assailant.

All of which is street legal. Reasonable deception, the courts call it. After all, what could be more reasonable than deceiving someone who has taken a human life and is now lying about it?

The deception sometimes goes too far, or at least it sometimes seems that way to those unfamiliar with the process. Not long ago, several veteran homicide detectives in Detroit were publicly upbraided and disciplined by their superiors for using the office Xerox machine as a polygraph device. It seems that the detectives, when confronted with a statement of dubious veracity, would sometimes adjourn to the Xerox room and load three sheets of paper into the feeder.

"Truth," said the first.

"Truth," said the second.

"Lie," said the third.

Then the suspect would be led into the room and told to put his hand against the side of the machine. The detectives would ask the man's name, listen to the answer, then hit the copy button.

Truth.

And where do you live?

Truth again.

And did you or did you not kill Tater, shooting him down like a dog in the 1200 block of North Durham Street?

Lie. Well, well: You lying motherfucker.

In Baltimore, the homicide detectives read newspaper accounts of the Detroit controversy and wondered why anyone had a problem. Polygraph by copier was an old trick; it had been attempted on more than one occasion in the sixth-floor Xerox room. Gene Constantine, a veteran of Stanton's shift, once gave a mindless wonder the coordination test for drunk drivers ("Follow my finger with your eyes, but don't move your head . . . Now stand on one foot"), then loudly declared that the man's performance indicated obvious deception.

"You flunked," Constantine told him. "You're lying."

Convinced, the suspect confessed.

Variations on the theme are limited only by a detective's imagination and his ability to sustain the fraud. But every bluff carries a corresponding risk, and a detective who tells a suspect his fingerprints are all over a crime scene loses all hope if the man knows he was wearing gloves. An interrogation room fraud is only as good as the material from which it was constructed— or, for that matter, as good as the suspect is witless—and a detective who underestimates his prey or overestimates his knowledge of the crime will lose precious credibility. Once a detective claims knowledge of a fact that the suspect knows to be untrue, the veil has been lifted, and the investigator is instead revealed as the liar.

Only when everything else in the repertoire fails does a detective resort to rage. It might be a spasm limited to a well-chosen sentence or two, or an extended tantrum punctuated by the slamming of a metal door or the drop kick of a chair, perhaps even a rant delivered as part of a good-cop, bad-cop melodrama, although that particular routine has worn thin with the years. Ideally, the shouting should be loud enough to suggest the threat of violence but restrained enough to avoid any action that could jeopardize the statement: Tell the court why you felt threatened. Did the detective hit you? Did he attempt to hit you? Did he threaten to hit you? No, but he slammed his hand down on the table, real loud.

Oh my. Motion to suppress denied.

What a good detective will not do in this more enlightened age is beat his suspect, at least not for the purpose of obtaining a statement. A suspect who swings on a homicide detective, who raves and kicks furniture, who tries to fight off a pair of handcuffs, will receive as comprehensive an ass-kicking as he would out on the street, but as a function of interrogation, physical assault is not part of the arsenal. In Baltimore, that has been true for at least fifteen years.

Simply put, the violence isn't worth the risk—not only the risk that the statement obtained will later be ruled inadmissible, but the risk to a detective's career and pension. It would be another thing entirely in those instances in which an officer or an officer's family member is the victim. In those cases, a good detective will anticipate the accusation by photographing a suspect after interrogation, to show an absence of injuries and to prove that any beating received prior to the suspect's arrival at the city jail had nothing to do with what occurred in the homicide unit.

But those are rare cases and, for the vast majority of murders, there is little for a detective to take personally. He doesn't know the dead man, he just met the suspect and he doesn't live anywhere near the street where the violence occurred. From that perspective, what civil servant in his right mind is going to risk his entire career to prove that on the night of March 7, 1988, in some godforsaken tract of West Baltimore, a drug dealer, Stinky, shot a dope fiend, Pee Wee, over a $35 debt?

Still, circuit court juries often prefer to think in conspiratorial terms about back rooms and hot lights and rabbit punches to a suspect's kidneys. A Baltimore detective once lost a case because the defendant testified that his confession was obtained only after he had been mauled by two detectives who beat him with a phone book. The detective was sequestered and did not hear that testimony, but when he took the stand, the defense attorney asked what items were in the room during the interrogation.

"The table. Chairs. Some papers. An ashtray."

"Was there a phone book in the room?"

The detective thought about it and remembered that yes, they had used a phone book to look up an address. "Yeah," he acknowledged. "A yellow pages phone book."

Only when the defense attorney looked approvingly at the jury did the cop realize that something was wrong. After the not guilty verdict, the detective swore he would never again begin an interview until he had cleared the room of every unnecessary item.

The passage of time can also damage the credibility of a confession. In the privacy of the interrogation room, it requires hours of prolonged effort to break a man to a point where he's willing to admit a criminal act, yet at some point those hours begin to cast doubt on the statement itself. Even under the best conditions, four to six hours of interrogation are required to break a suspect down, and eight or ten or twelve hours can be justified as long as the man is fed and allowed the use of a bathroom. But after a suspect has spent more than twelve hours in an isolated chamber without benefit of counsel, even a sympathetic judge will have qualms about calling a confession or statement truly voluntary.

And how does a detective know he has the right man? Nervousness, fear, confusion, hostility, a story that changes or contradicts itself—all are signs that the man in an interrogation room is lying, particularly in the eyes of someone as naturally suspicious as a detective. Unfortunately, these are also signs of a human being in a state of high stress, which is pretty much where people find themselves after being accused of a capital crime. Terry McLarney once mused that the best way to unsettle a suspect would be to post in all three interrogation rooms a written list of those behavior patterns that indicate deception:

Uncooperative.

Too cooperative.

Talks too much.

Talks too little.

Gets his story perfectly straight.

Fucks his story up.

Blinks too much, avoids eye contact.

Doesn't blink. Stares.

And yet if the signs along the way are ambiguous, there can be no mistaking that critical moment, that light that shines from the other end of the tunnel when a guilty man is about to give it up. Later, after he's initialed each page and is alone again in the cubicle, there will be only exhaustion and, in some cases, depression. If he gets to brooding, there might even be a suicide attempt.

But that is epilogue. The emotive crest of a guilty man's performance comes in those cold moments before he opens his mouth and reaches for the Out. Just before a man gives up life and liberty in an interrogation room, his body acknowledges the defeat: His eyes are glazed, his jaw is slack, his body lists against the nearest wall or table edge. Some put their heads against the tabletop to steady themselves. Some become physically sick, holding their stomachs as if the problem were digestive; a few actually vomit.

At that critical moment, the detectives tell their suspects that they really are sick—sick of lying, sick of hiding. They tell them it's time to turn over a new leaf, that they'll only begin to feel better when they start to tell the truth. Amazingly enough, many of them actually believe it. As they reach for the ledge of that high window, they believe every last word of it.

"He came at you, right?"

"Yeah, he came at me."

The Out leads in.

From *Boys in Zinc*

SVETLANA ALEXIYEVICH

❧

Svetlana Alexiyevich combines Martha Gellhorn's relentless focus on the horror of war with Henry Mayhew's gift for editing interviews into powerful testimony. She is the author of *War's Unwomanly Face,* which documents Russian women's memories of World War II. *Boys in Zinc* is a similar book, based on interviews with those involved directly (as serving members of the armed forces) or indirectly (as wives or mothers) with the Soviet intervention in Afghanistan. More recently she has written, but so far been unable to publish, a book of interviews with people who were driven to attempt suicide during and after the collapse of communism in Russia.

Svetlana Alexiyevich's books have been received by some with immense admiration for her ability to cut through the cant and hypocrisy of official distortion, revealing the grim reality of lives scarred by war and deceit. Others have been enraged, and she has been the recipient of many death threats. In 1995 she faced prosecution in Belarus, where she lives, on a charge of fostering "antinational sentiments."

Her translator, Dr. Arch Tait, is the UK editor of *Glas: New Russian Writing,* a book series that publishes short prose by contemporary Russian authors in English translation. His latest book translation is of Vladimir Makanin's *Baize-Covered Table with Decanter* (Readers International, London, 1995), which won the Booker Russian Novel Prize. He teaches Russian literature at the University of Birmingham, United Kingdom.

—K. K.

❧

In 1986 I had decided not to write about war again. For a long time after I finished my book *War's Unwomanly Face* I couldn't bear to see a child with a bleeding nose. I suppose each of us has a measure of protection against pain; mine had been exhausted.

Two events changed my mind.

I was driving out to a village and I gave a lift to a schoolgirl. She had been

536

shopping in Minsk, and carried a bag with chickens' heads sticking out. In the village we were met by her mother, who was standing crying at the garden gate. The girl ran to her.

The mother had received a letter from her son Andrey. The letter was sent from Afghanistan. "They'll bring him back like they brought Fyodorina's Ivan," she said, "and dig a grave to put him in. Look what he writes. 'Mum, isn't it great! I'm a paratrooper . . .'"

And then there was another incident. An army officer with a suitcase was sitting in the half-empty waiting-room of the bus station in town. Next to him a thin boy with a crew-cut was digging in the pot of a rubber plant with a table fork. Two country women sat down beside the men and asked who they were. The officer said he was escorting home a private soldier who had gone mad. "He's been digging all the way from Kabul with whatever he can get his hands on, a spade, a fork, a stick, a fountain pen." The boy looked up. His pupils were so dilated they seemed to take up the whole of his eyes.

And at that time people continued to talk and write about our internationalist duty, the interests of state, our southern borders. The censors saw to it that reports of the war did not mention our fatalities. There were only rumours of notifications of death arriving at rural huts and of regulation zinc coffins delivered to prefabricated flats. I had not meant to write about war again, but I found myself in the middle of one.

For the next three years I spoke to many people at home and in Afghanistan. Every confession was like a portrait. They are not documents; they are images. I was trying to present a history of feelings, not the history of the war itself. What were people thinking? What made them happy? What were their fears? What stayed in their memory?

The war in Afghanistan lasted twice as long as the Second World War, but we know only so much as it is safe for us to know. It is no longer a secret that every year for ten years, 100,000 Soviet troops went to fight in Afghanistan. Officially, 50,000 men were killed or wounded. You can believe that figure if you will. Everybody knows what we are like at sums. We haven't yet finished counting and burying all those who died in the Second World War.

In what follows, I haven't given people's real names. Some asked for the confidentiality of the confessional, others I don't feel I can expose to a witch-hunt. We are still so close to the war that there is nowhere for anyone to hide.

One night I was asleep when my telephone rang.

"Listen," he began, without identifying himself, "I've read your garbage. If you so much as print another word . . ."

"Who are you?"

"One of the guys you're writing about. God, I hate pacifists! Have you ever been up a mountain in full marching kit? Been in an armoured personnel carrier when the temperature's seventy centigrade? Like hell you have. Fuck off! It's ours! It's got sod all to do with you."

I asked him again who he was.

"Leave it out, will you! My best friend—like a brother he was—and I brought him back from a raid in a cellophane bag. He'd been flayed, his head had been severed, his arms, his legs, his dick all cut off . . . He could have written about it, but you can't. The truth was in that cellophane sack. Fuck the lot of you!" He hung up; the sound in the receiver was like an explosion.

He might have been my most important witness.

A WIFE

"Don't worry if you don't get any letters," he wrote. "Carry on writing to the old address." Then nothing for two months. I never dreamed he was in Afghanistan. I was getting suitcases ready to go to see him at his new posting.

He didn't write about being in a war. Said he was getting a sun-tan and going fishing. He sent a photo of himself sitting on a donkey with his knees on the sand. It wasn't until he came home on leave that I knew he was in a war. He never used to spoil our daughter, never showed any fatherly feelings, perhaps because she was small. Now he came back and sat for hours looking at her, and his eyes were so sad it was frightening. In the mornings he'd get up and take her to the kindergarten; he liked carrying her on his shoulders. He'd collect her in the evening. Occasionally we went to the theatre or the cinema, but all he really wanted to do was to stay at home.

He couldn't get enough loving. I'd be getting ready to go to work or getting his dinner in the kitchen, and he even grudged that time. "Sit over here with me. Forget cutlets today. Ask for a holiday while I'm home." When it was time for him to get the plane he missed it deliberately so we would have an extra two days. The last night he was so good I was in tears. I was crying, and he was saying nothing, just looking and looking at me. Then he said, "Tamara, if you ever have another man, don't forget this."

I said, "Don't talk soft! They'll never kill you. I love you too much for them to be able to."

He laughed. "Forget it. I'm a big lad."

We talked of having more children, but he said he didn't want any more now. "When I come back you can have another. How would you manage with them on your own?"

When he was away I got used to the waiting, but if I saw a funeral car in town I'd feel ill, I'd want to scream and cry. I'd run home, the icon would be hanging there, and I'd get down on my knees and pray, "Save him for me, God! Don't let him die."

I went to the cinema the day it happened. I sat there looking at the screen and seeing nothing. I was really jumpy. It was as if I was keeping someone waiting or there was somewhere I had to go. I barely stuck it out to the end of the programme. Looking back, I think that it must have been during the battle.

It was a week before I heard anything. All of that week I'd start reading a book and put it down. I even got two letters from him. Usually I'd have been really pleased—I'd have kissed them—but this time they just made me wonder how much longer I was going to have to wait for him.

The ninth day after he was killed a telegram arrived at five in the morning. They just shoved it under the door. It was from his parents: "Come over. Petya dead." I screamed so much that it woke the baby. I had no idea what I should do or where I should go. I hadn't got any money. I wrapped our daughter in a red blanket and went out to the road. It was too early for the buses, but a taxi stopped.

"I need to go to the airport," I told the taxi-driver.

He told me he was going off duty and shut the car door.

"My husband has been killed in Afghanistan."

He got out without saying anything, and helped me in. We drove to the house of a friend of mine and she lent me some money. At the airport they said there were no tickets for Moscow, and I was scared to take the telegram out of my bag to show them. Perhaps it was all a mistake. I kept telling myself if I could just carry on thinking he was alive, he would be. I was crying and everybody was looking at me. They put me on a freight plane taking a cargo of sweetcorn to Moscow, from there I got a connection to Minsk. I was still 150 kilometres from Starye Dorogi where Petya's parents lived. None of the taxi drivers wanted to drive there even though I begged and begged. I finally got to Starye Dorogi at two o'clock in the morning.

"Perhaps it isn't true?"

"It's true, Tamara, it's true."

In the morning we went to the Military Commissariat. They were very formal. "You will be notified when it arrives." We waited for two more days before we rang the Provincial Military Commissariat at Minsk. They told us that it would be best if we came to collect my husband's body ourselves. When we got to Minsk, the official told us that the coffin had been sent on to Baranovichi by mistake. Baranovichi was another 100 kilometres and when we got to the airport there it was after working hours and there was nobody about, except for a night watchman in his hut.

"We've come to collect . . ."

"Over there," he pointed over to a far corner. "See if that box is yours. If it is, you can take it."

There was a filthy box standing outside with "Senior Lieutenant Dovnar" scrawled on it in chalk. I tore a board away from where the window should be in a coffin. His face was in one piece, but he was lying in there unshaven, and nobody had washed him. The coffin was too small and there was a bad smell. I couldn't lean down to kiss him. That's how they gave my husband back to me. I got down on my knees before what had once been the dearest thing in the world to me.

His was the first coffin to come back to my home town, Yazyl. I still remember the horror in people's eyes. When we buried him, before they could draw up the bands with which they had been lowering him, there was a terrible crash of thunder. I remember the hail crunching under foot like white gravel.

I didn't talk much to his father and mother. I thought his mother hated me because I was alive, and he was dead. She thought I would remarry. Now, she says, "Tamara, you ought to get married again," but then I was afraid to meet her eye. Petya's father almost went out of his mind. "The bastards! To put a boy like that in his grave! They murdered him!" My mother-in-law and I tried to tell him they'd given Petya a medal, that we needed Afghanistan to defend our southern borders, but he didn't want to hear. "The bastards! They murdered him!"

The worst part was later, when I had to get used to the thought that there was nothing, no one for me to wait for any more. I would wake up terrified, drenched with sweat, thinking Petya would come back, and not know where his wife and child live now. All I had left were memories of good times.

The day we met, we danced together. The second day we went for a stroll in the park, and the next day he proposed. I was already engaged and I told him the application was lying in the registry office. He went away and wrote to me in huge letters which took up the whole page: "Aaaaargh!"

We got married in the winter, in my village. It was funny and rushed. At Epiphany, when people guess their fortunes, I'd had a dream which I told my mother about in the morning. "Mum, I saw this really good-looking boy. He was standing on a bridge, calling me. He was wearing a soldier's uniform, but when I came towards him he began to go away until he disappeared completely."

"Don't marry a soldier. You'll be left on your own," my mother told me.

Petya had two days' leave. "Let's go to the Registry Office," he said, even before he'd come in the door.

They took one look at us in the Village Soviet and said, "Why wait two months. Go and get the brandy. We'll do the paperwork." An hour later we were husband and wife. There was a snowstorm raging outside.

"Where's the taxi for your new wife, bridegroom?"

"Hang on!" He went out and stopped a Belarus tractor for me.

For years I dreamed of us getting on that tractor, driving along in the snow.

The last time Petya came home on leave the flat was locked. He hadn't sent a telegram to warn me that he was coming, and I had gone to my friend's flat to celebrate her birthday. When he arrived at the door and heard the music and saw everyone happy and laughing, he sat down on a stool and cried. Every day of his leave he came to work to meet me. He told me, "When I'm coming to see you at work my knees shake as if we had a date." I remember we went swimming together one day. We sat on the bank and built a fire. He looked at me and said, "You can't imagine how much I don't want to die for someone else's country."

I was twenty-four when he died. In those first months I would have married any man who wanted me. I didn't know what to do. Life was going on all around me the same as before. One person was building a *dacha*, one was buying a car; someone had got a new flat and needed a carpet or a hotplate for the kitchen. In the last war everybody was grief stricken, the whole country. Everybody had lost someone, and they knew what they had lost them for. All the women cried together. There are a hundred people in the catering college where I work and I am the only one who lost her husband in a war the rest of them have only read about in the newspapers. When I first heard them saying on television that the war in Afghanistan had been a national disgrace, I wanted to break the screen. I lost my husband for a second time that day.

A Private Soldier

The only training we got before we took the oath was that twice they took us down the firing-range. The first time we went there they issued us with nine rounds; the second time we all got to throw a grenade.

They lined us up on the square and read out the order: "You're going to the Democratic Republic of Afghanistan to do your internationalist duty. Anyone who doesn't want to go, take two paces forward." Three lads did. The unit commander shoved them back in line with a knee up the backside. "Just checking morale." They gave us two days' rations and a leather belt, and we were off. Nobody said a word. The flight seemed to take an age. I saw mountains through the plane window. Beautiful! They were the first mountains any of us had ever seen. We were all from round Pskov, where there are only woodlands and clearings. We got out in Shin Dand. I remembered the date: 19 December 1980.

They took a look at me. "One metre eighty: reconnaissance company. They can use lads your size."

We went to Herat to build a firing-range. We were digging, hauling stones for a foundation. I tiled a roof and did some joinery. Some of us hadn't fired a single shot before the first battle. We were hungry the whole time. There were two fifty-litre vats in the kitchen: one for soup, the other for mash or barley porridge. We had one can of mackerel between four, and the label said, "Date of manufacture, 1956; shelf-life eighteen months." In a year and a half, the only time I wasn't hungry was when I was wounded. Otherwise you were always thinking of ways to get something to eat. We were so desperate for fruit that we'd slip over into the Afghans' orchards knowing that they'd shoot at us. We asked our parents to send citric acid in their letters so that we could dissolve it in water and drink it. It was so sour that it burned your stomach.

Before our first battle they played the Soviet national anthem. The deputy political commander gave us a talk. I remember he said we'd only beaten the Americans here by one hour, and everybody was waiting to welcome us back home as heroes.

I had no idea how to kill. Before the army I was a racing cyclist. I'd never so much as seen a real knife fight, and here I was, driving along on the back of an armoured personnel carrier. I hadn't felt like this before: powerful, strong and secure. The hills suddenly looked low, the irrigation ditches small, the trees few and far between. After half an hour I was so relaxed I felt like a tourist, taking a look at a foreign country.

We drove over a ditch on a little clay bridge: I remember being amazed it could take the weight of several tons of metal. Suddenly there was an explosion and the APC in front had got a direct hit from a grenade launcher. Men I knew were already being carried away, like stuffed animals with their arms dangling. I couldn't make sense of this new, frightening world. We sent all our mortars into where the firing had come from, several mortars to every homestead. After the battle we scraped our own guys off the armour plate with spoons. There weren't any identification discs for fatalities; I suppose they thought they might fall into the wrong hands. It was like in the song: *We don't live in a house on a street, Our address is the USSR.* So we just spread a tarpaulin over the bodies, a "communal grave." War hadn't even been declared; we were fighting a war that did not exist.

A MOTHER

I sat by Sasha's coffin saying, "Who is it? Is that you, son?" I just kept repeating over and over, "Is that you?" They decided I was out of my mind. Later on, I wanted to know how my son had died. I went to the Military Commissariat and the commissar started shouting at me, telling me it was a state secret that my son had died, that I shouldn't run around telling everyone.

My son was in the Vitebsk parachute division. When I went to see him take his oath of allegiance, I didn't recognize him; he stood so tall.

"Hey, how come I've got such a small mum?"

"Because I miss you and I've stopped growing."

He bent down and kissed me, and somebody took a photograph. It's the only photograph of him as a soldier that I've got.

After the oath he had a few hours free time. We went to the park and sat down on the grass. He took his boots off because his feet were all blistered and bleeding. The previous day his unit had been on a fifty kilometre forced march and there hadn't been any size forty-six boots, so they had given him forty-fours.

"We had to run with rucksacks filled with sand. What do you reckon? Where did I come?"

"Last, probably, with those boots."

"Wrong, mum. I was first. I took the boots off and ran. And I didn't tip sand out like some of the others."

That night, they let the parents sleep inside the unit on mats laid out in the sports hall, but we didn't lie down until far into the night, instead we wandered round the barracks where our sons were asleep. I hoped I would get to see him when they went to do their morning gymnastics but they were all running in identical striped vests and I missed him, didn't catch a last glimpse of him. They all went to the toilet in a line, in a line to do their gymnastics, in a line to the canteen. They didn't let them do anything on their own because, when the boys had heard they were being sent to Afghanistan, one hanged himself in the toilet and two others slashed their wrists. They were under guard.

His second letter began, "Greetings from Kabul . . ." I screamed so loudly that the neighbours ran in. It was the first time since Sasha was born that I was sorry I had not got married and had no one to look after me.

Sasha used to tease me. "Why don't you get married, Mum?"

"Because you'd be jealous."

He'd laugh and say nothing. We were going to live together for a long, long time to come.

I got a few more letters and then there was silence, such a long silence I wrote to the commander of his unit. Straight away Sasha wrote back to me, "Mum, please don't write to the commander again. I couldn't write to you. I got my hand stung by a wasp. I didn't want to ask someone else to write, because you'd have been worried by the different handwriting." I knew immediately that he had been wounded, and now if even a day went by without a letter from him my legs would give way under me. One of his letters was very cheerful. "Hurray, hurray! We escorted a column back to the Union. We went with them as far as the frontier. They wouldn't let us go any further, but at least we got a distant look at our homeland. It's the best country in the world." In his last letter he wrote, "If I last the summer, I'll be back."

On 29 August I decided summer was over. I bought Sasha a new suit and a pair of shoes, which are still in the wardrobe now. The next day, before I went to work I took off my ear-rings and my ring. For some reason I couldn't bear to wear them. That was the day on which he was killed.

When they brought the zinc coffin into the room, I lay on top of it and measured it again and again. One metre, two metres. He was two metres tall. I measured with my hands to make sure the coffin was the right size for him. The coffin was sealed, so I couldn't kiss him one last time, or touch him, I didn't even know what he was wearing, I just talked to the coffin like a mad-woman.

I said I wanted to choose the place in the cemetery for him myself. They gave me two injections, and I went there with my brother. There were "Afghan" graves on the main avenue.

"Lay my son here too. He'll be happier among his friends."

I can't remember who was there with us. Some official. He shook his head. "We are not permitted to bury them together. They have to be dispersed throughout the cemetery."

They say there was a case where they brought a coffin back to a mother, and she buried it, and a year later her son came back alive. He'd only been wounded. I never saw my son's body, or kissed him goodbye. I'm still waiting.

A Nurse

Every day I was there I told myself I was a fool to come. Especially at night, when I had no work to do. All I thought during the day was "How can I help them all?" I couldn't believe anybody would make the bullets they were using. Whose idea were they? The point of entry was small, but inside, their intestines, their liver, their spleen were all ripped and torn apart. As if it wasn't enough to kill or wound them, they had to be put through that kind of agony as well. They always cried for their mothers when they were in pain, or frightened. I never heard them call for anyone else.

They told us it was a just war. We were helping the Afghan people to put an end to feudalism and build a socialist society. Somehow they didn't get round to mentioning that our men were being killed. For the whole of the first month I was there they just dumped the amputated arms and legs of our soldiers and officers, even their bodies, right next to the tents. It was something I would hardly have believed if I had seen it in films about the Civil War. There were no zinc coffins then: they hadn't got round to manufacturing them.

Twice a week we had political indoctrination. They went on about our sacred duty, and how the border must be inviolable. Our superior ordered us to inform on every wounded soldier, every patient. It was called monitoring the state of morale: the army must be healthy! We weren't to feel compassion. But we did feel compassion: it was the only thing that held everything together.

A Regimental Press Officer

I will begin at the point where everything fell apart.

We were advancing on Jalalabad and a little girl of about seven years old was standing by the roadside. Her arm had been smashed and was held on only by a thread, as if she were a torn rag doll. She had dark eyes like olives, and they were fixed on me. I jumped down from the vehicle to take her in my arms and carry her to our nurses, but she sprang back terrified and screaming like a small animal. Still screaming she ran away, her little arm dangling and looking as though it would come off completely. I ran after her shouting, caught up with her and pressed her to me, stroking her. She was biting and scratching, trembling all over, as if some wild animal had seized her. It was only then that the thought struck me like a thunderbolt: she didn't believe I wanted to help her; she thought I wanted to kill her. The way she ran away, the way she shuddered, how afraid she was of me are things I'll never forget.

I had set out for Afghanistan with idealism blazing in my eyes. I had been told that the Afghans needed me, and I believed it. While I was there I never dreamed about the war, but now every night I am back running after that little girl with her olive eyes, and her little arm dangling as if it's going to fall off any moment.

Out there you felt quite differently about your country. "The Union," we called it. It seemed there was something great and powerful behind us, something which would always stand up for us. I remember, though, the evening after one battle—there had been losses, men killed and men seriously injured—we plugged in the television to forget about it, to see what was going on in the Union. A mammoth new factory had been built in Siberia; the Queen of England had given a banquet in honour of some VIP; youths in Voronezh had raped two schoolgirls for the hell of it; a prince had been killed in Africa. The country was going about its business and we felt completely useless. Someone had to turn the television off, before we shot it to pieces.

It was a mothers' war. They were in the thick of it. The people at large didn't suffer, they didn't know what was going on. They were told we were fighting bandits. In nine years a regular army of 100,000 troops couldn't beat some ragged bandits? An army with the latest technology. (God help anyone who got in the way of an artillery bombardment with our Hail or Hurricane rocket launchers: the telegraph poles flew like matchsticks.) The "bandits" had only old Maxim machine-guns we had seen in films, the Stingers and Japanese machine guns came later. We'd bring in prisoners, emaciated people with big, peasant hands. They were no bandits. They were the people of Afghanistan.

The war had its own ghastly rules: if you were photographed or if you shaved before a battle, you were dead. It was always the blue-eyed heroes who were the first to be killed: you'd meet one of those types and before you knew it, he was dead. People mostly got killed either in their first months when they were too curious, or towards the end when they'd lost their sense of caution and become stupid. At night you'd forget where you were, who you were, what you were doing there. No one could sleep during the last six or eight weeks before they went home.

Here in the Union we are like brothers. A young guy going down the street on crutches with a shiny medal can only be one of us. You might only sit down on a bench and smoke a cigarette together, but you feel as if you've been talking to each other the whole day.

The authorities want to use us to clamp down on organized crime. If there is any trouble to be broken up, the police send for "the Afghans." As far as they are concerned we are guys with big fists and small brains who nobody likes. But surely if your hand hurts you don't put it in the fire, you look after it until it gets better.

A MOTHER

I skip along to the cemetery as if I'm on my way to meet someone. I feel I'm going to visit my son. Those first days I stayed there all night. It wasn't frightening. I'm waiting for the spring, for a little flower to burst through to me out of the ground. I planted snowdrops, so I would have a greeting from my son as early as possible. They come to me from down there, from him.

I'll sit with him until evening and far on into the night. Sometimes I don't realize I've started wailing until I scare the birds, a whole squall of crows, circling and flapping above me until I come to my senses and stop. I've gone there every day for four years, in the evening if not in the morning. I missed eleven days when I was in hospital, then I ran away in the hospital gown to see my son.

He called me "Mother mine," and "Angel mother mine." "Well, angel mother mine, your son has been accepted by the Smolensk Military Academy. I trust you are pleased." He sat down at the piano and sang.

> Gentlemen officers, princes indeed!
> If I'm not first among them,
> I'm one of their breed.

My father was a regular officer who died in the defence of Leningrad. My grandfather was an officer too. My son was made to be a military man—he had the bearing, so tall and strong. He should have been a hussar with white gloves, playing cards.

Everybody wanted to be like him. Even I, his own mother, would imitate him. I would sit down at the piano the way he did, and sometimes start walking the way he did, especially after he was killed. I so much want him always to be present in me.

When he first went to Afghanistan, he didn't write for ages. I waited and waited for him to come home on leave. Then one day the telephone rang at work.

"Angel mother mine, I am home."

I went to meet him off the bus. His hair had gone grey. He didn't admit he wasn't on leave, that he'd asked to be let out of hospital for a couple of days to see his mother. He'd got hepatitis, malaria and everything else rolled into one but he warned his sister not to tell me. I went into his room again before I went off to work, to see him sleeping. He opened his eyes. I asked him why he was not asleep, it was so early. He said he'd had a bad dream.

We went with him as far as Moscow. It was lovely, sunny May weather, and the trees were in bloom. I asked him what it was like over there.

"Mother mine, Afghanistan is something we have no business to be doing." He looked only at me, not at anyone else. "I don't want to go back into that hole. I really do not." He walked away, but turned round, "It's as simple as that, Mum." He never said "Mum." The woman at the airport desk was in tears watching us.

When I woke up on 7 July I hadn't been crying. I stared glassily at the ceiling. He had woken me, as if he had come to say goodbye. It was eight o'clock. I had to get ready to go to work. I was wandering with my dress from the bathroom to the sitting-room, from one room to another. For some reason I couldn't bear to put that light-coloured dress on. I felt dizzy, and couldn't see people properly. Everything was blurred. I grew calmer towards lunch-time, towards midday.

The seventh day of July. He had seven cigarettes in his pocket, seven matches. He had taken seven pictures with his camera. He had written seven letters to me, and seven to his girlfriend. The book on his bedside table was open at page seven. It was Kobo Abe's *Containers of Death*.

He had three or four seconds in which he could have saved himself. They were hurtling over a precipice in a vehicle. He couldn't be the first to jump out. He never could.

From Deputy Regimental Commander for Political Affairs, Major S. R. Sinelnikov. In fulfilment of my duty as a soldier, I have to inform you that Senior Lieutenant Valerii Gennadievich Volovich was killed today at 1045 hours.

The whole city already knew all about it. In the Officers' Club they'd put up black crêpe and his photograph. The plane bringing his coffin was due at any minute, but nobody had told me a thing. They couldn't bring themselves to speak. At work everybody's faces were tear-stained. I asked, "What has happened?"

They tried to distract me in various ways. A friend came round, then finally a doctor in a white coat arrived. I told him he was crazy, that boys like my son did not get killed. I started hammering the table. I ran over to the window and started beating the glass. They gave me an injection. I kept on shouting. They gave me another injection, but that had no effect, either; I was screaming, "I want to see him, take me to my son." Eventually they had to take me.

There was a long coffin. The wood was unplaned, and written on it in large letters in yellow paint was "Volovich." I had to find him a place in the cemetery, somewhere dry, somewhere nice and dry. If that meant a fifty rouble bribe, fine. Here, take it, only make sure it's a good place, nice and dry. Inside I knew how disgusting that was, but I just wanted a nice dry place for him. Those first nights I didn't leave him. I stayed there. They would take me off home, but I would come back.

When I go to see him I bow, and when I leave I bow again. I never get cold even in freezing temperatures; I write my letters there; I am only ever at home when I have visitors. When I walk back to my house at night the streetlamps are lit, the cars have their headlamps on. I feel so strong that I am not afraid of anything.

Only now am I waking from my sorrow which is like waking from sleep. I want to know whose fault this was. Why doesn't anybody say anything? Why aren't we being told who did it? Why aren't they being put on trial?

I greet every flower on his grave, every little root and stem. "Have you come from there? Do you come from him? You have come from my son."

Holiday Pageant:
The Importance of Being Bluebell

MICHAEL WINERIP

Who would have thought that something original could still be done with the newspaper column? And with a Christmas angle, no less! Michael Winerip, at the time a suburban correspondent for the *New York Times,* began writing a three-times-a-week column for the paper in 1987, and the results were something to see. Winerip is a prodigious reporter who would conduct dozens of interviews for a piece, constructing from them a gem of observation, pacing, and language.

Winerip is famous among journalists for his ability in eliciting, spotting, and using good quotes; "The Importance of Being Bluebell" is full of them. ("People I didn't even know came up to me!") But more striking and much more daring is his use of proper names. In a mere 800 words, he formally introduces the reader to no fewer than nineteen characters—Dean Moriano and Jose Coons and Lisa Panzarita and all the rest. Where conventional feature-writing wisdom would rule this out as needlessly confusing to the reader, Winerip brilliantly builds those wonderful names into a poem of ethnic diversity and (that Christmas angle) holiday brotherhood for all.

—B. Y.

Albertson, L. I.—When 8-year-old Joey Floccari heard he was to be Bluebell in the holiday pageant, he nearly dropped his walker. He was filled with joy. All the way home on the bus for the handicapped, he sang: "Somewhere out there beneath the pale moonlight, someone's thinkin' of me and loving me tonight!" At home, he said, "Mom I saw Miss Leonard and she asked me to be Bluebell and do you want to hear it?" Before Antonietta Floccari could say, Joey was singing another chorus of "Somewhere."

Jose Coons was the Sun, a big dancing part. "Setting the table for dinner, he'd leap from the kitchen to the dining room," said his father, Robert. "I'd see his feet enter the room first."

"I'd look up," said his mother, Regina, "and Jose was flying by."

Karen Seeburger practiced being the Moon, the entire first grade practiced waving their lamé stars. At school, people who had seen rehearsals were talking. "There's a little kid who plays Bluebell, a little guardian angel," said Mike Lamb, the lighting designer. "Wait until you see him—he has no arms, no legs, he sings like Ethel Merman!"

The day of the pageant, the gym at the state Human Resources School for the physically handicapped was mobbed. Melissa Male, Allison Coleman and Lisa Panzarita, all chorus members, had decorated their wheelchair spokes with tinsel and ribbon. "I heard someone has lights on their walker," said Tyree Simpson. It was Merry Stanley, whose mother had hooked up a special battery pack. Dean Mariano, 10, wore a red tie. "I thought I might look a little better," he said.

The pageant director, Mary Leonard, was madly wheeling around in her chair. "I have a favor to ask," she said to the chorus. "At the beginning of Jose's dance, bow your heads. I'd really appreciate it—you look very beautiful." And she sped off.

Everywhere you turned, there were little angels with white construction-paper wings. Jean Crocket said, "You know where you stand?"

"In the center," said the Sun.

"You got it, toots," said Mrs. Crockett. "Thirty seconds!" someone shouted. "Oh God!" said the Sun. Born with a deformed face, without even a nose, he has had 30 reconstructive operations. As a little boy, the Sun wouldn't look at himself in the mirror. This was new, dancing in front of a crowded gym in a yellow sweatsuit.

The play Miss Leonard wrote wasn't religious, the word Christmas wasn't spoken, and yet somehow it felt more like Christmas than the whole Roosevelt Field mall. It was about a little boy, the captain of his school writing club, who has a chance to send a letter about peace to the United Nations, but is more interested in toys. His mother scolds him, but you know the old saying, "Gimme a break, Ma!" So Father Time—Stan Lewis the gym teacher—decides to send an angel, Bluebell, to set the boy straight. When Bluebell gets word he must go down to earth, he protests, "But I'll be so lonely there." These may be the truest words written in years. An angel come to earth in 1987 would be a mighty lonely fellow.

The audience thought so too, because they clapped, and they kept clapping in all the right places.

It's funny how you can sometimes watch a featured performer in a $30-million Hollywood spectacular complete with Dolby sound and you're bored stiff. And then three-foot-tall Joey Floccari puts on his artifical legs, his construction-paper wings, and stands alone, center stage, leaning on his walker, belting out "Somewhere"—and the whole gym is crying.

"When I heard what came out of him," said Mrs. Coons. "I was looking all over to see where that big voice came from."

"I was crying," said Jane Kalberer.

"You too?" said Pamela Allori.

Everyone was on best behavior. When the angels were done, they sat quietly on a blue gym mat, and gave their halos to Addie Syverson, a teacher's aid, for safekeeping.

It took Bluebell over an hour to straighten out the materialistic boy's priorities. By 3:05, he was done, but before he went back to heaven, he did a reprise of "Somewhere," and it was Ethel Merman and a thousand sniffles all over again. Miss Leonard knows when she has a good thing going.

The curtain went down and the parents rushed up. Bluebell, the angels, the Sun, the Moon—they were all stars. Jose said: "After the performance I didn't know what people would say, then they said it was great! People I don't even know came up to me."

He said he wasn't interested in this as a career. "I'm not the type to perform in front of people," he said. "I don't want people watching me." He said he planned to go to college and become an accountant.

Permissions

Index